BUSINESS LAW

TEXT AND CASES

An Accelerated Course

Fourteenth Edition

Roger LeRoy Miller
Institute for University Studies
Arlington, Texas

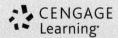

CENGAGE
Learning·

Australia · Brazil · Mexico · Singapore · United Kingdom · United States

CENGAGE
Learning®

Business Law
TEXT AND CASES

An Accelerated Course

Fourteenth Edition

Roger LeRoy Miller

Vice President for Social Science and Qualitative Business: *Erin Joyner*

Product Director: *Jason Fremder*

Senior Product Manager: *Vicky True-Baker*

Managing Content Developer: *Suzanne Wilder*

Content Developer: *Sarah Huber*

Product Assistant: *Christian Wood*

Marketing Director: *Kristen Hurd*

Marketing Manager: *Katie Jergens*

Marketing Coordinator: *Casey Binder*

Production Director: *Sharon Smith*

Senior Content Project Manager: *Ann Borman*

Digital Content Specialist: *Charles Nichols*

Manufacturing Planner: *Kevin Kluck*

Senior Inventory Analyst: *Terina Bradley*

Senior IP Director: *Julie Geagan-Chavez*

IP Analyst: *Jennifer Nonenmacher*

IP Project Manager: *Reba Frederics*

Senior Art Director: *Michelle Kunkler*

Interior and Cover Designer: *Harasymczuk Design*

Design Elements:
linen texture: Lisa-Blue/iStockphoto; justice scales: imagedb.com/Shutterstock; gavel: koosen/Shutterstock; media network: solarseven/Shutterstock; building windows: Nneirda/Shutterstock; puzzle icon: Shebeko/Shutterstock; spotlight: Ivan Lord/Shutterstock; ethics scale: Lightspring/Shutterstock; magnifying glass icon: sergign/Shutterstock; globe: mj007/Shutterstock; compass: Taddeus/Shutterstock; Insight Global globe: evantravels/Shutterstock

Printed in the United States of America
Print Number: 01   Print Year: 2016

For product information and technology assistance, contact us at
**Cengage Learning Customer & Sales Support,
1-800-354-9706**
For permission to use material from this text or product, submit all requests online at
www.cengage.com/permissions.
Further permissions questions can be emailed to
permissionrequest@cengage.com.

Library of Congress Control Number: 2016957208

Student Edition ISBN: 978-1-305-96729-8

Cengage Learning
20 Channel Center Street
Boston, MA 02210
USA

Cengage Learning is a leading provider of customized learning solutions with employees residing in nearly 40 different countries and sales in more than 125 countries around the world. Find your local representative at **www.cengage.com.**

Cengage Learning products are represented in Canada by Nelson Education, Ltd.

To learn more about Cengage Learning Solutions, visit **www.cengage.com.**

Purchase any of our products at your local college store or at our preferred online store **www.cengagebrain.com.**

Brief Contents

Contents

Concept Summaries

Exhibits

Preface

The study of business law and the legal environment of business has universal applicability. A student entering any field of business must have at least a passing understanding of business law in order to function in the real world. *Business Law: Text and Cases: An Accelerated Course,* Fourteenth Edition, provides the information that students need in an interesting and contemporary way.

Additionally, students preparing for a career in accounting, government and political science, economics, and even medicine can use much of the information they learn in a business law and legal environment course. In fact, every individual throughout his or her lifetime can benefit from knowledge of contracts, intellectual property and internet law, agency relationships, and other business law topics. Consequently, I have fashioned this text as a useful "tool for living" for all of your students (including those taking the revised 2017 CPA exam).

Business Law: An Accelerated Course is an exciting textbook made specifically for those instructors who teach a one-semester course of business law. For the Fourteenth Edition, I have spent a great deal of effort making this best-selling text more modern, exciting, and visually appealing than ever before. I have added sixteen new features and thirty-six new cases. The text also contains more than a hundred new highlighted and numbered *Cases in Point* and *Examples,* and sixty new case problems. Special pedagogical elements within the text focus on legal, ethical, global, and corporate issues while addressing core curriculum requirements.

Highlights of the Fourteenth Edition

Instructors have come to rely on the coverage, accuracy, and applicability of *Business Law: An Accelerated Course.* To make sure that this text engages your students, solidifies their understanding of legal concepts, and provides the best teaching tools available, it now offers the following.

A Variety of New and Exciting Features

The Fourteenth Edition of *Business Law: An Accelerated Course* is filled with many new features specifically designed to cover current legal topics of high interest. Each feature is related to a topic discussed in the text and ends with *Critical Thinking* or *Business Questions.* **Suggested answers to all the *Critical Thinking* and *Business Questions* are included in the *Solutions Manual* for this text.**

1. ***Ethics Today*** These features focus on the ethical aspects of a topic discussed in the text to emphasize that ethics is an integral part of a business law course. Examples include:
   - *Stare Decisis* versus Spiderman (Chapter 1)
   - When Is Impossibility of Performance a Valid Defense? (Chapter 11)
   - Is It Fair to Classify Uber and Lyft Drivers as Independent Contractors? (Chapter 17)
2. ***Global Insight*** These features illustrate how other nations deal with specific legal concepts to give students a sense of the global legal environment. Subjects include:
   - Does Cloud Computing Have a Nationality? (Chapter 19)
3. **NEW *Digital Update*** These features are designed to examine cutting-edge cyberlaw topics, such as the following:
   - Revenge Porn and Invasion of Privacy (Chapter 4)
   - Should Employees Have a "Right of Disconnecting"? (Chapter 6)
   - Monitoring Employees' Social Media—Right or Wrong? (Chapter 14)
4. ***Managerial Strategy*** These features emphasize the management aspects of business law and the legal environment. Topics include:
   - Marriage Equality and the Constitution (Chapter 2)
   - Should You Consent to Have Your Business Case Decided by a U.S. Magistrate Judge? (Chapter 3)
   - The Criminalization of American Business (Chapter 5)

Entire Chapter on Internet Law, Social Media, and Privacy

For the Fourteenth Edition, I continue to include a whole chapter (Chapter 14) on *Internet Law, Social Media, and Privacy.* Social media have entered the mainstream and become a part of everyday life for many businesspersons. In this special chapter, I give particular emphasis to the legal issues surrounding the Internet, social media, and privacy. I also recognize this trend throughout the text by incorporating the Internet and social media as they relate to the topics under discussion.

Highlighted and Numbered *Examples* and *Case in Point* Illustrations

Many instructors use cases and examples to illustrate how the law applies to business. Students understand legal concepts better in the context of their real-world application. Therefore, for this edition of *Business Law: An Accelerated Course,* I have expanded the number of highlighted numbered *Examples* and *Cases in Point* in every chapter. I have added 88 new *Cases in Point* and 31 new *Examples.*

Examples illustrate how the law applies in a specific situation. *Cases in Point* present the facts and issues of an actual case and then describe the court's decision and rationale. These two features are uniquely designed and consecutively numbered throughout each chapter for easy reference. The *Examples* and *Cases in Point* are integrated throughout the text to help students better understand how courts apply legal principles in the real world.

New Cases and Case Problems

For the Fourteenth Edition of *Business Law: An Accelerated Course,* I have added 36 new cases and 60 new case problems, most from 2016 and 2015. The new cases and case problems have been carefully selected to illustrate important points of law and to be of high interest to students and instructors. I have made it a point to find recent cases that enhance learning and are relatively easy to understand.

1. **Spotlight Cases and Classic Cases.** Certain cases and case problems that are exceptionally good teaching cases are labeled as *Spotlight Cases* and *Spotlight Case Problems.* Examples include *Spotlight on Amazon, Spotlight on Beer Labels, Spotlight on Gucci, Spotlight on Nike,* and *Spotlight on the Seattle Mariners.* Instructors will find these *Spotlight Cases* useful to illustrate the legal concepts under discussion, and students will enjoy studying the cases because they

involve interesting and memorable facts. Other cases have been chosen as *Classic Cases* because they establish a legal precedent in a particular area of law.

2. **Critical Thinking Section.** Each case concludes with a *Critical Thinking* section, which normally includes two questions. The questions may address *Legal Environment, E-Commerce, Economic, Environmental, Ethical, Global, Political,* or *Technological* issues, or they may ask *What If the Facts Were Different?* Each *Classic Case* has a section titled *Impact of This Case on Today's Law* and one *Critical Thinking* question.

3. **Longer Excerpts for *Case Analysis.*** I have also included one longer case excerpt in every chapter—labeled *Case Analysis*—followed by three *Legal Reasoning Questions.* The questions are designed to guide students' analysis of the case and build their legal reasoning skills. These *Case Analysis* cases may be used for case-briefing assignments and are also tied to the *Special Case Analysis* questions found in selected chapters of the text.

Suggested answers to all case-ending questions and case problems are included in the *Solutions Manual* for this text.

Business Case Problem with Sample Answer in Each Chapter

In response to those instructors who would like students to have sample answers available for some of the questions and case problems, I include a *Business Case Problem with Sample Answer* in each chapter. The *Business Case Problem with Sample Answer* is based on an actual case, and students can find a sample answer at the end of the text. **Suggested answers to the *Business Case Problems with Sample Answers* are provided in Appendix C at the end of the text and in the *Solutions Manual* for this text.**

New Exhibits and Concept Summaries

For this edition, I have spent considerable effort reworking and redesigning all of the exhibits and *Concept Summaries* in the text to achieve better clarity and more visual appeal. In addition, I have added new exhibits and *Concept Summaries.*

Special Case Analysis Questions

For selected chapters of the text, I provide a *Special Case Analysis* question that is based on the *Case Analysis* excerpt in that chapter. These special questions appear in the *Business Case Problems* at the ends of selected chapters.

The *Special Case Analysis* questions are designed to build students' analytical skills. They test students' ability to perform IRAC (Issue, Rule, Application, and Conclusion) case analysis. Students must identify the legal issue presented in the chapter's *Case Analysis* case, understand the rule of law, determine how the rule applies to the facts of the case, and describe the court's conclusion. Instructors can assign these questions as homework or use them in class to elicit student participation and teach case analysis. **Suggested answers to the *Special Case Analysis* questions can be found in the *Solutions Manual* for this text.**

Reviewing Features in Every Chapter

In the Fourteenth Edition of *Business Law: An Accelerated Course,* I continue to offer a *Reviewing* feature at the end of every chapter to help solidify students' understanding of the chapter materials. Each *Reviewing* feature presents a hypothetical scenario and then asks a series of questions that require students to identify the issues and apply the legal concepts discussed in the chapter.

These features are designed to help students review the chapter topics in a simple and interesting way and see how the legal principles discussed in the chapter affect the world in which they live. An instructor can use these features as the basis for in-class discussion or encourage students to use them for self-study prior to completing homework assignments. **Suggested answers to the questions posed in the *Reviewing* features can be found in the *Solutions Manual* for this text.**

Two *Issue Spotters*

At the conclusion of each chapter, I have included a special section with two *Issue Spotters* related to the chapter's topics. These questions facilitate student learning and review of the chapter materials. **Suggested answers to the *Issue Spotters* in every chapter are provided in Appendix B at the end of the text and in the *Solutions Manual* for this text.**

Legal Reasoning Group Activities

For instructors who want their students to engage in group projects, each chapter of the Fourteenth Edition includes a special *Legal Reasoning Group Activity.* Each activity begins by describing a business scenario and then poses several specific questions pertaining to the scenario.

Each question is to be answered by a different group of students based on the information in the chapter. These projects may be used in class to spur discussion or as homework assignments. **Suggested answers to the *Legal Reasoning Group Activities* are included in the *Solutions Manual* for this text.**

Supplements/Digital Learning Systems

Business Law: An Accelerated Course, Fourteenth Edition, provides a comprehensive supplements package designed to make the tasks of teaching and learning more enjoyable and efficient. The following supplements and exciting new digital products are offered in conjunction with the text.

MindTap

MindTap for *Business Law: An Accelerated Course,* Fourteenth Edition, is a fully online, highly personalized learning experience built upon Cengage Learning content. MindTap combines student learning tools—such as readings, multimedia, activities, and assessments from CengageNOW—into a singular Learning Path that intuitively guides students through their course.

Instructors can personalize the experience by customizing authoritative Cengage Learning content and learning tools. MindTap offers instructors the ability to add their own content in the Learning Path with apps that integrate into the MindTap framework seamlessly with Learning Management Systems (LMS).

MindTap includes:

- **An Interactive book with Whiteboard Videos and Interactive Cases.**
- **Automatically graded homework** with the following consistent question types:

  - **Worksheets**—Interactive Worksheets prepare students for class by ensuring reading and comprehension.
  - **Video Activities**—Real-world video exercises make business law engaging and relevant.
  - **Brief Hypotheticals**—These applications provide students practice in spotting the issue and applying the law in the context of a short, factual scenario.

- **Case Problem Analyses**—These promote deeper critical thinking and legal reasoning by guiding students step-by-step through a case problem and then adding in a critical thinking section based on "What If the Facts Were Different?" These now include a third section, a writing component, which requires students to demonstrate their ability to forecast the legal implications of real-world business scenarios.
- **Personalized Student Plan with multimedia study tools and videos.**
- **New Adaptive Test Prep** helps students study for exams.
- **Test Bank.**
- **Reporting and Assessment options.**

By using the MindTap system, students can complete the assignments online and can receive instant feedback on their answers. Instructors can utilize Mind-Tap to upload their course syllabi, create and customize homework assignments, and keep track of their students' progress. By hiding, rearranging, or adding content, instructors control what students see and when they see it to match the Learning Path to their course syllabus exactly. Instructors can also communicate with their students about assignments and due dates, and create reports summarizing the data for an individual student or for the whole class.

Cengage Learning Testing Powered by Cognero

Cengage Learning Testing Powered by Cognero is a flexible, online system that allows you to do the following:

- Author, edit, and manage *Test Bank* content from multiple Cengage Learning solutions.
- Create multiple test versions in an instant.
- Deliver tests from your LMS, your classroom, or wherever you want.

Start Right Away! *Cengage Learning Testing Powered by Cognero* works on any operating system or browser.

- No special installs or downloads are needed.
- Create tests from school, home, the coffee shop—anywhere with Internet access.

What Will You Find?

- *Simplicity at every step.* A desktop-inspired interface features drop-down menus and familiar intuitive tools that take you through content creation and management with ease.
- *Full-featured test generator.* Create ideal assessments with your choice of fifteen question types—including true/false, multiple choice, opinion scale/Likert, and essay). Multi-language support, an equation editor, and unlimited metadata help ensure your tests are complete and compliant.
- *Cross-compatible capability.* Import and export content to and from other systems.

Instructor's Companion Web Site

The Web site for the Fourteenth Edition of *Business Law: An Accelerated Course* can be found by going to www.cengagebrain.com and entering ISBN 9781305967298. The Instructor's Companion Web Site contains the following supplements:

- ***Instructor's Manual.*** Includes sections entitled "Additional Cases Addressing This Issue" at the end of selected case synopses.
- ***Solutions Manual.*** Provides answers to all questions presented in the text, including the questions in each case and feature, the *Issue Spotters,* the *Business Scenarios,* and the *Business Case Problems.*
- ***Test Bank.*** A comprehensive test bank that contains multiple-choice, true/false, and short essay questions.
- ***Case-Problem Cases.***
- ***Case Printouts.***
- ***PowerPoint Slides.***
- ***Lecture Outlines.***

For Users of the Thirteenth Edition

First of all, I want to thank you for helping make *Business Law* the best-selling business law text in America today. Second, I want to make you aware of the numerous additions and changes that I have made in this edition—many in response to comments from reviewers.

Every chapter of the Fourteenth Edition has been revised as necessary to incorporate new developments in the law or to streamline the presentations. Other major changes and additions for this edition include the following:

- Chapter 2 (Business and the Constitution)—The chapter has been revised and updated to be more business oriented. It has two new cases, four new *Cases in Point,* a new exhibit, and three new case problems. A *Managerial Strategy* feature on marriage equality and the constitution discusses United States Supreme Court decisions on this issue.

- Chapter 5 (Criminal Law and Cyber Crime)—This chapter includes three new cases, five new *Cases in Point,* three new examples, and four new case problems. A new *Managerial Strategy* feature discusses the criminalization of American business.

- Chapter 6 (Business Ethics)—This chapter contains two new cases, two new *Issue Spotters,* three new *Cases in Point* (including a case involving Tom Brady's suspension from the NFL as a result of "deflategate"), and three new case problems. The chapter includes a section on business ethics and social media, and discusses stakeholders and corporate social responsibility. The chapter also provides step-by-step guidance on making ethical business decisions and includes materials on global business ethics. A new *Digital Update* feature examines whether employees should have the right to disconnect from their electronic devices after work hours.

- Chapters 7 through 12 (the Contracts unit)—In this unit, I have added twelve new cases (including a *Spotlight Case* and several *Case Analysis* cases), twenty-four new *Cases in Point,* nine new *Examples,* and nineteen new case problems. I have also added new exhibits, graphic concept summaries, numbered lists, a new *Reviewing* feature, and a new *Digital Update* feature on when changes in social media terms of service can constitute a breach of contract. These updates clarify and enhance the already superb contract law coverage.

- Chapter 13 (Intellectual Property Rights)—The materials on intellectual property rights have been thoroughly revised and updated to reflect the most current laws and trends. The 2016 case involves the Hustler Club and a trademark infringement claim between brothers. A *Digital Update* feature examines the problem of patent trolls. There are

eleven new *Cases in Point,* including cases involving FedEx's color and logo, Google's digitalization of books, and how the Sherlock Holmes copyright fell into the public domain.

- Chapter 14 (Internet Law, Social Media, and Privacy)—This chapter, which was new to the last edition and covers legal issues that are unique to the Internet, has been thoroughly revised and updated for the Fourteenth Edition. It includes a new section on cyberstalking, two new cases, and a new *Digital Update* feature on whether employers can monitor employees' social media use.

- Chapter 15 (The Formation of Sales and Lease Contracts) and Chapter 16 (Performance, Breach, and Warranties in Sales and Lease Contracts)— I have streamlined and simplified the coverage of the Uniform Commercial Code and added three new cases. I have added twelve new *Cases in Point* and three new *Examples* in these chapters to increase student comprehension, as well as six new case problems.

- Chapter 17 (Agency Relationships in Business)— This chapter has been thoroughly updated to reflect the realities of the gig economy in which many people are working as independent contractors. A new *Ethics Today* feature continues that emphasis with a discussion of whether Uber and Lyft drivers should be considered employees rather than independent contractors. There are six new *Cases in Point,* five new *Examples,* and five new case problems to help students comprehend the important issues and liability in agency relationships.

- Chapter 18 (Small Businesses and Limited Liability Companies)—This chapter has been revised and updated to improve flow and clarity. I provide more practical information, six new *Cases in Point,* and two new *Examples.* All three cases presented are new and there is a new exhibit illustrating LLC management options. There is also a new *Digital Update* feature.

- Chapter 19 (Corporations)—There are two new cases, six new *Cases in Point* and two new *Examples.* A *Global Insight* feature examines whether cloud computing has a nationality. I also discuss crowdfunding and venture capital and have added five new case problems as well.

Acknowledgments for Previous Editions

Since this project began many years ago, a sizable number of business law professors and others have helped us in revising the book, including the following:

Jeffrey E. Allen
University of Miami

Judith Anshin
Sacramento City College

Thomas M. Apke
California State University, Fullerton

Raymond August
Washington State University

William Auslen
San Francisco City College

Mary B. Bader
Moorhead State University

Frank Bagan
County College of Morris

John J. Balek
Morton College, Illinois

Michael G. Barth
University of Phoenix

David L. Baumer
North Carolina State University

Barbara E. Behr
Bloomsburg University of Pennsylvania

Robert B. Bennett, Jr.
Butler University

Robert C. Bird
University of Connecticut

Heidi Boerstler
University of Colorado at Denver

Maria Kathleen Boss
California State University, Los Angeles

Lawrence J. Bradley
University of Notre Dame

Dean Bredeson
University of Texas at Austin

Kylar William Broadus, Esq.
Lincoln University in Missouri

Doug Brown
Montana State University

Kristi K. Brown
University of Texas at Austin

Elizabeth K. Brunn, Esq.
University of Baltimore;
University of Maryland
University College

William J. Burke
University of Massachusetts, Lowell

Kenneth Burns
University of Miami

Daniel R. Cahoy
Pennsylvania State University

Rita Cain
University of Missouri—Kansas City

Jeanne A. Calderon
New York University

Joseph E. Cantrell
DeAnza College, California

Donald Cantwell
University of Texas at Arlington

Arthur J. Casey
San Jose State University, College
of Business, Organization and
Management

Thomas D. Cavenagh
North Central College—Naperville,
Illinois

Robert Chatov
State University of New York, Buffalo

Corey Ciocchetti
University of Denver

Nanette C. Clinch
San Jose State University, California

Robert J. Cox
Salt Lake Community College

Thomas Crane
University of Miami

Angela Crossin
Purdue University, Calumet

Kenneth S. Culott
University of Texas at Austin

Larry R. Curtis
Iowa State University

Richard Dalebout
Brigham Young University

William H. Daughtrey, Jr.
Virginia Commonwealth University

Michael DeAngelis
University of Rhode Island

James Doering
University of Wisconsin, Green Bay

John V. Dowdy
University of Texas at Arlington

Michele A. Dunkerley
University of Texas at Austin

Julia M. Dunlap, Esq.
University of California, San Diego

Paul Dusseault
Herkimer Community
College (SUNY)

Maria Elena Ellison
Florida Atlantic University

Nena Ellison
Florida Atlantic University

O. E. Elmore
Texas A&M University

Robert J. Enders
California State Polytechnic
University, Pomona

Michael Engber
Ball State University

David A. Escamilla
University of Texas at Austin

Denise M. Farag
Linfield College

James S. Fargason
Louisiana State University

Frank S. Forbes
University of Nebraska at Omaha

Joe W. Fowler
Oklahoma State University

Stanley G. Freeman
University of South Carolina

Joan Gabel
Florida State University

Christ Gaetanos
State University of New York, Fredonia

Chester S. Galloway
Auburn University

Bob Garrett
American River College, California

Gary L. Giese
University of Colorado at Denver

Thomas Gossman
Western Michigan University

John D. Grigsby
Pennsylvania College of Technology

Dr. J. Keaton Grubbs
Stephen F. Austin State University

Patrick O. Gudridge
University of Miami School of Law

Paul Guymon
William Rainey Harper College

Jacqueline Hagerott
Franklin University

James M. Haine
University of Wisconsin, Stevens Point

Gerard Halpern
University of Arkansas

Christopher L. Hamilton
Golden West College, California

JoAnn W. Hammer
University of Texas at Austin

Charles Hartman
Wright State University, Ohio

Richard A. Hausler
University of Miami School of Law

Harry E. Hicks
Butler University, Indianapolis

Janine S. Hiller
Virginia Polytechnic Institute and State University

Rebecca L. Hillyer
Chemeketa Community College

E. Clayton Hipp, Jr.
Clemson University

Anthony H. Holliday, Jr.
Howard University

Telford Hollman
University of Northern Iowa

June A. Horrigan
California State University, Sacramento

John P. Huggard
North Carolina State University

Terry Hutchins
Pembroke State University, North Carolina

Robert Jesperson
University of Houston

Debra M. Johnson
Montana State University—Billings

Bryce J. Jones
Northeast Missouri State University

Margaret Jones
Southwest Missouri State College

Peter A. Karl III
SUNY Institute of Technology at Utica

Jack E. Karns
East Carolina University

Anne E. Kastle
Edmonds Community College

Tamra Kempf
University of Miami

Judith Kenney
University of Miami

Barbara Kincaid
Southern Methodist University

Carey Kirk
University of Northern Iowa

Nancy P. Klintworth
University of Central Florida

Kurtis P. Klumb
University of Wisconsin at Milwaukee

Kathleen M. Knutson
College of St. Catherine, St. Paul, Minnesota

Lisa Quinn Knych
Syracuse University, Whitman School of Management

Peter Kwiatkowski, Esq.
Baldwin Wallace University

Meg Costello Lambert
Oakland Community College—Auburn Hills Campus

Vonda M. Laughlin
Carson-Newman College

M. Alan Lawson
Mt. San Antonio College

Leslie E. Lenn
St. Edwards University

Susan Liebeler
Loyola University

Robert B. Long
Oakland Community College

Stuart MacDonald
University of Central Oklahoma

Thomas E. Maher
California State University, Fullerton

Sal Marchionna
Triton College, Illinois

Gene A. Marsh
University of Alabama

Michael Martin, J.D., M.B.A., LL.M.
University of Northern Colorado, Monfort College of Business

Karen Kay Matson
University of Texas at Austin

Woodrow J. Maxwell
Hudson Valley Community College, New York

Bruce E. May
University of South Dakota

Diane May
Winona State University, Minnesota

Gail McCracken
University of Michigan, Dearborn

John W. McGee
Southwest Texas State University

Cotton Meagher
University of Nevada at Las Vegas

Christopher Meakin
University of Texas at Austin

Roger E. Meiners
University of Texas at Arlington

Gerald S. Meisel
*Bergen Community College,
New Jersey*

Jennifer Merton, J.D.
University of Massachusetts at Amherst

Richard Mills
Cypress College

David Minars
City University of New York, Brooklyn

Leo Moersen
The George Washington University

Alan Moggio
Illinois Central College

Violet E. Molnar
Riverside City College

James E. Moon
Meyer, Johnson & Moon, Minneapolis

Melinda Ann Mora
University of Texas at Austin

Bob Morgan
Eastern Michigan University

Barry S. Morinaka
Baker College—Michigan

Melanie Morris
Raritan Valley Community College

Joan Ann Mrava
Los Angeles Southwest College

Dwight D. Murphey
Wichita State University

Daniel E. Murray
University of Miami School of Law

Paula C. Murray
University of Texas

Gregory J. Naples
Marquette University

George A. Nation III
Lehigh University

Caleb L. Nichols
Western Connecticut State University

John M. Norwood
University of Arkansas

Jamie O'Brien
University of Notre Dame

Dr. Kelly E. O'Donnell, J.C.D
*California Lutheran University,
Thousand Oaks, California*

Michael J. O'Hara
University of Nebraska at Omaha

Rick F. Orsinger
College of DuPage, Illinois

Daniel J. O'Shea
Hillsborough Community College

Thomas L. Palmer
Northern Arizona University

Charles M. Patten
University of Wisconsin, Oshkosh

Patricia Pattison
Texas State University, San Marcos

Peyton J. Paxson
University of Texas at Austin

Carlton Perkins
Texas Southern University

Darren A. Prum
The Florida State University

Ralph L. Quinones
University of Wisconsin, Oshkosh

Carol D. Rasnic
Virginia Commonwealth University

Marvin H. Robertson
Harding University

Bert K. Robinson
Kennesaw State University

Norberto Ruiz
Chabot College

Gary K. Sambol
Rutgers State University

Rudy Sandoval
University of Texas, San Antonio

Sidney S. Sappington
York College of Pennsylvania

Martha Sartoris
North Hennepin Community College

Barbara P. Scheller
Temple University

S. Alan Schlact
Kennesaw State University, Georgia

Lorne H. Seidman
University of Nevada at Las Vegas

Ira Selkowitz
University of Colorado at Denver

Roscoe B. Shain
Austin Peay University

Bennett D. Shulman
Lansing Community College, Michigan

S. Jay Sklar
Temple University

Dana Blair Smith
University of Texas at Austin

Michael Smydra
Oakland Community College—Royal Oak

Arthur Southwick
University of Michigan

Sylvia A. Spade
University of Texas at Austin

John A. Sparks
Grove City College, Pennsylvania

Robert D. Sprague
University of Wyoming

Elisabeth Sperow
*California Polytechnic University, San
Luis Obispo*

Brenda Steuer
North Harris College, Houston

Craig Stilwell
Michigan State University

Irwin Stotsky
University of Miami School of Law

Larry Strate
University of Nevada at Las Vegas

Charles R. B. Stowe
Sam Houston State University

Raymond Mason Taylor
North Carolina State University

Thomas F. Taylor
Campbell University

Ray Teske
University of Texas at San Antonio

H. Allan Tolbert
Central Texas College

Jesse C. Trentadue
University of North Dakota

Edwin Tucker
University of Connecticut

Gary Victor
Eastern Michigan University

William H. Volz
Wayne State University

David Vyncke
Scott Community College, Iowa

William H. Walker,
*Indiana University–Purdue University,
Fort Wayne*

Diana Walsh
County College of Morris

Robert J. Walter
University of Texas at El Paso

Gary Watson
California State University, Los Angeles

Katherine Hannan Wears, J.D.
Clarkson University School of Business

John L. Weimer
Nicholls State University, Louisiana

Marshall Wilkerson
University of Texas at Austin

Melanie Stallings Williams
California State University—Northridge

Arthur D. Wolfe
Michigan State University

Elizabeth A. Wolfe
University of Texas at Austin

Daniel R. Wrentmore
Santa Barbara City College

Eric D. Yordy
Northern Arizona University

Norman Gregory Young
*California State Polytechnic University,
Pomona*

Ronald C. Young
*Kalamazoo Valley Community College,
Michigan*

Bob Zaffram
*Erie Community College, Buffalo,
New York*

As in all past editions, I owe a debt of extreme gratitude to the numerous individuals who worked directly with me or at Cengage Learning. In particular, I wish to thank Vicky True-Baker, senior product manager; Suzanne Wilder, managing content developer; Sarah Huber, content developer; and Ann Borman, senior content project manager. I also thank Katie Jergens in marketing and Michelle Kunkler, art director. I am indebted as well to the staff at Lachina, the compositor, for accurately generating pages for this text and making it possible for me to meet an ambitious printing schedule.

I especially wish to thank Katherine Marie Silsbee for her management of the entire project, as well as for the application of her superb research and editorial skills. I also wish to thank William Eric Hollowell, who co-authored the *Instructor's Manual* and the *Test Bank,* for his excellent research efforts. I was fortunate enough to have the copyediting of Beverly Peavler and the proofreading services of Jeanne Yost. I am grateful for the efforts of Vickie Reierson and Roxanna Lee for their proofreading and other assistance, which helped to ensure an error-free text. Finally, I thank Suzanne Jasin of K & M Consulting for her many special efforts on this project.

Through the years, I have enjoyed an ongoing correspondence with many of you who have found points on which you wish to comment. I continue to welcome all comments and promise to respond promptly. By incorporating your ideas, I can continue to write a business law text that is best for you and best for your students.

R.L.M.

To Stephane Booz,

*Thanks for always
encouraging me
to do better.*

R.L.M.

The Legal Environment of Business

1. Law and Legal Reasoning

2. Business and the Constitution

3. Courts and Alternative Dispute Resolution

4. Tort Law

5. Criminal Law and Cyber Crime

6. Business Ethics

CHAPTER 1

Law and Legal Reasoning

One of the most important functions of law in any society is to provide stability, predictability, and continuity so that people can know how to order their affairs. If any society is to survive, its citizens must be able to determine what is legally right and legally wrong. They must know what sanctions will be imposed on them if they commit wrongful acts. If they suffer harm as a result of others' wrongful acts, they must know how they can seek compensation. By setting forth the rights, obligations, and privileges of citizens, the law enables individuals to go about their business with confidence and a certain degree of predictability.

Although law has various definitions, they all are based on the general observation that **law** consists of *enforceable rules governing relationships among individuals and between individuals and their society*. These "enforceable rules" may consist of unwritten principles of behavior established by a nomadic tribe. They may be set forth in a law code, such as the Code of Hammurabi in ancient Babylon (c. 1780 B.C.E.) or the law code of one of today's European nations. They may consist of written laws and court decisions created by modern legislative and judicial bodies, as in the United States. Regardless of how such rules are created, they all have one thing in common: they establish rights, duties, and privileges that are consistent with the values and beliefs of their society or its ruling group.

In this introductory chapter, we first look at an important question for any student reading this text: How does the legal environment affect business decision making? We next describe the major sources of American law, the common law tradition, and some basic schools of legal thought. We conclude the chapter with sections offering practical guidance on several topics, including how to find the sources of law discussed in this chapter (and referred to throughout the text) and how to read and understand court opinions.

1–1 Business Activities and the Legal Environment

Laws and government regulations affect almost all business activities—from hiring and firing decisions to workplace safety, the manufacturing and marketing of products, business financing, and more. To make good business decisions, a basic knowledge of the laws and regulations governing these activities is beneficial—if not essential.

Realize also that in today's business world, a knowledge of "black-letter" law and what conduct can lead to legal **liability** is not enough. Businesspersons must develop critical thinking and legal reasoning skills so that they can evaluate how various laws might apply to a given situation and determine the best course of action. Businesspersons are also expected to make ethical decisions. Thus, the study of business law necessarily involves an ethical dimension.

1–1a Many Different Laws May Affect a Single Business Decision

As you will note, each chapter in this text covers specific areas of the law and shows how the legal rules in each area affect business activities. Although compartmentalizing the law in this fashion promotes conceptual clarity, it does not indicate the extent to which a number of different laws may apply to just one decision. Exhibit 1–1 illustrates the various areas of the law that may influence business decision making.

■ **EXAMPLE 1.1** When Mark Zuckerberg started Facebook as a Harvard student, he probably did not imagine all the legal challenges his company would face as a result of his business decisions.

- Shortly after Facebook was launched, others claimed that Zuckerberg had stolen their ideas for a social networking site. Their claims involved alleged theft of intellectual property, fraudulent misrepresentation, and

EXHIBIT 1–1   Areas of the Law That Can Affect Business Decision Making

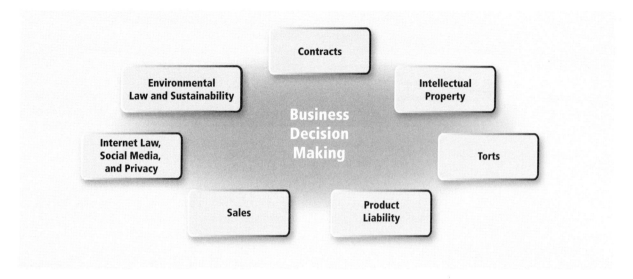

violations of partnership law and securities law. Facebook ultimately paid $65 million to settle those claims out of court.

- Facebook has been sued repeatedly for violating users' privacy (and federal laws) by tracking their Web site usage and by scanning private messages for purposes of data mining and user profiling. A class-action suit filed in Europe alleges that Facebook's data-use policies violate the law of the European Union. Facebook might have to pay millions in damages in this case.

- Facebook's business decisions have also come under scrutiny by federal regulators, such as the Federal Trade Commission (FTC). The company settled a complaint filed by the FTC alleging that Facebook had failed to keep "friends" lists and other user information private. ∎

1–1b Ethics and Business Decision Making

Merely knowing the areas of law that may affect a business decision is not sufficient in today's business world. Today, business decision makers need to consider not just whether a decision is legal, but also whether it is ethical.

Ethics generally is defined as the principles governing what constitutes right or wrong behavior. Often, as in several of the claims against Facebook discussed above, disputes arise in business because one party feels that he or she has been treated unfairly. Thus, the underlying

reason for bringing some lawsuits is a breach of ethical duties (such as when a partner or employee attempts to secretly take advantage of a business opportunity).

Throughout this text, you will learn about the relationship between the law and ethics, as well as about some of the types of ethical questions that arise in business. For instance, we often include *Ethical Questions* within the *Critical Thinking* sections of many of the cases presented in this text. In addition, *Ethics Today* features, which focus on ethical considerations in today's business climate, appear in selected chapters, including this chapter. Lastly, *A Question of Ethics* case problem is included at the end of every chapter to introduce you to the ethical aspects of specific cases involving real-life situations.

1–2 Sources of American Law

American law has numerous sources. Often, these sources of law are classified as either primary or secondary.

Primary sources of law, or sources that establish the law, include the following:

1. The U.S. Constitution and the constitutions of the various states.
2. Statutory law—including laws passed by Congress, state legislatures, or local governing bodies.
3. Regulations created by administrative agencies, such as the Federal Trade Commission.
4. Case law and common law doctrines.

We describe each of these important sources of law in the following pages.

Secondary sources of law are books and articles that summarize and clarify the primary sources of law. Examples include legal encyclopedias, treatises, articles in law reviews, and compilations of law, such as the *Restatements of the Law* (which will be discussed later). Courts often refer to secondary sources of law for guidance in interpreting and applying the primary sources of law discussed here.

1–2a Constitutional Law

The federal government and the states have separate written constitutions that set forth the general organization, powers, and limits of their respective governments. **Constitutional law** is the law as expressed in these constitutions.

According to Article VI of the U.S. Constitution, the Constitution is the supreme law of the land. As such, it is the basis of all law in the United States. A law in violation of the Constitution, if challenged, will be declared unconstitutional and will not be enforced, no matter what its source.

The Tenth Amendment to the U.S. Constitution reserves to the states all powers not granted to the federal government. Each state in the union has its own constitution. Unless it conflicts with the U.S. Constitution or a federal law, a state constitution is supreme within the state's borders.

1–2b Statutory Law

Laws enacted by legislative bodies at any level of government, such as statutes passed by Congress or by state legislatures, make up the body of law known as **statutory law.** When a legislature passes a statute, that statute ultimately is included in the federal code of laws or the relevant state code of laws.

Statutory law also includes local **ordinances**—regulations passed by municipal or county governing units to deal with matters not covered by federal or state law. Ordinances commonly have to do with city or county land use (zoning ordinances), building and safety codes, and other matters affecting the local community.

A federal statute, of course, applies to all states. A state statute, in contrast, applies only within the state's borders. State laws thus may vary from state to state. No federal statute may violate the U.S. Constitution, and no state statute or local ordinance may violate the U.S. Constitution or the relevant state constitution.

Uniform Laws During the 1800s, the differences among state laws frequently created difficulties for businesspersons conducting trade and commerce among the states. To counter these problems, a group of legal scholars and lawyers formed the National Conference of Commissioners on Uniform State Laws, or NCCUSL (**www.uniformlaws.org**), in 1892. The NCCUSL still exists today. Its object is to draft **uniform laws** (model statutes) for the states to consider adopting.

Each state has the option of adopting or rejecting a uniform law. *Only if a state legislature adopts a uniform law does that law become part of the statutory law of that state.* Note that a state legislature may adopt all or part of a uniform law as it is written, or the legislature may rewrite the law however the legislature wishes. Hence, even though many states may have adopted a uniform law, those states' laws may not be entirely "uniform."

The earliest uniform law, the Uniform Negotiable Instruments Law, was completed by 1896 and adopted in every state by the 1920s (although not all states used exactly the same wording). Over the following decades, other acts were drawn up in a similar manner. In all, more than two hundred uniform acts have been issued by the NCCUSL since its inception. The most ambitious uniform act of all, however, was the Uniform Commercial Code.

The Uniform Commercial Code One of the most important uniform acts is the Uniform Commercial Code (UCC), which was created through the joint efforts of the NCCUSL and the American Law Institute.[1] The UCC was first issued in 1952 and has been adopted in all fifty states,[2] the District of Columbia, and the Virgin Islands.

The UCC facilitates commerce among the states by providing a uniform, yet flexible, set of rules governing commercial transactions. Because of its importance in the area of commercial law, we will cite the UCC in this text. We also present Article 2 of the UCC in Appendix A. From time to time, the NCCUSL revises the articles contained in the UCC and submits the revised versions to the states for adoption.

1–2c Administrative Law

Another important source of American law is **administrative law,** which consists of the rules, orders, and decisions of administrative agencies. An **administrative agency** is a federal, state, or local government agency established to perform a specific function. Administrative law and procedures constitute a dominant element in the regulatory environment of business.

---

1. This institute was formed in the 1920s and consists of practicing attorneys, legal scholars, and judges.
2. Louisiana has not adopted Articles 2 and 2A (covering contracts for the sale and lease of goods), however.

Rules issued by various administrative agencies now affect almost every aspect of a business's operations. Regulations govern a business's capital structure and financing, its hiring and firing procedures, its relations with employees and unions, and the way it manufactures and markets its products. Regulations enacted to protect the environment also often play a significant role in business operations.

Federal Agencies At the national level, the cabinet departments of the executive branch include numerous **executive agencies.** The U.S. Food and Drug Administration, for instance, is an agency within the U.S. Department of Health and Human Services. Executive agencies are subject to the authority of the president, who has the power to appoint and remove their officers.

There are also major **independent regulatory agencies** at the federal level, such as the Federal Trade Commission, the Securities and Exchange Commission, and the Federal Communications Commission. The president's power is less pronounced in regard to independent agencies, whose officers serve for fixed terms and cannot be removed without just cause.

State and Local Agencies There are administrative agencies at the state and local levels as well. Commonly, a state agency (such as a state pollution-control agency) is created as a parallel to a federal agency (such as the Environmental Protection Agency). Just as federal statutes take precedence over conflicting state statutes, federal agency regulations take precedence over conflicting state regulations.

1–2d Case Law and Common Law Doctrines

The rules of law announced in court decisions constitute another basic source of American law. These rules include interpretations of constitutional provisions, of statutes enacted by legislatures, and of regulations created by administrative agencies.

Today, this body of judge-made law is referred to as **case law.** Case law—the doctrines and principles announced in cases—governs all areas not covered by statutory law or administrative law and is part of our common law tradition. We look at the origins and characteristics of the common law tradition in some detail in the pages that follow.

See Concept Summary 1.1 for a review of the sources of American law.

Concept Summary 1.1

Sources of American Law

Constitutional Law	• Law as expressed in the U.S. Constitution or state constitutions. • The U.S. Constitution is the supreme law of the land. • State constitutions are supreme within state borders to the extent that they do not conflict with the U.S. Constitution.
Statutory Law	• Statutes (including uniform laws) and ordinances enacted by federal, state, and local legislatures. • Federal statutes may not violate the U.S. Constitution. • State statutes and local ordinances may not violate the U.S. Constitution or the relevant state constitution.
Administrative Law	• The rules, orders, and decisions of federal, state, and local administrative agencies.
Case Law and Common Law Doctrines	• Judge-made law, including interpretations of constitutional provisions, of statutes enacted by legislatures, and of regulations created by administrative agencies.

1–3 The Common Law Tradition

Because of our colonial heritage, much of American law is based on the English legal system. Knowledge of this tradition is crucial to understanding our legal system today because judges in the United States still apply common law principles when deciding cases.

1–3a Early English Courts

After the Normans conquered England in 1066, William the Conqueror and his successors began the process of unifying the country under their rule. One of the means they used to do this was the establishment of the king's courts, or *curiae regis.*

Before the Norman Conquest, disputes had been settled according to the local legal customs and traditions in various regions of the country. The king's courts sought to establish a uniform set of customs for the country as a whole. What evolved in these courts was the beginning of the **common law**—a body of general rules that applied throughout the entire English realm. Eventually, the common law tradition became part of the heritage of all nations that were once British colonies, including the United States.

Courts of Law and Remedies at Law The early English king's courts could grant only very limited kinds of **remedies** (the legal means to enforce a right or redress a wrong). If one person wronged another in some way, the king's courts could award as compensation one or more of the following: (1) land, (2) items of value, or (3) money.

The courts that awarded this compensation became known as **courts of law,** and the three remedies were called **remedies at law.** (Today, the remedy at law normally takes the form of monetary **damages**—an amount given to a party whose legal interests have been injured.) This system made the procedure for settling disputes more uniform. When a complaining party wanted a remedy other than economic compensation, however, the courts of law could do nothing, so "no remedy, no right."

Courts of Equity When individuals could not obtain an adequate remedy in a court of law, they petitioned the king for relief. Most of these petitions were decided by an adviser to the king, called a *chancellor,* who had the power to grant new and unique remedies. Eventually, formal chancery courts, or **courts of equity,** were established. *Equity* is a branch of law—founded on notions of justice and fair dealing—that seeks to supply a remedy when no adequate remedy at law is available.

Remedies in Equity The remedies granted by the equity courts became known as **remedies in equity,** or equitable remedies. These remedies include specific performance, injunction, and rescission. *Specific performance* involves ordering a party to perform an agreement as promised. An *injunction* is an order to a party to cease engaging in a specific activity or to undo some wrong or injury. *Rescission* is the cancellation of a contractual obligation. We will discuss these and other equitable remedies in more detail in later chapters.

As a general rule, today's courts, like the early English courts, will not grant equitable remedies unless the remedy at law—monetary damages—is inadequate. ■ **EXAMPLE 1.2** Ted forms a contract (a legally binding agreement) to purchase a parcel of land that he thinks will be perfect for his future home. The seller **breaches** (fails to fulfill) this agreement. Ted could sue the seller for the return of any deposits or down payment he might have made on the land, but this is not the remedy he really wants. What Ted wants is to have a court order the seller to perform the contract. In other words, Ted will seek the equitable remedy of specific performance because monetary damages are inadequate in this situation. ■

Equitable Maxims In fashioning appropriate remedies, judges often were (and continue to be) guided by so-called **equitable maxims**—propositions or general statements of equitable rules. Exhibit 1–2 lists some important equitable maxims.

The last maxim listed in the exhibit—"Equity aids the vigilant, not those who rest on their rights"—merits special attention. It has become known as the equitable doctrine of **laches** (a term derived from the Latin *laxus,* meaning "lax" or "negligent"), and it can be used as a defense. A **defense** is an argument raised by the **defendant** (the party being sued) indicating why the **plaintiff** (the suing party) should not obtain the remedy sought. (Note that in equity proceedings, the party bringing a lawsuit is called the **petitioner,** and the party being sued is referred to as the **respondent.**)

The doctrine of laches arose to encourage people to bring lawsuits while the evidence was fresh. What constitutes a reasonable time, of course, varies according to the circumstances of the case. Time periods for different types of cases are now usually fixed by **statutes of limitations.** After the time allowed under a statute of limitations has expired, no action (lawsuit) can be brought, no matter how strong the case was originally.

EXHIBIT 1–2 Equitable Maxims

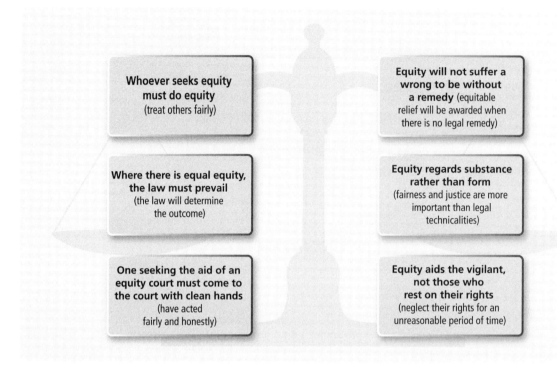

Whoever seeks equity
must do equity
(treat others fairly)

Equity will not suffer a
wrong to be without
a remedy (equitable
relief will be awarded when
there is no legal remedy)

Where there is equal equity,
the law must prevail
(the law will determine
the outcome)

Equity regards substance
rather than form
(fairness and justice are more
important than legal
technicalities)

One seeking the aid of an
equity court must come to
the court with clean hands
(have acted
fairly and honestly)

Equity aids the vigilant,
not those who
rest on their rights
(neglect their rights for an
unreasonable period of time)

1–3b Legal and Equitable Remedies Today

The establishment of courts of equity in medieval England resulted in two distinct court systems: courts of law and courts of equity. The courts had different sets of judges and granted different types of remedies. During the nineteenth century, however, most states in the United States adopted rules of procedure that resulted in the combining of courts of law and equity. A party now may request both legal and equitable remedies in the same action, and the trial court judge may grant either or both forms of relief.

The distinction between legal and equitable remedies remains relevant to students of business law, however, because these remedies differ. To seek the proper remedy for a wrong, you must know what remedies are available. Additionally, certain vestiges of the procedures used when there were separate courts of law and equity still exist. For instance, a party has the right to demand a jury trial in an action at law, but not in an action in equity. Exhibit 1–3 summarizes the procedural differences (applicable in most states) between an action at law and an action in equity.

1–3c The Doctrine of *Stare Decisis*

One of the unique features of the common law is that it is *judge-made* law. The body of principles and doctrines that form the common law emerged over time as judges decided legal controversies.

Case Precedents and Case Reporters When possible, judges attempted to be consistent and to base their decisions on the principles suggested by earlier cases. They sought to decide similar cases in a similar way, and they considered new cases with care because they knew that their decisions would make new law. Each interpretation became part of the law on the subject and thus served as a legal **precedent.** A precedent is a decision that furnishes an example or authority for deciding subsequent cases involving identical or similar legal principles or facts.

In the early years of the common law, there was no single place or publication where court opinions, or written decisions, could be found. By the fourteenth century, portions of the most important decisions from each year were being gathered together and recorded in *Year Books*, which became useful references for lawyers and judges. In the

EXHIBIT 1–3 Procedural Differences between Actions at Law and Actions in Equity

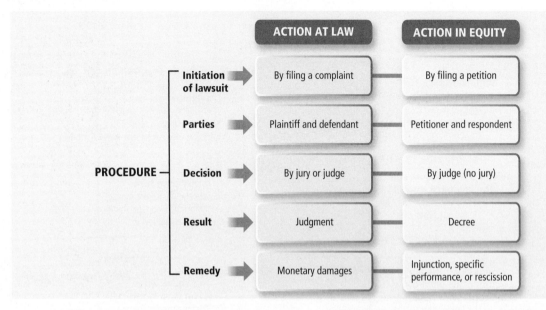

sixteenth century, the *Year Books* were discontinued, and other forms of case publication became available. Today, cases are published, or "reported," in volumes called **reporters,** or *reports*—and are also posted online. We describe today's case reporting system in detail later in this chapter.

Stare Decisis and the Common Law Tradition

The practice of deciding new cases with reference to former decisions, or precedents, became a cornerstone of the English and American judicial systems. The practice formed a doctrine known as ***stare decisis,***[3] a Latin phrase meaning "to stand on decided cases."

Under the doctrine of *stare decisis*, judges are obligated to follow the precedents established within their jurisdictions. The term *jurisdiction* refers to a geographic area in which a court or courts have the power to apply the law. Once a court has set forth a principle of law as being applicable to a certain set of facts, that court must apply the principle in future cases involving similar facts. Courts of lower rank (within the same jurisdiction) must do likewise. Thus, *stare decisis* has two aspects:

1. A court should not overturn its own precedents unless there is a compelling reason to do so.
2. Decisions made by a higher court are binding on lower courts.

Controlling Precedents Precedents that must be followed within a jurisdiction are called *controlling*

precedents. Controlling precedents are a type of binding authority. A **binding authority** is any source of law that a court must follow when deciding a case. Binding authorities include constitutions, statutes, and regulations that govern the issue being decided, as well as court decisions that are controlling precedents within the jurisdiction. United States Supreme Court case decisions, no matter how old, remain controlling until they are overruled by a subsequent decision of the Supreme Court or changed by further legislation or a constitutional amendment.

Stare Decisis and Legal Stability The doctrine of *stare decisis* helps the courts to be more efficient because, if other courts have analyzed a similar case, their legal reasoning and opinions can serve as guides. *Stare decisis* also makes the law more stable and predictable. If the law on a subject is well settled, someone bringing a case can usually rely on the court to rule based on what the law has been in the past. See this chapter's *Ethics Today* feature for a discussion of how courts often defer to case precedent even when they disagree with the reasoning in the case.

Although courts are obligated to follow precedents, sometimes a court will depart from the rule of precedent if it decides that the precedent should no longer be followed. If a court decides that a ruling precedent is simply incorrect or that technological or social changes have rendered the precedent inapplicable, the court might rule contrary to the precedent. Cases that overturn precedent often receive a great deal of publicity.

■ **CASE IN POINT 1.3** The United States Supreme Court expressly overturned precedent in the case of

---

3. Pronounced *ster*-ay dih-*si*-ses.

ETHICS TODAY · *Stare Decisis* versus Spider-Man

Supreme Court Justice Elena Kagan, in a recent decision involving Marvel Comics' Spider-Man, ruled that, "What we can decide, we can undecide. But *stare decisis* teaches that we should exercise that authority sparingly." Citing a Spider-Man comic book, she went on to say that "in this world, with great power there must also come—great responsibility."[a] In its decision in the case—*Kimble v. Marvel Entertainment, LLC*—the Supreme Court applied *stare decisis* and ruled against Stephen Kimble, the creator of a toy related to the Spider-Man figure.[b]

Can a Patent Involving Spider-Man Last Super Long?

A patent is an exclusive right granted to the creator of an invention. Under U.S. law, patent owners generally possess that right for twenty years. Patent holders can license the use of their patents as they see fit during that period. In other words, they can allow others (called *licensees*) to use their invention in return for a fee (called *royalties*).

More than fifty years ago, the Supreme Court ruled in its *Brulotte* decision that a licensee cannot be forced to pay royalties to a patent holder after the patent has expired.[c] So if a licensee signs a contract to continue to pay royalties after the patent has expired, the contract is invalid and thus unenforceable.

At issue in the *Kimble* case was a contract signed between Marvel Entertainment and Kimble, who had invented a toy made up of a glove equipped with a valve and a canister of pressurized foam. The patented toy allowed people to shoot fake webs intended to look like Spider-Man's. In 1990, Kimble tried to cut a deal with Marvel Entertainment concerning his toy, but he was unsuccessful. Then Marvel started selling its own version of the toy.

When Kimble sued Marvel for patent infringement, he won. The result was a settlement that involved a licensing agreement between Kimble and Marvel with a lump-sum payment plus a royalty to Kimble of 3 percent of all sales of the toy. The agreement did not specify an end date for royalty payments to Kimble, and Marvel later sued to have the payments stop after the patent expired, consistent with the Court's earlier *Brulotte* decision.

A majority of the Supreme Court justices agreed with Marvel. As Justice Kagan said in the opinion, "Patents endow their holders with certain super powers, but only for a limited time." The court further noted that the fifty-year-old *Brulotte* decision was perhaps based on what today is an outmoded understanding of economics. That decision, according to some, may even hinder competition and innovation. But "respecting *stare decisis* means sticking to some wrong decisions."

The Ethical Side

In a dissenting opinion, Supreme Court Justice Samuel A. Alito, Jr., said, "The decision interferes with the ability of parties to negotiate licensing agreements that reflect the true value of a patent, and it disrupts contractual expectations. *Stare decisis* does not require us to retain this baseless and damaging precedent. . . . *Stare decisis* is important to the rule of law, but so are correct judicial decisions."

In other words, *stare decisis* holds that courts should adhere to precedent in order to promote predictability and consistency. But in the business world, shouldn't parties to contracts be able to, for example, allow a patent licensee to make smaller royalty payments that exceed the life of the patent? Isn't that a way to reduce the yearly costs to the licensee? After all, the licensee may be cash-strapped in its initial use of the patent. Shouldn't the parties to a contract be the ones to decide how long the contract should last?

Critical Thinking *When is the Supreme Court justified in not following the doctrine of stare decisis?*

a. "Spider-Man," *Amazing Fantasy* No. 15 (1962), p. 13.
b. 576 U.S. ___, 135 S.Ct. 2401, 192 L.Ed.2d 463 (2015).
c. *Brulotte v. Thys Co.*, 379 U.S. 29, 85 S.Ct. 176 (1964).

Brown v. Board of Education of Topeka.[4] The Court concluded that separate educational facilities for whites and blacks, which it had previously upheld as constitutional,[5] were inherently unequal. The Supreme Court's departure from precedent in this case received a tremendous amount of publicity as people began to realize the ramifications of this change in the law. ■

Note that a lower court will sometimes avoid applying a precedent set by a higher court in its jurisdiction by

4. 347 U.S. 483, 74 S.Ct. 686, 98 L.Ed. 873 (1954).
5. See *Plessy v. Ferguson*, 163 U.S. 537, 16 S.Ct. 1138, 41 L.Ed. 256 (1896).

distinguishing the two cases based on their facts. When this happens, the lower court's ruling stands unless it is appealed to a higher court and that court overturns the decision.

When There Is No Precedent Occasionally, courts must decide cases for which no precedents exist, called *cases of first impression*. For instance, as you will read throughout this text, the Internet and certain other technologies have presented many new and challenging issues for the courts to decide.

■ **EXAMPLE 1.4** Google Glass is a Bluetooth-enabled, hands-free, wearable computer. A person using Google Glass can take photos and videos, surf the Internet, and do other things through voice commands. Many people expressed concerns about this new technology. Privacy advocates claimed that it is much easier to secretly film or photograph others with wearable video technology than with a camera or a smartphone. Indeed, numerous bars and restaurants, among others, banned the use of Google Glass to protect their patrons' privacy. Police officers were concerned about driver safety. A California woman was ticketed for wearing Google Glass while driving. But the court dismissed this case of first impression because it was not clear whether the device had been in operation at the time of the offense. ■

In deciding cases of first impression, courts often look at **persuasive authorities**—legal authorities that a court may consult for guidance but that are not binding on the court. A court may consider precedents from other jurisdictions, for instance, although those precedents are not binding. A court may also consider legal principles and policies underlying previous court decisions or existing statutes. Additionally, a court might look at issues of fairness, social values and customs, and public policy (governmental policy based on widely held societal values). Today, federal courts can also look at unpublished opinions (those not intended for publication in a printed legal reporter) as sources of persuasive authority.[6]

1-3d *Stare Decisis* and Legal Reasoning

In deciding what law applies to a given dispute and then applying that law to the facts or circumstances of the case, judges rely on the process of **legal reasoning.** Through the use of legal reasoning, judges harmonize their decisions with those that have been made before, as the doctrine of *stare decisis* requires.

Students of business law and the legal environment also engage in legal reasoning. For instance, you may be asked to provide answers for some of the case problems that appear at the end of every chapter in this text. Each problem describes the facts of a particular dispute and the legal question at issue. If you are assigned a case problem, you will be asked to determine how a court would answer that question, and why. In other words, you will need to give legal reasons for whatever conclusion you reach. We look next at the basic steps involved in legal reasoning and then describe some forms of reasoning commonly used by the courts in making their decisions.

Basic Steps in Legal Reasoning At times, the legal arguments set forth in court opinions are relatively simple and brief. At other times, the arguments are complex and lengthy. Regardless of the length of a legal argument, however, the basic steps of the legal reasoning process remain the same. These steps, which you can also follow when analyzing cases and case problems, form what is commonly referred to as the *IRAC method* of legal reasoning. IRAC is an acronym formed from the first letters of the words *Issue, Rule, Application*, and *Conclusion*. To apply the IRAC method, you ask the following questions:

1. **Issue**—*What are the key facts and issues?* Suppose that a plaintiff comes before the court claiming *assault* (words or acts that wrongfully and intentionally make another person fearful of immediate physical harm). The plaintiff claims that the defendant threatened her while she was sleeping. Although the plaintiff was unaware that she was being threatened, her roommate heard the defendant make the threat. The legal issue is whether the defendant's action constitutes the tort of assault, given that the plaintiff was unaware of that action at the time it occurred. (A tort is a wrongful act. As you will see later, torts fall under the governance of civil law rather than criminal law.)

2. **Rule**—*What rule of law applies to the case?* A rule of law may be a rule stated by the courts in previous decisions, a state or federal statute, or a state or federal administrative agency regulation. In our hypothetical case, the plaintiff **alleges** (claims) that the defendant committed a tort. Therefore, the applicable law is the common law of torts—specifically, tort law governing assault. Case precedents involving similar facts and issues thus would be relevant. Often, more than one rule of law will be applicable to a case.

3. **Application**—*How does the rule of law apply to the particular facts and circumstances of this case?* This step is often the most difficult because each case presents a unique set of facts, circumstances, and parties.

---

6. See Rule 32.1 of the Federal Rules of Appellate Procedure.

Although cases may be similar, no two cases are ever identical in all respects. Normally, judges (and lawyers and law students) try to find **cases on point**—previously decided cases that are as similar as possible to the one under consideration.

4. **Conclusion**—*What conclusion should be drawn?* This step normally presents few problems. Usually, the conclusion is evident if the previous three steps have been followed carefully.

There Is No One "Right" Answer Many people believe that there is one "right" answer to every legal question. In most legal controversies, however, there is no single correct result. Good arguments can usually be made to support either side of a legal controversy. Quite often, a case does not involve a "good" person suing a "bad" person. In many cases, both parties have acted in good faith in some measure or in bad faith to some degree. Additionally, each judge has her or his own personal beliefs and philosophy. At least to some extent, these personal factors shape the legal reasoning process. In short, the outcome of a particular lawsuit before a court cannot be predicted with certainty.

1–3e The Common Law Today

Today, the common law derived from judicial decisions continues to be applied throughout the United States. Common law doctrines and principles, however, govern only areas *not* covered by statutory or administrative law. In a dispute concerning a particular employment practice, for instance, if a statute regulates that practice, the statute will apply rather than the common law doctrine that applied before the statute was enacted. The common law tradition and its application are reviewed in Concept Summary 1.2.

Courts Interpret Statutes Even in areas governed by statutory law, judge-made law continues to be important because there is a significant interplay between statutory law and the common law. For instance, many statutes essentially codify existing common law rules, and regulations issued by various administrative agencies usually are based, at least in part, on common law principles. Additionally, the courts, in interpreting statutory law, often rely on the common law as a guide to what the legislators intended. Frequently, the applicability of a newly enacted statute does not become clear until a body of case law develops to clarify how, when, and to whom the statute applies.

Concept Summary 1.2

The Common Law Tradition

Origins of Common Law	The American legal system is based on the common law tradition, which originated in medieval England.
Legal and Equitable Remedies	Remedies at law (land, items of value, or money) and remedies in equity (including specific performance, injunction, and rescission of a contractual obligation) originated in the early English courts of law and courts of equity, respectively.
Case Precedents and the Doctrine of *Stare Decisis*	In the king's courts, judges attempted to make their decisions consistent with previous decisions, called precedents. This practice gave rise to the doctrine of *stare decisis*. This doctrine, which became a cornerstone of the common law tradition, obligates judges to abide by precedents established in their jurisdictions.
Common Law Today	The common law governs all areas not covered by statutory law or administrative laws. Courts interpret statutes and regulations.

Clearly, a judge's function is not to *make* the laws—that is the function of the legislative branch of government—but to interpret and apply them. From a practical point of view, however, the courts play a significant role in defining the laws enacted by legislative bodies, which tend to be expressed in general terms. Judges thus have some flexibility in interpreting and applying the law. It is because of this flexibility that different courts can, and often do, arrive at different conclusions in cases that involve nearly identical issues, facts, and applicable laws.

***Restatements of the Law* Clarify and Illustrate the Common Law** The American Law Institute (ALI) has published compilations of the common law called *Restatements of the Law*, which generally summarize the common law rules followed by most states. There are *Restatements of the Law* in the areas of contracts, torts, agency, trusts, property, restitution, security, judgments, and conflict of laws. The *Restatements,* like other secondary sources of law, do not in themselves have the force of law, but they are an important source of legal analysis and opinion. Hence, judges often rely on them in making decisions.

Many of the *Restatements* are now in their second, third, or fourth editions. We refer to the *Restatements* frequently in subsequent chapters of this text, indicating in parentheses the edition to which we are referring. For instance, we refer to the third edition of the *Restatement of the Law of Contracts* as simply the *Restatement (Third) of Contracts*.

1–4 Schools of Legal Thought

How judges apply the law to specific cases, including disputes relating to the business world, depends in part on their philosophical approaches to law. Thus, the study of law, or **jurisprudence,** involves learning about different schools of legal thought and how the approaches to law characteristic of each school can affect judicial decision making.

1–4a The Natural Law School

An age-old question about the nature of law has to do with the finality of a nation's laws. What if a particular law is deemed to be a "bad" law by a substantial number of the nation's citizens? Must they obey that law? According to the **natural law** theory, a higher, or universal, law exists that applies to all human beings. Each written law should reflect the principles inherent in natural law. If it does not, then it loses its legitimacy and need not be obeyed.

The natural law tradition is one of the oldest and most significant schools of jurisprudence. It dates back to the days of the Greek philosopher Aristotle (384–322

B.C.E.), who distinguished between natural law and the laws governing a particular nation. According to Aristotle, natural law applies universally to all humankind.

The notion that people have "natural rights" stems from the natural law tradition. Those who claim that a specific foreign government is depriving certain citizens of their human rights, for instance, are implicitly appealing to a higher law that has universal applicability.

The question of the universality of basic human rights also comes into play in the context of international business operations. U.S. companies that have operations abroad often hire foreign workers as employees. Should the same laws that protect U.S. employees apply to these foreign employees? This question is rooted implicitly in a concept of universal rights that has its origins in the natural law tradition.

1–4b The Positivist School

Positive law, or national law, is the written law of a given society at a particular time. In contrast to natural law, it applies only to the citizens of that nation or society. Those who adhere to **legal positivism** believe that there can be no higher law than a nation's positive law.

According to the positivist school, there are no "natural rights." Rather, human rights exist solely because of laws. If the laws are not enforced, anarchy will result. Thus, whether a law is "bad" or "good" is irrelevant. The law is the law and must be obeyed until it is changed—in an orderly manner through a legitimate lawmaking process. A judge who takes this view will probably be more inclined to defer to an existing law than would a judge who adheres to the natural law tradition.

1–4c The Historical School

The **historical school** of legal thought emphasizes the evolutionary process of law by concentrating on the origin and history of the legal system. This school looks to the past to discover what the principles of contemporary law should be. The legal doctrines that have withstood the passage of time—those that have worked in the past—are deemed best suited for shaping present laws. Hence, law derives its legitimacy and authority from adhering to the standards that historical development has shown to be workable. Followers of the historical school are more likely than those of other schools to strictly follow decisions made in past cases.

1–4d Legal Realism

In the 1920s and 1930s, a number of jurists and scholars, known as *legal realists*, rebelled against the historical approach to law. **Legal realism** is based on the idea that law is just one of many institutions in society and that it is shaped by social forces and needs. Because the law is a human enterprise, this school reasons that judges should take social and economic realities into account when deciding cases.

Legal realists also believe that the law can never be applied with total uniformity. Given that judges are human beings with unique personalities, value systems, and intellects, different judges will obviously bring different reasoning processes to the same case. Female judges, for instance, might be more inclined than male judges to consider whether a decision might have a negative impact on the employment of women or minorities.

Legal realism strongly influenced the growth of what is sometimes called the **sociological school,** which views law as a tool for promoting justice in society. In the 1960s, for instance, the justices of the United States Supreme Court helped advance the civil rights movement by upholding long-neglected laws calling for equal treatment for all Americans, including African Americans and other minorities. Generally, jurists who adhere to this philosophy of law are more likely to depart from past decisions than are jurists who adhere to other schools of legal thought.

Concept Summary 1.3 reviews the schools of jurisprudential thought.

1–5 Classifications of Law

The law may be broken down according to several classification systems. One system, for instance, divides law into substantive law and procedural law. **Substantive law** consists of all laws that define, describe, regulate, and create legal rights and obligations. **Procedural law** consists of all laws that outline the methods of enforcing the rights established by substantive law.

Note that many statutes contain both substantive and procedural provisions. ■ **EXAMPLE 1.5** A state law that provides employees with the right to *workers' compensation benefits* for on-the-job injuries is a substantive law because it creates legal rights. Procedural laws establish the method by which an employee must notify the employer about an on-the-job injury, prove the injury, and periodically submit additional proof to continue receiving workers' compensation benefits. ■

Other classification systems divide law into federal law and state law, private law (dealing with relationships between private entities) and public law (addressing the relationship between persons and their governments), and national law and international law. Here we look at still another classification system, which divides law into

---

Concept Summary 1.3

Schools of Jurisprudential Thought

Natural Law School	One of the oldest and most significant schools of legal thought. Those who believe in natural law hold that there is a universal law applicable to all human beings.
Positivist School	A school of legal thought centered on the assumption that there is no law higher than the laws created by the government.
Historical School	A school of legal thought that stresses the evolutionary nature of law and looks to doctrines that have withstood the passage of time for guidance in shaping present laws.
Legal Realism	A school of legal thought that advocates a less abstract and more realistic and pragmatic approach to the law and takes into account customary practices and the circumstances surrounding the particular transaction.

civil law and criminal law. We also explain what is meant by the term *cyberlaw*.

1–5a Civil Law and Criminal Law

Civil law spells out the rights and duties that exist between persons and between persons and their governments, as well as the relief available when a person's rights are violated. Typically, in a civil case, a private party sues another private party who has failed to comply with a duty. (Note that the government can also sue a party for a civil law violation.) Much of the law that we discuss in this text is civil law, including contract law and tort law.

Criminal law, in contrast, is concerned with wrongs committed *against the public as a whole*. Criminal acts are defined and prohibited by local, state, or federal government statutes. Criminal defendants are thus prosecuted by public officials, such as a district attorney (D.A.), on behalf of the state, not by their victims or other private parties. Some statutes, such as those protecting the environment or investors, have both civil and criminal provisions.

1–5b Cyberlaw

The use of the Internet to conduct business has led to new types of legal issues. In response, courts have had to adapt traditional laws to situations that are unique to our age. Additionally, legislatures at both the federal and the state levels have created laws to deal specifically with such issues.

Frequently, people use the term **cyberlaw** to refer to the emerging body of law that governs transactions conducted via the Internet. Cyberlaw is not really a classification of law, though, nor is it a new *type* of law. Rather, it is an informal term used to refer to both new laws and modifications of traditional laws that relate to the online environment. Throughout this book, you will read how the law in a given area is evolving to govern specific legal issues that arise in the online context.

1–6 How to Find Primary Sources of Law

This text includes numerous references, or *citations,* to primary sources of law—federal and state statutes, the U.S. Constitution and state constitutions, regulations issued by administrative agencies, and court cases. A **citation** identifies the publication in which a legal authority—such as a statute or a court decision or other source—can be found. In this section, we explain how you can use citations to find primary sources of law. Note

that in addition to being published in sets of books, as described next, most federal and state laws and case decisions are available online.

1–6a Finding Statutory and Administrative Law

When Congress passes laws, they are collected in a publication titled *United States Statutes at Large.* When state legislatures pass laws, they are collected in similar state publications. Most frequently, however, laws are referred to in their codified form—that is, the form in which they appear in the federal and state codes. In these codes, laws are compiled by subject.

United States Code The *United States Code* (U.S.C.) arranges all existing federal laws by broad subject. Each of the fifty-two subjects is given a title and a title number. For instance, laws relating to commerce and trade are collected in Title 15, "Commerce and Trade." Each title is subdivided by sections. A citation to the U.S.C. includes both title and section numbers. Thus, a reference to "15 U.S.C. Section 1" means that the statute can be found in Section 1 of Title 15. ("Section" may be designated by the symbol §, and "Sections," by §§.)

In addition to the print publication, the federal government provides a searchable online database at **www.gpo.gov**. It includes the *United States Code,* the U.S. Constitution, and many other federal resources. (Click on "Libraries" and then "Core Documents of Our Democracy" to find these resources.)

Commercial publications of federal laws and regulations are also available. For instance, Thomson Reuters publishes the *United States Code Annotated* (U.S.C.A.). The U.S.C.A. contains the official text of the U.S.C., plus notes (annotations) on court decisions that interpret and apply specific sections of the statutes. The U.S.C.A. also includes additional research aids, such as cross-references to related statutes, historical notes, and library references. A citation to the U.S.C.A. is similar to a citation to the U.S.C.: "15 U.S.C.A. Section 1."

State Codes State codes follow the U.S.C. pattern of arranging law by subject. They may be called codes, revisions, compilations, consolidations, general statutes, or statutes, depending on the preferences of the states.

In some codes, subjects are designated by number. In others, they are designated by name. ■ **EXAMPLE 1.6** "13 Pennsylvania Consolidated Statutes Section 1101" means that the statute can be found in Title 13, Section 1101, of the Pennsylvania code. "California Commercial Code Section 1101" means that the statute can be found under the subject heading "Commercial Code" of the California code in Section 1101. Abbreviations are often used. For example, "13 Pennsylvania Consolidated Statutes Section 1101" is abbreviated "13 Pa. C.S. § 1101," and "California Commercial Code Section 1101" is abbreviated "Cal. Com. Code § 1101." ■

Administrative Rules Rules and regulations adopted by federal administrative agencies are initially published in the *Federal Register,* a daily publication of the U.S. government. Later, they are incorporated into the *Code of Federal Regulations* (C.F.R.). The C.F.R. is available online on the government database (**www.gpo.gov**).

Like the U.S.C., the C.F.R. is divided into titles. Rules within each title are assigned section numbers. A full citation to the C.F.R. includes title and section numbers. ■ **EXAMPLE 1.7** A reference to "17 C.F.R. Section 230.504" means that the rule can be found in Section 230.504 of Title 17. ■

1–6b Finding Case Law

Before discussing the case reporting system, we need to look briefly at the court system. There are two types of courts in the United States, federal courts and state courts. Both systems consist of several levels, or tiers, of courts. *Trial courts*, in which evidence is presented and testimony given, are on the bottom tier. Decisions from a trial court can be appealed to a higher court, which commonly is an intermediate *court of appeals*, or *appellate court.* Decisions from these intermediate courts of appeals may be appealed to an even higher court, such as a state supreme court or the United States Supreme Court.

State Court Decisions Most state trial court decisions are not published in books (except in New York and a few other states, which publish selected trial court opinions). Decisions from state trial courts are typically filed in the office of the clerk of the court, where the decisions are available for public inspection. (Increasingly, they can be found online as well.)

Written decisions of the appellate, or reviewing, courts, however, are published and distributed (in print and online). As you will note, most of the state court cases presented in this textbook are from state appellate courts. The reported appellate decisions are published in volumes called *reports* or *reporters,* which are numbered consecutively. State appellate court decisions are found in the state reporters of that particular state. Official reports are published by the state, whereas unofficial reports are published by nongovernment entities.

Regional Reporters. State court opinions appear in regional units of the West's National Reporter System, published by Thomson Reuters. Most lawyers and libraries have these reporters because they report cases more quickly and are distributed more widely than the state-published reporters. In fact, many states have eliminated their own reporters in favor of the National Reporter System.

The National Reporter System divides the states into the following geographic areas: *Atlantic* (A., A.2d, or A.3d), *North Eastern* (N.E. or N.E.2d), *North Western* (N.W. or N.W.2d), *Pacific* (P., P.2d, or P.3d), *South Eastern* (S.E. or S.E.2d), *South Western* (S.W., S.W.2d, or S.W.3d), and *Southern* (So., So.2d, or So.3d). (The *2d* and *3d* in the preceding abbreviations refer to *Second Series* and *Third Series*, respectively.) The states included in each of these regional divisions are indicated in Exhibit 1–4, which illustrates the National Reporter System.

Case Citations. After appellate decisions have been published, they are normally referred to (cited) by the name of the case and the volume, name, and page number of the reporter(s) in which the opinion can be found. The citation first lists the state's official reporter (if different from the National Reporter System), then the National Reporter, and then any other selected reporter. (Citing a reporter by volume number, name, and page number, in that order, is common to all citations. The year that the decision was issued is often included at the end in parentheses.) When more than one reporter is cited for the same case, each reference is called a *parallel citation.*

Note that some states have adopted a "public domain citation system" that uses a somewhat different format for the citation. For instance, in Wisconsin, a Wisconsin Supreme Court decision might be designated "2016 WI 40," meaning that the case was decided in the year 2016 by the Wisconsin Supreme Court and was the fortieth decision issued by that court during that year. Parallel citations to the *Wisconsin Reports* and the *North Western Reporter* are still included after the public domain citation.

■ **EXAMPLE 1.8** Consider the following case citation: *Summerhill, LLC v. City of Meridan,* 162 Conn.App. 469, 131 A.3d. 1225 (2016). We see that the opinion in this case can be found in Volume 162 of the official *Connecticut Appellate Court Reports*, on page 469. The parallel citation is to Volume 131 of the *Atlantic Reporter, Third Series*, page 1225. ■

When we present opinions in this text, in addition to the reporter, we give the name of the court hearing the case and the year of the court's decision. Sample citations to state court decisions are explained in Exhibit 1–5.

EXHIBIT 1–4 National Reporter System—Regional/Federal

Regional Reporters	Coverage Beginning	Coverage
Atlantic Reporter (A., A.2d, or A.3d)	1885	Connecticut, Delaware, District of Columbia, Maine, Maryland, New Hampshire, New Jersey, Pennsylvania, Rhode Island, and Vermont.
North Eastern Reporter (N.E. or N.E.2d)	1885	Illinois, Indiana, Massachusetts, New York, and Ohio.
North Western Reporter (N.W. or N.W.2d)	1879	Iowa, Michigan, Minnesota, Nebraska, North Dakota, South Dakota, and Wisconsin.
Pacific Reporter (P., P.2d, or P.3d)	1883	Alaska, Arizona, California, Colorado, Hawaii, Idaho, Kansas, Montana, Nevada, New Mexico, Oklahoma, Oregon, Utah, Washington, and Wyoming.
South Eastern Reporter (S.E. or S.E.2d)	1887	Georgia, North Carolina, South Carolina, Virginia, and West Virginia.
South Western Reporter (S.W., S.W.2d, or S.W.3d)	1886	Arkansas, Kentucky, Missouri, Tennessee, and Texas.
Southern Reporter (So., So.2d, or So.3d)	1887	Alabama, Florida, Louisiana, and Mississippi.
Federal Reporters		
Federal Reporter (F., F.2d, or F.3d)	1880	U.S. Circuit Courts from 1880 to 1912; U.S. Commerce Court from 1911 to 1913; U.S. District Courts from 1880 to 1932; U.S. Court of Claims (now called U.S. Court of Federal Claims) from 1929 to 1932 and since 1960; U.S. Courts of Appeals since 1891; U.S. Court of Customs and Patent Appeals since 1929; U.S. Emergency Court of Appeals since 1943.
Federal Supplement (F.Supp., F.Supp.2d, or F.Supp.3d)	1932	U.S. Court of Claims from 1932 to 1960; U.S. District Courts since 1932; U.S. Customs Court since 1956.
Federal Rules Decisions (F.R.D.)	1939	U.S. District Courts involving the Federal Rules of Civil Procedure since 1939 and Federal Rules of Criminal Procedure since 1946.
Supreme Court Reporter (S.Ct.)	1882	United States Supreme Court since the October term of 1882.
Bankruptcy Reporter (Bankr.)	1980	Bankruptcy decisions of U.S. Bankruptcy Courts, U.S. District Courts, U.S. Courts of Appeals, and the United States Supreme Court.
Military Justice Reporter (M.J.)	1978	U.S. Court of Military Appeals and Courts of Military Review for the Army, Navy, Air Force, and Coast Guard.

NATIONAL REPORTER SYSTEM MAP

EXHIBIT 1–5 How to Read Citations

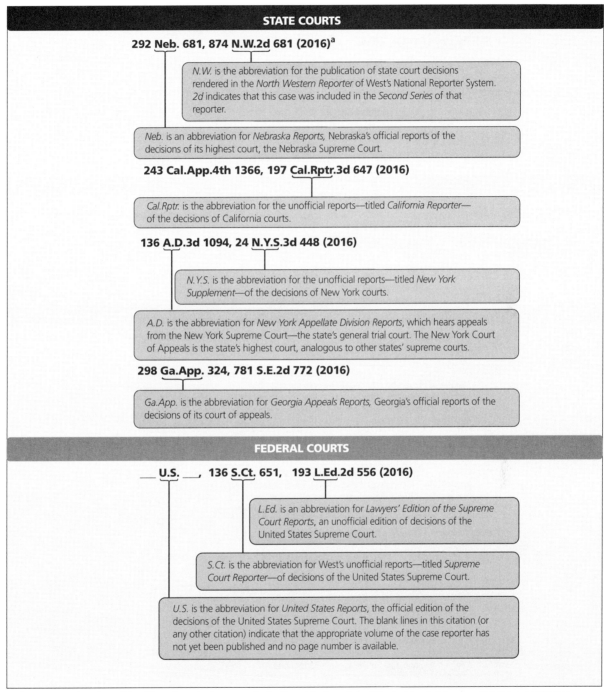

STATE COURTS

292 Neb. 681, 874 N.W.2d 681 (2016)[a]

N.W. is the abbreviation for the publication of state court decisions rendered in the *North Western Reporter* of West's National Reporter System. *2d* indicates that this case was included in the *Second Series* of that reporter.

Neb. is an abbreviation for *Nebraska Reports,* Nebraska's official reports of the decisions of its highest court, the Nebraska Supreme Court.

243 Cal.App.4th 1366, 197 Cal.Rptr.3d 647 (2016)

Cal.Rptr. is the abbreviation for the unofficial reports—titled *California Reporter*—of the decisions of California courts.

136 A.D.3d 1094, 24 N.Y.S.3d 448 (2016)

N.Y.S. is the abbreviation for the unofficial reports—titled *New York Supplement*—of the decisions of New York courts.

A.D. is the abbreviation for *New York Appellate Division Reports*, which hears appeals from the New York Supreme Court—the state's general trial court. The New York Court of Appeals is the state's highest court, analogous to other states' supreme courts.

298 Ga.App. 324, 781 S.E.2d 772 (2016)

Ga.App. is the abbreviation for *Georgia Appeals Reports,* Georgia's official reports of the decisions of its court of appeals.

FEDERAL COURTS

__ U.S. __, 136 S.Ct. 651, 193 L.Ed.2d 556 (2016)

L.Ed. is an abbreviation for *Lawyers' Edition of the Supreme Court Reports*, an unofficial edition of decisions of the United States Supreme Court.

S.Ct. is the abbreviation for West's unofficial reports—titled *Supreme Court Reporter*—of decisions of the United States Supreme Court.

U.S. is the abbreviation for *United States Reports*, the official edition of the decisions of the United States Supreme Court. The blank lines in this citation (or any other citation) indicate that the appropriate volume of the case reporter has not yet been published and no page number is available.

a. The case names have been deleted from these citations to emphasize the publications. It should be kept in mind, however, that the name of a case is as important as the specific page numbers in the volumes in which it is found. If a citation is incorrect, the correct citation may be found in a publication's index of case names. In addition to providing a check on errors in citations, the date of a case is important because the value of a recent case as an authority is likely to be greater than that of older cases from the same court.

Continued

EXHIBIT 1–5 How to Read Citations—Continued

FEDERAL COURTS (Continued)

809 F.3d 376 (7th Cir. 2016)

7th Cir. is an abbreviation denoting that this case was decided in the U.S. Court of Appeals for the Seventh Circuit.

___ F.Supp.3d ___ 2016 WL 466132 (E.D.Cal. 2016)

E.D.Cal. is an abbreviation indicating that the U.S. District Court for the Eastern District of California decided this case.

WESTLAW® CITATIONS[b]

2016 WL 66334

WL is an abbreviation for Westlaw. The number 2016 is the year of the document that can be found with this citation in the Westlaw database. The number 66334 is a number assigned to a specific document. A higher number indicates that a document was added to the Westlaw database later in the year.

STATUTORY AND OTHER CITATIONS

18 U.S.C. Section 1961(1)(A)

U.S.C. denotes *United States Code*, the codification of *United States Statutes at Large*. The number 18 refers to the statute's U.S.C. title number and 1961 to its section number within that title. The number 1 in parentheses refers to a subsection within the section, and the letter A in parentheses to a subsection within the subsection.

UCC 2–206(1)(b)

UCC is an abbreviation for *Uniform Commercial Code*. The first number 2 is a reference to an article of the UCC, and 206 to a section within that article. The number 1 in parentheses refers to a subsection within the section, and the letter b in parentheses to a subsection within the subsection.

Restatement (Third) of Torts, Section 6

Restatement (Third) of Torts refers to the third edition of the American Law Institute's *Restatement of the Law of Torts*. The number 6 refers to a specific section.

17 C.F.R. Section 230.505

C.F.R. is an abbreviation for *Code of Federal Regulations*, a compilation of federal administrative regulations. The number 17 designates the regulation's title number, and 230.505 designates a specific section within that title.

b. Many court decisions that are not yet published or that are not intended for publication can be accessed through Westlaw, an online legal database.

Federal Court Decisions Federal district (trial) court decisions are published unofficially in the *Federal Supplement* (F.Supp. or F.Supp.2d), and opinions from the circuit courts of appeals (reviewing courts) are reported unofficially in the *Federal Reporter* (F., F.2d, or F.3d). Cases concerning federal bankruptcy law are published unofficially in the *Bankruptcy Reporter* (Bankr. or B.R.).

The official edition of the United States Supreme Court decisions is the *United States Reports* (U.S.), which is published by the federal government. Unofficial editions of Supreme Court cases include the *Supreme Court Reporter* (S.Ct.) and the *Lawyers' Edition of the Supreme Court Reports* (L.Ed. or L.Ed.2d). Sample citations for federal court decisions are also listed and explained in Exhibit 1–5.

Unpublished Opinions Many court opinions that are not yet published or that are not intended for publication can be accessed through Thomson Reuters Westlaw® (abbreviated in citations as "WL"), an online legal database. When no citation to a published reporter is available for cases cited in this text, we give the WL citation (such as 2016 WL 145734, which means it was case number 145734 decided in the year 2016). In addition, federal appellate court decisions that are designated as unpublished may appear in the *Federal Appendix* (Fed.Appx.) of the National Reporter System.

Old Case Law On a few occasions, this text cites opinions from old, classic cases dating to the nineteenth century or earlier. Some of these are from the English courts. The citations to these cases may not conform to the descriptions just presented because the reporters in which they were originally published were often known by the names of the persons who compiled the reporters.

1–7 How to Read and Understand Case Law

The decisions made by the courts establish the boundaries of the law as it applies to almost all business relationships. It thus is essential that businesspersons know how to read and understand case law.

The cases that we present in this text have been condensed from the full text of the courts' opinions and are presented in a special format. In approximately two-thirds of the cases (including the cases designated as *Classic* and *Spotlight*), we have summarized the background and facts, as well as the court's decision and remedy, in our own words. In those cases, we have included only selected excerpts from the court's opinion ("In the Language of the Court"). In the remaining one-third of the cases (labeled "Case Analysis"), we have provided a longer excerpt from the court's opinion without summarizing the background and facts or decision and remedy.

The following sections provide useful insights into how to read and understand case law.

1–7a Case Titles and Terminology

The title of a case, such as *Adams v. Jones*, indicates the names of the parties to the lawsuit. The *v.* in the case title stands for *versus*, which means "against." In the trial court, Adams was the plaintiff—the person who filed the suit. Jones was the defendant.

If the case is appealed, however, the appellate court will sometimes place the name of the party appealing the decision first, so the case may be called *Jones v. Adams* if Jones appealed. Because some appellate courts retain the trial court order of names, it is often impossible to distinguish the plaintiff from the defendant in the title of a reported appellate court decision. You must carefully read the facts of each case to identify the parties.

The following terms, phrases, and abbreviations are frequently encountered in court opinions and legal publications.

Parties to Lawsuits The party initiating a lawsuit is referred to as the *plaintiff* or *petitioner*, depending on the nature of the action. The party against whom a lawsuit is brought is the *defendant* or *respondent*. Lawsuits frequently involve more than one plaintiff and/or defendant.

When a case is appealed from the original court or jurisdiction to another court or jurisdiction, the party appealing the case is called the **appellant.** The **appellee** is the party against whom the appeal is taken. (In some appellate courts, the party appealing a case is referred to as the *petitioner*, and the party against whom the suit is brought or appealed is called the *respondent*.)

Judges and Justices The terms *judge* and *justice* are usually synonymous and represent two designations given to judges in various courts. All members of the United States Supreme Court, for instance, are referred to as justices. Justice is the formal title often given to judges of appellate courts, although this is not always true. In New York, a justice is a judge of the trial court (called the Supreme Court), and a member of the Court of Appeals (the state's highest court) is called a judge.

The term *justice* is commonly abbreviated to J., and *justices*, to JJ. A United States Supreme Court case might refer to Justice Sotomayor as Sotomayor, J., or to Chief Justice Roberts as Roberts, C.J.

Decisions and Opinions Most decisions reached by reviewing, or appellate, courts are explained in written **opinions.** The opinion contains the court's reasons for its decision, the rules of law that apply, and the judgment. You may encounter several types of opinions as you read appellate cases, including the following:

- When all the judges (or justices) agree, a *unanimous opinion* is written for the entire court.
- When there is not unanimous agreement, a **majority opinion** is generally written. It outlines the views of the majority of the judges deciding the case.
- A judge who agrees (concurs) with the majority opinion as to the result but not as to the legal reasoning often writes a **concurring opinion.** In it, the judge sets out the reasoning that he or she considers correct.
- A **dissenting opinion** presents the views of one or more judges who disagree with the majority view.
- Sometimes, no single position is fully supported by a majority of the judges deciding a case. In this situation, we may have a **plurality opinion.** This is the opinion that has the support of the largest number of judges, but the group in agreement is less than a majority.
- Finally, a court occasionally issues a *per curiam* **opinion** (*per curiam* is Latin for "of the court"), which does not indicate which judge wrote the opinion.

1–7b Sample Court Case

To illustrate the various elements contained in a court opinion, we present an annotated court opinion in Exhibit 1–6. The opinion is from an actual case that the United States Court of Appeals for the Eleventh Circuit decided in 2016.

Background of the Case In December 1955, on a bus in Montgomery, Alabama, Rosa Parks refused to give up her seat to a white man in violation of the city's segregation law. This "courageous act" sparked the modern civil rights movement. Parks's role in "the most significant social movement in the history of the United States" has been chronicled in books and movies, and featured on

mementoes, some of which are offered for sale by Target Corp. The Rosa and Raymond Parks Institute for Self Development is a Michigan firm that owns the right to use Parks's name and likeness for commercial purposes. The Institute filed a suit in a federal district court against Target, alleging misappropriation in violation of the Institute's right of publicity. The court dismissed the complaint. The Institute appealed to the U.S. Court of Appeals for the Eleventh Circuit, arguing that Target's sales of books, movies, and other items that depict or discuss Rosa Parks and the modern civil rights movement violated Michigan law.

Editorial Practice You will note that triple asterisks (* * *) and quadruple asterisks (* * * *) frequently appear in the opinion. The triple asterisks indicate that we have deleted a few words or sentences from the opinion for the sake of readability or brevity. Quadruple asterisks mean that an entire paragraph (or more) has been omitted.

Additionally, when the opinion cites another case or legal source, the citation to the case or source has been omitted, again for the sake of readability and brevity. These editorial practices are continued in the other court opinions presented in this book. In addition, whenever we present a court opinion that includes a term or phrase that may not be readily understandable, a bracketed definition or paraphrase has been added.

Briefing Cases Knowing how to read and understand court opinions and the legal reasoning used by the courts is an essential step in undertaking accurate legal research. A further step is "briefing," or summarizing, the case.

Legal researchers routinely brief cases by reducing the texts of the opinions to their essential elements. Generally, when you brief a case, you first summarize the background and facts of the case, as the authors have done for most of the cases presented in this text. You then indicate the issue (or issues) before the court. An important element in the case brief is, of course, the court's decision on the issue and the legal reasoning used by the court in reaching that decision.

EXHIBIT 1–6 A Sample Court Case

This section contains the citation—the name of the case, the name of the court that heard the case, the year of the decision, and reporters in which the court's opinion can be found.	**Rosa and Raymond Parks Institute for Self Development v. Target Corporation** United States Court of Appeals, Eleventh Circuit, 812 F.3d 824 (2016).

This line provides the name of the judge (or justice) who authored the court's opinion.

ROSENBAUM, Circuit Judge:

* * * *

In December 1955, on a bus in Montgomery, Alabama, Parks refused to give up her seat to a white man in violation of the city's segregation law.

[Rosa] **Parks's courageous act** inspired the Montgomery Bus Boycott and served as the **impetus** for the **modern Civil Rights Movement,** transforming the nation. In response to Parks's arrest, for 381 days, 42,000 African–Americans boycotted Montgomery buses, until the United States Supreme Court held the Montgomery segregation law unconstitutional and ordered desegregation of the buses.

An *impetus* is a stimulus or a spark.

Parks's refusal to **cede** ground in the face of continued injustice has made her among the most revered heroines of our national story; her role in American history cannot be over-emphasized. Indeed, the United States Congress * * * has credited Parks with "igniting the most significant social movement in the history of the United States."

The *modern civil rights movement* (1954–1964) included mass demonstrations in which participants sought equality in public and private life at national, state, and local levels, as well as an end to state and local segregation and discrimination in schools, in the workplace and at the polls. The movement culminated in the enactment of two federal Civil Rights acts in 1957 and 1964.

So it is not surprising that authors would write about Parks's story and artists would celebrate it with their works. The commemoration and dissemination of Parks's journey continues to entrench and embolden our pursuit of justice. And it is in the general public interest to relentlessly preserve, spotlight, and recount the story of Rosa Parks and the Civil Rights Movement—even when that interest allegedly conflicts with an individual **right of publicity.**

To *cede* is to yield or surrender.

A *right of publicity* is a person's right to the use of his or her name and likeness for a commercial purpose.

I.

The Rosa and Raymond Parks Institute for Self Development (the "Institute") is a Michigan * * * corporation that owns the name and likeness of the late Rosa Parks * * *.

The court divides the opinion into three sections. The first section summarizes the factual background of the case.

Continued

EXHIBIT 1–6 A Sample Court Case—Continued

Target Corporation ("Target"), a national retail corporation headquartered in Minneapolis, Minnesota, operates more than 1,800 retail stores across the United States.

Target offered [for sale] seven books about Parks * * * , the * * * movie *The Rosa Parks Story,* and a * * * plaque that included * * * a picture of Parks.

* * * *

Misappropriation is the use of a person's name or likeness without his or her consent for a commercial purpose. This is commonly referred to as a violation of the individual's right of publicity.

* * * The Institute filed the underlying complaint in [a federal district court]. The Institute alleged claims for * * * **misappropriation** * * * for Target's sales of all items using the name and likeness of Rosa Parks.

Generally, the Institute complained that * * * Target had unfairly and "without the Institute's prior knowledge, or consent, used Parks's name, likeness, and image to sell products * * * for Target's own commercial advantage." * * * The district court dismissed the complaint, and this appeal followed.

The second major section of the opinion responds to the plaintiff's appeal.

II.

* * * In this case we apply * * * the **substantive law** of Michigan.

* * * *

Substantive law is law that defines the rights and duties of persons with respect to each other. A federal court exercising jurisdiction based on diversity of citizenship—as in this case, where the two corporate parties are "citizens" of different states—applies the substantive law of the state in which the court sits (except in cases governed by federal law or the United States Constitution).

Michigan's common-law right of publicity is founded upon the interest of the individual in the exclusive use of his own identity, in so far as it is represented by his name or likeness, and in so far as the use may be of benefit to him or to others. This * * * privacy right guards against the appropriation of the commercial value of a person's identity by using without consent the person's name, likeness, or other *indicia*

Indicia is a synonym for indications or signs.

of identity for the purpose of trade.

Privacy rights, however, are not absolute. * * * Individual rights must yield to the **qualified privilege** to communicate on matters of public interest.

Qualified privilege gives someone a limited right to act contrary to another person's right without the other person's having legal recourse for the act.

* * * *

In this context, *bona fide* means sincerely and honestly.

* * * The privilege attaches to matters of general public interest and extends to all communications made ***bona fide*** upon any subject matter where the party

EXHIBIT 1–6 A Sample Court Case—Continued

communicating has an interest or a [legal, moral, or social] duty to a person having

a corresponding interest or duty.

* * * *

Of course, it is beyond dispute that Rosa Parks is a figure of great historical

significance and the Civil Rights Movement a matter of legitimate and important

public interest. And it is **uncontested** that * * * the * * * books * * * and the movie are

all *bona fide* works * * * discussing Parks and her role in the Civil Rights Movement.

> Here, *uncontested* can mean unchallenged or accepted, as well as evident or obvious.

Similarly, the plaque depicts images and mentions dates and statements related

to Parks and the Civil Rights Movement, in an effort to convey a message concern-

ing Parks, her courage, and the results of her strength. Indeed, all of the works in

question communicate information, express opinions, recite grievances, and protest

claimed abuses on behalf of a movement whose existence and objectives continue to

be of the highest public interest and concern.

* * * *

* * * The Institute has not articulated any argument as to why Michigan's quali-

fied privilege for matters of public concern would not apply to these works, in light

of the conspicuous historical importance of Rosa Parks. Nor can we conceive of any.

* * * Indeed, it is difficult to conceive of a discussion of the Civil Rights Move-

ment without reference to Parks and her role in it. And Michigan law does not make

discussion of these topics of public concern contingent on paying a fee. As a result,

[the] books, the movie, and the plaque find protection in Michigan's qualified privi-

lege protecting matters of public interest.

> In the third major section of the opinion, the court states its decision.

[III.]

In short, the district court did not err in dismissing the Institute's complaint. The

district court's order is **AFFIRMED.**

> To *affirm* is to validate, to give legal force to.

Reviewing: Law and Legal Reasoning

Suppose that the California legislature passes a law that severely restricts carbon dioxide emissions from automobiles in that state. A group of automobile manufacturers files suit against the state of California to prevent the enforcement of the law. The automakers claim that a federal law already sets fuel economy standards nationwide and that fuel economy standards are essentially the same as carbon dioxide emission standards. According to the automobile manufacturers, it is unfair to allow California to impose more stringent regulations than those set by the federal law. Using the information presented in the chapter, answer the following questions.

1. Who are the parties (the plaintiffs and the defendant) in this lawsuit?
2. Are the plaintiffs seeking a legal remedy or an equitable remedy?
3. What is the primary source of the law that is at issue here?
4. Where would you look to find the relevant California and federal laws?

Debate This . . .   *Under the doctrine of* stare decisis, *courts are obligated to follow the precedents established in their jurisdiction unless there is a compelling reason not to. Should U.S. courts continue to adhere to this common law principle, given that our government now regulates so many areas by statute?*

Terms and Concepts

administrative agency 4
administrative law 4
allege 10
appellant 19
appellee 19
binding authority 8
breach 6
case law 5
case on point 11
citation 14
civil law 14
common law 6
concurring opinion 20
constitutional law 4
court of equity 6
court of law 6
criminal law 14
cyberlaw 14
damages 6

defendant 6
defense 6
dissenting opinion 20
equitable maxims 6
executive agency 5
historical school 12
independent regulatory agency 5
jurisprudence 12
laches 6
law 2
legal positivism 12
legal realism 13
legal reasoning 10
liability 2
majority opinion 20
natural law 12
opinion 20
ordinance 4
persuasive authority 10

per curiam opinion 20
petitioner 6
plaintiff 6
plurality opinion 20
precedent 7
procedural law 13
remedy 6
remedy at law 6
remedy in equity 6
reporter 8
respondent 6
sociological school 13
stare decisis 8
statute of limitations 6
statutory law 4
substantive law 13
uniform law 4

Issue Spotters

1. Under what circumstances might a judge rely on case law to determine the intent and purpose of a statute? (See *Sources of American Law.*)

2. After World War II, several Nazis were convicted of "crimes against humanity" by an international court. Assuming that these convicted war criminals had not disobeyed any law of their country and had merely been following their government's orders, what law had they violated? Explain. (See *Schools of Legal Thought.*)

• **Check your answers to the Issue Spotters against the answers provided in Appendix B at the end of this text.**

Business Scenarios

1–1. Binding versus Persuasive Authority. A county court in Illinois is deciding a case involving an issue that has never been addressed before in that state's courts. The Iowa Supreme Court, however, recently decided a case involving a very similar fact pattern. Is the Illinois court obligated to follow the Iowa Supreme Court's decision on the issue? If the United States Supreme Court had decided a similar case, would that decision be binding on the Illinois court? Explain. (See *The Common Law Tradition*.)

1–2. Sources of Law. This chapter discussed a number of sources of American law. Which source of law takes priority in the following situations, and why? (See *Sources of American Law*.)

(a) A federal statute conflicts with the U.S. Constitution.

(b) A federal statute conflicts with a state constitutional provision.

(c) A state statute conflicts with the common law of that state.

(d) A state constitutional amendment conflicts with the U.S. Constitution.

1–3. Stare Decisis. In this chapter, we stated that the doctrine of *stare decisis* "became a cornerstone of the English and American judicial systems." What does *stare decisis* mean, and why has this doctrine been so fundamental to the development of our legal tradition? (See *The Common Law Tradition*.)

Business Case Problems

1–4. Spotlight on AOL—Common Law. AOL, LLC, mistakenly made public the personal information of 650,000 of its members. The members filed a suit, alleging violations of California law. AOL asked the court to dismiss the suit on the basis of a "forum-selection clause" in its member agreement that designates Virginia courts as the place where member disputes will be tried. Under a decision of the United States Supreme Court, a forum-selection clause is unenforceable "if enforcement would contravene a strong public policy of the forum in which suit is brought." California courts have declared in other cases that the AOL clause contravenes a strong public policy. If the court applies the doctrine of *stare decisis*, will it dismiss the suit? Explain. [*Doe 1 v. AOL LLC*, 552 F.3d 1077 (9th Cir. 2009)] (See *The Common Law Tradition*.)

1–5. Business Case Problem with Sample Answer— Reading Citations. Assume that you want to read the entire court opinion in the case of *Equal Employment Opportunity Commission v. Autozone, Inc.*, 809 F.3d 916 (7th Cir. 2016). Refer to the subsection entitled "Finding Case Law" in this chapter, and then explain specifically where you would find the court's opinion. (See *How to Find Primary Sources of Law.*)

- For a sample answer to Problem 1–5, go to Appendix C at the end of this text.

1–6. A Question of Ethics—The Common Law Tradition. *On July 5, 1884, Dudley, Stephens, and Brooks—* *"all able-bodied English seamen"—and a teenage English boy were cast adrift in a lifeboat following a storm at sea. They had no water with them in the boat, and all they had for sustenance were two one-pound tins of turnips. On July 24, Dudley proposed that one of the four in the lifeboat be sacrificed to save the others. Stephens agreed with Dudley, but Brooks refused to consent—and the boy was never asked for his opinion. On July 25, Dudley killed the boy, and the three men then fed on the boy's body and blood. Four days later, a passing vessel rescued the men. They were taken to England and tried for the murder of the boy. If the men had not fed on the boy's body, they would probably have died of starvation within the four-day period. The boy, who was in a much weaker condition, would likely have died before the rest.* [Regina v. Dudley and Stephens, 14 Q.B.D. *(Queen's Bench Division, England) 273 (1884)]* (See *The Common Law Tradition*.)

(a) The basic question in this case is whether the survivors should be subject to penalties under English criminal law, given the men's unusual circumstances. Were the defendants' actions necessary but unethical? Explain your reasoning. What ethical issues might be involved here?

(b) Should judges ever have the power to look beyond the written "letter of the law" in making their decisions? Why or why not?

Legal Reasoning Group Activity

1–7. Court Opinions. Read through the subsection in this chapter entitled "Decisions and Opinions." (See *How to Read and Understand Case Law.*)

(a) One group will explain the difference between a concurring opinion and a majority opinion.

(b) Another group will outline the difference between a concurring opinion and a dissenting opinion.

(c) A third group will explain why judges and justices write concurring and dissenting opinions, given that these opinions will not affect the outcome of the case at hand, which has already been decided by majority vote.

CHAPTER 2

Business and the Constitution

L aws that govern business have their origin in the lawmaking authority granted by the U.S. Constitution, which is the supreme law in this country. Neither Congress nor any state may pass a law that is in conflict with the Constitution.

Constitutional disputes frequently come before the courts. For instance, numerous states challenged the Obama administration's Affordable Care Act on constitutional grounds. The United States Supreme Court decided in 2012 that the provisions of this law, which required most Americans to have health insurance by 2014, did not exceed the constitutional authority of the federal government. The Court's decision in the matter continues to have a significant impact on the business environment.

2-1 The Constitutional Powers of Government

Following the Revolutionary War, the states adopted the Articles of Confederation. The Articles created a *confederal form of government* in which the states had the authority to govern themselves and the national government could exercise only limited powers. Problems soon arose because the nation was facing an economic crisis and state laws interfered with the free flow of commerce. A national convention was called, and the delegates drafted the U.S. Constitution. This document, after its ratification by the states in 1789, became the basis for an entirely new form of government.

2-1a A Federal Form of Government

The new government created by the U.S. Constitution reflected a series of compromises made by the convention delegates on various issues. Some delegates wanted sovereign power to remain with the states. Others wanted the national government alone to exercise sovereign power. The end result was a compromise—a **federal form of government** in which the national government and the states *share* sovereign power.

Federal Powers The Constitution sets forth specific powers that can be exercised by the national (federal) government. It further provides that the national government has the implied power to undertake actions necessary to carry out its expressly designated powers (or *enumerated powers*). All other powers are expressly "reserved" to the states under the Tenth Amendment to the U.S. Constitution.

Regulatory Powers of the States As part of their inherent **sovereignty** (power to govern themselves), state governments have the authority to regulate certain affairs within their borders. As mentioned, this authority stems, in part, from the Tenth Amendment, which reserves all powers not delegated to the national government to the states or to the people.

State regulatory powers are often referred to as **police powers.** The term encompasses more than just the enforcement of criminal laws. Police powers also give state governments broad rights to regulate private activities to protect or promote the public order, health, safety, morals, and general welfare. Fire and building codes, antidiscrimination laws, parking regulations, zoning restrictions, licensing requirements, and thousands of other state statutes have been enacted pursuant to states' police powers. Local governments, such as cities, also exercise police powers.[1] Generally, state laws enacted

---

1. Local governments derive their authority to regulate their communities from the state, because they are creatures of the state. In other words, they cannot come into existence unless authorized by the state to do so.

pursuant to a state's police powers carry a strong presumption of validity.

2–1b Relations among the States

The U.S. Constitution also includes provisions concerning relations among the states in our federal system. Particularly important are the *privileges and immunities clause* and the *full faith and credit clause.*

The Privileges and Immunities Clause Article IV, Section 2, of the Constitution provides that the "Citizens of each State shall be entitled to all Privileges and Immunities of Citizens in the several States." This clause is often referred to as the interstate **privileges and immunities clause.**[2] It prevents a state from imposing unreasonable burdens on citizens of another state—particularly with regard to means of livelihood or doing business.

When a citizen of one state engages in basic and essential activities in another state (the "foreign state"), the foreign state must have a *substantial reason* for treating the nonresident differently than its own residents. Basic activities include transferring property, seeking employment, and accessing the court system. The foreign state must also establish that its reason for the discrimination is *substantially related* to the state's ultimate purpose in adopting the legislation or regulating the activity.[3]

The Full Faith and Credit Clause Article IV, Section 1, of the U.S. Constitution provides that "Full Faith and Credit shall be given in each State to the public Acts, Records, and judicial Proceedings of every other State." This clause, which is referred to as the **full faith and credit clause,** applies only to civil matters. It ensures that rights established under deeds, wills, contracts, and similar instruments in one state will be honored by other states. It also ensures that any judicial decision with respect to such property rights will be honored and enforced in all states.

The legal issues raised by same-sex marriage involve, among other things, the full faith and credit clause, because that clause requires each state to honor marriage decrees issued by another state. See this chapter's *Managerial Strategy* feature for a discussion of marriage equality laws.

The full faith and credit clause has contributed to the unity of American citizens because it protects their legal rights as they move about from state to state. It also protects the rights of those to whom they owe obligations, such as persons who have been awarded monetary damages by courts. The ability to enforce such rights is extremely important for the conduct of business in a country with a very mobile citizenry.

2–1c The Separation of Powers

To make it more difficult for the national government to use its power arbitrarily, the Constitution provided for three branches of government. The legislative branch makes the laws, the executive branch enforces the laws, and the judicial branch interprets the laws. Each branch performs a separate function, and no branch may exercise the authority of another branch.

Additionally, a system of **checks and balances** allows each branch to limit the actions of the other two branches, thus preventing any one branch from exercising too much power. Some examples of these checks and balances include the following:

1. The legislative branch (Congress) can enact a law, but the executive branch (the president) has the constitutional authority to veto that law.
2. The executive branch is responsible for foreign affairs, but treaties with foreign governments require the advice and consent of the Senate.
3. Congress determines the jurisdiction of the federal courts, and the president appoints federal judges, with the advice and consent of the Senate. The judicial branch has the power to hold actions of the other two branches unconstitutional.[4]

2–1d The Commerce Clause

To prevent states from establishing laws and regulations that would interfere with trade and commerce among the states, the Constitution expressly delegated to the national government the power to regulate interstate commerce. Article I, Section 8, of the U.S. Constitution explicitly permits Congress "[t]o regulate Commerce with foreign Nations, and among the several States, and with the Indian Tribes." This clause, referred to as the **commerce clause,** has had a greater impact on business than any other provision in the Constitution. The commerce clause provides the basis for the national government's extensive regulation of state and even local affairs.

---

2. Interpretations of this clause commonly use the terms *privilege* and *immunity* synonymously. Generally, the terms refer to certain rights, benefits, or advantages enjoyed by individuals.

3. This test was first announced in *Supreme Court of New Hampshire v. Piper,* 470 U.S. 274, 105 S.Ct. 1272, 84 L.Ed.2d 205 (1985). For another example, see *Lee v. Miner,* 369 F.Supp.2d 527 (D.Del. 2005).

4. The power of judicial review was established by the United States Supreme Court in *Marbury v. Madison,* 5 U.S. (1 Cranch) 137, 2 L.Ed. 60 (1803).

MANAGERIAL STRATEGY — Marriage Equality and the Constitution

The debate over same-sex marriage has been raging across the country for years. The legal issues raised by marriage equality involve privacy rights and equal protection. Although marriage equality may not appear at first glance to be business related, it is an important legal issue for managers. Companies like Barilla Pasta, Chick-fil-A, Exxon Mobil, and Target Corporation have lost significant business for purportedly supporting anti-gay organizations and legislation.

The Definition of Marriage

Before 1996, federal law did not define marriage, and the U.S. government recognized any marriage that was recognized by a state. Then Congress passed the Defense of Marriage Act (DOMA), which explicitly defined marriage as a union of one man and one woman. DOMA was later challenged, and a number of federal courts found it to be unconstitutional in the context of bankruptcy, public employee benefits, and estate taxes. In 2013, the United States Supreme Court struck down part of DOMA as unconstitutional.[a] Today, once again, no federal law defines marriage.

Bans on Same-Sex Marriage Eliminated by the Supreme Court

During this period, federal courts became increasingly likely to invalidate state bans on same-sex marriage. In 2013, a federal district court held that Utah's same-sex marriage ban was unconstitutional.[b] In 2014, federal district courts in Arkansas, Mississippi, and Oklahoma struck down state same-sex marriage bans.[c] Moreover, public sentiment on the issue had shifted, and more states recognized the rights of same-sex couples. By 2015, thirty-seven states, as well as the District of Columbia, had legalized same-sex marriage.

In 2015, the United States Supreme Court determined that the remaining state-level prohibitions on same-sex marriage were unconstitutional. In a landmark decision, the Court ruled that the Fourteenth Amendment requires individual states to (1) issue marriage licenses to same-sex couples and (2) recognize same-sex marriages performed in other states.[d]

The landmark Supreme Court decision requiring all states to recognize same-sex marriage means that businesses must make adjustments. Company policies need to be revised to specify how same-sex partners will be treated in terms of family and medical leave, health-insurance coverage, pensions, and other benefits.

Business Questions

1. *Can a business manager's religious beliefs legally factor into the business's hiring and treatment of same-sex partners? Why or why not?*
2. *Must business owners in all states provide the same benefits to employees in a same-sex union as they do to heterosexual couples?*

a. *Windsor v. United States,* ___ U.S. ___, 133 S.Ct. 2675, 186 L.Ed.2d 808 (2013).
b. *Kitchen v. Herbert,* 961 F.Supp.2d 1181 (D.Utah 2013).

c. *Campaign for Southern Equality v. Bryant,* 64 F.Supp.3d 906 (S.D. Miss. 2014); *Jernigan v. Crane,* 64 F.Supp.3d 1260 (E.D.Ark. 2014); and *Bishop v. U.S. ex rel. Holder,* 962 F.Supp.2d 1252 (N.D. Okla. 2014).
d. *Obergefell v. Hodges,* ___ U.S. ___, 135 S.Ct. 2584, 192 L.Ed.2d 609 (2015).

Initially, the courts interpreted the commerce clause to apply only to commerce between the states (*interstate* commerce) and not commerce within the states (*intrastate* commerce). That changed in 1824, however, when the United States Supreme Court decided the landmark case of *Gibbons v. Ogden.*[5] The Court held that commerce within the states could also be regulated by the national government as long as the commerce *substantially affected* commerce involving more than one state.

The Expansion of National Powers under the Commerce Clause As the nation grew and faced

new kinds of problems, the commerce clause became a vehicle for the additional expansion of the national government's regulatory powers. Even activities that seemed purely local in nature came under the regulatory reach of the national government if those activities were deemed to substantially affect interstate commerce. In 1942, the Supreme Court held that wheat production by an individual farmer intended wholly for consumption on his own farm was subject to federal regulation.[6]

The following *Classic Case* involved a challenge to the scope of the national government's constitutional authority to regulate local activities.

---

5. 22 U.S. (9 Wheat.) 1, 6 L.Ed. 23 (1824).

6. *Wickard v. Filburn,* 317 U.S. 111, 63 S.Ct. 82, 87 L.Ed. 122 (1942).

Heart of Atlanta Motel v. United States

Supreme Court of the United States, 379 U.S. 241, 85 S.Ct. 348, 13 L.Ed.2d 258 (1964).

Background and Facts In the 1950s, the United States Supreme Court ruled that racial segregation imposed by the states in school systems and other public facilities violated the Constitution. Privately owned facilities were not affected until Congress passed the Civil Rights Act of 1964, which prohibited racial discrimination in "establishments affecting interstate commerce."

The owner of the Heart of Atlanta Motel, in violation of the Civil Rights Act of 1964, refused to rent rooms to African Americans. The motel owner brought an action in a federal district court to have the Civil Rights Act declared unconstitutional on the ground that Congress had exceeded its constitutional authority to regulate commerce by enacting the statute.

The owner argued that his motel was not engaged in interstate commerce but was "of a purely local character." The motel, however, was accessible to state and interstate highways. The owner advertised nationally, maintained billboards throughout the state, and accepted convention trade from outside the state (75 percent of the guests were residents of other states).

The district court ruled that the act did not violate the Constitution and enjoined (prohibited) the owner from discriminating on the basis of race. The motel owner appealed. The case ultimately went to the United States Supreme Court.

In the Language of the Court

Mr. Justice *CLARKE* delivered the opinion of the Court.

* * * *

While the Act as adopted carried no congressional findings, the record of its passage through each house is replete with evidence of the burdens that discrimination by race or color places upon interstate commerce * * * . This testimony included the fact that our people have become increasingly mobile with millions of all races traveling from State to State; that Negroes in particular have been the subject of discrimination in transient accommodations, having to travel great distances to secure the same; that often they have been unable to obtain accommodations and have had to call upon friends to put them up overnight. * * * These exclusionary practices were found to be nationwide, the Under Secretary of Commerce testifying that there is "no question that this discrimination in the North still exists to a large degree" and in the West and Midwest as well * * * . This testimony indicated a qualitative as well as quantitative effect on interstate travel by Negroes. The former was the obvious impairment of the Negro traveler's pleasure and convenience that resulted when he continually was uncertain of finding lodging. As for the latter, there was evidence that this uncertainty stemming from racial discrimination had the effect of discouraging travel on the part of a substantial portion of the Negro community * * * . We shall not burden this opinion with further details since the voluminous testimony presents overwhelming evidence that discrimination by hotels and motels impedes interstate travel.

* * * *

It is said that the operation of the motel here is of a purely local character. But, assuming this to be true, "if it is interstate commerce that feels the pinch, it does not matter how local the operation that applies the squeeze." * * * *Thus the power of Congress to promote interstate commerce also includes the power to regulate the local incidents thereof, including local activities in both the States of origin and destination, which might have a substantial and harmful effect upon that commerce.* [Emphasis added.]

Decision and Remedy *The United States Supreme Court upheld the constitutionality of the Civil Rights Act of 1964. The power of Congress to regulate interstate commerce permitted the enactment of legislation that could halt local discriminatory practices.*

Impact of This Case on Today's Law *If the United States Supreme Court had invalidated the Civil Rights Act of 1964, the legal landscape of the United States would be much different today. The act prohibits discrimination based on race, color, national origin, religion, or gender in all "public accommodations," including hotels and restaurants.*

Case 2.1 Continues

Case 2.1 Continued

The act also prohibits discrimination in employment based on these criteria. Although state laws now prohibit many of these forms of discrimination as well, the protections available vary from state to state—and it is not certain whether such laws would have been passed had the outcome in this case been different.

Critical Thinking

- **What If the Facts Were Different?** *If this case had involved a small, private retail business that did not advertise nationally, would the result have been the same? Why or why not?*

The Commerce Clause Today Today, at least theoretically, the power over commerce authorizes the national government to regulate almost every commercial enterprise in the United States. The breadth of the commerce clause permits the national government to legislate in areas in which Congress has not explicitly been granted power. Only occasionally has the Supreme Court curbed the national government's regulatory authority under the commerce clause.[7]

The Supreme Court has, for instance, allowed the federal government to regulate noncommercial activities relating to medical marijuana that take place wholly within a state's borders. ■ **CASE IN POINT 2.1** More than half the states, including California, have adopted laws that legalize marijuana for medical purposes (and a handful of states now permit the recreational use of marijuana). Marijuana possession, however, is illegal under the federal Controlled Substances Act (CSA).[8] After the federal government seized the marijuana that two seriously ill California women were using on the advice of their physicians, the women filed a lawsuit. They argued that it was unconstitutional for the federal statute to prohibit them from using marijuana for medical purposes that were legal within the state.

The Supreme Court, though, held that Congress has the authority to prohibit the *intrastate* possession and noncommercial cultivation of marijuana as part of a larger regulatory scheme (the CSA).[9] In other words, the federal government may still prosecute individuals for possession of marijuana regardless of whether they reside in a state that allows the medical or recreational use of marijuana. ■

The "Dormant" Commerce Clause The Supreme Court has interpreted the commerce clause to mean that the national government has the *exclusive* authority to regulate commerce that substantially affects trade and commerce among the states. This express grant of authority to the national government is often referred to as the "positive" aspect of the commerce clause. But this positive aspect also implies a negative aspect—that the states do *not* have the authority to regulate interstate commerce. This negative aspect of the commerce clause is often referred to as the "dormant" (implied) commerce clause.

The dormant commerce clause comes into play when state regulations affect interstate commerce. In this situation, the courts weigh the state's interest in regulating a certain matter against the burden that the state's regulation places on interstate commerce. Because courts balance the interests involved, it is difficult to predict the outcome in a particular case. State laws that alter conditions of competition to favor in-state interests over out-of-state competitors in a market (such as wineries or construction workers) are usually invalidated, however.[10]

■ **CASE IN POINT 2.2** Maryland imposed personal income taxes on its residents at the state level and the county level. Maryland residents who paid income tax in another state were allowed a credit against the *state* portion of their Maryland taxes, but not the *county* portion. Several Maryland residents who had earned profits in and paid taxes to other states but had not received a credit against their county tax liability sued. They claimed that Maryland's system discriminated against intrastate commerce because those who earned income in other states paid more taxes than residents whose only income came from within Maryland. When the case reached the United States Supreme Court in 2015, the

---

7. See, for example, *United States v. Morrison*, 529 U.S. 598, 120 S.Ct. 1740, 146 L.Ed.2d 658 (2000), holding that the federal Violence Against Women Act violated Congress's commerce clause authority.

8. 21 U.S.C. Sections 801 *et seq.*

9. *Gonzales v. Raich*, 545 U.S. 1, 125 S.Ct. 2195, 162 L.Ed.2d 1 (2005).

10. See *Family Winemakers of California v. Jenkins*, 592 F.3d 1 (1st Cir. 2010); and *Tri-M Group, LLC v. Sharp*, 638 F.3d 406 (3d Cir. 2011).

Court held that Maryland's personal income tax scheme violated the dormant commerce clause.[11] ■

2–1e The Supremacy Clause and Federal Preemption

Article VI of the U.S. Constitution, commonly referred to as the **supremacy clause,** provides that the Constitution, laws, and treaties of the United States are "the supreme Law of the Land." When there is a direct conflict between a federal law and a state law, the state law is rendered invalid. Because some powers are *concurrent* (shared by the federal government and the states), however, it is necessary to determine which law governs in a particular circumstance.

Preemption When Congress chooses to act exclusively in a concurrent area, **preemption** occurs. In this circumstance, a valid federal statute or regulation will take precedence over a conflicting state or local law or regulation on the same general subject.

Congressional Intent Often, it is not clear whether Congress, in passing a law, intended to preempt an entire subject area. In these situations, the courts determine whether Congress intended to exercise exclusive power.

No single factor is decisive as to whether a court will find preemption. Generally, though, congressional intent to preempt will be found if a federal law regulating an activity is so pervasive, comprehensive, or detailed that the states have little or no room to regulate in that area. Also, when a federal statute creates an agency to enforce the law, matters that may come within the agency's jurisdiction will likely preempt state laws.

■ **CASE IN POINT 2.3** A man who alleged that he had been injured by a faulty medical device (a balloon catheter that was inserted into his artery following a heart attack) sued the manufacturer. The case ultimately came before the United States Supreme Court. The Court noted that the relevant federal law (the Medical Device Amendments of 1976) had included a preemption provision. Furthermore, the device had passed the U.S. Food and Drug Administration's rigorous premarket approval process. Therefore, the Court ruled that the federal regulation of medical devices preempted the man's state law claims.[12] ■

2–1f The Taxing and Spending Powers

Article I, Section 8, of the U.S. Constitution provides that Congress has the "Power to lay and collect Taxes, Duties, Imposts, and Excises." Section 8 further requires uniformity in taxation among the states, and thus Congress may not tax some states while exempting others.

In the distant past, if Congress attempted to regulate indirectly, by taxation, an area over which it had no authority, the courts would invalidate the tax. Today, however, if a tax measure is reasonable, it generally is held to be within the national taxing power. Moreover, the expansive interpretation of the commerce clause almost always provides a basis for sustaining a federal tax.

Article I, Section 8, also gives Congress its spending power—the power "to pay the Debts and provide for the common Defence and general Welfare of the United States." Congress can spend revenues not only to carry out its expressed powers but also to promote any objective it deems worthwhile, so long as it does not violate the Bill of Rights. The spending power necessarily involves policy choices, with which taxpayers (and politicians) may disagree.

2–2 Business and the Bill of Rights

The importance of a written declaration of the rights of individuals caused the first Congress of the United States to submit twelve amendments to the U.S. Constitution to the states for approval. Ten of these amendments, known as the **Bill of Rights,** were adopted in 1791 and embody a series of protections for the individual against various types of interference by the federal government.[13]

The protections guaranteed by these ten amendments are summarized in Exhibit 2–1. Some of these constitutional protections apply to business entities as well as individuals. For example, corporations exist as separate legal entities, or *legal persons,* and enjoy many of the same rights and privileges as *natural persons* do.

---

11. *Comptroller of Treasury of Maryland v. Wynne,* ___ U.S. ___, 135 S.Ct. 1787, 191 L.Ed.2d 813 (2015).
12. *Riegel v. Medtronic, Inc.,* 552 U.S. 312, 128 S.Ct. 999, 169 L.Ed.2d 892 (2008).

13. Another of these proposed amendments was ratified more than two hundred years later (in 1992) and became the Twenty-Seventh Amendment to the Constitution.

EXHIBIT 2–1 Protections Guaranteed by the Bill of Rights

First Amendment:	Guarantees the freedoms of religion, speech, and the press and the rights to assemble peaceably and to petition the government.
Second Amendment:	States that the right of the people to keep and bear arms shall not be infringed.
Third Amendment:	Prohibits, in peacetime, the lodging of soldiers in any house without the owner's consent.
Fourth Amendment:	Prohibits unreasonable searches and seizures of persons or property.
Fifth Amendment:	Guarantees the rights to *indictment* (formal accusation) by a grand jury, to due process of law, and to fair payment when private property is taken for public use. The Fifth Amendment also prohibits compulsory self-incrimination and double jeopardy (trial for the same crime twice).
Sixth Amendment:	Guarantees the accused in a criminal case the right to a speedy and public trial by an impartial jury and with counsel. The accused has the right to cross-examine witnesses against him or her and to solicit testimony from witnesses in his or her favor.
Seventh Amendment:	Guarantees the right to a trial by jury in a civil case involving at least twenty dollars.
Eighth Amendment:	Prohibits excessive bail and fines, as well as cruel and unusual punishment.
Ninth Amendment:	Establishes that the people have rights in addition to those specified in the Constitution.
Tenth Amendment:	Establishes that those powers neither delegated to the federal government nor denied to the states are reserved to the states and to the people.

2–2a Limits on Federal and State Governmental Actions

As originally intended, the Bill of Rights limited only the powers of the national government. Over time, however, the United States Supreme Court "incorporated" most of these rights into the protections against state actions afforded by the Fourteenth Amendment to the Constitution.

The Fourteenth Amendment The Fourteenth Amendment, passed in 1868 after the Civil War, provides, in part, that "[n]o State shall . . . deprive any person of life, liberty, or property, without due process of law." Starting in 1925, the Supreme Court began to define various rights and liberties guaranteed in the U.S. Constitution as constituting "due process of law," which was required of state governments under that amendment.

Today, most of the rights and liberties set forth in the Bill of Rights apply to state governments as well as the national government. In other words, neither the federal government nor state governments can deprive persons of those rights and liberties.

Judicial Interpretation The rights secured by the Bill of Rights are not absolute. Many of the rights

guaranteed by the first ten amendments are set forth in very general terms. The Second Amendment states that people have a right to keep and bear arms, but it does not describe the extent of this right. As the Supreme Court has noted, this right does not mean that people can "keep and carry any weapon whatsoever in any manner whatsoever and for whatever purpose."[14] Legislatures can prohibit the carrying of concealed weapons or certain types of weapons, such as machine guns.

Ultimately, the United States Supreme Court, as the final interpreter of the Constitution, gives meaning to these rights and determines their boundaries. Changing public views on controversial topics, such as privacy in an era of terrorist threats or the rights of gay men and lesbians, can affect the way the Supreme Court decides a case.

2–2b Freedom of Speech

A democratic form of government cannot survive unless people can freely voice their political opinions and criticize government actions or policies. Freedom of speech,

---

14. *District of Columbia v. Heller*, 554 U.S. 570, 128 S.Ct. 2783, 171 L.Ed.2d 637 (2008).

particularly political speech, is thus a prized right, and traditionally the courts have protected this right to the fullest extent possible.

Symbolic speech—gestures, movements, articles of clothing, and other forms of expressive conduct—is also given substantial protection by the courts. The Supreme Court has held that the burning of the American flag as part of a peaceful protest is a constitutionally protected form of expression.[15] Similarly, wearing a T-shirt with a photo of a presidential candidate is a constitutionally protected form of expression. ■ **EXAMPLE 2.4** As a form of expression, Nate has gang signs tattooed on his torso, arms, neck, and legs. If a reasonable person would interpret this conduct as conveying a message, then it might be a protected form of symbolic speech. ■

Reasonable Restrictions   A balance must be struck between a government's obligation to protect its citizens and those citizens' exercise of their rights. Expression—oral, written, or symbolized by conduct—is therefore subject to reasonable restrictions. Reasonableness is analyzed on a case-by-case basis.

Content-Neutral Laws. Laws that regulate the time, manner, and place, but not the content, of speech receive less scrutiny by the courts than do laws that restrict the content of expression. If a restriction imposed by the government is content neutral, then a court may allow it. To be content neutral, the restriction must be aimed at combatting some societal problem, such as crime or drug abuse, and not be aimed at suppressing the expressive conduct or its message.

Courts have often protected nude dancing as a form of symbolic expression but typically allow content-neutral laws that ban all public nudity. ■ **CASE IN POINT 2.5** Ria Ora was charged with dancing nude at an annual "anti-Christmas" protest in Harvard Square in Cambridge, Massachusetts, under a statute banning public displays of open and gross lewdness. Ora argued that the statute was overbroad and unconstitutional, and a trial court agreed. On appeal, however, a state appellate court upheld the statute as constitutional in situations in which there was an unsuspecting or unwilling audience.[16] ■

Laws That Restrict the Content of Speech. Any law that regulates the content of expression must serve a compelling state interest and must be narrowly written to achieve that interest. Under the **compelling government**

interest test, the government's interest is balanced against the individual's constitutional right to free expression. For the statute to be valid, there must be a compelling government interest that can be furthered only by the law in question.

The United States Supreme Court has held that schools may restrict students' speech at school events. ■ **CASE IN POINT 2.6** Some high school students held up a banner saying "Bong Hits 4 Jesus" at an off-campus but school-sanctioned event. The Supreme Court ruled that the school did not violate the students' free speech rights when school officials confiscated the banner and suspended the students for ten days. Because the banner could reasonably be interpreted as promoting drugs, the Court concluded that the school's actions were justified. Several justices disagreed, however, noting that the majority's holding creates an exception that will allow schools to censor any student speech that mentions drugs.[17] ■

Corporate Political Speech   Political speech by corporations also falls within the protection of the First Amendment. Many years ago, the United States Supreme Court struck down as unconstitutional a Massachusetts statute that prohibited corporations from making political contributions or expenditures that individuals were permitted to make.[18] The Court has also held that a law forbidding a corporation from including inserts with its bills to express its views on controversial issues violates the First Amendment.[19]

Corporate political speech continues to be given significant protection under the First Amendment. ■ **CASE IN POINT 2.7** In *Citizens United v. Federal Election Commission,*[20] the Supreme Court issued a landmark decision that overturned a twenty-year-old precedent on campaign financing. The case involved Citizens United, a nonprofit corporation that runs a *political action committee* (an organization that registers with the government and campaigns for or against political candidates).

Citizens United had produced a film called *Hillary: The Movie* that was critical of Hillary Clinton, who was seeking the Democratic nomination for presidential candidate. Campaign-finance law restricted Citizens United from broadcasting the movie. The Court ruled that these

---

15. *Texas v. Johnson,* 491 U.S. 397, 109 S.Ct. 2533, 105 L.Ed.2d 342 (1989).

16. *Commonwealth v. Ora,* 451 Mass. 125, 883 N.E.2d 1217 (2008).

17. *Morse v. Frederick,* 551 U.S. 393, 127 S.Ct. 2618, 168 L.Ed.2d 290 (2007).

18. *First National Bank of Boston v. Bellotti,* 435 U.S. 765, 98 S.Ct. 1407, 55 L.Ed.2d 707 (1978).

19. *Consolidated Edison Co. v. Public Service Commission,* 447 U.S. 530, 100 S.Ct. 2326, 65 L.Ed.2d 319 (1980).

20. 558 U.S. 310, 130 S.Ct. 876, 175 L.Ed.2d 753 (2010).

restrictions were unconstitutional and that the First Amendment prevents limits from being placed on independent political expenditures by corporations. ■

Commercial Speech The courts also give substantial protection to *commercial speech,* which consists of communications—primarily advertising and marketing—made by business firms that involve only their commercial interests. The protection given to commercial speech under the First Amendment is less extensive than that afforded to noncommercial speech, however.

A state may restrict certain kinds of advertising, for instance, in the interest of preventing consumers from being misled. States also have a legitimate interest in roadside beautification and therefore may impose restraints on billboard advertising. ■ **EXAMPLE 2.8** Café Erotica, a nude dancing establishment, sues the state after being denied a permit to erect a billboard along an interstate highway in Florida. Because the law directly advances a substantial government interest in highway beautification and safety, a court will likely find that it is not an unconstitutional restraint on commercial speech. ■

Generally, a restriction on commercial speech will be considered valid as long as it meets three criteria:

1. It must seek to implement a substantial government interest.
2. It must directly advance that interest.
3. It must go no further than necessary to accomplish its objective.

At issue in the following case was whether a government agency had unconstitutionally restricted commercial speech when it prohibited the inclusion of a certain illustration on beer labels.

Spotlight on Beer Labels

Case 2.2 Bad Frog Brewery, Inc. v. New York State Liquor Authority

United States Court of Appeals, Second Circuit, 134 F.3d 87 (1998).

Background and Facts Bad Frog Brewery, Inc., makes and sells alcoholic beverages. Some of the beverages feature labels that display a drawing of a frog making the gesture generally known as "giving the finger." Bad Frog's authorized New York distributor, Renaissance Beer Company, applied to the New York State Liquor Authority (NYSLA) for brand label approval, as required by state law before the beer could be sold in New York.

The NYSLA denied the application, in part, because "the label could appear in grocery and convenience stores, with obvious exposure on the shelf to children of tender age." Bad Frog filed a suit in a federal district court against the NYSLA, asking for, among other things, an injunction against the denial of the application. The court granted summary judgment in favor of the NYSLA. Bad Frog appealed to the U.S. Court of Appeals for the Second Circuit.

In the Language of the Court

Jon O. *NEWMAN,* Circuit Judge:
* * * *

* * * To support its asserted power to ban Bad Frog's labels [NYSLA advances] * * * the State's interest in "protecting children from vulgar and profane advertising" * * * .

[This interest is] substantial * * * . *States have a compelling interest in protecting the physical and psychological wellbeing of minors* * * * . [Emphasis added.]
* * * *

* * * NYSLA endeavors to advance the state interest in preventing exposure of children to vulgar displays by taking only the limited step of barring such displays from the labels of alcoholic beverages. *In view of the wide currency of vulgar displays throughout contemporary society, including comic books targeted directly at children, barring such displays from labels for alcoholic beverages cannot realistically be expected to reduce children's exposure to such displays to any significant degree.* [Emphasis added.]

* * * If New York decides to make a substantial effort to insulate children from vulgar displays in some significant sphere of activity, at least with respect to materials likely to be seen by children, NYSLA's label prohibition might well be found to make a justifiable contribution to the material

advancement of such an effort, but its currently isolated response to the perceived problem, applicable only to labels on a product that children cannot purchase, does not suffice. * * * A state must demonstrate that its commercial speech limitation is part of a substantial effort to advance a valid state interest, not merely the removal of a few grains of offensive sand from a beach of vulgarity.

* * * *

* * * Even if we were to assume that the state materially advances its asserted interest by shielding children from viewing the Bad Frog labels, it is plainly excessive to prohibit the labels from all use, including placement on bottles displayed in bars and taverns where parental supervision of children is to be expected. Moreover, to whatever extent NYSLA is concerned that children will be harmfully exposed to the Bad Frog labels when wandering without parental supervision around grocery and convenience stores where beer is sold, that concern could be less intrusively dealt with by placing restrictions on the permissible locations where the appellant's products may be displayed within such stores.

Decision and Remedy *The U.S. Court of Appeals for the Second Circuit reversed the judgment of the district court and remanded the case for the entry of a judgment in favor of Bad Frog. The NYSLA's ban on the use of the labels lacked a "reasonable fit" with the state's interest in shielding minors from vulgarity. In addition, the NYSLA had not adequately considered alternatives to the ban.*

Critical Thinking
- **What If the Facts Were Different?** *If Bad Frog had sought to use the offensive label to market toys instead of beer, would the court's ruling likely have been the same? Why or why not?*
- **Legal Environment** *Whose interests are advanced by the banning of certain types of advertising?*

Unprotected Speech The United States Supreme Court has made it clear that certain types of speech will not be protected under the First Amendment. Unprotected speech includes fighting words, or words that are likely to incite others to respond violently. It also includes speech that harms the good reputation of another, or defamatory speech. In addition, speech that violates criminal laws (threatening speech or possession of child pornography, for instance) is not constitutionally protected.

Threatening Speech. Note that in the case of threatening speech, the speaker must have posed a "true threat"—that is, must have meant to communicate a serious intent to commit an unlawful, violent act against a particular person or group. ■ **CASE IN POINT 2.9** After Anthony Elonis's wife, Tara, left him and took their two children, Elonis was upset and experienced problems at work. A coworker filed five sexual harassment reports against him. When Elonis posted a photograph of himself in a Halloween costume holding a toy knife to the coworker's neck, he was fired from his job. Elonis then began posting violent statements on his Facebook page, mostly focusing on his former wife and talking about killing her.

Elonis continued to post statements about killing his wife and eventually was arrested and prosecuted for his online posts. Elonis was convicted by a jury of violating a statute and ordered to serve time in prison. He appealed to the United States Supreme Court, which held that it is not enough that a reasonable person might view the defendant's Facebook posts as threats. Elonis must have intended to issue threats or known that his statements would be viewed as threats to be convicted of a crime. The Court reversed Elonis's conviction and remanded the case back to the lower court to determine if there was sufficient evidence of intent.[21] ■

Obscene Speech. The First Amendment, as interpreted by the Supreme Court, also does not protect obscene speech. Numerous state and federal statutes make it a crime to disseminate and possess obscene materials, including child pornography. Objectively defining obscene speech has proved difficult, however. It is even more difficult to prohibit the dissemination of obscenity and pornography online.

Most of Congress's attempts to pass legislation protecting minors from pornographic materials on the Internet have been struck down on First Amendment grounds when challenged in court. One exception is a law that requires public schools and libraries to install **filtering software** on computers to keep children from accessing adult content.[22] Such software is designed to

---

21. *Elonis v. United States*, ___ U.S. ___, 135 S.Ct. 2001, 192 L.Ed.2d 1 (2015).
22. Children's Internet Protection Act (CIPA), 17 U.S.C. Sections 1701–1741.

prevent persons from viewing certain Web sites based on a site's Internet address or its **meta tags,** or key words. The Supreme Court held that the act does not unconstitutionally burden free speech because it is flexible and libraries can disable the filters for any patrons who ask.[23]

Another exception is a law that makes it a crime to intentionally distribute *virtual child pornography*—which uses computer-generated images, not actual people—without indicating that it is computer-generated.[24] In a case challenging the law's constitutionality, the Supreme Court held that the statute is valid because it does not prohibit a substantial amount of protected speech.[25] Nevertheless, because of the difficulties of policing the Internet, as well as the constitutional complexities of prohibiting obscenity through legislation, online obscenity remains a legal issue.

2–2c Freedom of Religion

The First Amendment states that the government may neither establish any religion nor prohibit the free exercise of religious practices. The first part of this constitutional provision is referred to as the **establishment clause,** and the second part is known as the **free exercise clause**. Government action, both federal and state, must be consistent with this constitutional mandate.

The Establishment Clause The establishment clause prohibits the government from establishing a state-sponsored religion, as well as from passing laws that promote (aid or endorse) religion or show a preference for one religion over another. Although the establishment clause involves the separation of church and state, it does not require a complete separation.

Applicable Standard. Establishment clause cases often involve such issues as the legality of allowing or requiring school prayers, using state-issued vouchers to pay tuition at religious schools, and teaching creation theories versus evolution. Federal or state laws that do not promote or place a significant burden on religion are constitutional even if they have some impact on religion. For a government law or policy to be constitutional, it must not have the primary effect of promoting or inhibiting religion.

Religious Displays. Religious displays on public property have often been challenged as violating the establishment clause, and the United States Supreme Court has

ruled on a number of such cases. Generally, the Court has focused on the proximity of the religious display (such as a Christian Christmas symbol) to nonreligious symbols (such as reindeer and candy canes) or symbols from different religions (such as a menorah, a nine-branched candelabrum used in celebrating Hanukkah).

The Supreme Court took a slightly different approach when it held that public displays having historical, as well as religious, significance do not necessarily violate the establishment clause.[26] Still, historical significance must be carefully weighed against religious elements in establishment clause cases.

■ **CASE IN POINT 2.10** Mount Soledad is a prominent hill near San Diego. There has been a forty-foot cross on top of Mount Soledad since 1913. In the 1990s, a war memorial with six walls listing the names of veterans was constructed next to the cross. The site was privately owned until 2006, when Congress authorized the property's transfer to the federal government "to preserve a historically significant war memorial."

Steve Trunk and the Jewish War Veterans filed lawsuits claiming that the cross violated the establishment clause because it endorsed the Christian religion. A federal appellate court agreed, finding that the primary effect of the memorial as a whole sent a strong message of endorsement of Christianity and exclusion of non-Christian veterans. The court noted that although not all cross displays at war memorials violate the establishment clause, the cross in this case physically dominated the site. Additionally, it was originally dedicated to religious purposes, had a long history of religious use, and was the only portion visible to drivers on the freeway below.[27] ■

The Free Exercise Clause The free exercise clause guarantees that people can hold any religious beliefs they want or can hold no religious beliefs. The constitutional guarantee of personal freedom restricts only the actions of the government, however, and not those of individuals or private businesses.

Restrictions Must Be Necessary. The government must have a compelling state interest for restricting the free exercise of religion, and the restriction must be the only way to further that interest. ■ **CASE IN POINT 2.11** Gregory Holt, an inmate in an Arkansas state prison, was a devout Muslim who wished to grow a beard in accord with his religious beliefs. The Arkansas Department of

---

23. *United States v. American Library Association*, 539 U.S. 194, 123 S.Ct. 2297, 156 L.Ed.2d 221 (2003).

24. The Prosecutorial Remedies and Other Tools to End the Exploitation of Children Today Act (Protect Act), 18 U.S.C. Section 2252A(a)(5)(B).

25. *United States v. Williams,* 553 U.S. 285, 128 S.Ct. 1830, 170 L.Ed.2d 650 (2008).

26. *Van Orden v. Perry*, 545 U.S. 677, 125 S.Ct. 2854, 162 L.Ed.2d 607 (2005). The Court held that a six-foot-tall monument of the Ten Commandments on the Texas state capitol grounds did not violate the establishment clause because the Ten Commandments have historical significance.

27. *Trunk v. City of San Diego*, 629 F.3d 1099 (9th Cir. 2011).

Correction prohibited inmates from growing beards (except for medical reasons). Holt asked for an exemption to grow a half-inch beard on religious grounds, and prison officials denied his request. Holt filed a suit in a federal district court against Ray Hobbs, the director of the department, and others.

A federal statute prohibits the government from taking any action that substantially burdens the religious exercise of an institutionalized person unless the action constitutes the least restrictive means of furthering a compelling governmental interest. The defendants argued that beards compromise prison safety—a compelling government interest—because contraband can be hidden in them and because an inmate can quickly shave his beard to disguise his identity.

The district court dismissed Holt's suit, and the dismissal was affirmed on appeal. Holt then appealed to the United States Supreme Court. The Court noted that "an item of contraband would have to be very small indeed to

be concealed by a 1/2–inch beard." Moreover, the Court reasoned that the department could satisfy its security concerns by simply searching the beard, the way it already searches prisoners' hair and clothing. The Court concluded that the department's grooming policy, which prevented Holt from growing a half-inch beard, violated his right to exercise his religious beliefs.[28] ■

Restrictions Must Not Be a Substantial Burden. To comply with the free exercise clause, a government action must not place a substantial burden on religious practices. A burden is substantial if it pressures an individual to modify his or her behavior and to violate his or her beliefs.

At issue in the following case was whether forcing a state prison inmate to choose between daily nutrition and a religious practice is a substantial burden.

---

28. *Holt v. Hobbs*, ___ U.S. ___, 135 S.Ct. 853, 190 L.Ed.2d 747 (2015).

Case Analysis 2.3

Thompson v. Holm
United States Court of Appeals, Seventh Circuit, 809 F.3d 376 (2016).

In the Language of the Court
ROVNER, Circuit Judge.

Michael Thompson, a Muslim inmate incarcerated at Waupun Correctional Institution in Wisconsin, sued members of the prison staff for violating his right under the First Amendment to exercise his religion freely. The violation occurred, Thompson says, when for two days prison staff prevented him from fasting properly during Ramadan.

* * * A central religious practice of the Islamic faith is a sunrise-to-sunset fast during the month of Ramadan. The prison normally accommodates this practice by providing Ramadan "meal bags" at sunset to each Muslim prisoner listed as eligible. The prison's chaplain determines eligibility. Each Ramadan meal bag contains two meals: the post-sunset dinner and the next morning's pre-sunrise breakfast. A prisoner who eats at the prison cafeteria during Ramadan forfeits his right to the meal bags for the rest of the month-long fast. Thompson, a practicing Muslim, began fasting for Ramadan after sunrise on August 11—the first day of Ramadan. He

received his daily meal bags until August 21, about one-third into the month.

* * * Thompson says that shortly before August 21, as he was on his way back to his cell, Randall Lashock, a prison guard, handed him a meal bag. When Thompson arrived at his cell, he found that a guard had already left a meal bag for him there. Thompson could not leave his cell to return the extra bag without risking a conduct violation, so he left one of the two bags unopened for Lashock to retrieve. Lashock asserts that when he later retrieved that extra meal bag from Thompson's cell, he found Thompson eating from both bags.

Thompson received no meal bags on August 21 and 22. Lashock was supposed to deliver the Ramadan meal bags to every prisoner on the eligibility list. But on those two days, Lashock brought Thompson nothing, even though * * * he remained on the list. Receiving no meals, and learning from [prison guards] Bruce Bleich and Matthew Larson when he complained to them that he would have to go to the cafeteria if he wanted

to eat, Thompson felt pressure to break his fast by going to the cafeteria. But he knew that under the prison's policy he could not do that without forfeiting meal bags for the rest of the month-long fast. He also had hunger pangs and felt tired and unwell. Because of his hunger, exhaustion, and anxiety, he missed one of his morning prayers and did not properly experience Ramadan, which is meant to be a time of peace and focus.

* * * *

While he was receiving no meal bags, Thompson asked other prison officials to explain why Lashock was not bringing him food * * * . Bleich and Larson told him that Captain William Holm had ordered his name removed from the list because he had stolen a meal bag; they too refused to bring him any meals. But Holm * * * did not remove Thompson from the list and had no authority to do so; only the chaplain could do that.

* * * On August 23, Thompson received a Ramadan meal bag at sunset

Case 2.3 Continues

Case 2.3 Continued

and continued to receive a bag each day until the end of Ramadan.

Thompson [filed a suit in a federal district court against] Lashock, Holm, Bleich, and Larson * * * for violating his First Amendment rights, and the defendants moved for summary judgment. * * * They argued the lack of meal bags for two days did not substantially burden Thompson's free-exercise rights.

Thompson responded that the defendants unlawfully withheld his meal bags. * * * By forcing him to choose between adequate nutrition and a central tenet of his religion, the defendants substantially burdened his free-exercise rights.

[The court] granted the defendants' motion for summary judgment. The judge ruled that receiving no meal bags for just two days was not a substantial burden on Thompson's free-exercise rights because he kept fasting, praying, and reading the Koran.

On appeal Thompson challenges the entry of summary judgment.

We begin our analysis by asking whether the denial of meal bags substantially burdened Thompson's free exercise rights. The answer is yes. *Without the meal bags, Thompson was forced to choose between foregoing adequate nutrition or violating a central tenet of his religion. Facing that choice for "only" two days was not, as defendants argue, a "de minimis" [minimal] burden.* Not only did Thompson receive no proper meal for 55 hours, leaving him weak and tired, he did not know if he would ever be put back on the Ramadan list and get regular food. This uncertainty put pressure on him to resign himself to the cafeteria; the anxiety left him unable to practice Ramadan properly. [Emphasis added.]

* * * *

We next consider whether Thompson produced sufficient evidence that all the defendants were personally involved in imposing this burden. Once again, the answer is yes. We consider the defendants individually, beginning with

Lashock. He was responsible for delivering the meal bags to all inmates on the eligibility list. Yet he personally denied them to Thompson for two days even though * * * Thompson remained on the list. As to Holm, * * * Holm lied about whether he had removed Thompson from the meal list. Finally, as to Bleich and Larson, they also bear responsibility for depriving Thompson of his food. By (falsely) telling Thompson that Holm had removed him from the religious meal list, refusing to bring him any meals, and warning him to go to the cafeteria if he wanted to eat, * * * they were involved in a joint effort to pressure Thompson to break his fast.

* * * *

Accordingly, we VACATE the judgment. This case is REMANDED for further proceedings consistent with this order.

Legal Reasoning Questions

1. What is the standard for determining whether a restriction on a religious practice is constitutional under the First Amendment?

2. How did that standard apply to the prison guards' conduct in this case?

3. Were all of the guards personally involved in the alleged violation of the First Amendment? Explain.

Public Welfare Exception. When religious *practices* work against public policy and the public welfare, the government can act. For instance, the government can require that a child receive certain types of vaccinations or medical treatment if his or her life is in danger— regardless of the child's or parent's religious beliefs. When public safety is an issue, an individual's religious beliefs often have to give way to the government's interest in protecting the public.

■ **EXAMPLE 2.12** A woman of the Muslim faith may choose not to appear in public without a scarf, known as a *hijab*, over her head. Nevertheless, due to public safety concerns, many courts today do not allow the wearing of any headgear (hats or scarves) in courtrooms. ■

2–2d Searches and Seizures

The Fourth Amendment protects the "right of the people to be secure in their persons, houses, papers, and effects."

Before searching or seizing private property, law enforcement officers must usually obtain a **search warrant**—an order from a judge or other public official authorizing the search or seizure. Because of the strong government interest in protecting the public, however, a warrant normally is not required for seizures of spoiled or contaminated food. Nor are warrants required for searches of businesses in such highly regulated industries as liquor, guns, and strip mining.

To obtain a search warrant, law enforcement officers must convince a judge that they have reasonable grounds, or **probable cause,** to believe a search will reveal evidence of a specific illegality. To establish probable cause, the officers must have trustworthy evidence that would convince a reasonable person that the proposed search or seizure is more likely justified than not.

■ **CASE IN POINT 2.13** Citlalli Flores was driving across the border into the United States from Tijuana, Mexico, when a border protection officer became suspicious because she was acting nervous and looking around inside her car.

On further inspection, the officer found thirty-six pounds of marijuana hidden in the car's quarter panels. Flores claimed that she had not known about the marijuana.

Flores was arrested for importing marijuana into the United States. She then made two jail-recorded phone calls in which she asked her cousin to delete whatever he felt needed to be removed from Flores's Facebook page. The government got a warrant to search Flores's Facebook messages, where they found references to her "carrying" or "bringing" marijuana into the United States that day. Flores's Facebook posts were later used as evidence against her at trial, and she was convicted.

On appeal, the court held that the phone calls had given the officers probable cause to support a warrant to search Flores's social networking site for incriminating statements. Her conviction was affirmed.[29] ■

2–2e Self-Incrimination

The Fifth Amendment guarantees that no person "shall be compelled in any criminal case to be a witness against himself." Thus, in any court proceeding, an accused person cannot be forced to give testimony that might subject him or her to any criminal prosecution. The guarantee applies to both federal and state proceedings because the due process clause of the Fourteenth Amendment (discussed shortly) extends the protection to state courts.

The Fifth Amendment's guarantee against self-incrimination extends only to natural persons. Neither corporations nor partnerships receive Fifth Amendment protection. When a partnership is required to produce business records, it must therefore do so even if the information provided incriminates the individual partners of the firm. In contrast, sole proprietors and sole practitioners (those who individually own their businesses) cannot be compelled to produce their business records. These individuals have full protection against self-incrimination because they function in only one capacity, and there is no separate business entity.

2–3 Due Process and Equal Protection

Other constitutional guarantees of great significance to Americans are mandated by the *due process clauses* of the Fifth and Fourteenth Amendments and the *equal protection clause* of the Fourteenth Amendment.

2–3a Due Process

Both the Fifth and Fourteenth Amendments provide that no person shall be deprived "of life, liberty, or property, without due process of law." The **due process clause** of these constitutional amendments has two aspects—procedural and substantive. Note that the due process clause applies to "legal persons" (that is, corporations), as well as to individuals.

Procedural Due Process *Procedural* due process requires that any government decision to take life, liberty, or property must be made equitably. In other words, the government must give a person proper notice and an opportunity to be heard. Fair procedures must be used in determining whether a person will be subjected to punishment or have some burden imposed on her or him.

Fair procedure has been interpreted as requiring that the person have at least an opportunity to object to a proposed action before an impartial, neutral decision maker (who need not be a judge). ■ **EXAMPLE 2.14** Doyle Burns, a nursing student in Kansas, poses for a photograph standing next to a placenta used as a lab specimen. Although she quickly deletes the photo from her library, it ends up on Facebook. When the director of nursing sees the photo, Burns is expelled. She sues for reinstatement and wins. The school violated Burns's due process rights by expelling her from the nursing program for taking a photo without giving her an opportunity to present her side to school authorities. ■

Substantive Due Process *Substantive* due process focuses on the content of legislation rather than the fairness of procedures. Substantive due process limits what the government may do in its legislative and executive capacities. Legislation must be fair and reasonable in content and must further a legitimate governmental objective.

If a law or other governmental action limits a fundamental right, the state must have a legitimate and compelling interest to justify its action. Fundamental rights include interstate travel, privacy, voting, marriage and family, and all First Amendment rights. Thus, for instance, a state must have a substantial reason for taking any action that infringes on a person's free speech rights.

In situations not involving fundamental rights, a law or action does not violate substantive due process if it rationally relates to any legitimate government purpose. It is almost impossible for a law or action to fail the "rationality" test. Under this test, almost any business regulation will be upheld as reasonable.

---

29. *United States v. Flores*, 830 F.3d 1028 (9th Cir. 2015).

2–3b Equal Protection

Under the Fourteenth Amendment, a state may not "deny to any person within its jurisdiction the equal protection of the laws." The United States Supreme Court has interpreted the due process clause of the Fifth Amendment to make the **equal protection clause** applicable to the federal government as well. Equal protection means that the government cannot enact laws that treat similarly situated individuals differently.

Equal protection, like substantive due process, relates to the substance of a law or other governmental action. When a law or action limits the liberty of *all* persons, it may violate substantive due process. When a law or action limits the liberty of *some* persons but not others, it may violate the equal protection clause. ■ **EXAMPLE 2.15** If a law prohibits all advertising on the sides of trucks, it raises a substantive due process question. If the law makes an exception to allow truck owners to advertise their own businesses, it raises an equal protection issue. ■

In an equal protection inquiry, when a law or action distinguishes between or among individuals, the basis for the distinction—that is, the classification—is examined. Depending on the classification, the courts apply different levels of scrutiny, or "tests," to determine whether the law or action violates the equal protection clause. The courts use one of three standards: strict scrutiny, intermediate scrutiny, or the "rational basis" test.

Strict Scrutiny If a law or action prohibits or inhibits some persons from exercising a fundamental right, the law or action will be subject to "strict scrutiny" by the courts. Under this standard, the classification must be necessary to promote a *compelling state interest.*

Compelling state interests include remedying past unconstitutional or illegal discrimination but do not include correcting the general effects of "society's discrimination." ■ **EXAMPLE 2.16** For a city to give preference to minority applicants in awarding construction contracts, it normally must identify past unconstitutional or illegal discrimination against minority construction firms. Because the policy is based on suspect traits (race and national origin), it will violate the equal protection clause *unless* it is necessary to promote a compelling state interest. ■ Generally, few laws or actions survive strict-scrutiny analysis by the courts.

Intermediate Scrutiny Another standard, that of *intermediate scrutiny,* is applied in cases involving discrimination based on gender or legitimacy (children born out of wedlock). Laws using these classifications must be *substantially related to important government*

objectives. ■ **EXAMPLE 2.17** An important government objective is preventing illegitimate teenage pregnancies. Males and females are not similarly situated in this regard because only females can become pregnant. Therefore, a law that punishes men but not women for statutory rape will be upheld even though it treats men and women unequally. ■

The state also has an important objective in establishing time limits (called *statutes of limitation*) for how long after an event a particular type of action can be brought. Nevertheless, the limitation period must be substantially related to the important objective of preventing fraudulent or outdated claims. ■ **EXAMPLE 2.18** A state law requires illegitimate children to bring paternity suits within six years of their births in order to seek support from their fathers. A court will strike down this law if legitimate children are allowed to seek support from their parents at any time. Distinguishing between support claims on the basis of legitimacy is not related to the important government objective of preventing fraudulent or outdated claims. ■

The "Rational Basis" Test In matters of economic or social welfare, a classification will be considered valid if there is any conceivable *rational basis* on which the classification might relate to a legitimate government interest. It is almost impossible for a law or action to fail the rational basis test.

■ **CASE IN POINT 2.19** A Kentucky statute prohibits businesses that sell substantial amounts of staple groceries or gasoline from applying for a license to sell wine and liquor. A local grocer (Maxwell's Pic-Pac) filed a lawsuit against the state, alleging that the statute and the regulation were unconstitutional under the equal protection clause. The court applied the rational basis test and ruled that the statute and regulation were rationally related to a legitimate government interest in reducing access to products with high alcohol content.

The court cited the problems caused by alcohol, including drunk driving, and noted that the state's interest in limiting access to such products extends to the general public. Grocery stores and gas stations pose a greater risk of exposing members of the public to alcohol. For these and other reasons, the state can restrict these places from selling wine and liquor.[30] ■

2–4 Privacy Rights

The U.S. Constitution does not explicitly mention a general right to privacy. In a 1928 Supreme Court case,

---

30. *Maxwell's Pic-Pac, Inc. v. Dehner,* 739 F.3d 936 (6th Cir. 2014).

Olmstead v. United States,[31] Justice Louis Brandeis stated in his dissent that the right to privacy is "the most comprehensive of rights and the right most valued by civilized men." The majority of the justices at that time, however, did not agree with Brandeis.

It was not until the 1960s that the Supreme Court endorsed the view that the Constitution protects individual privacy rights. In a landmark 1965 case, *Griswold v. Connecticut,*[32] the Supreme Court held that a constitutional right to privacy was implied by the First, Third, Fourth, Fifth, and Ninth Amendments.

Today, privacy rights receive protection under various federal statutes as well the U.S. Constitution. State constitutions and statutes also secure individuals' privacy rights, often to a significant degree. Privacy rights are also protected to an extent under tort law, consumer law, and employment law.

2–4a Federal Privacy Legislation

In the last several decades, Congress has enacted a number of statutes that protect the privacy of individuals in various areas of concern. Most of these statutes deal with personal information collected by governments or private businesses.

In the 1960s, Americans were sufficiently alarmed by the accumulation of personal information in government files that they pressured Congress to pass laws permitting individuals to access their files. Congress responded by passing the Freedom of Information Act, which allows any person to request copies of any information on her or him contained in federal government files. Congress later enacted the Privacy Act, which also gives persons the right to access such information.

In the 1990s, responding to the growing need to protect the privacy of individuals' health records—particularly computerized records—Congress passed the Health Insurance Portability and Accountability Act (HIPAA).[33] This act defines and limits the circumstances in which an individual's "protected health information" may be used or disclosed by health-care providers, health-care plans, and others. These and other major federal laws protecting privacy rights are listed and briefly described in Exhibit 2–2.

---

31. 277 U.S. 438, 48 S.Ct. 564, 72 L.Ed. 944 (1928).
32. 381 U.S. 479, 85 S.Ct. 1678, 14 L.Ed.2d 510 (1965).

33. HIPAA was enacted as Pub. L. No. 104-191 (1996) and is codified in 29 U.S.C.A. Sections 1181 *et seq.*

EXHIBIT 2–2 Federal Legislation Relating to Privacy

Freedom of Information Act (1966)	Provides that individuals have a right to obtain access to information about them collected in government files.
Privacy Act (1974)	Protects the privacy of individuals about whom the federal government has information. Regulates agencies' use and disclosure of data, and gives individuals access to and a means to correct inaccuracies.
Electronic Communications Privacy Act (1986)	Prohibits the interception of information communicated by electronic means.
Health Insurance Portability and Accountability Act (1996)	Requires health-care providers and health-care plans to inform patients of their privacy rights and of how their personal medical information may be used. States that medical records may not be used for purposes unrelated to health care or disclosed without permission.
Financial Services Modernization Act (Gramm-Leach-Bliley Act) (1999)	Prohibits the disclosure of nonpublic personal information about a consumer to an unaffiliated third party unless strict disclosure and opt-out requirements are met.

2–4b The USA Patriot Act and the USA Freedom Act

The USA Patriot Act was passed by Congress in the wake of the terrorist attacks of September 11, 2001.[34] The Patriot Act has given government officials increased authority to monitor Internet activities (such as e-mail and Web site visits) and to gain access to personal financial information and student information. Law enforcement officials can track the telephone and e-mail communications of one party to find out the identity of the other party or parties. Privacy advocates argue that this law adversely affects the constitutional rights of all Americans, and it has been widely criticized in the media.

While the bulk of the Patriot Act is permanent law, its most controversial surveillance provisions had to be reauthorized every four years and expired in June 2015. Most of the expired provisions were restored by the USA Freedom Act, which extends surveillance authority through 2019.[35] The Freedom Act did amend a portion of the Patriot Act in an attempt to stop the National Security Agency (NSA) from collecting mass phone data. (Note, however, that the act still allows the data to be collected by private phone companies, and the NSA can obtain data about targeted individuals through these companies.)

---

34. The Uniting and Strengthening America by Providing Appropriate Tools Required to Intercept and Obstruct Terrorism Act of 2001, also known as the USA Patriot Act, was enacted as Pub. L. No. 107-56 (2001) and last reauthorized by Pub. L. No. 112-114 (2011).

35. The full title of this statute is Uniting and Strengthening America by Fulfilling Rights and Ending Eavesdropping, Dragnet-collection and Online Monitoring, H.R. 3361.

Reviewing: Business and the Constitution

A state legislature enacted a statute that required any motorcycle operator or passenger on the state's highways to wear a protective helmet. Jim Alderman, a licensed motorcycle operator, sued the state to block enforcement of the law. Alderman asserted that the statute violated the equal protection clause because it placed requirements on motorcyclists that were not imposed on other motorists. Using the information presented in the chapter, answer the following questions.

1. Why does this statute raise equal protection issues instead of substantive due process concerns?
2. What are the three levels of scrutiny that the courts use in determining whether a law violates the equal protection clause?
3. Which standard of scrutiny, or test, would apply to this situation? Why?
4. Applying this standard, is the helmet statute constitutional? Why or why not?

Debate This . . . *Legislation aimed at "protecting people from themselves" concerns the individual as well as the public in general. Protective helmet laws are just one example of such legislation. Should individuals be allowed to engage in unsafe activities if they choose to do so?*

Terms and Concepts

Bill of Rights 31
checks and balances 27
commerce clause 27
compelling government interest 33
due process clause 39
equal protection clause 40
establishment clause 36

federal form of government 26
filtering software 35
free exercise clause 36
full faith and credit clause 27
meta tag 36
police powers 26
preemption 31

privileges and immunities clause 27
probable cause 38
search warrant 38
sovereignty 26
supremacy clause 31
symbolic speech 33

Issue Spotters

1. Can a state, in the interest of energy conservation, ban all advertising by power utilities if conservation could be accomplished by less restrictive means? Why or why not? (See *Business and the Bill of Rights*.)

2. Suppose that a state imposes a higher tax on out-of-state companies doing business in the state than it imposes on in-state companies. Is this a violation of equal protection if the only reason for the tax is to protect the local firms from out-of-state competition? Explain. (See *The Constitutional Powers of Government*.)

• **Check your answers to the Issue Spotters against the answers provided in Appendix B at the end of this text.**

Business Scenarios

2–1. Commerce Clause. A Georgia state law requires the use of contoured rear-fender mudguards on trucks and trailers operating within Georgia state lines. The statute further makes it illegal for trucks and trailers to use straight mudguards. In approximately thirty-five other states, straight mudguards are legal. Moreover, in Florida, straight mudguards are explicitly required by law. There is some evidence suggesting that contoured mudguards might be a little safer than straight mudguards. Discuss whether this Georgia statute violates any constitutional provisions. (See *The Constitutional Powers of Government*.)

2–2. Equal Protection. With the objectives of preventing crime, maintaining property values, and preserving the quality of urban life, New York City enacted an ordinance to regulate the locations of adult entertainment establishments. The ordinance expressly applied to female, but not male, topless entertainment. Adele Buzzetti owned the Cozy Cabin, a New York City cabaret that featured female topless dancers. Buzzetti and an anonymous dancer filed a suit in a federal district court against the city, asking the court to block the enforcement of the ordinance. The plaintiffs argued, in part, that the ordinance violated the equal protection clause. Under the equal protection clause, what standard applies to the court's consideration of this ordinance? Under this test, how should the court rule? Why? (See *Due Process and Equal Protection*.)

Business Case Problems

2–3. Spotlight on Plagiarism—Due Process. The Russ College of Engineering and Technology of Ohio University announced in a press conference that it had found "rampant and flagrant plagiarism" in the theses of mechanical engineering graduate students. Faculty singled out for "ignoring their ethical responsibilities" included Jay Gunasekera, chair of the department. Gunasekera was prohibited from advising students. He filed a suit against Dennis Irwin, the dean of Russ College, for violating his due process rights. What does due process require in these circumstances? Why? [*Gunasekera v. Irwin,* 551 F.3d 461 (6th Cir. 2009)] (See *Due Process and Equal Protection.*)

2–4. Business Case Problem with Sample Answer— The Dormant Commerce Clause. In 2001, Puerto Rico enacted a law that requires specific labels on cement sold in Puerto Rico and imposes fines for any violations of these requirements. The law prohibits the sale or distribution of cement manufactured outside Puerto Rico that does not carry a required label warning that the cement may not be used in government-financed construction projects. Antilles Cement Corp., a Puerto Rican firm that imports foreign cement, filed a complaint in federal court, claiming that this law violated the dormant commerce clause. (The dormant commerce clause doctrine applies not only to commerce among the states and U.S. territories, but also to international commerce.) Did the 2001 Puerto Rican law violate the dormant commerce clause? Why or why not? [*Antilles Cement Corp. v. Fortuno,* 670 F.3d 310 (1st Cir. 2012)] (See *The Constitutional Powers of Government*.)

• **For a sample answer to Problem 2–4, go to Appendix C at the end of this text.**

2–5. Freedom of Speech. Mark Wooden sent an e-mail to an alderwoman for the city of St. Louis. Attached was a nineteen-minute audio file that compared her to the biblical character Jezebel. The audio said she was a "bitch in the Sixth Ward," spending too much time with the rich and powerful and too little time with the poor. In a menacing, maniacal tone, Wooden said that he was "dusting off a sawed-off shotgun," called himself a "domestic terrorist," and referred to the assassination of President John Kennedy, the murder of federal judge John Roll, and the shooting of Representative Gabrielle Giffords. Feeling threatened, the alderwoman called the police. Wooden was convicted of harassment under a state criminal statute. Was this conviction unconstitutional under the First Amendment? Discuss. [*State of Missouri v. Wooden,* 388 S.W.3d 522 (Mo. 2013)] (See *Business and the Bill of Rights*.)

2–6. Equal Protection. Abbott Laboratories licensed SmithKline Beecham Corp. to market an Abbott human immunodeficiency virus (HIV) drug in conjunction with one of SmithKline's drugs. Abbott then increased the price of its drug fourfold, forcing SmithKline to increase its prices and thereby driving business to Abbott's own combination drug. SmithKline filed a suit in a federal district court against Abbott. During jury selection, Abbott struck the only self-identified gay person among the potential jurors. (The pricing of HIV drugs is of considerable concern in the gay community.) Could the equal protection clause be applied to prohibit discrimination based on sexual orientation in jury selection? Discuss. [*SmithKline Beecham Corp. v. Abbott Laboratories,* 740 F.3d 471 (9th Cir. 2014)] (See *Due Process and Equal Protection.*)

2–7. Procedural Due Process. Robert Brown applied for admission to the University of Kansas School of Law. Brown answered "no" to questions on the application asking if he had a criminal history and acknowledged that a false answer constituted "cause for . . . dismissal." In fact, Brown had criminal convictions for domestic battery and driving under the influence. He was accepted for admission to the school. When school officials discovered his history, however, he was notified of their intent to dismiss him and given an opportunity to respond in writing. He demanded a hearing. The officials refused to grant Brown a hearing and then expelled him. Did the school's actions deny Brown due process? Discuss. [*Brown v. University of Kansas,* 599 Fed.Appx. 833 (10th Cir. 2015)] (See *Due Process and Equal Protection.*)

2–8. The Commerce Clause. Regency Transportation, Inc., operates a freight business throughout the eastern United States. Regency maintains its corporate headquarters, four warehouses, and a maintenance facility and terminal location for repairing and storing vehicles in Massachusetts. All of the vehicles in Regency's fleet were bought in other states. Massachusetts imposes a use tax on all taxpayers subject to its jurisdiction, including those that do business in interstate commerce, as Regency does. When Massachusetts imposed the tax on the purchase price of each tractor and trailer in Regency's fleet, the trucking firm challenged the assessment as discriminatory under the commerce clause. What is the chief consideration under the commerce clause when a state law affects interstate commerce?

Is Massachusetts's use tax valid? Explain. [*Regency Transportation, Inc. v. Commissioner of Revenue,* 473 Mass. 459, 42 N.E.3d 1133 (2016)] (See *The Constitutional Powers of Government.*)

2–9. A Question of Ethics—Defamation. *Aric Toll owns and manages the Balboa Island Village Inn, a restaurant and bar in Newport Beach, California. Anne Lemen lives across from the inn. Lemen complained to the authorities about the inn's customers, whom she called "drunks" and "whores." She referred to Aric's wife as "Madam Whore" and told neighbors that the owners were involved in illegal drugs and prostitution. Lemen told Ewa Cook, a bartender at the Inn, that Cook "worked for Satan." She repeated her statements to potential customers, and the inn's sales dropped more than 20 percent. The inn filed a suit against Lemen.* [Balboa Island Village Inn, Inc. v. Lemen, *40 Cal.4th 1141, 156 P.3d 339 (2007)]* (See *Business and the Bill of Rights.*)

(a) Are Lemen's statements about the inn's owners, customers, and activities protected by the U.S. Constitution? Should such statements be protected? In whose favor should the court rule? Why?

(b) Did Lemen behave unethically in the circumstances of this case? Explain.

2–10. Special Case Analysis—Freedom of Religion. Go to Case Analysis 2.3, *Thompson v. Holm.* Read the excerpt, and answer the following questions.

(a) Issue: The focus in this case was on an allegation of the violation of which clause of the U.S. Constitution, and by what means?

(b) Rule of Law: What is required to establish that this clause has been violated?

(c) Applying the Rule of Law: How did the court determine whether the claim of a violation was supported in this case?

(d) Conclusion: What did the federal appellate court conclude with respect to the plaintiff's claim, and what did the court order as the next step in the case?

Legal Reasoning Group Activity

2–11. Free Speech and Equal Protection. For many years, New York City has had to deal with the vandalism and defacement of public property caused by unauthorized graffiti. In an effort to stop the damage, the city banned the sale of aerosol spray-paint cans and broad-tipped indelible markers to persons under twenty-one years of age. The new rules also prohibited people from possessing these items on property other than their own. Within a year, five people under age twenty-one were cited for violations of these regulations, and 871 individuals were arrested for actually making graffiti.

Lindsey Vincenty and other artists wished to create graffiti on legal surfaces, such as canvas, wood, and clothing. Unable to buy supplies in the city or to carry them into the city from elsewhere, Vincenty and others filed a lawsuit on behalf of themselves and other young artists against Michael

Bloomberg, the city's mayor, and others. The plaintiffs claimed that, among other things, the new rules violated their right to freedom of speech.

(a) One group will argue in favor of the plaintiffs and provide several reasons why the court should hold that the city's new rules violate the plaintiffs' freedom of speech. (See *Business and the Bill of Rights.*)

(b) Another group will develop a counterargument that outlines the reasons why the new rules do not violate free speech rights. (See *Business and the Bill of Rights.*)

(c) A third group will argue that the city's ban violates the equal protection clause because it applies only to persons under age twenty-one. (See *Due Process and Equal Protection.*)

CHAPTER 3

Courts and Alternative Dispute Resolution

The United States has fifty-two court systems—one for each of the fifty states, one for the District of Columbia, and a federal system. Keep in mind that the federal courts are not superior to the state courts. They are simply an independent system of courts, which derives its authority from Article III, Section 2, of the U.S. Constitution. By the power given to it under the U.S. Constitution, Congress has extended the federal court system to U.S. territories such as Guam, Puerto Rico, and the Virgin Islands.[1]

As we shall see, the United States Supreme Court is the final controlling voice over all of these fifty-two systems, at least when questions of federal law are involved. The Supreme Court's decisions—whether on free speech and social media, health-care subsidies, environmental regulation, or same-sex marriage—represent the last word in the most controversial legal debates in our society. Nevertheless, many of the legal issues that arise in our daily lives, such as the use of social media by courts, employers, and law enforcement, have not yet come before the nation's highest court. The lower courts usually resolve such pressing matters, making these courts equally important in our legal system.

Although an understanding of our nation's court systems is beneficial for anyone, it is particularly crucial for businesspersons, who will likely face a lawsuit at some time during their careers. Anyone involved in business should be familiar with the basic requirements that must be met before a party can bring a lawsuit before a particular court.

---

1. In Guam and the Virgin Islands, territorial courts serve as both federal courts and state courts. In Puerto Rico, they serve only as federal courts.

3–1 The Judiciary's Role in American Government

The body of American law includes the federal and state constitutions, statutes passed by legislative bodies, administrative law, and the case decisions and legal principles that form the common law. These laws would be meaningless, however, without the courts to interpret and apply them. The essential role of the judiciary—the courts—in the American governmental system is to interpret the laws and apply them to specific situations.

3–1a Judicial Review

As the branch of government entrusted with interpreting the laws, the judiciary can decide, among other things, whether the laws or actions of the other two branches are constitutional. The process for making such a determination is known as **judicial review.** The power of judicial review enables the judicial branch to act as a check on the other two branches of government, in line with the system of checks and balances established by the U.S. Constitution.[2]

3–1b The Origins of Judicial Review in the United States

The power of judicial review is not mentioned in the U.S. Constitution (although many constitutional scholars believe that the founders intended the judiciary to have this power). The United States Supreme Court explicitly established this power in 1803 in the case *Marbury v. Madison*.[3] In that decision, the Court stated, "It is emphatically the province [authority] and duty of the Judicial Department to say what the law is. . . . If two laws conflict with each other, the courts must decide on

---

2. In a broad sense, judicial review occurs whenever a court "reviews" a case or legal proceeding—as when an appellate court reviews a lower court's decision. When discussing the judiciary's role in American government, however, the term *judicial review* refers to the power of the judiciary to decide whether the actions of the other two branches of government violate the U.S. Constitution.

3. 5 U.S. (1 Cranch) 137, 2 L.Ed. 60 (1803).

the operation of each. . . . [I]f both [a] law and the Constitution apply to a particular case, . . . the Court must determine which of these conflicting rules governs the case. This is of the very essence of judicial duty." Since the *Marbury v. Madison* decision, the power of judicial review has remained unchallenged. Today, this power is exercised by both federal and state courts.

3–2 Basic Judicial Requirements

Before a lawsuit can be brought before a court, certain requirements must be met. These requirements relate to jurisdiction, venue, and standing to sue. We examine each of these important concepts here.

3–2a Jurisdiction

In Latin, *juris* means "law," and *diction* means "to speak." Thus, "the power to speak the law" is the literal meaning of the term **jurisdiction.** Before any court can hear a case, it must have jurisdiction over the person (or company) against whom the suit is brought (the defendant) or over the property involved in the suit. The court must also have jurisdiction over the subject matter of the dispute.

Jurisdiction over Persons or Property Generally, a particular court can exercise *in personam* **jurisdiction** (personal jurisdiction) over any person or business that resides in a certain geographic area. A state trial court, for instance, normally has jurisdictional authority over residents (including businesses) of a particular area of the state, such as a county or district. A state's highest court (often called the state supreme court[4]) has jurisdictional authority over all residents within the state.

A court can also exercise jurisdiction over property that is located within its boundaries. This kind of jurisdiction is known as *in rem* **jurisdiction**, or "jurisdiction over the thing." ■ **EXAMPLE 3.1** A dispute arises over the ownership of a boat in dry dock in Fort Lauderdale, Florida. The boat is owned by an Ohio resident, over whom a Florida court normally cannot exercise personal jurisdiction. The other party to the dispute is a resident of Nebraska. In this situation, a lawsuit concerning the boat could be brought in a Florida state court on the basis of the court's *in rem* jurisdiction. ■

Long Arm Statutes and Minimum Contacts. Under the authority of a state **long arm statute,** a court can exercise personal jurisdiction over certain out-of-state defendants based on activities that took place within the state. Before a court can exercise jurisdiction, though, it must be demonstrated that the defendant had sufficient contacts, or *minimum contacts*, with the state to justify the jurisdiction.[5]

Generally, the minimum-contacts requirement means that the defendant must have sufficient connection to the state for the judge to conclude that it is fair for the state to exercise power over the defendant. For instance, if an out-of-state defendant caused an automobile accident within the state or breached a contract formed there, a court will usually find that minimum contacts exist to exercise jurisdiction over that defendant. Similarly, a state may exercise personal jurisdiction over a nonresident defendant that is sued for selling defective goods within the state.

■ **CASE IN POINT 3.2** An Xbox game system caught fire in Bonnie Broquet's home in Texas and caused substantial personal injuries. Broquet filed a lawsuit in a Texas court against Ji-Haw Industrial Company, a nonresident company that made the Xbox components. Broquet alleged that Ji-Haw's components were defective and had caused the fire. Ji-Haw argued that the Texas court lacked jurisdiction over it, but a state appellate court held that the Texas long arm statute authorized the exercise of jurisdiction over the out-of-state defendant.[6] ■

Corporate Contacts. Because corporations are considered legal persons, courts use the same principles to determine whether it is fair to exercise jurisdiction over a corporation. A corporation normally is subject to personal jurisdiction in the state in which it is incorporated, has its principal office, and/or is doing business.

Courts apply the minimum-contacts test to determine if they can exercise jurisdiction over out-of-state corporations. The minimum-contacts requirement is usually met if the corporation advertises or sells its products within the state, or places its goods into the "stream of commerce" with the intent that the goods be sold in the state. ■ **EXAMPLE 3.3** A business is incorporated under the laws of Maine but has a branch office and manufacturing plant in Georgia. The corporation also advertises and sells its products in Georgia. These activities would likely constitute sufficient contacts with the state of Georgia to allow a Georgia court to exercise jurisdiction over the corporation. ■

---

4. As will be discussed shortly, a state's highest court is often referred to as the state supreme court, but there are exceptions. For instance, in New York the supreme court is a trial court.

5. The minimum-contacts standard was first established in *International Shoe Co. v. State of Washington*, 326 U.S. 310, 66 S.Ct. 154, 90 L.Ed. 95 (1945).

6. *Ji-Haw Industrial Co. v. Broquet*, 2008 WL 441822 (Tex.App.—San Antonio 2008).

Some corporations do not sell or advertise their products in the general marketplace. Determining what constitutes minimum contacts in these situations can be more difficult. ■ **CASE IN POINT 3.4** Independence Plating Corporation is a New Jersey corporation that provides metal-coating services. Its only office and all of its personnel are located in New Jersey, and it does not advertise out of state. Independence had a long-standing business relationship with Southern Prestige Industries, Inc., a North Carolina company. Eventually, Southern Prestige filed suit in North Carolina against Independence for defective workmanship. Independence argued that North Carolina did not have jurisdiction over it, but the court held that Independence had sufficient minimum contacts with the state to justify jurisdiction. The two parties had exchanged thirty-two separate purchase orders in a period of less than twelve months.[7] ■

Jurisdiction over Subject Matter Subject-matter jurisdiction refers to the limitations on the types of cases a court can hear. Certain courts are empowered to hear certain kinds of disputes. In both the federal and the state court systems, there are courts of general (unlimited) jurisdiction and courts of limited jurisdiction.

A *court of general jurisdiction* can decide cases involving a broad array of issues. An example of a court of general jurisdiction is a state trial court or a federal district court.

In contrast, a *court of limited jurisdiction* can hear only specific types of cases. An example of a state court of limited jurisdiction is a probate court. **Probate courts** are state courts that handle only the disposition of a person's assets and obligations after that person's death, including issues relating to the custody and guardianship of children. An example of a federal court of limited subject-matter jurisdiction is a bankruptcy court. **Bankruptcy courts** handle only bankruptcy proceedings, which are governed by federal bankruptcy law.

A court's jurisdiction over subject matter is usually defined in the statute or constitution that created the court. In both the federal and the state court systems, a court's subject-matter jurisdiction can be limited by any of the following:

1. The subject of the lawsuit.
2. The sum in controversy.
3. Whether the case involves a felony (a serious type of crime) or a misdemeanor (a less serious type of crime).
4. Whether the proceeding is a trial or an appeal.

Original and Appellate Jurisdiction The distinction between courts of original jurisdiction and courts of appellate jurisdiction normally lies in whether the case is being heard for the first time. Courts having original jurisdiction are courts of the first instance, or trial courts. These are courts in which lawsuits begin, trials take place, and evidence is presented. In the federal court system, the *district courts* are trial courts. In the various state court systems, the trial courts are known by various names, as will be discussed shortly.

The key point here is that any court having original jurisdiction normally serves as a trial court. Courts having appellate jurisdiction act as reviewing, or appellate, courts. In general, cases can be brought before appellate courts only on appeal from an order or a judgment of a trial court or other lower courts.

Jurisdiction of the Federal Courts Because the federal government is a government of limited powers, the jurisdiction of the federal courts is limited. Federal courts have subject-matter jurisdiction in two situations: when a federal question is involved and when there is diversity of citizenship.

Federal Questions. Article III of the U.S. Constitution establishes the boundaries of federal judicial power. Section 2 of Article III states that "the judicial Power shall extend to all Cases, in Law and Equity, arising under this Constitution, the Laws of the United States, and Treaties made, or which shall be made, under their Authority."

In effect, this clause means that whenever a plaintiff's cause of action is based, at least in part, on the U.S. Constitution, a treaty, or a federal law, a **federal question** arises. Any lawsuit involving a federal question, such as a person's rights under the U.S. Constitution, can originate in a federal court. Note that in a case based on a federal question, a federal court will apply federal law.

Diversity of Citizenship. Federal district courts can also exercise original jurisdiction over cases involving **diversity of citizenship**. The most common type of diversity jurisdiction[8] requires *both* of the following:

1. The plaintiff and defendant must be residents of different states.
2. The dollar amount in controversy must exceed $75,000.

---

7. *Southern Prestige Industries, Inc. v. Independence Plating Corp.*, 690 S.E.2d 768 (N.C. 2010).

8. Diversity jurisdiction also exists in cases between (1) a foreign country and citizens of a state or of different states and (2) citizens of a state and citizens or subjects of a foreign country. Cases based on these types of diversity jurisdiction occur infrequently.

For purposes of diversity jurisdiction, a corporation is a citizen of both the state in which it is incorporated and the state in which its principal place of business is located.

A case involving diversity of citizenship can be filed in the appropriate federal district court. (If the case starts in a state court, it can sometimes be transferred, or "removed," to a federal court.) A large percentage of the cases filed in federal courts each year are based on diversity of citizenship. As noted before, a federal court will apply federal law in cases involving federal questions. In a case based on diversity of citizenship, in contrast, a federal court will apply the relevant state law (which is often the law of the state in which the court sits).

The following case focused on whether diversity jurisdiction existed. A boat owner was severely burned when his boat exploded after being overfilled with fuel at a marina in the U.S. Virgin Islands. The owner filed a suit in a federal district court against the marina and sought a jury trial. The defendant argued that a plaintiff in an admiralty, or maritime, case (a case based on something that happened at sea) does not have a right to a jury trial unless the court has diversity jurisdiction. The defendant claimed that because both parties were citizens of the Virgin Islands, the court had no such jurisdiction.

Case Analysis 3.1

Mala v. Crown Bay Marina, Inc.

United States Court of Appeals, Third Circuit, 704 F.3d 239 (2013).

In the Language of the Court

SMITH, Circuit Judge.

* * * *

Kelley Mala is a citizen of the United States Virgin Islands. * * * He went for a cruise in his powerboat near St. Thomas, Virgin Islands. When his boat ran low on gas, he entered Crown Bay Marina to refuel. Mala tied the boat to one of Crown Bay's eight fueling stations and began filling his tank with an automatic gas pump. Before walking to the cash register to buy oil, Mala asked a Crown Bay attendant to watch his boat.

By the time Mala returned, the boat's tank was overflowing and fuel was spilling into the boat and into the water. The attendant manually shut off the pump and acknowledged that the pump had been malfunctioning in recent days. Mala began cleaning up the fuel, and at some point, the attendant provided soap and water. Mala eventually departed the marina, but as he did so, the engine caught fire and exploded. Mala was thrown into the water and was severely burned. His boat was unsalvageable.

* * * Mala sued Crown Bay in the District Court of the Virgin Islands.

Mala's * * * complaint asserted * * * that Crown Bay negligently maintained its gas pump. [Negligence is the failure to exercise the standard of care that a reasonable person would exercise in similar circumstances. Negligence can form the basis for a legal claim.] The complaint also alleged that the District Court had admiralty and diversity jurisdiction over the case, and it requested a jury trial.

* * * *

* * * Crown Bay filed a motion to strike Mala's jury demand. Crown Bay argued that plaintiffs generally do not have a jury-trial right in admiralty cases—only when the court also has diversity jurisdiction. And Crown Bay asserted that the parties were not diverse in this case * * * . In response to this motion, the District Court ruled that both Mala and Crown Bay were citizens of the Virgin Islands. The court therefore struck Mala's jury demand, but nevertheless opted to empanel an advisory jury. [The court could accept or reject the advisory jury's verdict.]

* * * At the end of the trial, the advisory jury returned a verdict of $460,000 for Mala—$400,000 for pain and suffering and $60,000 in compensatory

damages. It concluded that Mala was 25 percent at fault and that Crown Bay was 75 percent at fault. The District Court ultimately rejected the verdict and entered judgment for Crown Bay.

* * * *

This appeal followed.

* * * *

Mala * * * argues that the District Court improperly refused to conduct a jury trial. This claim ultimately depends on whether the District Court had diversity jurisdiction.

The Seventh Amendment [to the U.S. Constitution] creates a right to civil jury trials in federal court: "In Suits at common law * * * the right of trial by jury shall be preserved." Admiralty suits are not "Suits at common law," which means that when a district court has only admiralty jurisdiction the plaintiff does not have a jury-trial right. But [a federal statute] allows plaintiffs to pursue state claims in admiralty cases as long as the district court also has diversity jurisdiction. In such cases [the statute] preserves whatever jury-trial right exists with respect to the underlying state claims.

Case 3.1 Continued

Mala argues that the District Court had both admiralty and diversity jurisdiction. As a preliminary matter, the court certainly had admiralty jurisdiction. The alleged tort occurred on navigable water and bore a substantial connection to maritime activity.

The grounds for diversity jurisdiction are less certain. *District courts have jurisdiction only if the parties are completely diverse. This means that no plaintiff may have the same state or territorial citizenship as any defendant.* The parties agree that Mala was a citizen of the Virgin Islands. [Emphasis added.]

Unfortunately for Mala, the District Court concluded that Crown Bay also was a citizen of the Virgin Islands. Mala rejects this conclusion.

Mala bears the burden of proving that the District Court had diversity jurisdiction. Mala failed to meet that burden because he did not offer evidence that Crown Bay was anything other than a citizen of the Virgin Islands. Mala contends that Crown Bay admitted to being a citizen of Florida, but Crown Bay actually denied Mala's allegation.

Absent evidence that the parties were diverse, we are left with Mala's allegations. *Allegations are insufficient at trial. And they are especially insufficient on appeal*, where we review the District Court's underlying factual findings for clear error. Under this standard, we will not reverse unless we are left with the definite and firm conviction that Crown Bay was in fact a citizen of Florida. Mala has not presented any credible evidence that Crown Bay was a citizen of Florida—much less evidence that would leave us with the requisite firm conviction. [Emphasis added.]

* * * Accordingly, the parties were not diverse and Mala does not have a jury-trial right.

* * * *

* * * For these reasons we will affirm the District Court's judgment.

Legal Reasoning Questions

1. What is "diversity of citizenship"?

2. How does the presence—or lack—of diversity of citizenship affect a lawsuit?

3. What did the court conclude with respect to the parties' diversity of citizenship in this case?

Exclusive versus Concurrent Jurisdiction When both federal and state courts have the power to hear a case, as is true in lawsuits involving diversity of citizenship, **concurrent jurisdiction** exists. When cases can be tried only in federal courts or only in state courts, **exclusive jurisdiction** exists.

Federal courts have exclusive jurisdiction in cases involving federal crimes, bankruptcy, most patent and copyright claims, suits against the United States, and some areas of admiralty law. State courts also have exclusive jurisdiction over certain subjects—for instance, divorce and adoption.

When concurrent jurisdiction exists, a party may choose to bring a suit in either a federal court or a state court. Many factors can affect a party's decision to litigate in a federal versus a state court. Examples include the availability of different remedies, the distance to the respective courthouses, or the experience or reputation of a particular judge.

For instance, if the dispute involves a trade secret, a party might conclude that a federal court—which has exclusive jurisdiction over copyrights and patents—would have more expertise in the matter. In contrast, a plaintiff might choose to litigate in a state court if the court has a reputation for awarding substantial amounts of damages or if the judge is perceived as being pro-plaintiff. The concepts of exclusive and concurrent jurisdiction are illustrated in Exhibit 3–1.

Jurisdiction in Cyberspace The Internet's capacity to bypass political and geographic boundaries undercuts the traditional basis on which courts assert personal jurisdiction. As discussed, for a court to compel a defendant to come before it, the defendant must have a sufficient connection—that is, minimum contacts—with the state. When a defendant's only contacts with the state are through a Web site, however, it can be difficult to determine whether these contacts are sufficient for a court to exercise jurisdiction.

The "Sliding-Scale" Standard. The courts have developed a "sliding-scale" standard to determine when they can exercise personal jurisdiction over an out-of-state defendant based on the defendant's Web activities. The sliding-scale standard identifies three types of Internet business contacts and outlines the following rules for jurisdiction:

1. When the defendant conducts substantial business over the Internet (such as contracts and sales), jurisdiction is proper.

2. When there is some interactivity through a Web site, jurisdiction may be proper, depending on the

EXHIBIT 3–1   Exclusive and Concurrent Jurisdiction

Exclusive Federal Jurisdiction
(cases involving federal crimes, federal antitrust law, bankruptcy, patents, copyrights, trademarks, suits against the United States, some areas of admiralty law, and certain other matters specified in federal statutes)

Concurrent Jurisdiction
(most cases involving federal questions, diversity-of-citizenship cases)

Exclusive State Jurisdiction
(cases involving all matters not subject to federal jurisdiction— for example, divorce and adoption cases)

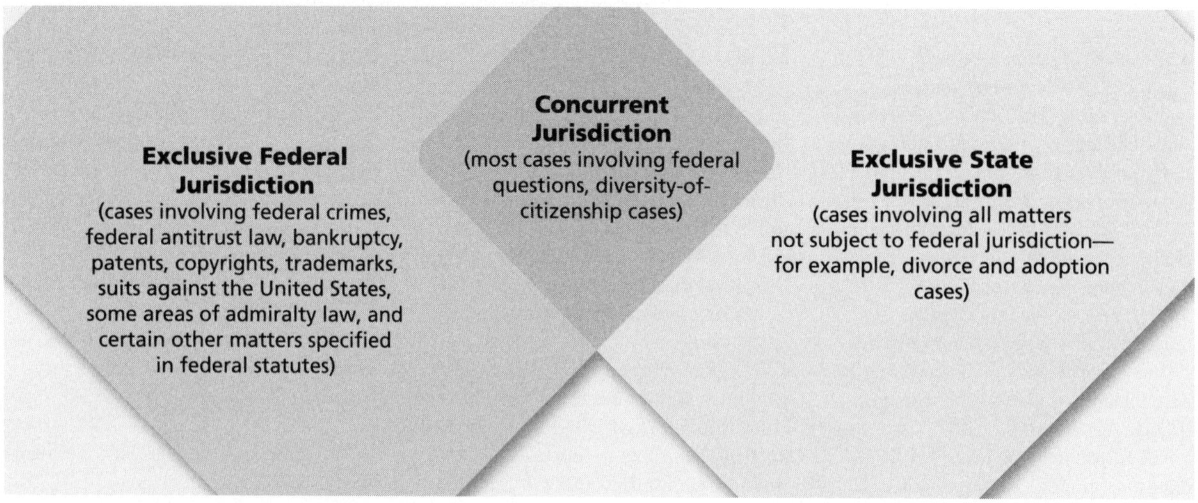

circumstances. Even a single contact can satisfy the minimum-contacts requirement in certain situations.

3. When a defendant merely engages in passive advertising on the Web, jurisdiction is never proper.[9] An Internet communication is typically considered passive if people have to voluntarily access it to read the message and active if it is sent to specific individuals.

■ **CASE IN POINT 3.5** Samantha Guffey lives in Oklahoma. She placed a winning bid on eBay for a used 2009 Volvo XC90 from Motorcars of Nashville, Inc. (MNI), a Tennessee corporation. Before she won the auction, she spoke with Otto Ostonakulov at the dealership. Later, Ostonakulov sent the necessary paperwork to Guffey in Oklahoma. She signed and returned it by mail, and he arranged for MNI to ship the Volvo to Oklahoma.

When the car was delivered to Guffey, she discovered it was not in the condition advertised. She filed a lawsuit in Oklahoma against MNI and Ostonakulov, alleging fraud and a violation of state consumer protection laws. Guffey's complaint alleged that the defendants were active "power sellers" on eBay, averaging twelve to twenty-five cars for sale every day. The sellers claimed that the Oklahoma court lacked jurisdiction over them, and a trial court dismissed the complaint. Guffey appealed. The reviewing court found that Oklahoma had jurisdiction because the sellers' "use of eBay to make multiple sales is systemic and appears to be a core part of their business." They had negotiated with Guffey directly to sell her a vehicle in Oklahoma and had regularly used eBay to sell vehicles to remote parties in the past.[10] ■

International Jurisdictional Issues. Because the Internet is international in scope, it obviously raises international jurisdictional issues. The world's courts seem to be developing a standard that echoes the requirement of minimum contacts applied by the U.S. courts.

Most courts are indicating that minimum contacts— doing business within the jurisdiction, for instance— are enough to compel a defendant to appear and that a physical presence in the country is not necessary. The effect of this standard is that a business firm has to comply with the laws in any jurisdiction in which it targets customers for its products. This situation is complicated by the fact that many countries' laws on particular issues—free speech, for instance—are very different from U.S. laws.

The following case illustrates how federal courts apply a sliding-scale standard to determine if they can exercise jurisdiction over a foreign defendant whose only contact with the United States is through a Web site.

---

9. For a leading case on this issue, see *Zippo Manufacturing Co. v. Zippo Dot Com, Inc.*, 952 F.Supp. 1119 (W.D.Pa. 1997).

10. *Guffey v. Ostonakulov*, 2014 OK 6, 321 P.3d 971 (Ok.Sup. 2014). Note that a single sale on eBay does not necessarily form the basis for jurisdiction. Jurisdiction depends on whether the seller regularly uses eBay as a means for doing business with remote buyers. See *Hinners v. Robey*, 336 S.W.3d 891 (Ky.Sup. 2008).

Spotlight on Gucci

Case 3.2 Gucci America, Inc. v. Wang Huoqing

United States District Court, Northern District of California, 2011 WL 30972 (2011).

Company Profile *Gucci America, Inc., a New York corporation headquartered in New York City, is part of Gucci Group, a global fashion firm with offices in China, France, Great Britain, Italy, and Japan. Gucci makes and sells high-quality luxury goods, including footwear, belts, sunglasses, handbags, wallets, jewelry, fragrances, and children's clothing. In connection with its products, Gucci uses twenty-one federally registered trademarks. Gucci also operates a number of boutiques, some of which are located in California.*

Background and Facts Wang Huoqing, a resident of the People's Republic of China, operates numerous Web sites. When Gucci discovered that Wang Huoqing's Web sites offered for sale counterfeit goods—products bearing Gucci's trademarks but not genuine Gucci articles—it hired a private investigator in San Jose, California, to buy goods from the Web sites. The investigator purchased a wallet that was labeled Gucci but was counterfeit.

Gucci filed a trademark infringement lawsuit against Wang Huoqing in a federal district court in California seeking damages and an injunction to prevent further infringement. Wang Huoqing was notified of the lawsuit via e-mail but did not appear in court. Gucci asked the court to enter a default judgment—that is, a judgment entered when the defendant fails to appear. First, however, the court had to determine whether it had personal jurisdiction over Wang Huoqing based on the Internet sales.

In the Language of the Court

Joseph C. *SPERO*, United States Magistrate Judge.

* * * *

* * * Under California's long-arm statute, federal courts in California may exercise jurisdiction to the extent permitted by the Due Process Clause of the Constitution. The Due Process Clause allows federal courts to exercise jurisdiction where * * * the defendant has had sufficient minimum contacts with the forum to subject him or her to the specific jurisdiction of the court. The courts apply a three-part test to determine whether specific jurisdiction exists:

(1) The nonresident defendant must do some act or consummate some transaction with the forum or perform some act by which he purposefully avails himself of the privilege of conducting activities in the forum, thereby invoking the benefits and protections of its laws; (2) the claim must be one which arises out of or results from the defendant's forum-related activities; and (3) exercise of jurisdiction must be reasonable.

* * * *

In order to satisfy the first prong of the test for specific jurisdiction, a defendant must have either purposefully availed itself of the privilege of conducting business activities within the forum or purposefully directed activities toward the forum. *Purposeful availment typically consists of action taking place in the forum that invokes the benefits and protections of the laws of the forum, such as executing or performing a contract within the forum.* To show purposeful availment, a plaintiff must show that the defendant "engage[d] in some form of affirmative conduct allowing or promoting the transaction of business within the forum state." [Emphasis added.]

"In the Internet context, the Ninth Circuit utilizes a sliding scale analysis under which 'passive' websites do not create sufficient contacts to establish purposeful availment, whereas interactive websites may create sufficient contacts, depending on how interactive the website is." * * * *Personal jurisdiction is appropriate where an entity is conducting business over the Internet and has offered for sale and sold its products to forum [California] residents.* [Emphasis added.]

Here, the allegations and evidence presented by Plaintiffs in support of the Motion are sufficient to show purposeful availment on the part of Defendant Wang Huoqing. Plaintiffs have alleged that Defendant operates "fully interactive Internet websites operating under the Subject Domain Names" and have presented evidence in the form of copies of web pages showing that the websites are, in fact, interactive.

Case 3.2 Continues

Case 3.2 Continued * * * Additionally, Plaintiffs allege Defendant is conducting counterfeiting and infringing activities within this Judicial District and has advertised and sold his counterfeit goods in the State of California. * * * Plaintiffs have also presented evidence of one actual sale within this district, made by investigator Robert Holmes from the website bag2do.cn.* * * Finally, Plaintiffs have presented evidence that Defendant Wang Huoqing owns or controls the twenty-eight websites listed in the Motion for Default Judgment. * * * Such commercial activity in the forum amounts to purposeful availment of the privilege of conducting activities within the forum, thus invoking the benefits and protections of its laws. Accordingly, the Court concludes that Defendant's contacts with California are sufficient to show purposeful availment.

Decision and Remedy *The U.S. District Court for the Northern District of California held that it had personal jurisdiction over the foreign defendant, Wang Huoqing. The court entered a default judgment against Wang Huoqing and granted Gucci an injunction.*

Critical Thinking
- **What If the Facts Were Different?** *Suppose that Gucci had not presented evidence that Wang Huoqing had made one actual sale through his Web site to a resident of the court's district (the private investigator). Would the court still have found that it had personal jurisdiction over Wang Huoqing? Why or why not?*
- **Legal Environment** *Is it relevant to the analysis of jurisdiction that Gucci America's principal place of business is in New York rather than California? Explain.*

Minimum Contacts and Smartphones. The widespread use of cellular phones, particularly smartphones, also complicates the determination of personal jurisdiction. People use their smartphones while traveling to make purchases, negotiate business deals, enter contracts, and download applications (apps). If a person traveling in another state (or nation) uses a smartphone to form a contract, does that forum have jurisdiction over the person? Is the party that creates an app subject to jurisdiction anywhere the app is downloaded or used? Because an app differs from a Web page, what degree of interactivity is required for apps to confer jurisdiction in the sliding-scale analysis? The courts will be addressing these questions in coming years and adapting traditional notions of jurisdiction to ever-changing technology.

Concept Summary 3.1 reviews the various types of jurisdiction, including jurisdiction in cyberspace.

3–2b Venue

Jurisdiction has to do with whether a court has authority to hear a case involving specific persons, property, or subject matter. **Venue**[11] is concerned with the most appropriate location for a trial. For instance, two state courts (or two federal courts) may have the authority to exercise jurisdiction over a case. Nonetheless, it may be more appropriate or convenient to hear the case in one court than in the other.

The concept of venue reflects the policy that a court trying a case should be in the geographic neighborhood (usually the county) where the incident occurred or where the parties reside. Venue in a civil case typically is where the defendant resides or does business, whereas venue in a criminal case normally is where the crime occurred.

In some cases, pretrial publicity or other factors may require a change of venue to another community, especially in criminal cases in which the defendant's right to a fair and impartial jury has been impaired. Note, though, that venue has lost some significance in today's world because of the Internet and 24/7 news reporting. Courts now rarely grant requests for a change of venue. Because everyone has instant access to all information about a purported crime, courts reason that no community is more or less informed or prejudiced for or against a defendant.

3–2c Standing to Sue

Before a party can bring a lawsuit to court, that party must have **standing to sue,** or a sufficient stake in a matter to justify seeking relief through the court system. Standing means that the party that filed the action in court has a legally protected interest at stake in the litigation. At times, a person can have standing to sue on behalf of another person, such as a minor (child) or a mentally incompetent person.

---

11. Pronounced *ven*-yoo.

Concept Summary 3.1

Jurisdiction

Personal

Exists when a defendant:
- Is located in the court's territorial boundaries.
- Qualifies under state long arm statutes.
- Is a corporation doing business within the state.
- Advertises, sells, or places goods into commerce within the state.

Property

- Exists when the property that is subject to a lawsuit is located within the court's territorial boundaries.

Subject Matter

Limits the court's jurisdictional authority to particular types of cases.
- *General jurisdiction*—Exists when a court can hear cases involving a broad array of issues.
- *Limited jurisdiction*—Exists when a court is limited to a specific subject matter, such as probate or divorce.

Original

- Exists with courts that have the authority to hear a case for the first time (trial courts, district courts).

Appellate

- Exists with courts of appeal and review. Generally, appellate courts do not have original jurisdiction.

Federal

A federal court can exercise jurisdiction:
- When the plaintiff's cause of action involves a federal question (is based at least in part on the U.S. Constitution, a treaty, or a federal law).
- In cases between citizens of different states (or cases involving U.S. citizens and foreign countries or their citizens) when the amount in controversy exceeds $75,000 (diversity-of-citizenship jurisdiction).

Concurrent

- Exists when both federal and state courts have authority to hear the same case.

Exclusive

- Exists when only state courts or only federal courts have authority to hear a case.

Cyberspace

- The courts have developed a sliding-scale standard to use in determining when jurisdiction over a Web site owner or operator in another state is proper.

Standing can be broken down into three elements:

1. *Harm.* The party bringing the action must have suffered harm—an invasion of a legally protected interest—or must face imminent harm. The controversy must be real and substantial rather than hypothetical.
2. *Causation.* There must be a causal connection between the conduct complained of and the injury.
3. *Remedy.* It must be likely, as opposed to merely speculative, that a favorable court decision will remedy the injury suffered.

■ **CASE IN POINT 3.6**   Harold Wagner obtained a loan through M.S.T. Mortgage Group to buy a house in Texas. After the sale, M.S.T. transferred its interest in the loan to another lender, which, in turn, assigned it to another lender (a common practice in the mortgage industry). Eventually, when Wagner failed to make the loan payments, CitiMortgage, Inc., notified him that it was going to foreclose on the property and sell the house.

Wagner filed a lawsuit, claiming that the lenders had improperly assigned the mortgage loan. In 2014, a federal district court ruled that Wagner lacked standing to contest the assignment. Under Texas law, only the parties directly involved in an assignment can challenge its validity. In this case, the assignment was between two lenders and did not directly involve Wagner.[12] ■

---

12. *Wagner v. CitiMortgage, Inc.*, 995 F.Supp.2d 621 (N.D.Tex. 2014).

3–3 The State and Federal Court Systems

Each state has its own court system. Additionally, there is a system of federal courts. The right-hand side of Exhibit 3–2 illustrates the basic organizational framework characteristic of the court systems in many states. The exhibit also shows how the federal court system is structured. We turn now to an examination of these court systems, beginning with the state courts.

3–3a The State Court Systems

No two state court systems are exactly the same. Typically, though, a state court system includes several levels, or tiers, of courts, as shown in Exhibit 3–2. State courts may include (1) trial courts of limited jurisdiction, (2) trial courts of general jurisdiction, (3) appellate courts (intermediate appellate courts), and (4) the state's highest court (often called the state supreme court).

Generally, any person who is a party to a lawsuit has the opportunity to plead the case before a trial court and then, if he or she loses, before at least one level of appellate court. If the case involves a federal statute or a federal constitutional issue, the decision of the state supreme court may be further appealed to the United States Supreme Court. Note that lawsuits can take years to resolve through the courts, especially since many states have experienced large cuts in court funding in recent years. In fact, the United States Supreme Court decided a

EXHIBIT 3–2   **The State and Federal Court Systems**

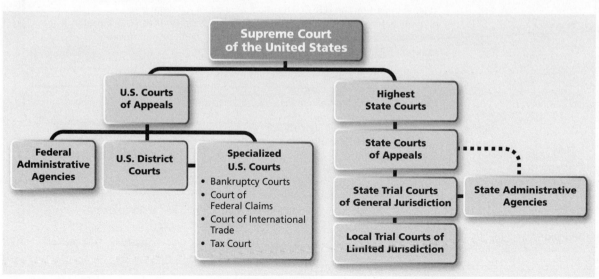

case in 2015 involving a trademark dispute that had been in the courts for more than sixteen years.[13]

The states use various methods to select judges for their courts. Usually, voters elect judges, but in some states judges are appointed. For instance, in Iowa, the governor appoints judges, and then the general population decides whether to confirm their appointment in the next general election. The states usually specify the number of years that judges will serve.

Trial Courts   Trial courts are exactly what their name implies—courts in which trials are held and testimony is taken. State trial courts have either general or limited jurisdiction, as defined earlier.

General Jurisdiction.   Trial courts that have general jurisdiction as to subject matter may be called county, district, superior, or circuit courts.[14] State trial courts of general jurisdiction have jurisdiction over a wide variety of subjects, including both civil disputes and criminal prosecutions. In some states, trial courts of general jurisdiction may hear appeals from courts of limited jurisdiction.

Limited Jurisdiction.   Courts of limited jurisdiction as to subject matter are generally inferior trial courts or minor judiciary courts. Limited jurisdiction courts might include local municipal courts (which could include separate traffic courts and drug courts) and domestic relations courts (which handle divorce and child-custody disputes).

Small claims courts are inferior trial courts that hear only civil cases involving claims of less than a certain amount, such as $5,000 (the amount varies from state to state). Procedures in small claims courts are generally informal, and lawyers are not required (in a few states, lawyers are not even allowed). Decisions of small claims

courts and municipal courts may sometimes be appealed to a state trial court of general jurisdiction.

A few states have also established Islamic law courts, which are courts of limited jurisdiction that serve the American Muslim community. These courts decide cases with reference to the *sharia*, a system of law used in most Islamic countries that is derived from the Qur'an and the sayings and doings of Muhammad and his followers.

Appellate, or Reviewing, Courts   Every state has at least one court of appeals (appellate court, or reviewing court), which may be an intermediate appellate court or the state's highest court. About three-fourths of the states have intermediate appellate courts.

Generally, courts of appeals do not conduct new trials, in which evidence is submitted to the court and witnesses are examined. Rather, an appellate court panel of three or more judges reviews the record of the case on appeal, which includes a transcript of the trial proceedings. The appellate court hears arguments from attorneys and determines whether the trial court committed an error.

Reviewing courts focus on questions of law, not questions of fact. A **question of fact** deals with what really happened in regard to the dispute being tried—such as whether a party actually burned a flag. A **question of law** concerns the application or interpretation of the law—such as whether flag-burning is a form of speech protected by the First Amendment to the U.S. Constitution. Only a judge, not a jury, can rule on questions of law.

Appellate courts normally defer (give significant weight) to the trial court's findings on questions of fact because the trial court judge and jury were in a better position to evaluate testimony. The trial court judge and jury can directly observe witnesses' gestures, demeanor, and other nonverbal behavior during the trial. An appellate court cannot.

In the following case, neither the administrative agency that initially ruled on the dispute nor the trial court to which the agency's decision was appealed made a finding on a crucial question of fact. Faced with that circumstance, what should a state appellate court do?

---

13. *B&B Hardware, Inc. v. Hargis Industries, Inc.,* ___ U.S. ___, 135 S.Ct. 1293, 191 L.Ed.2d 222 (2015).
14. The name in Ohio and Pennsylvania is Court of Common Pleas. The name in New York is Supreme Court, Trial Division.

Case 3.3

Johnson v. Oxy USA, Inc.

Court of Appeals of Texas, Houston—14th District, __ S.W.3d __ , 2016 WL 93559 (2016).

Background and Facts   Jennifer Johnson was working as a finance analyst for Oxy USA, Inc., when Oxy changed the job's requirements. To meet the new standards, Johnson took courses to become a certified public accountant. Oxy's "Educational Assistance Policy" was to reimburse employees for the

Case 3.3 Continues

Case 3.3 Continued   cost of such courses. Johnson further agreed that Oxy could withhold the reimbursed amount from her final paycheck if she quit Oxy within a year. When she resigned less than a year later, Oxy withheld that amount from her last check. Johnson filed a claim for the amount with the Texas Workforce Commission (TWC). The TWC ruled that she was not entitled to the unpaid wages. She filed a suit in a Texas state court against Oxy, alleging breach of contract. The court affirmed the TWC's ruling. Johnson appealed.

In the Language of the Court

Ken WISE, Justice

* * * *

* * * The trial court * * * held that Johnson's [claim for breach of contract was] barred by *res judicata* ["a matter judged"]. In a court of law, a claimant typically cannot pursue one remedy to an unfavorable outcome and then seek the same remedy in another proceeding before the same or a different tribunal. Res judicata *bars the relitigation of claims that have been finally adjudicated or that could have been litigated in the prior action.* [Emphasis added.]

Johnson argues that *res judicata* does not apply here because the TWC did not render a final judgment on the merits of her claim that Oxy misinterpreted its Educational Assistance Policy. Specifically, Johnson claims she was "denied the right of full adjudication of her claim because the TWC refused to consider her arguments at the administrative level as beyond its jurisdiction." To support this contention, Johnson points to the following excerpt from the * * * decision:

> * * * The TWC does not interpret contracts between employers and employee but only enforces the Texas Payday Law [the Texas state law that governs the timing of employees' paychecks]. * * * The question of whether the employer properly interpreted their policy on reimbursed educational expenses versus a business expense is a question for a different forum.

According to Johnson, this language shows that the TWC refused to consider the merits of the issue she raised as "beyond its reach." In contrast, the defendants contend that Johnson's claims are barred by *res judicata* because they are based on claims previously decided by the TWC.

* * * *

In Johnson's case, however, the TWC did not decide the key question of fact in dispute—whether Oxy violated its own Educational Assistance Policy when it withheld Johnson's final wages as reimbursement for the CPA courses. In fact, the TWC explicitly refused to do so, stating that the agency "does not interpret contracts between employers and employee." * * * Because this question goes to the heart of Johnson's breach of contract * * * claim, we hold that *res judicata* does not bar [that] claim. [Emphasis added.]

The defendants argue that because Johnson seeks to recover the same wages in this suit as she did in her claim with the TWC, *res judicata* must bar her common law cause of action. However, * * * *res judicata* would only bar a claim if TWC's order is considered final. * * * Here, the order in Johnson's case made no such findings with regard to the Educational Assistance Policy. The order expressly declined to address that issue. Therefore, * * * *res judicata* will not bar Johnson's breach of contract * * * claim.

Decision and Remedy   *A state intermediate appellate court reversed the lower court's decision. "The TWC did not decide the key question of fact in dispute—whether Oxy violated its own Educational Assistance Policy when it withheld Johnson's final wages. In fact, the TWC explicitly refused to do so, stating that the agency 'does not interpret contracts between employers and employee.'" The appellate court remanded the case for a trial on the merits.*

Critical Thinking

- **Legal Environment** *Who can decide questions of fact? Who can rule on questions of law? Why?*
- **Global** *In some cases, a court may be asked to determine and interpret the law of a foreign country. Some states consider the issue of what the law of a foreign country requires to be a question of fact. Federal rules of procedure provide that this issue is a question of law. Which position seems more appropriate? Why?*

Highest State Courts The highest appellate court in a state is usually called the supreme court but may be designated by some other name. For instance, in both New York and Maryland, the highest state court is called the Court of Appeals. The highest state court in Maine and Massachusetts is the Supreme Judicial Court. In West Virginia, it is the Supreme Court of Appeals.

The decisions of each state's highest court on all questions of state law are final. Only when issues of federal law are involved can the United States Supreme Court overrule a decision made by a state's highest court. ■ **EXAMPLE 3.7** A city enacts an ordinance that prohibits citizens from engaging in door-to-door advocacy without first registering with the mayor's office and receiving a permit. A religious group then sues the city, arguing that the law violates the freedoms of speech and religion guaranteed by the First Amendment. If the state supreme court upholds the law, the group could appeal the decision to the United States Supreme Court, because a constitutional (federal) issue is involved. ■

3–3b The Federal Court System

The federal court system is basically a three-tiered model consisting of (1) U.S. district courts (trial courts of general jurisdiction) and various courts of limited

---

MANAGERIAL STRATEGY

Should You Consent to Have Your Business Case Decided by a U.S. Magistrate Judge?

You have a strong case in a contract dispute with one of your business's suppliers. The supplier is located in another state. Your attorney did everything necessary to obtain your "day in court." The court in question is a federal district court. But you have just found out that your case may not be heard for several years— or even longer. Your attorney tells you that the case can be heard in just a few months if you consent to place it in the hands of a U.S. magistrate judge.[a] Should you consent?

A Short History of U.S. Magistrate Judges

Congress authorized the creation of a new federal judicial officer, the U.S. magistrate, in 1968 to help reduce delays in the U.S. district courts.[b] These junior federal officers were to conduct a wide range of judicial proceedings as set out by statute and as assigned by the district judges under whom they served. In 1979, Congress gave U.S. magistrates consent jurisdiction, which authorized them to conduct all civil trials as long as the parties consent.[c] Currently, magistrate judges dispose of over one million civil and criminal district court matters, which include motions and hearings.

The Selection and Quality of Magistrate Judges

As mentioned, federal district judges are nominated by the president, confirmed by the Senate, and appointed for life. In contrast, U.S. magistrate judges are selected by federal district court judges based on the recommenda-

tions of a merit screening committee. They serve an eight-year term (which can be renewed).

By statute, magistrate judges must be chosen through a merit selection process. Applicants are interviewed by a screening committee of lawyers and others from the district in which the position will be filled.[d] Political party affiliation plays no part in the process.

A variety of experienced attorneys, administrative law judges, state court judges, and others apply for magistrate judge positions. A typical opening receives about a hundred applicants. The merit selection panel selects the five most qualified, who are then voted on by federal district court judges.

Because the selection process for a magistrate judge is not the same as for a district judge, some critics have expressed concerns about the quality of magistrate judges. Some groups, such as People for the American Way, are not in favor of allowing magistrate judges the power to decide cases. These critics believe that because of their limited terms, they are not completely immune from outside pressure.

Business Questions

1. *If you were facing an especially complex legal dispute— one involving many facets and several different types of law—would you consent to allowing a U.S. magistrate judge to decide the case? Why or why not?*

2. *If you had to decide whether to allow a U.S. magistrate judge to hear your case, what information might you ask your attorney to provide concerning that individual?*

---

a. 28 U.S.C. Sec 636(c); *Roell v. Withrow*, 538 U.S. 580, 123 S.Ct. 1698, 155 L.Ed.2d 775 (2003).
b. Federal Magistrates Act, 82 Stat. 1107, October 17, 1968.
c. U.S.C. Section 636(c)(1).

d. 28 U.S.C. Section 631(b)(5).

jurisdiction, (2) U.S. courts of appeals (intermediate courts of appeals), and (3) the United States Supreme Court.

Unlike state court judges, who are usually elected, federal court judges—including the justices of the Supreme Court—are appointed by the president of the United States, subject to confirmation by the U.S. Senate. Federal judges receive lifetime appointments under Article III of the U.S. Constitution, which states that federal judges "hold their offices during good Behaviour." In the entire history of the United States, only seven federal judges have been removed from office through impeachment proceedings.

Certain federal court officers are not chosen in the way just described. This chapter's *Managerial Strategy* feature describes how U.S. magistrate judges are selected.

U.S. District Courts   At the federal level, the equivalent of a state trial court of general jurisdiction is the district court. U.S. district courts have original jurisdiction in matters involving a federal question and concurrent

jurisdiction with state courts when diversity jurisdiction exists. Federal cases typically originate in district courts. There are other federal courts with original, but special (or limited), jurisdiction, such as the federal bankruptcy courts and tax courts.

Every state has at least one federal district court. The number of judicial districts can vary over time, primarily owing to population changes and corresponding changes in caseloads. Today, there are ninety-four federal judicial districts. Exhibit 3–3 shows the boundaries of both the U.S. district courts and the U.S. courts of appeals.

U.S. Courts of Appeals   In the federal court system, there are thirteen U.S. courts of appeals—referred to as U.S. circuit courts of appeals. Twelve of these courts (including the Court of Appeals for the D.C. Circuit) hear appeals from the federal district courts located within their respective judicial circuits (shown in Exhibit 3–3).[15]

---

15. Historically, judges were required to "ride the circuit" and hear appeals in different courts around the country, which is how the name "circuit court" came about.

EXHIBIT 3–3   Geographic Boundaries of the U.S. Courts of Appeals and U.S. District Courts

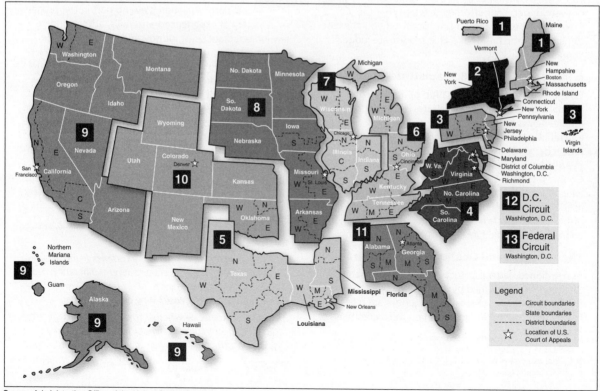

Source: Administrative Office of the United States Courts.

The Court of Appeals for the Thirteenth Circuit, called the Federal Circuit, has national appellate jurisdiction over certain types of cases, including those involving patent law and those in which the U.S. government is a defendant.

The decisions of a circuit court of appeals are binding on all courts within the circuit court's jurisdiction. These decisions are final in most cases, but appeal to the United States Supreme Court is possible.

The United States Supreme Court The highest level of the three-tiered federal court system is the United States Supreme Court. According to the U.S. Constitution, there is only one national Supreme Court. All other courts in the federal system are considered "inferior." Congress is empowered to create inferior courts as it deems necessary. The inferior courts that Congress has created include the second tier in our model—the U.S. circuit courts of appeals—as well as the district courts and the various federal courts of limited, or specialized, jurisdiction.

The United States Supreme Court consists of nine justices. Although the Supreme Court has original, or trial, jurisdiction in rare instances (set forth in Article III, Sections 1 and 2), most of its work is as an appeals court. The Supreme Court can review any case decided by any of the federal courts of appeals. It also has appellate authority over cases involving federal questions that have been decided in the state courts. The Supreme Court is the final authority on the Constitution and federal law.

Appeals to the Supreme Court. To bring a case before the Supreme Court, a party requests the Court to issue a writ of *certiorari*.[16] A **writ of *certiorari*** is an order issued by the Supreme Court to a lower court requiring the latter to send it the record of the case for review. The Court will not issue a writ unless at least four of the nine justices approve of it. This is called the **rule of four.**

Whether the Court will issue a writ of *certiorari* is entirely within its discretion, and most petitions for writs are denied. (Although thousands of cases are filed with the Supreme Court each year, it hears, on average, fewer than one hundred of these cases.)[17] A denial of the request to issue a writ of *certiorari* is not a decision on the merits of the case, nor does it indicate agreement with the lower court's opinion. Also, denial of the writ has no

value as a precedent. Denial simply means that the lower court's decision remains the law in that jurisdiction.

Petitions Granted by the Court. Typically, the Court grants petitions when cases raise important constitutional questions or when the lower courts have issued conflicting decisions on a significant issue. The justices, however, never explain their reasons for hearing certain cases and not others, so it is difficult to predict which type of case the Court might select.

Concept Summary 3.2 reviews the courts in the federal and state court systems.

3–4 Alternative Dispute Resolution

Litigation—the process of resolving a dispute through the court system—is expensive and time consuming. Litigating even the simplest complaint is costly, and because of the backlog of cases pending in many courts, several years may pass before a case is actually tried. For these and other reasons, more and more businesspersons are turning to **alternative dispute resolution (ADR)** as a means of settling their disputes.

The great advantage of ADR is its flexibility. Methods of ADR range from the parties sitting down together and attempting to work out their differences to multinational corporations agreeing to resolve a dispute through a formal hearing before a panel of experts. Normally, the parties themselves can control how they will attempt to settle their dispute. They can decide what procedures will be used, whether a neutral third party will be present or make a decision, and whether that decision will be legally binding or nonbinding. ADR also offers more privacy than court proceedings and allows disputes to be resolved relatively quickly.

Today, more than 90 percent of civil lawsuits are settled before trial using some form of ADR. Indeed, most states either require or encourage parties to undertake ADR prior to trial. Many federal courts have instituted ADR programs as well. In this section, we examine the basic forms of ADR.

3–4a Negotiation

The simplest form of ADR is **negotiation,** a process in which the parties attempt to settle their dispute informally, with or without attorneys to represent them. Attorneys frequently advise their clients to negotiate a settlement voluntarily before they proceed to trial. Parties may even try to negotiate a settlement during a trial or after the trial but before an appeal.

---

16. Pronounced sur-shee-uh-*rah*-ree.
17. From the mid-1950s through the early 1990s, the Supreme Court reviewed more cases per year than it has since then. In the Court's 1982–1983 term, for example, the Court issued written opinions in 151 cases. In contrast, during the Court's 2015–2016 term, the Court issued written opinions in only 81 cases.

Concept Summary 3.2

Types of Courts

Trial Courts	Trial courts are courts of original jurisdiction in which actions are initiated. • *State courts* —Courts of general jurisdiction can hear any case that has not been specifically designated for another court. Courts of limited jurisdiction include, among others, domestic relations courts, probate courts, municipal courts, and small claims courts. • *Federal courts* —The federal district court is the equivalent of the state trial court. Federal courts of limited jurisdiction include the bankruptcy courts and others shown in Exhibit 3–2.
Intermediate Appellate Courts	Courts of appeals are reviewing courts. Generally, appellate courts do not have original jurisdiction. • About three-fourths of the states have intermediate appellate courts. • In the federal court system, the U.S. circuit courts of appeals are the intermediate appellate courts.
Supreme Courts	The highest state court is that state's supreme court, although it may be called by some other name. • Appeal from state supreme courts to the United States Supreme Court is possible only if a federal question is involved. • The United States Supreme Court is the highest court in the federal court system and the final authority on the Constitution and federal law.

Negotiation traditionally involves just the parties themselves and (typically) their attorneys. The attorneys, though, are advocates—they are obligated to put their clients' interests first.

3–4b Mediation

In **mediation,** a neutral third party acts as a mediator and works with both sides in the dispute to facilitate a resolution. The mediator, who need not be a lawyer, usually charges a fee for his or her services (which can be split between the parties). States that require parties to undergo ADR before trial often offer mediation as one of the ADR options or (as in Florida) the only option.

During mediation, the mediator normally talks with the parties separately as well as jointly, emphasizes their points of agreement, and helps them to evaluate their options. Although the mediator may propose a solution (called a mediator's proposal), he or she does not make a decision resolving the matter.

One of the biggest advantages of mediation is that it is less adversarial than litigation. In mediation, the mediator takes an active role and attempts to bring the parties together so that they can come to a mutually satisfactory resolution. The mediation process tends to reduce the antagonism between the disputants, allowing them to resume their former relationship while minimizing hostility. For this reason, mediation is often the preferred form of ADR for disputes between business partners, employers and employees, or other parties involved in long-term relationships.

3–4c Arbitration

A more formal method of ADR is **arbitration,** in which an arbitrator (a neutral third party or a panel of experts) hears a dispute and imposes a resolution on the parties. Arbitration differs from other forms of ADR in that the third party hearing the dispute makes a decision for the parties. Exhibit 3–4 outlines the basic differences among the three traditional forms of ADR.

Usually, the parties in arbitration agree that the third party's decision will be *legally binding*, although the parties can also agree to *nonbinding* arbitration. In nonbinding arbitration, the parties can go forward with a lawsuit if they do not agree with the arbitrator's decision. Arbitration that is mandated by the courts often is not binding on the parties.

In some respects, formal arbitration resembles a trial, although usually the procedural rules are much less restrictive than those governing litigation. In a typical arbitration, the parties present opening arguments and ask for specific remedies. Both sides present evidence and may call and examine witnesses. The arbitrator then renders a decision.

The Arbitrator's Decision The arbitrator's decision is called an **award.** It is usually the final word on the matter. Although the parties may appeal an arbitrator's decision, a court's review of the decision will be much more restricted in scope than an appellate court's review of a trial court's decision. The general view is that because the parties were free to frame the issues and set the powers of the arbitrator at the outset, they cannot complain about the results. A court will set aside an award only in the event of one of the following:

1. The arbitrator's conduct or "bad faith" substantially prejudiced the rights of one of the parties.
2. The award violates an established public policy.
3. The arbitrator exceeded her or his powers—that is, arbitrated issues that the parties did not agree to submit to arbitration.

Arbitration Clauses Almost any commercial matter can be submitted to arbitration. Frequently, parties include an **arbitration clause** in a contract specifying that any dispute arising under the contract will be resolved through arbitration rather than through the court system. Parties can also agree to arbitrate a dispute *after* it arises.

Arbitration Statutes Most states have statutes (often based, in part, on the Uniform Arbitration Act) under which arbitration clauses will be enforced. Some state statutes compel arbitration of certain types of disputes, such as those involving public employees.

At the federal level, the Federal Arbitration Act (FAA), enacted in 1925, enforces arbitration clauses in contracts involving maritime activity and interstate commerce. As you will see in later chapters, the courts have defined *interstate commerce* broadly, and so arbitration

EXHIBIT 3–4 Basic Differences in the Traditional Forms of ADR

	Negotiation	**Mediation**	**Arbitration**
		Type of ADR	
Description	Parties meet informally with or without their attorneys and attempt to agree on a resolution. This is the simplest and least expensive method of ADR.	A neutral third party meets with the parties and emphasizes points of agreement to bring them toward resolution of their dispute, reducing hostility between the parties.	The parties present their arguments and evidence before an arbitrator at a formal hearing. The arbitrator renders a decision to resolve the parties' dispute.
Neutral Third Party Present?	No	Yes	Yes
Who Decides the Resolution?	The parties themselves reach a resolution.	The parties, but the mediator may suggest or propose a resolution.	The arbitrator imposes a resolution on the parties that may be either binding or nonbinding.

agreements involving transactions only slightly connected to the flow of interstate commerce may fall under the FAA. The FAA established a national policy favoring arbitration that the United States Supreme Court has continued to reinforce.[18]

■ **CASE IN POINT 3.8** Cleveland Construction, Inc. (CCI), was the general contractor on a project to build a grocery store in Houston, Texas. CCI hired Levco Construction, Inc., as a subcontractor. Their contract included an arbitration provision stating that any disputes would be resolved by arbitration in Ohio. When a dispute arose between the parties, Levco filed a suit against CCI in a Texas state court. CCI sought to compel arbitration in Ohio under the Federal Arbitration Act (FAA), but a Texas statute allows a party to void a contractual provision that requires arbitration outside Texas. Ultimately, a Texas appellate court held that the FAA preempted (took priority over) the state law. CCI could compel arbitration in Ohio.[19] ■

The Issue of Arbitrability The terms of an arbitration agreement can limit the types of disputes that the parties agree to arbitrate. Disputes can arise, however, when the parties do not specify limits or when the parties disagree on whether a particular matter is covered by their arbitration agreement.

When one party files a lawsuit to compel arbitration, it is up to the court to resolve the issue of *arbitrability*. That is, the court must decide whether the matter is one that must be resolved through arbitration. If the court finds that the subject matter in controversy is covered by the agreement to arbitrate, then it may compel arbitration.

Usually, a court will allow a claim to be arbitrated if the court finds that the relevant statute (the state arbitration statute or the FAA) does not exclude such claims. No party, however, will be ordered to submit a particular dispute to arbitration unless the court is convinced that the party has consented to do so. Additionally, the courts will not compel arbitration if it is clear that the arbitration rules and procedures are inherently unfair to one of the parties.

Mandatory Arbitration in the Employment Context A significant question for businesspersons has concerned mandatory arbitration clauses in employment contracts. Many employees claim they are at a disadvantage when they are forced, as a condition of being hired,

to agree to arbitrate all disputes and thus waive their rights under statutes designed to protect employees.

The United States Supreme Court, however, has held that mandatory arbitration clauses in employment contracts are generally enforceable. ■ **CASE IN POINT 3.9** In a landmark decision, *Gilmer v. Interstate Johnson Lane Corp.*,[20] the Supreme Court held that a claim brought under a federal statute prohibiting age discrimination could be subject to arbitration. The Court concluded that the employee had waived his right to sue when he agreed, as part of a required application to be a securities representative, to arbitrate "any dispute, claim, or controversy" relating to his employment. ■

Since the *Gilmer* decision, some courts have refused to enforce one-sided arbitration clauses.[21] Nevertheless, the policy favoring enforcement of mandatory arbitration agreements in employment contracts remains strong.

■ **CASE IN POINT 3.10** Stephanie Cruise was hired by Kroger Co. to work in its deli. Her job application had included a clause requiring arbitration of "employment-related disputes." When Cruise was fired four years later, she filed a lawsuit claiming that Kroger had violated a number of laws prohibiting employment discrimination. Kroger filed a motion to compel arbitration. A state appellate court concluded that the arbitration clause in the employment application established that the parties had agreed to arbitrate their "employment-related disputes." Cruise's claims fell within the meaning of that agreement, and therefore she was required to arbitrate.[22] ■

3–4d Other Types of ADR

The three forms of ADR just discussed are the oldest and traditionally the most commonly used forms. In addition, a variety of newer types of ADR have emerged, including those described here.

1. In **early neutral case evaluation,** the parties select a neutral third party (generally an expert in the subject matter of the dispute) and explain their respective positions to that person. The case evaluator assesses the strengths and weaknesses of each party's claims.

2. In a **mini-trial,** each party's attorney briefly argues the party's case before the other party and a panel of representatives from each side who have the authority to settle the dispute. Typically, a neutral third party (usually an expert in the area being disputed) acts as

---

18. See, for example, *AT&T Mobility LLC v. Concepcion*, 563 U.S. 333, 131 S.Ct. 1740, 179 L.Ed.2d 742 (2010).

19. *Cleveland Construction, Inc. v. Levco Construction, Inc.*, 359 S.W.3d 843 (Tex.App. 2012).

20. 500 U.S. 20, 111 S.Ct. 1647, 114 L.Ed.2d 26 (1991).

21. See, for example, *Mohamed v. Uber Technologies, Inc.*, 2015 WL 3749716 (N.D.Cal. 2015); *Macias v. Excel Building Services, LLC*, 767 F.Supp.2d 1002 (N.D.Cal. 2011).

22. *Cruise v. Kroger Co.*, 233 Cal.App.4th 390, 183 Cal.Rptr.3d 17 (2015).

an adviser. If the parties fail to reach an agreement, the adviser renders an opinion as to how a court would likely decide the issue.

3. Numerous federal courts hold **summary jury trials,** in which the parties present their arguments and evidence and the jury renders a verdict. The jury's verdict is not binding, but it does act as a guide to both sides in reaching an agreement during the mandatory negotiations that immediately follow the trial.

4. Other alternatives being employed by the courts include summary proceedings, which dispense with some formal court procedures, and the appointment of special masters to assist judges in deciding complex issues.

3–4e Providers of ADR Services

ADR services are provided by both government agencies and private organizations. A major provider of ADR services is the American Arbitration Association (AAA), which handles more than 200,000 claims a year in its numerous offices worldwide. Most of the largest U.S. law firms are members of this nonprofit association.

Cases brought before the AAA are heard by an expert or a panel of experts in the area relating to the dispute and are usually settled quickly. Generally, about half of the panel members are lawyers. To cover its costs, the AAA charges a fee, paid by the party filing the claim. In addition, each party to the dispute pays a specified amount for each hearing day, as well as a special additional fee in cases involving personal injuries or property loss.

Hundreds of for-profit firms around the country also provide dispute-resolution services. Typically, these firms hire retired judges to conduct arbitration hearings or otherwise assist parties in settling their disputes. The judges follow procedures similar to those of the federal courts and use similar rules. Usually, each party to the dispute pays a filing fee and a designated fee for a hearing session or conference.

3–4f Online Dispute Resolution

An increasing number of companies and organizations are offering dispute-resolution services using the Internet. The settlement of disputes in these forums is known as **online dispute resolution (ODR).** The disputes resolved have most commonly involved rights to domain names (Web site addresses) or the quality of goods sold via the Internet, including goods sold through Internet auction sites.

Rules being developed in online forums may ultimately become a code of conduct for everyone who does business in cyberspace. Most online forums do not automatically apply the law of any specific jurisdiction. Instead, results are often based on general, universal legal principles. As with most offline methods of dispute resolution, any party may appeal to a court at any time.

ODR may be best for resolving small- to medium-sized business liability claims, which may not be worth the expense of litigation or traditional ADR methods. In addition, some cities use ODR as a means of resolving claims against them. ■ **EXAMPLE 3.11** New York City uses Cybersettle.com to resolve auto accident, sidewalk, and other personal-injury claims made against the city. Parties with complaints submit their demands, and the city submits its offers confidentially online. If an offer exceeds a demand, the claimant keeps half the difference as a bonus, plus the original claim. ■

3–5 International Dispute Resolution

Businesspersons who engage in international business transactions normally take special precautions to protect themselves in the event that a party with whom they are dealing in another country breaches an agreement. Often, parties to international contracts include special clauses in their contracts providing for how disputes arising under the contracts will be resolved. Sometimes, international treaties (formal agreements among several nations) even require parties to arbitrate any disputes.

3–5a Forum-Selection and Choice-of-Law Clauses

Parties to international transactions often include forum-selection and choice-of-law clauses in their contracts. These clauses designate the jurisdiction (court or country) where any dispute arising under the contract will be litigated and which nation's law will be applied.

When an international contract does not include such clauses, any legal proceedings arising under the contract will be more complex and attended by much more uncertainty. For instance, litigation may take place in two or more countries, with each country applying its own national law to the particular transactions.

Furthermore, even if a plaintiff wins a favorable judgment in a lawsuit litigated in the plaintiff's country, the defendant's country could refuse to enforce the court's judgment. The judgment may be enforced in the defendant's country for reasons of courtesy. The United States, for instance, will generally enforce a foreign court's decision if it is consistent with U.S. national law and policy. Other nations, however, may not be as accommodating as the United States, and the plaintiff may be left empty-handed.

3–5b Arbitration Clauses

International contracts also often include arbitration clauses that require a neutral third party to decide any contract disputes. Many of the institutions that offer arbitration, such as the International Chamber of Commerce or the Hong Kong International Arbitration Centre, have formulated model clauses for parties to use. In international arbitration proceedings, the third party may be a neutral entity, a panel of individuals representing both parties' interests, or some other group or organization.

The United Nations Convention on the Recognition and Enforcement of Foreign Arbitral Awards[23] has been implemented in more than 145 countries, including the United States. This convention assists in the enforcement of arbitration clauses, as do provisions in specific treaties among nations. The American Arbitration Association provides arbitration services for international as well as domestic disputes.

---

23. June 10, 1958, 21 U.S.T. 2517, T.I.A.S. No. 6997 (the "New York Convention").

Reviewing: Courts and Alternative Dispute Resolution

Stan Garner resides in Illinois and promotes boxing matches for SuperSports, Inc., an Illinois corporation. Garner created the concept of "Ages" promotion—a three-fight series of boxing matches pitting an older fighter (George Foreman) against a younger fighter. The concept had titles for each of the three fights, including "Battle of the Ages." Garner contacted Foreman and his manager, who both reside in Texas, to sell the idea, and they arranged a meeting in Las Vegas, Nevada. During negotiations, Foreman's manager signed a nondisclosure agreement prohibiting him from disclosing Garner's promotional concepts unless the parties signed a contract. Nevertheless, after negotiations fell through, Foreman used Garner's "Battle of the Ages" concept to promote a subsequent fight. Garner filed a suit against Foreman and his manager in a federal district court located in Illinois, alleging breach of contract. Using the information presented in the chapter, answer the following questions.

1. On what basis might the federal district court in Illinois exercise jurisdiction in this case?
2. Does the federal district court have original or appellate jurisdiction?
3. Suppose that Garner had filed his action in an Illinois state court. Could an Illinois state court have exercised personal jurisdiction over Foreman or his manager? Why or why not?
4. Now suppose that Garner had filed his action in a Nevada state court. Would that court have had personal jurisdiction over Foreman or his manager? Explain.

Debate This ... *In this age of the Internet, when people communicate via e-mail, texts, tweets, Facebook, and Skype, is the concept of jurisdiction losing its meaning?*

Terms and Concepts

alternative dispute resolution (ADR) 59
arbitration 60
arbitration clause 61
award 61
bankruptcy court 47
concurrent jurisdiction 49
diversity of citizenship 47
early neutral case evaluation 62
exclusive jurisdiction 49

federal question 47
in personam jurisdiction 46
in rem jurisdiction 46
judicial review 45
jurisdiction 46
litigation 59
long arm statute 46
mediation 60
mini-trial 62
negotiation 59

online dispute resolution (ODR) 63
probate court 47
question of fact 55
question of law 55
rule of four 59
small claims court55
standing to sue 52
summary jury trial 63
venue 52
writ of *certiorari* 59

Issue Spotters

1. Sue uses her smartphone to purchase a video security system for her architectural firm from Tipton, Inc., a company located in a different state. The system arrives a month after the projected delivery date, is of poor quality, and does not function as advertised. Sue files a suit against Tipton in a state court. Does the court in Sue's state have jurisdiction over Tipton? What factors will the court consider in determining jurisdiction? (See *Basic Judicial Requirements.*)

2. The state in which Sue resides requires that her dispute with Tipton be submitted to mediation or nonbinding arbitration. If the dispute is not resolved, or if either party disagrees with the decision of the mediator or arbitrator, will a court hear the case? Explain. (See *Alternative Dispute Resolution.*)

- **Check your answers to the Issue Spotters against the answers provided in Appendix B at the end of this text.**

Business Scenarios

3–1. Standing. Jack and Maggie Turton bought a house in Jefferson County, Idaho, located directly across the street from a gravel pit. A few years later, the county converted the pit to a landfill. The landfill accepted many kinds of trash that cause harm to the environment, including major appliances, animal carcasses, containers with hazardous content warnings, leaking car batteries, and waste oil. The Turtons complained to the county, but the county did nothing. The Turtons then filed a lawsuit against the county alleging violations of federal environmental laws pertaining to groundwater contamination and other pollution. Do the Turtons have standing to sue? Why or why not? (See *Basic Judicial Requirements.*)

Business Case Problems

3–2. Venue. Brandy Austin used powdered infant formula manufactured by Nestlé USA, Inc., to feed her infant daughter. Austin claimed that a can of the formula was contaminated with *Enterobacter sakazakii* bacteria, causing severe injury to the infant. The bacteria can cause infections of the bloodstream and central nervous system—in particular, meningitis (inflammation of the tissue surrounding the brain or spinal cord). Austin filed an action against Nestlé in Hennepin County District Court in Minnesota. Nestlé argued for a change of venue because the alleged harm had occurred in South Carolina. Austin is a South Carolina resident and had given birth to her daughter in that state. Should the case be transferred to a South Carolina venue? Why or why not? [*Austin v. Nestlé USA, Inc.*, 677 F.Supp.2d 1134 (D.Minn. 2009)] (See *Basic Judicial Requirements.*)

3–3. Arbitration. PRM Energy Systems owned patents licensed to Primenergy to use in the United States. Their contract stated that "all disputes" would be settled by arbitration. Kobe Steel of Japan was interested in using the technology represented by PRM's patents. Primenergy agreed to let Kobe use the technology in Japan without telling PRM. When PRM learned about the secret deal, the firm filed a suit against Primenergy for fraud and theft. Does this dispute go to arbitration or to trial? Why? [*PRM Energy Systems v. Primenergy*, 592 F.3d 830 (8th Cir. 2010)] (See *Alternative Dispute Resolution.*)

3–4. Spotlight on the National Football League— Arbitration. Bruce Matthews played football for the Tennes-

 see Titans. As part of his contract, he agreed to submit any dispute to arbitration. He also agreed that Tennessee law would determine all matters related to workers' compensation. After Matthews retired, he filed a workers' compensation claim in California. The arbitrator ruled that Matthews could pursue his claim in California but only under Tennessee law. Should this award be set aside? Explain. [*National Football League Players Association v. National Football League Management Council*, 2011 WL 1137334 (S.D.Cal. 2011)] (See *Alternative Dispute Resolution.*)

3–5. Minimum Contacts. Seal Polymer Industries sold two freight containers of latex gloves to Med-Express, Inc., a company based in North Carolina. When Med-Express failed to pay the $104,000 owed for the gloves, Seal Polymer sued in an Illinois court and obtained a judgment against Med-Express. Med-Express argued that it did not have minimum contacts with Illinois because it was incorporated under North Carolina law and had its principal place of business in North Carolina. Therefore, the Illinois judgment based on personal jurisdiction was invalid. Was this argument alone sufficient to prevent the Illinois judgment from being collected against Med-Express in North Carolina? Why or why not? [*Seal Polymer Industries v. Med-Express, Inc.*, 725 S.E.2d 5 (N.C.App. 2012)] (See *Basic Judicial Requirements.*)

3–6. Arbitration. Horton Automatics and the Industrial Division of the Communications Workers of America, the union that represented Horton's workers, negotiated a collective bargaining agreement. If an employee's discharge for a workplace-rule violation was submitted to arbitration, the agreement limited the arbitrator to determining whether the rule was reasonable and whether the employee had violated it. When Horton discharged employee Ruben de la Garza, the union appealed to arbitration. The arbitrator found that de la Garza had violated a reasonable safety rule, but "was not totally convinced" that Horton should have treated the violation more seriously than other rule violations. The arbitrator ordered de la Garza reinstated. Can a court set aside this order? Explain. [*Horton Automatics v. The Industrial Division of the Communications Workers of America, AFL-CIO*, 2013 WL 59204 (5th Cir. 2013)] (See *Alternative Dispute Resolution*.)

3–7. Business Case Problem with Sample Answer—Corporate Contacts.

 LG Electronics, Inc., a South Korean company, and nineteen other foreign companies participated in the global market for cathode ray tube (CRT) products. CRTs were integrated as components in consumer goods, including television sets, and were sold for many years in high volume in the United States, including the state of Washington. The state filed a suit in a Washington state court against LG and the others, alleging a conspiracy to raise prices and set production levels in the market for CRTs in violation of a state consumer protection statute. The defendants filed a motion to dismiss the suit for lack of personal jurisdiction. Should this motion be granted? Explain. [*State of Washington v. LG Electronics, Inc.*, 341 P.3d 346 (Wash.App., Div. 1 2015)] (See *Basic Judicial Requirements*.)

- For a sample answer to Problem 3–7, go to Appendix C at the end of this text.

3–8. Appellate, or Reviewing, Courts.

Angelica Westbrook was employed as a collector for Franklin Collection Service, Inc. During a collection call, Westbrook told a debtor that a $15 processing fee was an "interest" charge. This violated company policy. Westbrook was fired. She filed a claim for unemployment benefits, which the Mississippi Department of Employment Security (MDES) approved. Franklin objected. At an MDES hearing, a Franklin supervisor testified that she had heard Westbrook make the false statement, although she admitted that there had been no similar incidents with Westbrook. Westbrook denied making the statement, but added that if she had said it, she did not remember it. The agency found that Franklin's reason for terminating Westbrook did not amount to the misconduct required to disqualify her for benefits and upheld the approval. Franklin appealed to a state intermediate appellate court. Is the court likely to uphold the agency's findings of fact? Explain. [*Franklin Collection Service, Inc. v. Mississippi Department of Employment Security*, 184 So.3d 330 (Miss.App. 2016)] (See *The State and Federal Court Systems*.)

3–9. A Question of Ethics—Agreement to Arbitrate.

 Nellie Lumpkin, who suffered from various illnesses, including dementia, was admitted to the Picayune Convalescent Center, a nursing home. Because of her mental condition, her daughter, Beverly McDaniel, filled out the admissions paperwork and signed the admissions agreement. It included a clause requiring parties to submit to arbitration any disputes that arose. After Lumpkin left the center two years later, she sued, through her husband, for negligent treatment and malpractice during her stay. The center moved to force the matter to arbitration. The trial court held that the arbitration agreement was not enforceable. The center appealed. [Covenant Health & Rehabilitation of Picayune, LP v. Lumpkin, 23 So.3d 1092 (Miss.App. 2009)] (See Alternative Dispute Resolution.)

(a) Should a dispute involving medical malpractice be forced into arbitration? This is a claim of negligent care, not a breach of a commercial contract. Is it ethical for medical facilities to impose such a requirement? Is there really any bargaining over such terms? Discuss fully.

(b) Should a person with limited mental capacity be held to an arbitration clause agreed to by the next of kin who signed on behalf of that person? Why or why not?

Legal Reasoning Group Activity

3–10. Access to Courts.

Assume that a statute in your state requires that all civil lawsuits involving damages of less than $50,000 be arbitrated. Such a case can be tried in court only if a party is dissatisfied with the arbitrator's decision. The statute also provides that if a trial does not result in an improvement of more than 10 percent in the position of the party who demanded the trial, that party must pay the entire cost of the arbitration proceeding. (See *Alternative Dispute Resolution*.)

(a) One group will argue that the state statute violates litigants' rights of access to the courts and trial by jury.

(b) Another group will argue that the statute does not violate litigants' right of access to the courts.

(c) A third group will evaluate how the determination on right of access would be changed if the statute was part of a pilot program that affected only a few judicial districts in the state.

CHAPTER 4

Tort Law

Part of doing business today—and, indeed, part of everyday life—is the risk of being involved in a lawsuit. The list of circumstances in which businesspersons can be sued is long and varied. A customer who is injured by a security guard at a business establishment, for instance, may sue the business owner, claiming that the security guard's conduct was intentionally wrongful. A person who slips and falls at a retail store may sue the company for negligence.

Any time that one party's allegedly wrongful conduct causes injury to another, an action may arise under the law of *torts* (the word *tort* is French for "wrong"). Through tort law, society compensates those who have suffered injuries as a result of the wrongful conduct of others. Many of the lawsuits brought by or against business firms are based on various tort theories.

4–1 The Basis of Tort Law

Two notions serve as the basis of all **torts:** wrongs and compensation. Tort law is designed to compensate those who have suffered a loss or injury due to another person's wrongful act. In a tort action, one person or group brings a lawsuit against another person or group to obtain compensation (monetary damages) or other relief for the harm suffered.

4–1a The Purpose of Tort Law

Generally, the purpose of tort law is to provide remedies for the violation of various *protected interests.* Society recognizes an interest in personal physical safety. Thus, tort law provides remedies for acts that cause physical injury or that interfere with physical security and freedom of movement. Society also recognizes an interest in protecting property, and tort law provides remedies for acts that cause destruction of or damage to property.

4–1b Damages Available in Tort Actions

Because the purpose of tort law is to compensate the injured party for the damage suffered, you need to have an understanding of the types of damages that plaintiffs seek in tort actions. Note that legal usage distinguishes between the terms *damage* and *damages. Damage* refers to harm or injury to persons or property, while **damages** refers to monetary compensation for such harm or injury.

Compensatory Damages A plaintiff is awarded **compensatory damages** to compensate or reimburse the plaintiff for actual losses. Thus, the goal is to make the plaintiff whole and put her or him in the same position that she or he would have been in had the tort not occurred. Compensatory damages awards are often broken down into *special damages* and *general damages.*

Special damages compensate the plaintiff for quantifiable monetary losses, such as medical expenses and lost wages and benefits (now and in the future). Special damages might also be awarded to compensate for extra costs, the loss of irreplaceable items, and the costs of repairing or replacing damaged property.

■ **CASE IN POINT 4.1** Seaway Marine Transport operates the *Enterprise,* a large cargo ship, which has twenty-two hatches for storing coal. When the *Enterprise* positioned itself to receive a load of coal on the shores of Lake Erie, in Ohio, it struck a land-based coal-loading machine operated by Bessemer & Lake Erie Railroad Company. A federal court found Seaway liable and awarded $522,000 in special damages to compensate Bessemer for the cost of repairing the damage to the loading boom.[1] ■

General damages compensate individuals (not companies) for the nonmonetary aspects of the harm suffered, such as pain and suffering. A court might award general damages for physical or emotional pain and suffering, loss of companionship, loss of consortium (losing

---

1. *Bessemer & Lake Erie Railroad Co. v. Seaway Marine Transport,* 357 F.3d 596 (6th Cir. 2010).

the emotional and physical benefits of a spousal relationship), disfigurement, loss of reputation, or loss or impairment of mental or physical capacity.

Punitive Damages Occasionally, the courts also award **punitive damages** in tort cases to punish the wrongdoer and deter others from similar wrongdoing. Punitive damages are appropriate only when the defendant's conduct was particularly egregious (flagrant) or reprehensible (blameworthy).

Usually, this means that punitive damages are available in *intentional* tort actions and only rarely in negligence lawsuits (negligence actions will be discussed later in this chapter). They may be awarded, however, in suits involving *gross negligence*. Gross negligence can be defined as an intentional failure to perform a manifest duty in reckless disregard of the consequences of such a failure for the life or property of another.

Courts exercise great restraint in granting punitive damages to plaintiffs in tort actions because punitive damages are subject to limitations under the due process clause of the U.S. Constitution. The United States Supreme Court has held that to the extent that an award of punitive damages is grossly excessive, it furthers no legitimate purpose and violates due process requirements.[2] Consequently, an appellate court will sometimes reduce the amount of punitive damages awarded to a plaintiff on the ground that it is excessive and thereby violates the due process clause.

Legislative Caps on Damages State laws may limit the amount of damages—both punitive and general—that can be awarded to the plaintiff. More than half of the states have placed caps ranging from $250,000 to $750,000 on noneconomic general damages (such as for pain and suffering), especially in medical malpractice suits. More than thirty states have limited punitive damages, with some imposing outright bans.

4–1c Classification of Torts

There are two broad classifications of torts: *intentional torts* and *unintentional torts* (torts involving negligence). The classification of a particular tort depends largely on how the tort occurs (intentionally or negligently) and the surrounding circumstances. Intentional torts result from the intentional violation of person or property (fault plus intent). Negligence results from the breach of a duty to act reasonably (fault without intent).

---

2. *State Farm Mutual Automobile Insurance Co. v. Campbell*, 538 U.S. 408, 123 S.Ct. 1513, 155 L.Ed.2d 585 (2003).

4–1d Defenses

Even if a plaintiff proves all the elements of a tort, the defendant can raise a number of legally recognized *defenses* (reasons why the plaintiff should not obtain damages). A successful defense releases the defendant from partial or full liability for the tortious act.

The defenses available may vary depending on the specific tort involved. A common defense to intentional torts against persons, for instance, is *consent*. When a person consents to the act that damages her or him, there is generally no liability. The most widely used defense in negligence actions is *comparative negligence*.

In addition, most states have a *statute of limitations* that establishes the time limit (often two years from the date of discovering the harm) within which a particular type of lawsuit can be filed. After that time period has run, the plaintiff can no longer file a claim.

4–2 Intentional Torts against Persons

An **intentional tort,** as the term implies, requires intent. The **tortfeasor** (the one committing the tort) must intend to commit an act, the consequences of which interfere with another's personal or business interests in a way not permitted by law. An evil or harmful motive is not required—in fact, the person committing the action may even have a beneficial motive for doing what turns out to be a tortious act.

In tort law, *intent* means only that the person intended the consequences of his or her act or knew with substantial certainty that specific consequences would result from the act. The law generally assumes that individuals intend the *normal* consequences of their actions. Thus, forcefully pushing another—even if done in jest—is an intentional tort (if injury results), because the object of a strong push can ordinarily be expected to fall down.

In addition, intent can be transferred when a defendant intends to harm one individual, but unintentionally harms a second person. This is called **transferred intent. ■ EXAMPLE 4.2** Alex swings a bat intending to hit Blake but misses and hits Carson instead. Carson can sue Alex for the tort of battery (discussed shortly) because Alex's intent to harm Blake can be transferred to Carson. ■

4–2a Assault

An **assault** is any intentional and unexcused threat of immediate harmful or offensive contact—words or acts that create a reasonably believable threat. An assault can occur even if there is no actual contact with the plaintiff, provided that the defendant's conduct creates a reasonable apprehension of imminent harm in the plaintiff. Tort law aims to protect individuals from having to expect harmful or offensive contact.

4–2b Battery

If the act that created the apprehension is *completed* and results in harm to the plaintiff, it is a **battery**—an unexcused and harmful or offensive physical contact *intentionally* performed. ■ **EXAMPLE 4.3** Ivan threatens Jean with a gun and then shoots her. The pointing of the gun at Jean is an assault. The firing of the gun (if the bullet hits Jean) is a battery. ■

The contact can be harmful, or it can be merely offensive (such as an unwelcome kiss). Physical injury need not occur. The contact can involve any part of the body or anything attached to it—for instance, a hat, a purse, or a jacket. The contact can be made by the defendant or by some force set in motion by the defendant, such as a rock thrown by the defendant. Whether the contact is offensive is determined by the *reasonable person standard*.[3]

If the plaintiff shows that there was contact, and the jury (or judge, if there is no jury) agrees that the contact was offensive, then the plaintiff has a right to compensation. A plaintiff may be compensated for the emotional harm or loss of reputation resulting from a battery, as well as for physical harm. A defendant may assert self-defense or defense of others in an attempt to justify his or her conduct.

4–2c False Imprisonment

False imprisonment is the intentional confinement or restraint of another person's activities without justification. False imprisonment interferes with the freedom to move without restraint. The confinement can be accomplished through the use of physical barriers, physical restraint, or threats of physical force. Moral pressure does not constitute false imprisonment. It is essential that the person being restrained does not wish to be restrained. (The plaintiff's consent to the restraint bars any liability.)

Businesspersons often face suits for false imprisonment after they have attempted to confine a suspected shoplifter for questioning. Under the "privilege to detain" granted to merchants in most states, a merchant can use *reasonable force* to detain or delay persons suspected of shoplifting and hold them for the police. Although laws pertaining to this privilege vary from state to state, generally any detention must be conducted in a *reasonable* manner and for only a *reasonable* length of time. Undue force or unreasonable detention can lead to liability for the business.

Cities and counties may also face lawsuits for false imprisonment if they detain individuals without reason. ■ **CASE IN POINT 4.4** Police arrested Adetokunbo Shoyoye for riding the subway without a ticket and for a theft that had been committed by someone who had stolen his identity. A court ordered him to be released, but a county employee mistakenly confused Shoyoye's paperwork with that of another person who was scheduled to be sent to state prison. As a result, instead of being released, Shoyoye was held in county jail for more than two weeks. Shoyoye later sued the county for false imprisonment and won.[4] ■

4–2d Intentional Infliction of Emotional Distress

The tort of *intentional infliction of emotional distress* involves an intentional act that amounts to extreme and outrageous conduct resulting in severe emotional distress to another. To be **actionable** (capable of serving as the ground for a lawsuit), the act must be extreme and outrageous to the point that it exceeds the bounds of decency accepted by society.

Outrageous Conduct Courts in most jurisdictions are wary of emotional distress claims and confine them to situations involving truly outrageous behavior. Generally, repeated annoyances (such as those experienced by a person who is being stalked), coupled with threats, are enough. Acts that cause indignity or annoyance alone usually are not sufficient.

■ **EXAMPLE 4.5** A father attacks a man who has had consensual sexual relations with the father's nineteen-year-old daughter. The father handcuffs the man to a steel pole and threatens to kill him unless he leaves town immediately. The father's conduct may be sufficiently extreme and outrageous to be actionable as an intentional infliction of emotional distress. ■

Limited by the First Amendment When the outrageous conduct consists of speech about a public figure,

---

3. The *reasonable person standard* is an "objective" test of how a reasonable person would have acted under the same circumstances. See "The Duty of Care and Its Breach" later in this chapter.

4. *Shoyoye v. County of Los Angeles*, 203 Cal.App.4th 947, 137 Cal.Rptr.3d 839 (2012).

the First Amendment's guarantee of freedom of speech also limits emotional distress claims.

■ **CASE IN POINT 4.6** *Hustler* magazine once printed a false advertisement that showed a picture of the late Reverend Jerry Falwell and described him as having lost his virginity to his mother in an outhouse while he was drunk. Falwell sued the magazine for intentional infliction of emotional distress and won, but the United States Supreme Court overturned the decision. The Court held that parodies of public figures are protected under the First Amendment from intentional infliction of emotional distress claims. (The Court uses the same standards that apply to public figures in defamation lawsuits, discussed next.)[5] ■

4–2e Defamation

The freedom of speech guaranteed by the First Amendment is not absolute. The courts are required to balance the vital guarantee of free speech against other pervasive

and strong social interests, including society's interest in preventing and redressing attacks on reputation.

Defamation of character involves wrongfully hurting a person's good reputation. The law imposes a general duty on all persons to refrain from making false, defamatory *statements of fact* about others. Breaching this duty in writing or other permanent form (such as a digital recording) involves the tort of **libel.** Breaching this duty orally involves the tort of **slander.** The tort of defamation also arises when a false statement of fact is made about a person's product, business, or legal ownership rights to property.

Establishing defamation involves proving the following elements:

1. The defendant made a false statement of fact.
2. The statement was understood as being about the plaintiff and tended to harm the plaintiff's reputation.
3. The statement was published to at least one person other than the plaintiff.
4. If the plaintiff is a public figure, she or he must also prove *actual malice,* discussed later in the chapter.

The following case involved the application of free speech guarantees to online reviews of professional services.

---

5. *Hustler Magazine, Inc. v. Falwell,* 485 U.S. 46, 108 S.Ct. 876, 99 L.Ed.2d 41 (1988). For another example of how the courts protect parody, see *Busch v. Viacom International, Inc.,* 477 F.Supp.2d 764 (N.D.Tex. 2007), involving a false endorsement of televangelist Pat Robertson's diet shake.

Case Analysis 4.1

Blake v. Giustibelli

District Court of Appeal of Florida, Fourth District, 41 Fla.L.Weekly D122, 182 So.3d 881 (2016).

In the Language of the Court
CIKLIN, C.J. [Chief Judge]

* * * *

[Ann-Marie] Giustibelli represented Copia Blake in a dissolution of marriage proceeding brought against Peter Birzon. After a breakdown in the attorney-client relationship between Giustibelli and her client[,] Blake, and oddly, Birzon as well, took to the Internet to post defamatory reviews of Giustibelli. In response, Giustibelli brought suit [in a Florida state court against Blake and Birzon], pleading a count for libel.

Blake's and Birzon's posted Internet reviews contained the following statements:

This lawyer represented me in my divorce. She was combative and

explosive and took my divorce to a level of anger which caused major suffering of my minor children. She insisted I was an emotionally abused wife who couldn't make rational decisions which caused my case to drag on in the system for a year and a half so her FEES would continue to multiply!! She misrepresented her fees with regards to the contract I initially signed. The contract she submitted to the courts for her fees were 4 times her original quote and pages of the original had been exchanged to support her claims, only the signature page was the same. Shame on me that I did not have an original copy, but like an idiot * * * I trusted my lawyer. Don't mistake sincerity for honesty because I assure you, that in this attorney's case, they are NOT the same thing. She absolutely perpetuates

the horrible image of attorneys who are only out for the money and themselves. Although I know this isn't the case and there are some very good honest lawyers out there, Mrs. Giustibelli is simply not one of the "good ones." Horrible horrible experience. Use anyone else, it would have to be a better result.

* * * *

No integrity. Will say one thing and do another. Her fees outweigh the truth. Altered her charges to 4 times the original quote with no explanation. Do not use her. Don't mistake sincerity for honesty. In her case, they're not at all the same. Will literally lie to your face if it means more money for her. Get someone else.

* * * Anyone else would do a superior effort for you.

* * * *

I accepted an initial VERY fair offer from my ex. Mrs. Giustibelli convinced me to "crush" him and that I could have permanent etc. Spent over a year (and 4 times her original estimate) to arrive at the same place we started at. Caused unnecessary chaos and fear with my kids, convinced me that my ex cheated (which he didn't), that he was hiding money (which he wasn't), and was mad at ME when I realized her fee circus had gone on long enough and finally said "stop." Altered her fee structures, actually replaced original documents with others to support her charges and generally gave the kind of poor service you only hear about. I'm not a disgruntled

ex-wife. I'm just the foolish person who believes that a person's word should be backed by integrity. Not even remotely true in this case. I've had 2 prior attorneys and never ever have I seen ego and monies be so blatantly out of control.

Both Blake and Birzon admitted to posting the reviews on various Internet sites. The evidence showed that Blake had agreed to pay her attorney the amount reflected on the written retainer agreement—$300 an hour. Blake and Birzon both admitted at trial that Giustibelli had not charged Blake four times more than what was quoted in the agreement. The court entered judgment in favor of Giustibelli and awarded punitive damages of $350,000.

On appeal, Blake and Birzon argue that their Internet reviews constituted

statements of opinion and thus were protected by the First Amendment and not actionable as defamation. We disagree. *An action for libel will lie for a false and unprivileged publication by letter, or otherwise, which exposes a person to distrust, hatred, contempt, ridicule or obloquy [censure or disgrace] or which causes such person to be avoided, or which has a tendency to injure such person in their office, occupation, business or employment.* [Emphasis added.]

Here, all the reviews contained allegations that Giustibelli lied to Blake regarding the attorney's fee. Two of the reviews contained the allegation that Giustibelli falsified a contract. These are factual allegations, and the evidence showed they were false.

* * * *

Affirmed.

Legal Reasoning Questions

1. What is the standard for the protection of free speech guaranteed by the First Amendment?

2. How did this standard apply to the statements posted online by Blake and Birzon?

3. The First Amendment normally protects statements of opinion, and this can be an effective defense against a charge of defamation. Does it seem reasonable to disregard this defense, however, if *any* assertion of fact within a statement of opinion is false? Explain.

Statement-of-Fact Requirement Often at issue in defamation lawsuits (including online defamation) is whether the defendant made a statement of fact or a *statement of opinion*. Statements of opinion normally are not actionable, because they are protected under the First Amendment.

In other words, making a negative statement about another person is not defamation unless the statement is false and represents something as a fact rather than a personal opinion. ■ **EXAMPLE 4.7** The statement "Lane cheats on his taxes," if false, can lead to liability for defamation. The statement "Lane is a jerk" cannot constitute defamation because it is clearly an opinion. ■

The Publication Requirement The basis of the tort of defamation is the publication of a statement or statements that hold an individual up to contempt, ridicule, or

hatred. *Publication* here means that the defamatory statements are communicated (either intentionally or accidentally) to persons other than the defamed party.

The courts have generally held that even dictating a letter to a secretary constitutes publication, although the publication may be privileged (a concept that will be explained shortly). Moreover, if a third party merely overhears defamatory statements by chance, the courts usually hold that this also constitutes publication. Defamatory statements made via the Internet are actionable as well. Note also that any individual who repeats or republishes defamatory statements normally is liable even if that person reveals the source of the statements.

■ **CASE IN POINT 4.8** Eddy Ramirez, a meat cutter at Costco Wholesale Corporation, was involved in a workplace incident with a coworker, and Costco gave him a notice of suspension. After an investigation in which coworkers were interviewed, Costco fired Ramirez. Ramirez sued, claiming that the suspension notice was defamatory. The court ruled in Costco's favor. Ramirez could not establish defamation, because he had not shown that the suspension notice was published to any third parties. Costco did nothing beyond what was necessary to investigate the events that led to Ramirez's termination.[6] ■

Damages for Libel Once a defendant's liability for libel is established, general damages are presumed as a matter of law. General damages are designed to compensate the plaintiff for nonspecific harms such as disgrace or dishonor in the eyes of the community, humiliation, injured reputation, and emotional distress—harms that are difficult to measure. In other words, to recover damages, the plaintiff need not prove that he or she was actually harmed in any specific way as a result of the libelous statement.

Damages for Slander In contrast to cases alleging libel, in a case alleging slander, the plaintiff must prove *special damages* to establish the defendant's liability. The plaintiff must show that the slanderous statement caused her or him to suffer actual economic or monetary losses.

Unless this initial hurdle of proving special damages is overcome, a plaintiff alleging slander normally cannot go forward with the suit and recover any damages. This requirement is imposed in slander cases because oral statements have a temporary quality. In contrast, a libelous (written) statement has the quality of permanence and can be circulated widely, especially through tweets and blogs. Also, libel usually results from some degree of deliberation by the author.

Slander *Per Se* Exceptions to the burden of proving special damages in cases alleging slander are made for certain types of slanderous statements. If a false statement constitutes "slander *per se*," it is actionable with no proof of special damages required. In most states, the following four types of declarations are considered to be slander *per se*:

1. A statement that another has a "loathsome" disease (such as a sexually transmitted disease).
2. A statement that another has committed improprieties while engaging in a profession or trade.
3. A statement that another has committed or has been imprisoned for a serious crime.

4. A statement that a person is unchaste or has engaged in serious sexual misconduct. (This usually applies only to unmarried persons and sometimes only to women.)

Defenses to Defamation Truth is normally an absolute defense against a defamation charge. In other words, if a defendant in a defamation case can prove that the allegedly defamatory statements of fact were true, normally no tort has been committed.

■ **CASE IN POINT 4.9** David McKee, a neurologist, went to examine a patient who had been transferred from the intensive care unit (ICU) to a private room. In the room were family members of the patient, including his son. The patient's son later made the following post on a "rate your doctor" Web site: "[Dr. McKee] seemed upset that my father had been moved [into a private room]. Never having met my father or his family, Dr. McKee said 'When you weren't in ICU, I had to spend time finding out if you transferred or died.' When we gaped at him, he said 'Well, 44 percent of hemorrhagic strokes die within 30 days. I guess this is the better option.'"

McKee filed suit for defamation but lost. The court found that all the statements made by the son were essentially true, and truth is a complete defense to a defamation action.[7] ■ In other words, true statements are not actionable no matter how disparaging. Even the presence of minor inaccuracies of expression or detail does not render basically true statements false.

Other defenses to defamation may exist if the speech is privileged or if it concerns a public figure. We discuss these defenses next. Note that the majority of defamation actions are filed in state courts, and state laws differ somewhat in the defenses they allow.

Privileged Communications. In some circumstances, a person will not be liable for defamatory statements because she or he enjoys a **privilege,** or immunity. Privileged communications are of two types: absolute and qualified.[8] Only in judicial proceedings and certain government proceedings is an *absolute privilege* granted. Thus, statements made by attorneys and judges in the courtroom during a trial are absolutely privileged, as are statements made by government officials during legislative debate.

---

6. *Ramirez v. Costco Wholesale Corp.,* 2014 WL 2696737 (Ct.Sup.Ct. 2014).

7. *McKee v. Laurion,* 825 N.W.2d 725 (Minn.Sup. 2013).
8. Note that the term *privileged communication* in this context is not the same as privileged communication between a professional, such as an attorney, and his or her client.

In other situations, a person will not be liable for defamatory statements because he or she has a *qualified, or conditional, privilege.* An employer's statements in written evaluations of employees, for instance, are protected by a qualified privilege. Generally, if the statements are made in good faith and the publication is limited to those who have a legitimate interest in the communication, the statements fall within the area of qualified privilege.

■ **EXAMPLE 4.10** Jorge has worked at Google for five years and is being considered for a management position. His supervisor, Lydia, writes a memo about Jorge's performance to those evaluating him for the position. The memo contains certain negative statements, which Lydia honestly believes are true. If Lydia limits the disclosure of the memo to company representatives, her statements will likely be protected by a qualified privilege. ■

Public Figures. Politicians, entertainers, professional athletes, and others in the public eye are considered **public figures.** Public figures are regarded as "fair game." False and defamatory statements about public figures that are published in the media will not constitute defamation unless the statements are made with **actual malice.**[9] To be made with actual malice, a statement must be made *with either knowledge of its falsity or a reckless disregard of the truth.*

Statements made about public figures, especially when they are communicated via a public medium, usually relate to matters of general interest. They are made about people who substantially affect all of us. Furthermore, public figures generally have some access to a public medium for answering belittling falsehoods about themselves. For these reasons, public figures have a greater burden of proof in defamation cases—to show actual malice—than do private individuals.

■ **CASE IN POINT 4.11** *In Touch* magazine published a story about a former call girl who claimed to have slept with legendary soccer player David Beckham more than once. Beckham sued *In Touch* magazine for libel, seeking $25 million in damages. He said that he had never met the woman, had not cheated on his wife with her, and had not paid her for sex. After months of litigation, a federal district court dismissed the case because Beckham could not show that the magazine had acted with actual malice. Whether or not the statements in the article were accurate, there was no evidence that the defendants had made the statements with knowledge of their falsity or reckless disregard for the truth.[10] ■

---

9. *New York Times Co. v. Sullivan,* 376 U.S. 254, 84 S.Ct. 710, 11 L.Ed.2d 686 (1964).
10. *Beckham v. Bauer Pub. Co., L.P.,* 2011 WL 977570 (2011).

4–2f Invasion of Privacy

A person has a right to solitude and freedom from prying public eyes—in other words, to privacy. The courts have held that certain amendments to the U.S. Constitution imply a right to privacy. Some state constitutions explicitly provide for privacy rights, as do a number of federal and state statutes.

Tort law also safeguards these rights through the tort of *invasion of privacy.* Generally, to sue successfully for an invasion of privacy, a person must have a reasonable expectation of privacy, and the invasion must be highly offensive. (See this chapter's *Digital Update* feature for a discussion of how invasion of privacy claims can arise when someone posts pictures or videos taken with digital devices.)

Invasion of Privacy under the Common Law
The following four acts qualify as an invasion of privacy under the common law:

1. *Intrusion into an individual's affairs or seclusion.* Invading someone's home or searching someone's briefcase or laptop without authorization is an invasion of privacy. This tort has been held to extend to eavesdropping by wiretap, unauthorized scanning of a bank account, compulsory blood testing, and window peeping. ■ **EXAMPLE 4.12** A female sports reporter for ESPN is digitally videoed while naked through the peephole in the door of her hotel room. She will probably win a lawsuit against the man who took the video and posted it on the Internet. ■

2. *False light.* Publication of information that places a person in a false light is also an invasion of privacy. For instance, writing a story that attributes to a person ideas and opinions not held by that person is an invasion of privacy. (Publishing such a story could involve the tort of defamation as well.) ■ **EXAMPLE 4.13** An Iowa newspaper prints an article saying that nineteen-year-old Yassine Alam is part of the terrorist organization Islamic State of Iraq (ISIL). Next to the article is a photo of Yassine's brother, Salaheddin. Salaheddin can sue the paper for putting him in a false light by using his photo. If the report is not true, and Yassine is not involved with ISIL, Yassine can sue the paper for defamation. ■

3. *Public disclosure of private facts.* This type of invasion of privacy occurs when a person publicly discloses private facts about an individual that an ordinary person would find objectionable or embarrassing. A newspaper account of a private citizen's sex life or financial affairs could be an actionable invasion of

DIGITAL UPDATE   Revenge Porn and Invasion of Privacy

Nearly every digital device today takes photos and videos at virtually no cost. Software allows the recording of conversations via Skype. Many couples immortalize their "private moments" using such digital devices. One partner may take a racy selfie and send it as an attachment to a text message to the other partner, for example.

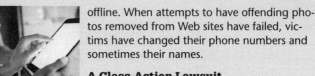

Occasionally, after a couple breaks off their relationship, one of them seeks a type of digital revenge. The result, called revenge porn, has been defined in the Cyber Civil Rights Initiative as "the online distribution of sexually explicit images of a non-consenting individual with the intent to humiliate that person."

Until relatively recently, few states had criminal statutes that covered revenge porn. Therefore, victims have sued on the basis of (1) invasion of privacy, (2) public disclosure of private facts, and (3) intentional infliction of emotional distress.

It Is More Than Just Pictures and Videos

Perhaps the worst form of revenge porn occurs when the perpetrator provides detailed information about the victim. Such information may include the victim's name, Facebook page, address, and phone number, as well as the victim's workplace and children's names. This information, along with the sexually explicit photos and videos, are posted on hosting Web sites. Many such Web sites have been shut down, as was the case with IsAnybodyDown? and Texxxan.com. But others are still active, usually with offshore servers and foreign domain name owners.

The Injurious Results of Revenge Porn

Of course, victims of revenge porn suffer extreme embarrassment. They may also have their reputations ruined. Some have lost their jobs. Others have been unable to obtain jobs because employers have seen their pictures online. A number of victims have been stalked in the physical world and harassed online and offline. When attempts to have offending photos removed from Web sites have failed, victims have changed their phone numbers and sometimes their names.

A Class-Action Lawsuit

Hollie Toups, along with twenty-two other female plaintiffs, sued the domain name registrar and Web hosting company GoDaddy in a Texas court. Although GoDaddy did not create the defamatory and offensive material at issue, GoDaddy knew of the content and did not remove it. The plaintiffs asserted causes of action "for intentional infliction of emotional distress," among other claims.

Additionally, the plaintiffs argued that "by its knowing participation in these unlawful activities, GoDaddy has also committed the intentional Texas tort of invasion of privacy . . . as well as intrusion on Plaintiffs' right to seclusion, the public disclosure of their private facts, [and] the wrongful appropriation of their names and likenesses. . . ." GoDaddy sought to dismiss the case, and an appeals court eventually granted the motion to dismiss.[a]

Another Texas woman had better luck. The woman's ex-boyfriend had uploaded videos of her to YouTube and other sites. At the time she made the complaint, revenge porn was not a crime in Texas. Nevertheless, in a jury trial in 2014, she won a $500,000 award. Since then, a handful of states have made revenge porn a crime. In 2015, a California man, Kevin Bollaert, was convicted for creating a revenge porn Web site and sentenced to serve eighteen years in prison.

Critical Thinking *Should domain name hosting companies be liable for revenge porn?*

---

a. *GoDaddy.com, LLC. v. Toups*, 429 S.W.3d 752 (Tex.App.—Beaumont 2014).

---

privacy. This is so even if the information revealed is true, because it should not be a matter of public concern.

4. *Appropriation of identity.* Using a person's name, picture, likeness, or other identifiable characteristic for commercial purposes without permission is also an invasion of privacy. An individual's right to privacy normally includes the right to the exclusive use of her or his identity. ■ **EXAMPLE 4.14** An advertising agency asks a singer with a distinctive voice and stage presence to take part in a marketing campaign for a new automobile. The singer rejects the offer. If the

agency then uses someone who imitates the singer's voice and dance moves in the ad, it will be actionable as an appropriation of identity. ■

Appropriation Statutes Most states today have codified the common law tort of appropriation of identity in statutes that establish the distinct tort of **appropriation,** or right of publicity. States differ as to the degree of likeness that is required to impose liability for appropriation, however.

Some courts have held that even when an animated character in a video or a video game is made to look like an actual person, there are not enough similarities to constitute appropriation. **■ CASE IN POINT 4.15** Robert Burck is a street entertainer in New York City who has become famous as "The Naked Cowboy." Burck performs wearing only a white cowboy hat, white cowboy boots, and white underwear. He carries a guitar strategically placed to give the illusion of nudity. Burck sued Mars, Inc., the maker of M&Ms candy, over a video it showed on billboards in Times Square that depicted a blue M&M dressed exactly like The Naked Cowboy. The court, however, held that the use of Burck's signature costume did not amount to appropriation.[11] ■

---

11. *Burck v. Mars, Inc.,* 571 F.Supp.2d 446 (S.D.N.Y. 2008).

4–2g Fraudulent Misrepresentation

A misrepresentation leads another to believe in a condition that is different from the condition that actually exists. Although persons sometimes make misrepresentations accidentally because they are unaware of the existing facts, the tort of **fraudulent misrepresentation (fraud),** involves *intentional* deceit for personal gain. The tort includes several elements:

1. A misrepresentation of material facts or conditions with knowledge that they are false or with reckless disregard for the truth.
2. An intent to induce another party to rely on the misrepresentation.
3. A justifiable reliance on the misrepresentation by the deceived party.
4. Damages suffered as a result of that reliance.
5. A causal connection between the misrepresentation and the injury suffered.

For fraud to occur, more than mere **puffery,** or *seller's talk,* must be involved. Fraud exists only when a person represents as a fact something he or she knows is untrue. For instance, it is fraud to claim that the roof of a building does not leak when one knows that it does. Facts are objectively ascertainable, whereas seller's talk (such as "I am the best accountant in town") is not, because the use of the word *best* is subjective.

In the following case, the court considered each of the elements of fraud.

Case 4.2

Revell v. Guido

New York Supreme Court, Appellate Division, Third Department, 124 A.D.3d 1006, 2 N.Y.S.3d 252 (2015).

Background and Facts Joseph Guido bought a parcel of land in Stillwater, New York, that contained nine rental houses. The houses shared a waste disposal system that was defective. Guido had a new septic system installed. When town officials discovered sewage on the property, Guido had the system partially replaced. Prospective buyers, including Danny Revell, were given a property information sheet that stated, "Septic system totally new—each field totally replaced." In response to a questionnaire from the buyers' bank, Guido denied any knowledge of environmental problems.

A month after the buyers bought the houses, the septic system failed and required substantial repairs. The lender foreclosed on the property. The buyers filed a suit in a New York state court against Guido and his firm, Real Property Solutions, LLC, alleging fraud. A jury found fraud and awarded damages. The court issued a judgment in the plaintiffs' favor. The defendants appealed.

In the Language of the Court

EGAN, Jr., J.: [Judge:]
    * * * *

    To prevail upon their cause of action for fraud, plaintiffs were required to establish that defendants, with the intent to deceive, misrepresented or omitted a material fact that they knew to be false and that plaintiffs,

Case 4.2 Continues

in turn, justifiably relied upon such misrepresentation or omission, thereby incurring damages. As to the misrepresentation element, plaintiffs point to the statement made on the property information sheet * * * , as well as Guido's responses to certain of the inquiries contained on the environmental questionnaire. In this regard, the record reflects that the [replacement] septic system * * * was not "totally new," as it retained the original pump house structure and, more to the point, utilized the holding tanks that originally were part of the system * * * . There also is no question that Guido provided false answers to various inquiries posed on the environmental questionnaire. For example, Guido disavowed any knowledge of "governmental notification relating to past or recurrent violations of environmental laws with respect to the property * * * "—despite having been advised by the Town of Stillwater * * * that partially treated sewage was discovered on the property. [Emphasis added.]

As to the intent element, * * * given the arguably cavalier [offhand] manner in which Guido completed the environmental questionnaire, as well as his extensive knowledge regarding the * * * problems with the original septic system * * * , the jury could properly find that Guido made the cited misrepresentations with the intent to deceive plaintiffs.

With respect to the issue of justifiable reliance, Revell * * * conducted a visual inspection of the property prior to making an offer and did not observe any conditions indicative of a problem with the septic system. * * * If a septic system was represented to be "totally new" and a visual inspection of the property did not reveal any red flags, [that is,] boggy areas, odors or liquids bubbling up to the surface, one would assume that the system was working properly. * * * The jury [could] find that plaintiffs' reliance upon the representation contained in the property information sheet was reasonable.
* * * *

Nor are we persuaded that plaintiffs failed to tender sufficient admissible proof to substantiate the damages awarded by the jury. During the trial, the parties stipulated to the admission into evidence of a binder containing, among other things, an abundance of receipts, invoices, billing statements and canceled checks detailing plaintiffs' expenditures related to the subject property—and plaintiffs' forensic accountant, in turn, utilized such documents to arrive at a damages figure. * * * We are satisfied that plaintiffs tendered sufficient admissible proof to sustain the damages awarded by the jury.

Decision and Remedy *The state intermediate appellate court affirmed the lower court's judgment in the plaintiffs' favor. The facts of the case and the plaintiffs' proof met all of the requirements for establishing fraud.*

Critical Thinking
- **Legal Environment** *Financing for the purchase of the property was conditioned on the bank's review of Guido's answers to the environmental questionnaire. How could the court conclude that the plaintiffs justifiably relied on misrepresentations made to the bank? Explain.*
- **What If the Facts Were Different?** *If a visual inspection of the property had revealed "boggy areas, odors or liquids bubbling up to the surface" indicating that the septic system was not working properly, would the outcome of this case have been different?*

Statement of Fact versus Opinion Normally, the tort of fraudulent misrepresentation occurs only when there is reliance on a *statement of fact.* Sometimes, however, reliance on a *statement of opinion* may involve the tort of fraudulent misrepresentation if the individual making the statement of opinion has superior knowledge of the subject matter. For instance, when a lawyer makes a statement of opinion about the law in a state in which the lawyer is licensed to practice, a court might treat it as a statement of fact.

Negligent Misrepresentation Sometimes, a tort action can arise from misrepresentations that are made negligently rather than intentionally. The key difference between intentional and negligent misrepresentation is whether the person making the misrepresentation had actual knowledge of its falsity. Negligent misrepresentation requires only that the person making the statement or omission did not have a reasonable basis for believing its truthfulness.

Liability for negligent misrepresentation usually arises when the defendant who made the misrepresentation owed a duty of care to the plaintiff to supply correct information. (We discuss the duty of care in more detail later in the chapter.) Statements or omissions made by attorneys and accountants to their clients, for instance, can lead to liability for negligent misrepresentation.

4–2h Abusive or Frivolous Litigation

Tort law recognizes that people have a right not to be sued without a legally just and proper reason, and therefore it protects individuals from the misuse of litigation. Torts related to abusive litigation include malicious prosecution and abuse of process. If a party initiates a lawsuit out of malice and without a legitimate legal reason, and ends up losing the suit, that party can be sued for *malicious prosecution. Abuse of process* can apply to any person using a legal process against another in an improper manner or to accomplish a purpose for which the process was not designed.

The key difference between the torts of abuse of process and malicious prosecution is the level of proof. Unlike malicious prosecution, abuse of process is not limited to prior litigation and does not require the plaintiff to prove malice. It can be based on the wrongful use of subpoenas, court orders to attach or seize real property, or other types of formal legal process.

Concept Summary 4.1 reviews intentional torts against persons.

Concept Summary 4.1

Intentional Torts against Persons

Assault and Battery	Any unexcused and intentional act that causes another person to be apprehensive of immediate harm is an assault. An assault resulting in physical contact is a battery.
False Imprisonment	An intentional confinement or restraint of another person's movement without justification.
Intentional Infliction of Emotional Distress	An intentional act that amounts to extreme and outrageous conduct resulting in severe emotional distress to another.
Defamation (Libel or Slander)	A false statement of fact, not made under privilege, that is communicated to a third person and that causes damage to a person's reputation. For public figures, the plaintiff must also prove that the statement was made with actual malice.
Invasion of Privacy	Publishing or otherwise making known or using information relating to a person's private life and affairs, with which the public has no legitimate concern, without that person's permission or approval.
Fraudulent Misrepresentation (Fraud)	A false representation made by one party, through misstatement of facts or through conduct, with the intention of deceiving another and on which the other reasonably relies to his or her detriment.
Abusive or Frivolous Litigation	The filing of a lawsuit without legitimate grounds and with malice. Alternatively, the use of a legal process in an improper manner.

4-2i Wrongful Interference

The torts known as *business torts* generally involve wrongful interference with another's business rights. Public policy favors free competition, and these torts protect against tortious interference with legitimate business. Business torts involving wrongful interference generally fall into two categories: interference with a contractual relationship and interference with a business relationship.

Wrongful Interference with a Contractual Relationship Three elements are necessary for wrongful interference with a contractual relationship to occur:

1. A valid, enforceable contract must exist between two parties.
2. A third party must know that this contract exists.
3. This third party must *intentionally induce* a party to the contract to breach the contract.

■ **CASE IN POINT 4.16** A landmark case in this area involved an opera singer, Joanna Wagner, who was under contract to sing for a man named Lumley for a specified period of years. A man named Gye, who knew of this contract, nonetheless "enticed" Wagner to refuse to carry out the agreement, and Wagner began to sing for Gye. Gye's action constituted a tort because it interfered with the contractual relationship between Wagner and Lumley. (Wagner's refusal to carry out the agreement also entitled Lumley to sue Wagner for breach of contract.)[12] ■

The body of tort law relating to wrongful interference with a contractual relationship has increased greatly in recent years. In principle, any lawful contract can be the basis for an action of this type. The contract could be between a firm and its employees or a firm and its customers. Sometimes, a competitor of a firm lures away one of the firm's key employees. In this situation, the original employer can recover damages from the competitor only if it can be shown that the competitor knew of the contract's existence and intentionally induced the breach.

Wrongful Interference with a Business Relationship Businesspersons devise countless schemes to attract customers. They are prohibited, however, from unreasonably interfering with another's business in their attempts to gain a greater share of the market.

There is a difference between *competitive practices* and *predatory behavior*—actions undertaken with the intention of unlawfully driving competitors completely out of the market. Attempting to attract customers in general is a legitimate business practice, whereas specifically

targeting the customers of a competitor is more likely to be predatory. A plaintiff claiming predatory behavior must show that the defendant used predatory methods to intentionally harm an established business relationship or gain a prospective economic advantage.

■ **EXAMPLE 4.17** A shopping mall contains two athletic shoe stores: Joe's and Ultimate Sport. Joe's cannot station an employee at the entrance of Ultimate Sport's to divert customers to Joe's by telling them that Joe's will beat Ultimate Sport's prices. This type of activity constitutes the tort of wrongful interference with a business relationship, which is commonly considered to be an unfair trade practice. If this activity were permitted, Joe's would reap the benefits of Ultimate Sport's advertising. ■

Defenses to Wrongful Interference A person will not be liable for the tort of wrongful interference with a contractual or business relationship if it can be shown that the interference was justified or permissible. Bona fide competitive behavior—such as marketing and advertising strategies—is a permissible interference even if it results in the breaking of a contract.

■ **EXAMPLE 4.18** Taylor Meats advertises so effectively that it induces Sam's Restaurant to break its contract with Burke's Meat Company. In that situation, Burke's Meat Company will be unable to recover against Taylor Meats on a wrongful interference theory. The public policy that favors free competition through advertising outweighs any possible instability that such competitive activity might cause in contractual relations. ■

4–3 Intentional Torts against Property

Intentional torts against property include trespass to land, trespass to personal property, conversion, and disparagement of property. These torts are wrongful actions that interfere with individuals' legally recognized rights with regard to their land or personal property.

The law distinguishes real property from personal property. *Real property* is land and things permanently attached to the land, such as a house. *Personal property* consists of all other items, including cash and securities (such as stocks and bonds).

4–3a Trespass to Land

A **trespass to land** occurs when a person, without permission, does any of the following:

---

12. *Lumley v. Gye*, 118 Eng.Rep. 749 (1853).

1. Enters onto, above, or below the surface of land that is owned by another.
2. Causes anything to enter onto land owned by another.
3. Remains on land owned by another or permits anything to remain on it.

Actual harm to the land is not an essential element of this tort, because the tort is designed to protect the right of an owner to exclusive possession.

Common types of trespass to land include walking or driving on another's land, shooting a gun over another's land, and throwing rocks at a building that belongs to someone else. Another common form of trespass involves constructing a building so that part of it extends onto an adjoining landowner's property.

Establishing Trespass Before a person can be a trespasser, the real property owner (or another person in actual and exclusive possession of the property, such as a renter) must establish that person as a trespasser. For instance, "posted" trespass signs expressly establish as a trespasser a person who ignores these signs and enters onto the property. A guest in your home is not a trespasser, unless he or she has been asked to leave and refuses. Any person who enters onto another's property to commit an illegal act (such as a thief entering a lumberyard at night to steal lumber) is impliedly a trespasser, with or without posted signs.

Liability for Harm At common law, a trespasser is liable for any damage caused to the property and generally cannot hold the owner liable for injuries that the trespasser sustains on the premises. This common law rule is being modified in many jurisdictions, however, in favor of a *reasonable duty of care* rule that varies depending on the status of the parties.

For instance, a landowner may have a duty to post a notice that guard dogs patrol the property. Also, if young children are attracted to the property by some object, such a swimming pool or a sand pile, and are injured, the landowner may be held liable (under the *attractive nuisance doctrine)*. Still, an owner can normally use reasonable force to remove a trespasser from the premises or detain the trespasser for a reasonable time without liability for damages.

Defenses against Trespass to Land One defense to a claim of trespass is to show that the trespass was warranted, such as when a trespasser enters a building to assist someone in danger. Another defense exists when the trespasser can show that she or he had a *license* to come onto the land.

A **licensee** is one who is invited (or allowed to enter) onto the property of another for the licensee's benefit. A person who enters another's property to read an electric meter, for example, is a licensee. When you purchase a ticket to attend a movie or sporting event, you are licensed to go onto the property of another to view that movie or event.

Note that licenses to enter onto another's property are *revocable* by the property owner. If a property owner asks an electric meter reader to leave and she or he refuses to do so, the meter reader at that point becomes a trespasser.

4–3b Trespass to Personal Property

Whenever any individual wrongfully takes or harms the personal property of another or otherwise interferes with the lawful owner's possession and enjoyment of personal property, **trespass to personal property** occurs. This tort may also be called *trespass to chattels* or *trespass to personalty*.[13] In this context, harm means not only destruction of the property, but also anything that diminishes its value, condition, or quality.

Trespass to personal property involves intentional meddling with a possessory interest (one arising from possession), including barring an owner's access to personal property. ■ **EXAMPLE 4.19** Kelly takes Ryan's business law book as a practical joke and hides it so that Ryan is unable to find it for several days before the final examination. Here, Kelly has engaged in a trespass to personal property (and also *conversion,* the tort discussed next). ■

If it can be shown that trespass to personal property was warranted, then a complete defense exists. Most states, for instance, allow automobile repair shops to hold a customer's car (under what is called an *artisan's lien*) when the customer refuses to pay for repairs already completed.

4–3c Conversion

Any act that deprives an owner of personal property or of the use of that property without the owner's permission and without just cause can constitute **conversion.** Even the taking of electronic records and data may form the basis of a conversion claim. Often, when conversion occurs, a trespass to personal property also occurs. The original taking of the personal property from the owner was a trespass. Wrongfully retaining the property is conversion.

---

13. Pronounced *per*-sun-ul-tee.

Failure to Return Goods   Conversion is the civil side of crimes related to theft, but it is not limited to theft. Even when the rightful owner consented to the initial taking of the property, so no theft or trespass occurred, a failure to return the property may still be conversion.   ■ **EXAMPLE 4.20**   Chen borrows Mark's iPad mini to use while traveling home from school for the holidays. When Chen returns to school, Mark asks for his iPad back, but Chen says that he gave it to his little brother for Christmas. In this situation, Mark can sue Chen for conversion, and Chen will have to either return the iPad or pay damages equal to its replacement value. ■

Intention   Conversion can occur even when a person mistakenly believed that she or he was entitled to the goods. In other words, good intentions are not a defense against conversion. Someone who buys stolen goods, for instance, may be sued for conversion even if he or she did not know the goods were stolen. If the true owner of the goods sues the buyer, the buyer must either return the property to the owner or pay the owner the full value of the property.

Conversion can also occur from an employee's unauthorized use of a credit card.   ■ **CASE IN POINT 4.21**   Nicholas Mora worked for Welco Electronics, Inc., but had also established his own company, AQM Supplies. Mora used Welco's credit card without permission and deposited more than $375,000 into AQM's account, which he then transferred to his personal account. Welco sued. A California court held that Mora was liable for conversion. The court reasoned that when Mora misappropriated Welco's credit card and used it, he took part of Welco's credit balance with the credit-card company.[14] ■

4–3d Disparagement of Property

Disparagement of property occurs when economically injurious falsehoods are made about another's product or property rather than about another's reputation (as in the tort of defamation). *Disparagement of property* is a general term for torts that can be more specifically referred to as *slander of quality* or *slander of title*.

Slander of Quality   The publication of false information about another's product, alleging that it is not what its seller claims, constitutes the tort of **slander of quality,** or **trade libel.** To establish trade libel, the plaintiff must prove that the improper publication caused a third

person to refrain from dealing with the plaintiff and that the plaintiff sustained economic damages (such as lost profits) as a result.

An improper publication may be both a slander of quality and a defamation of character. For instance, a statement that disparages the quality of a product may also, by implication, disparage the character of a person who would sell such a product.

Slander of Title   When a publication falsely denies or casts doubt on another's legal ownership of property, resulting in financial loss to the property's owner, the tort of **slander of title** occurs. Usually, this is an intentional tort in which someone knowingly publishes an untrue statement about another's ownership of certain property with the intent of discouraging a third person from dealing with the person slandered. For instance, it would be difficult for a car dealer to attract customers after competitors published a notice that the dealer's stock consisted of stolen automobiles.

See Concept Summary 4.2 for a review of intentional torts against property.

4–4 Unintentional Torts—Negligence

The tort of **negligence** occurs when someone suffers injury because of another's failure to live up to a required *duty of care*. In contrast to intentional torts, in torts involving negligence, the tortfeasor neither wishes to bring about the consequences of the act nor believes that they will occur. The person's conduct merely creates a risk of such consequences. If no risk is created, there is no negligence.

Moreover, the risk must be foreseeable. In other words, it must be such that a reasonable person engaging in the same activity would anticipate the risk and guard against it. In determining what is reasonable conduct, courts consider the nature of the possible harm.

Many of the actions giving rise to the intentional torts discussed earlier in the chapter constitute negligence if the element of intent is missing (or cannot be proved).   ■ **EXAMPLE 4.22**   Juan walks up to Maya and intentionally shoves her. Maya falls and breaks her arm as a result. In this situation, Juan is liable for the intentional tort of battery. If Juan carelessly bumps into Maya, however, and she falls and breaks her arm as a result, Juan's action constitutes negligence. In either situation, Juan has committed a tort. ■

Concept Summary 4.2

Intentional Torts against Property

Trespass to Land	The invasion of another's real property without consent or privilege. Once a person is expressly or impliedly established as a trespasser, the property owner has specific rights, which may include the right to detain or remove the trespasser.
Trespass to Personal Property	The intentional interference with an owner's right to use, possess, or enjoy his or her personal property without the owner's consent.
Conversion	The wrongful possession or use of another person's personal property without just cause.
Disparagement of Property	Any economically injurious falsehood that is made about another's product or property; an inclusive term for the torts of *slander of quality* and *slander of title*.

To succeed in a negligence action, the plaintiff must prove each of the following:

1. *Duty.* The defendant owed a duty of care to the plaintiff.
2. *Breach.* The defendant breached that duty.
3. *Causation.* The defendant's breach caused the plaintiff's injury.
4. *Damages.* The plaintiff suffered a legally recognizable injury.

4–4a The Duty of Care and Its Breach

Central to the tort of negligence is the concept of a **duty of care.** The basic principle underlying the duty of care is that people are free to act as they please so long as their actions do not infringe on the interests of others. When someone fails to comply with the duty to exercise reasonable care, a potentially tortious act may have been committed.

Failure to live up to a standard of care may be an act (accidentally setting fire to a building) or an omission (neglecting to put out a campfire). It may be a careless act or a carefully performed but nevertheless dangerous act that results in injury. In determining whether the duty of care has been breached, courts consider several factors:

1. The nature of the act (whether it is outrageous or commonplace).
2. The manner in which the act was performed (cautiously versus heedlessly).
3. The nature of the injury (whether it is serious or slight).

Creating even a very slight risk of a dangerous explosion might be unreasonable, whereas creating a distinct possibility of someone's burning his or her fingers on a stove might be reasonable.

The Reasonable Person Standard Tort law measures duty by the **reasonable person standard.** In determining whether a duty of care has been breached, the courts ask how a reasonable person would have acted in the same circumstances. The reasonable person standard is said to be objective. It is not necessarily how a particular person *would* act. It is society's judgment of how an ordinarily prudent person *should* act. If the so-called reasonable person existed, he or she would be careful, conscientious, even tempered, and honest.

The degree of care to be exercised varies, depending on the defendant's occupation or profession, her or his relationship with the plaintiff, and other factors. Generally, whether an action constitutes a breach of the duty of care is determined on a case-by-case basis. The outcome depends on how the judge (or jury) decides that a reasonable person in the position of the defendant would have acted in the particular circumstances of the case.

Note that the courts frequently use the reasonable person standard in other areas of law as well as in negligence cases. Indeed, the principle that individuals are required to exercise a reasonable standard of care in their activities is a pervasive concept in business law.

The Duty of Landowners Landowners are expected to exercise reasonable care to protect individuals coming onto their property from harm. In some jurisdictions, landowners may even have a duty to protect trespassers against certain risks. Landowners who rent or lease premises to tenants are expected to exercise reasonable care to ensure that the tenants and their guests are not harmed in common areas, such as stairways, entryways, and laundry rooms.

The Duty to Warn Business Invitees of Risks. Retailers and other business operators who explicitly or implicitly invite persons to come onto their premises have a duty to exercise reasonable care to protect these **business invitees.** The duty normally requires storeowners to warn business invitees of foreseeable risks, such as construction zones or wet floors, about which the owners knew or *should have known.*

■ **EXAMPLE 4.23** Liz enters Kwan's neighborhood market, slips on a wet floor, and sustains injuries as a result. If there was no sign or other warning that the floor was wet at the time Liz slipped, the owner, Kwan, would be liable for damages. A court would hold that Kwan was negligent because he failed to exercise a reasonable degree of care to protect customers against foreseeable risks about which he knew or should have known. That a patron might slip on the wet floor and be injured was a foreseeable risk, and Kwan should have taken care to avoid this risk or warn the customer of it. ■

A business owner also has a duty to discover and remove any hidden dangers that might injure a customer or other invitee. Hidden dangers might include uneven surfaces or defects in the pavement of a parking lot or a walkway, or merchandise that has fallen off shelves in a store.

Obvious Risks Provide an Exception. Some risks are so obvious that an owner need not warn of them. For instance, a business owner does not need to warn customers to open a door before attempting to walk through it. Other risks, however, even though they may seem obvious to a business owner, may not be so in the eyes of

another, such as a child. In addition, even if a risk is obvious, a business owner is not necessarily excused from the duty to protect customers from foreseeable harm from that risk.

■ **CASE IN POINT 4.24** Giorgio's Grill is a restaurant in Florida that becomes a nightclub after hours. At those times, traditionally, as the manager of Giorgio's knew, the staff and customers throw paper napkins into the air as the music plays. The napkins land on the floor, but no one picks them up. One night, Jane Izquierdo went to Giorgio's. Although she had been to the club on prior occasions and knew about the napkin-throwing tradition, she slipped and fell, breaking her leg. She sued Giorgio's for negligence, but lost at trial because a jury found that the risk of slipping on the napkins was obvious. A state appellate court reversed, however, holding that the obviousness of a risk does not discharge a business owner's duty to its invitees to maintain the premises in a safe condition.[15] ■

The Duty of Professionals Persons who possess superior knowledge, skill, or training are held to a higher standard of care than others. Professionals—including physicians, dentists, architects, engineers, accountants, and lawyers, among others—are required to have a standard minimum level of special knowledge and ability. In determining what constitutes reasonable care in the case of professionals, the law takes their training and expertise into account. Thus, an accountant's conduct is judged not by the reasonable person standard, but by the reasonable accountant standard.

If a professional violates his or her duty of care toward a client, the client may bring a suit against the professional, alleging **malpractice,** which is essentially professional negligence. For instance, a patient might sue a physician for *medical malpractice.* A client might sue an attorney for *legal malpractice.*

4–4b Causation

Another element necessary to a negligence action is *causation.* If a person breaches a duty of care and someone suffers injury, the person's act must have caused the harm for it to constitute the tort of negligence.

Courts Ask Two Questions In deciding whether the requirement of causation is met, the court must address two questions:

---

15. *Izquierdo v. Gyroscope, Inc.*, 946 So.2d 115 (Fla.App. 2007).

1. *Is there causation in fact?* Did the injury occur because of the defendant's act, or would it have occurred anyway? If the injury would not have occurred without the defendant's act, then there is causation in fact.

   Causation in fact usually can be determined by use of the *but for* test: "but for" the wrongful act, the injury would not have occurred. This test seeks to determine whether there was a cause-and-effect relationship between the act and the injury suffered. In theory, causation in fact is limitless. One could claim, for example, that "but for" the creation of the world, a particular injury would not have occurred. Thus, as a practical matter, the law has to establish limits, and it does so through the concept of proximate cause.

2. *Was the act the proximate, or legal, cause of the injury?* **Proximate cause,** or *legal cause*, exists when the connection between an act and an injury is strong enough to justify imposing liability. Proximate cause asks whether the injuries sustained were foreseeable or were too remotely connected to the incident to trigger liability. Judges use proximate cause to limit the scope of the defendant's liability to a subset of the total number of potential plaintiffs that might have been harmed by the defendant's actions.

   ■ **EXAMPLE 4.25** Ackerman carelessly leaves a campfire burning. The fire not only burns down the forest but also sets off an explosion in a nearby chemical plant that spills chemicals into a river, killing all the fish for twenty miles downstream and ruining the economy of a tourist resort. Should Ackerman be liable to the resort owners? To the tourists whose vacations were ruined? These are questions of proximate cause that a court must decide. ■

Both of these causation questions must be answered in the affirmative for liability in tort to arise. If there is causation in fact but a court decides that the defendant's action is not the proximate cause of the plaintiff's injury, the causation requirement has not been met. Therefore, the defendant normally will not be liable to the plaintiff.

Foreseeability Questions of proximate cause are linked to the concept of foreseeability because it would be unfair to impose liability on a defendant unless the defendant's actions created a foreseeable risk of injury. Generally, if the victim or the consequences of a harm done were unforeseeable, there is no proximate cause.

Probably the most cited case on the concept of foreseeability and proximate cause is the *Palsgraf* case, which established foreseeability as the test for proximate cause. ■ **CASE IN POINT 4.26** Helen Palsgraf was waiting for a train on a station platform. A man carrying a package was rushing to catch a train that was moving away from a platform across the tracks from Palsgraf. As the man attempted to jump aboard the moving train, he seemed unsteady and about to fall. A railroad guard on the car reached forward to grab him, and another guard on the platform pushed him from behind to help him board the train.

In the process, the man's package, which (unknown to the railroad guards) contained fireworks, fell on the railroad tracks and exploded. There was nothing about the package to indicate its contents. The repercussions of the explosion caused weighing scales at the other end of the train platform to fall on Palsgraf, causing injuries for which she sued the railroad company. At the trial, the jury found that the railroad guards had been negligent in their conduct. The railroad company appealed. New York's highest state court held that the railroad company was not liable to Palsgraf. The railroad had not been negligent toward her, because injury to her was not foreseeable.[16] ■

4–4c The Injury Requirement and Damages

For tort liability to arise, the plaintiff must have suffered a *legally recognizable* injury. To recover damages, the plaintiff must have suffered some loss, harm, wrong, or invasion of a protected interest. Essentially, the purpose of tort law is to compensate for legally recognized harms and injuries resulting from wrongful acts. If no harm or injury results from a given negligent action, there is nothing to compensate, and no tort exists.

For instance, if you carelessly bump into a passerby, who stumbles and falls as a result, you may be liable in tort if the passerby is injured in the fall. If the person is unharmed, however, there normally can be no lawsuit for damages, because no injury was suffered.

Compensatory damages are the norm in negligence cases. A court will award punitive damages only if the defendant's conduct was grossly negligent, reflecting an intentional failure to perform a duty with reckless disregard of the consequences to others.

4–4d Good Samaritan Statutes

Most states now have what are called **Good Samaritan statutes.**[17] Under these statutes, someone who is aided voluntarily by another cannot turn around and sue the "Good Samaritan" for negligence. These laws were passed largely to protect physicians and medical personnel who

---

16. *Palsgraf v. Long Island Railroad Co.,* 248 N.Y. 339, 162 N.E. 99 (1928).
17. These laws derive their name from the Good Samaritan story in the Bible. In the story, a traveler who had been robbed and beaten lay along the roadside, ignored by those passing by. Eventually, a man from the region of Samaria (the "Good Samaritan") stopped to render assistance to the injured person.

volunteer their services in emergency situations to those in need, such as individuals hurt in car accidents.

4–4e Dram Shop Acts

Many states have also passed **dram shop acts,**[18] under which a bar's owner or bartender may be held liable for injuries caused by a person who became intoxicated while drinking at the bar. The owner or bartender may also be held responsible for continuing to serve a person who was already intoxicated.

Some states' statutes also impose liability on *social hosts* (persons hosting parties) for injuries caused by guests who became intoxicated at the hosts' homes. Under these statutes, it is unnecessary to prove that the bar owner, bartender, or social host was negligent. ■ **EXAMPLE 4.27** Jane hosts a Super Bowl party at which Brett, a minor, sneaks alcoholic drinks. Jane is potentially liable for damages resulting from Brett's drunk driving after the party. ■

4–5 Defenses to Negligence

Defendants often defend against negligence claims by asserting that the plaintiffs have failed to prove

---

18. Historically, a dram was a small unit of liquid, and distilled spirits (strong alcoholic liquor) were sold in drams. Thus, a dram shop was a place where liquor was sold in drams.

the existence of one or more of the required elements for negligence. Additionally, there are three basic *affirmative* defenses in negligence cases (defenses that a defendant can use to avoid liability even if the facts are as the plaintiff states): *assumption of risk, superseding cause,* and *contributory and comparative negligence.*

4–5a Assumption of Risk

A plaintiff who voluntarily enters into a risky situation, knowing the risk involved, will not be allowed to recover. This is the defense of **assumption of risk,** which requires two elements:

1. Knowledge of the risk.
2. Voluntary assumption of the risk.

The defense of assumption of risk is frequently asserted when the plaintiff was injured during a recreational activity that involves known risk, such as skiing or skydiving. (Courts do not apply the assumption of risk doctrine in emergency situations.)

Assumption of risk can apply not only to participants in sporting events, but also to spectators and bystanders who are injured while attending those events. In the following *Spotlight Case,* the issue was whether a spectator at a baseball game voluntarily assumed the risk of being hit by an errant ball thrown while the players were warming up before the game.

Spotlight on the Seattle Mariners

Case 4.3 Taylor v. Baseball Club of Seattle, LP

Court of Appeals of Washington, 132 Wash.App. 32, 130 P.3d 835 (2006).

Background and Facts Delinda Taylor went to a Seattle Mariners baseball game at Safeco Field with her boyfriend and her two minor sons. Their seats were four rows up from the field along the right field foul line. They arrived more than an hour before the game so that they could see the players warm up and get their autographs. When she walked in, Taylor saw that a Mariners pitcher, Freddy Garcia, was throwing a ball back and forth with José Mesa right in front of their seats.

As Taylor stood in front of her seat, she looked away from the field, and a ball thrown by Mesa got past Garcia and struck her in the face, causing serious injuries. Taylor sued the Mariners for the allegedly negligent warm-up throw. The Mariners filed a motion for summary judgment in which they argued that Taylor, a longtime Mariners fan, was familiar with baseball and the inherent risk of balls entering the stands. Thus, the motion asserted, Taylor had assumed the risk of her injury. The trial court granted the motion and dismissed Taylor's case. Taylor appealed.

In the Language of the Court

DWYER, J. [Judge]

* * * *

* * * For many decades, courts have required baseball stadiums to screen some seats—generally those behind home plate—to provide protection to spectators who choose it.

Case 4.3 Continued

A sport spectator's assumption of risk and a defendant sports team's duty of care are accordingly discerned under the doctrine of primary assumption of risk. * * * "Implied *primary* assumption of risk arises where a plaintiff has impliedly consented (often in advance of any negligence by defendant) to relieve defendant of a duty to plaintiff regarding specific *known* and appreciated risks."

* * * *

Under this implied primary assumption of risk, defendant must show that plaintiff had full subjective understanding of the specific risk, both its nature and presence, and that he or she voluntarily chose to encounter the risk.

* * * It is undisputed that the warm-up is part of the sport, that spectators such as Taylor purposely attend that portion of the event, and that the Mariners permit ticket-holders to view the warm-up.

* * * We find the fact that Taylor was injured during warm-up is not legally significant because that portion of the event is necessarily incident to the game.

* * * *

Here, there is no evidence that the circumstances leading to Taylor's injury constituted an unusual danger. It is undisputed that it is the normal, every-day practice at all levels of baseball for pitchers to warm up in the manner that led to this incident. *The risk of injuries such as Taylor's are within the normal comprehension of a spectator who is familiar with the game.* Indeed, the possibility of an errant ball entering the stands is part of the game's attraction for many spectators. [Emphasis added.]

* * * The record contains substantial evidence regarding Taylor's familiarity with the game. She attended many of her sons' baseball games, she witnessed balls entering the stands, she had watched Mariners' games both at the Kingdome and on television, and she knew that there was no screen protecting her seats, which were close to the field. In fact, as she walked to her seat she saw the players warming up and was excited about being in an unscreened area where her party might get autographs from the players and catch balls.

Decision and Remedy *The state intermediate appellate court affirmed the lower court's judgment. As a spectator who chose to sit in an unprotected area of seats, Taylor voluntarily undertook the risk associated with being hit by an errant baseball thrown during the warm-up before the game.*

Critical Thinking

- **What If the Facts Were Different?** *Would the result in this case have been different if it had been Taylor's minor son, rather than Taylor herself, who had been struck by the ball? Should courts apply the doctrine of assumption of risk to children? Discuss.*
- **Legal Environment** *What is the basis underlying the defense of assumption of risk? How does that basis support the court's decision in this case?*

4–5b Superseding Cause

An unforeseeable intervening event may break the causal connection between a wrongful act and an injury to another. If so, the intervening event acts as a **superseding cause**—that is, it relieves the defendant of liability for injuries caused by the intervening event.

■ **EXAMPLE 4.28** While riding his bicycle, Derrick negligently runs into Julie, who is walking on the sidewalk. As a result of the impact, Julie falls and fractures her hip. While she is waiting for help to arrive, a small aircraft crashes nearby and explodes, and some of the fiery debris hits her, causing her to sustain severe burns. Derrick will be liable for the damages related to Julie's fractured hip, because the risk of injuring her with his bicycle was foreseeable. Normally, though, Derrick will not be liable for the burns caused by the plane crash, because he could not have foreseen the risk that a plane would crash nearby and injure Julie. ■

4–5c Contributory Negligence

All individuals are expected to exercise a reasonable degree of care in looking out for themselves. In the past, under the common law doctrine of **contributory negligence,** a plaintiff who was also negligent (who failed to exercise a reasonable degree of care) could not recover anything from the defendant. Under this rule, no matter how insignificant the plaintiff's negligence was relative to the defendant's negligence, the plaintiff would be precluded from recovering any damages. Today, only a few jurisdictions still follow this doctrine.

4–5d Comparative Negligence

In most states, the doctrine of contributory negligence has been replaced by a **comparative negligence** standard. Under this standard, both the plaintiff's and the defendant's negligence are computed, and the liability for damages is distributed accordingly.

Some jurisdictions have adopted a "pure" form of comparative negligence that allows the plaintiff to recover, even if the extent of his or her fault is greater than that of the defendant. Under pure comparative negligence, if the plaintiff was 80 percent at fault and the defendant 20 percent at fault, the plaintiff can recover 20 percent of his or her damages.

Many states' comparative negligence statutes, however, contain a "50 percent" rule that prevents the plaintiff from recovering any damages if she or he was more than 50 percent at fault. Under this rule, a plaintiff who was 35 percent at fault can recover 65 percent of his or her damages, but a plaintiff who was 65 percent (more than 50 percent) at fault can recover nothing.

Reviewing: Tort Law

Elaine Sweeney went to Ragged Mountain Ski Resort in New Hampshire with a friend. Elaine went snow tubing down a run designed exclusively for snow tubers. There were no Ragged Mountain employees present in the snow-tube area to instruct Elaine on the proper use of a snow tube. On her fourth run down the trail, Elaine crossed over the center line between snow-tube lanes, collided with another snow tuber, and was injured. Elaine filed a negligence action against Ragged Mountain seeking compensation for the injuries that she sustained. Two years earlier, the New Hampshire state legislature had enacted a statute that prohibited a person who participates in the sport of skiing from suing a ski-area operator for injuries caused by the risks inherent in skiing. Using the information presented in the chapter, answer the following questions.

1. What defense will Ragged Mountain probably assert?
2. The central question in this case is whether the state statute establishing that skiers assume the risks inherent in the sport bars Elaine's suit. What would your decision be on this issue? Why?
3. Suppose that the court concludes that the statute applies only to skiing and not to snow tubing. Will Elaine's lawsuit be successful? Explain.
4. Now suppose that the jury concludes that Elaine was partly at fault for the accident. Under what theory might her damages be reduced in proportion to the degree to which her actions contributed to the accident and her resulting injuries?

Debate This . . . *Each time a state legislature enacts a law that applies the assumption of risk doctrine to a particular sport, participants in that sport suffer.*

Terms and Concepts

actionable 69	contributory negligence 85	general damages 67
actual malice 73	conversion 79	Good Samaritan statute 83
assault 68	damages 67	intentional tort 68
assumption of risk 84	defamation 70	libel 70
battery 69	disparagement of property 80	licensee 79
business invitee 82	dram shop act 84	malpractice 82
causation in fact 83	duty of care 81	negligence 80
comparative negligence 86	fraudulent misrepresentation	privilege 72
compensatory damages 67	(fraud) 75	proximate cause 83

Issue Spotters

1. Jana leaves her truck's motor running while she enters a Kwik-Pik Store. The truck's transmission engages, and the vehicle crashes into a gas pump, starting a fire that spreads to a warehouse on the next block. The warehouse collapses, causing its billboard to fall and injure Lou, a bystander. Can Lou recover from Jana? Why or why not? (See *Unintentional Torts—Negligence*.)

2. A water pipe bursts, flooding a Metal Fabrication Company utility room and tripping the circuit breakers on a panel in the room. Metal Fabrication contacts Nouri, a licensed electrician with five years' experience, to check the damage and turn the breakers back on. Without testing for short circuits, which Nouri knows that he should do, he tries to switch on a breaker. He is electrocuted, and his wife sues Metal Fabrication for damages, alleging negligence. What might the firm successfully claim in defense? (See *Defenses to Negligence*.)

• **Check your answers to the Issue Spotters against the answers provided in Appendix B at the end of this text.**

Business Scenarios

4–1. Defamation. Richard is an employee of the Dun Construction Corp. While delivering materials to a construction site, he carelessly backs Dun's truck into a passenger vehicle driven by Green. This is Richard's second accident in six months. When the company owner, Dun, learns of this latest accident, a heated discussion ensues, and Dun fires Richard. Dun is so angry that he immediately writes a letter to the union of which Richard is a member and to all other construction companies in the community, stating that Richard is the "worst driver in the city" and that "anyone who hires him is asking for legal liability." Richard files a suit against Dun, alleging libel on the basis of the statements made in the letters. Discuss the results. (See *Intentional Torts against Persons*.)

4–2. Liability to Business Invitees. Kim went to Ling's Market to pick up a few items for dinner. It was a stormy day, and the wind had blown water through the market's door each time it opened. As Kim entered through the door, she slipped and fell in the rainwater that had accumulated on the floor. The manager knew of the weather conditions but had not posted any sign to warn customers of the water hazard. Kim injured her back as a result of the fall and sued Ling's for damages. Can Ling's be held liable for negligence? Discuss. (See *Unintentional Torts—Negligence*.)

Business Case Problems

4–3. Spotlight on Intentional Torts—Defamation.

 Sharon Yeagle was an assistant to the vice president of student affairs at Virginia Polytechnic Institute and State University (Virginia Tech). As part of her duties, Yeagle helped students participate in the Governor's Fellows Program. The *Collegiate Times*, Virginia Tech's student newspaper, published an article about the university's success in placing students in the program. The article's text surrounded a block quotation attributed to Yeagle with the phrase "Director of Butt Licking" under her name. Yeagle sued the *Collegiate Times* for defamation. She argued that the phrase implied the commission of sodomy and was therefore actionable. What is *Collegiate Times* defense to this claim? [*Yeagle v. Collegiate Times,* 497 S.E.2d 136 (Va. 1998)] (See *Intentional Torts against Persons*.)

4–4. Intentional Infliction of Emotional Distress. While living in her home country of Tanzania, Sophia Kiwanuka signed an employment contract with Anne Margareth Bakilana, a Tanzanian living in Washington, D.C. Kiwanuka traveled to the United States to work as a babysitter and maid in Bakilana's house. When Kiwanuka arrived, Bakilana confiscated her passport, held her in isolation, and forced her to work long hours under threat of having her deported. Kiwanuka worked seven days a week without breaks and was subjected to regular verbal and psychological abuse by Bakilana. Kiwanuka filed a complaint against Bakilana for intentional infliction of emotional distress, among other claims. Bakilana argued that Kiwanuka's complaint should be dismissed because the allegations were insufficient to show outrageous intentional conduct that resulted in severe emotional distress.

If you were the judge, in whose favor would you rule? Why? [*Kiwanuka v. Bakilana,* 844 F.Supp.2d 107 (D.D.C. 2012)] (See *Intentional Torts against Persons.*)

4–5. Business Case Problem with Sample Answer—Negligence.

 At the Weatherford Hotel in Flagstaff, Arizona, in Room 59, a balcony extends across thirty inches of the room's only window, leaving a twelve-inch gap with a three-story drop to the concrete below. A sign prohibits smoking in the room but invites guests to "step out onto the balcony" to smoke. Toni Lucario was a guest in Room 59 when she climbed out of the window and fell to her death. Patrick McMurtry, her estate's personal representative, filed a suit against the Weatherford. Did the hotel breach a duty of care to Locario? What might the Weatherford assert in its defense? Explain. [*McMurtry v. Weatherford Hotel, Inc.,* 231 Ariz. 244, 293 P.3d 520 (2013)] (See *Unintentional Torts—Negligence.*)

- **For a sample answer to Problem 4–5, go to Appendix C at the end of this text.**

4–6. Negligence.
Ronald Rawls and Zabian Bailey were in an auto accident in Bridgeport, Connecticut. Bailey rear-ended Rawls at a stoplight. Evidence showed it was more likely than not that Bailey failed to apply his brakes in time to avoid the collision, failed to turn his vehicle to avoid the collision, failed to keep his vehicle under control, and was inattentive to his surroundings. Rawls filed a suit in a Connecticut state court against his insurance company, Progressive Northern Insurance Co., to obtain benefits under an underinsured motorist clause, alleging that Bailey had been negligent. Could Rawls collect? Discuss. [*Rawls v. Progressive Northern Insurance Co.,* 310 Conn. 768, 83 A.3d 576 (2014)] (See *Unintentional Torts—Negligence.*)

4–7. Negligence.
Charles Robison, an employee of West Star Transportation, Inc., was ordered to cover an unevenly loaded flatbed trailer with a 150-pound tarpaulin (a waterproof cloth). The load included uncrated equipment and pallet crates of different heights, about thirteen feet off the ground at its highest point. While standing on the load, manipulating the tarpaulin without safety equipment or assistance, Robison fell and sustained a traumatic head injury. He filed a suit against West Star to recover for his injury. Was West Star "negligent in failing to provide a reasonably safe place to work," as Robison claimed? Explain. [*West Star Transportation, Inc. v. Robison,* 457 S.W.3d 178 (Tex.App.—Amarillo 2015)] (See *Unintentional Torts—Negligence.*)

4–8. Negligence.
DSC Industrial Supply and Road Rider Supply are located in North Kitsap Business Park in Seattle, Washington. Both firms are owned by Paul and Suzanne Marshall. The Marshalls had outstanding commercial loans from Frontier Bank. The bank dispatched one of its employees, Suzette Gould, to North Kitsap to "spread Christmas cheer" to the Marshalls as an expression of appreciation for their business. Approaching the entry to Road Rider, Gould tripped over a concrete "wheel stop" and fell, suffering a broken arm and a dislocated elbow. The stop was not clearly visible, it had not been painted a contrasting color, and it was not marked with a sign. Gould had not been aware of the stop before she tripped over it. Is North Kitsap liable to Gould for negligence? Explain. [*Gould v. North Kitsap Business Park Management, LLC,* 2016 WL 236455 (2016)] (See *Unintentional Torts—Negligence.*)

4–9. A Question of Ethics—Wrongful Interference.

 White Plains Coat & Apron Co. is a New York–based linen rental business. Cintas Corp. is a competitor. White Plains had five-year exclusive contracts with some of its customers. As a result of Cintas's soliciting of business, dozens of White Plains' customers breached their contracts and entered into rental agreements with Cintas. White Plains filed a suit against Cintas, alleging wrongful interference. [White Plains Coat & Apron Co. v. Cintas Corp., 8 N.Y.3d 422, 867 N.E.2d 381 (2007)] (See *Intentional Torts against Persons.*)

(a) What are the two important policy interests at odds in wrongful interference cases? Which of these interests should be accorded priority?

(b) The U.S. Court of Appeals for the Second Circuit asked the New York Court of Appeals to answer a question: Is a general interest in soliciting business for profit a sufficient defense to a claim of wrongful interference with a contractual relationship? What do you think? Why?

Legal Reasoning Group Activity

4–10. Negligence.
Donald and Gloria Bowden hosted a cookout at their home in South Carolina, inviting mostly business acquaintances. Justin Parks, who was nineteen years old, attended the party. Alcoholic beverages were available to all of the guests, even those who, like Parks, were between the ages of eighteen and twenty-one. Parks consumed alcohol at the party and left with other guests. One of these guests detained Parks at the guest's home to give Parks time to "sober up." Parks then drove himself from this guest's home and was killed in a one-car accident. At the time of death, he had a blood alcohol content of 0.291 percent, which exceeded the state's limit for driving a motor vehicle. Linda Marcum, Parks's mother, filed a suit in a South Carolina state court against the Bowdens and others, alleging that they were negligent. (See *Unintentional Torts—Negligence.*)

(a) The first group will present arguments in favor of holding the social hosts liable in this situation.

(b) The second group will formulate arguments against holding the social hosts liable based on principles in this chapter.

(c) The third group will determine the reasons why some courts do not treat social hosts the same as parents who serve alcoholic beverages to their underage children.

CHAPTER 5

Criminal Law and Cyber Crime

Criminal law is an important part of the legal environment of business. Society imposes a variety of sanctions to protect businesses from harm so that they can compete and flourish. These sanctions include damages for various types of tortious conduct, damages for breach of contract, and various equitable remedies. Additional sanctions are imposed under criminal law. Many statutes regulating business provide for criminal as well as civil penalties.

In this chapter, after explaining some essential differences between criminal law and civil law, we look at how crimes are classified and at the elements that must be present for criminal liability to exist. We then examine the various categories of crimes, the defenses that can be raised to avoid criminal liability, and the rules of criminal procedure.

We conclude the chapter with a discussion of crimes that occur in cyberspace, which are often called *cyber crimes.* Cyber attacks are becoming all too common—even e-mail and data of government agencies and of former U.S. presidents have been hacked.

5-1 Civil Law and Criminal Law

Civil law pertains to the duties that exist between persons or between persons and their governments. Criminal law, in contrast, has to do with crime. A **crime** can be defined as a wrong against society set forth in a statute and punishable by a fine and/or imprisonment—or, in some cases, death.

Because crimes are *offenses against society as a whole,* they are prosecuted by a public official, such as a district attorney (D.A.) or an attorney general (A.G.), not by the victims. Once a crime has been reported, the D.A.'s office decides whether to file criminal charges and to what extent to pursue the prosecution or carry out additional investigation.

5-1a Key Differences between Civil Law and Criminal Law

Because the state has extensive resources at its disposal when prosecuting criminal cases, there are numerous procedural safeguards to protect the rights of defendants. We look here at one of these safeguards—the higher burden of proof that applies in a criminal case—as well as the harsher sanctions for criminal acts compared with those for civil wrongs. Exhibit 5-1

summarizes these and other key differences between civil law and criminal law.

Burden of Proof In a civil case, the plaintiff usually must prove his or her case by a *preponderance of the evidence.* Under this standard, the plaintiff must convince the court that based on the evidence presented by both parties, it is more likely than not that the plaintiff's allegation is true.

In a criminal case, in contrast, the government must prove its case **beyond a reasonable doubt.** If the jury views the evidence in the case as reasonably permitting either a guilty or a not guilty verdict, then the jury's verdict must be not guilty. In other words, the government (prosecutor) must prove beyond a reasonable doubt that the defendant has committed every essential element of the offense with which she or he is charged.

Note also that in a criminal case, the jury's verdict normally must be unanimous—agreed to by all members of the jury—to convict the defendant.[1] (In a civil trial by jury, in contrast, typically only three-fourths of the jurors need to agree.)

---

1. A few states allow jury verdicts that are not unanimous. Arizona, for example, allows six of eight jurors to reach a verdict in criminal cases. Louisiana and Oregon have also relaxed the requirement of unanimous jury verdicts.

EXHIBIT 5–1   Key Differences between Civil Law and Criminal Law

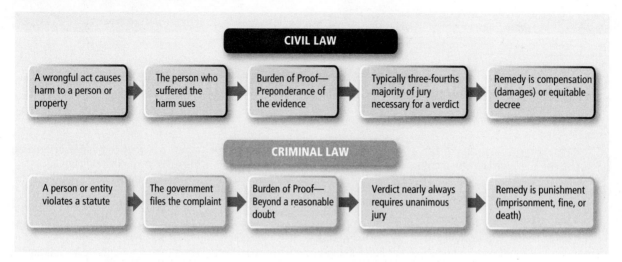

Criminal Sanctions The sanctions imposed on criminal wrongdoers are normally harsher than those applied in civil cases. Remember that the purpose of tort law is to enable a person harmed by a wrongful act to obtain compensation from the wrongdoer, rather than to punish the wrongdoer. In contrast, criminal sanctions are designed to punish those who commit crimes and to deter others from committing similar acts in the future.

Criminal sanctions include fines as well as the much stiffer penalty of the loss of one's liberty by incarceration in a jail or prison. Most criminal sanctions also involve probation and sometimes require performance of community service, completion of an educational or treatment program, or payment of restitution. The harshest criminal sanction is, of course, the death penalty.

5–1b Civil Liability for Criminal Acts

Some torts, such as assault and battery, provide a basis for a criminal prosecution as well as a civil action in tort. ■ **EXAMPLE 5.1** Jonas is walking down the street, minding his own business, when a person attacks him. In the ensuing struggle, the attacker stabs Jonas several times, seriously injuring him. A police officer restrains and arrests the assailant. In this situation, the attacker may be subject both to criminal prosecution by the state and to a tort lawsuit brought by Jonas to obtain compensation for his injuries. ■

Exhibit 5–2 illustrates how the same wrongful act can result in both a civil (tort) action and a criminal action against the wrongdoer.

5–1c Classification of Crimes

Depending on their degree of seriousness, crimes are classified as felonies or misdemeanors. **Felonies** are serious crimes punishable by death or by imprisonment for more than one year.[2] Many states also define different degrees of felony offenses and vary the punishment according to the degree.[3] For instance, most jurisdictions punish a burglary that involves forced entry into a home at night more harshly than a burglary that involves breaking into a nonresidential building during the day.

Misdemeanors are less serious crimes, punishable by a fine or by confinement for up to a year. **Petty offenses** are minor violations, such as jaywalking or violations of building codes, considered to be a subset of misdemeanors. Even for petty offenses, however, a guilty party can be put in jail for a few days, fined, or both, depending on state or local law. Whether a crime is a felony or a misdemeanor can determine in which court the case is tried and, in some states, whether the defendant has a right to a jury trial.

---

2. Federal law and most state laws use this definition, but there is some variation among states as to the length of imprisonment associated with a felony conviction.
3. Note that the Model Penal Code is not a uniform code and each state has developed its own set of laws governing criminal acts. Thus, types of crimes and prescribed punishments may differ from one jurisdiction to another.

EXHIBIT 5–2 Civil (Tort) Lawsuit and Criminal Prosecution for the Same Act

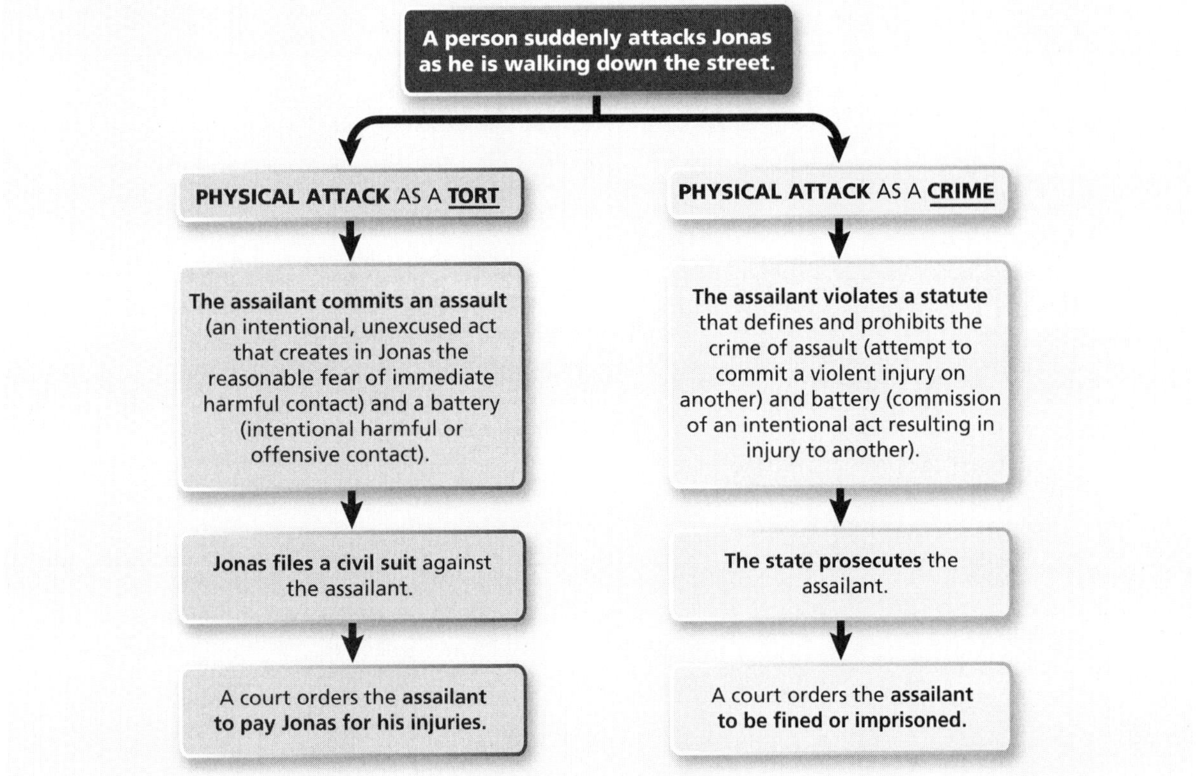

A person suddenly attacks Jonas as he is walking down the street.

PHYSICAL ATTACK AS A **TORT**

The assailant commits an assault (an intentional, unexcused act that creates in Jonas the reasonable fear of immediate harmful contact) and a battery (intentional harmful or offensive contact).

Jonas files a civil suit against the assailant.

A court orders the **assailant to pay Jonas for his injuries.**

PHYSICAL ATTACK AS A **CRIME**

The assailant violates a statute that defines and prohibits the crime of assault (attempt to commit a violent injury on another) and battery (commission of an intentional act resulting in injury to another).

The state prosecutes the assailant.

A court orders the **assailant to be fined or imprisoned.**

5–2 Criminal Liability

The following two elements normally must exist *simultaneously* for a person to be convicted of a crime:

1. The performance of a prohibited act *(actus reus)*.
2. A specified state of mind, or intent, on the part of the actor *(mens rea)*.

5–2a The Criminal Act

Every criminal statute prohibits certain behavior. Most crimes require an act of *commission*—that is, a person must *do* something in order to be accused of a crime. In criminal law, a prohibited act is referred to as the **actus reus**,[4] or guilty act. In some instances, an act of omission can be a crime, but only when a person has a legal duty to perform the omitted act, such as filing a tax return.

The guilty act requirement is based on one of the premises of criminal law—that a person should be punished for harm done to society. For a crime to exist, the guilty act must thus cause some harm to a person or to property. Thinking about killing someone or about stealing a car may be morally wrong, but the thoughts do no harm until they are translated into action.

Of course, a person can be punished for *attempting* murder or robbery, but normally only if he or she has taken substantial steps toward the criminal objective. Additionally, the person must have specifically intended to commit the crime to be convicted of an attempt.

5–2b State of Mind

Mens rea,[5] or wrongful mental state, also is typically required to establish criminal liability. The required mental state, or intent, is indicated in the applicable statute or law. Murder, for instance, involves the guilty act of

---

4. Pronounced *ak*-tuhs *ray*-uhs.

5. Pronounced *mehns ray*-uh.

killing another human being, and the guilty mental state is the desire, or intent, to take another's life. For theft, the guilty act is the taking of another person's property. The mental state involves both the awareness that the property belongs to another and the desire to deprive the owner of it.

Recklessness A court can also find that the required mental state is present when a defendant's acts are reckless or criminally negligent. A defendant is *criminally reckless* if he or she consciously disregards a substantial and unjustifiable risk.

    ■ **EXAMPLE 5.2** A fourteen-year-old New Jersey girl posts a Facebook message saying that she is going to launch a terrorist attack on her high school and asking if anyone wants to help. The police arrest the girl for the crime of making a terrorist threat. The statute requires the intent to commit an act of violence with "the intent to terrorize" or "in reckless disregard of the risk of causing" terror or inconvenience. Although the girl argues that she had no intent to cause harm, the police can prosecute her under the "reckless disregard" part of the statute. ■

Criminal Negligence *Criminal negligence* involves the mental state in which the defendant takes an unjustified, substantial, and foreseeable risk that results in harm. A defendant can be negligent even if she or he was not actually aware of the risk but *should have been aware* of it.[6]

    A homicide is classified as *involuntary manslaughter* when it results from an act of criminal negligence and there is no intent to kill. ■ **EXAMPLE 5.3** Dr. Conrad Murray, the personal physician of pop star Michael Jackson, was convicted of involuntary manslaughter for prescribing the drug that led to Jackson's sudden death. Murray had given Jackson propofol, a powerful anesthetic normally used in surgery, as a sleep aid on the night of his death, even though he knew that Jackson had already taken other sedatives. ■

Strict Liability and Overcriminalization An increasing number of laws and regulations impose criminal sanctions for strict liability crimes. Strict liability crimes are offenses that do not require a wrongful mental state to establish criminal liability.

    Proponents of strict liability criminal laws argue that they are necessary to protect the public and the environment. Critics say laws that criminalize conduct without requiring intent have led to *overcriminalization*. They argue that when the requirement of intent is removed,

people are more likely to commit crimes unknowingly—and perhaps even innocently. When an honest mistake can lead to a criminal conviction, the idea that crimes are a wrong against society is undermined.

Federal Crimes. The federal criminal code lists more than four thousand criminal offenses, many of which do not require a specific mental state. In addition, many of these rules do not require intent. See this chapter's *Managerial Strategy* feature for a discussion of how these laws and rules affect American businesspersons.

    ■ **EXAMPLE 5.4** Eddie Leroy Anderson, a retired logger and former science teacher, went digging for arrowheads with his son near a campground in Idaho. They did not realize that they were on federal land and that it is a felony to remove artifacts from federal land without a permit. Although the crime carries a penalty of as much as two years in prison, the father and son pleaded guilty, and each received a sentence of probation and a $1,500 fine. ■

    Strict liability crimes are particularly common in environmental laws, laws aimed at combatting illegal drugs, and other laws affecting public health, safety, and welfare. Under federal law, for instance, tenants can be evicted from public housing if one of their relatives or a guest used illegal drugs—regardless of whether the tenant knew about the drug activity.

State Crimes. Many states have also enacted laws that punish behavior as criminal without the need to show criminal intent. ■ **EXAMPLE 5.5** In Arizona, a hunter who shoots an elk outside the area specified by the hunting permit has committed a crime. The hunter can be convicted of the crime regardless of her or his intent or knowledge of the law. ■

5–2c Corporate Criminal Liability

A corporation is a legal entity created under the laws of a state. At one time, it was thought that a corporation could not incur criminal liability because, although a corporation is a legal person, it can act only through its agents (corporate directors, officers, and employees). Therefore, the corporate entity itself could not "intend" to commit a crime. Over time, this view has changed. Obviously, corporations cannot be imprisoned, but they can be fined or denied certain legal privileges (such as necessary licenses).

Liability of the Corporate Entity Today, corporations normally are liable for the crimes committed by their agents and employees within the course and scope of

---

6. Model Penal Code Section 2.02(2)(d).

MANAGERIAL STRATEGY — The Criminalization of American Business

What do Bank of America, Citigroup, JPMorgan Chase, and Goldman Sachs have in common? All paid hefty fines for purportedly misleading investors about mortgage-backed securities. In fact, these companies paid the government a total of $50 billion in fines. The payments were made in lieu of criminal prosecutions.

Today, several hundred thousand federal rules that apply to businesses carry some form of criminal penalty. That is in addition to more than four thousand federal laws, many of which carry criminal sanctions for their violation. From 2000 to the beginning of 2017, about 2,200 corporations either were convicted or pleaded guilty to violating federal statutes or rules.

Criminal Convictions

The first successful criminal conviction in a federal court against a company—the New York Central and Hudson River Railroad—was upheld by the Supreme Court in 1909 (the violation: cutting prices).[a] Many other successful convictions followed.

One landmark case developed the *aggregation test,* now called the Doctrine of Collective Knowledge.[b] This test aggregates the omissions and acts of two or more persons in a corporation, thereby constructing an *actus reus* and a *mens rea* out of the conduct and knowledge of several individuals.

Not all government attempts at applying criminal law to corporations survive. In 2013, for example, Sentinel Offender Services, LLC, prevailed on appeal. There was no actual evidence to show that the company had acted with specific intent to commit theft by deception.[c]

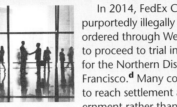

In 2014, FedEx Corporation was indicted for purportedly illegally shipping prescription drugs ordered through Web sites. FedEx has chosen to proceed to trial in the U.S. District Court for the Northern District of California in San Francisco.[d] Many companies, however, choose to reach settlement agreements with the government rather than fight criminal indictments.

Many Pay Substantial Fines in Lieu of Prosecution

More than three hundred corporations reached so-called non-prosecution agreements with the government from 2000 to the beginning of 2017. These agreements typically involve multimillion- or multibillion-dollar fines. This number does not include fines paid to the Environmental Protection Agency or to the Fish and Wildlife Service.

According to law professors Margaret Lemos and Max Minzner, "Public enforcers often seek large monetary awards for self-interested reasons divorced from the public interest and deterrents. The incentives are strongest when enforcement agencies are permitted to retain all or some of the proceeds of enforcement."[e]

Business Questions

1. *Why might a corporation's managers agree to pay a large fine rather than to be indicted and proceed to trial?*

2. *How does a manager determine the optimal amount of legal research to undertake to prevent her or his company from violating the many thousands of federal regulations?*

---

a. *New York Central and Hudson River Railroad v. United States,* 212 U.S. 481, 29 S.Ct. 304, 53 L.Ed 613 (1909).
b. *United States v. Bank of New England,* 821 F.2d 844 (1st Cir. 1987).
c. *McGee v. Sentinel Offender Services, LLC,* 719 F.3d 1236 (11th Cir. 2013).

d. *United States v. FedEx Corp.,* Case No. CR14-380 Northern District, California, July 17, 2014.
e. Margaret Lemos and Max Minzner, "For-Profit Public Enforcement," *Harvard Law Review 127,* January 17, 2014.

---

their employment.[7] For liability to be imposed, the prosecutor generally must show that the corporation could have prevented the act or that a supervisor authorized or had knowledge of the act. In addition, corporations can be criminally liable for failing to perform specific duties

imposed by law (such as duties under environmental laws or securities laws).

■ **CASE IN POINT 5.6** A prostitution ring, the Gold Club, was operating out of some motels in West Virginia. A motel manager, who was also a corporate officer, gave discounted rates to Gold Club prostitutes, and they paid him in cash. The corporation received a portion of the

---

7. See Model Penal Code Section 2.07.

funds generated by the Gold Club's illegal operations. A jury found that the corporation was criminally liable because a supervisor within the corporation—the motel manager—had knowledge of the prostitution activities and the corporation had allowed it to continue.[8] ◼

Liability of Corporate Officers and Directors Corporate directors and officers are personally liable for the crimes they commit, regardless of whether the crimes were committed for their private benefit or on the corporation's behalf. Additionally, corporate directors and officers may be held liable for the actions of employees under their supervision. Under the *responsible corporate officer* doctrine, a court may impose criminal liability on a corporate officer who participated in, directed, or merely knew about a given criminal violation.

◼ **CASE IN POINT 5.7** Austin DeCoster owned and controlled Quality Egg, LLC, an egg production and processing company with facilities across Iowa. His son Peter DeCoster was the chief operating officer. Due to unsanitary conditions in some of its facilities, Quality shipped and sold eggs that contained salmonella bacteria, which sickened thousands of people across the United States.

The federal government prosecuted the DeCosters under the responsible corporate officer doctrine, in part, for Quality's failure to comply with regulations on egg production facilities. The DeCosters ultimately pleaded guilty to violating three criminal statutes. But when they were ordered to serve three months in jail, the DeCosters challenged the sentence as unconstitutional. The court held that the sentence of incarceration was appropriate because the evidence suggested that the defendants knew about the unsanitary conditions in their processing plants.[9] ◼

5-3 Types of Crimes

Federal, state, and local laws provide for the classification and punishment of hundreds of thousands of different criminal acts. Generally, though, criminal acts fall into five broad categories: violent crime (crimes against persons), property crime, public order crime, white-collar crime, and organized crime. In addition, when crimes are committed in cyberspace rather the physical world, we often refer to them as cyber crimes.

5-3a Violent Crime

Certain crimes are called *violent crimes,* or crimes against persons, because they cause others to suffer harm or death. Murder is a violent crime. So is sexual assault, or rape. **Robbery**—defined as the taking of money, personal property, or any other article of value from a person by means of force or fear—is also a violent crime. Typically, states have more severe penalties for *aggravated robbery*—robbery with the use of a deadly weapon.

Assault and battery, which were discussed in the context of tort law, are also classified as violent crimes. ◼ **EXAMPLE 5.8** Former rap star Flavor Flav (whose real name is William Drayton) was arrested in Las Vegas on assault and battery charges. During an argument with his fiancée, Drayton allegedly threw her to the ground and then grabbed two kitchen knives and chased her son. ◼

Each violent crime is further classified by degree, depending on the circumstances surrounding the criminal act. These circumstances include the intent of the person committing the crime and whether a weapon was used. For crimes other than murder, the level of pain and suffering experienced by the victim is also a factor.

5-3b Property Crime

The most common type of criminal activity is property crime, in which the goal of the offender is some form of economic gain or the damaging of property. Robbery is a form of property crime, as well as a violent crime, because the offender seeks to gain the property of another.

Burglary Traditionally, **burglary** was defined as breaking and entering the dwelling of another at night with the intent to commit a felony. This definition was aimed at protecting an individual's home and its occupants.

Most state statutes have eliminated some of the requirements found in the common law definition. The time of day at which the breaking and entering occurs, for instance, is usually immaterial. State statutes frequently omit the element of breaking, and some states do not require that the building be a dwelling. When a deadly weapon is used in a burglary, the perpetrator can be charged with *aggravated burglary* and punished more severely.

The defendant in the following case challenged whether the evidence presented by the state was sufficient to support his conviction for burglary.

---

8. As a result of the convictions, the motel manager was sentenced to fifteen months in prison, and the corporation was ordered to forfeit the motel property. *United States v. Singh*, 518 F.3d 236 (4th Cir. 2008).
9. *United States v. Quality Egg, LLC*, 99 F.Supp.3d 920 (N.D. Iowa 2015).

State of Minnesota v. Smith

Court of Appeals of Minnesota, 2015 WL 303643 (2015).

Background and Facts Over a Labor Day weekend in Rochester, Minnesota, two homes and the Rochester Tennis Center, a business, were burglarized. One day later, at the nearby Bell Tower Inn, cleaning personnel found a garbage bag in the room of Albert Smith. The bag contained a passport that belonged to the owner of one of the burglarized homes and documents that belonged to the business.

Police officers arrested Smith. They found a Sentry safe stolen in one of the burglaries in Smith's room. A search of a bag in his possession revealed other stolen items, as well as burglary tools. Smith claimed that he had bought some of the items from a man named Mali and had bought other items on Craigslist. He said that he had found the documents from the tennis center in a dumpster. Convicted of burglary in a Minnesota state court, Smith appealed.

In the Language of the Court

CHUTICH, Judge.

* * * *

* * * Both burglarized homes and the burglarized business were within a few blocks of the hotel where Smith stayed over the Labor Day weekend, and each burglary occurred during the holiday weekend. In fact, two of the burglaries occurred in the morning and early evening of September 3. On the morning of September 4, only hours after two of the burglaries occurred, Smith possessed property stolen in each of the three burglaries. Some of the items found in Smith's possession were worthless to anyone but their owners, including a passport, a birth certificate, and property documents. In addition, the hotel manager saw Smith carrying the stolen Sentry safe into the hotel during the relevant time frame and identified the safe found in Smith's room as the Sentry safe. When the police confronted Smith in the hotel, he was carrying a bag that contained numerous stolen electronics and burglary tools, including a flashlight and gloves.

* * * Smith possessed property reported as stolen from both homes and the business, and the nature of several of the items he possessed suggested that they came directly from the burglaries. * * * The assortment of items found in Smith's possession, from the electronics to the financially worthless documents, as well as gloves and a flashlight, illustrate Smith's guilt of each of the burglaries. The mishmash of items found in defendant's possession looks like the raw loot that a thief quickly grabbed and made off with. Moreover, *the brief time that passed between the burglaries and the discovery of the stolen items in Smith's possession, along with the close proximity of the hotel to the burglarized homes and tennis center, are consistent with the findings that Smith was the thief.* [Emphasis added.]

Smith contends that a reasonable inference can be drawn from his alternate explanation of the events that is inconsistent with finding him guilty of the burglaries, namely that he obtained the valuable stolen items from Mali or from Craigslist, while he found the tennis club's records in a dumpster. The [trial] court, however, did not find Smith's testimony credible, determining that Smith "demonstrated a flexible approach to the truth—a looseness with the facts, in which the incriminatory truth is conceded only when and to the extent it is inescapable." Further, we consider it improbable, considering the timing and locations of the break-ins, that Smith came into possession of stolen items from a September 3 burglary by way of Mali, while finding additional stolen items from another September 3 burglary that same evening by fortuitously finding them in a dumpster. * * * The only rational hypothesis that can be drawn from the proved circumstances is that Smith committed the burglaries.

Decision and Remedy *A state intermediate appellate court affirmed Smith's conviction for burglary. The appellate court concluded that the circumstances "are consistent with guilt and inconsistent with any rational hypothesis except that of guilt."*

Critical Thinking

- **Social** *Who is in the best position to evaluate the credibility of the evidence and the witnesses in a case? Why?*

Larceny Under the common law, the crime of **larceny** involved the unlawful taking and carrying away of someone else's personal property with the intent to permanently deprive the owner of possession. Put simply, larceny is stealing, or theft. Whereas robbery involves force or fear, larceny does not. Therefore, picking pockets is larceny, not robbery. Similarly, an employee taking company products and supplies home for personal use without permission is committing larceny.

Most states have expanded the definition of property that is subject to larceny statutes. Stealing computer programs may constitute larceny even though the "property" is not physical (see the discussion of computer crime later in this chapter). The theft of natural gas, Internet access, or television cable service can also constitute larceny.

Obtaining Goods by False Pretenses Obtaining goods by means of false pretenses is a form of theft that involves trickery or fraud, such as using someone else's credit-card number without permission to purchase an iPad. Statutes dealing with such illegal activities vary widely from state to state. They often apply not only to property, but also to services and cash.

■ **CASE IN POINT 5.9** While Matthew Steffes was incarcerated, he started a scheme to make free collect calls from prison. (A *collect call* is a telephone call in which the calling party places a call at the called party's expense.) Steffes had his friends and family members set up new phone number accounts by giving false information to AT&T. This information included fictitious business names, as well as personal identifying information stolen from a health-care clinic. Once a new phone number was working, Steffes made unlimited collect calls to it without paying the bill until AT&T eventually shut down the account. For nearly two years, Steffes used sixty fraudulently obtained phone numbers to make hundreds of collect calls. The loss to AT&T was more than $28,000.

Steffes was convicted in a state court of theft by fraud of property in excess of $10,000. He appealed, arguing that he had not made false representations to AT&T. The Wisconsin Supreme Court affirmed his conviction. The court held that Steffes had made false representations to AT&T by providing fictitious business names and stolen personal identifying information to the phone company. He made these false representations so that he could make phone calls without paying for them, which deprived the company of its "property"—meaning its electricity.[10] ■

Theft Sometimes, state statutes consolidate the crime of obtaining goods by false pretenses with other property offenses, such as larceny and embezzlement (discussed shortly), into a single crime called simply "theft." Under such a statute, it is not necessary for a defendant to be charged specifically with larceny or obtaining goods by false pretenses. *Petty theft* is the theft of a small quantity of cash or low-value goods. *Grand theft* is the theft of a larger amount of cash or higher-value property.

Receiving Stolen Goods It is a crime to receive goods that a person knows or should have known were stolen or illegally obtained. To be convicted, the recipient of such goods need not know the true identity of the owner or the thief, and need not have paid for the goods. All that is necessary is that the recipient knows or should know that the goods are stolen, which implies an intent to deprive the true owner of those goods.

Arson The willful and malicious burning of a building (or, in some states, a vehicle or other item of personal property) is the crime of **arson.** At common law, arson applied only to burning down another person's house. The law was designed to protect human life. Today, arson statutes have been extended to cover the destruction of any building, regardless of ownership, by fire or explosion.

Every state has a special statute that covers the act of burning a building for the purpose of collecting insurance. (Of course, the insurer need not pay the claim when insurance fraud is proved.)

Forgery The fraudulent making or altering of any writing (including an electronic record) in a way that changes the legal rights and liabilities of another is **forgery.** ■ **EXAMPLE 5.10** Without authorization, Severson signs Bennett's name to the back of a check made out to Bennett and attempts to cash it. Severson is committing forgery. ■ Forgery also includes changing trademarks, falsifying public records, counterfeiting, and altering a legal document.

5–3c Public Order Crime

Historically, societies have always outlawed activities that are considered contrary to public values and morals. Today, the most common public order crimes include public drunkenness, prostitution, gambling, and illegal drug use. These crimes are sometimes referred to as *victimless crimes* because they normally harm only the offender. From a broader perspective, however, they are deemed detrimental to society as a whole because they

---

10. *State of Wisconsin v. Steffes,* 347 Wis.2d 683, 832 N.W.2d 101 (2013).

may create an environment that gives rise to property and violent crimes.

■ **EXAMPLE 5.11** A flight attendant observes a man and woman engaging in sex acts while on a flight to Las Vegas. A criminal complaint is filed, and the two defendants plead guilty in federal court to misdemeanor disorderly conduct. ■

5–3d White-Collar Crime

Crimes occurring in the business context are popularly referred to as *white-collar crimes,* although this is not an official legal term. Ordinarily, **white-collar crime** involves an illegal act or series of acts committed by an individual or business entity using some nonviolent means to obtain a personal or business advantage.

Usually, this kind of crime takes place in the course of a legitimate business occupation. Corporate crimes fall into this category. Certain property crimes, such as larceny and forgery, may also be white-collar crimes if they occur within the business context. The crimes discussed next normally occur only in the business context.

Embezzlement When a person who is entrusted with another person's property fraudulently appropriates it, **embezzlement** occurs. Embezzlement is not larceny, because the wrongdoer does not *physically* take the property from another's possession, and it is not robbery, because no force or fear is used.

Typically, embezzlement is carried out by an employee who steals funds a small amount at a time over a long period. Banks are particularly prone to this problem, but embezzlement can occur in any firm. In a number of businesses, corporate officers or accountants have fraudulently converted funds for their own benefit and then "fixed" the books to cover up their crimes.

Embezzlement occurs whether the embezzler takes the funds directly from the victim or from a third person. If the financial officer of a large corporation pockets checks from third parties that were given to her to deposit into the corporate account, she is embezzling.

The intent to return embezzled property—or its actual return—is not a defense to the crime of embezzlement, as the following *Spotlight Case* illustrates.

Spotlight on White-Collar Crime

Case 5.2 People v. Sisuphan
Court of Appeal of California, First District, 181 Cal.App.4th 800, 104 Cal.Rptr.3d 654 (2010).

Background and Facts Lou Sisuphan was the director of finance at a Toyota dealership. His responsibilities included managing the financing contracts for vehicle sales and working with lenders to obtain payments. Sisuphan complained repeatedly to management about the performance and attitude of one of the finance managers, Ian McClelland. The general manager, Michael Christian, would not terminate McClelland "because he brought a lot of money into the dealership."

One day, McClelland accepted $22,600 in cash and two checks totaling $7,275.51 from a customer in payment for a car. McClelland placed the cash, the checks, and a copy of the receipt in a large envelope. As he tried to drop the envelope into the safe through a mechanism at its top, the envelope became stuck. While McClelland went for assistance, Sisuphan wiggled the envelope free and kept it. On McClelland's return, Sisuphan told him that the envelope had dropped into the safe. When the payment turned up missing, Christian told all the managers he would not bring criminal charges if the payment was returned within twenty-four hours.

After the twenty-four-hour period had lapsed, Sisuphan told Christian that he had taken the envelope, and he returned the cash and checks to Christian. Sisuphan claimed that he had no intention of stealing the payment but had taken it to get McClelland fired. Christian fired Sisuphan the next day, and the district attorney later charged Sisuphan with embezzlement.

After a jury trial, Sisuphan was found guilty. Sisuphan appealed, arguing that the trial court had erred by excluding evidence that he had returned the payment. The trial court had concluded that the evidence was not relevant because return of the property is not a defense to embezzlement.

Case 5.2 Continues

Case 5.2 Continued

In the Language of the Court
JENKINS, J. [Judge]
* * * *

Fraudulent intent is an essential element of embezzlement. Although restoration of the property is not a defense, evidence of repayment may be relevant to the extent it shows that a defendant's intent at the time of the taking was not fraudulent. Such evidence is admissible "only when [a] defendant shows a relevant and probative [confirming] link in his subsequent actions from which it might be inferred his original intent was innocent." The question before us, therefore, is whether evidence that Sisuphan returned the money reasonably tends to prove he lacked the requisite intent at the time of the taking. [Emphasis added.]

Section 508 [of the California Penal Code], which sets out the offense of which Sisuphan was convicted, provides: "Every clerk, agent, or servant of any person who fraudulently appropriates to his own use, or secretes with a fraudulent intent to appropriate to his own use, any property of another which has come into his control or care by virtue of his employment * * * is guilty of embezzlement." Sisuphan denies he ever intended "to use the [money] to financially better himself, even temporarily" and contends the evidence he sought to introduce showed "he returned the [money] without having appropriated it to his own use in any way." He argues that this evidence negates fraudulent intent because it supports his claim that he took the money to get McClelland fired and acted "to help his company by drawing attention to the inadequacy and incompetency of an employee." We reject these contentions.

In determining whether Sisuphan's intent was fraudulent at the time of the taking, the issue is not whether he intended to spend the money, but whether he intended to use it for a purpose other than that for which the dealership entrusted it to him. *The offense of embezzlement contemplates a principal's entrustment of property to an agent for certain purposes and the agent's breach of that trust by acting outside his authority in his use of the property.* * * * Sisuphan's undisputed purpose—to get McClelland fired—was beyond the scope of his responsibility and therefore outside the trust afforded him by the dealership. Accordingly, even if the proffered [submitted] evidence shows he took the money for this purpose, it does not tend to prove he lacked fraudulent intent, and the trial court properly excluded this evidence. [Emphasis added.]

Decision and Remedy *The California appellate court affirmed the trial court's decision. The fact that Sisuphan had returned the payment was irrelevant. He was guilty of embezzlement.*

Critical Thinking

- **Legal Environment** *Why was Sisuphan convicted of embezzlement instead of larceny? What is the difference between these two crimes?*
- **Ethical** *Given that Sisuphan returned the cash, was it fair of the dealership's general manager to terminate Sisuphan's employment? Why or why not?*

Mail and Wire Fraud Among the most potent weapons against white-collar criminals are the federal laws that prohibit mail fraud[11] and wire fraud.[12] These laws make it a federal crime to devise any scheme that uses U.S. mail, commercial carriers (FedEx, UPS), or wire (telegraph, telephone, television, the Internet, e-mail) with the intent to defraud the public. These laws are often applied when persons send out advertisements or e-mails with the intent to fraudulently obtain cash or property by false pretenses.

■ **CASE IN POINT 5.12** Cisco Systems, Inc., offers a warranty program to authorized resellers of Cisco parts.

Iheanyi Frank Chinasa and Robert Kendrick Chambliss devised a scheme to intentionally defraud Cisco with respect to this program and to obtain replacement parts to which they were not entitled. The two men planned and used specific language in numerous e-mails and Internet service requests that they sent to Cisco to convince Cisco to ship them new parts via commercial carriers. Ultimately, Chinasa and Chambliss were convicted of mail and wire fraud and of conspiracy to commit mail and wire fraud.[13] ■

---

11. The Mail Fraud Act, 18 U.S.C. Sections 1341–1342.
12. 18 U.S.C. Section 1343.

13. *United States v. Chinasa*, 789 F.Supp.2d 691 (E.D.Va. 2011). See also *United States v. Lyons*, 569 F.3d 995 (9th Cir. 2009).

The maximum penalty under these statutes is substantial. Persons convicted of mail, wire, and Internet fraud may be imprisoned for up to twenty years and/or fined. If the violation affects a financial institution or involves fraud in connection with emergency disaster-relief funds, the violator may be fined up to $1 million, imprisoned for up to thirty years, or both.

Bribery   The crime of bribery involves offering to give something of value to a person in an attempt to influence that person in a way that serves a private interest. Three types of bribery are considered crimes: bribery of public officials, commercial bribery, and bribery of foreign officials.

The bribe itself can be anything the recipient considers to be valuable, but the defendant must have intended it as a bribe. Realize that the *crime of bribery occurs when the bribe is offered*—it is not required that the bribe be accepted. *Accepting a bribe* is a separate crime.

Commercial bribery involves corrupt dealings between private persons or businesses. Typically, people make commercial bribes to obtain proprietary information, cover up an inferior product, or secure new business. Industrial espionage sometimes involves commercial bribes. ■ **EXAMPLE 5.13** Kent Peterson works at the firm of Jacoby & Meyers. He offers to pay Laurel, an employee in a competing firm, to give him that firm's trade secrets and pricing schedules. Peterson has committed commercial bribery. ■ So-called kickbacks, or payoffs for special favors or services, are a form of commercial bribery in some situations.

Bankruptcy Fraud   Federal bankruptcy law allows individuals and businesses to be relieved of oppressive debt through bankruptcy proceedings. Numerous white-collar crimes may be committed during the many phases of a bankruptcy action. A creditor may file a false claim against the debtor, which is a crime. Also, a debtor may fraudulently transfer assets to favored parties before or after the bankruptcy is filed. For instance, a company-owned automobile may be "sold" at a bargain price to a trusted friend or relative. Closely related to the crime of fraudulent transfer of property is the crime of fraudulent concealment of property, such as the hiding of gold coins.

Insider Trading   An individual who obtains "inside information" about the plans of a publicly listed corporation can often make stock-trading profits by purchasing or selling corporate securities based on this information. *Insider trading* is a violation of securities law. Basically, a person who possesses inside information and has a duty not to disclose it to outsiders may not trade on that information. A person may not profit from the purchase or sale of securities based on inside information until the information is made available to the public.

Theft of Trade Secrets and Other Intellectual Property   The Economic Espionage Act[14] makes the theft of trade secrets a federal crime. The act also makes it a federal crime to buy or possess another person's trade secrets, knowing that the trade secrets were stolen or otherwise acquired without the owner's authorization.

Violations of the Economic Espionage Act can result in steep penalties: imprisonment for up to ten years and a fine of up to $500,000. A corporation or other organization can be fined up to $5 million. Additionally, any property acquired as a result of the violation, such as airplanes and automobiles, is subject to criminal forfeiture, or seizure by the government. Similarly, any property used in the commission of the violation is subject to forfeiture.

5–3e Organized Crime

White-collar crime takes place within the confines of the legitimate business world. *Organized crime,* in contrast, operates *illegitimately* by, among other things, providing illegal goods and services. Traditionally, organized crime has been involved in gambling, prostitution, illegal narcotics, counterfeiting, and loan sharking (lending funds at higher-than-legal interest rates), along with more recent ventures into credit-card scams and cyber crime.

Money Laundering   The profits from organized crime and illegal activities amount to billions of dollars a year. These profits come from illegal drug transactions and, to a lesser extent, from racketeering, prostitution, and gambling. Under federal law, banks, savings and loan associations, and other financial institutions are required to report currency transactions involving more than $10,000. Consequently, those who engage in illegal activities face difficulties in depositing their cash profits from illegal transactions.

As an alternative to storing the cash from illegal transactions in a safe-deposit box, wrongdoers and racketeers often launder "dirty" money through legitimate businesses to make it "clean." **Money laundering** is engaging in financial transactions to conceal the identity, source, or destination of illegally gained funds.

■ **EXAMPLE 5.14** Leo Harris, a successful drug dealer, becomes a partner with a restaurateur. Little by little, the restaurant shows increasing profits. As a partner in the

---

14. 18 U.S.C. Sections 1831–1839.

restaurant, Harris is able to report the "profits" of the restaurant as legitimate income on which he pays federal and state taxes. He can then spend those funds without worrying that his lifestyle may exceed the level possible with his reported income. ■

Racketeering To curb the entry of organized crime into the legitimate business world, Congress enacted the Racketeer Influenced and Corrupt Organizations Act (RICO).[15] The statute makes it a federal crime to:

1. Use income obtained from racketeering activity to purchase any interest in an enterprise.
2. Acquire or maintain an interest in an enterprise through racketeering activity.
3. Conduct or participate in the affairs of an enterprise through racketeering activity.
4. Conspire to do any of the preceding activities.

Broad Application of RICO. The broad language of RICO has allowed it to be applied in cases that have little or nothing to do with organized crime. RICO incorporates by reference twenty-six separate types of federal crimes and nine types of state felonies.[16] If a person commits two of these offenses, he or she is guilty of "racketeering activity."

Under the criminal provisions of RICO, any individual found guilty is subject to a fine of up to $25,000 per violation, imprisonment for up to twenty years, or both. Additionally, any assets (property or cash) that were acquired as a result of the illegal activity or that were "involved in" or an "instrumentality of" the activity are subject to government forfeiture.

Civil Liability. In the event of a RICO violation, the government can seek not only criminal penalties but also civil penalties. The government can, for instance, seek the divestiture of a defendant's interest in a business or the dissolution of the business. (Divestiture refers to the taking of possession—or forfeiture—of the defendant's interest and its subsequent sale.)

Moreover, in some cases, the statute allows private individuals to sue violators and potentially recover three times their actual losses (treble damages), plus attorneys' fees, for business injuries caused by a RICO violation. This is perhaps the most controversial aspect of RICO and one that continues to cause debate in the nation's federal courts. The prospect of receiving treble damages in civil RICO lawsuits has given plaintiffs a financial incentive to pursue businesses and employers for violations.

See Concept Summary 5.1 for a review of the different types of crimes.

5–4 Defenses to Criminal Liability

Persons charged with crimes may be relieved of criminal liability if they can show that their criminal actions were justified under the circumstances. In certain situations, the law may also allow a person to be excused from criminal liability because she or he lacks the required mental state. We look at several defenses to criminal liability here.

Note that procedural violations (such as obtaining evidence without a valid search warrant) may also operate as defenses. Evidence obtained in violation of a defendant's constitutional rights may not be admitted in court. If the evidence is suppressed, then there may be no basis for prosecuting the defendant.

5–4a Justifiable Use of Force

Probably the best-known defense to criminal liability is **self-defense.** Other situations, however, also justify the use of force: the defense of one's dwelling, the defense of other property, and the prevention of a crime. In all of these situations, it is important to distinguish between deadly and nondeadly force. *Deadly force* is likely to result in death or serious bodily harm. *Nondeadly force* is force that reasonably appears necessary to prevent the imminent use of criminal force.

Generally speaking, people can use the amount of nondeadly force that seems necessary to protect themselves, their dwellings, or other property, or to prevent the commission of a crime. Deadly force can be used in self-defense only when the defender *reasonably believes* that imminent death or grievous bodily harm will otherwise result. In addition, normally the attacker must be using unlawful force, and the defender must not have initiated or provoked the attack.

Many states are expanding the situations in which the use of deadly force can be justified. Florida, for instance, allows the use of deadly force to prevent the commission of a "forcible felony," including robbery, carjacking, and sexual battery.

5–4b Necessity

Sometimes, criminal defendants can be relieved of liability by showing **necessity**—that a criminal act was

---

15. 18 U.S.C. Sections 1961–1968.
16. See 18 U.S.C. Section 1961(1)(A). The crimes listed in this section include murder, kidnapping, gambling, arson, robbery, bribery, extortion, money laundering, securities fraud, counterfeiting, dealing in obscene matter, dealing in controlled substances (illegal drugs), and a number of others.

Concept Summary 5.1

Types of Crimes

Violent Crime	Crimes that cause others to suffer harm or death, such as murder, assault and battery, and robbery.
Property Crime	Crimes in which the goal of the offender is some form of economic gain or the damaging of property. Property crime includes theft-related offenses such as burglary, larceny, and forgery.
Public Order Crime	Crimes that are contrary to public values and morals, such as public drunkenness and prostitution.
White-Collar Crime	An illegal act or series of acts committed by an individual or business entity using some nonviolent means to obtain a personal or business advantage. These crimes are usually committed in the course of a legitimate occupation. Examples include embezzlement, bribery, and fraud.
Organized Crime	Crime conducted by groups operating illegitimately to provide illegal goods and services, such as narcotics. Organized crime may also include money laundering and racketeering.

necessary to prevent an even greater harm. ■ **EXAMPLE 5.15** Jake Trevor is a convicted felon and, as such, is legally prohibited from possessing a firearm. While he and his wife are in a convenience store, a man draws a gun, points it at the cashier, and demands all the cash in the register. Afraid that the man will start shooting, Trevor grabs the gun and holds onto it until police arrive. In this situation, if Trevor is charged with possession of a firearm, he can assert the defense of necessity. ■

5–4c Insanity

A person who suffers from a mental illness may be incapable of the state of mind required to commit a crime. Thus, insanity may be a defense to a criminal charge. Note that an insanity defense does not enable a person to avoid imprisonment. It simply means that if the defendant successfully proves insanity, she or he will be placed in a mental institution.

■ **EXAMPLE 5.16** James Holmes opened fire with an automatic weapon in a crowded Colorado movie theater during a screening of *The Dark Knight Rises,* killing twelve people and injuring seventy. Holmes had been a graduate student but had suffered from mental health problems and had left school. Before the incident, he had no criminal history. Holmes's attorneys asserted the defense of insanity to try to avoid a possible death sentence. Although a jury ultimately rejected the defense and convicted Holmes of multiple counts of murder in 2015, he was sentenced to life in prison rather than death. If the insanity defense had been successful, Holmes would have been confined to a mental institution, not a prison. ■

Model Penal Code The courts have had difficulty deciding what the test for legal insanity should be. Federal courts and some states use the substantial-capacity test set forth in the Model Penal Code:

> A person is not responsible for criminal conduct if at the time of such conduct as a result of mental disease or defect he or she lacks substantial capacity either to appreciate the wrongfulness of his [or her] conduct or to conform his [or her] conduct to the requirements of the law.

***M'Naghten* and Other Tests** Some states use the *M'Naghten* test.[17] Under this test, a person is not responsible if, at the time of the offense, he or she did not know the nature and quality of the act or did not know that the act was wrong. Other states use the irresistible-impulse test. A person operating under an irresistible impulse may know an act is wrong but cannot refrain from doing it.

Under any of these tests, proving insanity is extremely difficult. For this reason, the insanity defense is rarely used and usually is not successful. Four states have abolished the insanity defense.

5–4d Mistake

Everyone has heard the saying "Ignorance of the law is no excuse." Ordinarily, ignorance of the law or a mistaken idea about what the law requires is not a valid defense. A *mistake of fact,* however, as opposed to a *mistake of law,* can normally excuse criminal responsibility if it negates the mental state necessary to commit a crime.

■ **EXAMPLE 5.17** Oliver Wheaton mistakenly walks off with Julie Tyson's briefcase. If Wheaton genuinely thought that the case was his, there is no theft. Theft requires knowledge that the property belongs to another. (If Wheaton's act causes Tyson to incur damages, however, she may sue him in a civil tort action for trespass to personal property or conversion.) ■

5–4e Duress

Duress exists when the *wrongful threat* of one person induces another person to perform an act that he or she would not otherwise have performed. In such a situation, duress is said to negate the mental state necessary to commit a crime because the defendant was forced or compelled to commit the act.

Duress can be used as a defense to most crimes except murder. Both the definition of duress and the types of crimes that it can excuse vary among the states, however. Generally, to successfully assert duress as a defense, the defendant must reasonably have believed that he or she was in immediate danger, and the jury (or judge) must conclude that the defendant's belief was reasonable.

5–4f Entrapment

Entrapment is a defense designed to prevent police officers or other government agents from enticing persons

to commit crimes in order to later prosecute them for those crimes. In the typical entrapment case, an undercover agent *suggests* that a crime be committed and somehow pressures or induces an individual to commit it. The agent then arrests the individual for the crime.

For entrapment to be considered a defense, both the suggestion and the inducement must take place. The defense is not intended to prevent law enforcement agents from setting a trap for an unwary criminal. Rather, its purpose is to prevent them from pushing the individual into a criminal act. The crucial issue is whether the person who committed a crime was predisposed to commit the illegal act or did so only because the agent induced it.

5–4g Statute of Limitations

With some exceptions, such as the crime of murder, statutes of limitations apply to crimes just as they do to civil wrongs. In other words, the government must initiate criminal prosecution within a certain number of years. If a criminal action is brought after the statutory time period has expired, the accused person can raise the statute of limitations as a defense.

The running of the time period in a statute of limitations may be *tolled*—that is, suspended or stopped temporarily—if the defendant is a minor or is not in the jurisdiction. When the defendant reaches the age of majority or returns to the jurisdiction, the statutory time period begins to run again.

5–4h Immunity

Accused persons are understandably reluctant to give information if it will be used to prosecute them, and they cannot be forced to do so. The privilege against **self-incrimination** is guaranteed by a clause in the Fifth Amendment to the U.S. Constitution. The clause reads "nor shall [any person] be compelled in any criminal case to be a witness against himself."

When the state wishes to obtain information from a person accused of a crime, the state can grant *immunity* from prosecution. Alternatively, the state can agree to prosecute the accused for a less serious offense in exchange for the information. Once immunity is given, the person has an absolute privilege against self-incrimination and therefore can no longer refuse to testify on Fifth Amendment grounds.

Often, a grant of immunity from prosecution for a serious crime is part of the **plea bargaining** between the defending and prosecuting attorneys. The defendant

---

17. A rule derived from *M'Naghten's* Case, 8 Eng.Rep. 718 (1843).

may be convicted of a lesser offense, while the state uses the defendant's testimony to prosecute accomplices for serious crimes carrying heavy penalties.

5–5 Criminal Procedures

Criminal law brings the force of the state, with all of its resources, to bear against the individual. Criminal procedures are designed to protect the constitutional rights of individuals and to prevent the arbitrary use of power on the part of the government.

The U.S. Constitution provides specific safeguards for those accused of crimes. The United States Supreme Court has ruled that most of these safeguards apply not only in federal court but also in state courts by virtue of the due process clause of the Fourteenth Amendment. These protections include the following:

1. The Fourth Amendment protection from unreasonable searches and seizures.
2. The Fourth Amendment requirement that no warrant for a search or an arrest be issued without probable cause.
3. The Fifth Amendment requirement that no one be deprived of "life, liberty, or property without due process of law."
4. The Fifth Amendment prohibition against **double jeopardy** (trying someone twice for the same criminal offense).[18]
5. The Fifth Amendment requirement that no person be required to be a witness against (incriminate) himself or herself.
6. The Sixth Amendment guarantees of a speedy trial, a trial by jury, a public trial, the right to confront witnesses, and the right to a lawyer at various stages in some proceedings.
7. The Eighth Amendment prohibitions against excessive bail and fines and against cruel and unusual punishment.

5–5a Fourth Amendment Protections

The Fourth Amendment protects the "right of the people to be secure in their persons, houses, papers, and effects." Before searching or seizing private property, normally law enforcement officers must obtain a **search warrant**—an order from a judge or other public official authorizing the search or seizure.

Advances in technology allow the authorities to track phone calls and vehicle movements with greater ease and precision. The use of such technology can constitute a search within the meaning of the Fourth Amendment. ■ **CASE IN POINT 5.18** Antoine Jones owned and operated a nightclub in the District of Columbia. Government agents suspected that he was also trafficking in narcotics. As part of their investigation, agents obtained a warrant to attach a global positioning system (GPS) device to Jones's wife's car, which Jones regularly used. The warrant authorized installation in the District of Columbia within ten days, but agents installed the device on the eleventh day in Maryland.

The agents then tracked the vehicle's movement for about a month, eventually arresting Jones for possession and intent to distribute cocaine. Jones was convicted. He appealed, arguing that the government did not have a valid warrant for the GPS tracking. The United States Supreme Court held that the attachment of a GPS tracking device to a suspect's vehicle does constitute a Fourth Amendment search. The Court did not rule on whether the search in this case was unreasonable, however, and allowed Jones's conviction to stand.[19] ■

Probable Cause To obtain a search warrant, law enforcement officers must convince a judge that they have reasonable grounds, or **probable cause,** to believe a search will reveal a specific illegality. Probable cause requires the officers to have trustworthy evidence that would convince a reasonable person that the proposed search or seizure is more likely justified than not.

■ **CASE IN POINT 5.19** Based on a tip that Oscar Gutierrez was involved in drug trafficking, law enforcement officers went to his home with a drug-sniffing dog. The dog alerted officers to the scent of narcotics at the home's front door. Officers knocked for fifteen minutes, but no one answered. Eventually, they entered and secured the men inside the home. They then obtained a search warrant based on the dog's positive alert. Officers found eleven pounds of methamphetamine in the search, and Gutierrez was convicted.

On appeal, a court held that the search was permissible because the evidence of the drug-sniffing dog's positive alert for the presence of drugs established probable cause for the warrant.[20] The court noted that a recent

---

18. The prohibition against double jeopardy does not preclude the crime victim from bringing a *civil* suit against that same person to recover damages, however. Additionally, a state's prosecution of a crime will not prevent a separate federal prosecution of the same crime, and vice versa.

19. *United States v. Jones,* __ U.S. __, 132 S.Ct. 945, 181 L.Ed.2d 911 (2012).
20. *United States v. Gutierrez,* 760 F.3d 750 (7th Cir. 2014).

United States Supreme Court decision would have prohibited the search. In that decision, the Court held that police officers cannot bring drug-sniffing dogs onto the front porch of a person's home without a warrant.[21] But the officers' conduct in this case had occurred before the Supreme Court's decision, so the officers could reasonably rely on the sniff evidence. ∎

Scope of Warrant The Fourth Amendment prohibits general warrants. It requires a specific description of what is to be searched or seized. General searches through a person's belongings are impermissible. The search cannot extend beyond what is described in the warrant. Nevertheless, if a warrant is issued for a person's residence, items in that residence may be searched even if they do not belong to that individual.

Reasonable Expectation of Privacy The Fourth Amendment protects only against searches that violate a person's *reasonable expectation of privacy*. A reasonable expectation of privacy exists if (1) the individual actually expects privacy and (2) the person's expectation is one that society as a whole would consider legitimate.

∎ **CASE IN POINT 5.20** Angela Marcum was the drug court coordinator responsible for collecting money for the District Court of Pittsburg County, Oklahoma. She was romantically involved with James Miller, an assistant district attorney. The state charged Marcum with obstructing an investigation of suspected embezzlement and offered in evidence text messages sent and received by her and Miller. The state had obtained a search warrant and collected the records of the messages from U.S. Cellular, Miller's phone company.

Marcum filed a motion to suppress the messages, which the court granted. The state appealed. A state intermediate appellate court reversed the lower court's judgment. Marcum had no reasonable expectation of privacy in U.S. Cellular's records of her text messages in Miller's account. "Once the messages were both transmitted and received, the expectation of privacy was lost."[22] ∎

5–5b The Exclusionary Rule

Under what is known as the **exclusionary rule,** any evidence obtained in violation of the constitutional rights spelled out in the Fourth, Fifth, and Sixth Amendments generally is not admissible at trial. All evidence derived from the illegally obtained evidence is known as the "fruit of the poisonous tree," and it normally must also be excluded from the trial proceedings. For instance, if a confession is obtained after an illegal arrest, the arrest is the "poisonous tree," and the confession, if "tainted" by the arrest, is the "fruit."

The purpose of the exclusionary rule is to deter police from conducting warrantless searches and engaging in other misconduct. The rule can sometimes lead to injustice, however. If evidence of a defendant's guilt was obtained improperly (without a valid search warrant, for instance), it normally cannot be used against the defendant in court.

5–5c The *Miranda* Rule

In *Miranda v. Arizona,*[23] a landmark case decided in 1966, the United States Supreme Court established the rule that individuals who are arrested must be informed of certain constitutional rights. Suspects must be informed of their Fifth Amendment right to remain silent and their Sixth Amendment right to counsel. If the arresting officers fail to inform a criminal suspect of these constitutional rights, any statements the suspect makes normally will not be admissible in court.

Although the Supreme Court's decision in the *Miranda* case was controversial, it has survived several attempts by Congress to overrule it. Over time, however, the Supreme Court has made a number of exceptions to the *Miranda* ruling.

For instance, the Court has recognized a "public safety" exception that allows certain statements to be admitted even if the defendant was not given *Miranda* warnings. A defendant's statements that reveal the location of a weapon would be admissible under this exception.

Additionally, a suspect must unequivocally and assertively ask to exercise her or his right to counsel in order to stop police questioning. Saying "Maybe I should talk to a lawyer" during an interrogation after being taken into custody is not enough.

5–5d Criminal Process

A criminal prosecution differs significantly from a civil case in several respects. These differences reflect the desire to safeguard the rights of the individual against the state. Exhibit 5–3 summarizes the major steps in processing a criminal case, several of which we discuss here.

---

21. *Florida v. Jardines,* 569 U.S. 1, 133 S.Ct. 1409, 185 L.Ed.2d 495 (2013).
22. *State of Oklahoma v. Marcum,* 319 P.3d 681 (2014).

23. 384 U.S. 436, 86 S.Ct. 1602, 16 L.Ed.2d 694 (1966).

EXHIBIT 5–3 Major Procedural Steps in a Criminal Case

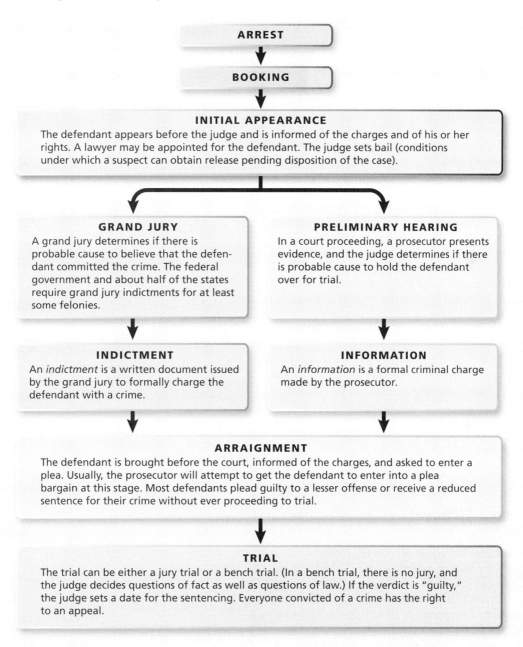

ARREST

BOOKING

INITIAL APPEARANCE
The defendant appears before the judge and is informed of the charges and of his or her rights. A lawyer may be appointed for the defendant. The judge sets bail (conditions under which a suspect can obtain release pending disposition of the case).

GRAND JURY
A grand jury determines if there is probable cause to believe that the defendant committed the crime. The federal government and about half of the states require grand jury indictments for at least some felonies.

PRELIMINARY HEARING
In a court proceeding, a prosecutor presents evidence, and the judge determines if there is probable cause to hold the defendant over for trial.

INDICTMENT
An *indictment* is a written document issued by the grand jury to formally charge the defendant with a crime.

INFORMATION
An *information* is a formal criminal charge made by the prosecutor.

ARRAIGNMENT
The defendant is brought before the court, informed of the charges, and asked to enter a plea. Usually, the prosecutor will attempt to get the defendant to enter into a plea bargain at this stage. Most defendants plead guilty to a lesser offense or receive a reduced sentence for their crime without ever proceeding to trial.

TRIAL
The trial can be either a jury trial or a bench trial. (In a bench trial, there is no jury, and the judge decides questions of fact as well as questions of law.) If the verdict is "guilty," the judge sets a date for the sentencing. Everyone convicted of a crime has the right to an appeal.

Arrest Before a warrant for arrest can be issued, there must be probable cause to believe that the individual in question has committed a crime. Note that probable cause involves a substantial likelihood that the person has committed a crime, not just a possibility. Arrests can be made without a warrant if there is no time to obtain one, but the action of the arresting officer is still judged by the standard of probable cause.

Indictment or Information Individuals must be formally charged with having committed specific crimes before they can be brought to trial. If issued by a grand jury, such a charge is called an **indictment.**[24] A **grand jury** does not determine the guilt or innocence of an accused party. Rather, its function is to hear the state's evidence and to determine whether a reasonable basis (probable cause) exists for believing that a crime has been committed and that a trial ought to be held. For less serious crimes, an individual may be formally charged with a crime by an **information,** or criminal complaint, issued by a government prosecutor.

Trial At a criminal trial, the accused person does not have to prove anything. The entire burden of proof is on the prosecutor (the state). The prosecution must show that, based on all the evidence, the defendant's guilt is established *beyond a reasonable doubt.* If there is reasonable doubt as to whether a criminal defendant committed the crime with which she or he has been charged, then the verdict must be "not guilty." Returning a verdict of "not guilty" is not the same as stating that the defendant is innocent. It merely means that not enough evidence was properly presented to the court to prove guilt beyond a reasonable doubt.

At the conclusion of the trial, a convicted defendant will be sentenced by the court. The U.S. Sentencing Commission performs the task of standardizing sentences for *federal* crimes. The commission's guidelines establish a range of possible penalties, but judges are allowed to depart from the guidelines if circumstances warrant. Sentencing guidelines also provide for enhanced punishment for white-collar crimes, violations of the Sarbanes-Oxley Act, and violations of securities laws.[25]

5–6 Cyber Crime

The U.S. Department of Justice broadly defines **computer crime** as any violation of criminal law that involves knowledge of computer technology for its perpetration, investigation, or prosecution. Many computer crimes fall under the broad label of **cyber crime,** which describes any criminal activity occurring via a computer in the virtual community of the Internet.

Most cyber crimes are simply existing crimes, such as fraud and theft, in which the Internet is the instrument of wrongdoing. Here, we look at several types of activities that constitute cyber crimes against persons or property.

5–6a Cyber Fraud

Fraud is any misrepresentation knowingly made with the intention of deceiving another and on which a reasonable person would and does rely to her or his detriment. **Cyber fraud** is fraud committed over the Internet. Cyber scams have been estimated to affect over 1.5 million people worldwide every day.[26] Scams that were once conducted solely by mail or phone can now be found online, and new technology has led to increasingly more creative ways to commit fraud.

Advance Fee and Online Auction Fraud Two widely reported forms of cyber crime are *advance fee fraud* and *online auction fraud.* In the simplest form of advance fee fraud, consumers order and pay for items, such as automobiles or antiques, that are never delivered. Online auction fraud is also fairly straightforward. A person lists an expensive item for auction, on either a legitimate or a fake auction site, and then refuses to send the product after receiving payment. Or, as a variation, the wrongdoer may send the purchaser an item that is worth less than the one offered in the auction.

■ **CASE IN POINT 5.21**   Jeremy Jaynes grossed more than \$750,000 per week selling nonexistent or worthless products such as "penny stock pickers" and "Internet history erasers." By the time he was arrested, he had amassed an estimated \$24 million from his various fraudulent schemes.[27] ■

Consumer Protections The larger online auction sites, such as eBay, try to protect consumers against such schemes by providing warnings about deceptive sellers or offering various forms of insurance. It is nearly impossible to completely block fraudulent auction activity on the Internet, however. Because users can assume multiple identities, it is very difficult to pinpoint fraudulent sellers—they will simply change their screen names with each auction.

5–6b Cyber Theft

In cyberspace, thieves are not subject to the physical limitations of the "real" world. A thief can steal data stored in a networked computer with Internet access from anywhere on the globe. Only the speed of the connection and the thief's computer equipment limit the quantity of data that can be stolen.

---

24. Pronounced in-*dyte*-ment.
25. The sentencing guidelines were amended in 2003, as required under the Sarbanes-Oxley Act of 2002, to impose stiffer penalties for corporate securities fraud.

26. *2013 Norton Report* (Mountain View, Calif.: Symantec, 2014), pg. 8.
27. *Jaynes v. Commonwealth of Virginia,* 276 Va. 443, 666 S.E.2d 303 (2008).

Identity Theft Not surprisingly, there has been a marked increase in identity theft in recent years. **Identity theft** occurs when the wrongdoer steals a form of identification—such as a name, date of birth, or Social Security number—and uses the information to access the victim's financial resources. According to the federal government, about 7 percent of Americans have been victims of identity theft.

More than half of identity thefts involve the misappropriation of an existing credit-card account. In most situations, the legitimate holders of credit cards are not held responsible for the costs of purchases made with a stolen number. The loss is born by the businesses and banks.

The Internet has provided relatively easy access to private data that includes credit-card numbers and more. Frequent Web surfers surrender a wealth of information about themselves. Web sites use "cookies" to collect data on those who visit their sites and make purchases. Often, sites store information such as the consumer's name, e-mail address, and credit-card number. Identity thieves may be able to steal this information by fooling a Web site into thinking that they are the true account holders.

In addition, people often enter important personal information, such as their birthdays, hometowns, or employers, on social media sites. Identity thieves can use such information to convince a third party to reveal someone's Social Security or bank account number.

Identity theft can be committed in the course of pursuing other criminal objectives. In the following case, for example, the defendant was charged with identity theft in connection with the filing of five thousand false income tax returns to obtain refunds. He challenged his conviction on these charges and sought a new trial.

Case Analysis 5.3

United States v. Warner

United States Court of Appeals, Eleventh Circuit, 2016 WL 403166 (2016).

In the Language of the Court

PER CURIAM [By the Whole Court]:

* * * *

A [federal district court] jury convicted Mauricio Warner on all 50 counts of an indictment that charged him with obtaining individuals' identities and using such identities to file over 5,000 false income tax returns resulting in millions of dollars in refunds that were deposited in bank accounts Warner controlled. [The court sentenced Warner to prison for a total of 240 months.] He now appeals his convictions. He seeks the vacation of his convictions and a new trial on the grounds that the District Court abused its discretion (1) in refusing to permit a polygraph examiner to testify to the results of a polygraph examination he administered to Warner; (2) admitting into evidence government Exhibits 500 and 500A, spreadsheets of fraudulently submitted tax returns, as business records; and (3) permitting each juror to have a copy of the indictment throughout trial.

* * * *

A district court's decision to admit or exclude expert testimony under Federal Rule of Evidence 702 is reviewed for abuse of discretion, which is the standard we apply in reviewing evidentiary rulings in general. *A district court abuses its discretion when it applies the wrong law, follows the wrong procedure, bases its decision on clearly erroneous facts, or commits a clear error in judgment.* [Emphasis added.]

Federal Rule of Evidence 702 provides that an expert witness may testify in the form of an opinion if the expert's specialized knowledge will assist the trier of fact to understand the evidence or to determine a fact at issue.

The results of a polygraph examination are not inadmissible *per se*. The trial judge in the exercise of discretion may admit the results of such examination to impeach or corroborate witness testimony.

The District Court did not abuse its discretion in concluding that the polygraph examination was inadmissible under Rule 702. The question

posed by the examiner addressed an issue that was to be decided by the jury, that is, whether Warner knowingly filed tax returns without the individuals' authority or knowing that they were not entitled to the refund requested. Since Warner took the stand and answered the same questions, the jury was capable of determining his credibility without the aid of an expert.

* * * *

Federal Rule of Evidence 1006 authorizes the admission into evidence of a summary of voluminous business records but only where the originals or duplicates of those originals are available for examination or copying by the other party.

The business record exception to the hearsay rule under Federal Rule of Evidence 803(6) states, in relevant part, that a record will be admitted if:

(A) the record was made at or near the time by—or from information transmitted by—someone with knowledge;

Case 5.3 Continues

(B) the record was kept in the course of a regularly conducted activity of a business, organization, occupation, or calling, whether or not for profit;

(C) making the record was a regular practice of that activity;

(D) all these conditions are shown by the testimony of the custodian or another qualified witness * * *;

(E) the opponent does not show that the source of information or the method of circumstances of preparation indicate a lack of trustworthiness.

Rule 803(6) requires that both the underlying records and the report summarizing those records be prepared and maintained for business purposes in the ordinary course of business and not for purposes of litigation. * * * *The touchstone of admissibility under Rule 803(6) is reliability, and a trial judge has broad discretion to determine the admissibility of such evidence.* [Emphasis added.]

Computer-generated business records are admissible under the following circumstances: (1) the records must be kept pursuant to some routine procedure designed to assure their accuracy, (2) they must be created for motives that would tend to assure accuracy (preparation for litigation, for example, is not such a motive), and (3) they must not themselves be mere accumulations of hearsay or uninformed opinion.

* * * A typed summary of handwritten business records created solely for litigation [is] inadmissible hearsay evidence. [This is] distinguishable from * * * records [that consist of] electronically stored information and the summary [is] simply a printout of that information.

* * * *

* * * Airline check-in and reservation records and flight manifests that [are] kept in the ordinary course of business and printed at the government's request [for a trial are admissible]. Computer data compiled and presented in computer printouts prepared specifically for trial is admissible under Rule 803(6), even though the printouts themselves are not kept in the ordinary course of business.

We find no abuse of discretion in admitting government Exhibits 500 and 500A under Rule 803(6). Although the spreadsheets were formatted to be easier to understand and printed for litigation, the underlying records were kept in the ordinary course of business and the data was not modified or combined when entered into the spreadsheet.

* * * *

The decision to provide the jury with a copy of an indictment is committed to the district court's sound discretion.

As a general rule, a trial court may, in the exercise of discretion, allow the indictment to be taken into the jury room. Likewise, a court may provide the jury copies of the indictment before trial, provided that the court gives specific instructions that the indictment is not evidence.

There was no abuse of discretion here. The court specifically instructed the jurors on two separate occasions that the indictment was not evidence or proof of any guilt. Even if the court's lack of contemporaneous instructions was error, it was harmless.

For the foregoing reasons, Warner's convictions are

AFFIRMED.

Legal Reasoning Questions

1. What three reasons did the defendant assert to support a request for a new trial?

2. What standard applies to an appellate court's consideration of a contention that a trial court's evidentiary ruling was in error?

3. What were the appellate court's conclusions with respect to the trial court's rulings in this case? What reasons support these conclusions?

Password Theft The more personal information a cyber criminal obtains, the easier it is for him or her to find a victim's online user name at a particular Web site. Once the online user name has been compromised, it is easier to steal the victim's password, which is often the last line of defense to financial information.

Numerous software programs aid identity thieves in illegally obtaining passwords. A technique called *keystroke logging,* for instance, relies on software that embeds itself in a victim's computer and records every keystroke made on that computer. User names and passwords are then recorded and sold to the highest bidder. Internet users should also be wary of any links contained within e-mails sent from unknown sources. These links can sometimes be used to illegally obtain personal information.

Phishing A form of identity theft known as **phishing** has added a different wrinkle to the practice. In a phishing attack, the perpetrator "fishes" for financial data and passwords from consumers by posing as a legitimate business, such as a bank or credit-card company. The "phisher" sends an e-mail asking the recipient to update or confirm vital information. Often, the e-mail includes a threat that an account or some other service will be discontinued if the information is not provided. Once the unsuspecting individual enters the information, the phisher can sell it or use it to masquerade as that person or to drain his or her bank or credit account.

■ **EXAMPLE 5.22** Customers of Wells Fargo Bank received official-looking e-mails telling them to type in personal information in an online form to complete a mandatory installation of a new Internet security certificate. But the Web site was bogus. When people filled out the forms, their computers were infected and funneled their data to a computer server. The cyber criminals then sold the data. ■ Phishing scams have also spread to text messaging and social networking sites.

5–6c Hacking

A **hacker** is someone who uses one computer to break into another. The danger posed by hackers has increased significantly because of **botnets,** or networks of computers that have been appropriated by hackers without the knowledge of their owners. A hacker may secretly install a program on thousands, even millions, of personal computer "robots," or "bots." The program, in turn, allows the hacker to forward transmissions to an even larger number of systems.

■**EXAMPLE 5.23** Almost as soon as Apple, Inc., introduced a new mobile-payment system in late 2014, cyber thieves began hacking into the company's smartphones and tablets to make purchases with stolen credit-card numbers. At about the same time, cyber criminals were stealing the credit-card data of at least 60 million Home Depot customers and illegally accessing the financial information of 76 million JPMorgan Chase clients. In 2015, hackers stole the personal information of 19.7 million individuals from the U.S. Office of Personnel Management's background-investigation databases.

It has also been demonstrated that hackers can take over the dashboard computer systems that control cars— General Motors' OnStar system, for example. This risk of takeover extends to numerous wireless-enabled medical devices in use today, such as pacemakers, insulin pumps, and neurostimulators. A criminal could hack someone's car or pacemaker with the intent of causing the person harm. ■

Malware Botnets are one of the latest forms of **malware,** a term that refers to any program that is harmful to a computer or, by extension, a computer user. Malware can be programmed to perform a number of functions, such as prompting host computers to continually "crash" and reboot or otherwise infecting the systems.

One type of malware is a **worm**—a software program that is capable of reproducing itself as it spreads from one computer to the next. The Conficker worm, for instance, spread to more than a million personal computers around the world within a three-week period. It was transmitted to some computers through the use of Facebook and Twitter.

A **virus,** another form of malware, is also able to reproduce itself, but must be attached to an "infested" host file to travel from one computer network to another. For instance, hackers are now capable of corrupting banner ads that use Adobe's Flash Player. When an Internet user clicks on the banner ad, a virus is installed.

■ **EXAMPLE 5.24** During the 2013 holiday season, a group of Eastern European hackers managed to gain access to Target's computer system. Once "inside," these hackers infected the in-store devices that Target customers use to swipe their credit and debit cards with "memory scraper" malware nicknamed Kaptoxa. Over the course of several weeks, the malware was used to steal the credit- and debit-card data of as many as 40 million Target customers. Personal data such as passwords, phone numbers, and addresses were stolen from at least 70 million more customers. Some experts estimate that the incident resulted in billions of dollars in losses to consumers, their banks, and others. ■

Service-Based Hacking Today, many companies offer "software as a service." Instead of buying software to install on a computer, the user connects to Web-based software. The user can then write e-mails, edit spreadsheets, or perform other tasks using his or her Web browser.

Cyber criminals have adapted this distribution method to provide "crimeware as a service." A would-be thief no longer has to be a computer hacker to create a botnet or steal banking information and credit-card numbers. He or she can rent the online services of cyber criminals to do the work for a small price. Fake security software (also known as scareware) is a common example. The thief can even target individual groups, such as U.S. physicians or British attorneys.

Cyberterrorism Cyberterrorists, as well as hackers, may target businesses. The goals of a hacking operation might include a wholesale theft of data, such as a merchant's customer files, or the monitoring of a computer to discover a business firm's plans and transactions. A cyberterrorist might also want to insert false codes or data. For instance, the processing control system of a food manufacturer could be changed to alter the levels of ingredients so that consumers of the food would become ill.

A cyberterrorist attack on a major financial institution, such as the New York Stock Exchange or a large bank, could leave securities or money markets in flux. Such an attack could seriously affect U.S. citizens, business operations, and national security.

5–6d Prosecuting Cyber Crime

Cyber crime has raised new issues in the investigation of crimes and the prosecution of offenders. Determining the "location" of a cyber crime and identifying a criminal in cyberspace present significant challenges for law enforcement.

Jurisdiction and Identification Challenges A threshold issue is, of course, jurisdiction. Each state and nation has jurisdiction, or authority, over crimes committed within its boundaries. But geographic boundaries simply do not apply in cyberspace. A person who commits an act against a business in California, where the act is a cyber crime, might never have set foot in California. Instead, the perpetrator might reside in another state, or even another nation, where the act may not be a crime. Indeed, many cyber crimes emanate from Russia and China.

Identifying the wrongdoer can also be difficult. Cyber criminals do not leave physical traces, such as fingerprints or DNA samples, as evidence of their crimes. Even electronic "footprints" can be hard to find and follow. For instance, cyber criminals may employ software such as Tor to mask their IP addresses (codes that identify individual computers) and the IP addresses of those with whom they communicate. Law enforcement has to hire computer forensic experts to bypass the software and track down the criminal. For these reasons, laws written to protect physical property are often difficult to apply in cyberspace.

The Computer Fraud and Abuse Act Perhaps the most significant federal statute specifically addressing cyber crime is the Counterfeit Access Device and Computer Fraud and Abuse Act.[28] This act is commonly known as the Computer Fraud and Abuse Act (CFAA).

Among other things, the CFAA provides that a person who accesses a computer online, without authority, to obtain classified, restricted, or protected data (or attempts to do so) is subject to criminal prosecution. Such data could include financial and credit records, medical records, legal files, military and national security files, and other confidential information. The data can be located in government or private computers. The crime has two elements: accessing a computer without authority and taking data.

The theft is a felony if it is committed for a commercial purpose or for private financial gain, or if the value of the stolen data (or computer time) exceeds $5,000. Penalties include fines and imprisonment for up to twenty years. A person who violates the CFAA can also be sued in a civil action for damages.

---

28. 18 U.S.C. Section 1030.

Reviewing: Criminal Law and Cyber Crime

Edward Hanousek worked for Pacific & Arctic Railway and Navigation Company (P&A) as a roadmaster of the White Pass & Yukon Railroad in Alaska. Hanousek was responsible "for every detail of the safe and efficient maintenance and construction of track, structures and marine facilities of the entire railroad," including special projects. One project was a rock quarry, known as "6-mile," above the Skagway River. Next to the quarry, and just beneath the surface, ran a high-pressure oil pipeline owned by Pacific & Arctic Pipeline, Inc., P&A's sister company. When the quarry's backhoe operator punctured the pipeline, an estimated 1,000 to 5,000 gallons of oil were discharged into the river. Hanousek was charged with negligently discharging a harmful quantity of oil into a navigable water of the United States in violation of the criminal provisions of the Clean Water Act (CWA). Using the information presented in the chapter, answer the following questions.

1. Did Hanousek have the required mental state *(mens rea)* to be convicted of a crime? Why or why not?
2. Which theory discussed in the chapter would enable a court to hold Hanousek criminally liable for violating the statute if he participated in, directed, or merely knew about the specific violation?
3. Could the backhoe operator who punctured the pipeline also be charged with a crime in this situation? Explain.
4. Suppose that at trial, Hanousek argued that he should not be convicted because he was not aware of the requirements of the CWA. Would this defense be successful? Why or why not?

Debate This . . . *Because of overcriminalization, particularly by the federal government, Americans may be breaking the law regularly without knowing it. Should Congress rescind many of the more than four thousand federal crimes now on the books?*

Terms and Concepts

actus reus 91	beyond a reasonable doubt 89	burglary 94
arson 96	botnet 109	computer crime 106

Issue Spotters

1. Dana takes her roommate's credit card without permission, intending to charge expenses that she incurs on a vacation. Her first stop is a gas station, where she uses the card to pay for gas. With respect to the gas station, has she committed a crime? If so, what is it? (See *Types of Crimes.*)

2. Without permission, Ben downloads consumer credit files from a computer belonging to Consumer Credit Agency. He then sells the data to Dawn. Has Ben committed a crime? If so, what is it? (See *Cyber Crime.*)

• **Check your answers to the Issue Spotters against the answers provided in Appendix B at the end of this text.**

Business Scenarios

5–1. Types of Cyber Crimes. The following situations are similar, but each represents a variation of a particular crime. Identify the crime and point out the differences in the variations. (See *Cyber Crime.*)

(a) Chen, posing fraudulently as Diamond Credit Card Co., sends an e-mail to Emily, stating that the company has observed suspicious activity in her account and has frozen the account. The e-mail asks her to reregister her credit-card number and password to reopen the account.

(b) Claiming falsely to be Big Buy Retail Finance Co., Conner sends an e-mail to Dino, asking him to confirm or update his personal security information to prevent his Big Buy account from being discontinued.

(c) Felicia posts her résumé on GotWork.com, an online job-posting site, seeking a position in business and managerial finance and accounting. Hayden, who misrepresents himself as an employment officer with International Bank & Commerce Corp., sends her an e-mail asking for more personal information.

5–2. Cyber Scam. Kayla, a student at Learnwell University, owes $20,000 in unpaid tuition. If Kayla does not pay the tuition, Learnwell will not allow her to graduate. To obtain the funds to pay the debt, she sends e-mails to people that she does not personally know asking for financial help to send Milo, her disabled child, to a special school. In reality, Kayla has no children. Is this a crime? If so, which one? (See *Cyber Crime.*)

Business Case Problems

5–3. Credit-Card Theft. Jacqueline Barden was shopping for school clothes with her children when her purse and automobile were taken. In Barden's purse were her car keys, credit and debit cards, and the children's Social Security cards and birth certificates, which were needed for enrollment at school. Immediately after the purse and car were stolen, Rebecca Mary Turner attempted to use Barden's credit card at a local Exxon gas station, but the card was declined. The gas station attendant recognized Turner because she had previously written bad checks and used credit cards that did not belong to her.

Turner was later arrested while attempting to use one of Barden's checks to pay for merchandise at a Wal-Mart—where the clerk also recognized Turner from prior criminal activity. Turner claimed that she had not stolen Barden's purse or car. Instead, she said that a friend had told her he had some checks and credit cards and asked her to try using them at Wal-Mart. Turner was convicted at trial. She appealed, claiming that there was insufficient evidence that she committed credit- and debit-card theft. Was the evidence sufficient to uphold her conviction? Why or why not? [*Turner v. State of Arkansas*, 2012 Ark.App. 150 (2012)] (See *Types of Crimes.*)

5–4. Business Case Problem with Sample Answer— Criminal Liability. During the morning rush hour, David Green threw bottles and plates from a twenty-sixth-floor hotel balcony overlooking Seventh Avenue in New York City. A video of the incident also showed him doing cartwheels while holding a beer bottle and sprinting toward the balcony while holding a glass steadily in his hand. When he saw police on the street below and on the roof of the building across the street, he suspended his antics but resumed tossing objects off the balcony after the police left. He later admitted that he could recall what he had done, but claimed to have been intoxicated and said his only purpose was to amuse himself and his friends. Did Green have the mental state required to establish criminal liability? Discuss. [*State of New York v. Green,* 104 A.D.3d 126, 958 N.Y.S.2d 138 (1 Dept. 2013)] (See *Criminal Liability.*)

- **For a sample answer to Problem 5–4, go to Appendix C at the end of this text.**

5–5. White-Collar Crime. Matthew Simpson and others created and operated a series of corporate entities to defraud telecommunications companies, creditors, credit reporting agencies, and others. Through these entities, Simpson and his confederates used routing codes and spoofing services to make long-distance calls appear to be local. They stole other firms' network capacity and diverted payments to themselves. They leased goods and services without paying for them. To hide their association with their corporate entities and with each other, they used false identities, addresses, and credit histories, and issued false bills, invoices, financial statements, and credit references. Did these acts constitute mail and wire fraud? Discuss. [*United States v. Simpson,* 741 F.3d 539 (5th Cir. 2014)] (See *Types of Crimes.*)

5–6. Defenses to Criminal Liability. George Castro told Ambrosio Medrano that a bribe to a certain corrupt Los Angeles County official would buy a contract with the county hospitals. To share in the deal, Medrano recruited Gustavo Buenrostro. In turn, Buenrostro contacted his friend James Barta, the owner of Sav–Rx, which provides prescription benefit management services. Barta was asked to pay a "finder's fee" to Castro. He did not pay, even after frequent e-mails and calls with deadlines and ultimatums delivered over a period of months. Eventually, Barta wrote Castro a Sav–Rx check for $6,500, saying that it was to help his friend Buenrostro. Castro was an FBI agent, and the county official and contract were fictional. Barta was charged with conspiracy to commit bribery. At trial, the government conceded that Barta was not predisposed to commit the crime.

Could he be absolved of the charge on a defense of entrapment? Explain. [*United States v. Barta,* 776 F.3d 931 (7th Cir. 2015)] (See *Defenses to Criminal Liability.*)

5–7. Criminal Procedures. Federal officers obtained a warrant to arrest Kateena Norman on charges of credit-card fraud and identity theft. Evidence of the crime included videos, photos, and a fingerprint on a fraudulent check. A previous search of Norman's house had uncovered credit cards, new merchandise, and identifying information for other persons. An Internet account registered to the address had been used to apply for fraudulent credit cards, and a fraudulently obtained rental car was parked on the property. As the officers arrested Norman outside her house, they saw another woman and a caged pit bull inside. They further believed that Norman's boyfriend, who had a criminal record and was also suspected of identify theft, could be there. In less than a minute, the officers searched only those areas within the house in which a person could hide. Would it be reasonable to admit evidence revealed in this "protective sweep" during Norman's trial on the arrest charges? Discuss. [*United States v. Norman,* 2016 WL 324949 (11th Cir. 2016)] (See *Criminal Procedures.*)

5–8. A Question of Ethics—Criminal Process. *Gary* 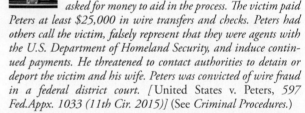 *Peters fraudulently told an undocumented immigrant that Peters could help him obtain lawful status. Peters said that he knew immigration officials and asked for money to aid in the process. The victim paid Peters at least $25,000 in wire transfers and checks. Peters had others call the victim, falsely represent that they were agents with the U.S. Department of Homeland Security, and induce continued payments. He threatened to contact authorities to detain or deport the victim and his wife. Peters was convicted of wire fraud in a federal district court. [*United States v. Peters, 597 Fed.Appx. 1033 (11th Cir. 2015)]* (See *Criminal Procedures.*)

(a) Peters had previously committed theft and fraud. The court stated, "This is the person he is. He steals from his relatives. He steals from his business partner. He steals from immigrants. He steals from anybody he comes into contact with." What does Peters's conduct indicate about his ethics?

(b) Peters's attorney argued that his client's criminal history was partially due to "difficult personal times" caused by divorce, illness, and job loss. Despite this claim, Peters was sentenced to forty-eight months imprisonment, which exceeded the federal sentencing guidelines but was less than the statutory maximum of twenty years. Was this sentence too harsh? Was it too lenient? Discuss.

Legal Reasoning Group Activity

5–9. Cyber Crime. Cyber crime costs consumers millions of dollars per year, and it costs businesses, including banks and other credit-card issuers, even more. Nonetheless, when cyber criminals are caught and convicted, they are rarely ordered to pay restitution or sentenced to long prison terms. (See *Cyber Crime.*)

(a) One group should argue that stiffer sentences would reduce the amount of cyber crime.

(b) A second group should determine how businesspersons can best protect themselves from cyber crime and avoid the associated costs.

CHAPTER 6

Business Ethics

One of the most complex issues businesspersons and corporations face is ethics. It is not as well defined as the law, and yet it can have substantial impacts on a firm's finances and reputation, especially when the firm is involved in a well-publicized scandal. Some scandals arise from activities that are legal, but are ethically questionable. Other scandals arise from conduct that is both illegal and unethical.

Consider, for example, Volkswagen's corporate executives, who were accused of cheating on the pollution emissions tests of millions of vehicles that were sold in the United States. Volkswagen admitted in 2015 that it had installed "defeat device" software in its diesel models. The software detected when the car was being tested and changed its performance to improve the test outcome. As a result, the diesel cars showed low emissions—a feature that made the cars more attractive to today's consumers. Ultimately, millions of Volkswagen vehicles were recalled, and the company suffered its first quarterly loss in fifteen years.

6-1 Business Ethics

At the most basic level, the study of **ethics** is the study of what constitutes right or wrong behavior. It is a branch of philosophy focusing on morality and the way moral principles are derived and implemented. Ethics has to do with the fairness, justness, rightness, or wrongness of an action.

The study of **business ethics** typically looks at the decisions businesses make or have to make and whether those decisions are right or wrong. It has to do with how businesspersons apply moral and ethical principles in making their decisions. Those who study business ethics also evaluate what duties and responsibilities exist or should exist for businesses.

6-1a Why Is Studying Business Ethics Important?

Over the last hundred years, the public perception of the corporation has changed from an entity that primarily generates revenues for its owners to an entity that participates in society as a corporate citizen. Originally, the only goal or duty of a corporation was to maximize profits. Although many people today may view this idea as greedy or inhumane, the rationale for the profit-maximization theory is still valid.

Profit Maximization In theory, if all firms strictly adhere to the goal of profit maximization, resources flow to where they are most highly valued by society. Corporations can focus on their strengths, and other entities that are better suited to deal with social problems and perform charitable acts can specialize in those activities. The government, through taxes and other financial allocations, can shift resources to those other entities to perform public services. Thus, in an ideal world, profit maximization leads to the most efficient allocation of scarce resources.

The Rise of Corporate Citizenship Over the years, as resources purportedly were not sufficiently reallocated to cover the costs of social needs, many people became dissatisfied with the profit-maximization theory. Investors and others began to look beyond profits and dividends and to consider the **triple bottom line**—a corporation's profits, its impact on people, and its impact on the planet. Magazines and Web sites began to rank companies based on their environmental impacts and their ethical decisions. The corporation came to be viewed as a "citizen" that was expected to participate in bettering communities and society.

Even so, many still believe that corporations are fundamentally profit-making entities that should have no responsibility other than profit maximization.

6–1b The Importance of Ethics in Making Business Decisions

Whether one believes in profit maximization or corporate citizenship, ethics is important in making business decisions. When making decisions, a business should evaluate:

1. The legal implications of each decision.
2. The public relations impact.
3. The safety risks for consumers and employees.
4. The financial implications.

This four-part analysis will assist the firm in making decisions that not only maximize profits but also reflect good corporate citizenship.

Long-Run Profit Maximization In attempting to maximize profits, corporate executives and employees have to distinguish between *short-run* and *long-run* profit maximization. In the short run, a company may increase its profits by continuing to sell a product even though it knows that the product is defective. In the long run, though, because of lawsuits, large settlements, and bad publicity, such unethical conduct will cause profits to suffer. Thus, business ethics is consistent only with long-run profit maximization. An overemphasis on short-term profit maximization is the most common reason that ethical problems occur in business.

■ **CASE IN POINT 6.1** When the powerful narcotic painkiller OxyContin was first marketed, its manufacturer, Purdue Pharma, claimed that it was unlikely to lead to drug addiction or abuse. Internal company documents later showed that the company's executives knew that OxyContin could be addictive, but kept this risk a secret to boost sales and maximize short-term profits.

Subsequently, Purdue Pharma and three former executives pleaded guilty to criminal charges that they had misled regulators, patients, and physicians about OxyContin's risks of addiction. Purdue Pharma agreed to pay $600 million in fines and other payments. The three former executives agreed to pay $34.5 million in fines and were barred from federal health programs for a period of fifteen years. Thus, the company's focus on maximizing profits in the short run led to unethical conduct that hurt profits in the long run.[1] ■

---

1. *United States v. Purdue Frederick Co.*, 495 F.Supp.2d 569 (W.D.Va. 2007).

The Internet Can Ruin Reputations In the past, negative information or opinions about a company might remain hidden. Now, however, cyberspace provides a forum where disgruntled employees, unhappy consumers, or special interest groups can post derogatory remarks. Thus, the Internet has increased the potential for a major corporation (or other business) to suffer damage to its reputation or loss of profits through negative publicity.

Wal-Mart and Nike in particular have been frequent targets for advocacy groups that believe those corporations exploit their workers. Although some of these assertions may be unfounded or exaggerated, the courts generally have refused to consider them *defamatory* (a tort giving rise to a civil lawsuit). Most courts regard online attacks as expressions of opinion protected by the First Amendment. Even so, corporations often incur considerable expense in running marketing campaigns to thwart bad publicity and may even face legal costs if the allegations lead to litigation.

Image Is Everything The study of business ethics is concerned with the purposes of a business and how that business achieves those purposes. Thus, business ethics is concerned not only with the image of the business, but also with the impact that the business has on the environment, customers, suppliers, employees, and the global economy.

Unethical corporate decision making can negatively affect suppliers, consumers, the community, and society as a whole. It can also have a negative impact on the reputation of the company and the individuals who run that company. Hence, an in-depth understanding of business ethics is important to the long-run viability of any corporation today.

6–1c The Relationship of Law and Ethics

Because the law does not codify all ethical requirements, compliance with the law is not always sufficient to determine "right" behavior. Laws have to be general enough to apply in a variety of circumstances. Laws are broad in their purpose and their scope. They prohibit or require certain actions to avoid significant harm to society.

When two competing companies secretly agree to set prices on products, for instance, society suffers harm—typically, the companies will charge higher prices than they could if they continued to compete. This harm inflicted on consumers has negative consequences for the economy, and so colluding to set prices is an illegal activity. Similarly, when a company is preparing to issue stock, the law requires certain disclosures to potential investors. This requirement is meant to prevent harms that come with uninformed investing. Such harms occurred in the 1920s and may have contributed to the stock market crash and the Great Depression.

Moral Minimum Compliance with the law is sometimes called the **moral minimum.** If people and entities merely comply with the law, they are acting at the lowest ethical level society will tolerate. The study of ethics goes beyond those legal requirements to evaluate what is right for society. The following case illustrates some consequences of a businessperson's failure to meet the moral minimum.

Case 6.1

Scott v. Carpanzano
United States Court of Appeals, Fifth Circuit, 556 Fed.Appx. 288 (2014).

Background and Facts Rick Scott deposited $2 million into an escrow account maintained by a company owned by Salvatore Carpanzano. Immediately after the deposit was made, in violation of the escrow agreement, the funds were withdrawn. When Scott was unable to recover his money, he filed a suit against Salvatore Carpanzano and others, including Salvatore's daughter Carmela Carpanzano. In the complaint, Scott made no allegations of acts or knowledge on Carmela's part.

Salvatore failed to cooperate with discovery and did not respond to attempts to contact him by certified mail, regular mail, or e-mail. Salvatore also refused to make an appearance in the court and did not finalize a settlement negotiated between the parties' attorneys. Carmela denied that she was involved in her father's business or the Scott transaction. The court found that the defendants had intentionally failed to respond to the litigation and issued a judgment for more than $6 million in Scott's favor. The defendants appealed to the U.S. Court of Appeals for the Fifth Circuit.

In the Language of the Court
PER CURIAM [By the Whole Court].
    * * * *

A willful default is an *intentional failure to respond to litigation.* The district court found that [the] Defendants willfully defaulted based on evidence that the Defendants were aware of the proceedings against them and that [their] attorneys were specifically instructed not to enter an appearance [participate] in this case. [Emphasis added.]

The evidence substantially supports the district court's finding as to Mr. Carpanzano. First, Mr. Carpanzano's first attorney withdrew [from the case] because Mr. Carpanzano failed to cooperate with the discovery process and refused to appear as requested and ordered. Second, * * * Mr. Carpanzano instructed his second set of attorneys to negotiate settlement of this matter but not to enter an appearance in the district court. Significantly, Mr. Carpanzano never denies this allegation. Third, * * * Mr. Carpanzano and his attorneys were well aware that the case was proceeding toward default and * * * were in communication with each other during this time. Fourth, * * * once final execution of settlement papers was at hand, Mr. Carpanzano also ceased communication with his second set of attorneys and did not finalize the settlement. Finally, other than ambiguously suggesting that a health condition (unsupported by any evidence of what the condition was) and absence from the country (unsupported by any evidence that electronic communication was not possible from that country) prevented him from defending this action, Mr. Carpanzano offers no real reason why he did not answer the * * * complaint.
    * * * *

By contrast, the record does not support the district court's finding that * * * Ms. [Carmela] Carpanzano also willfully defaulted.

* * * Ms. Carpanzano repeatedly indicated that [she was] relying on Mr. Carpanzano * * * to make sure [her] interests were protected. Nothing in the record contradicts this assertion. While [her] reliance on Mr. Carpanzano acting with the attorneys he retained may have been negligent, it does not amount to an intentional failure to respond to litigation.

Case 6.1 Continues

Case 6.1 Continued

* * * *

* * * [Furthermore] the * * * complaint * * * contains no factual allegations of acts or omissions on the part of Ms. Carpanzano. It does not allege that she ever was in contact with Scott, that she was in control of the * * * escrow account, or that she wrongfully transferred any funds out of the account. Nor does it allege any intent or knowledge on the part of Ms. Carpanzano * * *. Indeed, an examination of the complaint reveals that there is not a sufficient basis in the pleadings for the judgment * * * entered against Ms. Carpanzano.

The defenses presented by Ms. Carpanzano to the district court assert that she had no knowledge of the details of her father's business transactions, she did not personally enter into any contracts with Scott or seek to defraud him, and * * * she had limited involvement in the facts of this case.

* * * *

* * * Even if Scott were able to prove the entirety of the * * * complaint, we fail to see how it would justify a judgment * * * against Ms. Carpanzano.

Decision and Remedy *The U.S. Court of Appeals for the Fifth Circuit affirmed the judgment against Salvatore, but reversed the decision against Carmela. Scott had made no allegations of acts on Carmela's part.*

Critical Thinking
- **Ethical** *Are Salvatore's actions likely to affect his business's ability to profit in the long run? Discuss.*
- **Legal Environment** *Did Carmela Carpanzano meet the minimum acceptable standard for ethical business behavior? Explain.*

Ethical Requirements The study of ethics goes beyond legal requirements to evaluate what is right for society. Businesspersons thus must remember that an action that is legal is not necessarily ethical. For instance, a company's refusal to negotiate liability claims for alleged injuries because of a faulty product is legal. But it may not be ethical if the reason the business refuses to negotiate is to increase the injured party's legal costs and force the person to drop a legitimate claim.

Private Company Codes of Ethics Most companies attempt to link ethics and law through the creation of internal codes of ethics. Company codes are not law. Instead, they are rules that the company sets forth that it can also enforce (by terminating an employee who does not follow them, for instance). Codes of conduct typically outline the company's policies on particular issues and indicate how employees are expected to act.
■ **EXAMPLE 6.2** Google's code of conduct starts with the motto "Don't be evil." The code then makes general statements about how Google promotes integrity, mutual respect, and the highest standard of ethical business conduct. Google's code also provides specific rules on a number of issues, such as privacy, drugs and alcohol, conflicts of interest, co-worker relationships, and confidentiality.

It even has a dog policy. The company takes a stand against employment discrimination that goes further than the law requires—it prohibits discrimination based on sexual orientation, gender identity or expression, and veteran status. ■

Industry Ethical Codes Numerous industries have also developed their own codes of ethics. The American Institute of Certified Public Accountants (AICPA) has a comprehensive Code of Professional Conduct for the ethical practice of accounting. The American Bar Association has model rules of professional conduct for attorneys, and the American Nurses Association has a code of ethics that applies to nurses. These codes can give guidance to decision makers facing ethical questions.

Violation of an industry code may result in discipline of an employee or sanctions against a company from the industry organization. Remember, though, that these internal codes are not laws, so their effectiveness is determined by the commitment of the industry or company leadership to enforcing the codes.
■ **CASE IN POINT 6.3** National Football League (NFL) rules require footballs to be inflated to a minimum air pressure (pounds per square inch, or psi) as measured by the referees. This rule gained attention when the New

England Patriots played the Indianapolis Colts for the American Football Conference championship in early 2015. After Tom Brady, the Patriots quarterback, threw a pass that was intercepted, officials became suspicious that the football was underinflated. The game continued after NFL officials verified the psi in all the footballs, and the Patriots won.

Nevertheless, allegations continued that Brady and the Patriots had deflated balls during the game—a controversy popularly known as "deflategate." The NFL performed an investigation, and after arbitration, the league announced that Brady would be suspended for four games. Brady appealed, and a federal district court vacated the arbitrator's decision to suspend, but a federal appellate court reinstated Brady's suspension in 2016. The reviewing court held that the arbitrator had grounds to suspend Brady for being generally aware that the team had intentionally released air from the game balls.[2] ∎

"Gray Areas" in the Law Because it is often highly subjective and subject to change over time without any sort of formal process, ethics is less certain than law. But the law can also be uncertain. Numerous "gray areas" in the law make it difficult to predict with certainty how a court will apply a given law to a particular action. In addition, laws frequently change.

6–2 Business Ethics and Social Media

Most young people may think of social media—Facebook, Flickr, Instagram, Tumblr, Twitter, Pinterest, Google+, LinkedIn, VR, and the like—as simply ways to communicate rapidly. Businesses, though, often face ethical issues with respect to these same social media platforms.

6–2a Hiring Procedures

In the past, to learn about a prospective employee, an employer would ask the candidate's former employers for references. Today, employers are likely to also conduct Internet searches to discover what job candidates have posted on their Facebook pages, blogs, and tweets.

On the one hand, job candidates may be judged by what they post on social media. On the other hand,

though, they may be judged because they *do not* participate in social media. Given that the vast majority of younger people do use social media, some employers have decided that the failure to do so raises a red flag. In either case, many people believe that judging a job candidate based on what she or he does outside the work environment is unethical.

6–2b The Use of Social Media to Discuss Work-Related Issues

Because so many Americans use social media daily, they often discuss work-related issues there. Numerous companies have strict guidelines about what is appropriate and inappropriate for employees to say when making posts on their own or others' social media accounts. A number of companies have fired employees for such activities as criticizing other employees or managers through social media outlets. Until recently, such disciplinary measures were considered ethical and legal.

Responsibility of Employers Today, in contrast, a ruling by the National Labor Relations Board (NLRB—the federal agency that investigates unfair labor practices) has changed the legality of such actions. ∎ **EXAMPLE 6.4** At one time, Costco's social media policy specified that its employees should not make statements that would damage the company, harm another person's reputation, or violate the company's policies. Employees who violated these rules were subject to discipline and could be fired.

The NLRB ruled that Costco's social media policy violated federal labor law, which protects employees' right to engage in "concerted activities." Employees can freely associate with each other and have conversations about common workplace issues without employer interference. This right extends to social media posts. Therefore, an employer cannot broadly prohibit its employees from criticizing the company or co-workers, supervisors, or managers via social media. ∎

Responsibility of Employees While most of the discussion in this chapter concerns the ethics of business management, employee ethics is also an important issue. For instance, is it ethical for employees to make negative posts in social media about other employees or, more commonly, about managers? After all, negative comments about managers reflect badly on those managers, who often are reluctant to respond via social media to such criticism. Disgruntled employees may exaggerate the negative qualities of managers whom they do not like.

---

2. *National Football League Management Council v. National Football League Players Association,* 820 F.3d 527 (2d Cir. 2016).

Some may consider the decision by the National Labor Relations Board outlined in *Example 6.4* to be too lenient toward employees and too stringent toward management. There is likely to be an ongoing debate about how to balance employees' right to free expression against employers' right to prevent the spreading of inaccurate negative statements across the Internet.

6-3 Ethical Principles and Philosophies

As Dean Krehmeyer, executive director of the Business Roundtable's Institute for Corporate Ethics, once said, "Evidence strongly suggests being ethical—doing the right thing—pays." Even if ethics "pays," though, instilling ethical business decision making into the fabric of a business organization is no small task.

How do business decision makers decide whether a given action is the "right" one for their firms? What ethical standards should be applied? Broadly speaking, **ethical reasoning**—the application of morals and ethics to a situation—applies to businesses just as it does to individuals. As businesses make decisions, they must analyze their alternatives in a variety of ways, one of which is the ethical implications of each alternative.

Generally, the study of ethics is divided into two major categories—duty-based ethics and outcome-based ethics. **Duty-based ethics** is rooted in the idea that every person has certain duties to others, including both humans and the planet. **Outcome-based ethics** focuses on the impacts of a decision on society or on key *stakeholders*.

6-3a Duty-Based Ethics

Duty-based ethics focuses on the obligations of the corporation. It deals with standards for behavior that traditionally were derived from revealed truths, religious authorities, or philosophical reasoning. These standards involve concepts of right and wrong, duties owed, and rights to be protected. Corporations today often describe these values or duties in their mission statements or strategic plans. Some companies base their statements on a nonreligious rationale, while others derive their values from religious doctrine.

Religious Ethical Principles Nearly every religion has principles or beliefs about how one should treat others. In the Judeo-Christian tradition, which is the

dominant religious tradition in the United States, the Ten Commandments of the Old Testament establish these fundamental rules for moral action. The principles of the Muslim faith are set out in the Qur'an, and Hindus find their principles in the four Vedas.

Religious rules generally are absolute with respect to the behavior of their adherents. ■ **EXAMPLE 6.5** The commandment "Thou shalt not steal" is an absolute mandate for a person who believes that the Ten Commandments reflect revealed truth. Even a benevolent motive for stealing (such as Robin Hood's) cannot justify the act because the act itself is inherently immoral and thus wrong. ■

For businesses, religious principles can be a unifying force for employees or a rallying point to increase employee motivation. They can also present problems, however, because different owners, suppliers, employees, and customers may have different religious backgrounds. Taking an action based on religious principles, especially when those principles address socially or politically controversial topics, can lead to negative publicity and even to protests or boycotts.

Principles of Rights Another view of duty-based ethics focuses on basic rights. The principle that human beings have certain fundamental rights (to life, freedom, and the pursuit of happiness, for example) is deeply embedded in Western culture.

Those who adhere to this **principle of rights,** or "rights theory," believe that a key factor in determining whether a business decision is ethical is how that decision affects the rights of others. These others include the firm's owners, its employees, the consumers of its products or services, its suppliers, the community in which it does business, and society as a whole.

Conflicting Rights. A potential dilemma for those who support rights theory is that they may disagree on which rights are most important. When considering all those affected by a business decision to downsize a firm, for example, how much weight should be given to employees relative to shareholders? Which employees should be laid off first—those with the highest salaries or those who have worked there for less time (and have less seniority)? How should the firm weigh the rights of customers relative to the community, or employees relative to society as a whole?

Resolving Conflicts. In general, rights theorists believe that whichever right is stronger in a particular circumstance takes precedence. ■ **EXAMPLE 6.6** Murray

Chemical Corporation has to decide whether to keep a chemical plant in Utah open, thereby saving the jobs of a hundred and fifty workers, or shut it down. Closing the plant will avoid contaminating a river with pollutants that might endanger the health of tens of thousands of people. In this situation, a rights theorist can easily choose which group to favor because the value of the right to health and well-being is obviously stronger than the basic right to work. Not all choices are so clear-cut, however. ■

Kantian Ethical Principles Duty-based ethical standards may also be derived solely from philosophical reasoning. The German philosopher Immanuel Kant (1724–1804) identified some general guiding principles for moral behavior based on what he thought to be the fundamental nature of human beings. Kant believed that human beings are qualitatively different from other physical objects and are endowed with moral integrity and the capacity to reason and conduct their affairs rationally.

People Are Not a Means to an End. Based on this view of human beings, Kant said that when people are treated merely as a means to an end, they are being treated as the equivalent of objects and are being denied their basic humanity. For instance, a manager who treats subordinates as mere profit-making tools is less likely to retain motivated and loyal employees than a manager who respects employees. Management research has shown that, in fact, employees who feel empowered to share their thoughts, opinions, and solutions to problems are happier and more productive.

Categorical Imperative. When a business makes unethical decisions, it often rationalizes its action by saying that the company is "just one small part" of the problem or that its decision has had "only a small impact." A central theme in Kantian ethics is that individuals should evaluate their actions in light of the consequences that would follow if everyone in society acted in the same way. This **categorical imperative** can be applied to any action.

■ **EXAMPLE 6.7** CHS Fertilizer is deciding whether to invest in expensive equipment that will decrease profits but will also reduce pollution from its factories. If CHS has adopted Kant's categorical imperative, the decision makers will consider the consequences if every company invested in the equipment (or if no company did so). If the result would make the world a better place (less polluted), CHS's decision would be clear. ■

6–3b Outcome-Based Ethics: Utilitarianism

In contrast to duty-based ethics, outcome-based ethics focuses on the consequences of an action, not on the nature of the action itself or on any set of preestablished moral values or religious beliefs. Outcome-based ethics looks at the impacts of a decision in an attempt to maximize benefits and minimize harms.

The premier philosophical theory for outcome-based decision making is **utilitarianism,** a philosophical theory developed by Jeremy Bentham (1748–1832) and modified by John Stuart Mill (1806–1873)—both British philosophers. "The greatest good for the greatest number" is a paraphrase of the major premise of the utilitarian approach to ethics.

Cost-Benefit Analysis Under a utilitarian model of ethics, an action is morally correct, or "right," when, among the people it affects, it produces the greatest amount of good for the greatest number or creates the least amount of harm for the fewest people. When an action affects the majority adversely, it is morally wrong. Applying the utilitarian theory thus requires the following steps:

1. A determination of which individuals will be affected by the action in question.
2. A **cost-benefit analysis,** which involves an assessment of the negative and positive effects of alternative actions on these individuals.
3. A choice among alternative actions that will produce maximum societal utility (the greatest positive net benefits for the greatest number of individuals).

Thus, if expanding a factory would provide hundreds of jobs but generate pollution that could endanger the lives of thousands of people, a utilitarian analysis would find that saving the lives of thousands creates greater good than providing jobs for hundreds.

Problems with the Utilitarian Approach There are problems with a strict utilitarian analysis. In some situations, an action that produces the greatest good for the most people may not seem to be the most ethical. ■ **EXAMPLE 6.8** Phazim Company is producing a drug that will cure a disease in 85 percent of patients, but the other 15 percent will experience agonizing side effects and a horrible, painful death. A quick utilitarian analysis would suggest that the drug should be produced and marketed because the majority of patients will benefit. Many people, however, have significant concerns about manufacturing a drug that will cause such harm to anyone. ■

6–3c Corporate Social Responsibility

In pairing duty-based concepts with outcome-based concepts, strategists and theorists developed the idea of the corporate citizen. **Corporate social responsibility (CSR)** combines a commitment to good citizenship with a commitment to making ethical decisions, improving society, and minimizing environmental impact.

CSR is a relatively new concept in the history of business, but a concept that becomes more important every year. Although CSR is not imposed on corporations by law, it does involve a commitment to self-regulation in a way that attends to the text and intent of the law as well as to ethical norms and global standards. A survey of U.S. executives undertaken by the Boston College Center for Corporate Citizenship found that more than 70 percent of those polled agreed that corporate citizenship must be treated as a priority. More than 60 percent said that good corporate citizenship added to their companies' profits.

CSR can be a successful strategy for companies, but corporate decision makers must not lose track of the two descriptors in the title: *corporate* and *social*. The company must link the responsibility of citizenship with the strategy and key principles of the business. Incorporating both the social and the corporate components of CSR and making ethical decisions can help companies grow and prosper. CSR is most successful when a company undertakes activities that are significant and related to its business operations.

The Social Aspects of CSR Because business controls so much of the wealth and power in this country, business has a responsibility to use that wealth and power in socially beneficial ways. Thus, the social aspect requires that corporations demonstrate that they are promoting goals that society deems worthwhile and are moving toward solutions to social problems. Companies may be judged on how much they donate to social causes, as well as how they conduct their operations with respect to employment discrimination, human rights, environmental concerns, and similar issues.

Some corporations publish annual social responsibility reports, which may also be called corporate sustainability (referring to the capacity to endure) or citizenship reports. ■ **EXAMPLE 6.9** The software company Symantec Corporation issues corporate responsibility reports to demonstrate its focus on critical environmental, social, and governance issues. In its 2014 report, Symantec pointed out that 88 percent of facilities it owns or leases on a long-term basis are certified as environmentally friendly by the LEED program. LEED stands for Leadership in Energy and Environmental Design. Certification requires the achievement of high standards for energy efficiency, material usage in construction, and other environmental qualities. ■

The Corporate Aspects of CSR Arguably, any socially responsible activity will benefit a corporation. A corporation may see an increase in goodwill from the local community for creating a park, for instance. A corporation that is viewed as a good citizen may see an increase in sales.

At times, the benefit may not be immediate. Constructing a new plant that meets the high LEED standards may cost more initially. Nevertheless, over the life of the building, the savings in maintenance and utilities may more than make up for the extra cost of construction.

Surveys of college students about to enter the job market confirm that young people are looking for socially responsible employers. Socially responsible activities may thus cost a corporation now, but may lead to more impressive and more committed employees. Corporations that engage in meaningful social activities retain workers longer, particularly younger ones.

■ **EXAMPLE 6.10** Pacific Gas and Electric (PG&E) in California sends its employees out on Earth Day to help clean and restore state parks. PG&E also provides free solar panels for new Habitat for Humanity homes and donates food to the needy. LinkedIn employees participate in an "InDay" every month to donate time and resources to the community. Zappos donates large amounts of its goods to charities and pays its employees for time off if they are volunteering. ■

Stakeholders One view of CSR stresses that corporations have a duty not just to shareholders, but also to other groups affected by corporate decisions—called **stakeholders.** The rationale for this "stakeholder view" is that, in some circumstances, one or more of these other groups may have a greater stake in company decisions than the shareholders do.

Under this approach, a corporation considers the impact of its decisions on its employees, customers, creditors, suppliers, and the community in which it operates. Stakeholders could also include advocacy groups such as environmental groups and animal rights groups. To avoid making a decision that may be perceived as unethical and result in negative publicity or protests, a corporation should consider the impact of its decision on the stakeholders.

The most difficult aspect of the stakeholder analysis is determining which group's interests should receive greater weight if the interests conflict. For instance, companies that are struggling financially sometimes lay off workers to reduce labor costs. But in recent years, some corporations have given greater weight to employees' interests and have found ways to avoid slashing their workforces. Companies finding alternatives to layoffs included Dell (extended unpaid holidays), Cisco Systems (four-day end-of-year shutdowns), Motorola (salary cuts), and Honda (voluntary unpaid vacation time).

6–4 Making Ethical Business Decisions

Even if officers, directors, and others in a company want to make ethical decisions, it is not always clear what is ethical in a given situation. Thinking beyond things that are easily measured, such as profits, can be challenging. Although profit projections are not always accurate, they are more objective than considering the personal impacts of decisions on employees, shareholders, customers, and the community. But this subjective component of decision making potentially has a great potential influence on a company's profits.

Companies once considered leaders in their industry, such as Enron and the worldwide accounting firm Arthur Andersen, were brought down by the unethical behavior of a few. A two-hundred-year-old British investment banking firm, Barings Bank, was destroyed by the actions of one employee and a few of his friends. Clearly, ensuring that all employees get on the ethical business decision-making "bandwagon" is crucial in today's fast-paced world.

Individuals entering the global corporate community, even in entry-level positions, must be prepared to make hard decisions. Sometimes, there is no "good" answer to the questions that arise. Therefore, it is important to have tools to help in the decision-making process and to create a framework for organizing those tools. Business decisions can be complex and may involve legal concerns, financial questions, possibly health and safety concerns, and ethical components.

6–4a A Systematic Approach

Organizing the ethical concerns and issues and approaching them systematically can help a businessperson eliminate various alternatives and identify the strengths and weaknesses of the remaining alternatives. Ethics consultant Leonard H. Bucklin of Corporate-Ethics.US™ has devised a procedure that he calls Business Process Pragmatism™. It involves five steps:

Step 1: Inquiry. First, the decision maker must understand the problem. This step involves identifying the parties involved (the stakeholders) and collecting the relevant facts. Once the ethical problem or problems are clarified, the decision maker lists any relevant legal and ethical principles that will guide the decision.

Step 2: Discussion. In this step, the decision maker lists possible actions. The ultimate goals for the decision are determined, and each option is evaluated using the laws and ethical principles listed in Step 1.

Step 3: Decision. In this step, those participating in the decision making work together to craft a consensus decision or consensus plan of action for the corporation.

Step 4: Justification. In this step, the decision maker articulates the reasons for the proposed action or series of actions. Generally, these reasons should come from the analysis done in Step 3. This step essentially results in documentation to be shared with stakeholders explaining why the proposal is an ethical solution to the problem.

Step 5: Evaluation. This final step occurs once the decision has been made and implemented. The solution should be analyzed to determine if it was effective. The results of this evaluation may be used in making future decisions.

6–4b The Importance of Ethical Leadership

Talking about ethical business decision making is meaningless if management does not set standards. Furthermore, managers must apply the same standards to themselves as they do to the company's employees. See this chapter's *Digital Update* feature for a discussion of an ethical dilemma that has arisen from the increased use of digital technology by employees after work hours.

Attitude of Top Management One of the most important ways to create and maintain an ethical

DIGITAL UPDATE   Should Employees Have a "Right of Disconnecting"?

Almost all jobs today involve digital technology, whether it be e-mail, Internet access, or smartphone use. Most employees, when interviewed, say that digital technology increases their productivity and flexibility.

The downside is what some call an "electronic leash"—meaning that employees are constantly connected and end up working when they are not "at work." Over one-third of full-time workers, for example, say that they frequently check e-mails outside normal working hours.

Do Workers Have the Right to Disconnect?

Because the boundaries between being "at work" and being "at leisure" can be so hazy, some labor unions in other countries have attempted to pass rules that allow employees to disconnect from e-mail and other work-related digital communication during nonworking hours. For instance, a French labor union representing high-tech workers signed an agreement with a large business association recognizing a "right of disconnecting." In Germany, Volkswagen and BMW no longer forward e-mail to staff from company servers after the end of the workday. Other German firms have declared that workers are not expected to check e-mail on weekends and holidays. The government is considering legislating such restrictions nationwide.

The Thorny Issue of Overtime and the Fair Labor Standards Act

Payment for overtime work is strictly regulated under the Fair Labor Standards Act (FLSA). According to the United States Supreme Court, in this context, *work* is "physical or mental exertion (whether burdensome or not) controlled or required by the employer and pursued necessarily for the benefit of the employer and his business."[a]

This definition was extended to off-duty work if such work is an "integral and indispensible part of [employees'] activities."[b]

Today's modern digital connectivity raises issues about the definition of *work*. Employees at several major companies, including Black & Decker, T-Mobile, and Verizon, have sued for unpaid overtime related to smartphone use. In another case, a police sergeant has sued the city of Chicago, claiming that he should have been paid overtime for hours spent using his personal digital assistant (PDA).[c] The police department issues PDAs to officers and requires them to respond to work-related text messages, e-mails, and voice mails not only while on duty, but also while off duty. Off-duty responses are not compensated by the city.

Not All Employees Demand the "Right to Disconnect"

According to a recent Gallup poll, 79 percent of full-time employees had either strongly positive or somewhat positive views of using computers, e-mail, tablets, and smartphones to work remotely outside of normal business hours. According to the same poll, 17 percent of them report "better overall lives" because of constant online connectivity with their work. Finally, working remotely after business hours apparently does not necessarily result in additional work-related stress.

Critical Thinking *From an ethical point of view, is there any difference between calling subordinates during off hours for work-related questions and sending them e-mails or text messages?*

a. *Tennessee Coal, Iron & R. Co. v. Muscoda Local No. 123*, 321 U.S. 590, 64 S.Ct. 698, 8 L.Ed. 949 (1944). Although Congress later passed a statute that superseded the holding in this case, the statute gave the courts broad authority to interpret the FLSA's definition of *work*. 29 U.S.C. Section 251(a). See *Integrity Staffing Solutions, Inc. v. Busk*, ___ U.S. ___, 135 S.Ct. 513, 190 L.Ed.2d 410 (2014).

b. *Steiner v. Mitchell*, 350 U.S. 247, 76 S.Ct. 330, 100 L.Ed. 267 (1956).

c. *Allen v. City of Chicago*, 2014 WL 5461856 (N.D.Ill. 2014).

workplace is for top management to demonstrate its commitment to ethical decision making. A manager who is not totally committed to an ethical workplace rarely succeeds in creating one. Management's behavior, more than anything else, sets the ethical tone of a firm. Employees take their cues from management.

Managers have found that discharging even one employee for ethical reasons has a tremendous impact as a deterrent to unethical behavior in the workplace. This is true even if the company has a written code of ethics. If management does not enforce the company code, the code is essentially nonexistent.

The administration of a university may have had a similar concept in mind in the following case when it applied the school's professionalism standard to a student who had engaged in serious misconduct.

Al-Dabagh v. Case Western Reserve University

United States Court of Appeals, Sixth Circuit, 777 F.3d 355 (2015).

Background and Facts The curriculum at Case Western Reserve University School of Medicine identifies nine "core competencies." At the top of the list is professionalism, which includes "ethical, honest, responsible and reliable behavior." The university's Committee on Students determines whether a student has met the professionalism requirements.

Amir Al-Dabagh enrolled at the school and did well academically. But he sexually harassed fellow students, often asked an instructor not to mark him late for class, received complaints from hospital staff about his demeanor, and was convicted of driving while intoxicated. The Committee on Students unanimously refused to certify him for graduation and dismissed him from the university.

He filed a suit in a federal district court against Case Western, alleging a breach of good faith and fair dealing. The court ordered the school to issue a diploma. Case Western appealed.

In the Language of the Court

SUTTON, Circuit Judge.

* * * *

* * * Case Western's student handbook * * * makes clear that the only thing standing between Al-Dabagh and a diploma is the Committee on Students' finding that he lacks professionalism. Unhappily for Al-Dabagh, that is an academic judgment. And *we can no more substitute our personal views for the Committee's when it comes to an academic judgment than the Committee can substitute its views for ours when it comes to a judicial decision.* [Emphasis added.]

* * * *

* * * *The Committee's professionalism determination is an academic judgment. That conclusion all but resolves this case. We may overturn the Committee only if it substantially departed from accepted academic norms when it refused to approve Al-Dabagh for graduation.* And given Al-Dabagh's track record—one member of the Committee does not recall encountering another student with Al-Dabagh's "repeated professionalism issues" in his quarter century of experience—we cannot see how it did. [Emphasis added.]

To the contrary, Al-Dabagh insists: The Committee's decision was a "punitive disciplinary measure" that had nothing to do with academics. * * * His argument fails to wrestle with the prominent place of professionalism in the university's academic curriculum—which itself is an academic decision courts may not lightly disturb.

Even if professionalism is an academic criterion, Al-Dabagh persists that the university defined it too broadly. As he sees it, the only professional lapses that matter are the ones linked to academic performance. That is not how we see it or for that matter how the medical school sees it. That many professionalism-related cases involve classroom incidents does not establish that only classroom incidents are relevant to the professionalism inquiry * * * . Our own standards indicate that professionalism does not end at the courtroom door. Why should hospitals operate any differently? As for the danger that an expansive view of professionalism might forgive, or provide a cloak for, arbitrary or discriminatory behavior, we see no such problem here. Nothing in the record suggests that the university had impermissible motives or acted in bad faith in this instance. And nothing in our deferential standard prevents us from invalidating genuinely objectionable actions when they occur.

Decision and Remedy *The U.S. Court of Appeals for the Sixth Circuit reversed the lower court's order to issue a diploma to Al-Dabagh. The federal appellate court found nothing to indicate that Case Western had "impermissible motives," acted in bad faith, or dealt unfairly with Al-Dabagh.*

Critical Thinking

• **What If the Facts Were Different?** *Suppose that Case Western had tolerated Al-Dabagh's conduct and awarded him a diploma. What impact might that had on other students at the school? Why?*

Behavior of Owners and Managers   Certain types of behavior on the part of managers and owners contribute to unethical behavior among employees. Managers who set unrealistic production or sales goals increase the probability that employees will act unethically. If a sales quota can be met only through high-pressure, unethical sales tactics, employees will try to act "in the best interest of the company" and will continue to behave unethically. A manager who looks the other way when she or he knows about an employee's unethical behavior also sets an example—one indicating that ethical transgressions will be accepted.

Business owners and managers sometimes take more active roles in fostering unethical and illegal conduct. This sort of misbehavior can have negative consequences for the owners and managers and their business. Not only can a court sanction them, but it can also issue an injunction that prevents them from engaging in similar patterns of conduct in the future.

■ **CASE IN POINT 6.11**   John Robert Johnson, Jr., took a truck that needed repair along with its fifteen-ton trailer to Bubba Shaffer, doing business as Shaffer's Auto and Diesel Repair, LLC. The truck was supposedly fixed, and Johnson paid the bill, but the truck continued to leak oil and water. Johnson returned the truck to Shaffer, who again claimed to have fixed the problem. Johnson paid the second bill. The problems with the truck continued, however, so Johnson returned the truck and trailer to Shaffer a third time.

Johnson was given a verbal estimate of $1,000 for the repairs, but Shaffer ultimately sent an invoice for $5,863. Johnson offered to settle for $2,480, the amount of the initial estimate ($1,000), plus the costs of parts and shipping. Shaffer refused the offer and would not return Johnson's truck or trailer until full payment was made. Shaffer retained possession for almost four years and also charged Johnson a storage fee of $50 a day and 18 percent interest on the $5,863. Johnson sued for unfair trade practices and won. The court awarded him $3,500 in damages plus attorneys' fees and awarded Shaffer $1,000 (the amount of his estimate).[3] ■

The following case further demonstrates the types of situations that can occur when management demonstrates a lack of concern about ethics.

---

3. *Johnson Construction Co. v. Shaffer*, 87 So.3d 203 (La.App. 2012).

Case Analysis 6.3

Moseley v. Pepco Energy Services, Inc.

United States District Court, District of New Jersey, 2011 WL 1584166 (2011).

In the Language of the Court
Joseph H. *RODRIGUEZ*, District Judge.

* * * Plaintiff Moseley is an employee of Defendant Pepco Energy Services, Inc. ("PES"). He has been employed by PES or its corporate predecessors for over twenty-five years. PES, a subsidiary of Defendant Pepco Holdings, Inc. ("PHI"), provides deregulated energy and energy-related services for residential, small business, and large commercial customers.
* * * *

In 1998, Thomas Herzog held the position of Vice President of CTS. * * * In or around 2002, CTS merged with Potomic Electric Power Company, Inc., and each company became a subsidiary of PHI. Following the merger, according to Plaintiff, he continued to work for PHI, still as Maintenance Manager at Midtown Thermal, until December 31, 2009.
* * * *

Following the 2002 merger with PHI, employees were required to complete an annual ethics survey. By March of 2007, Plaintiff and two co-workers had discussed their respective observations of Herzog's conduct, which they deemed questionable and possibly unethical. Specifically, they felt that Herzog improperly used company assets and improperly hired immediate family members and friends who did not appear on the payroll. The three decided to disclose this information on PHI's annual "Ethics Survey."

The three planned to reveal that Herzog employed his daughter, Laurie, as his secretary in the summer of 2005 and the beginning of 2006 without posting the position first and in violation of PHI's anti-nepotism policy.
* * * *

Next, Herzog hired his girlfriend's daughter as his secretary after his daughter had gone back to school. Plaintiff believed this was in violation of Company policy because the position again was not posted. Herzog also hired his son as a project manager, again through a third party independent contractor, Walter Ratai. Plaintiff thought this was wrong because (1) Herzog circumvented the Company's hiring process, (2) it violated Company policy, and (3) Herzog's son was being paid $75.00/hr, which was more than Plaintiff was making. * * *

In addition, Plaintiff had learned that Herzog was improperly using the Company's Eagles' tickets for personal use. Finally, Herzog had leased a new SUV with Company funds, but which was not approved by the Company.

* * * *

[After the surveys were completed, an] investigation ensued. Following the investigation, effective on or about May 10, 2007, Herzog was escorted out of the building. * * * On March 8, 2008, Plaintiff received his annual performance evaluation * * * ; for the first time in twenty-three years, Plaintiff's performance review was negative. Plaintiff feels that this negative performance review was a further act of retaliation for his disclosure of Herzog's conduct.

* * * *

On or about June 11, 2008 the Plant/Operations Manager position was posted * * * . Plaintiff applied for the position, but it was offered to [another person]. Plaintiff alleges that he "was not promoted to the position of Plant/Operations Manager despite his experience performing the job for the previous two and a half years, qualifications for same and seniority, as a direct and proximate result of his prior complaints and/or disclosures regarding the Herzog illegal conduct and activities."

* * * *

The New Jersey Legislature enacted the Conscientious Employee Protection Act (CEPA) to "protect and encourage employees to report illegal or unethical workplace activities." * * * CEPA prohibits a New Jersey employer from taking "retaliatory action" against an employee who objects to "any activity, policy or practice which the employee reasonably believes" is in violation of applicable law. * * * "To prevail on a claim under

this provision, a plaintiff must establish that: (1) he reasonably believed that [the complained-of] conduct was violating a law or rule or regulation promulgated pursuant to law; (2) he objected to the conduct; (3) an adverse employment action was taken against him; and (4) a causal connection exists between the whistleblowing activity and the adverse employment action.

* * * *

The first element of the prima facie case [a case sufficient to be sent to the jury] under CEPA is that the Plaintiff reasonably believed that the complained-of conduct (1) was violating a "law, rule, or regulation promulgated pursuant to law, including any violation involving deception of, or misrepresentation to, any shareholder, investor, client, patient, customer, employee, former employee, retiree or pensioner of the employer or any governmental entity"; or "(2) is fraudulent or criminal, including any activity, policy or practice of deception or misrepresentation which the employee reasonably believes may defraud any shareholder, investor, client, patient, customer, employee, former employee, retiree or pensioner of the employer or any governmental entity."

Although Defendants have argued that Plaintiff merely disclosed a violation of Company policy, Moseley has testified that in March 2007, he reported what he believed to be "unethical conduct, misappropriation of company funds, and theft" by his direct supervisor. * * * *Moreover, a plaintiff need not demonstrate that there was a violation of the law or fraud, but instead that he "reasonably believed" that to be the case.* The facts in this case support an objectively reasonable belief that a violation of law or

fraudulent conduct was being committed by Plaintiff's supervisor. [Emphasis added.]

Regarding the causal connection between Plaintiff's whistleblowing activity and the negative adverse employment actions taken against him, Plaintiff stresses that he was employed by the Defendants for twenty-five years without a negative employment evaluation or any form of discipline until immediately after he disclosed the wrongful conduct of his supervisor. Not only did Plaintiff then receive a negative performance evaluation, but the posted position of Plant Manager was given to [another], despite [the other's] alleged past negative history and despite that Plaintiff asserts he had been acting in that job for over two years. Plaintiff contends that this is sufficient evidence of pretext.

The Court is unable to find as a matter of law that Defendants' inferences prevail or that a jury could not reasonably adopt a contrary inference of retaliation. There are questions of fact as to how much the individuals responsible for Plaintiff's negative performance evaluations knew about Plaintiff's complaints. "[A] finding of the required causal connection may be based solely on circumstantial evidence that the person ultimately responsible for an adverse employment action was aware of an employee's whistle-blowing activity." Because jurors may infer a causal connection from the surrounding circumstances, as well as temporal proximity, the Court will not grant summary judgment. [Emphasis added.]

* * * *

IT IS ORDERED on this 26th day of April, 2011 that Defendants' motion for summary judgment is hereby DENIED.

Legal Reasoning Questions

1. Using duty-based ethical principles, what facts or circumstances in this case would lead Moseley to disclose Herzog's behavior?

2. Using outcome-based ethical principles, what issues would Moseley have to analyze in making the decision to report Herzog's behavior? What would be the risks to Moseley? The benefits?

3. Under the Business Process Pragmatism™ steps, what alternatives might Moseley have had in this situation?

The Sarbanes-Oxley Act Congress enacted the Sarbanes-Oxley Act[4] to help reduce corporate fraud and unethical management decisions. The act requires companies to set up confidential systems so that employees and others can "raise red flags" about suspected illegal or unethical auditing and accounting practices.

Some companies have implemented online reporting systems to accomplish this goal. In one such system, employees can click on an on-screen icon that anonymously links them with NAVEX Global, an organization based in Oregon. Through NAVEX Global, employees can report suspicious accounting practices, sexual harassment, and other possibly unethical behavior. NAVEX, in turn, alerts management personnel or the audit committee at the designated company to the possible problem.

6–5 Global Business Ethics

Just as different religions have different moral codes, different countries, regions, and even states have different ethical expectations and priorities. Some of these differences are based in religious values, whereas others are cultural in nature. Such differences make it even more difficult to determine what is ethical in a particular situation. For instance, in certain countries the consumption of alcohol is forbidden for religious reasons. It would be considered unethical for a U.S. business to produce alcohol in those countries and employ local workers to assist in alcohol production.

International transactions often involve issues related to employment and financing. Congress has addressed some of these issues, not eliminating the ethical components but clarifying some of the conflicts between the ethics of the United States and the ethics of other nations. For instance, the Civil Rights Act and the Foreign Corrupt Practices Act have clarified the U.S. ethical position on employment issues and bribery in foreign nations. (Other nations, including Mexico, have also enacted laws that prohibit bribery.)

6–5a Monitoring the Employment Practices of Foreign Suppliers

Many businesses contract with companies in developing nations to produce goods, such as shoes and clothing, because the wage rates in those nations are significantly lower than those in the United States. But what if one of those contractors hires women and children at below-minimum-wage rates or requires its employees to work long hours in a workplace full of health hazards? What if the company's supervisors routinely engage in workplace conduct that is offensive to women? What if plants located abroad routinely violate labor and environmental standards?

■ **EXAMPLE 6.12** Pegatron Corporation, a company based in China, manufactures and supplies parts to Apple, Inc., for iPads and other Apple products. After an explosion at a Pegatron factory in Shanghai, allegations surfaced that the conditions at the factory violated labor and environmental standards. Similar allegations were made about other Apple suppliers.

Apple started to evaluate practices at companies in its supply chain and to communicate its ethics policies to them. Its audits revealed numerous violations. Apple released a list of its suppliers for the first time and issued a lengthy "Supplier Responsibility Report" detailing supplier practices. Numerous facilities had withheld worker pay as a disciplinary measure. Some had falsified pay records and forced workers to use machines without safeguards. Others had engaged in unsafe environmental practices, such as dumping wastewater on neighboring farms. Apple terminated its relationship with one supplier and turned over its findings to the Fair Labor Association for further inquiry. ■

Given today's global communications network, few companies can assume that their actions in other nations will go unnoticed by "corporate watch" groups that discover and publicize unethical corporate behavior. As a result, U.S. businesses today usually take steps to avoid such adverse publicity—either by refusing to deal with certain suppliers or by arranging to monitor their suppliers' workplaces to make sure that the employees are not being mistreated.

6–5b The Foreign Corrupt Practices Act

Another ethical problem in international business dealings has to do with the legitimacy of certain side payments to government officials. In the United States, the majority of contracts are formed within the private sector. In many foreign countries, however, government officials make the decisions on most major construction and manufacturing contracts because of extensive government regulation and control over trade and industry.

Side payments to government officials in exchange for favorable business contracts are not unusual in such countries, nor have they been considered unethical. In the past, U.S. corporations doing business in these nations largely followed the dictum "When in Rome, do as the Romans do."

In the 1970s, however, the U.S. media uncovered a number of business scandals involving large side

---

4. 15 U.S.C. Sections 7201 *et seq.*

payments by U.S. corporations to foreign representatives for the purpose of securing advantageous international trade contracts. In response to this unethical behavior, Congress passed the Foreign Corrupt Practices Act[5] (FCPA), which prohibits U.S. businesspersons from bribing foreign officials to secure beneficial contracts.

Prohibition against the Bribery of Foreign Officials

The first part of the FCPA applies to all U.S. companies and their directors, officers, shareholders, employees, and agents. This part prohibits the bribery of most officials of foreign governments if the purpose of the payment is to motivate the official to act in his or her official capacity to provide business opportunities.

The FCPA does not prohibit payments made to minor officials whose duties are ministerial. A ministerial action is a routine activity, such as the processing of paperwork, with little or no discretion involved in the action. These payments are often referred to as "grease," or facilitating payments. They are meant to accelerate the performance of administrative services that might otherwise be carried out at a slow pace. Thus, for instance, if a firm makes a payment to a minor official to speed up an import licensing process, the firm has not violated the FCPA.

Generally, the act, as amended, permits payments to foreign officials if such payments are lawful within the foreign country. Payments to private foreign companies or other third parties are permissible—unless the U.S. firm knows that the payments will be passed on to a foreign government in violation of the FCPA. The U.S. Department of Justice also uses the FCPA to prosecute foreign companies suspected of bribing officials outside the United States.

Accounting Requirements

In the past, bribes were often concealed in corporate financial records. Thus, the second part of the FCPA is directed toward accountants.

All companies must keep detailed records that "accurately and fairly" reflect their financial activities. Their accounting systems must provide "reasonable assurance" that all transactions entered into by the companies are accounted for and legal. These requirements assist in detecting illegal bribes. The FCPA prohibits any person from making false statements to accountants or false entries in any record or account.

■ **CASE IN POINT 6.13**   Noble Corporation, an international provider of offshore drilling services and equipment, was operating some drilling rigs offshore in Nigeria. Mark Jackson and James Ruehlen were officers at Noble. The U.S. government accused Noble of bribing Nigerian government officials and charged Jackson and Ruehlen individually with violating the FCPA's accounting provisions. Jackson and Ruehlen allegedly assisted in the bribery because they repeatedly allowed allegedly illegal payments to be posted on Noble's books as legitimate operating expenses.[6] ■

Penalties for Violations

The FCPA provides that business firms that violate the act may be fined up to $2 million. Individual officers or directors who violate the FCPA may be fined up to $100,000 (the fine cannot be paid by the company) and may be imprisoned for up to five years. These statutory amounts can be significantly increased under the Alternative Fines Act[7] (up to twice the amount of any gain that the defendant obtained by making the corrupt payment).

Today, the U.S. government is actively seeking out violators and has around 150 FCPA investigations going on at any given time. In recent years, a high percentage of the total fines imposed by the Department of Justice have come from FCPA cases.

---

5. 15 U.S.C. Sections 78dd-1 *et seq.*

6. *S.E.C. v. Jackson*, 908 F.Supp.2d 834 (S.D.Tex.—Houston Div. 2012).
7. 18 U.S.C. Section 3571.

Reviewing: Business Ethics

James Stilton is the chief executive officer (CEO) of RightLiving, Inc., a company that buys life insurance policies at a discount from terminally ill persons and sells the policies to investors. RightLiving pays the terminally ill patients a percentage of the future death benefit (usually 65 percent) and then sells the policies to investors for 85 percent of the value of the future benefit. The patients receive the cash to use for medical and other expenses. The investors are "guaranteed" a positive return on their investment, and RightLiving profits on the difference between the purchase and sale prices. Stilton is aware that some sick patients might obtain insurance policies through fraud (by not revealing the illness on the insurance application). Insurance companies that discover this will cancel the policy and refuse to pay.

Continues

Stilton believes that most of the policies he has purchased are legitimate, but he knows that some probably are not. Using the information presented in this chapter, answer the following questions.

1. Would a person who adheres to the principle of rights consider it ethical for Stilton not to disclose the potential risk of cancellation to investors? Why or why not?
2. Using Immanuel Kant's categorical imperative, are the actions of RightLiving, Inc., ethical? Why or why not?
3. Under utilitarianism, are Stilton's actions ethical? Why or why not? What difference does it make if most of the policies are legitimate?
4. Using the Business Process Pragmatism™ steps discussed in this chapter, discuss the decision process Stilton should use in deciding whether to disclose the risk of fraudulent policies to potential investors.

> **Debate This** . . . *Executives in large corporations are ultimately rewarded if their companies do well, particularly as evidenced by rising stock prices. Consequently, should we let those who run corporations decide what level of negative side effects of their goods or services is "acceptable"?*

Terms and Concepts

business ethics 113
categorical imperative 119
corporate social responsibility (CSR) 120
cost-benefit analysis 119

duty-based ethics 118
ethical reasoning 118
ethics 113
moral minimum 115
outcome-based ethics 118

principle of rights 118
stakeholders 120
triple bottom line 113
utilitarianism 119

Issue Spotters

1. Acme Corporation decides to respond to what it sees as a moral obligation to correct for past discrimination by adjusting pay differences among its employees. Does this raise an ethical conflict between Acme and its employees? Between Acme and its shareholders? Explain your answers. (See *Making Ethical Business Decisions*.)

2. Delta Tools, Inc., markets a product that under some circumstances is capable of seriously injuring consumers. Does Delta have an ethical duty to remove this product from the market, even if the injuries result only from misuse? Why or why not? (See *Making Ethical Business Decisions*.)

• **Check your answers to the Issue Spotters against the answers provided in Appendix B at the end of this text.**

Business Scenarios

6–1. Business Ethics. Jason Trevor owns a commercial bakery in Blakely, Georgia, that produces a variety of goods sold in grocery stores. Trevor is required by law to perform internal tests on food produced at his plant to check for contamination. On three occasions, the tests of food products containing peanut butter were positive for salmonella contamination. Trevor was not required to report the results to U.S. Food and Drug Administration officials, however, so he did not. Instead, Trevor instructed his employees to simply repeat the tests until the results were negative. Meanwhile, the products that had originally tested positive for salmonella were eventually shipped out to retailers.

Five people who ate Trevor's baked goods that year became seriously ill, and one person died from a salmonella infection. Even though Trevor's conduct was legal, was it unethical for him to sell goods that had once tested positive for salmonella? Why or why not? (See *Business Ethics*.)

Business Case Problems

6–2. Spotlight on Pfizer, Inc.—Corporate Social Responsibility. Methamphetamine (meth) is an addictive drug made chiefly in small toxic labs (STLs) in homes, tents, barns, or hotel rooms. The manufacturing process is dangerous and often results in explosions, burns, and toxic fumes. Government entities spend time and resources to find and destroy STLs, imprison meth dealers and users, treat addicts, and provide services for affected families. Meth cannot be made without ingredients that are also used in cold and allergy medications. Arkansas has one of the highest numbers of STLs in the United States. To recoup the costs of fighting the meth epidemic, twenty counties in Arkansas filed a suit against Pfizer, Inc., which makes cold and allergy medications. What is Pfizer's ethical responsibility here, and to whom is it owed? Why? [*Ashley County, Arkansas v. Pfizer, Inc.,* 552 F.3d. 659 (8th Cir. 2009)] (See *Ethical Principles and Philosophies.*)

6–3. Business Case Problem with Sample Answer— Online Privacy. Facebook, Inc., launched a program called 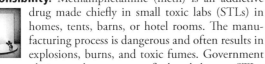 "Beacon" that automatically updated the profiles of users on Facebook's social networking site when those users had any activity on Beacon "partner" sites. For example, one partner site was Blockbuster.com. When a user rented or purchased a movie through Blockbuster.com, the user's Facebook profile would be updated to share the purchase. The Beacon program was set up as a default setting, so users never consented to the program, but they could opt out. What are the ethical implications of an opt-in program versus an opt-out program in social media? [*Lane v. Facebook, Inc.,* 696 F.3d 811 (9th Cir. 2011)] (See *Business Ethics and Social Media.*)

• **For a sample answer to Problem 6–3, go to Appendix C at the end of this text.**

6–4. Business Ethics on a Global Scale. After the fall of the Soviet Union, the new government of Azerbaijan began converting certain state-controlled industries to private ownership. Ownership in these companies could be purchased through a voucher program. Frederic Bourke, Jr., and Viktor Kozeny wanted to purchase the Azerbaijani oil company, SOCAR, but it was unclear whether the Azerbaijani president would allow SOCAR to be put up for sale. Kozeny met with one of the vice presidents of SOCAR (who was also the son of the president of Azerbaijan) and other Azerbaijani leaders to discuss the sale of SOCAR. To obtain their cooperation, Kozeny set up a series of parent and subsidiary companies through which the Azerbaijani leaders would eventually receive two-thirds of the SOCAR profits without ever investing any of their own funds. In return, the Azerbaijani leaders would attempt to use their influence to convince the president to put SOCAR up for sale. Assume that Bourke and Kozeny are operating out of a U.S. company. Discuss the ethics of this scheme, both in terms of the Foreign Corrupt Practices Act (FCPA) and as a general ethical issue. What duties did Kozeny have under the FCPA? [*United States v. Kozeny,* 667 F.3d 122 (2d Cir. 2011)] (See *Making Ethical Business Decisions.*)

6–5. Business Ethics. Mark Ramun worked as a manager for Allied Erecting and Dismantling Co., where he had a tense relationship with his father, who was Allied's president. After more than ten years, Mark left Allied, taking 15,000 pages of Allied's documents on DVDs and CDs, which constituted trade secrets. Later, he joined Genesis Equipment & Manufacturing, Inc., a competitor. Genesis soon developed a piece of equipment that incorporated elements of Allied equipment. How might business ethics have been violated in these circumstances? Discuss. [*Allied Erecting and Dismantling Co. v. Genesis Equipment & Manufacturing, Inc.,* 511 Fed.Appx. 398 (6th Cir. 2013)] (See *Business Ethics.*)

6–6. Business Ethics. Stephen Glass made himself infamous as a dishonest journalist by fabricating material for more than forty articles for *The New Republic* magazine and other publications. He also fabricated supporting materials to delude *The New Republic*'s fact checkers. At the time, he was a law student at Georgetown University. Once suspicions were aroused, Glass tried to avoid detection. Later, Glass applied for admission to the California bar. The California Supreme Court denied his application, citing "numerous instances of dishonesty and disingenuousness" during his "rehabilitation" following the exposure of his misdeeds. How do these circumstances underscore the importance of ethics? Discuss. [*In re Glass,* 58 Cal.4th 500, 316 P.3d 1199 (2014)] (See *Business Ethics.*)

6–7. Business Ethics. Operating out of an apartment in Secane, Pennsylvania, Hratch Ilanjian convinced Vicken Setrakian, the president of Kenset Corp., that he was an international businessman who could help Kenset turn around its business in the Middle East. At Ilanjian's insistence, Setrakian provided confidential business documents. Claiming that they had an agreement, Ilanjian demanded full, immediate payment and threatened to disclose the confidential information to a Kenset supplier if payment was not forthcoming. Kenset denied that they had a contract and filed a suit in a federal district court against Ilanjian, seeking return of the documents. During discovery, Ilanjian was uncooperative. Who behaved unethically in these circumstances? Explain. [*Kenset Corp. v. Ilanjian,* 600 Fed.Appx. 827 (3rd Cir. 2015)] (See *Business Ethics.*)

6–8. Business Ethics. Priscilla Dickman worked as a medical technologist at the University of Connecticut Health Center. Dickman's supervisor received complaints that she was getting nonbusiness-related phone calls and was absent from her work area when she should have been working. Based on e-mails and other documents found on Dickman's work computer, the state investigated her for violations of state law. She was convicted of conducting "personal business for financial gain on state time utilizing state resources." Separate criminal investigations resulted in convictions for forgery and filing an unrelated fraudulent insurance claim. She "retired" from her job and filed a claim with the state of Connecticut against the health center, alleging that her former employer had initiated the investigations to harass her and force her to quit. For lack of "credible evidence or legal support," the claim was dismissed. Which of these acts, if any, were unethical? Why? [*Dickman v. University of Connecticut Health Center,* 162 Conn.App. 441, 132 A.3d 739 (2016)] (See *Business Ethics.*)

6–9. A Question of Ethics—Consumer Rights. *Best Buy,* *a national electronics retailer, offered a credit card that allowed users to earn "reward points" that could be redeemed for discounts on Best Buy goods. After reading a newspaper advertisement for the card, Gary Davis applied for, and was given, a credit card. As part of the application process, he visited a Web page containing Frequently Asked Questions as well as terms and conditions for the card. He clicked on a button affirming that he understood the terms and conditions. When Davis received his card, it came with seven brochures about the card and the reward point program. As he read the brochures, he discovered that a $59 annual fee would be charged for the card. Davis went back to the Web pages he had*

visited and found a statement that the card "may" have an annual fee. Davis sued, claiming that the company did not adequately disclose the fee. [Davis v. HSBC Bank Nevada, N.A., *691 F.3d 1152 (9th Cir. 2012)]* (See *Business Ethics.*)

(a) Online applications frequently have click-on buttons or check boxes for consumers to acknowledge that they have read and understand the terms and conditions of applications or purchases. Often, the terms and conditions are so long that they cannot all be seen on one screen and users must scroll to view the entire document. Is it unethical for companies to put terms and conditions, especially terms that may cost the consumer, in an electronic document that is too long to read on one screen? Why or why not? Does this differ from having a consumer sign a hard-copy document with terms and conditions printed on it? Why or why not?

(b) The Truth-in-Lending Act requires that credit terms be clearly and conspicuously disclosed in application materials. Assuming that the Best Buy credit-card materials had sufficient legal disclosures, discuss the ethical aspects of businesses strictly following the language of the law as opposed to following the intent of the law.

Legal Reasoning Group Activity

6–10. Global Business Ethics. Pfizer, Inc., developed a new antibiotic called Trovan (trovafloxacinmesylate). Tests showed that in animals Trovan had life-threatening side effects, including joint disease, abnormal cartilage growth, liver damage, and a degenerative bone condition. Several years later, an epidemic of bacterial meningitis swept across Nigeria. Pfizer sent three U.S. physicians to test Trovan on children who were patients in Nigeria's Infectious Disease Hospital. Pfizer did not obtain the patients' consent, alert them to the risks, or tell them that Médecins Sans Frontières (Doctors without Borders) was providing an effective conventional treatment at the same site. Eleven children died in the experiment, and others were left blind, deaf, paralyzed, or brain damaged. Rabi

Abdullahi and other Nigerian children filed a suit in a U.S. federal court against Pfizer, alleging a violation of a customary international law norm prohibiting involuntary medical experimentation on humans. (See *Global Business Ethics.*)

(a) One group should use the principles of ethical reasoning discussed in this chapter to develop three arguments that Pfizer's conduct was a violation of ethical standards.

(b) A second group should take a pro-Pfizer position and argue that the company did not violate any ethical standards (and counter the first group).

(c) A third group should come up with proposals for what Pfizer might have done differently to avert the consequences.

Contracts

AN ACCELERATED COURSE · MILLER

CHAPTER 7

Nature and Terminology

Contract law deals with, among other things, the formation and keeping of promises. A **promise** is a declaration by a person (the *promisor*) to do or not to do a certain act. As a result, the person to whom the promise is made (the *promisee*) has a right to expect or demand that something either will or will not happen in the future.

Like other types of law, contract law reflects our social values, interests, and expectations at a given point in time. It shows, for instance, to what extent our society allows people to make promises or commitments that are legally binding. It distinguishes between promises that create only *moral* obligations (such as a promise to take a friend to lunch) and promises that are legally binding (such as a promise to pay for items ordered online).

Contract law also demonstrates which excuses our society accepts for breaking certain types of promises.

In addition, it indicates which promises are considered to be contrary to public policy—against the interests of society as a whole—and therefore legally invalid. When the person making a promise is a child or is mentally incompetent, for instance, a question will arise as to whether the promise should be enforced. Resolving such questions is the essence of contract law.

7–1 An Overview of Contract Law

Before we look at the numerous rules that courts use to determine whether a particular promise will be enforced, it is necessary to understand some fundamental concepts of contract law. In this section, we describe the sources and general function of contract law and introduce the objective theory of contracts.

7–1a Sources of Contract Law

The common law governs all contracts except when it has been modified or replaced by statutory law, such as the Uniform Commercial Code (UCC), or by administrative agency regulations. Contracts relating to services, real estate, employment, and insurance, for instance, generally are governed by the common law of contracts.

Contracts for the sale and lease of goods, however, are governed by the UCC—to the extent that the UCC has modified general contract law. In the discussion of general contract law that follows, we indicate in footnotes the areas in which the UCC has significantly altered common law contract principles.

7–1b The Function of Contract Law

No aspect of modern life is entirely free of contractual relationships. You acquire rights and obligations, for example, when you borrow funds, buy or lease a house, obtain insurance, and purchase goods or services. Contract law is designed to provide stability and predictability, as well as certainty, for both buyers and sellers in the marketplace.

Contract law assures the parties to private agreements that the promises they make will be enforceable. Clearly, many promises are kept because the parties involved feel a moral obligation to keep them or because keeping a promise is in their mutual self-interest. The **promisor** (the person making the promise) and the **promisee** (the person to whom the promise is made) may also decide to honor their agreement for other reasons. In business agreements, the rules of contract law are often followed to avoid potential disputes.

By supplying procedures for enforcing private contractual agreements, contract law provides an essential condition for the existence of a market economy. Without a legal framework of reasonably assured expectations within which to make long-run plans, businesspersons would be able to rely only on the good faith of others.

Duty and good faith are usually sufficient to obtain compliance with a promise. When price changes or adverse economic factors make contract compliance costly, however, these elements may not be enough. Contract law is necessary to ensure compliance with a promise or to entitle the innocent party to some form of relief.

7–1c The Definition of a Contract

A **contract** is "a promise or a set of promises for the breach of which the law gives a remedy, or the performance of which the law in some way recognizes as a duty."[1] Put simply, a contract is an agreement that can be enforced in court. It is formed by two or more parties who agree to perform or to refrain from performing some act now or in the future.

Generally, contract disputes arise when there is a promise of future performance. If the contractual promise is not fulfilled, the party who made it is subject to the sanctions of a court. That party may be required to pay damages for failing to perform the contractual promise. In a few instances, the party may be required to perform the promised act.

7–1d The Objective Theory of Contracts

In determining whether a contract has been formed, the element of intent is of prime importance. In contract law, intent is determined by what is called the **objective theory of contracts,** not by the personal or subjective intent, or belief, of a party.

The theory is that a party's intention to enter into a legally binding agreement, or contract, is judged by outward, objective facts. The facts are as interpreted by a *reasonable* person, rather than by the party's own secret, subjective intentions. Objective facts may include:

1. What the party said when entering into the contract.
2. How the party acted or appeared (intent may be manifested by conduct as well as by oral or written words).
3. The circumstances surrounding the transaction.

■ **CASE IN POINT 7.1** Pan Handle Realty, LLC, built a luxury home in Westport, Connecticut. Robert Olins signed a lease for the property and gave Pan Handle a check for the amount of the annual rent—$138,000. Olins planned to move into the home on January 28, but on January 27, Olins's bank informed Pan Handle that payment had been stopped on the rental check. Olins then told Pan Handle that he was "unable to pursue any further interest in the property."

When Pan Handle was not able to find a new tenant, it filed a lawsuit in a Connecticut state court against Olins, alleging that he had breached the lease. Olins argued that when he signed the lease, he did not intend to be bound by it. The court ruled in Pan Handle's favor and awarded $138,000 in damages, plus $8,000 for utilities, interest, and attorneys' fees. The decision was affirmed on appeal. The objective fact, as supported by the evidence, was that the parties intended to be bound by the lease when they signed it. The fact that Olins had a change of heart after signing the contract was irrelevant.[2] ■

7–2 Elements of a Contract

The many topics that will be discussed in the following chapters on contract law require an understanding of the basic elements of a valid contract and the way in which a contract is created. It is also necessary to understand the types of circumstances in which even legally valid contracts will not be enforced.

7–2a Requirements of a Valid Contract

The following list briefly describes the four requirements that must be met before a valid contract exists. If any of these elements is lacking, no contract will have been formed. (Each requirement will be explained more fully in subsequent chapters.)

1. *Agreement.* An agreement to form a contract includes an *offer* and an *acceptance.* One party must offer to enter into a legal agreement, and another party must accept the terms of the offer.
2. *Consideration.* Any promises made by the parties to the contract must be supported by legally sufficient and bargained-for *consideration* (something of value received or promised, such as money, to convince a person to make a deal).
3. *Contractual capacity.* Both parties entering into the contract must have the contractual *capacity* to do so. The law must recognize them as possessing characteristics that qualify them as competent parties.
4. *Legality.* The contract's purpose must be to accomplish some goal that is legal and not against public policy.

---

1. *Restatement (Second) of Contracts,* Section 1. *Restatements of the Law* are scholarly books that restate the existing common law principles distilled from court opinions as sets of rules on particular topics. Courts often refer to the *Restatements* for guidance. The *Restatement* dealing with contracts will be referred to throughout the material on contract law. *Second* in the title indicates that this *Restatement* is in its second edition. A third edition is being drafted.

2. *Pan Handle Realty, LLC v. Olins,* 140 Conn.App. 556, 59 A.3d 842 (2013).

An agreement to form a contract can modify the terms of a previous contract. When a dispute concerns whether this occurred, the offer and acceptance of both agreements can be reviewed to determine their effect. As in every case involving a contract, the parties' *subjective* beliefs with respect to the terms are irrelevant, particularly in the absence of any evidence to support those beliefs. At issue in the following case was the effect of an offer and acceptance on a previous agreement between a university and an associate professor.

Case Analysis 7.1

Weston v. Cornell University

New York Supreme Court, Appellate Division, Third Department, 136 A.D.3d 1094, 24 N.Y.S.3d 448 (2016).

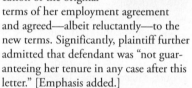

In the Language of the Court

ROSE, J. [Judge]
* * * *

Defendant [Cornell University in Ithaca, New York] appointed plaintiff [Leslie Weston] to an associate professorship in 1998 for an initial term of five years. The 1998 offer letter described the position as being "with tenure," but it stated that, although no problems were anticipated, the offer of tenure would have to be confirmed by defendant's review process shortly after plaintiff's arrival on campus. For a variety of reasons, plaintiff delayed her tenure submission for five years and, when she finally submitted it, she was not awarded tenure. In 2003, defendant gave plaintiff a two-year extension of her appointment, this time as an "associate professor without tenure," to allow her an opportunity to improve and resubmit her tenure package. Plaintiff resubmitted her request for tenure in 2005, but it was again denied, resulting in her eventual termination. Plaintiff then commenced this action [in a New York state court] seeking * * * to recover for breach of contract. * * * Following the completion of discovery, defendant moved for summary judgment dismissing the complaint * * * . The Supreme Court [a New York state trial court] denied that portion of the motion seeking dismissal of the breach of contract claim. Defendant now appeals.

Contrary to defendant's argument, Supreme Court properly found that issues of fact exist as to whether defendant's 1998 offer letter reflects an intent to assure plaintiff that she would be granted tenure. * * * The terms of the letter are ambiguous. Accordingly, Supreme Court properly relied upon extrinsic evidence to determine the parties' intent.[a] Based upon the affidavit of the then-chair of defendant's department who hired plaintiff and wrote the 1998 offer letter, as well as correspondence from the dean and associate dean of the college in which plaintiff's department was located, Supreme Court appropriately declined to award summary judgment to defendant with respect to the 1998 offer of tenure.

However, we must agree with defendant's alternative argument that the terms of its original offer were materially modified by plaintiff's acceptance of its 2003 offer to extend her appointment. *Defendant's 2003 letter offering to extend her appointment unambiguously replaced the "with tenure" language contained in the 1998 offer letter by restating her job title as "associate professor without tenure."* Defendant also points to plaintiff's deposition testimony, in which she explicitly acknowledged that she

---

a. *Extrinsic evidence*, which is evidence outside the contract itself, will be discussed later in this chapter.

understood the 2003 letter to be a modification of the original terms of her employment agreement and agreed—albeit reluctantly—to the new terms. Significantly, plaintiff further admitted that defendant was "not guaranteeing her tenure in any case after this letter." [Emphasis added.]

In response to this *prima facie* showing by defendant, plaintiff contends that, regardless of what she agreed to in 2003, her oft-repeated assertions of her belief that defendant still owed her tenure based upon the original letter suffice to preclude summary judgment. Aside from plaintiff's own opinions on the matter, however, there is nothing in the record to indicate that any alleged guarantee of tenure remained beyond the date of the 2003 letter. Accordingly, we find that plaintiff's subjective beliefs and unsupported arguments regarding the 2003 modification of her employment agreement are insufficient to raise triable issues of fact to defeat defendant's motion for summary judgment dismissing the breach of contract cause of action.

ORDERED that the order is modified * * * by reversing so much thereof as partially denied defendant's motion for summary judgment; said motion granted in its entirety and breach of contract cause of action dismissed.

Legal Reasoning Questions

1. What did the plaintiff seek in this action? What was the legal ground for her claim? What was her principal contention regarding the offers and acceptances at the center of this case?

2. Why did the trial court deny the defendant's motion for summary judgment to dismiss the plaintiff's claim?

3. Why did the appellate court modify the trial court's denial of the defendant's motion?

7–2b Defenses to the Enforceability of a Contract

Even if all of the requirements listed above are satisfied, a contract may be unenforceable if the following requirements are not met. These requirements typically are raised as *defenses* to the enforceability of an otherwise valid contract.

1. *Voluntary consent.* The consent of both parties must be voluntary. For instance, if a contract was formed as a result of fraud, undue influence, mistake, or duress, the contract may not be enforceable.
2. *Form.* The contract must be in whatever form the law requires. Some contracts must be in writing to be enforceable.

7–3 Types of Contracts

There are many types of contracts. They are categorized based on legal distinctions as to their formation, performance, and enforceability.

7–3a Contract Formation

Contracts can be classified according to how and when they are formed. Exhibit 7–1 shows three such classifications, and the following subsections explain them in greater detail.

Bilateral versus Unilateral Contracts Every contract involves at least two parties. The **offeror** is the party making the offer. The **offeree** is the party to whom the offer is made. Whether the contract is classified as *bilateral* or *unilateral* depends on what the offeree must do to accept the offer and bind the offeror to a contract.

Bilateral Contracts. If the offeree can accept simply by promising to perform, the contract is a **bilateral contract.** Hence, a bilateral contract is a "promise for a promise." No performance, such as payment of funds or delivery of goods, need take place for a bilateral contract to be formed. The contract comes into existence at the moment the promises are exchanged.

■ **EXAMPLE 7.2** Jacob offers to buy Ann's smartphone for $200. Jacob tells Ann that he will give her the $200 for the smartphone next Friday, when he gets paid. Ann accepts Jacob's offer and promises to give him the smartphone when he pays her on Friday. Jacob and Ann have formed a bilateral contract. ■

Unilateral Contracts. If the offer is phrased so that the offeree can accept the offer only by completing the contract performance, the contract is a **unilateral contract.** Hence, a unilateral contract is a "promise for an act." In other words, a unilateral contract is formed not at the moment when promises are exchanged but at the moment when the contract is *performed.*

■ **EXAMPLE 7.3** Reese says to Celia, "If you drive my car from New York to Los Angeles, I'll give you $1,000." Only on Celia's completion of the act—bringing the car to Los Angeles—does she fully accept Reese's offer to pay $1,000. If she chooses not to accept the offer to drive the car to Los Angeles, there are no legal consequences. ■

Contests, Lotteries, and Prizes. Contests, lotteries, and other competitions involving prizes are examples of offers

EXHIBIT 7–1   Classifications Based on Contract Formation

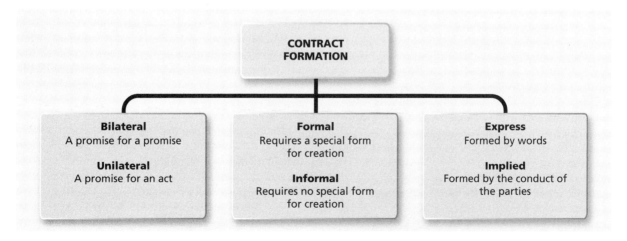

to form unilateral contracts. If a person complies with the rules of the contest—such as by submitting the right lottery number at the right place and time—a unilateral contract is formed. The organization offering the prize is then bound to a contract to perform as promised in the offer. If the person fails to comply with the contest rules, however, no binding contract is formed.

■ **CASE IN POINT 7.4** John Rogalski entered a poker tournament sponsored by Little Poker League (LPL) that lasted several months. During the final event, all contestants signed an agreement that said LPL would pay the tournament winner's entry fee and travel expenses to the World Series of Poker (WSOP). The agreement also stated that if the winner did not attend the WSOP, he or she would relinquish the WSOP seat and return the expense money to LPL.

Rogalski won and accepted $2,500 for travel-related expenses from the sponsor, but he did not attend the WSOP. He then filed a suit for $10,000 against LPL, arguing that it had advertised that the winner could choose to receive the cash value of the prizes ($12,500) instead of going to the WSOP. Rogalski claimed that he had accepted LPL's offer by participating in the tournament. The court rejected this argument and found in favor of LPL. The contract was formed when Rogalski signed the WSOP agreement. Under the contest rules as stated in that agreement, Rogalski had to return the $2,500 to LPL.[3] ■

Revocation of Offers for Unilateral Contracts. A problem arises in unilateral contracts when the promisor attempts to *revoke* (cancel) the offer after the promisee has begun performance but before the act has been completed. ■ **EXAMPLE 7.5** Seiko offers to buy Jin's sailboat, moored in San Francisco, on delivery of the boat to Seiko's dock in Newport Beach, three hundred miles south of San Francisco. Jin rigs the boat and sets sail. Shortly before his arrival at Newport Beach, Jin receives a message from Seiko withdrawing her offer. Has the offer been terminated? ■

In contract law, offers are normally *revocable* (capable of being taken back, or canceled) until accepted. Thus, under the traditional view of unilateral contracts, Seiko's revocation would terminate the offer. Because Seiko's offer was to form a unilateral contract, only Jin's delivery of the sailboat at her dock would have been an acceptance.

Because of the harsh effect on the offeree of the revocation of an offer to form a unilateral contract, the modern-day view is different. Today, once performance has been *substantially* undertaken, the offeror cannot

revoke the offer. Thus, in *Example 7.5*, even though Jin has not yet accepted the offer by complete performance, Seiko is normally prohibited from revoking it. Jin can deliver the boat and bind Seiko to the contract.

Formal versus Informal Contracts Another classification system divides contracts into formal contracts and informal contracts. **Formal contracts** are contracts that require a special form or method of creation (formation) to be enforceable.[4] One example is *negotiable instruments,* which include checks, drafts, promissory notes, bills of exchange, and certificates of deposit. Negotiable instruments are formal contracts because, under the Uniform Commercial Code (UCC), a special form and language are required to create them.

Letters of credit, which are frequently used in international sales contracts, are another type of formal contract. Letters of credit are agreements to pay contingent on the purchaser's receipt of invoices and *bills of lading* (documents evidencing receipt of, and title to, goods shipped).

Informal contracts (also called *simple contracts*) include all other contracts. No special form is required (except for certain types of contracts that must be in writing), as the contracts are usually based on their substance rather than their form. Typically, businesspersons put their contracts in writing (including electronic records) to ensure that there is some proof of a contract's existence should disputes arise.

Express versus Implied Contracts Contracts may also be categorized as *express* or *implied*. In an **express contract,** the terms of the agreement are fully and explicitly stated in words, oral or written. A signed lease for an apartment or a house is an express written contract. If one classmate calls another on the phone and agrees to buy her textbooks from last semester for $200, an express oral contract has been made.

A contract that is implied from the conduct of the parties is called an **implied contract** (or sometimes an *implied-in-fact contract*). This type of contract differs from an express contract in that the conduct of the parties, rather than their words, creates and defines the terms of the contract.

Requirements for Implied Contracts. For an implied contract to arise, certain requirements must be met. Normally, if the following conditions exist, a court will hold that an implied contract was formed:

---

3. *Rogalski v. Little Poker League, LLC*, 2011 WL 589636 (Minn.App. 2011).

4. See *Restatement (Second) of Contracts*, Section 6, which explains that formal contracts include (1) contracts under seal, (2) recognizances, (3) negotiable instruments, and (4) letters of credit.

1. The plaintiff furnished some service or property.
2. The plaintiff expected to be paid for that service or property, and the defendant knew or should have known that payment was expected.
3. The defendant had a chance to reject the services or property and did not.

■ EXAMPLE 7.6 Alex, a small-business owner, needs an accountant to complete his tax return. He drops by a local accountant's office, explains his situation to the accountant, and learns what fees she charges. The next day, he returns and gives the receptionist all of the necessary documents to complete his return. Then he walks out without saying anything further to the accountant. In this situation, Alex has entered into an implied contract to pay the accountant the usual fees for her services. The contract is implied because of Alex's conduct and hers. She expects to be paid for completing the tax return, and by bringing in the records she will need to do the job, Alex has implied an intent to pay her. ■

Mixed Contracts with Express and Implied Terms.
Note that a contract may be a mixture of an express contract and an implied contract. In other words, a contract may contain some express terms and some implied terms. During the construction of a home, for instance, the homeowner often asks the builder to make changes in the original specifications.

■ CASE IN POINT 7.7 Lamar Hopkins hired Uhrhahn Construction & Design, Inc., for several projects in building his home. For each project, the parties signed a written contract that was based on a cost estimate and specifications and that required changes to the agreement to be in writing. While the work was in progress, however, Hopkins repeatedly asked Uhrhahn to deviate from the contract specifications, which Uhrhahn did. None of these requests was made in writing.

One day, Hopkins asked Uhrhahn to use Durisol blocks instead of the cinder blocks specified in the original contract, indicating that the cost would be the same. Uhrhahn used the Durisol blocks but demanded extra payment when it became clear that the Durisol blocks were more complicated to install. Although Hopkins had paid for the other deviations from the contract that he had orally requested, he refused to pay Uhrhahn for the substitution of the Durisol blocks. Uhrhahn sued for breach of contract. The court found that Hopkins, through his conduct, had waived the provision requiring written contract modification and created an implied contract to pay the extra cost of installing the Durisol blocks.[5] ■

Among other implied terms, all contracts include an implied covenant of good faith and fair dealing. This implied term requires the parties to perform in accord with the contract and the parties' reasonable expectations under it. In the following case, the plaintiff claimed that the defendant had breached both the express terms of the parties' contract and the implied covenant of good faith and fair dealing.

---

5. *Uhrhahn Construction & Design, Inc. v. Hopkins*, 179 P.3d 808 (Utah App. 2008).

Case 7.2

Vukanovich v. Kine

Court of Appeals of Oregon, 268 Or.App. 623, 342 P.3d 1075 (2015).

Background and Facts Mark Vukanovich and Larry Kine agreed under a "Letter of Understanding" to work together to buy a certain parcel of real property in Eugene, Oregon, from Umpqua Bank. They expressly agreed to develop the property and to split the cost and profits equally. Vukanovich shared confidential financial information with Kine that he would not otherwise have shared. The bank agreed to accept $1.6 million for the property, and a closing date was set. Kine then said that he no longer wanted to pursue the deal with Vukanovich or to buy the property. The closing did not occur.

A month later, without Vukanovich's knowledge, Kine made a new offer to buy the property. At about the same time, Vukanovich made his own new offer. The bank accepted Kine's offer. Vukanovich filed a suit in an Oregon state court against Kine, alleging breach of contract. The jury returned a verdict in favor of Vukanovich, awarding him $686,000 on the breach of contract claim and other damages, but the court entered a judgment in favor of Kine. Vukanovich appealed.

In the Language of the Court

LAGESEN, J. [Judge]

* * * *

Case 7.2 Continues

Case 7.2 Continued

*** *Plaintiff's claim for breach of contract was predicated [based] on the theory that defendant breached both the express terms of the parties' "Letter of Understanding" and the implied covenant of good faith and fair dealing, damaging plaintiff by cutting plaintiff *** out of an ownership interest in the property and the profits generated by the property.* [Emphasis added.]

*** Based on the evidence presented at trial, the jury could permissibly find that plaintiff and defendant entered into a contract to buy the property together and that defendant breached the express terms of that contract when, after the bank accepted the parties' joint offer to purchase the property ***, defendant refused to close on the purchase and subsequently repudiated [renounced] the contract, even though defendant had the capacity to close the agreed upon *** purchase of the property. The jury also could permissibly find that defendant lied to plaintiff about the reasons for not closing the *** purchase of the property from the bank and used confidential information provided by plaintiff to develop a more lucrative plan for the property that cut out plaintiff, thereby breaching the implied covenant of good faith and fair dealing. Finally, the jury could find that defendant's breaches damaged plaintiff—that, but for those breaches, the *** purchase would have been completed, and plaintiff would have been a part owner of the property and would have been entitled to a share of the profits that the property was expected to earn.

*** Defendant argues that *** after the agreement was undisputedly terminated ***, both plaintiff and defendant made separate attempts to purchase the property. Defendant contends that his efforts to purchase the property after the contract was terminated could not constitute a breach of the parties' contract because, at that point in time, both parties understood that the agreement was over and were engaging in similar conduct.

The problem with defendant's argument is that plaintiff ultimately did not predicate his breach of contract claim on defendant's conduct of purchasing the property separately from plaintiff. Although the complaint identified defendant's separate purchase of the property as "among" the breaches committed by defendant, plaintiff's focus at trial *** was on *** defendant's refusal to complete the purchase of the property with plaintiff, his surreptitious [secret] use of the information that plaintiff had provided him to devise a more favorable transaction for himself ***, and his lies to plaintiff about his reasons for not closing the deal. It is the evidence of that conduct, not the evidence of defendant's conduct following the termination of the contract, that permits the finding that defendant breached the parties' contract, damaging plaintiff by causing the planned *** purchase of the property to fail.

Decision and Remedy *A state intermediate appellate court reinstated the jury verdict. The court ruled that there was sufficient evidence to permit the jury to find that Kine had "breached both the express terms of the parties' Letter of Understanding and the implied covenant of good faith and fair dealing."*

Critical Thinking
- **Economic** *What did the amount of the jury's award of $686,000 in damages represent? Explain.*

7–3b Contract Performance

Contracts are also classified according to the degree to which they have been performed. A contract that has been fully performed on both sides is called an **executed contract.** A contract that has not been fully performed by the parties is called an **executory contract.** If one party has fully performed but the other has not, the contract is said to be executed on the one side and executory on the other, but the contract is still classified as executory.

■ **EXAMPLE 7.8** Jackson, Inc., agreed to buy ten tons of coal from the Northern Coal Company. Northern delivered the coal to Jackson's steel mill, where it is being burned. At this point, the contract is executed on the part of Northern and executory on Jackson's part. After Jackson pays Northern, the contract will be executed on both sides. ■

7–3c Contract Enforceability

A **valid contract** has the elements necessary to entitle at least one of the parties to enforce it in court. Those elements, as mentioned earlier, consist of (1) an agreement (offer and acceptance), (2) supported by legally sufficient consideration, (3) made by parties who have the legal capacity to enter into the contract, and (4) a legal purpose.

As you can see in Exhibit 7–2, valid contracts may be enforceable, voidable, or unenforceable. Additionally, a contract may be referred to as a *void contract*. We look next at the meaning of the terms *voidable, unenforceable,* and *void* in relation to contract enforceability.

Voidable Contracts A **voidable contract** is a valid contract but one that can be avoided at the option of one or both of the parties. The party having the option can elect either to avoid any duty to perform or to *ratify* (make valid) the contract. If the contract is avoided, both parties are released from it. If it is ratified, both parties must fully perform their respective legal obligations.

For instance, contracts made by minors generally are voidable at the option of the minor (with certain exceptions). Contracts made by mentally incompetent persons and intoxicated persons may also be voidable. Additionally, contracts entered into under fraudulent conditions are voidable at the option of the defrauded party. Contracts entered into under legally defined duress or undue influence are also voidable.

Unenforceable Contracts An **unenforceable contract** is one that cannot be enforced because of certain legal defenses against it. It is not unenforceable because a party failed to satisfy a legal requirement of the contract. Rather, it is a valid contract rendered unenforceable by

some statute or law. For instance, certain contracts must be in writing, and if they are not, they will not be enforceable except in certain exceptional circumstances.

Void Contracts A **void contract** is no contract at all. The terms *void* and *contract* are contradictory. None of the parties have any legal obligations if a contract is void. A contract can be void because one of the parties was determined by a court to be mentally incompetent, for instance, or because the purpose of the contract was illegal.

To review the various types of contracts, see Concept Summary 7.1.

7–4 Quasi Contracts

Express contracts and implied contracts are actual or true contracts formed by the words or actions of the parties. **Quasi contracts,** or contracts *implied in law,* are not actual contracts. Rather, they are fictional contracts that courts can impose on the parties "as if" the parties had entered into an actual contract. (The word *quasi* is Latin for "as if.")

Quasi contracts are equitable rather than legal contracts. Usually, they are imposed to avoid the *unjust enrichment* of one party at the expense of another. The doctrine of unjust enrichment is based on the theory that individuals should not be allowed to profit or enrich themselves inequitably at the expense of others.

EXHIBIT 7–2 Enforceable, Voidable, Unenforceable, and Void Contracts

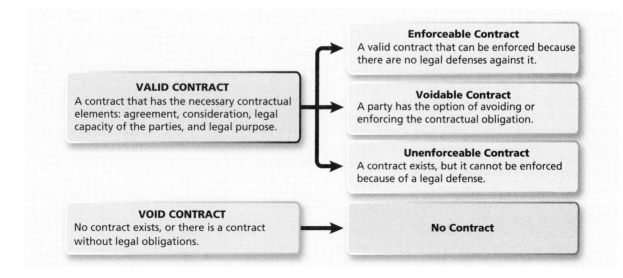

Concept Summary 7.1

Types of Contracts

Formation
- *Bilateral*—A promise for a promise.
- *Unilateral*—A promise for an act—that is, acceptance is the completed performance of the act.
- *Formal*—Requires a special form for creation.
- *Informal*—Requires no special form for creation.
- *Express*—Formed by words, such as oral, written, or a combination.
- *Implied*—Formed by the conduct of the parties.

Performance
- *Executed*—A fully performed contract.
- *Executory*—A contract not fully performed.

Enforceability
- *Valid*—The contract has the necessary contractual elements: agreement (offer and acceptance), consideration, legal capacity of the parties, and legal purpose.
- *Voidable*—One party has the option of avoiding or enforcing the contractual obligation.
- *Unenforceable*—A contract exists, but it cannot be enforced because of a legal defense.
- *Void*—No contract exists, or there is a contract without legal obligations.

■ **CASE IN POINT 7.9** Seawest Services Association operated a water distribution system that served homes inside a housing development (full members) and some homes located outside the subdivision (limited members). Both full and limited members paid water bills and assessments for work performed on the water system when necessary.

The Copenhavers purchased a home outside the housing development. They did not have an express contract with Seawest, but they paid water bills for eight years and paid one $3,950 assessment for water system upgrades. After a dispute arose, the Copenhavers refused to pay their water bills and assessments. Seawest sued. The court found that the Copenhavers had a quasi contract with Seawest and were liable. The Copenhavers had enjoyed the benefits of Seawest's water services and had even paid for them prior to their dispute. In addition, "the Copenhavers would be unjustly enriched if they could retain benefits provided by Seawest without paying for them."[6] ■

7–4a Limitations on Quasi-Contractual Recovery

Although quasi contracts exist to prevent unjust enrichment, the party obtaining the enrichment is not held liable in some situations. In general, a party who has conferred a benefit on someone else unnecessarily or as a result of misconduct or negligence cannot invoke the principle of quasi contract. The enrichment in those situations will not be considered "unjust."

■ **CASE IN POINT 7.10** Michael Plambeck owned two chiropractic clinics in Kentucky that treated many patients injured in car accidents, including some who were customers of State Farm Automobile Insurance Company. All of the clinics' treating chiropractors were licensed to practice in Kentucky, but Plambeck (the owner) was not. Plambeck was a licensed chiropractor in another state but had allowed his Kentucky license to lapse because he was not treating any patients. Plambeck did not realize that Kentucky state law required him to be licensed as the owner of the clinics.

When State Farm discovered that Plambeck was not licensed in Kentucky, it filed a suit against the clinics

---

6. *Seawest Services Association v. Copenhaver*, 166 Wash.App. 1006 (2012).

seeking to recover payments it had made on behalf of its customers. The trial court awarded State Farm $577,124 in damages for unjust enrichment, but the appellate court reversed. The court reasoned that State Farm had a legal duty to pay for the chiropractic treatment of its customers and could not avoid paying for the services because the clinics' owner was not licensed. The payments did not constitute unjust enrichment, because the patients had, in fact, received treatment by licensed chiropractors.[7] ■

7–4b When an Actual Contract Exists

The doctrine of quasi contract generally cannot be used when there is an *actual contract* that covers the matter in controversy. A remedy already exists if a party is unjustly enriched as a result of a breach of contract: the non-breaching party can sue the breaching party for breach of contract.

■ **EXAMPLE 7.11** Fung contracts with Cameron to deliver a furnace to a building owned by Grant. Fung delivers the furnace, but Cameron never pays Fung. Grant has been unjustly enriched in this situation, to be sure. Fung, however, cannot recover from Grant in quasi contract, because Fung had an actual contract with Cameron. Fung already has a remedy—he can sue for breach of contract to recover the price of the furnace from Cameron. The court does not need to impose a quasi contract in this situation to achieve justice. ■

---

7. *State Farm Automobile Insurance Co. v. Newburg Chiropractic, P.S.C.*, 741 F.3d 661 (6th Cir. 2013).

7–5 Interpretation of Contracts

Sometimes, parties agree that a contract has been formed but disagree on its meaning or legal effect. One reason this may happen is that one of the parties is not familiar with the legal terminology used in the contract. To an extent, *plain language* laws (enacted by the federal government and a majority of the states) have helped to avoid this difficulty. Sometimes, though, a dispute may arise over the meaning of a contract simply because the rights or obligations under the contract are not expressed clearly—no matter how "plain" the language used.

In this section, we look at some common law rules of contract interpretation. These rules, which have evolved over time, provide the courts with guidelines for deciding disputes over how contract terms or provisions should be interpreted. Exhibit 7–3 provides a brief graphic summary of how these rules are applied.

7–5a The Plain Meaning Rule

When a contract's writing is clear and unequivocal, a court will enforce it according to its obvious terms. The meaning of the terms must be determined from the *face of the instrument*—from the written document alone. This is sometimes referred to as the *plain meaning rule*. The words—and their plain, ordinary meaning—determine the intent of the parties at the time that they entered into the contract. A court is bound to give effect to the contract according to this intent.

EXHIBIT 7–3 Rules of Contract Interpretation

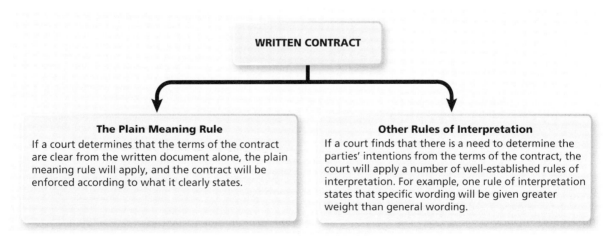

WRITTEN CONTRACT

The Plain Meaning Rule
If a court determines that the terms of the contract are clear from the written document alone, the plain meaning rule will apply, and the contract will be enforced according to what it clearly states.

Other Rules of Interpretation
If a court finds that there is a need to determine the parties' intentions from the terms of the contract, the court will apply a number of well-established rules of interpretation. For example, one rule of interpretation states that specific wording will be given greater weight than general wording.

Ambiguity A court will consider a contract to be unclear, or ambiguous, in the following situations:

1. When the intent of the parties cannot be determined from the contract's language.
2. When the contract lacks a provision on a disputed term.
3. When a term is susceptible to more than one interpretation.
4. When there is uncertainty about a provision.

Extrinsic Evidence If a contract term is ambiguous, a court may interpret the ambiguity against the party who drafted the term. The court may also consider *extrinsic evidence* when a term is ambiguous. **Extrinsic evidence** is any evidence not contained in the document itself—such as the testimony of parties and witnesses, additional agreements or communications, or other relevant information.

The admissibility of extrinsic evidence can significantly affect the court's interpretation of ambiguous contractual provisions and thus the outcome of litigation. When a contract is clear and unambiguous, a court cannot consider extrinsic evidence. The following case illustrates these points.

Spotlight on Columbia Pictures

Case 7.3 Wagner v. Columbia Pictures Industries, Inc.

California Court of Appeal, Second District, 146 Cal.App.4th 586, 52 Cal.Rptr.3d 898 (2007).

Background and Facts Actor Robert Wagner entered into an agreement with Spelling-Goldberg Productions (SGP) "relating to *Charlie's Angels* (herein called the 'series')." The contract entitled Wagner to 50 percent of the net profits that SGP received from broadcasting the series and from all ancillary, music, and subsidiary rights in connection with the series. SGP hired Ivan Goff and Ben Roberts to write the series, under a contract subject to the Writers Guild of America Minimum Basic Agreement (MBA).[a] The MBA stipulates that the writer of a television show retains the right to make and market films based on the material, subject to the producer's right to buy this right if the writer decides to sell it within five years.

The first *Charlie's Angels* episode aired in 1976. In 1982, SGP sold its rights to the series to Columbia Pictures Industries, Inc. Thirteen years later, Columbia bought the movie rights to the material from Goff's and Roberts's heirs. In 2000 and 2003, Columbia produced and distributed two *Charlie's Angels* films. Wagner filed a suit in a California state court against Columbia, claiming a share of the profits from the films. The court granted Columbia's motion for summary judgment. Wagner appealed to a state intermediate appellate court.

In the Language of the Court
JOHNSON, Acting P.J. [Presiding Judge]
* * * *

Wagner contends the "subsidiary rights" provision in the agreement with SGP entitles him * * * to 50 percent of the net profits from the two "Charlie's Angels" films.
* * * *

Wagner introduced evidence of the history of the negotiations underlying the "Charlie's Angels" contract in support of his [contention].

This history begins with a contract the Wagners [Wagner and his wife, Natalie Wood] entered into with SGP to star in a television movie-of-the-week, "Love Song." As compensation for Wagner and Wood acting in "Love Song," SGP agreed to pay them a fixed amount plus one-half the net profits * * * .
* * * *

In the * * * "Love Song" contract net profits were not limited to monies received "for the right to exhibit the Photoplay." Instead they were defined as the net of "all monies received by Producer as consideration for the right to exhibit the Photoplay, and exploitation of all ancillary, music and subsidiary rights in connection therewith."
* * * *

---

a. The Writers Guild of America is an association of screen and television writers that negotiates industry-wide agreements with motion picture and television producers.

Case 7.3 Continued

Wagner's argument is simple and straightforward. The net profits provision in the "Love Song" agreement was intended to give the Wagners a one-half share in the net profits received by SGP "from all sources" without limitation as to source or time. The "Charlie's Angels" agreement was based on the "Love Song" agreement and defines net profits in identical language. Therefore, the "Charlie's Angels" agreement should also be interpreted as providing the Wagners with a 50 percent share in SGP's income "from all sources" without limitation as to source or time. Since Columbia admits it stands in SGP's shoes with respect to SGP's obligations under the "Charlie's Angels" agreement, Columbia is obligated to pay Wagner * * * 50 percent of the net profits derived from the "Charlie's Angels" movies.

* * * *

The problem with Wagner's extrinsic evidence is that it does not explain the ["Charlie's Angels"] contract language, it contradicts it. *Under the parol evidence rule,*[b] *extrinsic evidence is not admissible to contradict express terms in a written contract or to explain what the agreement was. The agreement is the writing itself. Parol evidence cannot be admitted to show intention independent of an unambiguous written instrument.* [Emphasis added.]

Even if the Wagners and SGP intended the Wagners would share in the net profits "from any and all sources" they did not say so in their contract. What they said in their contract was the Wagners would share in "all monies actually received by Producer, as consideration for the right to exhibit photoplays of the series, and from the exploitation of all ancillary, music and subsidiary rights in connection therewith." For a right to be "subsidiary" or "ancillary," meaning supplementary or subordinate, there must be a primary right to which it relates. The only primary right mentioned in the contract is "the right to exhibit photoplays of the series." Thus the Wagners were entitled to share in the profits from the exploitation of the movie rights to "Charlie's Angels" if those rights were exploited by Columbia as ancillary or subsidiary rights of its primary "right to exhibit photoplays of the series" but not if those rights were acquired by Columbia independently from its right to exhibit photoplays.

Decision and Remedy *The state intermediate appellate court affirmed the lower court's summary judgment in favor of Columbia. The contract "unambiguously" stated the conditions under which the parties were to share the films' profits, and those conditions had not occurred.*

Critical Thinking

- **What If the Facts Were Different?** *How might the result in this case have been different if the court had admitted Wagner's evidence of the* Love Song *contract?*
- **Legal Environment** *Under what circumstances would Wagner have been entitled to a share of the profits from the* Charlie's Angels *movies even though the evidence of the* Love Song *contract was irrelevant?*

---

b. The *parol evidence rule* prohibits the parties from introducing in court evidence of an oral agreement that contradicts the written terms of a contract.

7–5b Other Rules of Interpretation

Generally, a court will interpret the language to give effect to the parties' intent as *expressed in their contract.* This is the primary purpose of the rules of interpretation—to determine the parties' intent from the language used in their agreement and to give effect to that intent. A court normally will not make or remake a contract, nor will it interpret the language according to what the parties *claim* their intent was when they made it.

Rules the Courts Use The courts use the following rules in interpreting contractual terms:

1. As far as possible, a reasonable, lawful, and effective meaning will be given to all of a contract's terms.
2. A contract will be interpreted as a whole. Individual, specific clauses will be considered subordinate to the contract's general intent. All writings that are a part of the same transaction will be interpreted together.
3. Terms that were the subject of separate negotiation will be given greater consideration than standardized terms and terms that were not negotiated separately.
4. A word will be given its ordinary, commonly accepted meaning, and a technical word or term will be given its technical meaning, unless the parties clearly intended something else.

5. Specific and exact wording will be given greater consideration than general language.

6. Written or typewritten terms will prevail over pre-printed ones.

7. Because a contract should be drafted in clear and unambiguous language, a party who uses ambiguous expressions is held to be responsible for the ambiguities. Thus, when the language has more than one meaning, it will be interpreted against the party who drafted the contract.

8. Evidence of *usage of trade, course of dealing,* and *course of performance* may be admitted to clarify the meaning of an ambiguously worded contract.

Express Terms Usually Given the Most Weight

Express terms (terms expressly stated in the contract) are given the greatest weight, followed by course of performance, course of dealing, and custom and usage of trade—in that order. When considering custom and usage, a court will look at the trade customs and usage common to the particular business or industry and to the locale in which the contract was made or is to be performed.

■ **CASE IN POINT 7.12** Jessica Robbins bought a house in Tennessee. U.S. Bank financed the purchase, and Tennessee Farmers Mutual Insurance Company issued the homeowner's insurance policy. The policy included a clause that promised payment to the bank for losses unless the loss was due to an "increase in hazard" about which the bank knew but did not tell the insurer. When Robbins fell behind on her mortgage payments, the bank started foreclosure proceedings. No one told the insurer. Robbins filed for bankruptcy, which postponed foreclosure.

Meanwhile, the house was destroyed in a fire. The bank filed a claim under the policy, but the insurer refused to pay because it had not been told by the bank of an "increase in hazard"—the foreclosure. The bank then filed a lawsuit. The court found that the plain meaning of the words "increase in hazard" in the policy referred to physical conditions on the property that posed a risk, not to events such as foreclosure. Thus, the bank was not required to notify the insurer under the terms of the policy, and the lack of notice did not invalidate the coverage.[8] ■

---

8. *U.S. Bank, N.A. v. Tennessee Farmers Mutual Insurance Co.*, 277 S.W.3d 381 (Tenn.Sup.Ct. 2009).

Reviewing: Nature and Terminology

Mitsui Bank hired Ross Duncan as a branch manager in one of its Southern California locations. At that time, Duncan received an employee handbook informing him that Mitsui would review his performance and salary level annually. In 2016, Mitsui decided to create a new lending program to help financially troubled businesses stay afloat. It hired Duncan to be the credit development officer (CDO) and gave him a written compensation plan. Duncan's compensation was to be based on the program's success and involved a bonus and commissions based on the volume of new loans and sales. The written plan also stated, "This compensation plan will be reviewed and potentially amended after one year and will be subject to such review and amendment annually thereafter."

Duncan's efforts as CDO were successful, and the program he developed grew to represent 25 percent of Mitsui's business in 2016 and 40 percent in 2017. Nevertheless, Mitsui refused to give Duncan a raise in 2016. Mitsui also amended his compensation plan to significantly reduce his compensation and to change his performance evaluation schedule to every six months. When he had still not received a raise by 2018, Duncan resigned as CDO and filed a lawsuit alleging breach of contract. Using the information presented in the chapter, answer the following questions.

1. What are the four requirements of a valid contract?
2. Did Duncan have a valid contract with Mitsui for employment as CDO? If so, was it a bilateral or a unilateral contract?
3. What are the requirements of an implied contract?
4. Can Duncan establish an implied contract based on the employment manual or the written compensation plan? Why or why not?

Debate This . . . *Companies should be able to make or break employment contracts whenever and however they wish.*

Terms and Concepts

bilateral contract 135
contract 133
executed contract 138
executory contract 138
express contract 136
extrinsic evidence 142
formal contract 136

implied contract 136
informal contract 136
objective theory of contracts 133
offeree 135
offeror 135
promise 132
promisee 132

promisor 132
quasi contract 139
unenforceable contract 139
unilateral contract 135
valid contract 138
void contract 139
voidable contract 139

Issue Spotters

1. Dyna tells Ed that she will pay him $1,000 to set fire to her store so that she can collect under a fire insurance policy. Ed sets fire to the store, but Dyna refuses to pay. Can Ed recover? Why or why not? (See *Elements of a Contract.*)

2. Alison receives a notice of property taxes due from a local tax collector. The notice is for tax on Jerry's property, but Alison believes that the tax is on her property and pays it. Can Alison recover from Jerry the amount that she paid? Why or why not? (See *Quasi Contracts.*)

• **Check your answers to the Issue Spotters against the answers provided in Appendix B at the end of this text.**

Business Scenarios

7–1. Unilateral Contract. Rocky Mountain Races, Inc., sponsors the "Pioneer Trail Ultramarathon," with an advertised first prize of $10,000. The rules require the competitors to run 100 miles from the floor of Blackwater Canyon to the top of Pinnacle Mountain. The rules also provide that Rocky reserves the right to change the terms of the race at any time. Monica enters the race and is declared the winner. Rocky offers her a prize of $1,000 instead of $10,000. Did Rocky and Monica have a contract? Explain. (See *Types of Contracts.*)

7–2. Implied Contract. Janine was hospitalized with severe abdominal pain and placed in an intensive care unit. Her doctor told the hospital personnel to order around-the-clock nursing care for Janine. At the hospital's request, a nursing services firm, Nursing Services Unlimited, provided two weeks of in-hospital care and, after Janine was sent home, an additional two weeks of at-home care. During the at-home period of care, Janine was fully aware that she was receiving the benefit of the nursing services. Nursing Services later billed Janine $4,000 for the nursing care, but Janine refused to pay on the ground that she had never contracted for the services, either orally or in writing. In view of the fact that no express contract was ever formed, can Nursing Services recover the $4,000 from Janine? If so, under what legal theory? Discuss. (See *Types of Contracts.*)

Business Case Problems

7–3. Spotlight on Taco Bell—Implied Contract.

Thomas Rinks and Joseph Shields developed Psycho Chihuahua, a caricature of a Chihuahua dog with a "do-not-back-down" attitude. They promoted and marketed the character through their company, Wrench, L.L.C. Ed Alfaro and Rudy Pollak, representatives of Taco Bell Corp., learned of Psycho Chihuahua and met with Rinks and Shields to talk about using the character as a Taco Bell "icon." Wrench sent artwork, merchandise, and marketing ideas to Alfaro, who promoted the character within Taco Bell. Alfaro asked Wrench to propose terms for Taco Bell's use of Psycho Chihuahua. Taco Bell did not accept Wrench's terms, but Alfaro continued to promote the character within the company.

Meanwhile, Taco Bell hired a new advertising agency, which proposed an advertising campaign involving a Chihuahua. When Alfaro learned of this proposal, he sent the Psycho Chihuahua materials to the agency. Taco Bell made a Chihuahua the focus of its marketing but paid nothing to Wrench. Wrench filed a suit against Taco Bell in a federal court claiming that it had an implied contract with Taco Bell and that Taco Bell breached that contract. Do these facts satisfy the requirements for an implied contract? Why or why not? [*Wrench, L.L.C. v. Taco Bell Corp.,* 256 F.3d 446 (6th Cir. 2001), *cert.* denied, 534 U.S. 1114, 122 S.Ct. 921, 151 L.Ed.2d 805 (2002)] (See *Types of Contracts.*)

7–4. Business Case Problem with Sample Answer—Quasi Contract. Robert Gutkowski, a sports marketing

expert, met numerous times with George Steinbrenner, the owner of the New York Yankees, to discuss the Yankees Entertainment and Sports Network (YES). Gutkowski was paid as a consultant. Later, he filed a suit, seeking an ownership share in YES. There was no written contract for the share, but he claimed that there were discussions about his being a part owner. Does Gutkowski have a valid claim for payment? Discuss. [*Gutkowski v. Steinbrenner,* 680 F.Supp.2d 602 (S.D.N.Y. 2010)] (See *Quasi Contracts.*)

• **For a sample answer to Problem 7–4, go to Appendix C at the end of this text.**

7–5. Quasi Contract. Kim Panenka asked to borrow $4,750 from her sister, Kris, to make a mortgage payment. Kris deposited a check for that amount into Kim's bank account. Hours later, Kim asked to borrow another $1,100. Kris took a cash advance on her credit card and deposited this amount into Kim's account. When Kim did not repay the amounts, Kris filed a suit, arguing that she had "loaned" Kim the money. Can the court impose a contract between the sisters? Explain. [*Panenka v. Panenka,* 331 Wis.2d 731, 795 N.W.2d 493 (2011)] (See *Quasi Contracts.*)

7–6. Implied Contracts. Ralph Ramsey insured his car with Allstate Insurance Co. He also owned a house on which he maintained a homeowner's insurance policy with Allstate. Bank of America had a mortgage on the house and paid the insurance premiums on the homeowner's policy from Ralph's account. After Ralph died, Allstate canceled the car insurance. Ralph's son Douglas inherited the house. The bank continued to pay the premiums on the homeowner's policy, but from Douglas's account, and Allstate continued to renew the insurance. When a fire destroyed the house, Allstate denied coverage, however, claiming that the policy was still in Ralph's name. Douglas filed a suit in a federal district court against the insurer. Was Allstate liable under the homeowner's policy? Explain. [*Ramsey v. Allstate Insurance Co.,* 514 Fed.Appx. 554 (6th Cir. 2013)] (See *Types of Contracts.*)

7–7. Quasi Contracts. Lawrence M. Clarke, Inc., was the general contractor for construction of a portion of a sanitary sewer system in Billings, Michigan. Clarke accepted Kim Draeger's proposal to do the work for a certain price. Draeger arranged with two subcontractors to work on the project. The work provided by Draeger and the subcontractors proved unsatisfactory. All of the work fell under Draeger's contract with Clarke. Clarke filed a suit in a Michigan state court against Draeger, seeking to recover damages on a theory of quasi contract. The court awarded Clarke $900,000 in damages on that theory. A state intermediate appellate court reversed this award. Why? [*Lawrence M. Clarke, Inc. v. Draeger,* 2015 WL 205182 (Mich.App. 2015)] (See *Quasi Contracts.*)

7–8. Interpretation of Contracts. Lehman Brothers, Inc. (LBI), wrote a letter to Mary Ortegón offering her employment as LBI's "Business Chief Administrative Officer in Its Fixed Income Division." The offer included a salary of $150,000 per year and an annual "minimum bonus" of $350,000. The letter stated that the bonus would be paid unless Ortegón resigned or was terminated for certain causes. In other words, the bonus was not a "signing" bonus—it was clearly tied to her performance on the job. Ortegón accepted the offer. Before she started work, however, LBI rescinded it. Later, LBI filed for bankruptcy in a federal court. Ortegón filed a claim with the court for the amount of the bonus on the ground that LBI had breached its contract with her by not paying it. Can extrinsic evidence be admitted to interpret the meaning of the bonus term? Explain. [*Ortegón v. Giddens,* 638 Fed.Appx. 47 (2d Cir. 2016)] (See *Interpretation of Contracts.*)

7–9. A Question of Ethics—Unilateral Contracts.

 International Business Machines Corp. (IBM) hired Niels Jensen in 2000 as a software sales representative. According to the brochure on IBM's "Sales Incentive Plan" (SIP), "the more you sell, the more earnings for you." But "the SIP program does not constitute a promise by IBM. IBM reserves the right to modify the program at any time." Jensen was given a "quota letter" that said he would be paid $75,000 as a base salary and, if he attained his quota, an additional $75,000 as incentive pay. Jensen closed a deal worth more than $24 million to IBM. When IBM paid him less than $500,000 as a commission, Jensen filed a suit. He argued that the SIP was a unilateral offer that became a binding contract when he closed the sale. [Jensen v. International Business Machines Corp., *454 F.3d 382 (4th Cir. 2006)*] (See *Types of Contracts.*)

(a) Would it be fair to the employer for the court to hold that the SIP brochure and the quota letter created a unilateral contract if IBM did not *intend* to create such a contract? Would it be fair to the employee to hold that *no* contract was created? Explain.

(b) The "Sales Incentives" section of IBM's brochure included a clause providing that "management will decide if an adjustment to the payment is appropriate" when an employee closes a large transaction. Does this affect your answers to the questions above? From an ethical perspective, would it be fair to hold that a contract exists despite these statements? Why or why not?

Legal Reasoning Group Activity

7–10. Contracts. Review the basic requirements for a valid contract listed at the beginning of this chapter. Now consider the relationship created when a student enrolls in a college or university. (See *Elements of a Contract.*)

(a) One group should analyze and discuss whether a contract has been formed between the student and the college or university.

(b) A second group should assume that there is a contract and explain whether it is bilateral or unilateral.

CHAPTER 8

Agreement in Traditional and E-Contracts

Contract law developed over time to meet society's need to know with certainty what kinds of promises, or contracts, will be enforced and the point at which a valid and binding contract is formed. For a contract to be considered valid and enforceable, four basic requirements—agreement, consideration, contractual capacity, and legality—must be met. In this chapter, we look closely at the first of these requirements, *agreement*.

Agreement is required to form a contract, whether it is formed in the traditional way (on paper) or online.

In today's world, many contracts are formed via the Internet. We discuss online offers and acceptances and examine some laws that have been created to apply to electronic contracts, or *e-contracts*, in the latter part of this chapter.

8–1 Agreement

An essential element for contract formation is **agreement**—the parties must agree on the terms of the contract and manifest to each other their *mutual assent* (agreement) to the same bargain. Ordinarily, agreement is evidenced by two events: an *offer* and an *acceptance.* One party offers a certain bargain to another party, who then accepts that bargain.

An agreement does not necessarily have to be in writing. Both parties, however, must manifest their assent, or voluntary consent, to the same bargain. Once an agreement is reached, if the other elements of a contract (consideration, capacity, and legality—discussed in the next chapter) are present, a valid contract is formed. Generally, the contract creates enforceable rights and duties between the parties.

Because words often fail to convey the precise meaning intended, the law of contracts generally adheres to the *objective theory of contracts.* Under this theory, a party's words and conduct are held to mean whatever a reasonable person in the offeree's position would think they meant.

8–1a Requirements of the Offer

An **offer** is a promise or commitment to do or refrain from doing some specified action in the future. The party making an offer is called the *offeror,* and the party to whom the offer is made is called the *offeree.* Under the common law, three elements are necessary for an offer to be effective:

1. The offeror must have a serious intention to become bound by the offer.
2. The terms of the offer must be reasonably certain, or definite, so that the parties and the court can ascertain the terms of the contract.
3. The offer must be communicated to the offeree.

Once an effective offer has been made, the offeree's acceptance of that offer creates a legally binding contract (providing the other essential elements for a valid and enforceable contract are present).

Intention The first requirement for an effective offer is a serious intent on the part of the offeror. Serious intent is not determined by the subjective intentions, beliefs, and assumptions of the offeror. Rather, it is determined by what a reasonable person in the offeree's position would conclude that the offeror's words and actions meant. Offers made in obvious anger, jest, or undue excitement do not meet the serious-and-objective-intent test. A reasonable person would realize that such offers were not made seriously. Because these offers are not effective, an offeree's acceptance does not create an agreement.

■ **EXAMPLE 8.1** Linda and Dena ride to school each day in Dena's new automobile, which has a market value of $20,000. One cold morning, they get into the car, but the car will not start. Dena yells in anger, "I'll sell this car to anyone for $500!" Linda drops $500 on Dena's lap. A reasonable person—taking into consideration Dena's frustration and the obvious difference in value between the market price of the car and the proposed purchase price—would realize that Dena's offer was not made with serious and objective intent. No agreement is formed. ∎

In the classic case presented next, the court considered whether an offer made "after a few drinks" met the serious-and-objective-intent requirement.

Lucy v. Zehmer

Supreme Court of Appeals of Virginia, 196 Va. 493, 84 S.E.2d 516 (1954).

Background and Facts W. O. Lucy, the plaintiff, filed a suit against A. H. and Ida Zehmer, the defendants, to compel the Zehmers to transfer title of their property, known as the Ferguson Farm, to the Lucys (W. O. and his wife) for $50,000, as the Zehmers had allegedly agreed to do. Lucy had known A. H. Zehmer for fifteen or twenty years and for the last eight years or so had been anxious to buy the Ferguson Farm from him. One night, Lucy stopped to visit the Zehmers in the combination restaurant, filling station, and motor court they operated. While there, Lucy tried to buy the Ferguson Farm once again. This time he tried a new approach. According to the trial court transcript, Lucy said to Zehmer, "I bet you wouldn't take $50,000 for that place." Zehmer replied, "Yes, I would too; you wouldn't give fifty." Throughout the evening, the conversation returned to the sale of the Ferguson Farm for $50,000. All the while, the men continued to drink whiskey and engage in light conversation.

Eventually, Lucy enticed Zehmer to write up an agreement to the effect that the Zehmers would sell the Ferguson Farm to Lucy for $50,000 complete. Later, Lucy sued Zehmer to compel him to go through with the sale. Zehmer argued that he had been drunk and that the offer had been made in jest and hence was unenforceable. The trial court agreed with Zehmer, and Lucy appealed.

In the Language of the Court

BUCHANAN, J. [Justice] delivered the opinion of the court.

* * * *

In his testimony, Zehmer claimed that he "was high as a Georgia pine," and that the transaction "was just a bunch of two doggoned drunks bluffing to see who could talk the biggest and say the most." That claim is inconsistent with his attempt to testify in great detail as to what was said and what was done.

* * * *

The appearance of the contract, the fact that it was under discussion for forty minutes or more before it was signed; Lucy's objection to the first draft because it was written in the singular, and he wanted Mrs. Zehmer to sign it also; the rewriting to meet that objection and the signing by Mrs. Zehmer; the discussion of what was to be included in the sale, the provision for the examination of the title, the completeness of the instrument that was executed, the taking possession of it by Lucy with no request or suggestion by either of the defendants that he give it back, are facts which furnish persuasive evidence that the execution of the contract was a serious business transaction rather than a casual, jesting matter as defendants now contend.

* * * *

In the field of contracts, as generally elsewhere, *we must look to the outward expression of a person as manifesting his intention rather than to his secret and unexpressed intention.* The law imputes to a person an intention corresponding to the reasonable meaning of his words and acts. [Emphasis added.]

* * * *

Whether the writing signed by the defendants and now sought to be enforced by the complainants was the result of a serious offer by Lucy and a serious acceptance by the defendants, or was a serious offer by Lucy and an acceptance in secret jest by the defendants, in either event it constituted a binding contract of sale between the parties.

Case 8.1 Continued

Decision and Remedy *The Supreme Court of Appeals of Virginia determined that the writing was an enforceable contract and reversed the ruling of the lower court. The Zehmers were required by court order to follow through with the sale of the Ferguson Farm to the Lucys.*

Impact of This Case on Today's Law *This is a classic case in contract law because it illustrates so clearly the objective theory of contracts with respect to determining whether a serious offer was intended. Today, the courts continue to apply the objective theory of contracts and routinely cite* Lucy v. Zehmer *as a significant precedent in this area.*

Critical Thinking

- **What If the Facts Were Different?** *Suppose that the day after Lucy signed the purchase agreement, he decided that he did not want the farm after all, and Zehmer sued Lucy to perform the contract. Would this change in the facts alter the court's decision that Lucy and Zehmer had created an enforceable contract? Why or why not?*

Situations in Which Intent May Be Lacking

The concept of intention can be further clarified by looking at statements that are *not* offers and situations in which the parties' intent to be bound might be questionable.

1. *Expressions of opinion.* An expression of opinion is not an offer. It does not indicate an intention to enter into a binding agreement.

2. *Statements of future intent.* A statement of an intention to do something in the future (such as "I plan to sell my Verizon stock") is not an offer.

3. *Preliminary negotiations.* A request or invitation to negotiate is not an offer. It only expresses a willingness to discuss the possibility of entering into a contract. Statements such as "Will you sell your farm?" or "I wouldn't sell my car for less than $8,000" are examples.

4. *Invitations to bid.* When a government entity or private firm needs to have construction work done, contractors are invited to submit bids. The invitation to submit bids is not an offer. The bids that contractors submit are offers, however, and the government entity or private firm can bind the contractor by accepting the bid.

5. *Advertisements and price lists.* In general, representations made in advertisements and price lists are treated not as offers to contract but as invitations to negotiate.[1]

6. *Live and online auctions.* In a live auction, a seller "offers" goods for sale through an auctioneer, but this is not an offer to form a contract. Rather, it is an invitation asking bidders to submit offers. In the context of an auction, a bidder is the offeror, and the auctioneer is the offeree. The offer is accepted when the auctioneer strikes the hammer.

The most familiar type of auction today takes place online through Web sites like eBay and eBid. "Offers" to sell an item on these sites generally are treated as invitations to negotiate. Unlike live auctions, online auctions are automated. Buyers can enter incremental bids on an item (without approving each price increase) up to a specified amount or without a limit.

Agreements to Agree. Traditionally, agreements to agree—that is, agreements to agree to the material terms of a contract at some future date—were not considered to be binding contracts. The modern view, however, is that agreements to agree may be enforceable agreements (contracts) if it is clear that the parties intended to be bound by the agreements. In other words, under the modern view the emphasis is on the parties' intent rather than on form.

■ **CASE IN POINT 8.2** After a person was injured and nearly drowned on a water ride at one of its amusement parks, Six Flags, Inc., filed a lawsuit against the manufacturer that had designed the ride. The defendant manufacturer claimed that the parties did not have a binding contract but had only engaged in preliminary negotiations that were never formalized in a construction contract.

The court, however, held that the evidence was sufficient to show an intent to be bound. The evidence included a faxed document specifying the details of the water ride, along with the parties' subsequent actions (having begun construction and written notes on the faxed document). The manufacturer was required to provide insurance for the water ride at Six Flags. In addition, its insurer was required to defend Six Flags in the personal-injury lawsuit that arose out of the incident.[2] ■

---

1. *Restatement (Second) of Contracts*, Section 26, Comment b.

2. *Six Flags, Inc. v. Steadfast Insurance Co.*, 474 F.Supp.2d 201 (D.Mass. 2007).

Preliminary Agreements. Increasingly, the courts are holding that a preliminary agreement constitutes a binding contract if the parties have agreed on all essential terms and no disputed issues remain to be resolved. In contrast, if the parties agree on certain major terms but leave other terms open for further negotiation, a preliminary agreement is not binding. The parties are bound only in the sense that they have committed themselves to negotiate the undecided terms in good faith in an effort to reach a final agreement.

In the following *Spotlight Case,* a dispute arose over an agreement to settle a case during the trial. One party claimed that the agreement, which was formed via e-mail, was binding. The other party claimed that the e-mail exchange was merely an agreement to work out the terms of a settlement in the future. Can an exchange of e-mails create a complete and unambiguous agreement?

Spotlight on Amazon.com

Case 8.2 Basis Technology Corp. v. Amazon.com, Inc.
Appeals Court of Massachusetts, 71 Mass.App.Ct. 29, 878 N.E.2d 952 (2008).

Background and Facts Basis Technology Corporation created software and provided technical services for a Japanese-language Web site belonging to Amazon.com, Inc. The agreement between the two companies allowed for separately negotiated contracts for additional services that Basis might provide to Amazon. At the end of 1999, Basis and Amazon entered into stock-purchase agreements. Later, Basis sued Amazon for various claims involving these securities and for failure to pay for services performed by Basis that were not included in the original agreement. During the trial, the two parties appeared to reach an agreement to settle out of court via a series of e-mail exchanges outlining the settlement. When Amazon reneged, Basis served a motion to enforce the proposed settlement. The trial judge entered a judgment against Amazon, which appealed.

In the Language of the Court
SIKORA, J. [Judge]

* * * *

* * * On the evening of March 23, after the third day of evidence and after settlement discussions, Basis counsel sent an e-mail with the following text to Amazon counsel:

> [Amazon counsel]—This e-mail confirms the essential business terms of the settlement between our respective clients * * *. Basis and Amazon agree that they promptly will take all reasonable steps to memorialize in a written agreement, to be signed by individuals authorized by each party, the terms set forth below, as well as such other terms that are reasonably necessary to make these terms effective.
>
> * * * *
>
> [Amazon counsel], please contact me first thing tomorrow morning if this e-mail does not accurately summarize the settlement terms reached earlier this evening.
> See you tomorrow morning when we report this matter settled to the Court.

At 7:26 A.M. on March 24, Amazon counsel sent an e-mail with a one-word reply: "correct." Later in the morning, in open court and on the record, both counsel reported the result of a settlement without specification of the terms.

On March 25, Amazon's counsel sent a facsimile of the first draft of a settlement agreement to Basis's counsel. The draft comported with all the terms of the e-mail exchange, and added some implementing and boilerplate [standard contract provisions] terms.

* * * *

[Within a few days, though,] the parties were deadlocked. On April 21, Basis served its motion to enforce the settlement agreement. Amazon opposed. * * * The motion and opposition presented the issues whether the e-mail terms were sufficiently complete and definite to form an agreement and whether Amazon had intended to be bound by them.

* * * *

We examine the text of the terms for the incompleteness and indefiniteness charged by Amazon. *Provisions are not ambiguous simply because the parties have developed different interpretations of them.* [Emphasis added.]

Case 8.2 Continued

* * * * We must interpret the document as a whole. In the preface to the enumerated terms, Basis counsel stated that the "e-mail confirms the essential business terms of the settlement between our respective clients," and that the parties "agree that they promptly will take all reasonable steps to memorialize" those terms. Amazon counsel concisely responded, "correct." Thus the "essential business terms" were resolved. The parties were proceeding to "memorialize" or record the settlement terms, not to create them.

* * * *

To ascertain intent, a court considers the words used by the parties, the agreement taken as a whole, and surrounding facts and circumstances. The essential circumstance of this disputed agreement is that it concluded a trial.

* * * As the trial judge explained in her memorandum of decision, she "terminated" the trial; she did not suspend it for exploratory negotiations. She did so in reliance upon the parties' report of an accomplished agreement for the settlement of their dispute.

* * * *

In sum, the deliberateness and the gravity attributable to a report of a settlement, especially during the progress of a trial, weigh heavily as circumstantial evidence of the intention of a party such as Amazon to be bound by its communication to the opposing party and to the court.

Decision and Remedy *The Appeals Court of Massachusetts affirmed the trial court's finding that Amazon intended to be bound by the terms of the March 23 e-mail. That e-mail constituted a complete and unambiguous statement of the parties' desire to be bound by the settlement terms.*

Critical Thinking
- **What If the Facts Were Different?** *Assume that, instead of exchanging e-mails, the attorneys for both sides had agreed by telephone to all of the terms actually included in their e-mail exchanges. Would the court have ruled differently? Why or why not?*
- **Legal Environment** *What does the result in this case suggest that a businessperson should do before agreeing to a settlement of a legal dispute?*

Definiteness of Terms The second requirement for an effective offer involves the definiteness of its terms. An offer must have reasonably definite terms so that a court can determine if a breach has occurred and give an appropriate remedy.[3] The specific terms required depend, of course, on the type of contract. Generally, a contract must include the following terms, either expressed in the contract or capable of being reasonably inferred from it:

1. The identification of the parties.
2. The identification of the object or subject matter of the contract (also the quantity, when appropriate), including the work to be performed, with specific identification of such items as goods, services, and land.
3. The consideration to be paid.
4. The time of payment, delivery, or performance.

An offer may invite an acceptance to be worded in such specific terms that the contract is made definite. ■**EXAMPLE 8.3** Nintendo of America, Inc., contacts your Play 2 Win Games store and offers to sell "from one to twenty-five Nintendo 3DS.XL gaming systems for $75 each. State number desired in acceptance." You agree to buy twenty systems. Because the quantity is specified in the acceptance, the terms are definite, and the contract is enforceable. ■

When the parties have clearly manifested their intent to form a contract, courts sometimes are willing to supply a missing term in a contract, especially a sales contract.[4] But a court will not rewrite a contract if the parties' expression of intent is too vague or uncertain to be given any precise meaning.

Communication The third requirement for an effective offer is communication—the offer must be communicated to the offeree. Ordinarily, one cannot agree to a bargain without knowing that it exists. ■ **CASE IN POINT 8.4** Adwoa Gyabaah was hit by a bus owned by Rivlab Transportation Corporation. Gyabaah filed a suit in a New York state court against the bus company. Rivlab's

---

3. *Restatement (Second) of Contracts*, Section 33.

4. See UCC 2–204. Article 2 of the UCC modifies general contract law by requiring *less* specificity, or definiteness of terms, in sales and lease contracts.

insurer offered to tender the company's policy limit of $1 million in full settlement of Gyabaah's claims. On the advice of her attorney, Jeffrey Aronsky, Gyabaah signed a release (a contract forfeiting the right to pursue a legal claim) to obtain the settlement funds.

The release, however, was not sent to Rivlab or its insurer, National Casualty. Moreover, Gyabaah claimed that she had not decided whether to settle. Two months later, Gyabaah changed lawyers and changed her mind about signing the release. Her former attorney, Aronsky, filed a motion to enforce the release so that he could obtain his fees from the settlement funds. The court denied the motion, and Aronsky appealed. The reviewing court held that there was no binding settlement agreement. The release was never delivered to Rivlab or its insurer nor was acceptance of the settlement offer otherwise communicated to them.[5] ■

8–1b Termination of the Offer

The communication of an effective offer to an offeree gives the offeree the power to transform the offer into a binding, legal obligation (a contract) by an acceptance. This power of acceptance does not continue forever, though. It can be terminated either by action of the parties or by operation of law.

Termination by Action of the Parties An offer can be terminated by action of the parties in any of three ways: by revocation, by rejection, or by counteroffer.

Revocation. The offeror's act of revoking, or withdrawing, an offer is known as **revocation.** Unless an offer is irrevocable, the offeror usually can revoke the offer, as long as the revocation is communicated to the offeree before the offeree accepts. Revocation may be accomplished by either of the following:

1. Express repudiation of the offer (such as "I withdraw my previous offer of October 17").
2. Performance of acts that are inconsistent with the existence of the offer and are made known to the offeree (for instance, selling the offered property to another person in the offeree's presence).

In most states, a revocation becomes effective when the offeree or the offeree's *agent* (a person acting on behalf of the offeree) actually receives it. Therefore, a revocation sent via FedEx on April 1 and delivered at the offeree's residence or place of business on April 3 becomes effective on April 3. An offer made to the general public can

be revoked in the same manner in which it was originally communicated. For instance, an offer made on specific Web sites or in particular newspapers can be revoked on the same Web sites or in the same newspapers.

Irrevocable Offers. Although most offers are revocable, some can be made irrevocable—that is, they cannot be revoked. One form of irrevocable offer is an **option contract.** An option contract is created when an offeror promises to hold an offer open for a specified period of time in return for a payment (consideration) given by the offeree. An option contract takes away the offeror's power to revoke the offer for the period of time specified in the option.

Option contracts are frequently used in conjunction with the sale or lease of real estate. ■ **EXAMPLE 8.5** Tyler agrees to lease a house from Jackson, the property owner. The lease contract includes a clause stating that Tyler is paying an additional $15,000 for an option to purchase the property within a specified period of time. If Tyler decides not to purchase the house after the specified period has lapsed, he loses the $15,000, and Jackson is free to sell the property to another buyer. ■

Rejection. If the offeree rejects the offer—by words or by conduct—the offer is terminated. Any subsequent attempt by the offeree to accept will be construed as a new offer, giving the original offeror (now the offeree) the power of acceptance.

Like a revocation, a rejection of an offer is effective only when it is actually received by the offeror or the offeror's agent. ■ **EXAMPLE 8.6** Goldfinch Farms offers to sell specialty Maitake mushrooms to a Japanese buyer, Kinoko Foods. If Kinoko rejects the offer by sending a letter via U.S. mail, the rejection will not be effective (and the offer will not be terminated) until Goldfinch receives the letter. ■

Merely inquiring about the "firmness" of an offer does not constitute rejection. ■ **EXAMPLE 8.7** Raymond offers to buy Francie's digital pen for $100. She responds, "Is that your best offer?" A reasonable person would conclude that Francie has not rejected the offer but has merely made an inquiry. Francie could still accept and bind Raymond to the $100 price. ■

Counteroffer. A **counteroffer** is a rejection of the original offer and the simultaneous making of a new offer. ■ **EXAMPLE 8.8** Burke offers to sell his home to Lang for $270,000. Lang responds, "Your price is too high. I'll offer to purchase your house for $250,000." Lang's response is a counteroffer because it rejects Burke's offer to sell at $270,000 and creates a new offer by Lang to purchase the home for $250,000. ■

At common law, the **mirror image rule** requires the offeree's acceptance to match the offeror's offer exactly—to

---

5. *Gyabaah v. Rivlab Transportation Corp.*, 102 A.D.3d 451, 958 N.Y.S.2d 109 (N.Y.A.D. 2013).

mirror the offer. Any change in, or addition to, the terms of the original offer automatically terminates that offer and substitutes the counteroffer. The counteroffer, of course, need not be accepted, but if the original offeror does accept the terms of the counteroffer, a valid contract is created.[6]

Termination by Operation of Law The power of the offeree to transform the offer into a binding, legal obligation can be terminated by operation of law through the occurrence of any of the following events:

1. Lapse of time.
2. Destruction of the specific subject matter of the offer.
3. Death or incompetence of the offeror or the offeree.
4. Supervening illegality of the proposed contract. (A statute or court decision that makes an offer illegal automatically terminates the offer.)

Lapse of Time. An offer terminates automatically by law when the period of time *specified in the offer* has passed. If the offer states that it will be left open until a particular date, then the offer will terminate at midnight on that day. If the offer states that it will be open for a number of days, this time period normally begins to run when the offeree *receives* the offer (not when it is formed or sent).

If the offer does not specify a time for acceptance, the offer terminates at the end of a *reasonable* period of time. What constitutes a reasonable period of time depends on the subject matter of the contract, business and market conditions, and other relevant circumstances. An offer to sell farm produce, for instance, will terminate sooner than an offer to sell farm equipment. Farm produce is perishable and is also subject to greater fluctuations in market value.

Destruction, Death, or Incompetence. An offer is automatically terminated if the specific subject matter of the offer (such as a smartphone or a house) is destroyed before the offer is accepted.[7] Notice of the destruction is not required for the offer to terminate.

An offeree's power of acceptance is also terminated when the offeror or offeree dies or is legally incapacitated—*unless the offer is irrevocable.* ■ **EXAMPLE 8.9** Sybil Maven offers to sell commercial property to Westside Investment for $2 million. In June, Westside pays Maven $5,000 in exchange for her agreement to hold the offer open for ten months (forming an option contract). If Maven dies in July, her offer is not terminated, because it is irrevocable. Westside can purchase the property from Maven's estate at any time within the ten-month period. ■

In contrast, a revocable offer is personal to both parties and cannot pass to the heirs, guardian, or the estate of either party. This rule applies whether or not the other party had notice of the death or incompetence.

Supervening Illegality. A statute or court decision that makes an offer illegal automatically terminates the offer.[8] ■ **EXAMPLE 8.10** Lee offers to lend Kim $10,000 at an annual interest rate of 15 percent. Before Kim can accept the offer, a law is enacted that prohibits interest rates higher than 8 percent. Lee's offer is automatically terminated. (If the statute is enacted after Kim accepts the offer, a valid contract is formed, but the contract may still be unenforceable.) ■

Concept Summary 8.1 reviews the ways in which an offer can be terminated.

---

6. The mirror image rule has been greatly modified in regard to sales contracts. Section 2–207 of the UCC provides that a contract is formed if the offeree makes a definite expression of acceptance (such as signing a form in the appropriate location), even though the terms of the acceptance modify or add to the terms of the original offer.

7. *Restatement (Second) of Contracts*, Section 36.
8. *Restatement (Second) of Contracts*, Section 36.

Concept Summary 8.1

Methods by Which an Offer Can Be Terminated

By Action of the Parties	• Revocation • Rejection • Counteroffer
By Operation of Law	• Lapse of time • Destruction of the subject matter • Death or incompetence of the offeror or offeree • Supervening illegality

8–1c Acceptance

Acceptance is a voluntary act by the offeree that shows assent (agreement) to the terms of an offer. The offeree's act may consist of words or conduct. The acceptance must be unequivocal and must be communicated to the offeror.

Generally, only the person to whom the offer is made or that person's agent can accept the offer and create a binding contract. (See this chapter's *Digital Update* feature for a discussion of how parties can sometimes inadvertently accept a contract via e-mail or instant messages.)

DIGITAL UPDATE   Can Your E-Mails or Instant Messages Create a Valid Contract?

Instant messaging and e-mailing are among the most common forms of informal communication. Not surprisingly, parties considering an agreement often exchange offers and counteroffers via e-mail (and, to a lesser extent, instant messaging). The parties may believe that these informal electronic exchanges are for negotiation purposes only. But such communications can lead to the formation of valid contracts.

E-Mails and Settlements

After automobile accidents, the parties' attorneys sometimes exchange e-mails as part of the negotiation process. For instance, John Forcelli, who was injured in an automobile accident, sued the owner of the vehicle, Gelco Corporation. While the suit was pending, Gelco's insurance company's representative orally offered Forcelli a $230,000 settlement, which Forcelli accepted. The representative then sent an e-mail confirming the terms of the settlement, and Forcelli signed a notarized release.

A few days later, however, a New York trial court (unaware of the settlement) granted Gelco's motion for summary judgment and dismissed Forcelli's claims. Gelco then tried to rescind the settlement, claiming that the e-mail did not constitute a binding written settlement agreement. The trial court ruled against Gelco, and an appeal followed. The reviewing court affirmed. The e-mail contained all the necessary elements of contract.[a]

"Accidental" Contracts via E-Mails

When a series of e-mails signal intent to be bound, a contract may be formed, even though some language in the e-mails may be careless or accidental. What matters is whether a court determines that it is reasonable for the receiving party to believe that there is an agreement.

Indeed, e-mail contracting has become so common that only unusually strange circumstances will cause a

court to reject such contracts.[b] Furthermore, under the Uniform Electronic Transactions Act (UETA), a contract "may not be denied legal effect solely because an electronic record was used in its formation." Most states have adopted this act, at least in part. (The UETA is discussed later in this chapter.)

Instant Messaging Can Create Valid Contract Modifications

Like e-mail exchanges, instant messaging conversations between individuals in the process of negotiations can result in the formation (or modification) of a contract. One case involved an online marketing service, CX Digital Media, Inc., which provides clients with advertising referrals from its network of affiliates.

CX Digital charges a fee for its services based on the number of referrals. One of its clients was Smoking Everywhere, Inc., a seller of electronic cigarettes. While the two companies were negotiating a change in contract terms via instant messaging, the issue of the maximum number of referrals per day came up. A CX Digital employee sent an instant message to a Smoking Everywhere executive asking about the maximum number. The executive responded, "NO LIMIT," and CX Digital's employee replied, "Awesome!"

After that, CX Digital referred a higher volume of sales leads than it had previously. Smoking Everywhere refused to pay for these additional referrals, claiming that the instant messaging chat did not constitute an enforceable modification of the initial contract. At trial, CX Digital prevailed. Smoking Everywhere had to pay more than $1 million for the additional sales leads.[c]

Critical Thinking *How can a company structure e-mail negotiations to avoid "accidentally" forming a contract?*

---

a. *Forcelli v. Gelco Corporation,* 109 A.D.3d 244, 972 N.Y.S.2d 570 (2013).

b. See, for example, *Beastie Boys v. Monster Energy Co.,* 983 F.Supp.2d 338 (S.D.N.Y. 2013).

c. *CX Digital Media, Inc. v. Smoking Everywhere, Inc.,* 2011 WL 1102782 (S.D.Fla. 2011).

Unequivocal Acceptance   To exercise the power of acceptance effectively, the offeree must accept unequivocally. This is the *mirror image rule* previously discussed. An acceptance may be unequivocal even though the offeree expresses dissatisfaction with the contract. For instance, "I accept the offer, but can you give me a better price?" or "I accept, but please send a written contract" is an effective acceptance. (Notice how important each word is!)

An acceptance cannot impose new conditions or change the terms of the original offer. If it does, the acceptance may be considered a counteroffer, which is a rejection of the original offer. For instance, the statement "I accept the offer but only if I can pay on ninety days' credit" is a counteroffer and not an unequivocal acceptance.

Note that even when the additional terms are construed as a counteroffer, the other party can accept the terms by words or by conduct.   ■ **CASE IN POINT 8.11** Lagrange Development is a nonprofit corporation in Ohio that acquires and rehabilitates real property. Sonja Brown presented Lagrange with a written offer to buy a particular house for $79,900. Lagrange's executive director, Terry Glazer, penciled in modifications to the offer—an increased purchase price of $84,200 and a later date for acceptance. Glazer initialed the changes and signed the document.

Brown initialed the date change but not the price increase, and did not sign the revised document. Nevertheless, Brown went through with the sale and received ownership of the property. When a dispute later arose as to the purchase price, a court found that Glazer's modification of the terms had constituted a counteroffer, which Brown had accepted by performance. Therefore, the contract was enforceable for the modified price of $84,200.[9]   ■

Silence as Acceptance   Ordinarily, silence cannot constitute acceptance, even if the offeror states, "By your silence and inaction, you will be deemed to have accepted this offer." An offeree should not be obligated to act affirmatively to reject an offer when no consideration (nothing of value) has passed to the offeree to impose such a duty.

In some instances, however, the offeree does have a duty to speak, and her or his silence or inaction will operate as an acceptance. Silence can constitute an acceptance when the offeree has had prior dealings with the offeror.   ■ **EXAMPLE 8.12**   Marabel's restaurant routinely receives shipments of produce from a certain supplier. That supplier notifies Marabel's that it is raising its prices because its crops were damaged by a late freeze. If the restaurant does not respond in any way, the silence may operate as an acceptance, and the supplier will be justified in continuing regular shipments.   ■

Communication of Acceptance   Whether the offeror must be notified of the acceptance depends on the nature of the contract. In a unilateral contract, the full performance of some act is called for. Acceptance is usually evident, and notification is therefore unnecessary (unless the law requires it or the offeror asks for it). In a bilateral contract, in contrast, communication of acceptance is necessary, because acceptance is in the form of a promise. The bilateral contract is formed when the promise is made rather than when the act is performed.

■ **CASE IN POINT 8.13**   Powerhouse Custom Homes, Inc., owed $95,260 to 84 Lumber Company under a credit agreement. When Powerhouse failed to pay, 84 Lumber filed a suit to collect. During mediation, the parties agreed to a deadline for objections to whatever agreement they might reach. If there were no objections, the agreement would be binding.

Powerhouse then offered to pay less than the amount owed, but 84 Lumber did not respond. Powerhouse later argued that 84 Lumber had accepted the offer by not objecting to it within the deadline. The court ruled in 84 Lumber's favor for the entire amount of the debt. To form a contract, an offer must be accepted unequivocally. Powerhouse made an offer, but 84 Lumber did not communicate acceptance. Therefore, the parties did not reach an agreement on settlement.[10]   ■

At issue in the following case was the validity and enforceability of a waiver of liability on the back page of a gym's membership agreement. In this case, the court had to determine whether the circumstances indicated that the offeree's acceptance of the agreement was unequivocal and clearly communicated.

---

9. *Brown v. Lagrange Development Corp.*, 2015 -Ohio- 133 (Ohio App. 2015).

10. *Powerhouse Custom Homes, Inc. v. 84 Lumber Co.*, 307 Ga.App. 605, 705 S.E.2d 704 (2011).

Hinkal v. Pardoe

Superior Court of Pennsylvania, 2016 PA Super 11, 133 A.3d 738 (2016).

In the Language of the Court

Opinion by *STABILE*, J. [Judge]

* * * *

[Melinda Hinkal filed a suit in a Pennsylvania state court against personal trainer Gavin Pardoe and Gold's Gym, Inc., alleging that] she sustained a serious neck injury while using a piece of exercise equipment under * * * Pardoe's direction [at Gold's Gym. Hinkal] alleges that she suffered a rupture of the C5 disc in her neck requiring two separate surgeries. [Gold's and Pardoe] filed a Motion for Summary Judgment [asserting] that as a member of Gold's Gym [Hinkal] signed * * * a Membership Agreement [that] contains legally valid "waiver of liability" provisions, which in turn, bar [her] claims.

The trial court concluded that the waiver language set forth in Gold's Membership Agreement was valid and enforceable.

[Hinkal] filed a timely appeal to this [state intermediate appellate] Court.

* * * *

* * * Appellant [Hinkal] questions whether the waiver on the back page of her membership agreement is valid and enforceable. The language on the back page of the agreement reads in pertinent part as follows:

WAIVER OF LIABILITY; ASSUMPTION OF RISK: Member acknowledges that the use of Gold's Gym's facilities, equipment, services and programs involves an inherent risk of personal injury to Member. * * * Member voluntarily agrees to assume all risks of personal injury to Member * * * and waives any and all claims or actions that Member may have against Gold's Gym * * * and any * * * employees * * * for * * * injuries arising from

use of any exercise equipment * * * in supervised or unsupervised activities.

The Gold's Gym Membership Agreement signed by Appellant further instructs:

Do not sign this Agreement until you have read both sides. The terms on each side of this form are a part of this Agreement. * * * By signing this Agreement, Member acknowledges that This Agreement is a contract that will become legally binding upon its acceptance.

The signature line follows immediately and the words "Notice: See other side for important information" appear in bold typeface below the signature line.

* * * *

* * * Appellant * * * asserts that her claim is not barred by the "exclusion clause" on the back of the membership agreement. * * * Appellant contends the waiver is invalid because the waiver language appeared on the back of the agreement, she never read or was told to read the back of the agreement, and the clause was not "brought home" to her in a way that could suggest she was aware of the clause and its contents. However, * * * Appellant admitted she did not read the agreement prior to signing it. * * * Her failure to read her agreement does not render it either invalid or unenforceable. *The law of Pennsylvania is clear. One who is about to sign a contract has a duty to read that contract first.* * * * It is well established that, in the absence of fraud, the failure to read a contract before signing it is an unavailing excuse or defense and cannot justify an avoidance, modification or nullification of the contract. [Emphasis added.]

[To support her claim, Appellant cites *Beck-Hummel v. Ski Shawnee, Inc.*,

a previous case before this court, but] the signed Gold's Gym membership agreement cannot be compared in any way to the unread and unsigned disclaimer on a ski facility ticket in [*Beck-Hummel.*]

* * * *

* * * In [*Beck-Hummel,*] the release provision was contained on the face of an entry ticket purchased for use of a ski facility. The ticket did not require a signature or an express acknowledgment that its terms were read and accepted before using the facility. Nothing about the ticket ensured that a purchaser would be aware of its release provision. The purchasers were mere recipients of the document. In short, there was not sufficient evidence to find conclusively that there was a meeting of the minds that part of the consideration for use of the facility was acceptance of a release provision. In stark contrast, here there is a written, signed and acknowledged agreement between the parties.

* * * *

Here, without reading it, Appellant signed the membership agreement, which included an unambiguous directive not to sign before reading both sides, a clear pronouncement that the terms on both sides of the form are part of the agreement, and a straightforward statement that the agreement constitutes the entire agreement between the parties. * * * We find no genuine issue as to any material fact or any error in the lower court's determination that the waiver was valid and enforceable. Appellant is not entitled to relief based on [this] issue.

* * * *

Order affirmed.

Legal Reasoning Questions

1. What indicated that the terms in the agreement at issue in this case were accepted?

2. What were the appellant's arguments in support of her claim? Which of those contentions did the court imply was irrelevant? Why?

3. How did the court distinguish its conclusion in this case from its decision in *Beck-Hummel*?

Mode and Timeliness of Acceptance In bilateral contracts, acceptance must be timely. The general rule is that acceptance in a bilateral contract is timely if it is made before the offer is terminated. Problems may arise, though, when the parties involved are not dealing face to face. In such situations, the offeree should use an authorized mode of communication.

The Mailbox Rule. Acceptance takes effect, thus completing formation of the contract, at the time the offeree sends or delivers the communication via the mode expressly or impliedly authorized by the offeror. This is the so-called **mailbox rule,** also called the *deposited acceptance rule,* which the majority of courts follow. Under this rule, if the authorized mode of communication is the mail, then an acceptance becomes valid when it is dispatched (placed in the control of the U.S. Postal Service)—*not* when it is received by the offeror. (Note, however, that if the offer stipulates when acceptance will be effective, then the offer will not be effective until the time specified.)

The mailbox rule does not apply to instantaneous forms of communication, such as when the parties are dealing face to face, by telephone, by fax, and (usually) by e-mail. Under the Uniform Electronic Transactions Act, e-mail is considered sent when it either leaves the control of the sender or is received by the recipient. This rule takes the place of the mailbox rule when the parties have agreed to conduct transactions electronically and allows an e-mail acceptance to become effective when sent.

Authorized Means of Acceptance. A means of communicating acceptance can be expressly authorized by the offeror or impliedly authorized by the facts and circumstances of the situation.[11] An acceptance sent by means not expressly or impliedly authorized normally is not effective until it is received by the offeror.

When an offeror specifies how acceptance should be made (for instance, by overnight delivery), *express authorization* is said to exist. The contract is not formed unless the offeree uses that specified mode of acceptance. Moreover, both offeror and offeree are bound in contract the moment this means of acceptance is employed. ■ **EXAMPLE 8.14** Motorola Mobility, Inc., offers to sell 144 Atrix 4G smartphones and 72 Lapdocks to Call Me Plus phone stores. The offer states that Call Me Plus must accept the offer via FedEx overnight delivery. The acceptance is effective (and a binding contract is formed) the moment that Call Me Plus gives the overnight envelope containing the acceptance to the FedEx driver. ■

If the offeror does not expressly authorize a certain mode of acceptance, then acceptance can be made by *any reasonable means.*[12] Courts look at the prevailing business usages and the surrounding circumstances to determine whether the mode of acceptance used was reasonable.

Usually, the offeror's choice of a particular means in making the offer implies that the offeree can use the *same or a faster means* for acceptance. Thus, if the offer is made via Priority U.S. mail, it would be reasonable to accept the offer via Priority mail or by a faster method, such as overnight delivery.

Substitute Method of Acceptance. Sometimes, the offeror authorizes a particular method of acceptance, but the offeree accepts by a different means. In that situation, the acceptance may still be effective if the substituted method serves the same purpose as the authorized means.

Acceptance by a substitute method is not effective on dispatch, however. No contract will be formed until the acceptance is received by the offeror. ■ **EXAMPLE 8.15** Bennion's offer specifies acceptance via FedEx overnight delivery, but the offeree accepts instead by overnight delivery from UPS. The substitute method of acceptance will still be effective, but not until the offeror (Bennion) receives it from UPS. ■

8–2 Agreement in E-Contracts

Numerous contracts are formed online. Electronic contracts, or **e-contracts,** must meet the same basic requirements (agreement, consideration, contractual capacity, and legality) as paper contracts. Disputes concerning e-contracts, however, tend to center on contract terms and whether the parties voluntarily agreed to those terms.

Online contracts may be formed not only for the sale of goods and services but also for *licensing.* The "sale" of software generally involves a license, or a right to use the software, rather than the passage of title (ownership rights) from the seller to the buyer. ■ **EXAMPLE 8.16** Lauren wants to obtain software that will allow her to work on spreadsheets on her smartphone. She goes online and purchases GridMagic. During the transaction, she clicks on several on-screen "I agree" boxes to indicate her understanding that she is purchasing only the right to use the software, not ownership rights. After she agrees to these terms (the licensing agreement), she can download the software. ■

As you read through the following subsections, you will see that we typically refer to the offeror and the

---

11. *Restatement (Second) of Contracts,* Section 30, provides that an offer invites acceptance "by any medium reasonable in the circumstances," unless the offer specifies the means of acceptance.

12. *Restatement (Second) of Contracts,* Section 30. This is also the rule under UCC 2–206(1)(a).

offeree as a *seller* and a *buyer.* Keep in mind, though, that in many online transactions these parties would be more accurately described as a *licensor* and a *licensee.*

8–2a Online Offers

Sellers doing business via the Internet can protect themselves against contract disputes and legal liability by creating offers that clearly spell out the terms that will govern their transactions if the offers are accepted. All important terms should be conspicuous and easy to view.

Displaying the Offer The seller's Web site should include a hypertext link to a page containing the full contract so that potential buyers are made aware of the terms to which they are assenting. The contract generally must be displayed online in a readable format, such as a twelve-point typeface. All provisions should be reasonably clear.

Provisions to Include An important point to keep in mind is that the offeror (the seller) controls the offer and thus the resulting contract. The seller should therefore anticipate the terms he or she wants to include in a contract and provide for them in the offer. In some instances, a standardized contract form may suffice.

At a minimum, an online offer should include the following provisions:

1. *Acceptance of terms.* A clause that clearly indicates what constitutes the buyer's agreement to the terms of the offer, such as a box containing the words "I accept" that the buyer can click.
2. *Payment.* A provision specifying how payment for the goods (including any applicable taxes) must be made.
3. *Return policy.* A statement of the seller's refund and return policies.
4. *Disclaimer.* Disclaimers of liability for certain uses of the goods. For instance, an online seller of business forms may add a disclaimer that the seller does not accept responsibility for the buyer's reliance on the forms rather than on an attorney's advice.
5. *Limitation on remedies.* A provision specifying the remedies available to the buyer if the goods are found to be defective or if the contract is otherwise breached. Any limitation of remedies should be clearly spelled out.
6. *Privacy policy.* A statement indicating how the seller will use the information gathered about the buyer.
7. *Dispute resolution.* Provisions relating to dispute settlement, which we examine more closely in the following section.

Dispute-Settlement Provisions Online offers frequently include provisions relating to dispute settlement. For instance, an offer might include an arbitration clause specifying that any dispute arising under the contract will be arbitrated in a designated forum. The parties might also select the forum and the law that will govern any disputes.

Forum-Selection Clause. Many online contracts contain a **forum-selection clause** indicating the forum, or location (such as a court or jurisdiction), in which contract disputes will be resolved. Significant jurisdictional issues may arise when parties are at a great distance, as they often are when they form contracts via the Internet. A forum-selection clause will help to avert future jurisdictional problems and also help to ensure that the seller will not be required to appear in court in a distant state.

■ **CASE IN POINT 8.17** Scott Rosendahl enrolled in an online college, Ashford University. He claimed that the school's adviser had told him that Ashford offered one of the cheapest undergraduate degree programs in the country. In fact, it did not. Rosendahl later sued the school, claiming that it had violated unfair competition laws and false advertising laws and had engaged in fraud and negligent misrepresentation.

The university argued that its enrollment agreement clearly contained a requirement that all disputes be arbitrated. Rosendahl, like other students, had electronically assented to this agreement when he enrolled. Ashford presented the online application forms to the court, and the court dismissed Rosendahl's lawsuit. Rosendahl had agreed to arbitrate any disputes he had with Ashford.[13] ■

Choice-of-Law Clause. Some online contracts may also include a *choice-of-law clause,* specifying that any contract dispute will be settled according to the law of a particular jurisdiction, such as a state or country. Choice-of-law clauses are particularly common in international contracts, but they may also appear in e-contracts to specify which state's laws will govern in the United States.

8–2b Online Acceptances

The *Restatement (Second) of Contracts,* which is a compilation of common law contract principles, states that parties may agree to a contract "by written or spoken words or by other action or by failure to act."[14] The Uniform Commercial Code (UCC), which governs sales contracts, has a similar provision. Section 2–204 of the UCC states

---

13. *Rosendahl v. Bridgepoint Education, Inc.,* 2012 WL 667049 (S.D.Cal. 2012).
14. *Restatement (Second) of Contracts,* Section 19.

that any contract for the sale of goods "may be made in any manner sufficient to show agreement, including conduct by both parties which recognizes the existence of such a contract." The courts have used these provisions in determining what constitutes an online acceptance.

Click-On Agreements The courts have concluded that the act of clicking on a box labeled "I accept" or "I agree" can indicate acceptance of an online offer. The agreement resulting from such an acceptance is often called a **click-on agreement** (sometimes referred to as a *click-on license* or *click-wrap agreement*). Exhibit 8–1 shows a portion of a typical click-on agreement that accompanies a software package.

Generally, the law does not require that the parties have read all of the terms in a contract for it to be effective. Therefore, clicking on a box that states "I agree" to certain terms can be enough. The terms may be contained on a Web site through which the buyer is obtaining goods or services. They may also appear on a screen when software is downloaded from the Internet.

■ **CASE IN POINT 8.18** The "Terms of Use" that govern Facebook users' accounts include a forum-selection clause that provides for the resolution of all disputes in a court in Santa Clara County, California. To sign up for a Facebook account, a person must click on a box indicating that he or she has agreed to this term.

Mustafa Fteja was an active user of facebook.com when his account was disabled. He sued Facebook in a federal court in New York, claiming that it had disabled his Facebook page without justification and for discriminatory reasons. Facebook filed a motion to transfer the case to California under the forum-selection clause. The court found that the clause in Facebook's online contract was binding and transferred the case. When Fteja clicked on the button to accept the contract terms, he agreed to resolve all disputes with Facebook in Santa Clara County, California.[15] ■

Shrink-Wrap Agreements With a **shrink-wrap agreement** (or *shrink-wrap license*), the terms are expressed inside the box in which the goods are packaged. (The term *shrink-wrap* refers to the plastic that covers the box.) Usually, the party who opens the box is told that she or he agrees to the terms by keeping whatever is in the box. Similarly, when a purchaser opens a software package, he or she agrees to abide by the terms of the limited license agreement.

■ **EXAMPLE 8.19** Ava orders a new iMac from Big Ed's Electronics, which ships it to her. Along with the iMac, the box contains an agreement setting forth the terms of the sale, including what remedies are available.

---

15. *Fteja v. Facebook, Inc.*, 841 F.Supp.2d 829 (S.D.N.Y. 2012).

EXHIBIT 8–1   A Click-On Agreement Sample

This exhibit illustrates an online offer to form a contract. To accept the offer, the user simply scrolls down the page and clicks on the "Accept and Install" button.

The document also states that Ava's retention of the iMac for longer than thirty days will be construed as an acceptance of the terms. ■

In most instances, a shrink-wrap agreement is not between a retailer and a buyer, but is between the manufacturer of the hardware or software and the ultimate buyer-user of the product. The terms generally concern warranties, remedies, and other issues associated with the use of the product.

Shrink-Wrap Agreements and Enforceable Contract Terms. In some cases, the courts have enforced the terms of shrink-wrap agreements in the same way as the terms of other contracts. These courts have reasoned that by including the terms with the product, the seller proposed a contract. The buyer could accept this contract by using the product after having an opportunity to read the terms. Thus, a buyer's failure to object to terms contained within a shrink-wrapped software package may constitute an acceptance of the terms by conduct.

Shrink-Wrap Terms That May Not Be Enforced. Sometimes, however, the courts have refused to enforce certain terms included in shrink-wrap agreements because the buyer did not expressly consent to them. An important factor is when the parties formed their contract.

If a buyer orders a product over the telephone, for instance, and is not informed of an arbitration clause or a forum-selection clause at that time, the buyer clearly has not expressly agreed to these terms. If the buyer discovers the clauses *after* the parties have entered into a contract, a court may conclude that those terms were proposals for additional terms and were not part of the contract.

Browse-Wrap Terms Like the terms of click-on agreements, **browse-wrap terms** can occur in transactions conducted over the Internet. Unlike click-on agreements, however, browse-wrap terms do not require Internet users to assent to the terms before downloading or using certain software. In other words, a person can install the software without clicking "I agree" to the terms of a license. Browse-wrap terms are often unenforceable because they do not satisfy the agreement requirement of contract formation.[16]

■ **EXAMPLE 8.20** BrowseNet Corporation provides free downloadable "QuickLoad" software on its Web site. The site refers to a license agreement but the user does not have to view it or agree to its terms before downloading the software. One of the license terms requires all disputes to be submitted to arbitration in California. If a user sues BrowseNet in Washington State, the arbitration clause might not be enforceable, because users were not required to indicate their assent to the agreement. ■

8–2c Federal Law on E-Signatures and E-Documents

An **e-signature** has been defined as "an electronic sound, symbol, or process attached to or logically associated with a record and executed or adopted by a person with the intent to sign the record."[17] In 2000, Congress enacted the Electronic Signatures in Global and National Commerce Act (E-SIGN Act).[18]

The E-SIGN Act provides that no contract, record, or signature may be "denied legal effect" solely because it is in electronic form. In other words, under this law, an electronic signature is as valid as a signature on paper, and an e-document can be as enforceable as a paper one. For an e-signature to be enforceable, however, the contracting parties must have agreed to use electronic signatures. For an electronic document to be valid, it must be in a form that can be retained and accurately reproduced.

E-Signature Technologies Electronic documents can be signed in a number of ways. E-signature technologies include encrypted digital signatures, names intended as signatures at the end of e-mail messages, and clicks on a Web page if the clicks include some means of identification.

Note that although courts do not question that documents can be signed electronically under the E-SIGN Act, some courts will question the validity of the signatures themselves. For instance, a court might find that a typed name at the bottom of e-mail is not admissible as the person's signature. For this reason, many businesses use special software, such as DocuSign or EchoSign, that is designed to create an e-signature that looks similar to a person's handwritten signature.

Exclusions The E-SIGN Act does not apply to all types of documents. Documents that are exempt include court papers, divorce decrees, evictions, foreclosures, health-insurance terminations, prenuptial agreements, and wills. Also, the only agreements governed by the UCC that fall under this law are those covered by Articles 2 and 2A (sales and lease contracts) and UCC 1–107 and 1–206.

---

16. See, for example, *Waldman v. New Chapter, Inc.*, 714 F.Supp.2d 398 (2010).

17. This definition is from the Uniform Electronic Transactions Act, discussed later in this chapter.
18. 15 U.S.C. Sections 7001 *et seq.*

Despite these limitations, the E-SIGN Act has significantly expanded online contracting.

8–2d Partnering Agreements

One way that online sellers and buyers can prevent disputes over signatures in their e-contracts, as well as disputes over the terms and conditions of those contracts, is to form partnering agreements. In a **partnering agreement,** a seller and a buyer who frequently do business with each other agree in advance on the terms and conditions that will apply to all transactions subsequently conducted electronically. The partnering agreement can also establish special access and identification codes to be used by the parties when transacting business electronically.

A partnering agreement reduces the likelihood that contract disputes will arise because the parties have agreed in advance to the terms and conditions that will accompany each sale. Furthermore, if a dispute does arise, a court or arbitration forum will be able to refer to the partnering agreement when determining the parties' intent.

8–3 The Uniform Electronic Transactions Act

The National Conference of Commissioners on Uniform State Laws and the American Law Institute promulgated the Uniform Electronic Transactions Act (UETA) in 1999. The UETA has been adopted, at least in part, by forty-eight states, resulting in more uniformity among state laws governing electronic transactions. Among other things, the UETA declares that a signature may not be denied legal effect or enforceability solely because it is in electronic form.

The primary purpose of the UETA is to remove barriers to e-commerce by giving the same legal effect to electronic records and signatures as is given to paper documents and signatures. As mentioned, the UETA broadly defines an *e-signature* as "an electronic sound, symbol, or process attached to or logically associated with a record and executed or adopted by a person with the intent to sign the record."[19] A **record** is "information that is inscribed on a tangible medium or that is stored in an electronic or other medium and is retrievable in perceivable [visual] form."[20]

8–3a The Scope and Applicability of the UETA

The UETA does not create new rules for electronic contracts. Rather, it establishes that records, signatures, and contracts may not be denied enforceability solely due to their electronic form.

The UETA does not apply to all writings and signatures. It covers only electronic records and electronic signatures *relating to a transaction.* A *transaction* is defined as an interaction between two or more people relating to business, commercial, or governmental activities.[21] The act specifically does not apply to wills or testamentary trusts or to transactions governed by the UCC (other than those covered by Articles 2 and 2A).[22] In addition, the provisions of the UETA allow the states to exclude its application to other areas of law.

8–3b The Federal E-SIGN Act and the UETA

Earlier, we discussed the provisions of the federal E-SIGN Act. Congress passed the E-SIGN Act in 2000, a year after the UETA was presented to the states for adoption. Thus, a significant issue was to what extent the federal E-SIGN Act preempted the UETA as adopted by the states.

The E-SIGN Act[23] explicitly provides that if a state has enacted the uniform version of the UETA, that law is not preempted by the E-SIGN Act. In other words, if the state has enacted the UETA without modification, state law will govern. The problem is that many states have enacted nonuniform (modified) versions of the UETA, usually to exclude other areas of state law from the UETA's terms. The E-SIGN Act specifies that those exclusions will be preempted to the extent that they are inconsistent with the E-SIGN Act's provisions.

The E-SIGN Act explicitly allows the states to enact alternative requirements for the use of electronic records or electronic signatures. Generally, however, the requirements must be consistent with the provisions of the E-SIGN Act, and the state must not give greater legal status or effect to one specific type of technology. Additionally, state laws that include alternative requirements, if enacted after the adoption of the E-SIGN Act, must specifically refer to the E-SIGN Act. The relationship between the UETA and the E-SIGN Act is illustrated in Exhibit 8–2.

---

19. UETA 102(8).
20. UETA 102(15).

21. UETA 2(12) and 3.
22. UETA 3(b).
23. 15 U.S.C. Section 7002(2)(A)(i).

EXHIBIT 8–2 The E-SIGN Act and the UETA

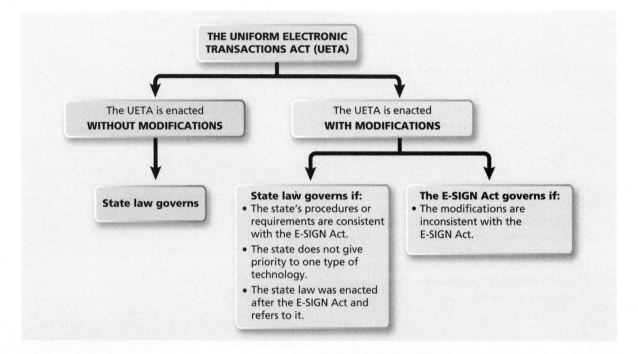

8-3c Highlights of the UETA

The UETA does not apply to a transaction unless each of the parties has previously agreed to conduct transactions by electronic means. The agreement may be explicit, or it may be implied by the conduct of the parties and the surrounding circumstances.[24] It may sometimes be reasonable to infer that a person who gives out a business card with an e-mail address on it has consented to transact business electronically, for instance. Agreement may also be inferred from an e-mail or even a verbal communication between the parties.

A person who has agreed to an electronic transaction can withdraw his or her consent and refuse to conduct further business electronically. In addition, the parties can agree to opt out of all or some of the terms of the UETA. If they do not do so, then the UETA terms will govern their electronic transactions.

Attribution of Signatures Under the UETA, if an electronic record or signature is the act of a particular person, the record or signature may be attributed to that person. If a person types her or his name at the bottom of an e-mail purchase order, for instance, that name qualifies as

---

24. UETA 5(b), and Comment 4B.

a "signature." The signature is therefore attributed to the person whose name appears on the purchase order.

The UETA does not contain any express provisions about what constitutes fraud or whether an agent is authorized to enter into a contract. Under the UETA, other state laws control if any issues relating to agency, authority, forgery, or contract formation arise. If existing state law requires a document to be notarized, the UETA provides that this requirement is satisfied by the electronic signature of a notary public or other person authorized to verify signatures.

The Effect of Errors The UETA encourages, but does not require, the use of security procedures (such as encryption) to verify changes to electronic documents and to correct errors.

The parties themselves may agree to use a security procedure. If they do, and if one party does not follow the procedure and thus fails to detect an error, the party that followed procedure can legally avoid the effect of the error. When the parties have not agreed to use a security procedure, then other state laws (including contract law governing mistakes) will determine the effect of the error.

To avoid the effect of errors, a party must promptly notify the other party of the error and of her or his intent not to be bound by the error. In addition, the party must take reasonable steps to return any benefit received. Parties cannot avoid a transaction if they have benefited.

Timing An electronic record is considered *sent* when it is properly directed to the intended recipient in a form readable by the recipient's computer system. Once the electronic record leaves the control of the sender or comes under the control of the recipient, the UETA deems it to have been sent. An electronic record is considered *received* when it enters the recipient's processing system in a readable form—*even if no individual is aware of its receipt.*

8–4 International Treaties Affecting E-Contracts

Much of the e-commerce conducted on a worldwide basis involves buyers and sellers from the United States.

The preeminence of U.S. law in this area is likely to be challenged in the future, however, as Internet use continues to expand worldwide. Already, several international organizations have created their own regulations for global Internet transactions.

The United Nations Convention on the Use of Electronic Communications in International Contracts improves commercial certainty by determining an Internet user's location for legal purposes. The convention also establishes standards for creating functional equivalence between electronic communications and paper documents. In addition, it provides that e-signatures will be treated as the equivalent of signatures on paper documents.

Another treaty relevant to e-contracts is the Hague Convention on the Choice of Court Agreements. Although it does not specifically mention e-commerce, this convention provides more certainty regarding jurisdiction and recognition of judgments by other nations' courts, thereby facilitating both offline and online transactions.

Reviewing: Agreement in Traditional and E-Contracts

Shane Durbin wanted to have a recording studio custom-built in his home. He sent invitations to a number of local contractors to submit bids on the project. Rory Amstel submitted the lowest bid, which was $20,000 less than any of the other bids Durbin received. Durbin called Amstel to ascertain the type and quality of the materials that were included in the bid and to find out if he could substitute a superior brand of acoustic tiles for the same bid price. Amstel said he would have to check into the price difference. The parties also discussed a possible start date for construction.

Two weeks later, Durbin changed his mind and decided not to go forward with his plan to build a recording studio. Amstel filed a suit against Durbin for breach of contract. Using the information presented in the chapter, answer the following questions.

1. Did Amstel's bid meet the requirements of an offer? Explain.
2. Was there an acceptance of the offer? Why or why not?
3. Suppose that the court determines that the parties did not reach an agreement. Further suppose that Amstel, in anticipation of building Durbin's studio, had purchased materials and refused other jobs so that he would have time in his schedule for Durbin's project. Under what theory discussed in the chapter might Amstel attempt to recover these costs?
4. How is an offer terminated? Assuming that Durbin did not inform Amstel that he was rejecting the offer, was the offer terminated at any time described here? Explain.

Debate This . . . *The terms and conditions in click-on agreements are so long and detailed that no one ever reads the agreements. Therefore, the act of clicking on "I agree" is not really an acceptance.*

Terms and Concepts

acceptance 154	browse-wrap terms 160	counteroffer 152
agreement 147	click-on agreement 159	e-contract 157

Issue Spotters

1. Fidelity Corporation offers to hire Ron to replace Monica, who has given Fidelity a month's notice of intent to quit. Fidelity gives Ron a week to decide whether to accept. Two days later, Monica decides not to quit and signs an employment contract with Fidelity for another year. The next day, Monica tells Ron of the new contract. Ron immediately faxes a formal letter of acceptance to Fidelity. Do Fidelity and Ron have a contract? Why or why not? (See *Agreement*.)

2. Applied Products, Inc., does business with Beltway Distributors, Inc., online. Under the Uniform Electronic Transactions Act, what determines the effect of the electronic documents evidencing the parties' deal? Is a party's "signature" necessary? Explain. (See *The Uniform Electronic Transactions Act*.)

• **Check your answers to the Issue Spotters against the answers provided in Appendix B at the end of this text.**

Business Scenarios

8–1. Agreement. Ball e-mails Sullivan and inquires how much Sullivan is asking for a specific forty-acre tract of land Sullivan owns. Sullivan responds, "I will not take less than $60,000 for the forty-acre tract as specified." Ball immediately sends Sullivan a fax stating, "I accept your offer for $60,000 for the forty-acre tract as specified." Discuss whether Ball can hold Sullivan to a contract for the sale of the land. (See *Agreement*.)

8–2. Offer and Acceptance. Schmidt, the owner of a small business, has a large piece of used farm equipment for sale. He offers to sell the equipment to Barry for $10,000. Discuss the legal effects of the following events on the offer: (See *Agreement*.)

(a) Schmidt dies prior to Barry's acceptance, and at the time he accepts, Barry is unaware of Schmidt's death.

(b) The night before Barry accepts, fire destroys the equipment.

(c) Barry pays $100 for a thirty-day option to purchase the equipment. During this period, Schmidt dies, and later Barry accepts the offer, knowing of Schmidt's death.

(d) Barry pays $100 for a thirty-day option to purchase the equipment. During this period, Barry dies, and Barry's estate accepts Schmidt's offer within the stipulated time period.

Business Case Problems

8–3. Spotlight on Crime Stoppers—Communication.
 The Baton Rouge Crime Stoppers (BCS) offered a reward for information about the "South Louisiana Serial Killer." The information was to be provided via a hot line. Dianne Alexander had survived an attack by a person suspected of being the killer. She identified a suspect in a police photo lineup and later sought to collect the reward. BCS refused to pay because she had not provided information to them via the hot line. Had Alexander complied with the terms of the offer? Explain. [*Alexander v. Lafayette Crime Stoppers, Inc.,* 38 So.3d 282 (La. App. 3 Dist. 2010) (See *Agreement*.)

8–4. Business Case Problem with Sample Answer—Online Acceptances. Heather Reasonover opted to try
 Internet service from Clearwire Corp. Clearwire sent her a confirmation e-mail and a modem. When Reasonover plugged in the modem, an "I accept terms" box appeared. Without clicking on the box, Reasonover quit the page. She had not seen Clearwire's "Terms of Service," accessible only through its Web site. Although the e-mail she received and the printed materials included with the model included URLs to the company's Web site, neither URL gave direct access to the "Terms of Service." A clause in the "Terms of Service" required subscribers to submit any dispute to arbitration. Is Reasonover bound to this clause? Why or why not? [*Kwan v. Clearwire Corp.,* 2012 WL 32380 (W.D.Wash. 2012)] (See *Agreement in E-Contracts*.)

• **For a sample answer to Problem 8–4, go to Appendix C at the end of this text.**

8–5. Acceptance. Judy Olsen, Kristy Johnston, and their mother, Joyce Johnston, owned seventy-eight acres of real property on Eagle Creek in Meagher County, Montana. When Joyce died, she left her interest in the property to Kristy. Kristy wrote to Judy, offering to buy Judy's interest or to sell her own interest to Judy. The letter said to "please respond to Bruce Townsend." In a letter to Kristy—not to Bruce—Judy accepted Kristy's offer to sell her interest. By that time, however, Kristy had made the same offer to sell her interest to their brother, Dave, and he had accepted. Did Judy and Kristy have an enforceable, binding contract? Or did Kristy's offer specifying one exclusive mode of acceptance mean that Judy's reply was not effective? Discuss. [*Olsen v. Johnston,* 368 Mont. 347, 301 P.3d 791 (2013)] (See *Agreement.*)

8–6. Agreement. Amy Kemper was seriously injured when her motorcycle was struck by a vehicle driven by Christopher Brown. Kemper's attorney wrote to Statewide Claims Services, the administrator for Brown's insurer, asking for "all the insurance money that Mr. Brown had under his insurance policy." In exchange, the letter indicated that Kemper would sign a "limited release" on Brown's liability, provided that it did not include any language requiring her to reimburse Brown or his insurance company for any of their incurred costs. Statewide then sent a check and release form to Kemper, but the release demanded that Kemper "place money in an escrow account in regards to any and all liens pending." Kemper refused the demand, claiming that Statewide's response was a counteroffer rather than an unequivocal acceptance of the settlement offer. Did Statewide and Kemper have an enforceable agreement? Discuss. [*Kemper v. Brown,* 325 Ga.App. 806, 754 S.E.2d 141 (2014)] (See *Agreement.*)

8–7. Requirements of the Offer. Technical Consumer Products, Inc. (TCP), makes and distributes energy-efficient lighting products. Emily Bahr was TCP's district sales manager in Minnesota, North Dakota, and South Dakota when the company announced the details of a bonus plan. A district sales manager who achieved 100 percent year-over-year sales growth and a 42 percent gross margin would earn 200 percent of his or her base salary as a bonus. TCP retained absolute discretion to modify the plan. Bahr's base salary was $42,500. Her final sales results for the year showed 113 percent year-over-year sales growth and a 42 percent gross margin. She anticipated a bonus of $85,945, but TCP could not afford to pay the bonuses as planned, and Bahr received only $34,229. In response to Bahr's claim for breach of contract, TCP argued that the bonus plan was too indefinite to be an offer. Is TCP correct? Explain. [*Bahr v. Technical Consumer Products, Inc.,* 601 Fed.Appx. 359 (6th Cir. 2015)] (See *Agreement.*)

8–8. Acceptance. Altisource Portfolio Solutions, Inc., is a global corporation that provides real property owners with a variety of services, including property preservation—repairs, debris removal, and so on. Lucas Contracting, Inc., is a small trade contractor in Carrollton, Ohio. On behalf of Altisource, Berghorst Enterprises, LLC, hired Lucas to perform preservation work on certain foreclosed properties in eastern Ohio.

When Berghorst did not pay for the work, Lucas filed a suit in an Ohio state court against Altisource. Before the trial, Lucas e-mailed the terms of a settlement. The same day, Altisource e-mailed a response that did not challenge or contradict Lucas's proposal and indicated agreement to it. Two days later, however, Altisource forwarded a settlement document that contained additional terms. Which proposal most likely satisfies the element of agreement to establish a contract? Explain. [*Lucas Contracting, Inc. v. Altisource Portfolio Solutions, Inc.,* __ Ohio App.3d __, 2016 -Ohio- 474, __ N.E.2d __ (2016)] (See *Agreement.*)

8–9. A Question of Ethics—E-Contract Disputes.
 Dewayne Hubbert, Elden Craft, Chris Grout, and Rhonda Byington bought computers from Dell Corp. through its Web site. Before buying, Hubbert and the others configured their own computers. To make a purchase, each buyer completed forms on five Web pages. On each page, Dell's "Terms and Conditions of Sale" were accessible by clicking on a blue hyperlink. A statement on three of the pages read, "All sales are subject to Dell's Term[s] and Conditions of Sale," but a buyer was not required to click an assent to the terms to complete a purchase. The terms were also printed on the backs of the invoices and on separate documents contained in the shipping boxes with the computers. Among those terms was a "Binding Arbitration" clause.

*The computers contained Pentium 4 microprocessors, which Dell advertised as the fastest, most powerful Intel Pentium processors then available. In 2002, Hubbert and the others filed a suit in an Illinois state court against Dell, alleging that this marketing was false, misleading, and deceptive. The plaintiffs claimed that the Pentium 4 microprocessor was slower and less powerful, and provided poorer performance, than either a Pentium III or an AMD Athlon, and at a greater cost. Dell asked the court to compel arbitration. [*Hubbert v. Dell Corp.,* 359 Ill.App.3d 976, 835 N.E.2d 113, 296 Ill.Dec. 258 (5 Dist. 2005)] (See *Agreement in E-Contracts.*)*

(a) Should the court enforce the arbitration clause in this case? If you were the judge, how would you rule on this issue?

(b) Do you think shrink-wrap, click-on, and browse-wrap terms impose too great a burden on purchasers? Why or why not?

(c) An ongoing complaint about shrink-wrap, click-on, and browse-wrap terms is that sellers (often large corporations) draft them and buyers (typically individual consumers) do not read them. Should purchasers be bound in contract by terms that they have not even read? Why or why not?

Legal Reasoning Group Activity

8–10. E-Contracts. To download a specific application (app) to your smartphone or tablet device, usually you have to check a box indicating that you agree to the company's terms and conditions. Most individuals do so without ever reading those terms and conditions. Print out a specific set of terms and conditions from a downloaded app to use in this assignment. (See *Agreement in E-Contracts.*)

(a) One group will determine which of these terms and conditions are favorable to the company.

(b) Another group will determine which of these terms and conditions conceivably will be favorable to the individual.

(c) A third group will determine which terms and conditions, on net, favor the company too much.

CHAPTER 9

Consideration, Capacity, and Legality

Courts generally want contracts to be enforceable, and much of the law is devoted to aiding the enforceability of contracts. Before a court will enforce a contractual promise, however, it must be convinced that there was some exchange of consideration underlying the bargain. Furthermore, *freedom of contract*—that is, the concept that all individuals are legally entitled to form contracts without any governmental restriction—is not absolute.

In other words, not all people can make legally binding contracts at all times. For instance, contracts entered into by persons lacking the capacity to do so may be voidable. Similarly, contracts calling for the performance of an act that is against the law are illegal and thus *void*, meaning that they are not contracts at all.

In this chapter, we first examine the requirement of consideration and then look at contractual capacity and legality.

9–1 Consideration

The fact that a promise has been made does not mean the promise can or will be enforced. Under Roman law, a promise was not enforceable without a *causa*—that is, a reason for making the promise that was also deemed to be a sufficient reason for enforcing it.

Under the common law, a primary basis for the enforcement of promises is consideration. **Consideration** usually is defined as the value given in return for a promise (in a bilateral contract) or in return for a performance (in a unilateral contract). It is the inducement, price, or motive that causes a party to enter into an agreement.

As long as consideration is present, the courts generally do not interfere with contracts based on the amount of consideration paid. It is up to the contracting parties to determine how much their bargain is worth.

9–1a Elements of Consideration

Often, consideration is broken down into two parts: (1) something of *legally sufficient value* must be given in exchange for the promise, and (2) there must be a *bargained-for* exchange.

Legally Sufficient Value To be legally sufficient, consideration must be something of value in the eyes of the law. The "something of legally sufficient value" may consist of the following:

1. A promise to do something that one has no prior legal duty to do.
2. The performance of an action that one is otherwise not obligated to undertake.
3. The refraining from an action that one has a legal right to undertake (called a **forbearance**).

Consideration in bilateral contracts normally consists of a promise in return for a promise. In a contract for the sale of goods, for instance, the seller promises to ship specific goods to the buyer, and the buyer promises to pay for those goods. Each of these promises constitutes consideration for the contract.

In contrast, unilateral contracts involve a promise in return for a performance (an action). ■ **EXAMPLE 9.1** Anita says to her neighbor, "When you finish painting the garage, I will pay you $800." Anita's neighbor paints the garage. The act of painting the garage is the consideration that creates Anita's contractual obligation to pay her neighbor $800. ■

Bargained-for Exchange The second element of consideration is that it must provide the basis for the bargain struck between the contracting parties. That is, the item of value must be given or promised by the promisor (offeror) in return for the promisee's promise, performance, or promise of performance.

This element of bargained-for exchange distinguishes contracts from gifts. ■ **EXAMPLE 9.2** Sheng-Li says to his son, "In consideration of the fact that you are not as wealthy as your brothers, I will pay you $5,000." The fact that the word *consideration* is used does not, by itself, mean that consideration has been given. Indeed, Sheng-Li's promise is not enforceable, because the son does not have to do anything in order to receive the $5,000 promised. Because the son does not need to give Sheng-Li something of legal value in return for his promise, there is no bargained-for exchange. Rather, Sheng-Li has simply stated his motive for giving his son a gift. ■

Sometimes, employers offer to cover the costs of employment-related education for their employees. The employees may then be required to repay their employers for all or a portion of the costs. At the center of the dispute in the following case was an agreement signed by an employee to reimburse his employer for educational costs. The question was whether the agreement met the requirement of a bargained-for exchange.

Case Analysis 9.1

USS–POSCO Industries v. Case

California Court of Appeal, First District, Division 1, 244 Cal.App.4th 197, 197 Cal.Rptr.3d 791 (2016).

In the Language of the Court

BANKE, J. [Judge]
    * * * *

[USS–POSCO Industries (UPI) in Pittsburg, California,] hired [Floyd] Case in 2007. He initially worked as an entry-level Laborer and Side Trim Operator. As a condition of employment, Case joined Local 1440 of the United Steelworkers of America.

UPI faced a shortage of skilled Maintenance Technical Electrical (MTE) workers. To address this, UPI, after consultation with Local 1440, decided to implement a Learner Program. Thus, in June 2008, the company and Local 1440 entered into a Memorandum of Understanding (MOU) stating UPI would train up to 10 current employees, while continuing to pay their wages and benefits, in an effort to qualify them as MTEs. UPI and the union recognized "that, due to the strong demand for Maintenance Technician Electrical [workers] the Company needs to retain successful candidates as employees for a reasonable period of time in order to recoup its substantial $46,000 investment in their training." UPI and the union therefore agreed UPI "may require candidates in the Learner Program to sign [a] Reimbursement Agreement that would require reimbursement for a portion of the training should a candidate voluntarily terminate employment

within 30 months of completion of the Learner Program."

The Learner Program required 135 weeks of instruction, 90 weeks of on the job training and 45 weeks of classroom work (partially courses at a local community college, partially other courses). The goal was to complete training within 162 weeks, or just over three years. If a participant successfully completed the program and then passed UPI's MTE test, he or she would be assigned to an MTE vacancy.

The MTE position and Learner Program aligned with Case's desire to work as an engineer. Case understood joining the Learner Program was voluntary. He also understood he did not need to go through the Learner Program or a similar formal educational program to obtain an MTE position. * * * A prospect could simply take and pass UPI's MTE test. However, Case did not attempt the test prior to participating in the Learner Program because he did not think he had the knowledge to pass. He was also unsure if he would pass if he undertook a self-study program. In any case, the Learner Program allowed him to get trained during the workday instead of after hours, and it would lead to higher pay. Accordingly, he applied for the program and was one of [the] selected participants.

Case was informed of the reimbursement obligation during a training session

for prospective participants. A presentation slide entitled "Repayment Agreement" told prospects they would "sign an agreement to reimburse a portion of their training cost should they voluntarily terminate employment within 30 months of program completion." The slide, consistent with the MOU, indicated the obligation would be "$46,000 prorated over 30 months."

Case was subsequently presented with a written reimbursement agreement and signed it without objection. Under that one-page agreement, Case acknowledged UPI would pay his "wages, benefits and training expenses" while he was in the Learner Program, but there would be no guarantee participation in the program would insure promotion, transfer, or continued employment with UPI. He further agreed that if he was fired for cause or voluntarily left UPI within 30 months after completing the program, he would, absent a compelling hardship such as a serious injury or family death, refund $30,000 of the expense of his training, less $1,000 per month of subsequent service at UPI.

Two months after completing the Learner Program and obtaining an MTE position, Case left UPI for Lawrence Livermore National Laboratory to work as a high voltage electrician.
    * * * *

Case 9.1 Continues

When Case refused to reimburse UPI, the company filed the instant lawsuit [in a California state court] alleging breach of contract * * *. UPI sought damages of $28,000—that is, $1,000 per month that remained in Case's 30-month earn-back period.

Case, in turn, filed a cross-complaint. [He] alleged the [reimbursement] agreement was unlawful because * * * it lacked consideration.

UPI subsequently moved for summary judgment on its complaint and Case's cross-complaint, asserting the reimbursement agreement was valid.

The trial court granted UPI's motion, and the parties thereafter stipulated to a judgment in favor of UPI in the amount of $28,000 plus prejudgment interest and costs. [The court also awarded UPI attorneys' fees of $80,000.]

[Case appealed the judgment to a state intermediate appellate court.]

Case maintains the reimbursement agreement * * * lacked consideration because UPI had no obligation to keep Case employed and, thus, no obligation to provide education, which Case views as "the only possible consideration listed in the Reimbursement Agreement." Case's view of the bargained-for exchange is too constrained.

On entering the program, Case held a new position of Learner, which meant he would remain on UPI's payroll while *additionally* getting classroom and on-the-job training, the costs of which UPI would front. While Case was not guaranteed a promotion, transfer, or continued employment, exactly the same had been true with respect to his previous position. The exchange, frankly, is

obvious: Case got continued wages and fronted education costs, and UPI got Case's agreement to repay those costs if he both completed the training and left the company before it could benefit from the investment. *That either Case or UPI could have terminated the agreement by ending the employment relationship at some point during the educational program does not render illusory the parties' bargained-for exchange*—or require us to ignore the substantial benefits Case obtained every day he spent on the payroll receiving advanced training with no upfront cost and potentially no cost at all to him. [Emphasis added.]

* * * *

The summary judgment in favor of UPI is affirmed.

Legal Reasoning Questions

1. What did Case view as "the only possible consideration" for his agreement to reimburse UPI for some of the cost of his employment-related education?

2. How did the court interpret Case's view of "the only possible consideration"? Why?

3. If UPI had simply offered to pay its employees' wages and training expenses during their participation in a program of instruction "subject entirely and exclusively to UPI's approval," would the element of bargained-for exchange have been met? Explain.

9–1b Adequacy of Consideration

Adequacy of consideration involves how much consideration is given. Essentially, adequacy of consideration concerns the fairness of the bargain.

The General Rule On the surface, when the items exchanged are of unequal value, fairness would appear to be an issue. Normally, however, a court will not question the adequacy of consideration based solely on the comparative value of the things exchanged.

In other words, the determination of whether consideration exists does not depend on a comparison of the values of the things exchanged. Something need not be of direct economic or financial value to be considered legally sufficient consideration. In many situations, the exchange of promises and potential benefits is deemed to be sufficient consideration.

Under the doctrine of freedom of contract, courts leave it up to the parties to decide what something is

worth, and parties are usually free to bargain as they wish. If people could sue merely because they had entered into an unwise contract, the courts would be overloaded with frivolous suits.

When Voluntary Consent May Be Lacking When there is a large disparity in the amount or value of the consideration exchanged, it may raise a red flag for a court to look more closely at the bargain. Shockingly inadequate consideration can indicate that fraud, duress, or undue influence was involved. ■ **EXAMPLE 9.3** Spencer pays $500 for an iPhone 7 that he later discovers is a fake (counterfeit). Because the device is not authentic, he could claim that there was no valid contract because of inadequate consideration and fraud. ■

Disparity in the consideration exchanged may also cause a judge to question whether the contract is so one sided that it is *unconscionable*.[1] For instance, an

---

1. Pronounced un-*kon*-shun-uh-bul.

experienced appliance dealer induces a consumer to sign a contract written in complicated legal language. If the contract requires the consumer to pay twice the market value of the appliance, the disparity in value may indicate that the sale involved undue influence or fraud. A judge would thus want to make sure that the person voluntarily entered into this agreement.[2]

Concept Summary 9.1 provides a review of the main aspects of consideration.

9–1c Agreements That Lack Consideration

Sometimes, one of the parties (or both parties) to an agreement may think that consideration has been exchanged when in fact it has not. Here, we look at some situations in which the parties' promises or actions do not qualify as contractual consideration.

Preexisting Duty Under most circumstances, a promise to do what one already has a legal duty to do does not constitute legally sufficient consideration. The preexisting legal duty may be imposed by law or may arise out of a previous contract. A sheriff, for instance, has a duty to investigate crime and to arrest criminals. Hence, a sheriff cannot collect a reward for providing information leading to the capture of a criminal.

Likewise, if a party is already bound by contract to perform a certain duty, that duty cannot serve as consideration

for a second contract. ■ **EXAMPLE 9.4** Ajax Contractors begins construction on a seven-story office building and after three months demands an extra $75,000 on its contract. If the extra $75,000 is not paid, the contractor will stop working. The owner of the land, finding no one else to complete the construction, agrees to pay the extra $75,000. The agreement is unenforceable because it is not supported by legally sufficient consideration. Ajax Contractors had a preexisting contractual duty to complete the building. ■

Unforeseen Difficulties. The rule regarding preexisting duty is meant to prevent extortion and the so-called holdup game. Nonetheless, if, during performance of a contract, extraordinary difficulties arise that were totally unforeseen at the time the contract was formed, a court may allow an exception to the rule. The key is whether the court finds that the modification is fair and equitable in view of circumstances not anticipated by the parties when the contract was made.[3]

Suppose that in *Example 9.4*, Ajax Contractors had asked for the extra $75,000 because it encountered a rock formation that no one knew existed. If the landowner agrees to pay the extra $75,000 to excavate the rock and the court finds that it is fair to do so, Ajax Contractors can enforce the agreement. If rock formations are common in the area, however, the court may determine that the contractor should have known of the risk. In that situation, the court may choose to apply the preexisting

---

2. For an example of an unconscionable home loan contract, see *Orcilla v. Big Sur, Inc.,* 244 Cal.App.4th 982, 198 Cal.Rptr.3d 715 (2016).

3. *Restatement (Second) of Contracts*, Section 73.

Concept Summary 9.1

Consideration

Elements of Consideration	Consideration is the value given in exchange for a promise that is necessary to form a contract. Consideration is often broken down into two elements: • *Legal value*—Something of legally sufficient value must be given in exchange for a promise. This may consist of a promise, a performance, or a forbearance. • *Bargained-for exchange*—There must be a bargained-for exchange.
Adequacy of Consideration	• Adequacy of consideration relates to how much consideration is given and whether a fair bargain was reached. • Courts will inquire into the adequacy of consideration (if the consideration is legally sufficient) only when fraud, undue influence, duress, or the lack of a bargained-for exchange may be involved.

duty rule and prevent Ajax Contractors from obtaining the extra $75,000.

Rescission and New Contract. The law recognizes that two parties can mutually agree to rescind, or cancel, their contract, at least to the extent that it is *executory* (still to be carried out). **Rescission**[4] is the unmaking of a contract so as to return the parties to the positions they occupied before the contract was made.

Sometimes, parties rescind a contract and make a new contract at the same time. When this occurs, it is often difficult to determine whether there was consideration for the new contract, or whether the parties had a pre-existing duty under the previous contract. If a court finds there was a preexisting duty, then the new contract will be invalid because there was no consideration.

Past Consideration Promises made in return for actions or events that have already taken place are unenforceable. These promises lack consideration in that the element of bargained-for exchange is missing. In short, you can bargain for something to take place now or in the future but not for something that has already taken place. Therefore, **past consideration** is no consideration.

■ **CASE IN POINT 9.5** Jamil Blackmon became friends with Allen Iverson when Iverson was a high school student who showed tremendous promise as an athlete. One evening, Blackmon suggested that Iverson use "The Answer" as a nickname in the summer league basketball tournaments. Blackmon said that Iverson would be "The Answer" to all of the National Basketball Association's woes. Later that night, Iverson said that he would give Blackmon 25 percent of any proceeds from the merchandising of products that used "The Answer" as a logo or a slogan. Because Iverson's promise was made in return for past consideration, it was unenforceable. In effect, Iverson stated his intention to give Blackmon a gift.[5] ■

Illusory Promises If the terms of the contract express such uncertainty of performance that the promisor has not definitely promised to do anything, the promise is said to be *illusory*—without consideration and unenforceable. A promise is illusory when it fails to bind the promisor.

■ **EXAMPLE 9.6** The president of Tuscan Corporation says to her employees, "If profits continue to be high, everyone will get a 10 percent bonus at the end of the year—if management agrees." This is an *illusory promise,*

or no promise at all, because performance depends solely on the discretion of management. There is no bargained-for consideration. The statement indicates only that management may or may not do something in the future. Therefore, even though the employees work hard and profits remain high, the company is not obligated to pay the bonus now or later. ■

Option-to-Cancel Clauses. Sometimes, option-to-cancel clauses in contracts present problems in regard to consideration. When the promisor has the option to cancel the contract before performance has begun, the promise is illusory.

■ **EXAMPLE 9.7** Abe contracts to hire Chris for one year at $5,000 per month, reserving the right to cancel the contract at any time. On close examination of these words, you can see that Abe has not actually agreed to hire Chris, as Abe could cancel without liability before Chris started performance. This contract is therefore illusory.

But if Abe instead reserves the right to cancel the contract at any time *after* Chris has begun performance by giving Chris *thirty days' notice,* the promise is not illusory. Abe, by saying that he will give Chris thirty days' notice, is relinquishing the opportunity (legal right) to hire someone else instead of Chris for a thirty-day period. If Chris works for one month and Abe then gives him thirty days' notice, Chris has an enforceable claim for two months' salary ($10,000). ■

Exhibit 9–1 illustrates some common situations in which promises or actions do not constitute contractual consideration.

Requirements and Output Contracts. Problems with consideration may also arise in other types of contracts because of uncertainty of performance. Uncertain performance is characteristic of requirements and output contracts, for instance. In a *requirements contract,* a buyer and a seller agree that the buyer will purchase from the seller all of the goods of a designated type that the buyer needs, or requires. In an *output contract,* the buyer and seller agree that the buyer will purchase from the seller all of what the seller produces, or the seller's output.

9–1d Settlement of Claims

Businesspersons and others often enter into contracts to settle legal claims. It is important to understand the nature of consideration given in these kinds of settlement agreements, or contracts. A claim may be settled through an *accord and satisfaction,* a *release,* or a *covenant not to sue.*

---

4. Pronounced reh-*sih*-zhen.
5. *Blackmon v. Iverson,* 324 F.Supp.2d 602 (E.D.Pa. 2003).

EXHIBIT 9–1 Examples of Agreements That Lack Consideration

PREEXISTING DUTY
When a person already has a legal duty to perform an action, there is no legally sufficient consideration.

Example: A firefighter cannot receive a cash reward from a business owner for putting out a fire in a downtown commercial district. As a city employee, the firefighter had a duty to extinguish the fire.

PAST CONSIDERATION
When a person makes a promise in return for actions or events that have already taken place, there is no consideration.

Example: A real estate agent sold a friend's house without charging a commission, and in return, the friend promises to give the agent $1,000. The friend's promise is simply an intention to give a gift.

ILLUSORY PROMISES
When a person expresses contract terms with such uncertainty that the terms are not definite, the promise is illusory.

Example: A storeowner promises a $500 bonus to each employee who works Christmas Day, as long as the owner feels that they did their jobs well. The owner's promise is just a statement of something she may or may not do in the future.

Accord and Satisfaction In an **accord and satisfaction,** a debtor offers to pay, and a creditor accepts, a lesser amount than the creditor originally claimed was owed. The *accord* is the agreement. In the accord, one party undertakes to give or perform, and the other to accept, in satisfaction of a claim, something other than that on which the parties originally agreed. *Satisfaction* is the performance (usually payment) that takes place after the accord is executed.

A basic rule is that there can be no satisfaction unless there is first an accord. In addition, for accord and satisfaction to occur, the amount of the debt *must be in dispute.*

Liquidated Debts. If a debt is *liquidated,* accord and satisfaction cannot take place. A **liquidated debt** is one whose amount has been ascertained, fixed, agreed on, settled, or exactly determined.

■ **EXAMPLE 9.8** Barbara Kwan signs an installment loan contract with her bank. In the contract, Kwan agrees to pay a set rate of interest on a specified amount of borrowed funds at monthly intervals for two years. Because both parties know the precise amount of the total obligation, it is a liquidated debt. ■

In the majority of states, a creditor's acceptance of a lesser sum than the entire amount of a liquidated debt is *not* satisfaction, and the balance of the debt is still legally owed. The reason for this rule is that the debtor has given no consideration to satisfy the obligation of paying the balance to the creditor. The debtor had a preexisting legal obligation to pay the entire debt. (Of course, even with liquidated debts, creditors often do negotiate debt settlement agreements with debtors for a lesser amount than

was originally owed. Creditors sometimes even forgive, or write off, a liquidated debt as uncollectable.)

Unliquidated Debts. An **unliquidated debt** is the opposite of a liquidated debt. The amount of the debt is *not* settled, fixed, agreed on, ascertained, or determined, and reasonable persons may differ over the amount owed. In these circumstances, acceptance of a lesser sum operates as satisfaction, or discharge, of the debt because there is valid consideration. The parties give up a legal right to contest the amount in dispute.

Release A **release** is a contract in which one party forfeits the right to pursue a legal claim against the other party. It bars any further recovery beyond the terms stated in the release.

A release will generally be binding if it meets the following requirements:

1. The agreement is made in good faith (honestly).
2. The release contract is in a signed writing (required in many states).
3. The contract is accompanied by consideration.[6]

Clearly, an individual is better off knowing the extent of his or her injuries or damages before signing a release. ■ **EXAMPLE 9.9** Lupe's car is damaged in an automobile accident caused by Dexter's negligence. Dexter offers to give her $3,000 if she will release him from

---

6. Under the Uniform Commercial Code (UCC), a written, signed waiver or renunciation by an aggrieved party discharges any further liability for a breach, even without consideration.

further liability resulting from the accident. Lupe agrees and signs the release.

If Lupe later discovers that it will cost $4,200 to repair her car, she normally cannot recover the additional amount from Dexter. Lupe is limited to the $3,000 specified in the release. Lupe and Dexter voluntarily agreed to the terms in the release, which was in a signed writing, and sufficient consideration was present. The consideration was the legal right Lupe forfeited to sue to recover damages, should they be more than $3,000, in exchange for Dexter's promise to give her $3,000. ■

Covenant Not to Sue Unlike a release, a **covenant not to sue** does not always bar further recovery. The parties simply substitute a contractual obligation for some other type of legal action based on a valid claim. Suppose that, in *Example 9.9*, Lupe agrees with Dexter not to sue for damages in a tort action if he will pay for the damage to her car. If Dexter fails to pay for the repairs, Lupe can bring an action against him for breach of contract.

As the following case illustrates, a covenant not to sue can form the basis for a dismissal of the claims of either party to the covenant.

Spotlight on Nike

Case 9.2 Already, LLC v. Nike, Inc.

Supreme Court of the United States, __ U.S. __, 133 S.Ct. 721, 184 L.Ed.2d 553 (2013).

Background and Facts Nike, Inc., designs, makes, and sells athletic footwear, including a line of shoes known as "Air Force 1." Already, LLC, also designs and markets athletic footwear, including the "Sugar" and "Soulja Boy" lines. Nike filed a suit in a federal district court against Already, alleging that Soulja Boys and Sugars infringed the Air Force 1 trademark. Already filed a counterclaim, contending that the Air Force 1 trademark was invalid. While the suit was pending, Nike issued a covenant not to sue. Nike promised not to raise any trademark claims against Already or any affiliated entity based on Already's existing footwear designs or any future Already designs that constituted a "colorable imitation" of Already's current products. Nike then filed a motion to dismiss its own claims and to dismiss Already's counterclaim. Already opposed the dismissal of its counterclaim, but the court granted Nike's motion. The U.S. Court of Appeals for the Second Circuit affirmed. Already appealed to the United States Supreme Court.

In the Language of the Court

Chief Justice *ROBERTS* delivered the opinion of the Court.

* * * *

* * * A defendant cannot automatically moot a case simply by ending its unlawful conduct once sued. [A matter is *moot* if it involves no actual controversy for the court to decide, and federal courts will dismiss moot cases.] Otherwise, a defendant could engage in unlawful conduct, stop when sued to have the case declared moot, then pick up where he left off, repeating this cycle until he achieves all his unlawful ends. Given this concern, * * * *a defendant claiming that its voluntary compliance moots a case bears the formidable burden of showing that it is absolutely clear the allegedly wrongful behavior could not reasonably be expected to recur.* [This is the voluntary cessation test. Emphasis added.]

* * * *

We begin our analysis with the terms of the covenant:

[Nike] unconditionally and irrevocably covenants to refrain from making *any* claim(s) or demand(s) * * * against Already or *any* of its * * * related business entities * * * [including] distributors * * * and employees of such entities and *all* customers * * * on account of any *possible* cause of action based on or involving trademark infringement * * * relating to the NIKE Mark based on the appearance of *any* of Already's current and/or previous footwear product designs, and *any* colorable imitations thereof, regardless of whether that footwear is produced * * * or otherwise used in commerce.

The breadth of this covenant suffices to meet the burden imposed by the voluntary cessation test.

In addition, Nike originally argued that the Sugars and Soulja Boys infringed its trademark; in other words, Nike believed those shoes were "colorable imitations" of the Air Force 1s. Nike's covenant now

Case 9.2 Continued

allows Already to produce all of its existing footwear designs—including the Sugar and Soulja Boy—and any "colorable imitation" of those designs. * * * It is hard to imagine a scenario that would potentially infringe Nike's trademark and yet not fall under the covenant. Nike, having taken the position in court that there is no prospect of such a shoe, would be hard pressed to assert the contrary down the road. If such a shoe exists, the parties have not pointed to it, there is no evidence that Already has dreamt of it, and we cannot conceive of it. It sits, as far as we can tell, on a shelf between Dorothy's ruby slippers and Perseus's winged sandals.

* * * *

* * * Given the covenant's broad language, and given that Already has asserted no concrete plans to engage in conduct not covered by the covenant, we can conclude the case is moot because the challenged conduct cannot reasonably be expected to recur.

Decision and Remedy *The United States Supreme Court affirmed the judgment of the lower court. Under the covenant not to sue, Nike could not file a claim for trademark infringement against Already, and Already could not assert that Nike's trademark was invalid.*

Critical Thinking
- **Economic** *Why would any party agree to a covenant not to sue?*
- **Legal Environment** *Which types of contracts are similar to covenants not to sue? Explain.*

9-1e Exceptions to the Consideration Requirement

There are some exceptions to the rule that only promises supported by consideration are enforceable. The following types of promises may be enforced despite the lack of consideration:

1. Promises that induce detrimental reliance, under the doctrine of *promissory estoppel*.
2. Promises to pay debts that are barred by a statute of limitations.
3. Promises to make charitable contributions.

Promissory Estoppel Sometimes, individuals rely on promises to their detriment, and their reliance may form a basis for a court to infer contract rights and duties. Under the doctrine of **promissory estoppel** (also called *detrimental reliance*), a person who has reasonably and substantially relied on the promise of another may be able to obtain some measure of recovery.

Promissory estoppel is applied in a wide variety of contexts in which a promise is otherwise unenforceable, such as when a promise is made *without consideration*. Under this doctrine, a court may enforce an otherwise unenforceable promise to avoid the injustice that would otherwise result.

Requirements to Establish Promissory Estoppel. For the promissory estoppel doctrine to be applied, the following elements are required:

1. There must be a clear and definite promise.
2. The promisor should have expected that the promisee would rely on the promise.
3. The promisee reasonably relied on the promise by acting or refraining from some act.
4. The promisee's reliance was definite and resulted in substantial detriment.
5. Enforcement of the promise is necessary to avoid injustice.

If these requirements are met, a promise may be enforced even though it is not supported by consideration.[7] In essence, the promisor will be **estopped** (prevented) from asserting the lack of consideration as a defense.

Promissory estoppel is similar in some ways to the doctrine of quasi contract. In both situations, a court, acting in the interests of equity, imposes contract obligations on the parties to prevent unfairness even though no actual contract exists. The difference is that with quasi contract, no promise was made at all. In contrast, with promissory estoppel, an unenforceable promise was made and relied on but not performed.

---

7. *Restatement (Second) of Contracts*, Section 90.

Application of the Doctrine. Promissory estoppel was originally applied to situations involving promises of gifts and of donations to charities. Later, courts began to apply the doctrine to avoid inequity or hardship in other situations, including business transactions, some employment relationships, and even disputes among family members.

■ **CASE IN POINT 9.10** Jeffrey and Kathryn Dow owned 125 acres of land in Corinth, Maine. The Dows regarded the land as their children's heritage, and the subject of the children's living on the land was often discussed within the family. With the Dows' permission, their daughter Teresa installed a mobile home and built a garage on the land. After Teresa married Jarrod Harvey, the Dows agreed to finance the construction of a house on the land for the couple. When Jarrod died in a motorcycle accident, however, Teresa financed the house with his life insurance proceeds. The construction cost about $200,000. Her father, Jeffrey, performed a substantial amount of carpentry and other work on the house.

Teresa then asked her parents for a deed to the property so that she could obtain a mortgage. They refused. Teresa sued her parents for promissory estoppel. Maine's highest court ruled in favor of Teresa's promissory estoppel claim. The court reasoned that the Dows' support and encouragement of their daughter's construction of a house on the land "conclusively demonstrated" their intent to transfer. For years, they had made general promises to convey the land to their children, including Teresa. Teresa had reasonably relied on their promise in financing construction of a house to her detriment ($200,000). The court concluded that enforcing the promise was the only way to avoid injustice in this situation.[8] ■

Promises to Pay Debts Barred by a Statute of Limitations Statutes of limitations in all states require a creditor to sue within a specified period to recover a debt. If the creditor fails to sue in time, recovery of the debt is barred by the statute of limitations.

A debtor who promises to pay a previous debt even though recovery is barred by the statute of limitations makes an enforceable promise. *The promise needs no consideration.* (Some states, however, require that it be in writing.) In effect, the promise extends the limitations period, and the creditor can sue to recover the entire debt or at least the amount promised. The promise can be implied if the debtor acknowledges the barred debt by making a partial payment.

Charitable Subscriptions A charitable subscription is a promise to make a donation to a religious, educational, or charitable institution. Traditionally, such promises were unenforceable because they are not supported by legally sufficient consideration. A gift, after all, is the opposite of bargained-for consideration. The modern view, however, is to make exceptions to the general rule by applying the doctrine of promissory estoppel.

■ **EXAMPLE 9.11** A church solicits and receives pledges (commitments to contribute funds) from church members to erect a new church building. On the basis of these pledges, the church purchases land, hires architects, and makes other contracts that change its position. Because of the church's detrimental reliance, a court may enforce the pledges under the theory of promissory estoppel. Alternatively, a court may find consideration in the fact that each promise was made in reliance on the other promises of support or that the church trustees, by accepting the subscriptions, impliedly promised to complete the proposed undertaking. ■

9–2 Contractual Capacity

In addition to agreement and consideration, for a contract to be deemed valid, the parties to the contract must have **contractual capacity**—the legal ability to enter into a contractual relationship. Courts generally presume the existence of contractual capacity, but in some situations, as when a person is young or mentally incompetent, capacity may be lacking or questionable.

A person who has been determined by a court to be mentally incompetent, for instance, cannot form a legally binding contract with another party. In other situations, a party may have the capacity to enter into a valid contract but also have the right to avoid liability under it. Minors—or *infants*, as they are commonly referred to in legal terminology—usually are not legally bound by contracts.

In this section, we look at the effect of youth (minority), intoxication, and mental incompetence on contractual capacity.

9–2a Minors

Today, in almost all states, the **age of majority** (when a person is no longer a minor) for contractual purposes is eighteen years.[9] In addition, some states provide for the termination of minority on marriage.

Minority status may also be terminated by a minor's **emancipation,** which occurs when a child's parent or

---

8. *Harvey v. Dow*, 2011 ME 4, 11 A.3d 303 (2011).

9. The age of majority may still be twenty-one for other purposes, such as the purchase and consumption of alcohol.

legal guardian relinquishes the legal right to exercise control over the child. Normally, minors who leave home to support themselves are considered emancipated. Several jurisdictions permit minors themselves to petition a court for emancipation. For business purposes, a minor may petition a court to be treated as an adult.

The general rule is that a minor can enter into any contract that an adult can, except contracts prohibited by law for minors (such as contracts to purchase tobacco or alcoholic beverages). A contract entered into by a minor, however, is voidable at the option of that minor, subject to certain exceptions. To exercise the option to avoid a contract, a minor need only manifest (clearly show) an intention not to be bound by it. The minor "avoids" the contract by disaffirming it.

Disaffirmance The legal avoidance, or setting aside, of a contractual obligation is referred to as **disaffirmance.** To disaffirm, a minor must express his or her intent, through words or conduct, not to be bound to the contract. The minor must disaffirm the entire contract, not merely a portion of it. For instance, the minor cannot decide to keep part of the goods purchased under a contract and return the remaining goods.

■ **CASE IN POINT 9.12** Fifteen-year-old Morgan Kelly was a cadet in her high school's Navy Junior Reserve Officer Training Corps. As part of the program, she visited a U.S. Marine Corps training facility. To enter the camp, she was required to sign a waiver that exempted the Marines from all liability for any injuries arising from her visit.

While participating in activities on the camp's confidence-building course, Kelly fell from the "Slide for Life" and suffered serious injuries. She filed a suit to recover her medical costs. The Marines asserted that she had signed their waiver of liability. Kelly claimed that she had disaffirmed the waiver when she filed suit. The court ruled in Kelly's favor. Liability waivers are generally enforceable contracts, but a minor can avoid a contract by disaffirming it.[10] ■

Note that an adult who enters into a contract with a minor cannot avoid his or her contractual duties on the ground that the minor can do so. Unless the minor exercises the option to disaffirm the contract, the adult party normally is bound by it. On disaffirming a contract, a minor normally can recover any property that he or she transferred to the adult as consideration, even if the property is in the possession of a third party.[11]

The question in the following case was whether a minor had effectively disaffirmed an agreement to arbitrate with her employer.

---

10. *Kelly v. United States*, 809 F.Supp.2d 429 (E.D.N.C. 2011).
11. Section 2–403(1) of the Uniform Commercial Code (UCC) allows an exception if the third party is a "good faith purchaser for value."

Case 9.3

PAK Foods Houston, LLC v. Garcia
Court of Appeals of Texas, Houston (14th District), 433 S.W.3d 171 (2014).

Background and Facts S.L., a female sixteen-year-old minor, worked at a KFC Restaurant operated by PAK Foods Houston, LLC. PAK Foods' policy was to resolve any dispute with an employee through arbitration. At the employer's request, S.L. signed an acknowledgment of this policy. S.L. was injured on the job and subsequently terminated her employment. S.L.'s mother, Marissa Garcia, filed a suit on S.L.'s behalf in a Texas state court against PAK Foods to recover the medical expenses for the injury. PAK Foods filed a motion to compel arbitration. The court denied the motion. "To the extent any agreement to arbitrate existed between S.L. and PAK Foods Houston, LLC, S.L. voided such agreement by filing this suit." PAK Foods appealed.

In the Language of the Court
Martha Hill *JAMISON*, Justice.
* * * *

* * * It is undisputed S.L. was a 16-year-old minor when the arbitration agreement was executed and she remained a minor during her employment by PAK Foods, including at the time of her injury. In Texas, the age of majority is 18 years.

It has long been the law in Texas that a contract executed by a minor is not void, but it is voidable by the minor. * * * *[A minor's contracts] may be either disaffirmed by the minor or ratified after the minor reaches majority. This means that the minor may set aside the entire contract at her option.* [Emphasis added.]

Appellees assert that S.L. elected to void any agreement to arbitrate by filing the underlying suit.

Case 9.3 Continues

* * * *

PAK Foods argues that * * * S.L. was an at-will employee and did not execute an employment contract. PAK Foods also notes that S.L. did not notify PAK Foods prior to filing suit that she was voiding the arbitration agreement. These distinctions do not alter the settled law that a minor may void a contract at her election. The arbitration agreement is a contract with a minor, S.L., who had the option to disaffirm the contract.

While appellees assert that S.L. voided the agreement by filing suit, the mere filing of suit may not necessarily disaffirm an arbitration agreement. A party may file suit but later determine arbitration is appropriate. Here, appellees' original petition does not expressly disaffirm an agreement to arbitrate; the petition is silent about arbitration. However, appellees' response filed in opposition to the motion to compel arbitration is a definitive disaffirmance of any agreement to arbitrate. The response states in relevant part:

> S.L. was a minor at the time of her employment. * * * Contracts such as this Arbitration Agreement are voidable at her instance, and may be disaffirmed or repudiated by her or her guardian, * * * . Thus as S.L.'s disaffirmance of the Arbitration agreement has manifestly occurred with her termination of employment and election to file suit, she cannot be bound by the terms of the Arbitration Agreement.

S.L. was still a minor when she objected to arbitration and elected to void the contract. The record contains sufficient evidence of her election to support the trial court's fact finding. The trial court also did not abuse its discretion in concluding as a matter of law that S.L.'s action voided the contract.

Decision and Remedy *A state intermediate appellate court affirmed the decision of the lower court. A minor may disaffirm a contract at his or her option. S.L. opted to disaffirm the agreement to arbitrate by terminating her employment and filing the lawsuit.*

Critical Thinking

- **Legal Environment** *Could PAK Foods successfully contend that S.L.'s minority does not bar enforcement of the arbitration agreement because medical expenses are necessaries[a]? Discuss.*
- **Ethical** *Is it fair that a minor can work for an employer yet not be bound by a contract with the employer? Why or why not?*

---

a. *Necessaries* are basic needs, such as food, clothing, shelter, and medical services. As you will read shortly, minors can disaffirm contracts for necessaries but remain liable for the value of goods or services.

Disaffirmance within a Reasonable Time. A contract can ordinarily be disaffirmed at any time during minority or for a reasonable period after the minor reaches the age of majority.[12] What constitutes a "reasonable" time may vary, depending on the jurisdiction and to what extent the contract has been performed.

Minors' Obligations on Disaffirmance. Although all states' laws permit minors to disaffirm contracts, states differ on the extent of a minor's obligations on disaffirmance. Courts in most states hold that the minor need only return the goods (or other consideration) subject to the contract, provided the goods are in the minor's

possession or control. Even if the minor returns damaged goods, the minor often is entitled to disaffirm the contract and obtain a full refund of the purchase price.

A growing number of states place an additional duty of restitution on the minor to restore the adult party to the position she or he held before the contract was made. These courts may hold a minor responsible for damage, ordinary wear and tear, and depreciation of goods that the minor used prior to disaffirmance.

■ **EXAMPLE 9.13** Sixteen-year-old Paul Dodson buys a pickup truck from a used-car dealer. The truck develops mechanical problems nine months later, but Dodson continues to drive it until it stops running. Then Dodson disaffirms the contract and attempts to return the truck to the dealer for a full refund. Dodson lives in a state that imposes a duty of restitution on minors. Therefore, he

---

12. In some states, a minor who enters into a contract for the sale of land cannot disaffirm the contract until she or he reaches the age of majority.

can disaffirm the contract but will not be entitled to a full refund of the purchase price. Dodson can only recover the fair market value of the truck in its current condition. ■

Exceptions to a Minor's Right to Disaffirm

State courts and legislatures have carved out several exceptions to the minor's right to disaffirm. For public-policy reasons, some contracts, such as marriage contracts and contracts to enlist in the armed services, cannot be avoided.

In addition, although ordinarily minors can disaffirm contracts even when they have misrepresented their age, a growing number of states have enacted laws to prohibit disaffirmance in such situations. Other states prohibit disaffirmance by minors who misrepresented their age while engaged in business as an adult.

Finally, a minor who enters into a contract for necessaries may disaffirm the contract but remains liable for the reasonable value of the goods. **Necessaries** are basic needs, such as food, clothing, shelter, and medical services. What is a necessary for one minor, however, may be a luxury for another, depending on the minors' customary living standard. Contracts for necessaries are enforceable only to the level of value needed to maintain the minor's standard of living.

Ratification In contract law, **ratification** is the act of accepting and giving legal force to an obligation that previously was not enforceable. A minor who has reached the age of majority can ratify a contract expressly or impliedly.

Express ratification takes place when the individual, on reaching the age of majority, states orally or in writing that he or she intends to be bound by the contract. *Implied* ratification takes place when the minor, on reaching the age of majority, indicates an intent to abide by the contract.

■ **EXAMPLE 9.14**   Lin enters into a contract to sell her laptop to Andrew, a minor. If, on reaching the age of majority, Andrew e-mails Lin stating that he still agrees to buy the laptop, he has *expressly* ratified the contract. If, instead, Andrew takes possession of the laptop as a minor and continues to use it well after reaching the age of majority, he has *impliedly* ratified the contract. ■

If a minor fails to disaffirm a contract within a reasonable time after reaching the age of majority, then the court must determine whether the conduct constitutes ratification or disaffirmance. Typically, courts presume that executed contracts (fully performed contracts) are ratified and that executory contracts (contracts not yet fully performed by both parties) are disaffirmed.

Parents' Liability As a general rule, parents are not liable for contracts made by minor children acting on their own, except contracts for necessaries, which parents are legally required to provide. As a consequence, businesses ordinarily require parents to cosign any contract made with a minor. The parents then become personally obligated under the contract to perform the conditions of the contract, even if their child avoids liability.

Concept Summary 9.2 reviews the rules relating to contracts by minors.

Concept Summary 9.2

Contracts by Minors

The General Rule	• Contracts entered into by minors are *voidable* at the option of the minor.
Rules of Disaffirmance	• A minor may disaffirm the contract at any time while still a minor and within a reasonable time after reaching the age of majority. • Most states do not require restitution.
Exceptions to Basic Rules of Disaffirmance	• *Misrepresentation of age (or fraud)*—In many jurisdictions, misrepresentation of age prohibits the right of disaffirmance. • *Necessaries*—Minors remain liable for the reasonable value of necessaries (goods and services). • *Ratification*—After reaching the age of majority, a person can ratify a contract that he or she formed as a minor, thereby becoming fully liable for it.

9–2b Intoxication

Intoxication is a condition in which a person's normal capacity to act or think is inhibited by alcohol or some other drug. A contract entered into by an intoxicated person can be either voidable or valid (and thus enforceable). If the person was sufficiently intoxicated to lack mental capacity, then the agreement may be voidable even if the intoxication was purely voluntary. If, despite intoxication, the person understood the legal consequences of the agreement, the contract will be enforceable.

Courts look at objective indications of the intoxicated person's condition to determine if he or she possessed or lacked the required capacity. It is difficult to prove that a person's judgment was so severely impaired that he or she could not comprehend the legal consequences of entering into a contract. Therefore, courts rarely permit contracts to be avoided due to intoxication.

Disaffirmance If a contract is voidable because one party was intoxicated, that person has the option of disaffirming it while intoxicated and for a reasonable time after becoming sober. The person claiming intoxication typically must be able to return all consideration received unless the contract involved necessaries. Contracts for necessaries are voidable, but the intoxicated person is liable in quasi contract for the reasonable value of the consideration received.

Ratification An intoxicated person, after becoming sober, may ratify a contract expressly or impliedly, just as a minor may do on reaching majority. Implied ratification occurs when a person enters into a contract while intoxicated and fails to disaffirm the contract within a *reasonable* time after becoming sober. Acts or conduct inconsistent with an intent to disaffirm—such as the continued use of property purchased under a voidable contract—will also ratify the contract.

See Concept Summary 9.3 for a review of the rules relating to contracts by intoxicated persons.

9–2c Mental Incompetence

Contracts made by mentally incompetent persons can be void, voidable, or valid. We look here at the circumstances that determine when each of these classifications applies.

When the Contract Will Be Void If a court has previously determined that a person is mentally incompetent, any contract made by that person is void—no contract exists. On determining that someone is mentally incompetent, the court appoints a guardian to represent the individual. Only the guardian can enter into binding legal obligations on behalf of the mentally incompetent person.

Concept Summary 9.3

Contracts by Intoxicated Persons

The General Rules	• If a person was sufficiently intoxicated to lack the mental capacity to comprehend the legal consequences of entering into the contract, the contract may be *voidable* at the option of the intoxicated person. • If, despite intoxication, the person understood these legal consequences, the contract will be enforceable.
Rules of Disaffirmance	• An intoxicated person may disaffirm the contract at any time while intoxicated and for a reasonable time after becoming sober but must make full restitution. • Contracts for necessaries are voidable, but the intoxicated person is liable for the reasonable value of the goods or services.
Ratification	• After becoming sober, a person can ratify a contract that she or he formed while intoxicated, thereby becoming fully liable for it.

When the Contract Will Be Voidable If a court has not previously judged a person to be mentally incompetent but the person was incompetent at the time the contract was formed, the contract may be voidable. The contract is voidable if the person did not know he or she was entering into the contract or lacked the mental capacity to comprehend its nature, purpose, and consequences. In such situations, the contract is voidable (or can be ratified) at the option of the mentally incompetent person but not at the option of the other party.

■ **EXAMPLE 9.15** Larry agrees to sell his stock in Google, Inc., to Sergey for substantially less than its market value. At the time of the deal, Larry is confused about the purpose and details of the transaction, but he has not been declared incompetent. Nonetheless, if a court finds that Larry did not understand the nature and consequences of the contract due to a lack of mental capacity, he can avoid the sale. ■

When the Contract Will Be Valid A contract entered into by a mentally ill person (not previously declared incompetent) may be valid if the person had capacity *at the time the contract was formed.* Some people who are incompetent due to age or illness have *lucid intervals*—periods during which their intelligence, judgment, and will are temporarily restored. During such intervals, they will be considered to have legal capacity to enter into contracts.

See Concept Summary 9.4 for a review of the rules relating to contracts entered into by mentally incompetent persons.

9–3 Legality

After agreement, consideration, and contractual capacity, legality is the fourth requirement for a valid and enforceable contract to exist. **Legality** means that a contract must be formed for a legal purpose.

A contract to do something that is prohibited by federal or state statutory law is illegal and, as such, void from the outset and thus unenforceable. Additionally, a contract to commit a tortious act (such as an agreement to engage in defamation or fraud) is contrary to public policy and therefore illegal and unenforceable.

9–3a Contracts Contrary to Statute

Statutes often set forth rules specifying what may be included in contracts and what is prohibited. We now examine several ways in which contracts may be contrary to statute and thus illegal.

Contracts to Commit a Crime Any contract to commit a crime is in violation of a statute. Thus, a contract to sell illegal drugs in violation of criminal laws is unenforceable, as is a contract to hide a corporation's violation of securities laws or environmental regulations.

Sometimes, the object or performance of a contract is rendered illegal by a statute *after* the parties entered into the contract. In that situation, the contract is considered to be discharged (terminated) by law.

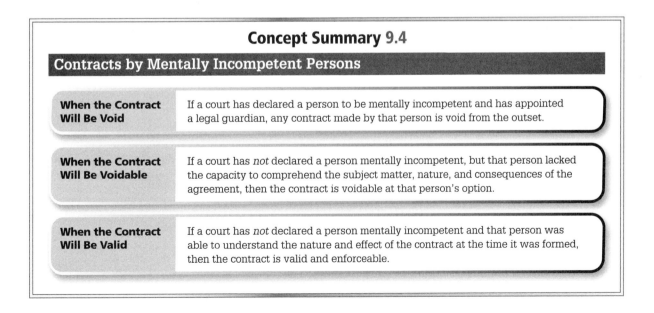

Concept Summary 9.4

Contracts by Mentally Incompetent Persons

When the Contract Will Be Void	If a court has declared a person to be mentally incompetent and has appointed a legal guardian, any contract made by that person is void from the outset.
When the Contract Will Be Voidable	If a court has *not* declared a person mentally incompetent, but that person lacked the capacity to comprehend the subject matter, nature, and consequences of the agreement, then the contract is voidable at that person's option.
When the Contract Will Be Valid	If a court has *not* declared a person mentally incompetent and that person was able to understand the nature and effect of the contract at the time it was formed, then the contract is valid and enforceable.

Usury Almost every state has a statute that sets the maximum rate of interest that can be charged for different types of transactions, including ordinary loans. A lender who makes a loan at an interest rate above the lawful maximum commits **usury.**

Although usurious contracts are illegal, most states simply limit the interest that the lender may collect on the contract to the lawful maximum interest rate in that state. In a few states, the lender can recover the principal amount of the loan but no interest. In addition, states can make exceptions to facilitate business transactions. For instance, many states exempt corporate loans from the usury laws, and nearly all states allow higher-interest-rate loans for borrowers who could not otherwise obtain loans.

Gambling Gambling is the creation of risk for the purpose of assuming it. Any scheme that involves the distribution of property by chance among persons who have paid valuable consideration for the opportunity (chance) to receive the property is gambling.

Traditionally, the states deemed gambling contracts illegal and thus void. Today, many states allow (and regulate) certain forms of gambling, such as horse racing, video poker machines, and charity-sponsored bingo. In addition, nearly all states allow state-operated lotteries and gambling on Native American reservations. Even in states that permit certain types of gambling, though, courts often find that gambling contracts are illegal.

■ **CASE IN POINT 9.16** Video poker machines are legal in Louisiana, but their use requires the approval of the state video gaming commission. Gaming Venture, Inc., did not obtain this approval before agreeing with Tastee Restaurant Corporation to install poker machines in some of its restaurants. For this reason, when Tastee allegedly reneged on the deal by refusing to install the machines, a state court held that their agreement was an illegal gambling contract and therefore void.[13] ■

Licensing Statutes All states require members of certain professions—including physicians, lawyers, real estate brokers, accountants, architects, electricians, and stockbrokers—to have licenses. Some licenses are obtained only after extensive schooling and examinations, which indicate to the public that a special skill has been acquired. Others require only that the applicant be of good moral character and pay a fee.

Whether a contract with an unlicensed person is legal and enforceable depends on the purpose of the licensing statute. If the statute's purpose is to protect the public from unauthorized practitioners (such as unlicensed attorneys and electricians), then a contract involving an unlicensed practitioner is generally illegal and unenforceable.

■ **CASE IN POINT 9.17** Cecil McNatt contracted with Jane Vestal to build Henderson Villa, an assisted-living facility in Tennessee, for $1.4 million. Three days later, McNatt formed a joint venture with Burton Construction Company to build two assisted-living facilities, including Henderson Villa. Burton was licensed under the state's Contractors Licensing Act, but McNatt was not. During the construction of Henderson Villa, McNatt remained on-site, selecting, supervising, and paying the subcontractors.

Following the project's completion, Vestal refused to pay the balance owed on the contract. McNatt filed a suit in a Tennessee state court against Vestal to collect. She filed a counterclaim, alleging breach of contract for his lack of a state contractor's license. The court dismissed her claim and awarded McNatt $96,280.11 in damages. Vestal appealed. A state intermediate appellate court reversed the lower court's finding that McNatt had not violated the state Contractors Licensing Act and reduced the amount of his award. The appellate court affirmed the judgment as modified and remanded the case for further proceedings.[14]

9–3b Contracts Contrary to Public Policy

Although contracts involve private parties, some are not enforceable because of the negative impact they would have on society. These contracts are said to be *contrary to public policy.* Examples include a contract to commit an immoral act, such as selling a child, and a contract that prohibits marriage. Business contracts that may be against public policy include contracts in restraint of trade and unconscionable contracts or clauses.

Contracts in Restraint of Trade The United States has a strong public policy favoring competition in the economy. Thus, contracts in restraint of trade (anti-competitive agreements) generally are unenforceable because they are contrary to public policy. Typically, such contracts also violate one or more federal or state antitrust statutes.[15]

An exception is recognized when the restraint is reasonable and is contained in an ancillary (secondary or subordinate) clause in a contract. Such restraints often

13. *Gaming Venture, Inc. v. Tastee Restaurant Corp.*, 996 So.2d 515 (La.App. 5th Cir. 2008).

14. *McNatt v. Vestal,* __ S.W.3d __, 2016 WL 659847 (Tenn.App. 2016).
15. Federal statutes include the Sherman Antitrust Act, the Clayton Act, and the Federal Trade Commission Act.

are included in contracts for the sale of an ongoing business and in employment contracts.

Covenants Not to Compete and the Sale of an Ongoing Business.

Many contracts involve a type of restraint called a **covenant not to compete,** or a restrictive covenant (promise). A covenant not to compete may be created when a merchant who sells a store agrees not to open a new store in a certain geographic area surrounding the old business. Such an agreement enables the seller to sell, and the purchaser to buy, the goodwill and reputation of an ongoing business without having to worry that the seller will open a competing business a block away. Provided the restrictive covenant is reasonable and is an ancillary part of the sale of an ongoing business, it is enforceable.

Covenants Not to Compete in Employment Contracts.

Sometimes, agreements not to compete (also referred to as *noncompete agreements*) are included in employment contracts. People in middle- or upper-level management positions commonly agree not to work for competitors or start competing businesses for a specified period of time after termination of employment.

Noncompete agreements are legal in most states so long as the specified period of time (of restraint) is not excessive in duration and the geographic restriction is reasonable. What constitutes a reasonable time period may be shorter in the online environment than in conventional employment contracts. Because the geographical restrictions apply worldwide, the time restrictions may be shorter.

A restraint that is found to be overly broad will not be enforced. ■ **CASE IN POINT 9.18** An insurance firm in New York City, Brown & Brown, Inc., hired Theresa Johnson to perform actuarial analysis. On her first day of work, Johnson was asked to sign a nonsolicitation covenant. The covenant prohibited her from soliciting or servicing any of Brown's clients for two years after the termination of her employment.

Less than five years later, when Johnson's employment with Brown was terminated, she went to work for Lawley Benefits Group, LLC. Brown sued to enforce the covenant. A state appellate court ruled that the covenant was overly broad and unenforceable. It attempted to restrict Johnson from working for any of Brown's clients, without regard to whether she had had a relationship with those clients.[16] ■

Enforcement Issues.

The laws governing the enforceability of covenants not to compete vary significantly from state to state. California prohibits the enforcement of covenants not to compete altogether. In some states, including Texas, such a covenant will not be enforced unless the employee has received some benefit in return for signing the noncompete agreement. This is true even if the covenant is reasonable as to time and area. (When a current employee is required to sign a noncompete agreement, for instance, his or her employment is not sufficient consideration for the agreement, because the individual is already employed. To be valid, the agreement requires new consideration.) If the employee receives no benefit, the covenant will be deemed void.

Occasionally, depending on the jurisdiction, courts will *reform* covenants not to compete. If a covenant is found to be unreasonable in time or geographic area, the court may convert the terms into reasonable ones and then enforce the reformed covenant. Such court actions present a problem, though, in that the judge implicitly becomes a party to the contract. Consequently, courts usually resort to contract **reformation** only when necessary to prevent undue burdens or hardships.

Unconscionable Contracts or Clauses

A court ordinarily does not look at the fairness or equity of a contract (or inquire into the adequacy of consideration). Persons are assumed to be reasonably intelligent, and the courts will not come to their aid just because they have made unwise or foolish bargains.

In certain circumstances, however, bargains are so oppressive that the courts relieve innocent parties of part or all of their duties. Such bargains are deemed **unconscionable**[17] because they are so unscrupulous or grossly unfair as to be "void of conscience." A contract can be unconscionable on either procedural or substantive grounds, as illustrated in Exhibit 9–2. The Uniform Commercial Code (UCC) incorporates the concept of unconscionability in its provisions regarding the sale and lease of goods.[18]

Procedural Unconscionability.

Procedural unconscionability often involves inconspicuous print, unintelligible language ("legalese"), or the lack of an opportunity to read the contract or ask questions about its meaning. This type of unconscionability typically arises when a party's lack of knowledge or understanding of the contract terms deprived him or her of any meaningful choice.

Procedural unconscionability can also occur when there is such disparity in bargaining power between the two parties that the weaker party's consent is not

---

16. *Brown & Brown, Inc. v. Johnson,* 115 A.D.3d 52, 980 N.Y.S.2d 631 (2014).

17. Pronounced un-*kon*-shun-uh-bul.

18. See UCC 2–302 and 2A–719.

EXHIBIT 9-2 Unconsciionability

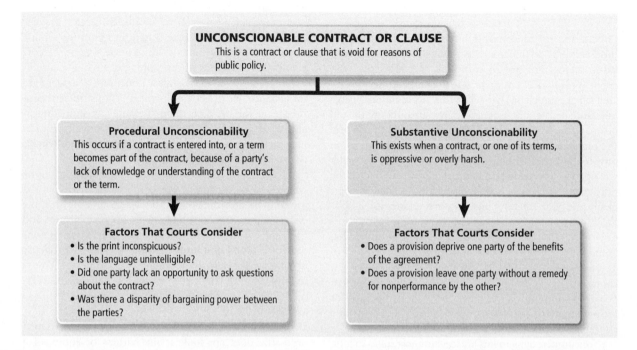

UNCONSCIONABLE CONTRACT OR CLAUSE
This is a contract or clause that is void for reasons of public policy.

Procedural Unconscionability
This occurs if a contract is entered into, or a term becomes part of the contract, because of a party's lack of knowledge or understanding of the contract or the term.

Factors That Courts Consider
- Is the print inconspicuous?
- Is the language unintelligible?
- Did one party lack an opportunity to ask questions about the contract?
- Was there a disparity of bargaining power between the parties?

Substantive Unconscionability
This exists when a contract, or one of its terms, is oppressive or overly harsh.

Factors That Courts Consider
- Does a provision deprive one party of the benefits of the agreement?
- Does a provision leave one party without a remedy for nonperformance by the other?

voluntary. This type of situation often involves an *adhesion* contract, which is a contract written exclusively by one party and presented to the other on a take-it-or-leave-it basis.[19] In other words, the party to whom the contract is presented (usually a buyer or borrower) has no opportunity to negotiate its terms.

Not all adhesion contracts are unconscionable, only those that unreasonably favor the drafter. ■ **CASE IN POINT 9.19** Tiffany Brinkley committed to take six real estate investment training sessions at a cost of $4,195. She paid $850 and signed a retail installment contract promising to pay monthly payments on the balance to Monterey Financial Services. The contract contained an arbitration agreement. When a dispute arose, Brinkley stopped making payments and filed a lawsuit against Monterey in a California state court.

Monterey filed a motion to arbitrate, which the trial court granted. Brinkley appealed. She argued that the arbitration clause was procedurally unconscionable because it was part of an adhesion contract. The court, though, found that the arbitration clause was enforceable and dismissed the lawsuit. The court held that the "purported lack of meaningful choice did not render the

arbitration provision in retail installment contract procedurally unconscionable."[20] ■

Substantive Unconscionability. *Substantive* unconscionability occurs when contracts, or portions of contracts, are oppressive or overly harsh. Courts generally focus on provisions that deprive one party of the benefits of the agreement or leave that party without a remedy for nonperformance by the other.

Substantive unconscionability can arise in a wide variety of business contexts. For instance, a contract clause that gives the business entity unconstrained access to the courts but requires the other party to arbitrate any dispute with the firm may be unconscionable.

Exculpatory Clauses Often closely related to the concept of unconscionability are **exculpatory clauses,** which release a party from liability in the event of monetary or physical injury *no matter who is at fault.* Indeed, courts sometimes refuse to enforce such clauses on the ground that they are unconscionable.

19. For a classic case involving an adhesion contract, see *Henningsen v. Bloomfield Motors, Inc.*, 32 N.J. 358, 161 A.2d 69 (1960).

20. *Brinkley v. Monterey Financial Services, Inc.,* 242 Cal.App.4th 314, 196 Cal.Rptr.3d 1 (2015). See also *Louisiana Extended Care Centers, LLC v. Bindon*, 180 So.3d 791 (2015).

Violations of Public Policy. Most courts view exculpatory clauses with disfavor. Exculpatory clauses found in rental agreements for commercial property are frequently held to be contrary to public policy, and such clauses are almost always unenforceable in residential property leases. Courts also usually hold that exculpatory clauses are against public policy in the employment context. Thus, employers frequently cannot enforce exculpatory clauses in contracts with employees or independent contractors to avoid liability for work-related injuries.

■ **CASE IN POINT 9.20** Crum Motor Sales entered into an agreement with Martin County Coal Corporation to service Martin Coal's pickup trucks and light-duty vehicles. The parties agreed that when vehicles needed service, Crum Motor would pick up the vehicles from Martin Coal's mining site, repair them, and then bring them back. Martin Coal required Crum Motor to sign an indemnification agreement (exculpatory clause) for all injuries sustained on the mining site and to have insurance coverage.

A few years later, Philip Crum (an employee of Crum Motor) was driving on a road on the mining site when a falling boulder crushed the cab of his pickup. He was seriously injured and spent the rest of the year in a hospital and rehabilitation facility. Philip Crum and Crum Motor sued Martin Coal for negligence in maintaining the road and the site. Martin Coal counterclaimed, arguing that it was not liable under the indemnification agreement.

Crum Motor's insurance provider (Universal Underwriters) declined to represent the company in the lawsuit. Eventually, Martin Coal settled with Philip Crum and Crum Motor for $3.65 million and filed a suit against Universal Underwriters for that same amount. The court held that the indemnification agreement between Crum Motor and Martin Coal was against public policy and void. Therefore, Martin Coal was responsible for paying the settlement, not Crum Motor's insurance provider.[21] ■

Enforcement of Exculpatory Clauses. Courts do enforce exculpatory clauses if they are reasonable, do not violate public policy, and do not protect parties from liability for intentional misconduct. The language used must not be ambiguous, and the parties must have been in relatively equal bargaining positions.

Businesses such as health clubs, racetracks, amusement parks, skiing facilities, horse-rental operations, golf-cart concessions, and skydiving organizations frequently use exculpatory clauses to limit their liability for patrons' injuries. Because these services are not essential, the companies offering them have no relative advantage in bargaining strength, and anyone contracting for their services does so voluntarily. Courts also may enforce reasonable exculpatory clauses in loan documents, real estate contracts, and trust agreements.

See this chapter's *Managerial Strategy* feature for more about exculpatory clauses that will not be considered unconscionable.

Discriminatory Contracts Contracts in which a party promises to discriminate on the basis of race, color, national origin, religion, gender, age, or disability are contrary to both statute and public policy. They are also unenforceable.[22] For instance, if a property owner promises in a contract not to sell the property to a member of a particular race, the contract is unenforceable. The public policy underlying these prohibitions is very strong, and the courts are quick to invalidate discriminatory contracts.

Exhibit 9–3 illustrates the types of contracts that may be illegal because they are contrary to statute or public policy.

9–3c Effect of Illegality

In general, an illegal contract is void—that is, the contract is deemed never to have existed, and the courts will not aid either party. In most illegal contracts, both parties are considered to be equally at fault—*in pari delicto*.[23] If the contract is executory (not yet fulfilled), neither party can enforce it. If it has been executed, neither party can recover damages.

Usually, the courts are not concerned if one wrongdoer in an illegal contract is unjustly enriched at the expense of the other. The main reason for this hands-off attitude is the belief that a plaintiff who has broken the law by entering into an illegal bargain should not be allowed to obtain help from the courts. Another justification is the hoped-for deterrent effect. A plaintiff who suffers a loss because of an illegal bargain will presumably be deterred from entering into similar illegal bargains in the future.

There are, however, exceptions to the general rule that neither party to an illegal bargain can sue for breach and neither party can recover for performance rendered. We look at these exceptions next.

Justifiable Ignorance of the Facts Sometimes, one of the parties to a contract has no reason to know that the contract is illegal and thus is relatively innocent.

---

21. *Martin County Coal Corp. v. Universal Underwriters Ins. Co.*, 727 F.3d 589 (6th Cir. 2013).

22. The major federal statute prohibiting discrimination is the Civil Rights Act of 1964, 42 U.S.C. Sections 2000e–2000e-17.

23. Pronounced in-*pah*-ree deh-*lick*-tow.

MANAGERIAL STRATEGY

Creating Liability Waivers That Are Not Unconscionable

Blanket liability waivers that absolve a business from virtually every event, even those caused by the business's own negligence, are usually unenforceable because they are unconscionable. Exculpatory waivers are common, nonetheless. We observe such waivers in gym memberships, on ski lift tickets, on admissions tickets to sporting events, and in simple contracts for the use of campgrounds.

Typically, courts view liability waivers as voluntarily bargained for whether or not they have been read. Thus, a waiver included in the fine print on the back of an admission ticket or on an entry sign to a stadium may be upheld. In general, if such waivers are unambiguous and conspicuous, the assumption is that patrons have had a chance to read them and have accepted their terms.

Activities with Inherent Risks

Cases challenging liability waivers have been brought against skydiving operations, skiing operations, bobsledding operations, white-water rafting companies, and health clubs. For example, in *Bergin v. Wild Mountain, Inc.,*[a] an appellate court in Minnesota upheld a ski resort's liability waiver.

In that case, the plaintiff hit a snowmaking mound, which was "an inherent risk of skiing." Before the accident, the plaintiff had stated that he knew "that an inherent risk of serious injury in downhill skiing was hitting snowmaking mounds." Furthermore, he had not rejected the season pass that contained the

resort's exculpatory clause. Thus, the ski resort prevailed.

Overly Broad Waivers

While most liability waivers have survived legal challenges, some have not. In *Bagley v. Mt. Bachelor, Inc.,*[b] the Supreme Court of Oregon ruled against a ski resort's "very broad" liability waiver. The case involved an eighteen-year-old, Myles Bagley, who was paralyzed from the waist down after a snowboarding accident at Mt. Bachelor ski resort. The season pass that Bagley signed included a liability waiver. The waiver stated that the signer agreed not to sue the resort for injury even if "caused by negligence."

Bagley argued that the resort had created a dangerous condition because of the way it had set up a particular ski jump. He sued for $21.5 million and eventually won the right to go forward with his lawsuit. The Oregon Supreme Court found that, for various reasons, enforcement of the release would have been unconscionable. "Because the release is unenforceable, genuine issues of fact exist that preclude summary judgment in defendant's favor."

Business Questions

1. *If you are running a business, why would you opt to include overly broad waivers in your contracts with customers?*
2. *Under what circumstances would you, as a business owner, choose to aggressively defend your business against a customer's liability lawsuit?*

a. 2014 WL 996788 (Minn.App. 2014).

b. 356 Or. 543, 340 P.3d 27 (2014).

That party can often recover any benefits conferred in a partially executed contract. In this situation, the courts will not enforce the contract but will allow the parties to return to their original positions.

Sometimes, a court may permit an innocent party who has fully performed under the contract to enforce the contract against the guilty party. ■ **EXAMPLE 9.21** A trucking company contracts with Gillespie to carry crates filled with goods to a specific destination for the normal fee of $5,000. The trucker delivers the crates and later finds out that they contained illegal goods. Although the law specifies that the shipment, use, and sale of the goods were illegal, the trucker, being an innocent party, can still legally collect the $5,000 from Gillespie. ■

Members of Protected Classes When a statute is clearly designed to protect a certain class of people, a member of that class can enforce a contract in violation of the statute even though the other party cannot. ■ **EXAMPLE 9.22** Statutes prohibit certain employees (such as flight attendants and pilots) from working more than a certain number of hours per month. An employee who is required to work more than the maximum can recover for those extra hours of service. ■

Other examples of statutes designed to protect a particular class of people are state statutes that regulate the sale of insurance. If an insurance company violates a statute when selling insurance, the purchaser can still enforce the policy and recover from the insurer.

EXHIBIT 9–3 Contract Legality

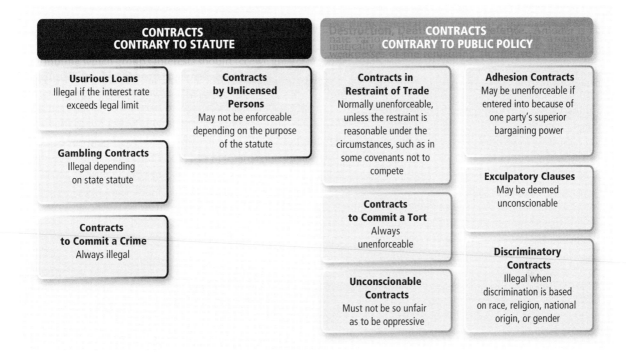

Withdrawal from an Illegal Agreement If the illegal part of a bargain has not yet been performed, the party rendering performance can withdraw from the contract and recover the performance or its value. ■ **EXAMPLE 9.23** Sam and Jim decide to wager (illegally) on the outcome of a boxing match. Each deposits its cash with a stakeholder, who agrees to pay the winner of the bet. At this point, each party has performed part of the agreement. Before payment occurs, either party is entitled to withdraw from the bargain by giving notice of repudiation to the stakeholder. ■

Contract Illegal through Fraud, Duress, or Undue Influence Often, one party to an illegal contract is more at fault than the other. When one party uses fraud, duress, or undue influence to induce another party to enter into an illegal bargain, the second party will be allowed to recover for the performance or its value.

Severable, or Divisible, Contracts A contract that is *severable,* or divisible, consists of distinct parts that can be performed separately, with separate consideration provided for each part. With an *indivisible* contract, in contrast, complete performance by each party is essential, even if the contract contains a number of seemingly separate provisions.

If a contract is divisible into legal and illegal portions, a court may enforce the legal portion but not the illegal one, so long as the illegal portion does not affect the essence of the bargain. This approach is consistent with the courts' basic policy of enforcing the legal intentions of the contracting parties whenever possible.

■ **EXAMPLE 9.24** Cole signs an employment contract that includes an overly broad and thus illegal covenant not to compete. In that situation, a court might allow the employment contract to be enforceable but reform the unreasonably broad covenant by converting its terms into reasonable ones. Alternatively, the court could declare the covenant illegal (and thus void) and enforce the remaining employment terms. ■

A contract clause stating that the parties intend the contract terms to be enforced to "the fullest extent possible" indicates that the parties regard their contract as divisible. In the event of a dispute, the parties intend that the court will strike out the illegal terms and enforce the rest.

Reviewing: Consideration, Capacity, and Legality

Renee Beaver started racing go-karts competitively in 2016, when she was fourteen. Many of the races required her to sign an exculpatory clause to participate, which she or her parents regularly signed. In 2018, right before her sixteenth birthday, Renee participated in the annual Elkhart Grand Prix, a series of races in Elkhart, Indiana. During the event in which she drove, a piece of foam padding used as a course barrier was torn from its base and ended up on the track. A portion of the padding struck Beaver in the head, and another portion was thrown into oncoming traffic, causing a multikart collision during which she sustained severe injuries. Beaver filed an action against the race organizers for negligence. The race organizers could not locate the exculpatory clause that Beaver had supposedly signed. The organizers argued that she must have signed one to enter the race, but even if she had not signed one, her actions showed her intent to be bound by its terms. Using the information presented in the chapter, answer the following questions.

1. Did Beaver have the contractual capacity to enter a contract with an exculpatory clause? Why or why not?
2. Assuming that Beaver did, in fact, sign the exculpatory clause, did she later disaffirm or ratify the contract? Explain.
3. Now assume that Beaver stated that she was eighteen years old at the time she signed the exculpatory clause. How might this affect her ability to disaffirm or ratify the contract?
4. If Beaver did not actually sign the exculpatory clause, could a court conclude that she impliedly accepted its terms by participating in the race? Why or why not?

Debate This . . . *After agreeing to an exculpatory clause or purchasing some item, minors often seek to avoid the contracts. Today's minors are far from naïve and should not be allowed to avoid their contractual obligations.*

Terms and Concepts

accord and satisfaction 171	estopped 173	ratification 177
age of majority 174	exculpatory clause 182	reformation 181
consideration 166	forbearance 166	release 171
contractual capacity 174	legality 179	rescission 170
covenant not to compete 181	liquidated debt 171	unconscionable 181
covenant not to sue 172	necessaries 177	unliquidated debt 171
disaffirmance 175	past consideration 170	usury 180
emancipation 174	promissory estoppel 173	

Issue Spotters

1. Joan, who is sixteen years old, moves out of her parents' home and signs a one-year lease for an apartment at Kenwood Apartments. Joan's parents tell her that she can return to live with them at any time. Unable to pay the rent, Joan moves back to her parents' home two months later. Can Kenwood enforce the lease against Joan? Why or why not? (See *Contractual Capacity*.)

2. Before Maria starts her first year of college, Fred promises to give her $5,000 when she graduates. She goes to college, borrowing and spending far more than $5,000. At the beginning of the spring semester of her senior year, she reminds Fred of the promise. Fred sends her a note that says, "I revoke the promise." Is Fred's promise binding? Explain. (See *Consideration*.)

- **Check your answers to the Issue Spotters against the answers provided in Appendix B at the end of this text.**

Business Scenarios

9–1. Preexisting Duty. Tabor is a buyer of file cabinets manufactured by Martin. Martin's contract with Tabor calls for delivery of fifty file cabinets at $40 per cabinet in five equal installments. After delivery of two installments (twenty cabinets), Martin informs Tabor that because of inflation, Martin is losing money. Martin will promise to deliver the remaining thirty cabinets only if Tabor will pay $50 per cabinet. Tabor agrees in writing to do so. Discuss whether Martin can legally collect the additional $100 on delivery to Tabor of the next installment of ten cabinets. (See *Consideration*.)

9–2. Capacity. Joanne is a seventy-five-year-old widow who survives on her husband's small pension. Joanne has become increasingly forgetful, and her family worries that she may have Alzheimer's disease (a brain disorder that seriously affects a person's ability to carry out daily activities). No physician has diagnosed her, however, and no court has ruled on her legal competence. One day while she is out shopping, Joanne stops by a store that is having a sale on pianos and enters into a fifteen-year installment contract to buy a grand piano. When the piano arrives the next day, Joanne seems confused and repeatedly asks the delivery person why a piano is being delivered. Joanne claims that she does not recall buying a piano. Explain whether this contract is void, voidable, or valid. Can Joanne avoid her contractual obligation to buy the piano? If so, how? (See *Contractual Capacity*.)

9–3. Accord and Satisfaction. Merrick grows and sells blueberries. Maine Wild Blueberry Co. agreed to buy all of Merrick's crop under a contract that left the price unliquidated. Merrick delivered the berries, but a dispute arose over the price. Maine Wild sent Merrick a check with a letter stating that the check was the "final settlement." Merrick cashed the check but filed a suit for breach of contract, claiming that he was owed more. What will the court likely decide in this case? Why? (See *Consideration*.)

Business Case Problems

9–4. Statute of Limitations. Leonard Kranzler loaned Lewis Saltzman $100,000. Saltzman made fifteen payments on the loan, but this did not repay the entire amount. More than ten years after the date of the loan, but less than two years after the date of the last payment, Kranzler filed a suit against Saltzman to recover the outstanding balance. Saltzman claimed that the suit was barred by a ten-year statute of limitations. Does Kranzler need to prove a new promise with new consideration to collect the unpaid debt? Explain. [*Kranzler v. Saltzman,* 407 Ill.App.3d 24, 942 N.E.2d 722, 347 Ill. Dec. 519 (1 Dist. 2011)] (See *Exceptions to the Consideration Requirement*.)

9–5. Adhesion Contracts. David Desgro hired Paul Pack to inspect a house that Desgro wanted to buy. Pack had Desgro sign a standard-form contract that included a twelve-month limit for claims based on the agreement. Pack reported that the house had no major problems, but after Desgro bought it, he discovered issues with the plumbing, insulation, heat pump, and floor support. Thirteen months after the inspection, Desgro filed a suit in a Tennessee state court against Pack. Was Desgro's complaint filed too late, or was the contract's twelve-month limit unenforceable? Discuss. [*Desgro v. Pack,* 2013 WL 84899 (Tenn.App. 2013)] (See *Legality*.)

9–6. Business Case Problem with Sample Answer—Consideration. Citynet, LLC, established an employee incentive plan "to enable the Company to attract and retain experienced individuals." The plan provided that a participant who left Citynet's employment was entitled to "cash out" his or her entire vested balance. (When an employee's rights to a particular benefit become *vested,* they belong to that employee and cannot be taken away. The vested balance refers to the part of an account that goes with the employee if he or she leaves the company.) When Citynet employee Ray Toney terminated his employment, he asked to redeem his vested balance, which amounted to $87,000.48. Citynet refused, citing a provision of the plan that limited redemptions to no more than 20 percent annually. Toney filed a suit in a West Virginia state court against Citynet, alleging breach of contract. Citynet argued that the plan was not a contract but a discretionary bonus over which Citynet had sole discretion. Was the plan a contract? If so, what was the consideration? [*Citynet, LLC v. Toney,* 235 W.Va. 79, 772 S.E.2d 36 (2015)] (See *Consideration*.)

• **For a sample answer to Problem 9–6, go to Appendix C at the end of this text.**

9–7. Agreements That Lack Consideration. Arkansas-Missouri Forest Products, LLC (Ark-Mo), sells supplies to make wood pallets. Blue Chip Manufacturing (BCM) makes pallets. Mark Garnett, an owner of Ark-Mo, and Stuart Lerner, an owner of BCM, went into business together. Garnett and Lerner agreed that Ark-Mo would have a 30-percent ownership interest in their future projects. When Lerner formed Blue Chip Recycling, LLC (BCR), to manage a pallet repair facility in California, however, he allocated only a 5-percent interest to Ark-Mo. Garnett objected. In a "Telephone Deal," Lerner then promised Garnett that Ark-Mo would receive a 30-percent interest in their future projects in the Midwest, and Garnett agreed to forgo an ownership interest in BCR. But when Blue Chip III, LLC (BC III), was formed to operate a repair facility in the Midwest, Lerner told Garnett that he "was not getting anything." Ark-Mo filed a suit in a Missouri state court against Lerner, alleging breach of contract. Was there consideration to support the Telephone Deal? Explain.

[Arkansas-Missouri Forest Products, LLC v. Lerner, 486 S.W.3d 438 (Mo.App. E.D. 2016)] (See *Consideration.*)

9–8. Legality. Sue Ann Apolinar hired a guide through Arkansas Valley Adventures, LLC, for a rafting excursion on the Arkansas River. At the outfitter's office, Apolinar signed a release that detailed potential hazards and risks, including "overturning," "unpredictable currents," "obstacles" in the water, and "drowning." The release clearly stated that her signature discharged Arkansas Valley from liability for all claims arising in connection with the trip. On the river, while attempting to maneuver around a rapid, the raft capsized. The current swept Apolinar into a logjam where, despite efforts to save her, she drowned. Her son, Jesus Espinoza, Jr., filed a suit in a federal district court against the rafting company, alleging negligence. What are the arguments for and against enforcing the release that Apolinar signed? Discuss. [*Espinoza v. Arkansas Valley Adventures, LLC,* 809 F.3d 1150 (10th Cir. 2016)] (See *Legality.*)

9–9. A Question of Ethics—Promissory Estoppel.

 Claudia Aceves borrowed from U.S. Bank to buy a home. Two years later, she could no longer afford the monthly payments. The bank notified her that it planned to foreclose on her home. (Foreclosure is a process that allows a lender to repossess and sell the property that secures a loan.) Aceves filed for bankruptcy. The bank offered to modify Aceves's mortgage if she would forgo bankruptcy. She agreed. Once she withdrew the filing, however, the bank foreclosed. [*Aceves v. U.S. Bank, N.A.,* 192 Cal.App.4th 218, 120 Cal.Rptr.3d 507 (2 Dist. 2011)] (See *Consideration.*)

(a) Could Aceves succeed on a claim of promissory estoppel? Why or why not?

(b) Did Aceves or U.S. Bank behave unethically? Discuss.

Legal Reasoning Group Activity

9–10. Covenants Not to Compete. Assume that you are part of a group of executives at a large software corporation. The company is considering whether to incorporate covenants not to compete into its employment contracts. You know that there are some issues with the enforceability of these covenants, and you want to make an informed decision. (See *Legality.*)

(a) One group should make a list of what interests are served by enforcing covenants not to compete.

(b) A second group should create a list of what interests are served by refusing to enforce covenants not to compete.

(c) A third group should consider whether a court should reform (and then enforce) a covenant not to compete that it determines is illegal. The group should create an argument for and an argument against reformation.

CHAPTER 10

Defenses to Contract Enforceability

An otherwise valid contract may still be unenforceable if the parties have not genuinely agreed to its terms. A lack of *voluntary consent* (assent) can be used as a defense to the contract's enforceability.

Voluntary consent may be lacking because of a mistake, misrepresentation, undue influence, or duress—in other words, because there is no true "meeting of the minds." Generally, a party who demonstrates that he or she did not truly agree to the terms of a contract has a choice. That party can choose either to carry out the contract or to rescind (cancel) it and thus avoid the entire transaction.

A contract that is otherwise valid may still be unenforceable if it is not in the proper form. Certain types of contracts are required to be in writing or evidenced by a memorandum or an electronic record. An agreement subject to the writing requirement does not necessarily have to be written on paper. An exchange of e-mails that evidences the parties' contract can be sufficient, provided that they are "signed," or agreed to, by the party against whom enforcement is sought.

10-1 Mistakes

We all make mistakes, so it is not surprising that mistakes are made when contracts are formed. In certain circumstances, contract law allows a contract to be avoided on the basis of mistake.

It is important to distinguish between *mistakes of fact* and *mistakes of value or quality*. Only a mistake of fact makes a contract voidable. Also, the mistake must involve some *material fact*—a fact that a reasonable person would consider important when determining his or her course of action.

Mistakes of fact occur in two forms—*bilateral* and *unilateral*. A unilateral mistake is made by only *one* of the parties. A bilateral, or mutual, mistake is made by *both* of the contracting parties. We look next at these two types of mistakes and illustrate them graphically in Exhibit 10–1.

10-1a Unilateral Mistakes of Fact

A **unilateral mistake** is made by only one of the parties. In general, a unilateral mistake does not give the mistaken party any right to relief from the contract. Normally, the contract is enforceable.

■ **EXAMPLE 10.1** Elena intends to sell her jet ski for $2,500. When she learns that Chin is interested in buying a used jet ski, she sends him an e-mail offering to sell the jet ski to him. When typing the e-mail, however, she mistakenly keys in the price of $1,500. Chin immediately sends Elena an e-mail reply accepting her offer. Even though Elena intended to sell her personal jet ski for $2,500, she has made a unilateral mistake and is bound by the contract to sell it to Chin for $1,500. ■

This general rule has at least two exceptions.[1] The contract may not be enforceable if:

1. The *other* party to the contract knows or should have known that a mistake of fact was made.
2. The error was due to a *substantial* mathematical mistake in addition, subtraction, division, or multiplication and was made inadvertently and without gross (extreme) negligence. If, for instance, a contractor's bid was significantly low because he or she made a mistake in addition when totaling the estimated costs, any contract resulting from the bid normally may be rescinded.

---

1. The *Restatement (Second) of Contracts*, Section 153, liberalizes the general rule to take into account the modern trend of allowing avoidance even though only one party has been mistaken.

EXHIBIT 10–1 Mistakes of Fact

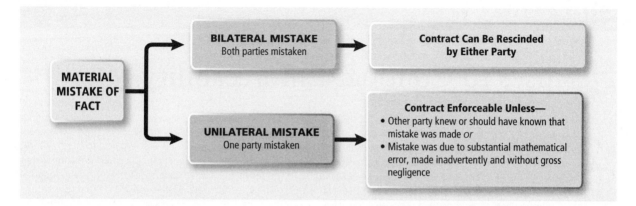

Of course, in both situations, the mistake must still involve some material fact.

10–1b Bilateral (Mutual) Mistakes of Fact

A **bilateral mistake** is a "mutual misunderstanding concerning a basic assumption on which the contract was made."[2] Note that, as with unilateral mistakes, the mistake must be about a material fact.

Either Party Can Rescind the Contract When both parties are mistaken about the same material fact, the contract can be rescinded by either party. ■ **CASE IN POINT 10.2** Coleman Holdings LP bought a parcel of real estate subject to setback restrictions imposed in a document entitled "Partial Release of Restrictions" that effectively precluded building a structure on the property. Lance and Joanne Eklund offered to buy the parcel from Coleman, intending to combine it with an adjacent parcel and build a home. Coleman gave the Eklunds a title report that referred to the "Partial Release of Restrictions," but they were not given a copy of the release.

Mistakenly believing that the document released restrictions on the property, the Eklunds did not investigate further. Meanwhile, Coleman also mistakenly believed that the setback restrictions had been removed. After buying the property and discovering the restrictions, the Eklunds filed a suit in a Nevada state court against Coleman, seeking rescission of the sale. The court ordered the deal rescinded. The Nevada Supreme Court affirmed the order. "The parties made a mutual mistake in their mutual belief that the parcel had no setback restrictions."[3] ■

When the Parties Reasonably Interpret a Term Differently A word or term in a contract may be subject to more than one reasonable interpretation. If the parties to the contract attach materially different meanings to the term, a court may allow the contract to be rescinded because there has been no true "meeting of the minds."

■ **CASE IN POINT 10.3** L&H Construction Company contracted with Circle Redmont, Inc., to make a cast-iron staircase and a glass flooring system. Redmont's original proposal was to "engineer, fabricate, and install" the staircase and flooring system, but installation was later dropped from the deal as a cost-cutting measure. The final contract stated that payment was due on "Supervision of Installation," although "install" appeared elsewhere in the contract. L&H insisted that installation was included and sued Redmont. The court found that the word *install* in the phrase "engineer, fabricate, and install" was the result of a mutual mistake. Both parties understood that Redmont would only supervise the installation, not perform it. Therefore, Redmont was not required to install the staircase and flooring.[4] ■

10–1c Mistakes of Value

If a mistake concerns the future market value or quality of the object of the contract, the mistake is one of *value,* and the contract normally is enforceable. ■ **EXAMPLE 10.4** Sung buys a violin from Bev for $250. Although the violin is very old, neither party believes that it is valuable. Later, however, an antiques dealer informs the parties that the violin is rare and worth thousands of dollars. Here, both parties were mistaken, but the mistake is a mistake of *value* rather than a mistake of *fact*. Because

---

2. *Restatement (Second) of Contracts,* Section 152.
3. *Coleman Holdings Limited Partnership v. Eklund,* 2015 WL 428567 (Nev. Sup.Ct. 2015).

4. *L&H Construction Co. v. Circle Redmont, Inc.,* 55 So.3d 630 (Fla.App. 2011).

mistakes of value do not warrant contract rescission, Bev cannot rescind the contract. ■

The reason that mistakes of value do not affect the enforceability of contracts is that value is variable. Depending on the time, place, and other circumstances, the same item may be worth considerably different amounts. When parties form a contract, their agreement establishes the value of the object of their transaction—for the moment. Each party is considered to have assumed the risk that the value will change in the future or prove to be different from what he or she thought. Without this rule, almost any party who did not receive what she or he considered a fair bargain could argue mistake.

10–2 Fraudulent Misrepresentation

Although fraud is a tort, the presence of fraud also affects the authenticity of the innocent party's consent to the contract. When an innocent party is fraudulently induced to enter into a contract, the contract usually can be avoided, because that party has not *voluntarily* consented to its terms.[5] The innocent party can either rescind the contract and be restored to her or his original position or enforce the contract and seek damages for any harms resulting from the fraud.

Generally, fraudulent misrepresentation refers only to misrepresentation that is consciously false and is intended to mislead another. The person making the fraudulent misrepresentation knows or believes that the assertion is false or knows that she or he does not have a basis (stated or implied) for the assertion.[6] Typically, fraudulent misrepresentation consists of the following elements:

1. A misrepresentation of a material fact must occur.
2. There must be an intent to deceive.
3. The innocent party must justifiably rely on the misrepresentation.
4. To collect damages, a party must have been harmed as a result of the misrepresentation.

Like other actions based in the common law, a cause of action based on fraud can be subject to a statute of limitations. Of course, a cause based on a statute can also be subject to a statute of limitations. The limitations periods governing these actions may be different. In the following case, the issue was which limit to apply to a specific fraud claim—the three-year limit that applied to certain statute-based actions or the six-year limit that applied to common law actions.

---

5. *Restatement (Second) of Contracts*, Sections 163 and 164.

6. *Restatement (Second) of Contracts*, Section 162.

Case 10.1

Schneiderman v. Trump Entrepreneur Initiative, LLC

New York Supreme Court, Appellate Division, First Department, 137 A.D.3d 409, 26 N.Y.S.3d 66 (2016).

Background and Facts Donald Trump and Michael Sexton formed Trump University, LLC—later known as Trump Entrepreneur Initiative, LLC (TEI)—to sell courses in real estate investing. To attract students, Trump made a promotional video. In it, he said, "We're going to have professors that are absolutely terrific—terrific people, terrific brains, successful, the best. . . . All people that are hand-picked by me."

New York Attorney General Eric Schneiderman brought a proceeding in a New York state court against TEI, Trump, and Sexton, alleging that they had operated an illegal educational institution between 2005 and 2011. The attorney general sought an injunction, damages, penalties, and restitution under a state statute that provided for these remedies in cases of "persistent fraud." TEI was charged with intentionally misleading more than 5,000 students, including over 600 New York residents, into paying as much as $35,000 each to participate in its programs. Among other things, according to the attorney general, Trump did not handpick the instructors as he claimed.

The court dismissed the claim on the ground that it exceeded a three-year limit imposed on all statutory causes of action. The court also held that the specific statute did not provide the state with an independent cause of action for fraud. The attorney general appealed.

In the Language of the Court
MAZZARELLI, J.P. [Justice Presiding], RENWICK, SAXE, MOSKOWITZ, J.J. [Justices]
* * * *
* * * [New York] Executive Law Section 63(12) states, in relevant part:

Case 10.1 Continues

Case 10.1 Continued

Whenever any person shall engage in repeated fraudulent or illegal acts or otherwise demonstrate persistent fraud or illegality in the carrying on, conducting or transaction of business, the attorney general may apply * * * to the supreme court of the state of New York * * * for an order enjoining the continuance of such business activity or of any fraudulent or illegal acts and directing restitution and damages * * * and the court may award [such] relief * * * as it may deem proper.

* * * *

[In its ruling, the lower court cited *People v. Charles Schwab & Co., Inc.,* 109 A.D.3d 445, 971 N.Y.S.2d 267 (1 Dept. 2013).] In *Charles Schwab,* the Attorney General had brought an enforcement action asserting claims under Section 63(12) * * *. The court dismissed the Section 63(12) claim.

On appeal to this Court, * * * we found that the court had properly dismissed that claim, stating that the section does not create independent claims, but merely authorizes the Attorney General to seek injunctive and other relief * * * in cases involving persistent fraud.

Although the holding of *Charles Schwab* purported to be based on the [New York] Court of Appeals' ruling in *State v. Cortelle Corp.,* 38 N.Y.2d 83, 378 N.Y.S.2d 654, 341 N.E.2d 223 (1975), *Cortelle* does not, in fact, hold that the Attorney General cannot bring a standalone cause of action for fraud under Executive Law Section 63(12).

* * * *

In *Cortelle,* the Court of Appeals [found] that * * * causes of action [under Section 63(12)] addressing * * * allegedly fraudulent practices did not rely on liabilities, penalties, or forfeitures created or imposed by statute. *Specifically, Section 63(12) did not make unlawful the alleged fraudulent practices, but only provided standing in the Attorney General to seek redress and additional remedies for recognized wrongs which pre-existed the statute.* [Emphasis added.]

* * * *

* * * Other New York courts addressing that issue * * * have generally allowed for independent causes of action for fraud under Section 63(12).

* * * *

Thus, *Charles Schwab* does not comport with prevailing authority.

* * * Hence, we hold that the Attorney General is, in fact, authorized to bring a cause of action for fraud under Section 63(12).

Decision and Remedy *A state intermediate appellate court reversed the lower court's dismissal of the fraud claim, holding that the three-year limit on statutory causes of action did not apply. Because material issues of fact still existed as to that claim, however, the court remanded the case for further proceedings.*

Critical Thinking
- **Legal Environment** *The statute at the center of this case provides for remedies that may not be available at common law. Why would those additional remedies be sought, and when would they most likely be awarded?*
- **What If the Facts Were Different?** *Suppose that Trump University, or Trump Entrepreneur Initiative, had offered courses in real estate investing only online. Would the result in this case have been different? Explain.*

10–2a Misrepresentation Has Occurred

The first element of proving fraud is to show that misrepresentation of a material fact has occurred. This misrepresentation can occur by words or actions. For instance, the statement "This sculpture was created by Michelangelo" is a misrepresentation of fact if another artist sculpted the statue. Similarly, if a customer asks to see only paintings by Jasper Johns and the gallery owner immediately leads the customer to paintings that were not done by Johns, the owner's actions can be a misrepresentation.

Misrepresentation by Conduct Misrepresentation also occurs when a party takes specific action to conceal a fact that is material to the contract.[7] Therefore, if a seller, by her or his actions, prevents a buyer from learning of

7. *Restatement (Second) of Contracts,* Section 160.

some fact that is material to the contract, such behavior constitutes misrepresentation by conduct.

■ **CASE IN POINT 10.5** Actor Tom Selleck contracted to purchase a horse named Zorro for his daughter from Dolores Cuenca. Cuenca acted as though Zorro were fit to ride in competitions, when in reality the horse was unfit for this use because of a medical condition. Selleck filed a lawsuit against Cuenca for wrongfully concealing the horse's condition and won. A jury awarded Selleck more than $187,000 for Cuenca's misrepresentation by conduct.[8] ■

Statements of Opinion versus Statements of Fact

Statements of opinion and representations of future facts (predictions) generally are not subject to claims of fraud. Statements such as "This land will be worth twice as much next year" and "This car will last for years and years" are statements of opinion, not fact. A fact is objective and verifiable, whereas an opinion is usually subject to debate. Contracting parties should know the difference and should not rely on statements of opinion.

Here, as in other areas of contract law, every person is expected to exercise care and judgment when entering into contracts. The law will not come to the aid of one who simply makes an unwise bargain. Nevertheless, in certain situations, such as when a naïve purchaser relies on an opinion from an expert, the innocent party may be entitled to rescission or reformation. (*Reformation* occurs when a court alters the terms of a contract to prevent undue hardships or burdens.)

■ **CASE IN POINT 10.6** In a classic case, an instructor at an Arthur Murray dance school told Audrey Vokes, a widow without family, that she had the potential to become an accomplished dancer. The instructor sold her 2,302 hours of dancing lessons for a total amount of $31,090.45 (equivalent to $146,000 in 2018). When it became clear to Vokes that she did not, in fact, have the potential to be an excellent dancer, she sued the school for fraudulent misrepresentation. The court held that because the dance school had superior knowledge about dance potential, the instructor's statements could be considered statements of fact rather than opinion.[9] ■

Misrepresentation of Law

Misrepresentation of law *ordinarily* does not entitle a party to relief from a contract. ■ **EXAMPLE 10.7** Camara has a parcel of property that she is trying to sell to Pike. Camara knows that a local ordinance prohibits the construction of anything higher than three stories on the property. Nonetheless, she tells Pike, "You can build a condominium a hundred stories high on this land if you want to." Pike buys the land and later discovers that Camara's statement was false. Normally, Pike cannot avoid the contract, because people are assumed to know local zoning laws. ■

Exceptions to this rule occur when the misrepresenting party is in a profession that is known to require greater knowledge of the law than the average citizen possesses. For instance, if Camara, in *Example 10.7*, had been a lawyer or a real estate broker, her willful misrepresentation of the area's zoning laws probably would have constituted fraud.

Misrepresentation by Silence

Ordinarily, neither party to a contract has a duty to come forward and disclose facts. Therefore, courts typically do not set aside contracts because a party did not volunteer pertinent information. ■ **EXAMPLE 10.8** Jim is selling a car that has been in an accident and has been repaired. He does not need to volunteer this information to a potential buyer. If, however, the purchaser asks Jim if the car has had extensive bodywork and he lies, he has committed a fraudulent misrepresentation. ■

In general, if a seller knows of a serious potential problem that the buyer cannot reasonably be expected to discover, the seller may have a duty to speak. Usually, the seller must disclose only **latent defects**—that is, defects that could not readily be ascertained. Because a buyer of a house could easily discover the presence of termites through an inspection, for instance, termites may not qualify as a latent defect. Also, when the parties are in a *fiduciary relationship*—one of trust, such as partners, physician and patient, or attorney and client—they have a duty to disclose material facts. Failure to do so may constitute fraud.

10–2b Intent to Deceive

The second element of fraud is knowledge on the part of the misrepresenting party that facts have been falsely represented. This element, normally called *scienter*,[10] or "guilty knowledge," signifies that there was an *intent to deceive.*

Scienter clearly exists if a party knows that a fact is not as stated, such as when a person lies on an employment application. *Scienter* also exists if a party makes a statement that he or she believes is not true or makes a statement recklessly, without regard to whether it is true or false. Finally, this element is met if a party says or implies that a statement is made on some basis, such as personal knowledge or personal investigation, when it is not.

8. *Selleck v. Cuenca*, Case No. GIN056909, North County of San Diego, California, decided September 9, 2009.
9. *Vokes v. Arthur Murray, Inc.*, 212 So.2d 906 (Fla.App. 1968).
10. Pronounced sy-*en*-ter.

Innocent Misrepresentation What if a person makes a statement that she or he believes to be true but that actually misrepresents material facts? In this situation, the person is guilty only of an **innocent misrepresentation,** not of fraud. When an innocent misrepresentation occurs, the aggrieved party can rescind the contract but usually cannot seek damages.

■ **EXAMPLE 10.9** Parris tells Roberta that a tract of land contains 250 acres. Parris is mistaken—the tract contains only 215 acres—but Parris had no knowledge of the mistake. Roberta relies on the statement and contracts to buy the land. Even though the misrepresentation is innocent, Roberta can avoid the contract if the misrepresentation is material. ■

Negligent Misrepresentation Sometimes, a party makes a misrepresentation through carelessness, believing the statement is true, which can constitute **negligent misrepresentation.** Negligent misrepresentation occurs if the party does not exercise reasonable care in uncovering or disclosing facts, or use the skill and competence required by his or her business or profession.

In almost all states, such negligent misrepresentation is equal to *scienter,* or knowingly making a misrepresentation. In effect, negligent misrepresentation is treated as fraudulent misrepresentation, even though the misrepresentation was not purposeful. In negligent misrepresentation, culpable ignorance of the truth supplies the intention to mislead, even if the defendant can claim, "I didn't know."

10-2c Justifiable Reliance on the Misrepresentation

The third element of fraud is reasonably *justifiable reliance* on the misrepresentation of fact. The deceived party must have a justifiable reason for relying on the misrepresentation. Also, the misrepresentation must be an important factor (but not necessarily the sole factor) in inducing the deceived party to enter into the contract. Reliance is not justified if the innocent party knows the true facts or relies on obviously extravagant statements (such as "this pickup truck will get fifty miles to the gallon").

■ **EXAMPLE 10.10** Meese, a securities broker, offers to sell BIM stock to Packer. Meese assures Packer that BIM shares are blue chip securities—that is, they are stable, have limited risk, and yield a good return on investment over time. In reality, Meese knows nothing about the quality of BIM stock and does not believe the truth of what he is saying. Thus, Meese's statement is an intentional misrepresentation of a material fact. If Packer is induced by Meese's statement to enter into a contract to buy the stock, he probably can avoid the contract. Packer justifiably relied on his broker's misrepresentation of material fact. ■

The same rule applies to defects in property sold. If the defects would be obvious on inspection, the buyer cannot justifiably rely on the seller's representations. If the defects are hidden or latent, as previously discussed, the buyer is justified in relying on the seller's statements.

In the following case, the receiver for a car wash assured the buyer that the property would be "appropriately winterized," but it was not. Was the buyer justified in relying on the seller's representations? (A *receiver,* also called a *trustee,* is an independent, impartial party appointed by a bankruptcy court to manage property in bankruptcy and dispose of it in an orderly manner for the benefit of the creditors.)

Case Analysis 10.2

Cronkelton v. Guaranteed Construction Services, LLC

Court of Appeals of Ohio, Third District, 988 N.E.2d 656, 2013 -Ohio- 328 (2013).

In the Language of the Court

PRESTON, P.J. [Presiding Judge]
* * * *

The case before this Court stems from a real estate transaction for a foreclosed car wash in Bellefontaine, Ohio. [A court had appointed Patrick Shivley to be a receiver for the protection of the property, which was offered for sale by Huntington Bank. Clifford] Cronkelton filed a complaint against appellants [Guaranteed Construction Services, LLC, and Shivley] in the Logan County Court of Common Pleas following his purchase of the car wash. Cronkelton asserted * * * fraud.

* * * *

* * * The trial court held a jury trial on the fraud claim. The jury returned a verdict for Cronkelton.

* * * The trial court filed its judgment entry recording the jury's verdict for Cronkelton and awarding Cronkelton $43,671 in compensatory damages, $66,000

in punitive damages, and $30,000 for attorney fees. [Guaranteed Construction Services and Shivley filed an appeal.]

* * * *

* * * [At the trial] Cronkelton testified that he first inspected the foreclosed car wash at the end of November 2009. At that time, Cronkelton tested the equipment and knew that some of the pieces of equipment were fully functioning and some were not. * * * Shortly thereafter, Cronkelton called Shivley to discuss the winterization of the property. Cronkelton testified:

> So I called him, said, hey, it's going to freeze here this week. * * * It's supposed to get down to like ten degrees, have you got it winterized, you know. If it's not winterized, I'm not interested in the property. If it freezes, I'm not interested in the property at all. And he guaranteed me. He said, no, it will be taken care of. We don't have a problem. That's my job as receiver. I'll take care of it.

After the phone call, Shivley sent Cronkelton an e-mail dated December 7, 2009 that stated:

> As per our phone conversation Guaranteed [Construction Services] will winterize the Car Wash with the anticipation of reopening the wash in the near future. Within this Winterization we will put antifreeze and secure floor heating as well as blow water out of all lines in self serve bays as well as empty tanks, etc. We will leave the heat on at a minimal level in the pump room. * * * We will complete all of this on Wednesday, December 9, 2009.

[Guaranteed Construction Services hired Strayer Company to winterize the property. But on December 10, Strayer's owner sent a memo to Guaranteed Construction Services and Shivley stating that the building was not designed to be winterized and that the only way to avoid problems was to leave the heat on. Shivley knew Huntington Bank had shut off the heat because the property was not generating income. In March 2010, Shivley informed Huntington of damage to the property as a result of freezing. Shivley did not share any of this information with Cronkelton.]

Cronkelton testified that they closed on the property in June and he received the keys at that time. Cronkelton testified that he immediately went to the property:

> I opened the door, and the huge canisters that I was telling you about were all busted. The tops had been exploded off the top of them. * * * You could see pipes that were busted * * * . So it was clear at that time that this whole thing had froze up, and the extent of the damage could not even be, you know, detailed at that point.

* * * *

* * * Appellants argue Cronkelton unjustifiably relied on Shivley's statements about the car wash's condition because Cronkelton had the opportunity to inspect the property prior to closing.

* * * *

* * * Whether or not reliance on a material misrepresentation was justified under the facts of a case is a question for the trier of fact. Consequently, we must determine whether the jury's decision is supported by competent, credible evidence.

In the present case, it is undisputed that the damage caused by freezing was open and obvious upon inspection, that Cronkelton did inspect the property in November 2009, and that he could have inspected the property again before signing the purchase agreement. Cronkelton testified regarding why he did not inspect the property after November 2009:

> * * * [Shivley] wrote me this e-mail, guaranteed me it was taken care of in detail what he was going to do, so I had no reason. And because * * * he was appointed by the Court, I don't know how much more I could have done to know that I could trust him.

* * * The jury found that Cronkelton had reasonably relied on Shivley's representations.

The jury's finding was supported by competent, credible evidence. * * * *When determining whether reliance is justifiable, courts consider the various circumstances involved, such as the nature of the transaction, the form and materiality of the transaction, the form and materiality of the representation, the relationship of the parties, the respective intelligence, experience, age, and mental and physical condition of the parties, and their respective knowledge and means of knowledge.* [Emphasis added.]

Cronkelton relied on representations made by Shivley * * *. As a receiver, Shivley had a fiduciary duty to the assets under his control. Under the circumstances of this case, Cronkelton had a reasonable basis to believe that Shivley, who was acting as an arm of the court, would take the promised steps to winterize the property.

* * * *

* * * We affirm the judgment of the trial court.

Legal Reasoning Questions

1. In evaluating a claim of fraud, what factors does a court consider in determining whether reliance was justifiable?

2. In this case, what did the jury find with respect to the plaintiff's claim of reliance? What was the appellate court's opinion of this finding?

3. Did Shivley's misrepresentations rise to the level of fraud? Explain.

10–2d Injury to the Innocent Party

Most courts do not require a showing of injury when the action is to rescind the contract. These courts hold that because rescission returns the parties to the positions they held before the contract was made, a showing of injury to the innocent party is unnecessary.

In contrast, to recover damages caused by fraud, proof of harm is universally required. The measure of damages is ordinarily equal to the property's value had it been delivered as represented, less the actual price paid for the property. (Additionally, because fraud actions necessarily involve wrongful conduct, courts may also sometimes award punitive damages, which are not ordinarily available in contract actions.)

10–3 Undue Influence

Undue influence arises from relationships in which one party can greatly influence another party, thus overcoming that party's free will. A contract entered into under excessive or undue influence lacks voluntary consent and is therefore voidable.[11]

10–3a One Party Dominates the Other

In various types of relationships, one party may have the opportunity to dominate and unfairly influence another party. Minors and elderly people, for instance, are often under the influence of guardians (persons who are legally responsible for them). If a guardian induces a young or elderly ward (a person whom the guardian looks after) to enter into a contract that benefits the guardian, the guardian may have exerted undue influence. Undue influence can arise from a number of fiduciary relationships, such as physician-patient, parent-child, husband-wife, or guardian-ward situations.

The essential feature of undue influence is that the party being taken advantage of does not, in reality, exercise free will in entering into a contract. It is not enough that a person is elderly or suffers from some physical or mental impairment. There must be clear and convincing evidence that the person did not act out of her or his free will.[12] Similarly, the existence of a fiduciary relationship alone is insufficient to prove undue influence.[13]

10–3b Presumption of Undue Influence in Certain Situations

When the dominant party in a fiduciary relationship benefits from that relationship, a presumption of undue influence arises. The dominant party must exercise the utmost good faith in dealing with the other party. When a contract enriches the dominant party, the court will often *presume* that the contract was made under undue influence.

■ **EXAMPLE 10.11** Erik is the guardian for Kinsley, his ward. Erik is the dominant party in this relationship. On Kinsley's behalf, he enters into a contract from which he benefits financially. If Kinsley challenges the contract, the court will likely presume that the guardian has taken advantage of his ward. To rebut (refute) this presumption, Erik has to show that he made full disclosure to Kinsley and that consideration was present. He must also show that Kinsley received, if available, independent and competent advice before completing the transaction. Unless the presumption can be rebutted, the contract will be rescinded. ■

10–4 Duress

Agreement to the terms of a contract is not voluntary if one of the parties is *forced* into the agreement. The use of threats to force a party to enter into a contract constitutes **duress.** Similarly, the use of blackmail or extortion to induce consent to a contract is duress. Duress is both a defense to the enforcement of a contract and a ground for the rescission of a contract.

10–4a The Threatened Act Must Be Wrongful or Illegal

To establish duress, there must be proof of a threat to do something that the threatening party has no right to do. Generally, for duress to occur, the threatened act must be wrongful or illegal. It also must render the person who is threatened incapable of exercising free will. A threat to exercise a legal right, such as the right to sue someone, ordinarily does not constitute duress.

10–4b Economic Duress

Economic need generally is not sufficient to constitute duress, even when one party exacts a very high price for an item that the other party needs. If the party exacting

---

11. *Restatement (Second) of Contracts*, Section 177.
12. See, for example, *Ayers v. Shaffer*, 286 Va. 212, 748 S.E.2d 83 (2013).
13. See, for example, *Sleepy Hollow Ranch LLC v. Robinson*, 373 S.W.3d 485 (Mo.App. 2012).

the price also creates the need, however, *economic duress* may be found.[14]

■ **EXAMPLE 10.12**   The Internal Revenue Service (IRS) assesses a large tax and penalty against Weller. Weller retains Eyman, the accountant who prepared the tax returns on which the assessment was based, to challenge the assessment. Two days before the deadline for filing a reply with the IRS, Eyman declines to represent Weller unless he signs a very expensive contingency-fee agreement for the services.

In this situation, a court might find that the agreement is unenforceable because of economic duress. Eyman threatened only to withdraw his services, something that he was legally entitled to do. However, he delayed the withdrawal until two days before the IRS deadline. It would have been impossible at that late date to obtain adequate representation elsewhere. Therefore, Weller can argue that he was forced either to sign the contract or to lose his right to challenge the IRS assessment. ■

See Concept Summary 10.1 for a review of the factors that may indicate a lack of voluntary consent.

10–5 The Statute of Frauds— Writing Requirement

Every state has a statute that stipulates what types of contracts must be in writing. We refer to such a statute as the **Statute of Frauds.** The origins of these statutes can be traced to an early English law. The law established that certain types of contracts, to be enforceable, had to be evidenced by a writing and signed by the party against whom enforcement was sought.

Today, each state has a statute modeled after the English act, although the statutes vary slightly from state to state. All states require certain types of contracts to be in writing or evidenced by a written memorandum or an

---

14. For a decision discussing the requirements for establishing economic duress, see *Cate Street Capital, Inc. v. DG Whitefield, LLC,* 2014 WL 8382756 (N.H.Super. 2014).

Concept Summary 10.1

Factors That May Indicate a Lack of Voluntary Consent

Mistakes	• *Unilateral mistake*—Generally, the mistaken party is bound by the contract, unless the other party knows or should have known of the mistake, or the mistake is an inadvertent and substantial mathematical error that is committed without gross negligence. • *Bilateral (mutual) mistake*—If both parties are mistaken about a material fact, either party can avoid the contract. If the mistake relates to the value or quality of the subject matter, either party can enforce the contract.
Fraudulent Misrepresentation	• A misrepresentation of a material fact has occurred. • There has been an intent to deceive. • The innocent party has justifiably relied on the misrepresentation. • To collect damages, a party must have been harmed as a result of the misrepresentation.
Undue Influence and Duress	• *Undue influence*—Arises from special relationships, in which one party's free will has been overcome by the undue influence of another. Usually, the contract is voidable. • *Duress*—Defined as the use of threats to force a party to enter into a contract out of fear; for example, the threat of violence or economic pressure. The party forced to enter into the contract can rescind the contract.

electronic record. In addition, the party or parties against whom enforcement is sought must have signed the contract, unless certain exceptions apply.

The actual name of the Statute of Frauds is misleading because the statute does not apply to fraud. Rather, it denies enforceability to certain contracts that do not comply with its writing requirements. The primary purpose of the statute is to prevent harm to innocent parties by requiring written evidence of agreements concerning important transactions. A contract that is oral when it is required to be in writing is normally voidable by a party who later does not wish to follow through with the agreement.

The following types of contracts are generally required to be in writing or evidenced by a written memorandum or electronic record:

1. Contracts involving interests in land.
2. Contracts that cannot *by their terms* be performed within one year from the day after the date of formation.
3. Collateral, or secondary, contracts, such as promises to answer for the debt or duty of another and promises by the administrator or executor of an estate to pay a debt of the estate personally—that is, out of her or his own pocket.
4. Promises made in consideration of marriage.
5. Under the Uniform Commercial Code (UCC), contracts for the sale of goods priced at $500 or more.

10–5a Contracts Involving Interests in Land

A contract calling for the sale of land is not enforceable unless it is in writing or evidenced by a written memorandum. Land is *real property* and includes all physical objects that are permanently attached to the soil, such as buildings, fences, trees, and the soil itself.

The Statute of Frauds operates as a *defense* to the enforcement of an oral contract for the sale of land. ■ **EXAMPLE 10.13** Skylar contracts orally to sell his property in Fair Oaks to Beth. If he later decides not to sell, under most circumstances, Beth cannot enforce the contract. ■

The Statute of Frauds also requires written evidence of contracts for the transfer of other interests in land, such as mortgage agreements and leases. Similarly, an agreement that includes an option to purchase real property must be in writing for the option to be enforced.

Generally, for a land sale contract to be enforceable under the Statute of Frauds, the contract must describe the property being transferred with sufficient certainty for it to be identified. ■ **CASE IN POINT 10.14** Talat

Solaiman and Sabina Chowdhury agreed to buy a convenience store and gas station owned by Mohammad Salim for $975,000 and gave Salim a $25,000 security deposit. They signed a handwritten contract, which was later typed up, but the contract described the property only by its street address (199 Upper Riverdale Road, Jonesboro, GA 30236).

When Solaiman and Chowdhury decided not to go through with the deal, Salim kept their deposit and filed a breach of contract lawsuit. The court held that the parties' purchase agreement was unenforceable because it did not sufficiently describe the real property to be purchased. To comply with the Statute of Frauds, "a contract must describe the property . . . with the same degree of certainty as that required in a deed conveying realty." Therefore, the contract was void, and Salim had to return the buyers' security deposit.[15] ■

10–5b The One-Year Rule

A contract that cannot, *by its own terms,* be performed within one year *from the day after* the contract is formed must be in writing to be enforceable.[16] The reason for this rule is that the parties' memory of their contract's terms is not likely to be reliable for longer than a year. Disputes are unlikely to occur until some time after the contracts are made, and if the terms have not been put into writing, resolving such disputes is difficult.

Time Period Starts the Day after the Contract Is Formed The one-year period begins to run *the day after the contract is made.* ■ **EXAMPLE 10.15** Superior University forms a contract with Kimi San stating that San will teach three courses in history during the coming academic year (September 15 through June 15). If the contract is formed in March, it must be in writing to be enforceable—because it cannot be performed within one year. If the contract is not formed until July, however, it does not have to be in writing to be enforceable—because it can be performed within one year. ■

Must Be Objectively Impossible to Perform within One Year The test for determining whether an oral contract is enforceable under the one-year rule is whether performance is *possible* within one year. It does not matter whether the agreement is *likely* to be performed during that period.

---

15. *Salim v. Solaiman,* 302 Ga.App. 607, 691 S.E.2d 389 (2010). See also *Sloop v. Kiker,* 2016 Ark. App. 125 (2016).
16. *Restatement (Second) of Contracts,* Section 130.

When performance of a contract is objectively impossible during the one-year period, the contract must be in writing (or a record) to be enforceable. ■ **EXAMPLE 10.16** A contract to provide five crops of tomatoes to be grown on a specific farm in Illinois would be objectively impossible to perform within one year. No farmer in Illinois can grow five crops of tomatoes in a single year. ■

If performance is possible within one year under the contract's terms, the contract does not fall under the Statute of Frauds and need not be in writing. ■ **EXAMPLE 10.17** Janine enters into a contract to create a carving of President Barack Obama's face on a mountainside, similar to the carvings of other presidents' faces on Mount Rushmore. It is technically possible—although not very likely—that the contract could be performed within one year. (Mount Rushmore took over fourteen years to complete.) Therefore, Janine's contract need not be in writing to be enforceable. ■

Exhibit 10–2 graphically illustrates the one-year rule.

10–5c Collateral Promises

A **collateral promise,** or secondary promise, is one that is ancillary (subsidiary) to a principal transaction or primary contractual relationship. In other words, a collateral promise is one made by a third party to assume the debts or obligations of a primary party to a contract if that party does not perform. Any collateral promise of this nature falls under the Statute of Frauds and therefore must be in writing to be enforceable.

Primary versus Secondary Obligations To understand this concept, it is important to distinguish between primary and secondary promises and obligations. A promise to pay another person's debt (or other obligation) that is *not conditioned on the person's failure to pay (or perform)* is a primary obligation. A promise to pay another's debt *only if that party fails to pay* is a secondary obligation. A contract in which a party assumes a primary obligation normally does not need to be in writing to be enforceable, whereas a contract assuming a secondary obligation does.

■ **EXAMPLE 10.18** Connor tells Leanne Lu, an orthodontist, that he will pay for the services provided for Connor's niece, Allison. Because Connor has assumed direct financial responsibility for his niece's debt, this is a primary obligation and need not be in writing to be enforceable. In contrast, if Connor commits to paying Allison's orthodontist bill only if her mother does not, it is a secondary obligation. In that situation, Lu must have a signed writing or record proving that Connor assumed this secondary obligation for it to be enforced. ■

An Exception—The "Main Purpose" Rule An oral promise to answer for the debt of another is covered by the Statute of Frauds *unless* the guarantor's main purpose in incurring a secondary obligation is to secure a personal benefit. This type of contract need not be in writing.[17] The assumption is that a court can infer from

---

17. *Restatement (Second) of Contracts,* Section 116.

EXHIBIT 10–2 The One-Year Rule

Under the Statute of Frauds, contracts that by their terms are impossible to perform within one year from the day after the date of contract formation must be in writing to be enforceable. Put another way, if it is at all possible to perform an oral contract within one year from the day after the contract is made, the contract will fall outside the Statute of Frauds and be enforceable.

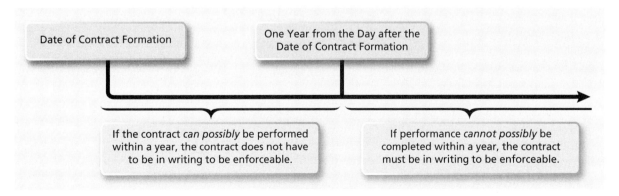

the circumstances of a particular case whether the "leading objective" of the guarantor was to secure a personal benefit.

■ **EXAMPLE 10.19** Carlie Braswell contracts with Winsom Manufacturing Company to have some machines custom-made for her factory. She promises Newform Supply, Winsom's supplier, that if Newform continues to deliver the materials to Winsom for the production of the custom-made machines, she will guarantee payment. This promise need not be in writing because Braswell's main purpose in forming the contract is to secure a benefit for herself. ■

10–5d Promises Made in Consideration of Marriage

A unilateral promise to make a monetary payment or to give property in consideration of a promise to marry must be in writing. In other words, if a mother promises to pay a man $20,000 if he marries her daughter, that promise must be in writing to be enforceable. ■ **EXAMPLE 10.20** Evan promises to buy Celeste a condo in Maui if she marries him. Celeste would need written evidence of Evan's promise to enforce it. ■

The same rule applies to **prenuptial agreements**—agreements made before marriage that define each partner's ownership rights in the other partner's property. Prenuptial agreements must be in writing to be enforceable. ■ **EXAMPLE 10.21** Before marrying country singer Keith Urban, actress Nicole Kidman entered into a prenuptial agreement with him. Kidman agreed that if the couple divorced, she would pay Urban $640,000 for every year they had been married, unless Urban had started to use drugs again. In that event, he would receive nothing. ■

10–5e Contracts for the Sale of Goods

The Uniform Commercial Code (UCC) includes Statute of Frauds provisions that require written evidence or an electronic record of a contract for the sale of goods priced at $500 or more. (This low threshold amount may be increased in the future.)

A writing that will satisfy the UCC requirement need only state the quantity term (6,000 boxes of cotton gauze, for instance). The contract will not be enforceable for any quantity greater than that set forth in the writing.

Other agreed-on terms can be omitted or stated imprecisely in the writing, as long as they adequately reflect both parties' intentions. A written memorandum or series of communications evidencing a contract will suffice, provided that the writing is signed by the party against whom enforcement is sought. The writing normally need not designate the buyer or the seller, the terms of payment, or the price.

10–5f Exceptions to the Writing Requirement

Exceptions to the writing requirement are made in certain circumstances. We describe those situations here.

Partial Performance When a contract has been partially performed and the parties cannot be returned to their positions prior to the contract's formation, a court may grant *specific performance.* Specific performance is an equitable remedy that requires performance of the contract according to its precise terms. Courts may sometimes grant specific performance of an oral contract. The parties must prove that an oral contract existed, of course.

In cases involving oral contracts for the transfer of interests in land, courts usually look at whether justice is better served by enforcing the oral contract when partial performance has taken place. For instance, if the purchaser has paid part of the price, taken possession, and made valuable improvements to the property, a court may grant specific performance.

In some states, mere reliance on certain types of oral contracts is enough to remove them from the Statute of Frauds. Under the UCC, an oral contract for the sale of goods is enforceable to the extent that a seller accepts payment or a buyer accepts delivery of the goods [UCC 2-201(3)(c)]. ■ **EXAMPLE 10.22** Cooper orders twenty chairs from an online seller. After ten chairs have been delivered and accepted, Cooper repudiates (denies the existence of) the contract. In that situation, the seller can enforce the contract (and obtain payment) to the extent of the ten chairs already accepted by Cooper. ■

Admissions If a party against whom enforcement of an oral contract is sought "admits" under oath that a contract for sale was made, the contract will be enforceable.[18] The party's admission can occur at any stage of the court proceedings, such as during a deposition or other discovery, pleadings, or testimony.

If a party admits a contract subject to the UCC, the contract is enforceable, but only to the extent of the quantity admitted [UCC 2–201(3)(b)]. ■ **EXAMPLE 10.23** Rachel, the president of Bistro Corporation,

---

18. *Restatement (Second) of Contracts*, Section 133.

admits under oath that an oral agreement was made with Commercial Kitchens, Inc., to buy certain equipment for $10,000. A court will enforce the agreement only to the extent admitted ($10,000), even if Commercial Kitchens claims that the agreement involved $20,000 worth of equipment. ■

Promissory Estoppel   An oral contract that would otherwise be unenforceable under the Statute of Frauds may be enforced in some states under the doctrine of promissory estoppel. Recall that if a person justifiably relies on another's promise to his or her detriment, a court may *estop* (prevent) the promisor from denying that a contract exists. Section 139 of the *Restatement (Second) of Contracts* provides that in these circumstances, an oral promise can be enforceable notwithstanding the Statute of Frauds.

For the promise to be enforceable, the promisee must have justifiably relied on it to her or his detriment, and the reliance must have been foreseeable to the person making the promise. In addition, there must be no way to avoid injustice except to enforce the promise. (Note the similarities between promissory estoppel and the doctrine of partial performance discussed previously. Both require reasonable reliance and operate to estop a party from claiming that no contract exists.)

Special Exceptions under the UCC   Special exceptions to the writing requirement apply to sales contracts. Oral contracts for customized goods may be enforced in certain circumstances. Another exception has to do with oral contracts *between merchants* that have been confirmed in a written memorandum. We will examine these exceptions in more detail when we discuss the UCC's Statute of Frauds provisions in a later chapter.

Exhibit 10–3 graphically summarizes how certain business contracts fall under the Statute of Frauds and the various exceptions that apply.

10–5g Sufficiency of the Writing

A written contract or memorandum will satisfy the writing requirement, as will an electronic record that evidences the agreement and is signed by the party against whom enforcement is sought. The signature need not be placed at the end of the document but can be anywhere in the writing. A signature can consist of a typed name or even just initials.

A writing can consist of any order confirmation, invoice, sales slip, check, fax, or e-mail—or such items in combination. The written contract need not consist of a single document in order to constitute an enforceable contract. One document may incorporate another

EXHIBIT 10–3   Business Contracts and the Writing Requirement

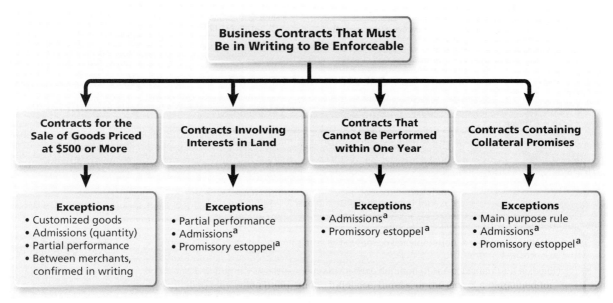

a. Some states follow Section 133 (on admissions) and Section 139 (on promissory estoppel) of the *Restatement (Second) of Contracts.*

document by expressly referring to it. Several documents may form a single contract if they are physically attached (such as by staple or paper clip) or even if they are only placed in the same envelope.

A memorandum or note evidencing an oral contract need only contain the essential terms of the contract, not every term. There must, of course, also be some indication that the parties voluntarily agreed to the terms. Under the UCC, a writing evidencing a contract for the sale of goods need only state the quantity and be signed by the party against whom enforcement is sought.

Under most state laws, the writing must also name the parties and identify the subject matter, the consideration, and the essential terms with reasonable certainty. In addition, contracts for the sale of land often are required to state the price and describe the property with sufficient clarity to allow it to be determined without reference to outside sources. Note that because only the party against whom enforcement is sought must have signed the writing, a contract may be enforceable by one of its parties but not by the other.

10–6 The Parol Evidence Rule

Sometimes, a written contract does not include—or contradicts—an oral understanding reached by the parties before or at the time of contracting. For instance, a landlord might tell a person who agrees to rent an apartment that cats are allowed, whereas the lease contract clearly states that no pets are permitted. In deciding such disputes, the courts look to a common law rule called the *parol evidence rule*

Under the **parol evidence rule,** if a court finds that a written contract represents the complete and final statement of the parties' agreement, it will not allow either party to present parol evidence. *Parol evidence* is testimony or other evidence of communications between the parties that is not contained in the contract itself. A party normally *cannot* present any evidence of the following if that evidence contradicts or varies the terms of the written contract:

1. Negotiations prior to contract formation.
2. Agreements prior to contract formation.
3. Oral agreements contemporaneous with (at the same time as) contract formation.[19]

10–6a Exceptions to the Parol Evidence Rule

Because of the rigidity of the parol evidence rule, the courts have created the following exceptions:

1. *Contracts subsequently modified.* Evidence of any subsequent modification (oral or written) of a written contract can be introduced in court. Oral modifications may not be enforceable under the Statute of Frauds, however (for instance, a modification that increases the price of the goods being sold to more than $500). Also, oral modifications will not be enforceable if the original contract provides that any modification must be in writing [UCC 2-209(2)(3)].
2. *Voidable or void contracts.* Oral evidence can be introduced in all cases to show that the contract was voidable or void (for example, induced by mistake, fraud, or misrepresentation). The reason is simple: if deception led one of the parties to agree to the terms of a written contract, oral evidence attesting to the fraud should not be excluded. Courts frown on bad faith and are quick to allow such evidence when it establishes fraud.
3. *Contracts containing ambiguous terms.* When the terms of a written contract are ambiguous and require interpretation, evidence is admissible to show the meaning of the terms. ■ **CASE IN POINT 10.24** Pamela Watkins bought a home from Sandra Schexnider. Their agreement stated that Watkins would make payments on the mortgage until the note was paid in full, when "the house" would become hers. The agreement also stipulated that she would pay for insurance on "the property." The home was destroyed in a hurricane, and the insurance proceeds paid off the mortgage. Watkins claimed that she owned the land, but Schexnider argued that she had sold only the house. The court found that because "the house" term in the contract was ambiguous, parol evidence was admissible. The court also concluded that the parties had intended to transfer ownership of both the house and the land, and ordered that title to the property be transferred to Watkins.[20] ■
4. *Incomplete contracts.* When the written contract is incomplete in that it lacks one or more of the essential terms, the courts allow additional evidence to "fill in the gaps."
5. *Prior dealing, course of performance, or usage of trade.* Under the UCC, evidence can be introduced to explain or supplement a written contract by showing a prior dealing, course of performance, or usage of trade [UCC 1–205, 2–202]. This is because when

---

19. *Restatement (Second) of Contracts*, Section 213.

20. *Watkins v. Schexnider*, 31 So.3d 609 (La.App. 3 Cir. 2010).

buyers and sellers deal with each other over extended periods of time, certain customary practices develop. These practices are often overlooked in writing the contract, so courts allow the introduction of evidence to show how the parties have acted in the past. Usage of trade—practices and customs generally followed in a particular industry—can also shed light on the meaning of certain contract provisions. Thus, evidence of trade usage may be admissible. We will discuss these terms in further detail later in the context of sales contracts.

6. *Contracts subject to an orally agreed-on condition precedent.* Sometimes the parties agree that a condition must be fulfilled before a party is required to perform the contract. This is called a *condition precedent.* If the parties have orally agreed on a condition precedent that does not conflict with the terms of their written agreement, a court may allow parol evidence to prove the oral condition. The parol evidence rule does not apply here because the existence of the entire written contract is subject to an orally agreed-on condition. Proof of the condition does not alter or modify the written terms but affects the *enforceability* of the written contract.

7. *Contracts with an obvious or gross clerical (or typographic) error that clearly would not represent the agreement of the parties.* Parol evidence is admissible to correct an obvious typographic error. ■ **EXAMPLE 10.25** Davis agrees to lease office space from Stone Enterprises for $3,000 per month. The signed written lease provides for a monthly payment of $300 rather than the $3,000 agreed to by the parties. Because the error is obvious, Stone Enterprises will be allowed to admit parol evidence to correct the mistake. ■

In the following case, an appellate court considered whether the trial court should have admitted parol evidence regarding the terms of an apartment lease.

Case 10.3

Frewil, LLC v. Price

Court of Appeals of South Carolina, 411 S.C. 525, 769 S.E.2d 250 (2015).

Background and Facts Madison Price and Carter Smith were planning to attend the College of Charleston in South Carolina. They contacted Frewil, LLC, about renting an apartment at the beginning of the fall semester. They asked if the apartment had a washer/dryer and dishwasher, and were told yes. The lease did not expressly state that the unit contained those appliances, but it provided that any overflow from a washing machine or dishwasher was the responsibility of the tenant and that the dishwasher had to be clean for a refund of the security deposit.

When Price and Smith arrived to move in, the apartment had no washer/dryer or dishwasher and no connections for them. The students found housing elsewhere. Frewil filed a suit in a South Carolina state court against Price and Smith, claiming breach of contract. The defendants sought to introduce parol evidence to challenge Frewil's claim. The court denied the request and issued a judgment in Frewil's favor. Price and Smith appealed.

In the Language of the Court
KONDUROS, J. [Judge]
＊ ＊ ＊ ＊

＊ ＊ ＊ If a writing, on its face, appears to express the whole agreement between the parties, parol evidence cannot be admitted to add another term thereto. However, *where a contract is silent as to a particular matter, and ambiguity thereby arises, parol evidence may be admitted to supply the deficiency and establish the true intent. For, generally, parol evidence is admissible to show the true meaning of an ambiguous written contract.* Such a contract is one capable of being understood in more ways than just one, or an agreement unclear in meaning because it expresses its purpose in an indefinite manner. When an agreement is ambiguous, the court may consider the circumstances surrounding its execution in determining the intent. Where the contract is susceptible of more than one interpretation, the ambiguity will be resolved against the party who prepared the contract. It would be virtually impossible for a contract to encompass all of the many possibilities which may be encountered by the parties. Indeed, neither law, nor equity, requires every term or condition to be set forth in a contract. If a situation is unaddressed in a contract,

Case 10.3 Continues

Case 10.3 Continued

the court may look to the circumstances surrounding the bargain as an aid in determining the parties' intent. [Emphasis added.]

In this case, the [lower] court relied upon * * * the lease itself to conclude the girls had breached the lease as a matter of law. However, if a contract is subject to more than one interpretation, it is ambiguous and parol evidence is admissible. Frewil contends, and the [lower] court found, the lease unambiguously states the unit does not contain a washer/dryer or dishwasher. However, the lease states any overflow from washing machines or dishwashers is the responsibility of the tenant. Additionally, the Security Deposit Agreement * * * indicates the dishwasher must be clean in order for the tenant to receive a return of the security deposit. The lease does not explicitly indicate what appliances are or are not in the unit. Because the lease is ambiguous on this point, parol evidence was admissible. As these appliances are mentioned and Price and Smith allege they were told the washer/dryer and dishwasher were included, the [lower] court erred in concluding the lease * * * precluded any challenge to Frewil's breach of contract claim as a matter of law.

Decision and Remedy   *A state intermediate appellate court reversed the judgment of the lower court. The court noted that "the lease was ambiguous thereby permitting the introduction of parol evidence."*

Critical Thinking

- **Economic**   *How does the parol evidence rule save time and money for the parties to a dispute and the court that hears it? Discuss.*

10–6b Integrated Contracts

In determining whether to allow parol evidence, courts consider whether the written contract is intended to be the complete and final statement of the terms of the agreement. If it is, the contract is referred to as an **integrated contract,** and extraneous evidence (evidence from outside the contract) is excluded.

■ **EXAMPLE 10.26**   TKTS, Inc., offers to sell Gwen season tickets to the Dallas Cowboys football games in Cowboys Stadium. Prices and seat locations are indicated in diagrams in a brochure that accompanies the offer. Gwen responds, listing her seat preference. TKTS sends her the tickets, along with a different diagram showing seat locations. Also enclosed is a document that reads, "This is the entire agreement of the parties," which Gwen signs and returns. When Gwen goes to the first game, she discovers that her seat is not where she expected, based on the brochure. Under the parol evidence rule, however, the brochure is not part of the parties' agreement. The

document that Gwen signed was identified as the parties' entire contract. Therefore, she cannot introduce in court any evidence of prior negotiations or agreements that contradict or vary the contract's terms. ■

A contract can be either completely or partially integrated. If it contains all of the terms of the parties' agreement, it is completely integrated. If it contains only some of the terms that the parties agreed on and not others, it is partially integrated. If the contract is only partially integrated, evidence of consistent additional terms is admissible to supplement the written agreement.[21] Note that for both completely and partially integrated contracts, courts exclude any evidence that *contradicts* the writing. Parol evidence is allowed only to add to the terms of a partially integrated contract. Exhibit 10–4 illustrates the relationship between integrated contracts and the parol evidence rule.

---

21. *Restatement (Second) of Contracts,* Section 216; and UCC 2–202.

EXHIBIT 10–4   The Parol Evidence Rule

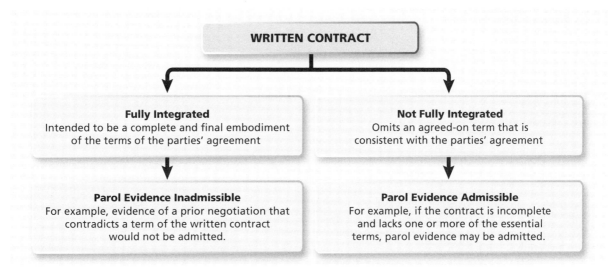

Reviewing: Defenses to Contract Enforceability

Chelene had been a caregiver for Marta's eighty-year-old mother, Janis, for nine years. Shortly before Janis passed away, Chelene convinced her to buy Chelene's house for Marta. The elderly woman died before the papers were signed, however. Four months later, Marta used her inheritance to buy Chelene's house without having it inspected. The house was built in the 1950s, and Chelene said it was in "perfect condition." Nevertheless, one year after the purchase, the basement started leaking. Marta had the paneling removed from the basement walls and discovered that the walls were bowed inward and cracked. Marta then had a civil engineer inspect the basement walls, and he found that the cracks had been caulked and painted over before the paneling was installed. He concluded that the "wall failure" had existed "for at least thirty years" and that the basement walls were "structurally unsound." Using the information presented in the chapter, answer the following questions.

1. Can Marta avoid the contract on the ground that both parties made a mistake about the condition of the house? Explain.
2. Can Marta sue Chelene for fraudulent misrepresentation? Why or why not? What element or elements might be lacking?
3. Now assume that Chelene knew that the basement walls were cracked and bowed and that she had hired someone to install paneling before she offered to sell the house. Did she have a duty to disclose this defect to Marta? Could a court find that Chelene's silence in this situation constituted misrepresentation? Explain.
4. Can Marta obtain rescission of the contract based on undue influence? If the sale to Janis had been completed before her death, could Janis have obtained rescission based on undue influence? Explain.

Debate This . . .   *Many countries have eliminated the Statute of Frauds except for sales of real estate. The United States should do the same.*

Terms and Concepts

bilateral mistake 190	latent defect 193	Statute of Frauds 197
collateral promise 199	negligent misrepresentation 194	undue influence 196
duress 196	parol evidence rule 202	unilateral mistake 189
innocent misrepresentation 194	prenuptial agreement 200	voluntary consent 189
integrated contract 204	*scienter* 193	

Issue Spotters

1. In selling a house, Matt tells Ann that the wiring, fixtures, and appliances are of a certain quality. Matt knows nothing about the quality, but it is not as specified. Ann buys the house. On learning the true quality, Ann confronts Matt. He says he wasn't trying to fool her, he was only trying to make a sale. Can she rescind the deal? Why or why not? (See *Fraudulent Misrepresentation*.)

2. GamesCo orders $800 worth of game pieces from Midstate Plastic, Inc. Midstate delivers, and GamesCo pays for $450 worth. GamesCo then says it wants no more pieces from Midstate. GamesCo and Midstate have never dealt with each other before and have nothing in writing. Can Midstate enforce a deal for the full $800? Explain your answer. (See *The Statute of Frauds—Writing Requirement*.)

• **Check your answers to the Issue Spotters against the answers provided in Appendix B at the end of this text.**

Business Scenarios

10–1. Undue Influence. Juan is an elderly man who lives with his nephew, Samuel. Juan is totally dependent on Samuel's support. Samuel tells Juan that unless he transfers a tract of land he owns to Samuel for a price 35 percent below its market value, Samuel will no longer support and take care of him. Juan enters into the contract. Discuss fully whether Juan can set aside this contract. (See *Undue Influence*.)

10–2. Voluntary Consent. Discuss whether either of the following contracts will be unenforceable on the ground that voluntary consent is lacking:

(a) Simmons finds a stone in his pasture that he believes to be quartz. Jenson, who also believes that the stone is quartz, contracts to purchase it for $10. Just before delivery, the stone is discovered to be a diamond worth $1,000. (See *Mistakes*.)

(b) Jacoby's barn is burned to the ground. He accuses Goldman's son of arson and threatens to have the prosecutor bring a criminal action unless Goldman agrees to pay him $5,000. Goldman agrees to pay. (See *Duress*.)

Business Case Problems

10–3. Sufficiency of the Writing. Newmark & Co. Real Estate, Inc., contacted 2615 East 17 Street Realty, LLC, to lease certain real property on behalf of a client. Newmark e-mailed the landlord a separate agreement for the payment of Newmark's commission. The landlord e-mailed it back with a separate demand to pay the commission in installments. Newmark revised the agreement and e-mailed a final copy to the landlord. Does the agreement qualify as a writing under the Statute of Frauds? Explain. [*Newmark & Co. Real Estate, Inc. v. 2615 East 17 Street Realty, LLC*, 80 A.D.3d 476, 914 N.Y.S.2d 162 (1 Dept. 2011)] (See *The Statute of Frauds—Writing Requirement*.)

10–4. The Parol Evidence Rule. Rimma Vaks and her husband, Steven Mangano, executed a written contract with Denise Ryan and Ryan Auction Co. to auction their furnishings. The six-page contract provided a detailed summary of the parties' agreement. It addressed the items to be auctioned, how reserve prices would be determined, and the amount of Ryan's commission. When a dispute arose between the parties, Vaks and Mangano sued Ryan for breach of contract. Vaks and Mangano asserted that, before they executed the contract, Ryan made various oral representations that were inconsistent with the terms of their written agreement. Assuming that their written contract was valid, can Vaks and Mangano recover for breach of an oral contract? Why or why not? [*Vaks v. Ryan*, 2012 WL 194398 (Mass.App. 2012)] (See *The Parol Evidence Rule*.)

10–5. Promises Made in Consideration of Marriage. After twenty-nine years of marriage, Robert and Mary Lou Tuttle were divorced. They admitted in court that before they were married, they had signed a prenuptial agreement. They agreed that the agreement had stated that each would keep his or her own property and anything derived from that property. Robert came into the marriage owning farmland, while Mary Lou owned no real estate. During the marriage, ten different parcels of land, totaling about six hundred acres, were acquired, and two corporations, Tuttle Grain, Inc., and Tuttle

Farms, Inc., were formed. A copy of the prenuptial agreement could not be found. Can the court enforce the agreement without a writing? Why or why not? [*In re Marriage of Tuttle,* 2013 WL 164035 (Ill.App. 5 Dist. 2013)] (See *The Statute of Frauds—Writing Requirement.*)

10–6. Business Case Problem with Sample Answer— Fraudulent Misrepresentation.

 Joy Pervis and Brenda Pauley worked together as talent agents in Georgia. When Pervis "discovered" actress Dakota Fanning, Pervis sent Fanning's audition tape to Cindy Osbrink, a talent agent in California. Osbrink agreed to represent Fanning in California and to pay 3 percent of Osbrink's commissions to Pervis and Pauley, who agreed to split the payments equally. Six years later, Pervis told Pauley that their agreement with Osbrink had expired and there would be no more payments. Nevertheless, Pervis continued to receive payments from Osbrink. Each time Pauley asked about commissions, however, Pervis replied that she was not receiving any. Do these facts evidence fraud? Explain. [*In re Pervis,* 512 Bankr. 348 (N.D.Ga. 2014)] (See *Fraudulent Misrepresentation.*)

- **For a sample answer to Problem 10–6, go to Appendix C at the end of this text.**

10–7. Promises Made in Consideration of Marriage.
Before their marriage, Linda and Gerald Heiden executed a prenuptial agreement. The agreement provided that "no spouse shall have any right in the property of the other spouse, even in the event of the death of either party." The description of Gerald's separate property included a settlement from a personal injury suit. Twenty-four years later, Linda filed for divorce. The court ruled that the prenuptial agreement applied only in the event of death, not divorce, and entered a judgment that included a property division and spousal support award. The ruling disparately favored Linda, whose monthly income with spousal support would be $4,467, leaving Gerald with only $1,116. Did the court interpret the Heidens' prenuptial agreement correctly? Discuss. [*Heiden v. Heiden,* 2015 WL 849006 (Mich.App. 2015)] (See *The Statute of Frauds—Writing Requirement.*)

10–8. Fraudulent Misrepresentation.
Vianna Stibal owns and operates the ThetaHealing Institute of Knowledge (THInK) in Idaho Falls, Idaho. ThetaHealing is Stibal's "self-discovered" healing method. In her book *Go Up and Seek God,* Stibal stated that she had been diagnosed with cancer and had cured herself using ThetaHealing. But Stibal's representation that she cured herself of cancer was false, and she knew it—her medical records did not confirm a cancer diagnosis. Believing Stibal's claim, Kara Alexander traveled from New York to Idaho to pay for, and attend, classes in ThetaHealing from Stibal. Later, Alexander began to question the validity of her THInK degree. What are the elements of a cause of action for fraudulent misrepresentation? Do the facts in this situation meet these requirements? Discuss. [*Alexander v. Stibal,* 160 Idaho 10, 368 P.3d 630 (2016)] (See *Fraudulent Misrepresentation.*)

10–9. A Question of Ethics—Exceptions to the Writing Requirement.

 Madeline Castellotti was the sole shareholder of Whole Pies, Inc., which owns John's Pizzeria in New York City. Her other assets included a 51 percent interest in a real estate partnership, a residence on Staten Island, and various bank accounts. When Madeline's son, Peter Castellotti, was going through a divorce, Madeline wanted to prevent Peter's then-wife Rea from benefiting from any of Madeline's assets. With this purpose in mind, she removed Peter from her will, leaving her daughter Lisa Free as the sole beneficiary. Lisa orally agreed to provide Peter with half of the income generated by the assets after their mother's death if his divorce was still pending and to transfer half of the assets after the divorce was final. In reliance on those promises, Peter agreed to pay the property taxes for the estate. Madeline died and Peter paid the taxes, but Lisa reneged on the deal. Peter filed a suit in a New York state court against his sister to recover. [Castellotti v. Free, 138 A.D.3d 198, 27 N.Y.S.3d 507 (1 Dept. 2016)] (See *The Statute of Frauds—Writing Requirement.*)

(a) Should the court enforce the promise? On what legal theory?

(b) If the court enforces the promise, should Rea get a share of what Peter and his mother and sister were "hiding"? Discuss.

Legal Reasoning Group Activity

10–10. The Writing Requirement. Jason Novell, doing business as Novell Associates, hired Barbara Meade to work for him. The parties orally agreed on the terms of employment, including payment of a share of the company's income to Meade, but they did not put anything in writing. Two years later, Meade quit. Novell then told Meade that she was entitled to $9,602—25 percent of the difference between the accounts receivable and the accounts payable as of Meade's last day of work. Meade disagreed and demanded more than $63,500—25 percent of the revenue from all invoices, less the cost of materials and outside processing, for each of the years that she had worked for Novell. Meade filed a lawsuit against

Novell for breach of contract. (See *The Statute of Frauds—Writing Requirement.*)

(a) The first group should decide whether the parties had an enforceable contract.

(b) The second group should decide whether the parties' oral agreement falls within any exception to the Statute of Frauds.

(c) The third group should discuss how the lawsuit would be affected if Novell admitted that the parties had an oral contract under which Meade was entitled to 25 percent of the difference between accounts receivable and accounts payable as of the day Meade quit.

CHAPTER 11

Third Party Rights and Discharge

Once it has been determined that a valid and legally enforceable contract exists, attention can turn to the rights and duties of the parties to the contract. A contract is a private agreement between the parties who have entered into it, and traditionally these parties alone have rights and liabilities under the contract. This principle is referred to as **privity of contract.** A *third party*—one who is not a direct party to a particular contract—normally does not have rights under that contract.

There are exceptions to the rule of privity of contract. One exception allows a party to a contract to transfer the rights or duties arising from the contract to another person through an *assignment* (of rights) or a *delegation* (of duties). The other exception involves a *third party beneficiary contract*—a contract in which the parties to the contract intend that the contract benefit a third party. We look at these exceptions in the following pages.

We also examine how contractual obligations can be *discharged*.

Normally, contract discharge is accomplished by both parties performing the acts promised in the contract. Sometimes, however, the duty to perform under the contract is conditioned on a certain event, such as when an agreement to buy a house is conditioned on obtaining financing.

We will look at the effect of conditions, consider the degree of performance required to discharge a contractual obligation, and discuss some other ways in which contract discharge can occur.

11–1 Assignments and Delegations

In a bilateral contract, the two parties have corresponding rights and duties. One party has a *right* to require the other to perform some task, and the other has a *duty* to perform it. The transfer of contractual *rights* to a third party is known as an **assignment.** The transfer of contractual *duties* to a third party is known as a **delegation.** An assignment or a delegation occurs *after* the original contract was made.

11–1a Assignments

In an assignment, the party assigning the rights to a third party is known as the **assignor,**[1] and the party receiving the rights is the **assignee.**[2] When rights under a contract are assigned unconditionally, the rights of the assignor are extinguished.[3] The third party (the assignee) has a right

to demand performance from the other original party to the contract. The assignee takes only those rights that the assignor originally had, however.

Assignments are important because they are used in many types of business financing. Lending institutions, such as banks, frequently assign their rights to receive payments under their loan contracts to other firms, which pay for those rights. ■ **CASE IN POINT 11.1** Edward Hosch entered into four loan agreements with Citicapital Commercial Corporation to finance the purchase of heavy construction equipment. A few months later, Citicapital merged into Citicorp Leasing, Inc., which was then renamed GE Capital Commercial, Inc. One year later, GE Capital assigned the loans to Colonial Pacific Leasing Corporation.

When Hosch defaulted on the loans, Colonial Pacific provided a notice of default and demanded payment. Hosch failed to repay the loans, so Colonial Pacific sued to collect the amount due. The trial court granted summary judgment to Colonial Pacific, and Hosch appealed. The state appellate court affirmed. There was sufficient

---

1. Pronounced uh-*sye*-nore.
2. Pronounced uh-*sye*-nee.
3. *Restatement (Second) of Contracts,* Section 317.

evidence that the loans had been assigned to Colonial Pacific.[4] ∎

Billions of dollars change hands daily in the business world in the form of assignments of rights in contracts. If it were not possible to transfer contractual rights, many businesses could not continue to operate.

Rights That Cannot Be Assigned   As a general rule, all rights can be assigned. Exceptions are made, however, under certain circumstances, including the following:

1. The assignment is prohibited by statute.
2. The contract is personal.
3. The assignment significantly changes the risk or duties of the *obligor* (the person who is obligated to perform the duty).
4. The contract prohibits assignment.

When a Contract Is Personal in Nature.   If a contract is for personal services, the rights under the contract normally cannot be assigned unless all that remains is a monetary payment.[5] ∎ **EXAMPLE 11.2** Anton signs a contract to be a tutor for Marisa's children. Marisa then attempts to assign to Roberto (who also has children) her right to Anton's services. Roberto cannot enforce the contract against Anton. Roberto's children may be more difficult to tutor than Marisa's. Thus, if Marisa could assign her rights to Anton's services to Roberto, it would change the nature of Anton's obligation. Because personal services are unique to the person rendering them, rights to receive personal services are likewise unique and cannot be assigned. ∎

Note that when legal actions involve personal rights, they are considered personal in nature and cannot be assigned. For instance, personal-injury tort claims generally are nonassignable as a matter of public policy. Thus, if Elizabeth is injured by Randy's defamation, she cannot assign to someone else her right to sue Randy for damages.

When an Assignment Will Significantly Change the Risk or Duties of the Obligor.   A right cannot be assigned if the assignment will significantly increase or alter the risks to or the duties of the obligor.[6] ∎ **EXAMPLE 11.3** Larson owns a hotel. To insure it, he takes out a policy with Southeast Insurance. The policy insures against fire, theft, floods, and vandalism. Larson attempts to assign the insurance policy to Hewitt, who also owns a hotel.

The assignment is ineffective because it substantially alters Southeast Insurance's *duty of performance.* An insurance company evaluates the particular risk of a certain party and tailors its policy to fit that risk. If the policy is assigned to a third party, the insurance risk is materially altered because the insurance company may have no information on the third party. Therefore, the assignment will not operate to give Hewitt any rights against Southeast Insurance. ∎

When the Contract Prohibits Assignment.   When a contract specifically stipulates that a right cannot be assigned, then *ordinarily* it cannot be assigned. Note that restraints on the power to assign operate only against the parties themselves. They do not prohibit an assignment by operation of law, such as an assignment pursuant to bankruptcy or death.

Whether such an *antiassignment clause* is effective depends, in part, on how it is phrased. A contract that states that *any* assignment is void effectively prohibits any assignment. ∎ **EXAMPLE 11.4** Ramirez agrees to build a house for Carmen. Their contract states "This contract cannot be assigned by Carmen without Ramirez's consent. Any assignment without such consent renders the contract void." This antiassignment clause is effective, and Carmen cannot assign her rights without obtaining Ramirez's consent. ∎

The general rule that a contract can prohibit assignment has several exceptions:

1. A contract cannot prevent an assignment of the right to receive funds. This exception exists to encourage the free flow of funds and credit in modern business settings.
2. The assignment of rights in real estate often cannot be prohibited because such a prohibition is contrary to public policy in most states. Prohibitions of this kind are called restraints against **alienation** (transfer of land ownership).
3. The assignment of *negotiable instruments* (such as checks and promissory notes) cannot be prohibited.
4. In a contract for the sale of goods, the right to receive damages for breach of contract or payment of an account owed may be assigned even though the sales contract prohibits such an assignment [UCC 2–210(2)].

The lease and purchase agreement in the following case contained an antiassignment clause. The court had to decide whether the clause was enforceable.

---

4. *Hosch v. Colonial Pacific Leasing Corp.*, 313 Ga.App. 873, 722 S.E.2d 778 (2012).
5. *Restatement (Second) of Contracts*, Sections 317 and 318.
6. Section 2–210(2) of the Uniform Commercial Code (UCC).

Bass-Fineberg Leasing, Inc. v. Modern Auto Sales, Inc.

Court of Appeals of Ohio, Ninth District, Medina County, __ N.E.3d __, 2015 -Ohio- 46 (2015).

Background and Facts Bass-Fineberg Leasing, Inc., leased a tour bus to Modern Auto Sales, Inc., and Michael Cipriani. The lease included an option to buy the bus. The lease prohibited Modern Auto and Cipriani from assigning their rights without Bass-Fineberg's written consent. Later, Cipriani left the bus with Anthony Allie at BVIP Limo Services, Ltd., for repairs. Modern Auto and Cipriani did not pay for the repairs. At the same time, they defaulted on the lease payments to Bass-Fineberg.

While BVIP retained possession of the bus, Allie signed an agreement with Cipriani to buy it and to make an initial $5,000 payment to Bass-Fineberg. Bass-Fineberg filed an action in an Ohio state court against Modern Auto, Cipriani, BVIP, and Allie to regain possession of the bus. The court ordered the bus returned to Bass-Fineberg and the $5,000 payment refunded to Allie. All of the parties appealed.

In the Language of the Court

WHITMORE, Judge.

* * * *

* * * Bass-Fineberg argues that the purported contract between Cipriani and Allie was void because Cipriani could not assign his rights or obligations under the lease without the written consent of Bass-Fineberg. * * * BVIP responds that if the contract was void, then the parties should be returned to their pre-contract status, including refunding its $5,000 payment. We agree with Bass-Fineberg that there was not a valid contract between Allie and Cipriani, but we agree with BVIP as to the effect of that invalidity, namely that it was entitled to have its $5,000 returned.

Ohio enforces anti-assignment clauses where there is clear contractual language prohibiting an assignment. Violations of a non-assignment provision in a contract render the resulting agreement null and void. [Emphasis added.]

* * * *

The lease between Bass-Fineberg and Modern Auto and Cipriani contained the following provision:

MODERN AUTO AND CIPRIANI ACKNOWLEDGE THAT MODERN AUTO AND CIPRIANI MAY NOT ASSIGN OR IN ANY WAY TRANSFER OR DISPOSE OF ALL OR ANY PART OF MODERN AUTO AND CIPRIANI'S RIGHTS OR OBLIGATIONS UNDER THIS LEASE * * * WITHOUT BASS-FINEBERG'S PRIOR WRITTEN CONSENT.

This clear contractual language prohibited Modern Auto and Cipriani from transferring their rights or obligations under the lease agreement unless Bass-Fineberg consented in writing.

The purported agreement between Cipriani and Allie attempted to transfer Cipriani's right to purchase the bus to Allie and some of Cipriani's payment obligations to Allie. [David] Libman, Bass-Fineberg's lease sales manager, did not sign the agreement between Allie and Cipriani. Nor did the parties introduce evidence of anyone else from Bass-Fineberg providing written consent to the attempted assignment.

As the lease agreement prohibited an assignment without Bass-Fineberg's consent, the agreement between Cipriani and Allie was void. If a contract is void, then an obligation under it never existed. In such circumstances, the one who made a payment is entitled to a refund.

Decision and Remedy *A state intermediate appellate court affirmed the lower court's order. The contract between Cipriani and Allie was void because Cipriani could not assign his rights under the lease without Bass-Fineberg's written consent. Because the contract was void, the parties were to be returned to their pre-contract status, which included a refund of the $5,000 payment.*

Critical Thinking

• **Economic** *The repairs to the bus cost $1,341.50. Who should pay this amount? Why?*

Notice of Assignment Once a valid assignment of rights has been made, the assignee should notify the obligor of the assignment. Giving notice is not legally necessary to establish the validity of the assignment: an assignment is effective immediately, whether or not notice is given. Two major problems arise, however, when notice of the assignment is not given to the obligor.

Priority Issues. If the assignor assigns the same right to two different persons, the question arises as to which one has priority—that is, which one has the right to the performance by the obligor. The rule most often observed in the United States is that the first assignment in time is the first in right. Nevertheless, some states follow the English rule, which basically gives priority to the first assignee who gives notice.

■ **EXAMPLE 11.5** Jason owes Alexis $5,000 under a contract. Alexis first assigns the claim to Carmen, who does not give notice to Jason. Alexis then assigns it to Dorman, who notifies Jason. In most states, Carmen would have priority because the assignment to her was first in time. In some states, however, Dorman would have priority because he gave first notice. ■

Potential for Discharge by Performance to the Wrong Party. Until the obligor has notice of an assignment, the obligor can discharge his or her obligation by performance to the assignor (the *obligee*, or person to whom the duty is owed). Performance by the obligor to the assignor constitutes a discharge to the assignee. Once the obligor receives proper notice, however, only performance to the assignee can discharge the obligor's obligations.

■ **EXAMPLE 11.6** Assume that Alexis assigned to Carmen her right to collect $5,000 from Jason, and Carmen did not give notice to Jason. Jason subsequently pays Alexis the $5,000. Although the assignment was valid, Jason's payment to Alexis is a discharge of the debt. Carmen's failure to notify Jason of the assignment causes her to lose the right to collect the $5,000 from Jason. (Note that Carmen still has a claim against Alexis for the $5,000.) If Carmen had given Jason notice of the assignment, Jason's payment to Alexis would not have discharged the debt. ■

11–1b Delegations

Just as a party can transfer rights through an assignment, a party can also transfer duties. Duties are not assigned, however, they are *delegated*. The party delegating the duties is the **delegator,** and the party to whom the duties are delegated is the **delegatee.** Normally, a delegation of duties does not relieve the delegator of the obligation to perform in the event that the delegatee fails to do so.

No special form is required to create a valid delegation of duties. As long as the delegator expresses an intention to make the delegation, it is effective. The delegator need not even use the word *delegate*.

Duties That Cannot Be Delegated As a general rule, any duty can be delegated. There are, however, some exceptions to this rule. Delegation is prohibited in the following circumstances:

1. When special trust has been placed in the obligor or when performance depends on the personal skill or talents of the obligor. ■ **EXAMPLE 11.7** O'Brien, who is impressed with Brodie's ability to perform veterinary surgery, contracts with Brodie to have her perform surgery on O'Brien's prize-winning stallion in July. Brodie later decides that she would rather spend the summer at the beach, so she delegates her duties under the contract to Lopez, who is also a competent veterinary surgeon. The delegation is not effective without O'Brien's consent, no matter how competent Lopez is, because the contract is for *personal* performance. ■

2. When performance by a third party will vary materially from that expected by the obligee. ■ **EXAMPLE 11.8** Jared, a wealthy investor, established the company Heaven Sent to provide grants of capital to struggling but potentially successful businesses. Jared contracted with Merilyn, whose judgment Jared trusted, to select the recipients of the grants. Later, Merilyn delegated this duty to Donald. Jared did not trust Donald's ability to select worthy recipients. This delegation is not effective because it materially alters Jared's expectations under the contract with Merilyn. ■

3. When the contract expressly prohibits delegation. ■ **EXAMPLE 11.9** Stark, Ltd., contracts with Belisario, a certified public accountant, to perform its annual audits for five years. The contract prohibits delegation. Belisario cannot delegate the duty to perform the audit to another accountant—not even an accountant at the same firm. ■

Effect of a Delegation If a delegation of duties is enforceable, the obligee must accept performance from the delegatee. The obligee can legally refuse performance from the delegatee only if the duty is one that cannot be delegated. ■ **EXAMPLE 11.10** Bryan has a duty to pick up and deliver metal fabrication equipment to Alicia's property. Bryan delegates his duty to Liam. Alicia (the obligee) must accept performance from Liam (the delegatee). ■

A valid delegation of duties does not relieve the delegator of obligations under the contract. Although there are exceptions, generally the obligee can sue both the delegatee and the delegator for nonperformance. Therefore, in *Example 11.10,* if Liam (the delegatee) fails to perform, Bryan (the delegator) is still liable to Alicia, and Alicia normally can sue Bryan, Liam, or both.

Concept Summary 11.1 outlines the basic principles of the laws governing assignments and delegations.

11–1c Assignment of "All Rights"

When a contract provides for an "assignment of all rights," this wording may create both an assignment of rights and a delegation of duties.[7] Typically, this occurs when gen-

eral words are used, such as "I assign the contract" or "I assign all my rights under the contract." A court normally will construe such words as implying both an assignment of rights and a delegation of any duties of performance. Thus, the assignor remains liable if the assignee fails to perform the contractual obligations.

11–2 Third Party Beneficiaries

Another exception to the doctrine of privity of contract arises when the contract is intended to benefit a third party. The original parties to a contract can agree that the contract performance should be rendered to or directly benefit a third person. When this happens, the third person becomes an *intended* **third party beneficiary** of the contract. As the **intended beneficiary** of the contract,

7. *Restatement (Second) of Contracts*, Section 328; UCC 2–210(3), (4).

Concept Summary 11.1

Assignment and Delegations

Which Rights Can Be Assigned, and Which Duties Can Be Delegated?	All rights can be assigned *unless:* • A statute expressly prohibits assignment. • The contract is for personal services. • The assignment will materially alter the obligor's risk or duties. • The contract prohibits assignment. All duties can be delegated *unless:* • Performance depends on the obligor's personal skills or talents or special trust has been placed in the obligor. • Performance by a third party will materially vary from that expected by the obligee. • The contract prohibits delegation.
What If the Contract Prohibits Assignment or Delegation?	No rights can be assigned *except:* • Rights to receive funds. • Ownership rights in real estate. • Rights to negotiable instruments. • Rights to damages for breach of a sales contract or payments under a sales contract. No duties can be delegated.
What Is the Effect on the Original Party's Rights?	• On a valid assignment, effective immediately, the original party (assignor) no longer has any rights under the contract. • On a valid delegation, if the delegatee fails to perform, the original party (delegator) is liable to the obligee (who may also hold the delegatee liable).

the third party has legal rights and can sue the promisor directly for breach of the contract.

Who, though, is the promisor? In a bilateral contract, both parties to the contract make promises that can be enforced, so the court has to determine which party made the promise that benefits the third party. That person is the promisor. In effect, allowing a third party to sue the promisor directly circumvents the "middle person" (the promisee) and thus reduces the burden on the courts. Otherwise, the third party would sue the promisee, who would then sue the promisor.

■ **CASE IN POINT 11.11** The classic case that gave third party beneficiaries the right to bring a suit directly against a promisor was decided in 1859. The case involved three parties—Holly, Lawrence, and Fox. Holly had borrowed $300 from Lawrence. Shortly thereafter, Holly loaned $300 to Fox, who in return promised Holly that he would pay Holly's debt to Lawrence on the following day. When Lawrence failed to obtain the $300 from Fox, he sued Fox to recover the funds. The court had to decide whether Lawrence could sue Fox directly (rather than suing Holly). The court held that when "a promise [is] made for the benefit of another, he for whose benefit it is made may bring an action for its breach."[8] ■

11–2a Types of Intended Beneficiaries

The law traditionally recognized two types of intended third party beneficiaries: creditor beneficiaries and donee beneficiaries.

Creditor Beneficiary One type of intended beneficiary is a *creditor beneficiary.* Like the plaintiff in *Case in Point 11.11,* a creditor beneficiary benefits from a contract in which one party (the promisor) promises another party (the promisee) to pay a debt that the promisee owes to a third party (the creditor beneficiary).

■ **CASE IN POINT 11.12** Autumn Allan owned a condominium unit in a Texas complex located directly beneath a condo unit owned by Aslan Koraev and Ekaterina Nersesova. Over the course of two years, Allan's unit suffered eight incidents of water and sewage incursion as a result of plumbing problems and misuse of appliances in Koraev's unit. Allan sued Koraev for breach of contract and won.

Koraev appealed, arguing that he had no contractual duty to Allan. The court found that Allan was an intended third party beneficiary of the contract between Koraev and the condominium owners' association. Because the governing documents stated that each owner

had to comply strictly with their provisions, failure to comply created grounds for an action by the condominium association or by an aggrieved (wronged) owner. Here, Allan was clearly an aggrieved owner and could sue Koraev directly for his failure to perform his contract duties to the condominium association.[9] ■

Donee Beneficiary Another type of intended beneficiary is a *donee beneficiary.* When a contract is made for the express purpose of giving a *gift* to a third party, the third party (the donee beneficiary) can sue the promisor directly to enforce the promise.

The most common donee beneficiary contract is a life insurance contract. ■ **EXAMPLE 11.13** Ang (the promisee) pays premiums to Standard Life, a life insurance company. Standard Life (the promisor) promises to pay a certain amount upon Ang's death to anyone Ang designates as a beneficiary. The designated beneficiary is a donee beneficiary under the life insurance policy and can enforce the promise made by the insurance company to pay her or him on Ang's death. ■

The Modern View Most third party beneficiaries do not fit neatly into either the creditor beneficiary or the donee beneficiary category. Thus, the modern view adopted by the *Restatement (Second) of Contracts* does not draw clear lines between the types of intended beneficiaries. Today, courts frequently distinguish only between *intended beneficiaries* (who can sue to enforce contracts made for their benefit) and *incidental beneficiaries* (who cannot sue, as will be discussed shortly).

11–2b When the Rights of an Intended Beneficiary Vest

An intended third party beneficiary cannot enforce a contract against the original parties until the rights of the third party have *vested,* which means the rights have taken effect and cannot be taken away. Until these rights have vested, the original parties to the contract—the promisor and the promisee—can modify or rescind the contract without the consent of the third party.

When do the rights of third parties vest? The majority of courts hold that the rights vest when any of the following occurs:

1. When the third party demonstrates express consent to the agreement, such as by sending a letter, a note, or an e-mail acknowledging awareness of, and consent to, a contract formed for her or his benefit.

---

8. *Lawrence v. Fox,* 20 N.Y. 268 (1859).

9. *Allan v. Nersesova,* 307 S.W.3d 564 (Tx.App.—Dallas 2010).

2. When the third party materially alters his or her position in detrimental reliance on the contract. For instance, a person contracts to have a home built in reliance on the receipt of funds promised to him or her in a donee beneficiary contract.

3. When the conditions for vesting are satisfied. For instance, the rights of a beneficiary under a life insurance policy vest when the insured person dies.[10]

If the contract expressly reserves to the contracting parties the right to cancel, rescind, or modify the contract, the rights of the third party beneficiary are subject to any changes that result. If the original contract reserves the right to revoke the promise or change the beneficiary, the vesting of the third party's rights does not terminate that power. In most life insurance contracts, for instance, the policyholder reserves the right to change the designated beneficiary.

11–2c Incidental Beneficiaries

Sometimes, a third person receives a benefit from a contract even though that person's benefit is not the reason the contract was made. Such a person is known as an **incidental beneficiary.** Because the benefit is *unintentional,* an incidental beneficiary cannot sue to enforce the contract.

---

10. *Restatement (Second) of Contracts,* Section 311.

■ **CASE IN POINT 11.14** Spectators at the infamous boxing match in which Mike Tyson was disqualified for biting his opponent's ear sued Tyson and the fight's promoters for a refund on the basis of breach of contract. The spectators claimed that they were third party beneficiaries of the contract between Tyson and the fight's promoters. The court, however, held that the spectators could not sue because they were not in contractual privity with the defendants. Any benefits they received from the contract were incidental to the contract. According to the court, the spectators got what they paid for: "the right to view whatever event transpired."[11] ■

11–2d Intended versus Incidental Beneficiaries

In determining whether a third party beneficiary is an intended or an incidental beneficiary, the courts focus on intent, as expressed in the contract language and implied by the surrounding circumstances. Any beneficiary who is not deemed an intended beneficiary is considered incidental. Exhibit 11–1 illustrates the distinction between intended beneficiaries and incidental beneficiaries.

Although no single test can embrace all possible situations, courts often apply the *reasonable person* test: Would

---

11. *Castillo v. Tyson,* 268 A.D.2d 336, 701 N.Y.S.2d 423 (Sup.Ct.App.Div. 2000).

EXHIBIT 11–1 Third Party Beneficiaries

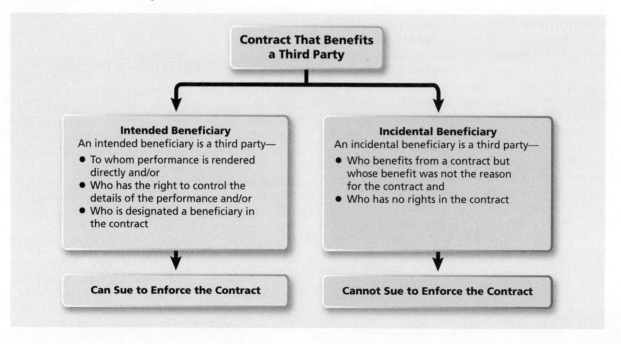

a reasonable person in the position of the beneficiary believe that the promisee intended to confer on the beneficiary the right to enforce the contract? In addition, the presence of one or more of the following factors strongly indicates that the third party is an intended beneficiary to the contract:

1. Performance is rendered directly to the third party.
2. The third party has the right to control the details of performance.
3. The third party is expressly designated as a beneficiary in the contract.

■ **CASE IN POINT 11.15** New York City decided to build a state-of-the-art forensic biology (DNA testing) laboratory next to Bellevue Hospital in Manhattan. The project was designed to be a fifteen-story structure with a two-level basement. The city turned the project over to the Dormitory Authority of the State of New York (DASNY), which oversees public projects. DASNY contracted with Perkins Eastman Architects, P.C., to provide architectural services for the project. Perkins hired Samson Construction Company to excavate the site and lay the foundation. Unfortunately, Samson's excavation of the site caused adjacent structures, including a building, sidewalks, roadbeds, sewers, and water systems, to "settle," sustaining about $37 million in damage.

DASNY and the city filed a suit in a New York state court against Samson and Perkins, alleging breach of contract. The lower court dismissed the claim, finding that because the city was not named in the contract between Samson and Perkins, it was not a third party beneficiary. A state intermediate appellate court reversed. "The City raised an issue of fact whether it is an intended third party beneficiary of the contract. The contract expressly states that a City agency will operate the DNA laboratory, and the City retained control over various aspects of the project."[12] ■

11-3 Contract Discharge

The most common way to **discharge,** or terminate, contractual duties is by the **performance** of those duties. For instance, a buyer and seller enter into an agreement via e-mail for the sale of a 2018 Lexus RX for $44,000. This contract will be discharged by performance when the buyer pays $44,000 to the seller and the seller transfers possession of the Lexus to the buyer.

In a perfect world, every party who signed a contract would perform his or her duties completely and in a timely fashion, thereby discharging the contract. The real world is more complicated. Events often occur that affect our performance or our ability to perform contractual duties. In addition, the duty to perform under a contract is not always *absolute.* It may instead be *conditioned* on the occurrence or nonoccurrence of a certain event. The legal environment of business requires the identification of some point at which the parties can reasonably know that their duties have ended.

11-3a Conditions of Performance

In most contracts, promises of performance are not expressly conditioned or qualified. Instead, they are *absolute promises.* They must be performed, or the parties promising the acts will be in breach of contract.
■ **EXAMPLE 11.16** Paloma Enterprises contracts to sell a truckload of organic produce to Tran for $10,000. The parties' promises are unconditional: Paloma will deliver the produce to Tran, and Tran will pay $10,000 to Paloma. The payment does not have to be made if the produce is not delivered. ■

In some situations, however, performance is *conditioned.* A **condition** is a qualification in a contract based on a possible future event. The occurrence or nonoccurrence of the event will trigger the performance of a legal obligation or terminate an existing obligation under a contract.[13] If the condition is not satisfied, the obligations of the parties are discharged.

Three types of conditions can be present in contracts: conditions *precedent,* conditions *subsequent,* and *concurrent* conditions. Conditions can also be classified as *express* or *implied.*

Conditions Precedent A condition that must be fulfilled before a party's performance can be required is called a **condition precedent.** The condition precedes the absolute duty to perform.

A contract to lease university housing, for instance, may be conditioned on the person's being a student at the university. ■ **CASE IN POINT 11.17** James Maciel leased an apartment in a university-owned housing facility for Regent University (RU) students in Virginia. The lease ran until the end of the fall semester. Maciel had an option to renew the lease semester by semester as long as he maintained his status as an RU student.

---

12. *Dormitory Authority of the State of New York v. Samson Construction Co.,* 137 A.D.3d 433, 27 N.Y.S.3d 114 (1 Dept. 2016).

13. The *Restatement (Second) of Contracts,* Section 224, defines a condition as "an event, not certain to occur, which must occur, unless its nonoccurrence is excused, before performance under a contract becomes due."

When Maciel told RU that he intended to withdraw, the university told him that he had to move out of the apartment by May 31, the final day of the semester. Maciel asked for two additional weeks, but the university denied the request. On June 1, RU changed the locks on the apartment. Maciel entered through a window and e-mailed the university that he planned to stay "for another one or two weeks." He was convicted of trespassing. He appealed, arguing that he had "legal authority" to occupy the apartment. The reviewing court affirmed his conviction. "Regent's deadline was consistent with the lease agreement, and Maciel's eligibility to reside in student housing was *conditioned* upon his status as a Regent student." In other words, being enrolled as a student in RU was a condition precedent to living in its student housing.[14] ∎

Life insurance contracts frequently specify that certain conditions, such as passing a physical examination, must be met before the insurance company will be obligated to perform under the contract. In addition, many contracts are conditioned on an independent appraisal of value.

Conditions Subsequent When a condition operates to terminate a party's absolute promise to perform, it is called a **condition subsequent.** The condition follows, or is subsequent to, the time at which the absolute duty to perform arose. If the condition occurs, the party's duty to perform is discharged. ∎ **EXAMPLE 11.18** A law firm hires Julie Mendez, a recent law school graduate. Their contract provides that the firm's obligation to continue employing Mendez is discharged if Mendez fails to pass the bar exam by her second attempt. This is a condition subsequent because a failure to pass the exam—and thus to obtain a license to practice law—would discharge a duty (employment) that has already arisen. ∎

Generally, conditions precedent are common, and conditions subsequent are rare. Indeed, the *Restatement (Second) of Contracts* does not use the terms *condition subsequent* and *condition precedent* but refers to both simply as conditions.[15]

Concurrent Conditions When each party's performance is conditioned on the other party's performance or tender of performance (offer to perform), **concurrent conditions** are present. These conditions exist only when the contract expressly or impliedly calls for the parties to perform their respective duties *simultaneously.*

---

14. *Maciel v. Commonwealth,* 2011 WL 65942 (Va.App. 2011).
15. *Restatement (Second) of Contracts,* Section 224.

∎ **EXAMPLE 11.19** If Janet Feibush promises to pay for goods when Hewlett-Packard delivers them, the parties' promises to perform are mutually dependent. Feibush's duty to pay for the goods does not become absolute until Hewlett-Packard either delivers or tenders the goods. Likewise, Hewlett-Packard's duty to deliver the goods does not become absolute until Feibush tenders or actually makes payment. Therefore, neither can recover from the other for breach without first tendering performance. ∎

Exhibit 11–2 reviews the types of conditions.

Express and Implied Conditions Conditions can also be classified as express or implied in fact. *Express conditions* are provided for by the parties' agreement. Although no particular words are necessary, express conditions are normally prefaced by the words *if, provided, after,* or *when.* For instance, most automobile insurance policies include what is known as a cooperation clause. This clause states that if the insured person is involved in an accident, he or she must cooperate with the insurance company in the defense of any claim or lawsuit.

Implied conditions are understood to be part of the agreement, but they are not found in the express language of the agreement. Courts may imply conditions from the purpose of the contract or from the intent of the parties. Conditions are often implied when they are inherent in the actual performance of the contract.

EXHIBIT 11–2 Conditions of Performance

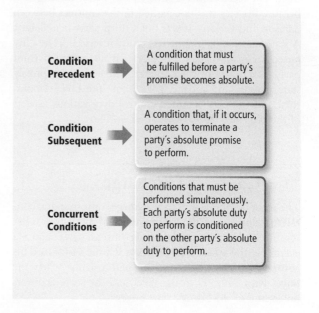

Condition Precedent → A condition that must be fulfilled before a party's promise becomes absolute.

Condition Subsequent → A condition that, if it occurs, operates to terminate a party's absolute promise to perform.

Concurrent Conditions → Conditions that must be performed simultaneously. Each party's absolute duty to perform is conditioned on the other party's absolute duty to perform.

11–3b Discharge by Performance

The great majority of contracts, as noted earlier, are discharged by performance. The contract comes to an end when both parties fulfill their respective duties by performing the acts they have promised.

Performance can also be accomplished by *tender.* **Tender** is an unconditional offer to perform by a person who is ready, willing, and able to do so. Therefore, a seller who places goods at the disposal of a buyer has tendered delivery and can demand payment. A buyer who offers to pay for goods has tendered payment and can demand delivery of the goods.

Once performance has been tendered, the party making the tender has done everything possible to carry out the terms of the contract. If the other party then refuses to perform, the party making the tender can sue for breach of contract. There are two basic types of performance—*complete performance* and *substantial performance.*

Complete Performance When a party performs exactly as agreed, there is no question as to whether the contract has been performed. When a party's performance is perfect, it is said to be complete. Normally, conditions expressly stated in a contract must fully occur in all respects for complete performance (strict performance) of the contract to take place. Any deviation breaches the contract and discharges the other party's obligation to perform.

Most construction contracts, for instance, require the builder to meet certain specifications. If the specifications are conditions, complete performance is required to avoid material breach (*material breach* will be discussed shortly). If the conditions are met, the other party to the contract must then fulfill her or his obligation to pay the builder.

If the parties to the contract did not expressly make the specifications a condition, however, and the builder fails to meet the specifications, performance is not complete. What effect does such a failure have on the other party's obligation to pay? The answer is part of the doctrine of *substantial performance.*

Substantial Performance A party who in good faith performs substantially all of the terms of a contract can enforce the contract against the other party under the doctrine of substantial performance. The basic requirements for performance to qualify as substantial performance are as follows:

1. The party must have performed in good faith. Intentional failure to comply with the contract terms is a breach of the contract.
2. The performance must not vary greatly from the performance promised in the contract. An omission, variance, or defect in performance is considered minor if it can easily be remedied by compensation (monetary damages).
3. The performance must create substantially the same benefits as those promised in the contract.

Courts Must Decide. Courts decide whether the performance was substantial on a case-by-case basis, examining all of the facts of the particular situation. ■ **CASE IN POINT 11.20** Eugene Pegg had been an electrician in North Dakota for thirty years and had brought a large customer, Sungold, with him through several employers. When an acquaintance, Kelly Kohn, started Kohn Electric, LLC, Pegg approached him to become partners.

Kohn and Pegg orally agreed that Pegg could become a partner in Kohn Electric if he contributed $10,000 in capital and the Sungold account. In return, Pegg was to receive 10 percent of the gross revenue generated by the Sungold account, among other things. Pegg paid $9,152.49 for a pickup truck titled in Kohn Electric's name and paid for tools and equipment for the business. Later, the relationship soured, and Pegg quit. Pegg sued in a state court to recover the proceeds due under the agreement. Kohn denied that they were partners, but he paid Pegg $9,152.49 for the truck.

The state court found that there was an oral partnership agreement and that Pegg had substantially performed by contributing the pickup and bringing in the Sungold account. Therefore, he was entitled to damages in an amount equal to 10 percent of the gross revenue generated from the Sungold account. The court's decision was affirmed on appeal.[16] ■

Effect on Duty to Perform. If one party's performance is substantial, the other party's duty to perform remains absolute. In other words, the parties must continue performing under the contract. For instance, the party who substantially performed is entitled to payment. If performance is not substantial, there is a material breach, and the nonbreaching party is excused from further performance.

---

16. *Pegg v. Kohn*, 861 N.W.2d 764, 2015 ND 79 (2015).

Measure of Damages. Because substantial performance is not perfect, the other party is entitled to damages to compensate for the failure to comply with the contract. The measure of the damages is the cost to bring the object of the contract into compliance with its terms, if that cost is reasonable under the circumstances.

What if the cost is unreasonable? Then the measure of damages is the difference in value between the performance rendered and the performance that would have been rendered if the contract had been performed completely.

■ **CASE IN POINT 11.21** In a classic case, the plaintiff, Jacob & Youngs, Inc., was a builder that had contracted with George Kent to construct a country residence for him. A specification in the building contract required that "all wrought-iron pipe must be well galvanized, lap welded pipe of the grade known as 'standard pipe' of Reading manufacture." Jacob & Youngs installed substantially similar pipe that was not of Reading manufacture. When Kent became aware of the difference, he ordered the builder to remove all of the plumbing and replace it with the Reading type. To do so would have required removing finished walls that encased the plumbing—an expensive and difficult task.

The builder explained that the plumbing was of the same quality, appearance, value, and cost as Reading pipe. When Kent nevertheless refused to pay the $3,483.46 still owed for the work, Jacob & Youngs sued to compel payment. The dispute ended up before the Court of Appeals of New York, the state's highest court, which concluded that "the measure of the allowance is not the cost of replacement, which would be great, but the difference in value, which would be either nominal or nothing." Therefore, New York's highest court held that Jacob & Youngs had substantially performed the contract.[17] ■

Performance to the Satisfaction of Another

Contracts often state that completed work must personally satisfy one of the parties or a third person. The question then is whether this satisfaction becomes a condition precedent, requiring actual personal satisfaction or approval for discharge, or whether the performance need only satisfy a *reasonable person.*

When the subject matter of the contract is *personal,* the obligation is conditional, and performance must actually satisfy the party specified in the contract. For instance, contracts for portraits, works of art, and tailoring are considered personal because they involve matters of personal taste. Therefore, only the personal satisfaction of the party fulfills the condition—unless the party expressing dissatisfaction is not acting in good faith.

Most other contracts need to be performed only to the satisfaction of a reasonable person unless they *expressly state otherwise.* When the subject matter of the contract is mechanical, such as installing a heat pump or building a fence, courts are more likely to find that the performance was satisfactory if a reasonable person would be satisfied with what was done.

Material Breach of Contract A **breach of contract**
is the nonperformance of a contractual duty. The breach is *material* when performance is not at least substantial.[18] As mentioned earlier, when there is a material breach, the nonbreaching party is excused from the performance of contractual duties. That party can also sue the breaching party for damages resulting from the breach.

■ **EXAMPLE 11.22** When country singer Garth Brooks's mother died, he donated $500,000 to a hospital in his hometown in Oklahoma to build a new women's health center named after his mother. After several years passed and the health center was not built, Brooks demanded a refund. The hospital refused, claiming that while it had promised to honor his mother in some way, it had not promised to build a women's health center. Brooks sued for breach of contract. A jury determined that the hospital's failure to build a women's health center and name it after Brooks's mother was a material breach of the contract. The jury awarded Brooks $1 million in damages. ■

Material versus Minor Breach. If the breach is *minor* (not material), the nonbreaching party's duty to perform is not entirely excused, but it can sometimes be suspended until the breach has been remedied. Once the minor breach has been cured, the nonbreaching party must resume performance of the contractual obligations.

Both parties in the following case were arguably in breach of their contract. Which party's breach was material?

---

17. *Jacob & Youngs v. Kent,* 230 N.Y. 239, 129 N.E. 889 (1921).

18. *Restatement (Second) of Contracts,* Section 241.

Kohel v. Bergen Auto Enterprises, L.L.C.

Superior Court of New Jersey, Appellate Division, 2013 WL 439970 (2013).

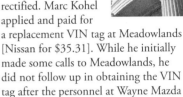

In the Language of the Court

PER CURIAM. [By the Whole Court]

* * * *

On May 24, 2010, plaintiffs Marc and Bree Kohel entered into a sales contract with defendant Bergen Auto Enterprises, L.L.C. d/b/a Wayne Mazda Inc. (Wayne Mazda), for the purchase of a used 2009 Mazda. Plaintiffs agreed to pay $26,430.22 for the Mazda and were credited $7,000 as a trade-in, for their 2005 Nissan Altima. As plaintiffs still owed $8,118.28 on the Nissan, Wayne Mazda assessed plaintiffs a net pay-off of this amount and agreed to remit the balance due to satisfy the outstanding lien.

Plaintiffs took possession of the Mazda with temporary plates and left the Nissan with defendant. A few days later, a representative of defendant advised plaintiffs that the Nissan's vehicle identification tag (VIN tag) was missing. The representative claimed it was unable to sell the car and offered to rescind the transaction. Plaintiffs refused.

When the temporary plates on the Mazda expired on June 24, 2010, defendant refused to provide plaintiffs with the permanent plates they had paid for. In addition, defendant refused to pay off plaintiffs' outstanding loan on the Nissan, as they had agreed. As a result, plaintiffs were required to continue to make monthly payments on both the Nissan and the Mazda.

On July 28, 2010, plaintiffs filed a complaint in [a New Jersey state court] against Wayne Mazda * * * . Plaintiffs alleged breach of contract.

* * * *

On February 2, 2012, the court rendered an oral decision finding that there was a breach of contract by Wayne Mazda * * * . On February 17, 2012, the court entered judgment in the amount of $5,405.17 in favor of plaintiffs against Wayne Mazda. [The defendant appealed to a state intermediate appellate court.]

* * * *

Defendant argues that plaintiffs' delivery of the Nissan without a VIN tag was, itself, a breach of the contract of sale and precludes a finding that defendant breached the contract. However, the trial court found that plaintiffs were not aware that the Nissan lacked a VIN tag when they offered it in trade. Moreover, defendant's representatives examined the car twice before accepting it in trade and did not notice the missing VIN until they took the car to an auction where they tried to sell it. *There is a material distinction in plaintiffs' conduct, which the court found unintentional, and defendant's refusal to release the permanent plates for which the plaintiffs had paid, an action the court concluded was done to maintain "leverage."* [Emphasis added.]

* * * The evidence * * * indicated that * * * the problem with the missing VIN tag could be rectified. Marc Kohel applied and paid for a replacement VIN tag at Meadowlands [Nissan for $35.31]. While he initially made some calls to Meadowlands, he did not follow up in obtaining the VIN tag after the personnel at Wayne Mazda began refusing to take his calls.

* * * The court concluded that "Wayne Mazda didn't handle this as—as adroitly [skillfully] as they could * * * ." Kevin DiPiano, identified in the complaint as the owner and/or CEO of Wayne Mazda, would not even take [the plaintiffs'] calls to discuss this matter. The court found:

> Mr. DiPiano could have been a better businessman, could have been a little bit more compassionate or at least responsive, you know? He was not. He acted like he didn't care. That obviously went a long way to infuriate the plaintiffs. I don't blame them for being infuriated.

* * * *

* * * Here, plaintiffs attempted to remedy the VIN tag issue but this resolution was frustrated by defendant's unreasonable conduct. We thus reject defendant's argument that plaintiffs' failure to obtain the replacement VIN tag amounted to a repudiation of the contract.

* * * *

Affirmed.

Legal Reasoning Questions

1. What is a material breach of contract? When a material breach occurs, what are the nonbreaching party's options?

2. What is a minor breach of contract? When a minor breach occurs, is the nonbreaching party excused from performance? Explain.

3. In this case, the defendant—Wayne Mazda—argued that the plaintiffs should not be granted relief for the defendant's breach. What were the defendant's main arguments in support of this position?

Underlying Policy. Note that any breach entitles the non-breaching party to sue for damages, but only a material breach discharges the nonbreaching party from the contract. The policy underlying these rules allows a contract to go forward when only minor problems occur but allows it to be terminated if major difficulties arise. Exhibit 11–3 reviews how performance can discharge a contract.

Anticipatory Repudiation Before either party to a contract has a duty to perform, one of the parties may refuse to carry out his or her contractual obligations. This is called **anticipatory repudiation**[19] of the contract.

When an anticipatory repudiation occurs, it is treated as a material breach of the contract, and the nonbreaching party is permitted to bring an action for damages immediately. The nonbreaching party can file suit even though the scheduled time for performance under the contract may still be in the future. Until the nonbreaching party treats an early repudiation as a breach, however, the repudiating party can retract the anticipatory repudiation by proper notice and restore the parties to their original obligations [UCC 2–611].

An anticipatory repudiation is treated as a present material breach for two reasons. First, the nonbreaching party should not be required to remain ready and willing to perform when the other party has already repudiated the contract. Second, the nonbreaching party should have the opportunity to seek a similar contract elsewhere and may have a duty to do so to minimize his or her loss.

Time for Performance If no time for performance is stated in a contract, a *reasonable time* is implied [UCC 2–204]. If a specific time is stated, the parties must usually perform by that time. Unless time is expressly stated to be vital, though, a delay in performance will not destroy the performing party's right to payment.

When time is expressly stated to be "of the essence," or vital, the parties normally must perform within the stated time period because the time element becomes a condition. Even when the contract states that time is of the essence, however, a court may find that a party who fails to complain about the other party's delay has waived the breach of the time provision.

11–3c Discharge by Agreement

Any contract can be discharged by agreement of the parties. The agreement can be contained in the original contract, or the parties can form a new contract for the express purpose of discharging the original contract.

Discharge by Mutual Rescission As mentioned in previous chapters, *rescission* is the process by which

---

19. *Restatement (Second) of Contracts*, Section 253; Section 2–610 of the Uniform Commercial Code (UCC).

EXHIBIT 11–3 Discharge by Performance

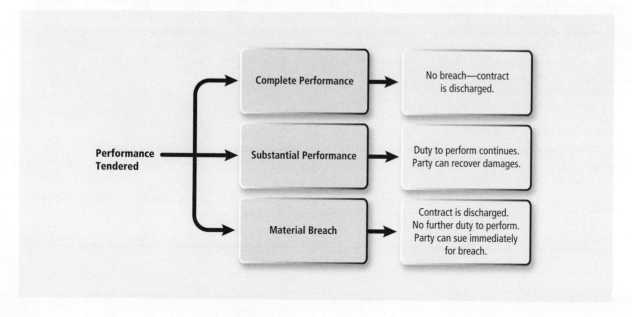

a contract is canceled or terminated and the parties are returned to the positions they occupied prior to forming it. For **mutual rescission** to take place, the parties must make another agreement that also satisfies the legal requirements for a contract. There must be an *offer,* an *acceptance,* and *consideration.* Ordinarily, if the parties agree to rescind the original contract, their promises not to perform the acts stipulated in the original contract will be legal consideration for the second contract (the rescission).

Agreements to rescind most executory contracts (in which neither party has performed) are enforceable, even if the agreement is made orally and even if the original agreement was in writing. Under the Uniform Commercial Code (UCC), however, agreements to rescind a sales contract must be in writing (or contained in an electronic record) when the contract requires a written rescission [UCC 2–209(2), (4)]. Agreements to rescind contracts involving transfers of realty also must be evidenced by a writing or record.

When one party has fully performed, an agreement to cancel the original contract normally will *not* be enforceable unless there is additional consideration. Because the performing party has received no consideration for the promise to call off the original bargain, additional consideration is necessary to support a rescission contract.

Discharge by Novation A contractual obligation may also be discharged through novation. A **novation** occurs when both of the parties to a contract agree to substitute a third party for one of the original parties. The requirements of a novation are as follows:

1. A previous valid obligation.
2. An agreement by all parties to a new contract.
3. The extinguishing of the old obligation (discharge of the prior party).
4. A new contract that is valid.

■ **EXAMPLE 11.23** Union Corporation contracts to sell its pharmaceutical division to British Pharmaceuticals, Ltd. Before the transfer is completed, Union, British Pharmaceuticals, and a third company, Otis Chemicals, execute a new agreement to transfer all of British Pharmaceuticals' rights and duties in the transaction to Otis Chemicals. As long as the new contract is supported by consideration, the novation will discharge the original contract (between Union and British Pharmaceuticals) and replace it with the new contract (between Union and Otis Chemicals). ■

A novation expressly or impliedly revokes and discharges a prior contract. The parties involved may expressly state in the new contract that the old contract is now discharged. If the parties do not expressly discharge the old contract, it will be impliedly discharged if the new contract's terms are inconsistent with the old contract's terms. It is this immediate discharge of the prior contract that distinguishes a novation from both an accord and satisfaction (discussed shortly) and an assignment of all rights.

Discharge by Settlement Agreement A compromise, or settlement agreement, that arises out of a genuine dispute over the obligations under an existing contract will be recognized at law. The agreement will be substituted as a new contract and will either expressly or impliedly revoke and discharge the obligations under the prior contract. In contrast to a novation, a substituted agreement does not involve a third party. Rather, the two original parties to the contract form a different agreement to substitute for the original one.

Discharge by Accord and Satisfaction In an accord and satisfaction, the parties agree to accept performance that is different from the performance originally promised. An *accord* is a contract to perform some act to satisfy an existing contractual duty that is not yet discharged. A *satisfaction* is the performance of the accord agreement. An accord and its satisfaction discharge the original contractual obligation.

Once the accord has been made, the original obligation is merely suspended until the accord agreement is fully performed. If it is not performed, the obligee (the one to whom performance is owed) can file a lawsuit based on either the original obligation or the accord. ■ **EXAMPLE 11.24** Felix has a judgment against Ling for $8,000. Later, both parties agree that the judgment can be satisfied by Ling's transfer of his automobile to Felix. This agreement to accept the auto in lieu of $8,000 in cash is the accord. If Ling transfers the car to Felix, the accord is fully performed, and the debt is discharged. If Ling refuses to transfer the car, the accord is breached. Because the original obligation was merely suspended, Felix can sue Ling to enforce the original judgment for $8,000 in cash or bring an action for breach of the accord. ■

11–3d Discharge by Operation of Law

Under specified circumstances, contractual duties may be discharged by operation of law. These circumstances include material alteration of the contract, the running of the statute of limitations, bankruptcy, and the impossibility or impracticability of performance.

Material Alteration of the Contract To discourage parties from altering written contracts, the law allows an innocent party to be discharged when the other party has materially altered a written contract without consent. For instance, suppose that a party alters a material term of a contract, such as the stated quantity or price, without the knowledge or consent of the other party. In this situation, the party who was unaware of the alteration can treat the contract as discharged.

Statutes of Limitations Statutes of limitations restrict the period during which a party can sue on a particular cause of action. After the applicable limitations period has passed, a suit can no longer be brought. The limitations period for bringing suits for breach of oral contracts usually is two to three years, and for written contracts, four to five years. Parties generally have ten to twenty years to file for recovery of amounts awarded in judgments, depending on state law.

Lawsuits for breach of a contract for the sale of goods usually must be brought within four years after the cause of action has accrued [UCC 2–725]. A cause of action for a sales contract generally accrues when the breach occurs, even if the aggrieved party is not aware of the breach. A breach of warranty normally occurs when the seller delivers the goods to the buyer. By their original agreement, the parties can reduce this four-year period to not less than one year, but they cannot agree to extend it.

Bankruptcy A proceeding in bankruptcy attempts to allocate the debtor's assets to the creditors in a fair and equitable fashion. Once the assets have been allocated, the debtor receives a **discharge in bankruptcy.** A discharge in bankruptcy ordinarily prevents the creditors from enforcing most of the debtor's contracts. Partial payment of a debt *after* discharge in bankruptcy will not revive the debt.

Impossibility of Performance After a contract has been made, supervening events (such as a fire) may make performance impossible in an objective sense. This is known as **impossibility of performance** and can discharge a contract. The doctrine of impossibility of performance applies only when the parties could not have reasonably foreseen, at the time the contract was formed, the event that rendered performance impossible. Performance may also become so difficult or costly due to some unforeseen event that a court will consider it commercially unfeasible, or impracticable, as will be discussed later in the chapter.

Objective impossibility ("It can't be done") must be distinguished from *subjective impossibility* ("I'm sorry, I simply can't do it"). An example of subjective impossibility occurs when a party cannot deliver goods on time because of freight car shortages or cannot make payment on time because the bank is closed. In effect, in each of these situations the party is saying, "It is impossible for *me* to perform," not "It is impossible for *anyone* to perform." Accordingly, such excuses do not discharge a contract, and the nonperforming party is normally held in breach of contract.

When Performance Is Impossible. Three basic types of situations may qualify as grounds for the discharge of contractual obligations based on impossibility of performance:[20]

1. *When one of the parties to a personal contract dies or becomes incapacitated prior to performance.* ■ **EXAMPLE 11.25** Frederic, a famous dancer, contracts with Ethereal Dancing Guild to play a leading role in its new ballet. Before the ballet can be performed, Frederic becomes ill and dies. His personal performance was essential to the completion of the contract. Thus, his death discharges the contract and his estate's liability for his nonperformance. ■

2. *When the specific subject matter of the contract is destroyed.* ■ **EXAMPLE 11.26** A-1 Farm Equipment agrees to sell Gunther the green tractor on its lot and promises to have the tractor ready for Gunther to pick up on Saturday. On Friday night, however, a truck veers off the nearby highway and smashes into the tractor, destroying it beyond repair. Because the contract was for this specific tractor, A-1's performance is rendered impossible owing to the accident. ■

3. *When a change in law renders performance illegal.* ■ **EXAMPLE 11.27** Hopper contracts with Playlist, Inc., to create a Web site through which users can post and share movies, music, and other forms of digital entertainment. Hopper goes to work. Before the site is operational, however, Congress passes the No Online Piracy in Entertainment (NOPE) Act. The NOPE Act makes it illegal to operate a Web site on which copyrighted works are posted without the copyright owners' consent. In this situation, the contract is discharged by operation of law. The purpose of the contract has been rendered illegal, and contract performance is objectively impossible. ■

The following case involved a financial institution participating in the federal Troubled Asset Relief Program (TARP). Could the institution assert TARP's prohibition on "golden parachute" payments as a defense to a breach of contract action brought by one of its former senior executive officers?

---

20. *Restatement (Second) of Contracts,* Sections 262–266; UCC 2–615.

Hampton Roads Bankshares, Inc. v. Harvard

Virginia Supreme Court, 291 Va. 42, 781 S.E.2d 172 (2016).

Background and Facts Scott Harvard was a senior executive officer of Hampton Roads Bankshares, Inc. (HRB), headquartered in Virginia Beach, Virginia. Harvard's employment contract included a "golden parachute"—a payment of approximately three times his average annual compensation if he quit.

In 2008, during the Great Recession, Congress enacted the Emergency Economic Stabilization Act (EESA) "to restore liquidity and stability to the financial system."[a] EESA included the Troubled Asset Relief Program (TARP), which allowed the government to buy "troubled assets" from financial institutions to promote market stability. TARP barred participating institutions from making golden parachute payments, defined as "any payment to a senior executive officer for departure from a company for any reason."

HRB participated in TARP. Later, Harvard quit the firm and filed a suit in a Virginia state court against HRB to obtain his golden parachute payment. The court ordered HRB to make the payment. HRB appealed to the Virginia Supreme Court.

In the Language of the Court

Opinion by Justice William C. *MIMS.*

 * * * *

The defense of impossibility of performance is an established principle of contract law. In Virginia, *it is well settled that where impossibility is due to domestic law, to the death or illness of one who by the terms of the contract was to do an act requiring his personal performance, or to the fortuitous destruction or change in the character of something to which the contract related, or which by the terms of the contract was made a necessary means of performance, the promisor will be excused, unless he either expressly agreed in the contract to assume the risk of performance, whether possible or not, or the impossibility was due to his fault.* [Emphasis added.]

Harvard does not dispute that EESA directly bars HRB from making the severance payment to Harvard upon the termination of his employment, because the payment falls within the definition of a prohibited "golden parachute payment." Moreover, Harvard does not suggest that HRB expressly agreed in the contract to assume the risk of performance, whether possible or not. Nor could he; the * * * Employment Agreement clearly places the risk of * * * the law regulating golden parachute payments on Harvard.

On December 31, 2008, Harvard agreed [with HRB to amend] the Employment Agreement [to provide that it] "will be interpreted, administered and construed to, comply with EESA."

By its plain language, the amended Employment Agreement must be read to comply with EESA. Nothing therein exempts the agreement from * * * EESA * * * or places the risk of performance * * * on HRB.

 * * * *

There is nothing in the record that would suggest HRB refused to make the golden parachute payment in bad faith. After Harvard terminated his employment, HRB sought guidance from [the U.S. Department of the] Treasury regarding its contractual obligation to make the disputed golden parachute payment, and whether it could perform that obligation in light of EESA. In response, Treasury provided informal guidance indicating that HRB could not make the payment and comply with EESA. Where, as here, the government has clearly expressed its intent to enforce the law, and the promisor cannot in good faith perform its contractual obligation without violating the law, the promisor is discharged from its obligation.

Decision and Remedy *The Virginia Supreme Court reversed the order of the lower court, which "erred when it ordered HRB to make the golden parachute payment despite the federal prohibition on such payments found in EESA." Under EESA, payment of the golden parachute would violate the law.*

Critical Thinking

- **Legal Environment** *What advantage does the discharge of a contractual obligation under the rule applied in this case offer to the contract's parties? Discuss.*
- **Ethical** *Did HRB violate any ethical duty by refusing to make Harvard's golden parachute payment? Explain.*

---

a. 12 U.S.C. Section 5201.

Temporary Impossibility. An occurrence or event that makes performance temporarily impossible operates to suspend performance until the impossibility ceases. Once the temporary event ends, the parties ordinarily must perform the contract as originally planned. ■ **EXAMPLE 11.28** Mindy and Lyn Carr contract to rent a sailboat from Key West Rentals for a month-long trip. The day before their trip is scheduled to begin, a hurricane hits the coast where the boat is docked, causing damage. The hurricane makes performance temporarily impossible, and the Carrs postpone their trip. Once the repairs are made to the dock and the boat, however, Key West Rentals would be required to perform the contract as originally planned. The Carrs have a right to rent the boat for a month for the previously agreed-on price. ■

Sometimes, the lapse of time and the change in circumstances surrounding the contract make it substantially more burdensome for the parties to perform the promised acts. In that situation, the contract is discharged. It can be difficult to predict how a court will—or should—rule on whether performance is impossible in a particular situation, as discussed in this chapter's *Ethics Today* feature.

Commercial Impracticability Courts may also excuse parties from their performance when it becomes much more difficult or expensive than the parties originally contemplated at the time the contract was formed.

For instance, a contract could be discharged because a party would otherwise have had to pay ten times more than the original estimate to perform the contract.

For someone to invoke the doctrine of **commercial impracticability** successfully, however, the anticipated performance must become *significantly* more difficult or costly.[21] In addition, the added burden of performing *must not have been foreseeable by the parties when the contract was made.*

Frustration of Purpose Closely allied with the doctrine of commercial impracticability is the doctrine of **frustration of purpose.** In principle, a contract will be discharged if supervening circumstances make it impossible to attain the purpose both parties had in mind when they made the contract. As with commercial impracticability and impossibility, the supervening event must not have been reasonably foreseeable at the time the contract was formed.

There are some differences between these doctrines, however. Commercial impracticability usually involves an event that increases the cost or difficulty of performance. In contrast, frustration of purpose typically involves an event that decreases the value of what a party receives under the contract.

---

21. *Restatement (Second) of Contracts*, Section 264.

ETHICS TODAY — When Is Impossibility of Performance a Valid Defense?

The doctrine of impossibility of performance is applied only when the parties could not have reasonably foreseen, at the time the contract was formed, the event or events that rendered performance impossible. In some cases, the courts may seem to go too far in holding that the parties should have foreseen certain events or conditions. Such a holding means that the parties cannot avoid their contractual obligations under the doctrine of impossibility of performance.

Actually, courts today are more likely to allow parties to raise this defense than were courts in the past, which rarely excused parties from performance under the impossibility doctrine. Indeed, until the latter part of the nineteenth century, courts were reluctant to

discharge a contract even when performance appeared to be impossible.

Generally, the courts must balance the freedom of parties to contract (and thereby assume the risks involved) against the injustice that may result when certain contractual obligations are enforced. If the courts allowed parties to raise impossibility of performance as a defense to contractual obligations more often, freedom of contract would suffer.

Critical Thinking *Why might those entering into contracts be worse off in the long run if the courts increasingly accepted impossibility of performance as a defense?*

Reviewing: Third Party Rights and Discharge

Val's Foods signs a contract to buy 1,500 pounds of basil from Sun Farms, a small organic herb grower, as long as an independent organization inspects the crop and certifies that it contains no pesticide or herbicide residue. Val's has a contract with several restaurant chains to supply pesto and intends to use Sun Farms' basil in the pesto to fulfill these contracts. While Sun Farms is preparing to harvest the basil, an unexpected hailstorm destroys half the crop. Sun Farms attempts to purchase additional basil from other farms, but it is late in the season, and the price is twice the normal market price. Sun Farms is too small to absorb this cost and immediately notifies Val's that it will not fulfill the contract. Using the information presented in the chapter, answer the following questions.

1. Suppose that the basil does not pass the chemical-residue inspection. Which concept discussed in the chapter might allow Val's to refuse to perform the contract in this situation?
2. Under which legal theory or theories might Sun Farms claim that its obligation under the contract has been discharged by operation of law? Discuss fully.
3. Suppose that Sun Farms contacts every basil grower in the country and buys the last remaining chemical-free basil anywhere. Nevertheless, Sun Farms is able to ship only 1,475 pounds to Val's. Would this fulfill Sun Farms' obligations to Val's? Why or why not?
4. Now suppose that Sun Farms sells its operations to Happy Valley Farms. As a part of the sale, all three parties agree that Happy Valley will provide the basil as stated under the original contract. What is this type of agreement called?

Debate This . . .   *The doctrine of commercial impracticability should be abolished.*

Terms and Concepts

alienation 209	condition precedent 215	incidental beneficiary 214
anticipatory repudiation 220	condition subsequent 216	intended beneficiary 212
assignee 208	delegatee 211	mutual rescission 221
assignment 208	delegation 208	novation 221
assignor 208	delegator 211	performance 215
breach of contract 218	discharge 215	privity of contract 208
commercial impracticability 224	discharge in bankruptcy 222	tender 217
concurrent conditions 216	frustration of purpose 224	third party beneficiary 212
condition 215	impossibility of performance 222	

Issue Spotters

1. Brian owes Jeff $100. Ed tells Brian to give him the $100 and he will pay Jeff. Brian gives Ed the $100. Ed never pays Jeff. Can Jeff successfully sue Ed for the $100? Why or why not? (See *Assignments and Delegations.*)
2. Ready Foods contracts to buy two hundred carloads of frozen pizzas from Stealth Distributors. Before Ready or Stealth starts performing, can the parties call off the deal? What if Stealth has already shipped the pizzas? Explain your answers. (See *Discharge by Performance.*)

- **Check your answers to the Issue Spotters against the answers provided in Appendix B at the end of this text.**

Business Scenarios

11–1. Assignment. Marsala, a college student, signs a one-year lease agreement that runs from September 1 to August 31. The lease agreement specifies that the lease cannot be assigned without the landlord's consent. In late May, Marsala decides not to go to summer school and assigns the balance of the lease (three months) to a close friend, Fred. The landlord objects to the assignment and denies Fred access to the apartment. Marsala claims that Fred is financially sound and should be allowed the full rights and privileges of an assignee. Discuss fully who is correct, the landlord or Marsala. (See *Assignments and Delegations.*)

11–2. Delegation. Inez has a specific set of plans to build a sailboat. The plans are detailed, and any boatbuilder can construct the boat. Inez secures bids, and the low bid is made by the Whale of a Boat Corp. Inez contracts with Whale to build the boat for $4,000. Whale then receives unexpected business from elsewhere. To meet the delivery date in the contract with Inez, Whale delegates its obligation to build the boat, without Inez's consent, to Quick Brothers, a reputable boatbuilder. When the boat is ready for delivery, Inez learns of the delegation and refuses to accept delivery, even though the boat is built to her specifications. Discuss fully whether Inez is obligated to accept and pay for the boat. Would your answer be any different if Inez had not had a specific set of plans but had instead contracted with Whale to design and build a sailboat for $4,000? Explain. (See *Assignments and Delegations.*)

Business Case Problems

11–3. Business Case Problem with Sample Answer—Third Party Beneficiary. David and Sandra Dess contracted with Sirva Relocation, LLC, to assist in selling their home. In their contract, the Desses agreed to disclose all information about the property on which Sirva "and other prospective buyers may rely in deciding whether and on what terms to purchase the Property." The Kincaids contracted with Sirva to buy the house. After the closing, they discovered dampness in the walls, defective and rotten windows, mold, and other undisclosed problems. Can the Kincaids bring an action against the Desses for breach of their contract with Sirva? Why or why not? [*Kincaid v. Dess,* 48 Kan.App.2d 640, 298 P.3d 358 (2013)] (See *Third Party Beneficiaries.*)

- For a sample answer to Problem 11–3, go to Appendix C at the end of this text.

11–4. Conditions of Performance. Russ Wyant owned Humble Ranch in Perkins County, South Dakota. Edward Humble, whose parents had previously owned the ranch, was Wyant's uncle. Humble held a two-year option to buy the ranch. The option included specific conditions. Once it was exercised, the parties had thirty days to enter into a purchase agreement, and the seller could become the buyer's lender by matching the terms of the proposed financing. After the option was exercised, the parties engaged in lengthy negotiations. Humble did not respond to Wyant's proposed purchase agreement nor advise him of available financing terms before the option expired, however. Six months later, Humble filed a suit against Wyant to enforce the option. Is Humble entitled to specific performance? Explain. [*Humble v. Wyant,* 843 N.W.2d 334 (S.Dak. 2014)] (See *Contract Discharge.*)

11–5. Discharge by Operation of Law. Dr. Jake Lambert signed an employment agreement with Baptist Health Services, Inc., to provide cardiothoracic surgery services to Baptist Memorial Hospital–North Mississippi, Inc., in Oxford, Mississippi. Complaints about Lambert's behavior arose almost immediately. He was evaluated by a team of doctors and psychologists, who diagnosed him as suffering from obsessive-compulsive personality disorder and concluded that he was unfit to practice medicine. Based on this conclusion, the hospital suspended his staff privileges. Citing the suspension, Baptist Health Services claimed that Lambert had breached his employment contract. What is Lambert's best defense to this claim? Explain. [*Baptist Memorial Hospital–North Mississippi, Inc. v. Lambert,* 157 So.3d 109 (Miss.App. 2015)] (See *Contract Discharge.*)

11–6. Third Party Beneficiaries. Randy Jones is an agent for Farmers Insurance Co. of Arizona. Through Jones, Robert and Marcia Murray obtained auto insurance with Farmers. On Jones's advice, the Murrays increased the policy's limits over the minimums required by the state of Arizona, except for uninsured/underinsured motorist coverage, for which Jones made no recommendation. Later, the Murrays' seventeen-year-old daughter, Jessyka, was in an accident that involved both an uninsured motorist and an underinsured motorist. She sustained a traumatic brain injury that permanently incapacitated her. Does Jessyka have standing to bring a claim against Jones and Farmers as a third party to her parents' contract for auto insurance? Explain. [*Lucas Contracting, Inc. v. Altisource Portfolio Solutions, Inc.,* __ N.E.2d __, 2016 -Ohio- 474 (Ohio App. 2016)] (See *Third Party Beneficiaries.*)

11–7. Conditions. H&J Ditching & Excavating, Inc., was hired by JRSF, LLC, to perform excavating and grading work on Terra Firma, a residential construction project in West Knox County, Tennessee. Cornerstone Community Bank financed the project with a loan to JRSF. As the work progressed, H&J received payments totaling 90 percent of the price on its contract. JRSF then defaulted on the loan from Cornerstone, and Cornerstone foreclosed and took possession of the property. H&J filed a suit in a Tennessee state court against the bank to recover the final payment on its contract. The bank responded that H&J had not received its payment because it had failed to obtain an engineer's certificate of final completion, a condition under its contract with JRSF. H&J responded that it had completed all the work it had contracted to do. What type of contract condition does obtaining the engineer's certificate represent? Is H&J entitled to the final payment? Discuss. [*H&J Ditching & Excavating, Inc. v. Cornerstone Community Bank,* __ S.W.3d __, 2016 WL 675554 (Tenn.App.—Knoxville 2016)] (See *Contract Discharge.*)

11–8. A Question of Ethics—Assignment and Delegation. *Premier Building & Development, Inc., entered into a listing agreement giving Sunset Gold Realty, LLC, the exclusive right to find a tenant for some commercial property. The terms of the listing agreement stated that it was binding on both parties and "their . . . assigns." Premier Building did not own the property at the time but had the option to purchase it. To secure financing for the project, Premier Building established a new company called Cobblestone Associates. Premier Building then bought the property and conveyed it to Cobblestone the same day. Meanwhile, Sunset Gold found a tenant for the property, and Cobblestone became the*

landlord. Cobblestone acknowledged its obligation to pay Sunset Gold for finding a tenant, but it later refused to pay Sunset Gold's commission. Sunset Gold then sued Premier Building and Cobblestone for breach of the listing agreement. [Sunset Gold Realty, LLC v. Premier Building & Development, Inc., *133 Conn. App. 445, 36 A.3d 243 (2012)*] (See *Assignments and Delegations.*)

(a) Is Premier Building relieved of its contractual duties if it assigned the contract to Cobblestone? Why or why not?

(b) Given that Sunset Gold performed its obligations under the listing agreement, did Cobblestone behave unethically in refusing to pay Sunset Gold's commission? Why or why not?

11–9. Special Case Analysis—Material Breach. Go to Case Analysis 11.2, *Kohel v. Bergen Auto Enterprises, L.L.C.* Read the excerpt, and answer the following questions.

(a) **Issue:** This case involved allegations of breach of contract involving which parties and for what actions?

(b) **Rule of Law:** What is the difference between a *material* breach and a *minor* breach of contract?

(c) **Applying the Rule of Law:** How did the court determine which party was in material breach of the contract in this case?

(d) **Conclusion:** Was the defendant liable for breach? Why or why not?

Legal Reasoning Group Activity

11–10. Anticipatory Repudiation. ABC Clothiers, Inc., has a contract with Taylor & Sons, a retailer, to deliver one thousand summer suits to Taylor's place of business on or before May 1. On April 1, Taylor receives a letter from ABC informing him that ABC will not be able to make the delivery as scheduled. Taylor is very upset, as he had planned a big ad campaign. (See *Contract Discharge.*)

(a) The first group will discuss whether Taylor can immediately sue ABC for breach of contract (on April 2).

(b) Now suppose that Taylor's son, Tom, tells his father that they cannot file a lawsuit until ABC actually fails to deliver the suits on May 1. The second group will decide who is correct, Taylor senior or Tom.

(c) Assume that Taylor & Sons can either file immediately or wait until ABC fails to deliver the goods. The third group will evaluate which course of action is better, given the circumstances.

CHAPTER 12

Breach of Contract and Remedies

When one party breaches a contract, the other party—the nonbreaching party—can choose one or more of several remedies. (Does changing terms of service on a social networking site constitute a breach of contract? See this chapter's *Digital Update* feature for a look at this issue.) A *remedy* is the relief provided for an innocent party when the other party has breached the contract. It is the means employed to enforce a right or to redress an injury.

The most common remedies available to a nonbreaching party include *damages, rescission* and *restitution, specific performance*, and *reformation*. Courts distinguish between *remedies at law* and *remedies in equity*. The remedy at law normally is monetary damages. Usually, a court will not award equitable remedies—such as rescission and restitution, specific performance, and reformation—unless the remedy at law is inadequate.

12-1 Damages

A breach of contract entitles the nonbreaching party to sue for monetary damages. In contract law, damages compensate the nonbreaching party for the loss of the bargain (whereas tort law damages compensate for harm suffered as a result of another's wrongful act). Often, courts say that innocent parties are to be placed in the position they would have occupied had the contract been fully performed.[1]

Realize at the outset, though, that collecting damages through a court judgment requires litigation, which can be expensive and time consuming. Also keep in mind that court judgments are often difficult to enforce, particularly if the breaching party does not have sufficient assets to pay the damages awarded. For these reasons, most parties settle their lawsuits for damages (or other remedies) prior to trial.

12-1a Types of Damages

There are four broad categories of damages:

1. Compensatory (to cover direct losses and costs).
2. Consequential (to cover indirect and foreseeable losses).

3. Punitive (to punish and deter wrongdoing).
4. Nominal (to recognize wrongdoing when no monetary loss is shown).

Compensatory and punitive damages were discussed in the context of tort law. Here, we look at these types of damages, as well as consequential and nominal damages, in the context of contract law.

Compensatory Damages Damages that compensate the nonbreaching party for the *loss of the bargain* are known as *compensatory damages*. These damages compensate the injured party only for damages actually sustained and proved to have arisen directly from the loss of the bargain caused by the breach of contract. They simply replace what was lost because of the wrong or damage and, for this reason, are often said to "make the person whole."

■ **CASE IN POINT 12.1** Janet Murley was the vice president of marketing at Hallmark Cards, Inc., until Hallmark eliminated her position as part of a corporate restructuring. Murley and Hallmark entered into a separation agreement under which she agreed not to work in the greeting card industry for eighteen months and not to disclose or use any of Hallmark's confidential information. In exchange, Hallmark gave Murley a $735,000 severance payment.

---

1. *Restatement (Second) of Contracts,* Section 347.

When Do Changes in Social Media Terms of Service Constitute a Breach of Contract?

Hundreds of millions of individuals use some form of social media. To do so, they must agree to certain terms of service.

The Terms of Service Are a Contract

When you use social media or other services on the Internet or download an app for a mobile device, you normally have to indicate that you accept the terms of service associated with that service or app. Of course, users rarely, if ever, actually read those terms. They simply click on "accept" and start using the service. By clicking on "accept," however, those users are entering into a contract.

Instagram Changes Its Terms of Service

A few years ago, Instagram changed its terms of service to give it the right to transfer and otherwise use content placed on the site by users. The new terms appeared to allow Instagram to do this without compensating users. The terms also limited users' ability to bring class-action lawsuits against Instagram, limited the damages they could recover to $100, and required arbitration of any disputes.

Lucy Funes, an Instagram user in California, filed a class-action lawsuit against Instagram on behalf of herself and other users.[a] The suit claimed breach of contract and breach of the covenant of good faith and fair dealing that a contract implies. Instagram subsequently modified the language that appeared to give it the right to use photos without compensation. It retained other controversial terms, however, including the mandatory arbitration clause and a provision allowing it to place ads in conjunction with user content.

a. *Funes v. Instagram, Inc.*, 3:12-CV06482-WHA (N.D.Cal. 2012). See also *Rodriguez v. Instagram, LLC*, 2013 WL 3732883 (N.D.Cal. 2013).

Instagram Seeks Dismissal of the Lawsuit

Funes contended that Instagram had breached their contract by changing its terms of service. Instagram argued that Funes could not claim breach of contract. The reason was that she—and other users—had been given thirty days' notice before the new terms of service took effect. Because Funes continued to use her account after that thirty-day period, Instagram maintained, in effect, she agreed to the new terms.

Instagram Changes Its Policies

Instagram continues to use its revised terms of service agreement. As mentioned, it abandoned some of its previous changes and denied any intention to sell user content. In the terms of service, Instagram states that it does "not claim ownership of any content user's post on or through the service."

Nonetheless, the terms state clearly that each user "hereby grants to Instagram a non-exclusive, fully paid and royalty-free, transferable, sublicensable, worldwide license to use content that the user posts." That means that Instagram can reassign the rights or relicense the work to any other party for free or for a fee. The user—anyone who posts on Instagram—need not be compensated or even given notice.

Critical Thinking *Within Instagram's current terms of service is the following statement: "we may not always identify paid services, sponsored content, or commercial communications as such." Is it ethical for Instagram to post advertisements without identifying them as advertisements? Discuss.*

After eighteen months, Murley took a job with Recycled Paper Greetings (RPG) for $125,000 and disclosed confidential Hallmark information to RPG. Hallmark sued for breach of contract and won. The jury awarded $860,000 in damages (the $735,000 severance payment and $125,000 that Murley received from RPG). Murley appealed. The appellate court held that Hallmark was entitled only to the return of the $735,000 severance payment. Hallmark was not entitled to the other $125,000 because that additional award would have left Hallmark better off than if Murley had not breached the contract.[2] ■

There is a two-step process to determine whether a breach of contract has resulted in compensable damages. First, it must be established that there was a contract between the parties and a breach of that contract. Next, it must be proved that the breach caused damages. The following case concerned the second step of this process.

2. *Hallmark Cards, Inc. v. Murley*, 703 F.3d 456 (8th Cir. 2013).

Baird v. Owens Community College

Court of Appeals of Ohio, Tenth District, Franklin County, __ N.E.2d __, 2016 -Ohio- 537 (2016).

In the Language of the Court

BRUNNER, J. [Judge]

* * * *

[Carrianne Baird and the other sixty-one] plaintiffs-appellants * * * are former students in the registered nursing program of defendant-appellee, Owens Community College. The college lost its accreditation from the National League for Nursing Accreditation Commission ("NLNAC") in 2009.[a] The program remains approved by the Ohio Board of Nursing, which permits successful graduates to take the National Council Licensure Examination ("NCLEX") for their nursing license. Although the college received notice via a letter dated July 27, 2009 that the accreditation had been denied, it did not formally notify its students until it issued a letter on September 26, 2009, after classes for the fall semester already had begun. The appellants sued [in an Ohio state court] for breach of contract.

* * * The court [did not determine whether there was a contract between the college and the students or whether such a contract was breached by the loss of accreditation, but only] concluded that the loss of accreditation did not affect the students' ability to take the state licensing examination, and therefore that appellants suffered no actual damages from the alleged breach of contract. [The court issued a summary judgment in favor of the college.]

* * * *

On appeal from the summary judgment against them, appellants [contend that] the trial court erred when it granted the Motion for Summary Judgment of the Defendant-Appellee because the evidence creates a genuine issue of material fact as to whether Appellee's breach of the contract caused damages.

* * * *

---

a. In 2013, the NLNAC changed its name and is now known as the Accreditation Commission for Education in Nursing.

After the appellee lost its NLNAC accreditation graduates feared that they would face barriers to licensing, employment or further education in their field. Some programs, including The Ohio State University RN [registered nursing] to BSN [bachelor of science in nursing] option, would accept only nurses who received an associate's degree or diploma in nursing from an institution with NLNAC accreditation. In support of their allegations of damages, appellants submitted the * * * testimony of various "sample plaintiffs." * * * Carianne Baird stated that she could not attend the University of Toledo's RN to MSN [master of science in nursing] program without submitting a "portfolio" that would not have been required if appellee had maintained its accreditation. Other institutions would not accept her for continuing nursing education because her associate's degree is not from an NLNAC accredited institution.

Kelsey Darbyshire testified * * * that Lima Memorial Hospital required applicants to have graduated from an accredited nursing school. She indicated on her application that she did not graduate from an accredited program, and had no response. Miracle Huffman * * * applied to the U.S. Department of Veterans Affairs for psychiatric nurse practitioner positions and has received no response. She testified that the Veterans Affairs requires an NLNAC accredited degree, and she does not have it.

* * * *

* * * None of the appellants submitted sufficient evidence of economic damages based on their rejection from specific employment or a higher degree program. *However, a claimant's inability to demonstrate a specific denial of employment due to the program's loss of accreditation does not defeat damages on account of lost earning capacity * * *. The measure of damages for impairment of earning capacity is the difference between the amount*

which the plaintiff was capable of earning before his injury and that which he is capable of earning thereafter. The claimant must offer sufficient proof of any future impairment and also sufficient evidence of the extent of prospective damages flowing from the impairment. In order to recover for impaired earning capacity, the plaintiff must prove by sufficient evidence that he is reasonably certain to incur such damages in the future. * * * The [lower] court * * * should have considered whether each of the appellants suffered impaired earning capacity or other compensable damages and what those damages would be to place them in the same position that they would have enjoyed if appellee had performed its contract. [Emphasis added.]

Since there exists a genuine issue of material fact concerning damages, the [lower] court * * * must also determine, in addition to whether any appellant can prove diminished earning capacity, whether any appellant produced sufficient evidence that appellee breached its contract with her or him.

When a student enrolls in a college or university, pays his or her tuition and fees, and attends such school, the resulting relationship may reasonably be construed as being contractual in nature. The terms of such a contract may be found in the college or university catalog, handbook, and/or other guidelines supplied to the students.

On the first page of the registered nursing section of the course book appellee provided to students, appellee listed its NLNAC accreditation foremost, and according to appellants, providing an NLNAC accredited education was part and parcel of appellee's "deal" with each of them. By contrast, appellee urges that a text box in another part of the course book contains a disclaimer for changes in circumstance, stating that it "reserves the right to modify rules, policies, fees, program requirements, course scheduling and courses offered during any specific semester, and any other matter, without notice."

Appellee submits that summary judgment should be affirmed on the * * * basis that this language effectively excludes the loss of NLNAC accreditation from the contractual relationship between it and its students. Without more evidence, or a more explicit disclaimer, we find that genuine issues remain to preclude summary judgment.

* * * *

* * * We remand this matter to the [lower] court * * * to ascertain as to each of the appellants whether the appellant has offered sufficient evidence to avoid summary judgment on whether appellee has breached its contract to her or him in losing its NLNAC accreditation, and if such a breach is determined from the evidence, whether she or he has set forth sufficient evidence to create a material issue of fact in support of a claim for diminished earning capacity.

Legal Reasoning Questions

1. In this case, what was the basis for the students' suit?

2. What was the college's argument against the students' allegations?

3. In whose favor did the court rule? Why? What remains to be determined?

Standard Measure. The standard measure of compensatory damages is the difference between the value of the breaching party's promised performance under the contract and the value of her or his actual performance. This amount is reduced by any loss that the injured party has avoided.

■ **EXAMPLE 12.2** Randall contracts to perform certain services exclusively for Hernandez during the month of March for $4,000. Hernandez cancels the contract and is in breach. Randall is able to find another job during March but can earn only $3,000. He can sue Hernandez for breach and recover $1,000 as compensatory damages. Randall can also recover from Hernandez the amount that he spent to find the other job. ■ Expenses that are caused directly by a breach of contract—such as those incurred to obtain performance from another source—are known as **incidental damages.**

Note that the measure of compensatory damages often varies by type of contract. Certain types of contracts deserve special mention.

Sale of Goods. In a contract for the sale of goods, the usual measure of compensatory damages is an amount equal to the difference between the contract price and the market price.[3] ■ **EXAMPLE 12.3** Medik Laboratories contracts to buy ten model UTS network servers from Cal Industries for $4,000 each. Cal Industries, however, fails to deliver the ten servers to Medik. The market price of the servers at the time Medik learns of the breach is $4,500. Therefore, Medik's measure of damages is $5,000 (10 × $500), plus any incidental damages (expenses) caused by the breach. ■

Sometimes, the buyer breaches when the seller has not yet produced the goods. In that situation, compensatory damages normally equal lost profits on the sale, not the difference between the contract price and the market price.

Sale of Land. Ordinarily, because each parcel of land is unique, the remedy for a seller's breach of a contract for a sale of real estate is specific performance. That is, the buyer is awarded the parcel of property for which she or he bargained. (*Specific performance* will be discussed more fully later in this chapter.) The majority of states follow this rule.

When the *buyer* is the party in breach, the measure of damages is typically the difference between the contract price and the market price of the land. The same measure is used when specific performance is not available (because the seller has sold the property to someone else, for example).

A minority of states apply a different rule when the seller breaches the contract and the breach is not deliberate (intentional).[4] These states limit the prospective buyer's damages to a refund of any down payment made plus any expenses incurred (such as fees for title searches, attorneys, and escrows). Thus, the minority rule

---

3. More specifically, the amount is the difference between the contract price and the market price at the time and place at which the goods were to be delivered or tendered. See Sections 2–708 and 2–713 of the Uniform Commercial Code (UCC).

4. "Deliberate" breaches include the seller's failure to convey (transfer title to) the land because the market price has gone up. "Nondeliberate" breaches include the seller's failure to convey the land because of a problem with the title. For instance, the discovery of an unknown easement that gives another party a right of use over the property would be a problem with the title.

effectively returns purchasers to the positions they occupied prior to the sale, rather than giving them the benefit of the bargain.

Construction Contracts. The measure of damages in a building or construction contract varies depending on which party breaches and when the breach occurs.

1. *Breach by owner.* The owner may breach at three different stages—before, during, or after performance. If the owner breaches *before performance has begun,* the contractor can recover only the profits that would have been made on the contract. (Profits equal the total contract price less the cost of materials and labor.) If the owner breaches *during performance,* the contractor can recover the profits plus the costs incurred in partially constructing the building. If the owner breaches *after the construction has been completed,* the contractor can recover the entire contract price, plus interest.

2. *Breach by contractor.* When the construction contractor breaches the contract—either by failing to begin construction or by stopping work partway through the project—the measure of damages is the cost of completion. The cost of completion includes reasonable compensation for any delay in performance. If the contractor finishes late, the measure of damages is the loss of use.

3. *Breach by both owner and contractor.* When the performance of both parties—the construction contractor and the owner—falls short of what their contract required, the courts attempt to strike a fair balance in awarding damages.

■ **CASE IN POINT 12.4** Jamison Well Drilling, Inc., contracted to drill a well for Ed Pfeifer for $4,130. Jamison drilled the well and installed a storage tank. The well did not comply with state health department requirements, however, and failed repeated tests for bacteria. The health department ordered the well to be abandoned and sealed. Pfeifer used the storage tank but paid Jamison nothing. Jamison filed a suit to recover. The court held that Jamison was entitled to $970 for the storage tank but was not entitled to the full contract price because the well was not usable.[5] ■

The rules concerning the measurement of damages in breached construction contracts are summarized in Exhibit 12–1.

Consequential Damages Foreseeable damages that result from a party's breach of contract are called **consequential damages,** or *special damages.* They differ from compensatory damages in that they are caused by special circumstances beyond the contract itself. They flow from the

---

5. *Jamison Well Drilling, Inc. v. Pfeifer,* 2011 -Ohio- 521 (2011).

EXHIBIT 12–1 Measurement of Damages—Breach of Construction Contracts

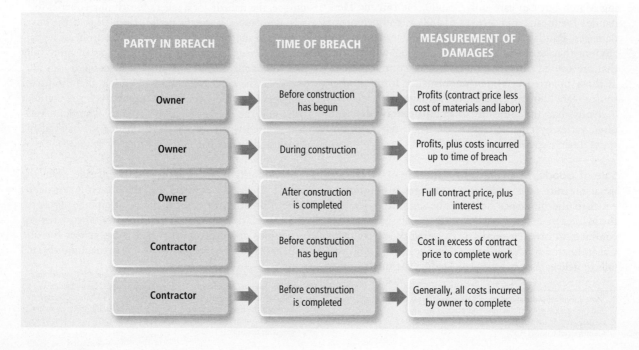

PARTY IN BREACH	TIME OF BREACH	MEASUREMENT OF DAMAGES
Owner	Before construction has begun	Profits (contract price less cost of materials and labor)
Owner	During construction	Profits, plus costs incurred up to time of breach
Owner	After construction is completed	Full contract price, plus interest
Contractor	Before construction has begun	Cost in excess of contract price to complete work
Contractor	Before construction is completed	Generally, all costs incurred by owner to complete

consequences, or results, of a breach. When a seller fails to deliver goods, knowing that the buyer is planning to use or resell those goods immediately, a court may award consequential damages for the loss of profits from the planned resale.

■ **EXAMPLE 12.5**   Marty contracts to buy a certain quantity of Quench, a specialty sports drink, from Nathan. Nathan knows that Marty has contracted with Ruthie to resell and ship the Quench within hours of its receipt. The beverage will then be sold to fans attending the Super Bowl. Nathan fails to deliver the Quench on time. Marty can recover the consequential damages—the loss of profits from the planned resale to Ruthie—caused by the nondelivery. (If Marty purchases Quench from another vender, he can also recover compensatory damages for any difference between the contract price and the market price.) ■

For the nonbreaching party to recover consequential damages, the breaching party must have known (or had reason to know) that special circumstances would cause the nonbreaching party to suffer an additional loss.[6]

Punitive Damages   Punitive damages are very seldom awarded in lawsuits for breach of contract. Because punitive damages are designed to punish a wrongdoer and set an example to deter similar conduct in the future, they have no legitimate place in contract law. A contract is simply a civil relationship between the parties. The law may compensate one party for the loss of the bargain—no more and no less. When a person's actions cause both a breach of contract and a tort (such as fraud), however, punitive damages may be available.

Nominal Damages   When no actual damage or financial loss results from a breach of contract and only a technical injury is involved, the court may award **nominal damages** to the innocent party. Awards of nominal damages are often small, such as one dollar, but they do establish that the defendant acted wrongfully. Most lawsuits for nominal damages are brought as a matter of principle under the theory that a breach has occurred and some damages must be imposed regardless of actual loss.

■ **EXAMPLE 12.6**   Jackson contracts to buy potatoes from Stanley at fifty cents a pound. Stanley breaches the contract and does not deliver the potatoes. In the meantime, the price of potatoes has fallen. Jackson is able to buy them in the open market at half the price he contracted for with Stanley. He is clearly better off

because of Stanley's breach. Thus, because Jackson sustained only a technical injury and suffered no monetary loss, he is likely to be awarded only nominal damages if he brings a suit for breach of contract. ■

12–1b Mitigation of Damages

In most situations, when a breach of contract occurs, the innocent injured party is held to a duty to mitigate, or reduce, the damages that he or she suffers. Under this doctrine of **mitigation of damages,** the duty owed depends on the nature of the contract.

Rental Agreements   Some states require a landlord to use reasonable means to find a new tenant if a tenant abandons the premises and fails to pay rent. If an acceptable tenant is found, the landlord is required to lease the premises to this tenant to mitigate the damages recoverable from the former tenant.

The former tenant is still liable for the difference between the amount of the rent under the original lease and the rent received from the new tenant. If the landlord has not taken reasonable steps to find a new tenant, a court will likely reduce any award made by the amount of rent the landlord could have received had he or she done so.

Employment Contracts   In the majority of states, a person whose employment has been wrongfully terminated owes a duty to mitigate the damages that he or she suffered. In other words, a wrongfully terminated employee has a duty to take a similar job if one is available.

If the employee fails to mitigate, the damages awarded will be equivalent to the person's former salary less the income he or she would have received in a similar job obtained by reasonable means. The employer has the burden of proving that such a job existed and that the employee could have been hired. Normally, the employee is under no duty to take a job of a different type and rank.

12–1c Liquidated Damages versus Penalties

A **liquidated damages** provision in a contract specifies that a certain dollar amount is to be paid in the event of a *future* default or breach of contract. (*Liquidated* means determined, settled, or fixed.)

Liquidated damages differ from penalties. Like liquidated damages, a **penalty** specifies a certain amount to be paid in the event of a default or breach of contract.

---

6. This rule was first enunciated in *Hadley v. Baxendale,* 156 Eng.Rep. 145 (1854).

Unlike liquidated damages, it is designed to penalize the breaching party, not to make the innocent party whole.

Liquidated damages provisions usually are enforceable. In contrast, if a court finds that a provision calls for a penalty, the agreement as to the amount will not be enforced. Recovery will be limited to actual damages.

Enforceability To determine if a particular provision is for liquidated damages or for a penalty, a court must answer two questions:

1. When the contract was entered into, was it apparent that damages would be difficult to estimate in the event of a breach?
2. Was the amount set as damages a reasonable estimate and not excessive?[7]

If the answers to both questions are yes, the provision normally will be enforced. If either answer is no, the provision usually will not be enforced.

In the following *Spotlight Case,* the court had to decide whether a clause in a contract was an enforceable liquidated damages provision or an unenforceable penalty.

---

7. *Restatement (Second) of Contracts,* Section 356(1).

Spotlight on Liquidated Damages

Case 12.2 Kent State University v. Ford
Court of Appeals of Ohio, Eleventh District, Portage County, 26 N.E.3d 868, 2015 -Ohio- 41 (2015).

Background and Facts Gene Ford signed a five-year contract with Kent State University in Ohio to work as the head coach for the men's basketball team. The contract provided that if Ford quit before the end of the term, he would pay liquidated damages to the school. The amount was to equal his salary ($300,000) multiplied by the number of years remaining on the contract. Laing Kennedy, Kent State's athletic director, told Ford that the contract would be renegotiated within a few years. Four years before the contract expired, however, Ford left Kent State and began to coach for Bradley University at an annual salary of $700,000. Kent State filed a suit in an Ohio state court against Ford, alleging breach of contract. The court enforced the liquidated damages clause and awarded the university $1.2 million. Ford appealed, arguing that the liquidated damages clause in his employment contract was an unenforceable penalty.

In the Language of the Court
Diane V. GRENDELL, J. [Judge]
* * * *

* * * The parties agreed on an amount of damages, stated in clear terms in Ford's * * * employment contract. * * * *It is apparent that such damages were difficult, if not impossible, to determine.* * * * The departure of a university's head basketball coach may result in a decrease in ticket sales, impact the ability to successfully recruit players and community support for the team, and require a search for both a new coach and additional coaching staff. Many of these damages cannot be easily measured or proven. This is especially true given the nature of how such factors may change over the course of different coaches' tenures with a sports program or team. [Emphasis added.]
* * * *

* * * Kennedy's statements to Ford that the contract would be renegotiated within a few years made it clear that Kent State desired Ford to have long-term employment, which was necessary to establish the stability in the program that would benefit recruitment, retention of assistant coaching staff, and community participation and involvement. The breach of the contract impacted all of these areas.
* * * *

Regarding the alleged unreasonableness of the damages, * * * based on the record, we find that the damages were reasonable. * * * Finding a coach of a similar skill and experience level as Ford, which was gained based partially on the investment of Kent State in his development, would have an increased cost. This is evident from the fact that Ford was able to more than double his yearly salary when hired

Case 12.2 Continued

by Bradley University. The salary Ford earned at Bradley shows the loss of market value in coaching experienced by Kent State, $400,000 per year, for four years. Although this may not have been known at the time the contract was executed, it could have been anticipated, and was presumably why Kent State wanted to renegotiate the contract * * * . There was also an asserted decrease in ticket sales, costs associated with the trips for the coaching search, and additional potential sums that may be expended.
* * * *

As discussed extensively above, there was justification for seeking liquidated damages to compensate for Kent State's losses, and, thus, there was a valid compensatory purpose for including the clause. * * * Given all of the circumstances and facts in this case, and the consideration of the factors above, we cannot find that the liquidated damages clause was a penalty. [Emphasis added.]

Decision and Remedy *A state intermediate appellate court affirmed the lower court's award. At the time Ford's contract was entered into, ascertaining the damages resulting from a breach was "difficult, if not impossible." The court found, "based on the record, . . . that the damages were reasonable." Thus, the clause was not a penalty—it had "a valid compensatory purpose."*

Critical Thinking
- **Cultural** *How does a college basketball team's record of wins and losses, and its ranking in its conference, support the court's decision in this case?*

Liquidated Damages Common in Certain Contracts Liquidated damages provisions are frequently used in construction contracts. For instance, a provision requiring a construction contractor to pay $300 for every day he or she is late in completing the project is a liquidated damages provision. Such provisions are also common in contracts for the sale of goods.[8] In addition, contracts with entertainers and professional athletes often include liquidated damages provisions.

12–2 Equitable Remedies

Sometimes, damages are an inadequate remedy for a breach of contract. In these situations, the nonbreaching party may ask the court for an equitable remedy. Equitable remedies include rescission and restitution, specific performance, and reformation.

12–2a Rescission and Restitution

Rescission is essentially an action to undo, or terminate, a contract—to return the contracting parties to the

positions they occupied prior to the transaction.[9] When fraud, a mistake, duress, undue influence, misrepresentation, or lack of capacity to contract is present, unilateral rescission is available. Rescission may also be available by statute.[10] The failure of one party to perform entitles the other party to rescind the contract. The rescinding party must give prompt notice to the breaching party.

Restitution Generally, to rescind a contract, both parties must make **restitution** to each other by returning goods, property, or funds previously conveyed.[11] If the property or goods can be returned, they must be. If the goods or property have been consumed, restitution must be made in an equivalent dollar amount.

Essentially, restitution involves the plaintiff's recapture of a benefit conferred on the defendant that has unjustly enriched her or him. ■ **EXAMPLE 12.7** Katie contracts with Mikhail to design a house for her. Katie pays Mikhail $9,000 and agrees to make two more payments of $9,000 (for a total of $27,000) as the design progresses. The next day, Mikhail calls Katie and tells

---

8. Section 2–718(1) of the UCC specifically authorizes the use of liquidated damages provisions.

9. The rescission discussed here is unilateral rescission, in which only one party wants to undo the contract. In mutual rescission, both parties agree to undo the contract. Mutual rescission discharges the contract. Unilateral rescission generally is available as a remedy for breach of contract.

10. Many states have statutes allowing individuals who enter "home solicitation contracts" to rescind those contracts within three business days for any reason. See, for example, California Civil Code Section 1689.5.

11. *Restatement (Second) of Contracts*, Section 370.

her that he has taken a position with a large architectural firm in another state and cannot design the house. Katie decides to hire another architect that afternoon. Katie can obtain restitution of the $9,000. ■

Restitution Is Not Limited to Rescission Cases
Restitution may be appropriate when a contract is rescinded, but the right to restitution is not limited to rescission cases. Because an award of restitution basically returns something to its rightful owner, a party can seek restitution in actions for breach of contract, tort actions, and other types of actions.

Restitution can be obtained, for instance, when funds or property have been transferred by mistake or because of fraud or incapacity. Similarly, restitution may be available when there has been misconduct by a party in a confidential or other special relationship. Even in criminal cases, a court can order restitution of funds or property obtained through embezzlement, conversion, theft, or copyright infringement.

As mentioned, one of the bases that a court may use to order the rescission of a contract is fraud. That was the ground for the order of rescission in the following case.

Case 12.3

Clara Wonjung Lee, DDS, Ltd. v. Robles
Appellate Court of Illinois, First District, 2014 WL 976776 (2014).

Background and Facts Clara Lee agreed to buy Rosalina Robles's dental practice and to lease her dental offices in Chicago, Illinois. The price was $267,000, with $133,500 allocated to goodwill—that is, the market value of the business's good reputation. After Lee took over the practice, *Chicago Magazine* and other local media revealed that Gary Kimmel, one of Robles's dentists, had illegally treated underage prostitutes in the practice's offices after hours. The media reported that Kimmel was under investigation by federal officials for this and other activities.

Lee filed a suit in an Illinois state court against Robles, seeking to rescind the contract. Lee alleged that Robles had deliberately withheld the information about Kimmel and that this information "adversely impacted the desirability and economic value of the practice." The court ruled in Lee's favor and awarded rescission and damages, which included the purchase price less Lee's unpaid rent and a portion of her income during her ownership of the practice. Robles appealed.

In the Language of the Court
Justice LIU delivered the judgment of the court:
* * * *

Section 6 of the Purchase Agreement required that Dr. Robles, as "seller, shall disclose to Dr. Lee, any material or significant information and/or charges that have occurred in the practice, (including but not limited to any pending litigation, actions, threatened actions by the Illinois State Board of Dental Examiners, or from any other governmental agency that materially alter the desirability or economic potential of the assets) up to the time of the date of transfer." *The question then was whether Dr. Robles had a duty to disclose the information she had about Dr. Kimmel's activities and the federal investigation to Dr. Lee.* Defendants offered no evidence to rebut the testimony of both Dr. Lee and [Bruce Lowery, a business appraiser], who indicated that such information would have been material to a reasonable dentist's decision to purchase the practice. Based on such evidence, we agree with the trial court's holding that information about Dr. Kimmel's activities and his association with the practice was material to Dr. Lee's decision to acquire the practice and to enter into the loan, and that Dr. Robles had a duty to disclose it to Dr. Lee under section 6 of the Purchase Agreement. [Emphasis added.]

* * * Defendants' actions were purposeful and not the result of any mistake or accident. Dr. Robles' nondisclosure was designed to prevent plaintiffs from gaining relevant information that may have caused them to not proceed with the sale transaction.

* * * Here, the trial judge had the opportunity to assess the credibility of the witnesses and to weigh the evidence presented at trial. In doing so, he concluded that Dr. Robles had knowledge of the investigations involving Dr. Kimmel's illicit use of the dental practice and that she deliberately withheld the information from Dr. Lee. Despite evidence that she had been interviewed by the FBI and by *Chicago*

Case 12.3 Continued

Magazine about Dr. Kimmel's activities, Dr. Robles testified that she was unaware of the nature of such activities. The * * * court characterized Dr. Robles' testimony as "incredible." We hold that no opposite conclusion is clearly evident from the record.

Accordingly, we find that the * * * court's judgment was consistent with the manifest weight of the evidence presented at trial.

Decision and Remedy *A state intermediate court affirmed the lower court's award of rescission and damages. Robles's nondisclosure was "designed to prevent Lee from gaining relevant information" that "would have been material to a reasonable dentist's decision to purchase the practice."*

Critical Thinking

- **Legal Environment** *When rescission is awarded, what is the measure of recovery? What did the recovery include in this case?*

12–2b Specific Performance

The equitable remedy of **specific performance** calls for the performance of the act promised in the contract. This remedy is attractive to a nonbreaching party because it provides the exact bargain promised in the contract. It also avoids some of the problems inherent in a suit for damages, such as collecting a judgment and arranging another contract. In addition, the actual performance may be more valuable than the monetary damages.

Normally, however, specific performance will not be granted unless the party's legal remedy (monetary damages) is inadequate.[12] For this reason, contracts for the sale of goods rarely qualify for specific performance. The legal remedy—monetary damages—is ordinarily adequate in such situations because substantially identical goods can be bought or sold in the market. Only if the goods are unique will a court grant specific performance. For instance, paintings, sculptures, or rare books or coins are so unique that monetary damages will not enable a buyer to obtain substantially identical substitutes in the market.

Sale of Land A court may grant specific performance to a buyer in an action for a breach of contract involving the sale of land. In this situation, the legal remedy of monetary damages may not compensate the buyer adequately. After all, every parcel of land is unique: the same land in the same location obviously cannot be obtained elsewhere. Only when specific performance is unavailable (such as when the seller has sold the property to someone else) will monetary damages be awarded instead.

A seller of land can also seek specific performance of the contract. ■ **CASE IN POINT 12.8** Developer Charles

Ghidorzi formed Crabtree Ridge, LLC, for the sole purpose of purchasing twenty-three acres of vacant land from Cohan Lipp, LLC. Crabtree signed a contract agreeing to pay $3.1 million for the land, which would be developed and paid for in three phases. When an environmental survey showed that the land might contain some wetlands that could not be developed, Crabtree backed out of the deal. Lipp sued Crabtree for breach of contract, seeking specific performance. The court held that Lipp was entitled to specific performance of the land-sale contract.[13] ■

Contracts for Personal Services Contracts for personal services require one party to work personally for another party. Courts generally refuse to grant specific performance of personal-service contracts. One reason is that to order a party to perform personal services against his or her will amounts to a type of involuntary servitude.[14]

Moreover, the courts do not want to monitor contracts for personal services, which usually require the exercise of personal judgment or talent. ■ **EXAMPLE 12.9** Nicole contracts with a surgeon to perform surgery to remove a tumor on her brain. If he refuses, the court would not compel (nor would Nicole want) the surgeon to perform under those circumstances. A court cannot ensure meaningful performance in such a situation.[15] ■

---

12. *Restatement (Second) of Contracts*, Section 359.

13. *Cohan Lipp, LLC v. Crabtree Ridge, LLC*, 358 Wis.2d 711, 856 N.W.2d 346 (2014).
14. Involuntary servitude, or slavery, is contrary to the public policy expressed in the Thirteenth Amendment to the U.S. Constitution. A court can, however, enter an order (injunction) prohibiting a person who breached a personal-service contract from engaging in similar contracts for a period of time in the future.
15. Similarly, courts often refuse to order specific performance of construction contracts because courts are not set up to operate as construction supervisors or engineers.

12–2c Reformation

Reformation is an equitable remedy used when the parties have *imperfectly* expressed their agreement in writing. Reformation allows a court to rewrite the contract to reflect the parties' true intentions.

Exhibit 12–2 graphically summarizes the remedies, including reformation, that are available to the nonbreaching party.

Fraud or Mutual Mistake Is Present Courts order reformation most often when fraud or mutual mistake (such as a clerical error) is present. Typically, a party seeks reformation so that some other remedy may then be pursued.

Written Contract Incorrectly States the Parties' Oral Agreement A court will also reform a contract when two parties enter into a binding oral contract but later make an error when they attempt to put the terms into writing. Normally, a court will allow into evidence the correct terms of the oral contract, thereby reforming the written contract.

Covenants Not to Compete Courts also may reform contracts that contain a written covenant not to compete. Such covenants are often included in contracts for the sale of ongoing businesses and in employment contracts. The agreements restrict the area and time in which one party can directly compete with the other party.

A covenant not to compete may be for a valid and legitimate purpose, but may impose unreasonable area or time restraints. In such instances, some courts will reform the restraints by making them reasonable and will then enforce the entire contract as reformed. Other courts will throw out the entire restrictive covenant as illegal. Thus, when businesspersons create restrictive covenants, they must make sure that the restrictions imposed are reasonable.

■ **CASE IN POINT 12.10** Cardiac Study Center, Inc., a medical practice group, hired Dr. Robert Emerick. Later, Emerick became a shareholder of Cardiac and signed an agreement that included a covenant not to compete. The covenant stated that a physician who left the group promised not to practice competitively in the surrounding area for a period of five years.

After Cardiac began receiving complaints from patients and other physicians about Emerick, it terminated his employment. Emerick sued Cardiac, claiming that the covenant not to compete that he had signed was unreasonable and should be declared illegal. Ultimately, a state appellate court held that the covenant was both reasonable and enforceable. Cardiac had a legitimate interest in protecting its existing client base and prohibiting Emerick from taking its clients.[16] ■

12–3 Recovery Based on Quasi Contract

In some situations, when no actual contract exists, a court may step in to prevent one party from being unjustly enriched at the expense of another party. Quasi contract

16. *Emerick v. Cardiac Study Center, Inc.,* 166 Wash.App. 1039 (2012).

EXHIBIT 12–2 Remedies for Breach of Contract

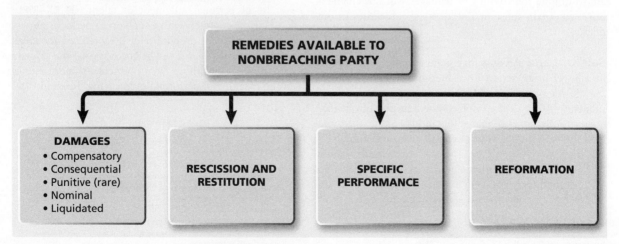

is a legal theory under which an obligation is imposed in the absence of an agreement.

The legal obligation arises because the law considers that the party accepting the benefits has made an implied promise to pay for them. Generally, when one party has conferred a benefit on another party, justice requires that the party receiving the benefit pay the reasonable value for it. The party conferring the benefit can recover in *quantum meruit,*[17] which means "as much as he or she deserves."

12–3a When Quasi Contract Is Used

Quasi contract allows a court to act as if a contract exists when there is no actual contract or agreement between the parties. Therefore, if the parties have entered into a contract concerning the matter in controversy, a court normally will not impose a quasi contract. A court can also use this theory when the parties entered into a contract, but it is unenforceable for some reason.

Quasi-contractual recovery is often granted when one party has partially performed under a contract that is unenforceable. It provides an alternative to suing for damages and allows the party to recover the reasonable value of the partial performance. Depending on the case, the amount of the recovery may be measured either by the benefit received or by the detriment suffered.

■ **EXAMPLE 12.11** Ericson contracts to build two oil derricks for Petro Industries. The derricks are to be built over a period of three years, but the parties do not make a written contract. Thus, the writing requirement will bar enforcement of the contract.[18] After Ericson completes one derrick, Petro Industries informs him that it will not pay for the derrick. Ericson can sue Petro Industries under the theory of quasi contract. ■

12–3b The Requirements of Quasi Contract

To recover under the theory of quasi contract, the party seeking recovery must show the following:

1. The party has conferred a benefit on the other party.
2. The party conferred the benefit with the reasonable expectation of being paid.
3. The party did not act as a volunteer in conferring the benefit.

4. The party receiving the benefit would be unjustly enriched if allowed to retain the benefit without paying for it.

Applying these requirements to *Example 12.11*, Ericson can sue in quasi contract because all of the conditions for quasi-contractual recovery have been fulfilled. Ericson conferred a benefit on Petro Industries by building the oil derrick. Ericson built the derrick with the reasonable expectation of being paid. He was not intending to act as a volunteer. The derrick conferred an obvious benefit on Petro Industries. Petro Industries would be unjustly enriched if it was allowed to keep the derrick without paying Ericson for the work. Therefore, Ericson should be able to recover in *quantum meruit* the reasonable value of the oil derrick that was built, which is ordinarily equal to its fair market value.

Concept Summary 12.1 reviews all of the equitable remedies, including quasi contract, that may be available in the event that a contract is breached.

12–4 Waiver of Breach

Under certain circumstances, a nonbreaching party may be willing to accept a defective performance of the contract. This knowing relinquishment of a legal right (that is, the right to require satisfactory and full performance) is called a **waiver.**

12–4a Consequences of a Waiver of Breach

When a waiver of a breach of contract occurs, the party waiving the breach cannot take any later action on it. In effect, the waiver erases the past breach, and the contract continues as if the breach had never occurred. Of course, the waiver of breach of contract extends only to the matter waived and not to the whole contract.

12–4b Reasons for Waiving a Breach

Businesspersons often waive breaches of contract to obtain whatever benefit is still possible out of the contract. ■ **EXAMPLE 12.12** A seller, Purdue Resources, contracts with a buyer, Bladco Enterprises, to deliver ten thousand tons of coal on or before November 1. The contract calls for Bladco to pay by November 10 for coal delivered. Because of a coal miners' strike, coal is hard to find. Purdue breaches the contract by not tendering delivery until November 5. Bladco will likely choose to waive the seller's breach, accept delivery of the coal, and pay as contracted. ■

---

17. Pronounced *kwahn*-tuhm *mehr*-oo-wit.
18. Contracts that by their terms cannot be performed within one year must be in writing to be enforceable.

Concept Summary 12.1

Equitable Remedies

Rescission and Restitution
- *Rescission*—A remedy whereby a contract is canceled and the parties are restored to the original positions that they occupied prior to the transaction.
- *Restitution*—When a contract is rescinded, both parties must make restitution to each other by returning the goods, property, or funds previously conveyed.

Specific Performance
- An equitable remedy calling for the performance of the act promised in the contract.
- Only available when monetary damages would be inadequate and never available in personal-service contracts.

Reformation
- An equitable remedy allowing a contract to be reformed, or rewritten, to reflect the parties' true intentions.
- Available when an agreement is imperfectly expressed in writing, such as when a mutual mistake has occurred.

Recovery Based on Quasi Contract
- An equitable theory under which a party who confers a benefit on another—with the reasonable expectation of being paid—can seek a court order for the fair market value of the benefit conferred.

12–4c Waiver of Breach and Subsequent Breaches

Ordinarily, a waiver by a contracting party will not operate to waive subsequent, additional, or future breaches of contract. This is always true when the subsequent breaches are unrelated to the first breach. ■ **EXAMPLE 12.13** Ashton owns a multimillion-dollar apartment complex that is under construction. Ashton allows the contractor to complete a stage of construction late. By doing so, Ashton waives his right to sue for the delay. Ashton does not, however, waive the right to sue for failure to comply with engineering specifications on the same job. ■

Pattern-of-Conduct Exception A waiver can extend to subsequent defective performance if a reasonable person would conclude that similar defective performance in the future will be acceptable. Therefore, a *pattern of conduct* that waives a number of successive breaches will operate as a continued waiver. To change this result, the nonbreaching party should give notice to the breaching party that full performance will be required in the future.

Effect on the Contract The party who has rendered defective or less-than-full performance remains liable for the damages caused by the breach of contract. In effect, the waiver operates to keep the contract going. The waiver prevents the nonbreaching party from declaring the contract at an end or rescinding the contract. The contract continues, but the nonbreaching party can recover damages caused by the defective or less-than-full performance.

12–5 Contract Provisions Limiting Remedies

A contract may include provisions stating that no damages can be recovered for certain types of breaches or that damages will be limited to a maximum amount. A contract may also provide that the only remedy for breach is replacement, repair, or refund of the purchase price. Finally, a contract may provide that one party can seek injunctive relief if the other party breaches the contract. Provisions stating that no damages can be recovered are called *exculpatory clauses*.

Provisions that affect the availability of certain remedies are called *limitation-of-liability clauses.*

12–5a The UCC Allows Sales Contracts to Limit Remedies

The Uniform Commercial Code (UCC) provides that in a contract for the sale of goods, remedies can be limited. We will examine the UCC provisions on limited remedies in a later chapter in the context of contracts for the sale or lease of goods.[19]

12–5b Enforceability of Limitation-of-Liability Clauses

Whether a limitation-of-liability clause in a contract will be enforced depends on the type of breach that is excused by the provision. Normally, a provision excluding liability for fraudulent or intentional injury will not be enforced. Likewise, a clause excluding liability for illegal acts, acts that are contrary to public policy, or violations of law

will not be enforced. A clause that excludes liability for negligence may be enforced in some situations when the parties have roughly equal bargaining positions.

■ **CASE IN POINT 12.14** Engineering Consulting Services, Ltd. (ECS), contracted with RSN Properties, Inc., a real estate developer. ECS was to perform soil studies for $2,200 and render an opinion on the use of septic systems in a particular subdivision being developed. A clause in the contract limited ECS's liability to RSN to the value of the engineering services or the sum of $50,000, whichever was greater.

ECS concluded that most of the lots were suitable for septic systems, so RSN proceeded with the development. RSN constructed the roads and water lines to the subdivision in reliance on ECS's conclusions, which turned out to be incorrect. RSN sued ECS for breach of contract and argued that the limitation of liability was against public policy and unenforceable. The court, however, enforced the limitation-of-liability clause as "a reasonable allocation of risks in an arm's-length business transaction."[20] ■

---

19. See UCC 2–719(1).

20. *RSN Properties, Inc. v. Engineering Consulting Services, Ltd.,* 301 Ga.App. 52, 686 S.E.2d 853 (2009).

Reviewing: Breach of Contract and Remedies

Kyle Bruno enters a contract with X Entertainment to be a stuntman in a movie. Bruno is widely known as the best motorcycle stuntman in the business, and the movie to be produced, *Xtreme Riders,* has numerous scenes involving high-speed freestyle street-bike stunts. Filming is set to begin August 1 and end by December 1 so that the film can be released the following summer. Both parties to the contract have stipulated that the filming must end on time to capture the profits from the summer movie market. The contract states that Bruno will be paid 10 percent of the net proceeds from the movie for his stunts.

The contract also includes a liquidated damages provision, which specifies that if Bruno breaches the contract, he will owe X Entertainment $1 million. In addition, the contract includes a limitation-of-liability clause stating that if Bruno is injured during filming, X Entertainment's liability is limited to nominal damages. Using the information presented in the chapter, answer the following questions.

1. One day, while Bruno is preparing for a difficult stunt, he gets into an argument with the director and refuses to perform any stunts at all. Can X Entertainment seek specific performance of the contract? Why or why not?
2. Suppose that while performing a high-speed wheelie on a motorcycle, Bruno is injured by the intentionally reckless act of an X Entertainment employee. Will a court be likely to enforce the limitation-of-liability clause? Why or why not?
3. What factors would a court consider to determine whether the $1 million liquidated damages provision constitutes valid damages or is a penalty?
4. Suppose that there was no liquidated damages provision (or the court refused to enforce it) and X Entertainment breached the contract. The breach caused the release of the film to be delayed until after summer. Could Bruno seek consequential (special) damages for lost profits from the summer movie market in that situation? Explain.

Debate This . . .   *Courts should always uphold limitation-of-liability clauses, whether or not the two parties to the contract had equal bargaining power.*

Terms and Concepts

consequential damages 232
incidental damages 231
liquidated damages 233
mitigation of damages 233

nominal damages 233
penalty 233
quantum meruit 239
reformation 238

restitution 235
specific performance 237
waiver 239

Issue Spotters

1. Greg contracts to build a storage shed for Haney, who pays Greg in advance, but Greg completes only half the work. Haney pays Ipswich $500 to finish the shed. If Haney sues Greg, what will be the measure of recovery? (See *Damages*.)

2. Lyle contracts to sell his ranch to Marley, who is to take possession on June 1. Lyle delays the transfer until August 1. Marley incurs expenses in providing for cattle that he bought for the ranch. When they made the contract, Lyle had no reason to know of the cattle. Is Lyle liable for Marley's expenses in providing for the cattle? Why or why not? (See *Damages*.)

• **Check your answers to the Issue Spotters against the answers provided in Appendix B at the end of this text.**

Business Scenarios

12–1. Liquidated Damages. Cohen contracts to sell his house and lot to Windsor for $100,000. The terms of the contract call for Windsor to pay 10 percent of the purchase price as a down payment. The terms further stipulate that if the buyer breaches the contract, Cohen will retain the deposit as liquidated damages. Windsor pays the deposit, but because her expected financing of the $90,000 balance falls through, she breaches the contract. Two weeks later, Cohen sells the house and lot to Ballard for $105,000. Windsor demands her $10,000 back, but Cohen refuses, claiming that Windsor's breach and the contract terms entitle him to keep the deposit. Discuss who is correct. (See *Damages*.)

12–2. Specific Performance. In which of the following situations would specific performance be an appropriate remedy? Discuss fully. (See *Equitable Remedies*.)

(a) Thompson contracts to sell her house and lot to Cousteau. Then, on finding another buyer willing to pay a higher purchase price, she refuses to deed the property to Cousteau.

(b) Amy contracts to sing and dance in Fred's nightclub for one month, beginning May 1. She then refuses to perform.

(c) Hoffman contracts to purchase a rare coin owned by Erikson, who is breaking up his coin collection. At the last minute, Erikson decides to keep his coin collection intact and refuses to deliver the coin to Hoffman.

Business Case Problems

12–3. Liquidated Damages and Penalties. Planned Pethood Plus, Inc., is a veterinarian-owned clinic. It borrowed $389,000 from KeyBank at an interest rate of 9.3 percent per year for ten years. The loan had a "prepayment penalty" clause that clearly stated that if the loan was repaid early, a specific formula would be used to assess a lump-sum payment to extinguish the obligation. The sooner the loan was paid off, the higher the prepayment penalty. After a year, the veterinarians decided to pay off the loan. KeyBank invoked a prepayment penalty of $40,525.92, which was equal to 10.7 percent of the balance due. The veterinarians sued, contending that the prepayment requirement was unenforceable because it was a penalty. The bank countered that the amount was not a penalty but liquidated damages and that the sum was reasonable. The trial court agreed with the bank, and the veterinarians appealed. Was the loan's prepayment charge reasonable, and should it have been enforced? Why or why not? [*Planned Pethood Plus, Inc. v. KeyCorp, Inc.,* 228 P.3d 262 (Colo.App. 2010)] (See *Damages*.)

12–4. Measure of Damages. Before buying a house, Dean and Donna Testa hired Ground Systems, Inc. (GSI), to inspect the sewage and water disposal system. GSI reported a split system with a watertight septic tank, a wastewater tank, a distribution box, and a leach field. The Testas bought the house. Later, Dean saw that the system was not as GSI described—there was no distribution box or leach field, and there was only one tank, which was not watertight. The Testas arranged for the installation of a new system and sold the house. Assuming that GSI is liable for breach of contract, what is the measure of damages? [*Testa v. Ground Systems, Inc.,* 206 N.J. 330, 20 A.3d 435 (App.Div. 2011)] (See *Damages*.)

12–5. Business Case Problem with Sample Answer— Consequential Damages. After submitting the high bid at a foreclosure sale, David Simard entered into a contract to purchase real property in Maryland for $192,000. Simard defaulted (failed to pay) on the contract. A state court ordered the property to be resold at Simard's expense, as required by state law. The property was then resold for $163,000, but the second purchaser also defaulted. The court then ordered a second resale, resulting in a final price of $130,000. Assuming that Simard is liable for consequential damages, what is the extent of his liability? Is he liable for losses and expenses related to the first resale? If so, is he also liable for losses and expenses related to the second resale? Why or why not? [*Burson v. Simard*, 35 A.3d 1154 (Md. 2012)] (See *Damages*.)

- **For a sample answer to Problem 12–5, go to Appendix C at the end of this text.**

12–6. Liquidated Damages. Cuesport Properties, LLC, sold a condominium in Anne Arundel County, Maryland, to Critical Developments, LLC. As part of the sale, Cuesport agreed to build a wall between Critical Developments' unit and an adjacent unit within thirty days of closing. If Cuesport failed to do so, it was to pay $126 per day until completion. This was an estimate of the amount of rent that Critical Developments would lose until the wall was finished and the unit could be rented. Actual damages were otherwise difficult to estimate at the time of the contract. The wall was built on time, but without a county permit, and it did not comply with the county building code. Critical Developments did not modify the wall to comply with the code until 260 days after the date of the contract deadline for completion of the wall. Does Cuesport have to pay Critical Developments $126 for each of the 260 days? Explain. [*Cuesport Properties, LLC v. Critical Developments, LLC*, 209 Md.App. 607, 61 A.3d 91 (2013)] (See *Damages*.)

12–7. Limitation-of-Liability Clauses. Mia Eriksson was a seventeen-year-old competitor in horseback-riding events. Her riding coach was Kristi Nunnink. Eriksson signed an agreement that released Nunnink from all liability except for damages caused by Nunnink's "direct, willful and wanton negligence." During an event at Galway Downs in Temecula, California, Eriksson's horse struck a hurdle. She fell from the horse and the horse fell on her, causing her death. Her parents, Karan and Stan Eriksson, filed a suit in a California state court against Nunnink for wrongful death. Is the limitation-of-liability agreement that Eriksson signed likely to be enforced in her parents' case? If so, how will it affect their claim? Explain. [*Eriksson v. Nunnink*, 233 Cal.App.4th 708, 183 Cal.Rptr.3d 234 (4 Dist. 2015)] (See *Contract Provisions Limiting Remedies*.)

12–8. Damages. Robert Morris was a licensed insurance agent working for his father's independent insurance agency when he contacted Farmers Insurance Exchange in Alabama about becoming a Farmers agent. According to Farmers' company policy, Morris was an unsuitable candidate due to his relationship with his father's agency. But no Farmers representative told Morris of this policy, and none of the documents that he signed expressed it. Farmers trained Morris and appointed him its agent. About three years later, however, Farmers terminated the appointment for "a conflict of interest because his father was in the insurance business." Morris filed a suit in an Alabama state court against Farmers, claiming that he had been fraudulently induced to leave his father's agency to work for Farmers. If Morris was successful, what type of damages was he most likely awarded? What was the measure of damages? Discuss. [*Farmers Insurance Exchange v. Morris*, __ So.3d __, 2016 WL 661671 (Ala. 2016)] (See *Damages*.)

12–9. A Question of Ethics—Remedies. *On a weekday,* *Tamara Cohen, a real estate broker, showed a town-house owned by Ray and Harriet Mayer to Jessica Seinfeld, the wife of comedian Jerry Seinfeld. On the weekend, when Cohen was unavailable because her religious beliefs prevented her from working, the Seinfelds revisited the townhouse on their own and agreed to buy it. The contract stated that the "buyers will pay buyer's real estate broker's fees." [Cohen v. Seinfeld, 15 Misc.3d 1118(A), 839 N.Y.S.2d 432 (Sup. 2007)] (See Equitable Remedies.)*

(a) Is Cohen entitled to payment even though she was not available to show the townhouse to the Seinfelds on the weekend? Explain.

(b) What obligation do parties involved in business deals owe to each other with respect to their religious beliefs? How might the situation in this case have been avoided?

Legal Reasoning Group Activity

12–10. Breach and Remedies. Frances Morelli agreed to sell Judith Bucklin a house in Rhode Island for $177,000. The sale was supposed to be closed by September 1. The contract included a provision that "if Seller is unable to convey good, clear, insurable, and marketable title, Buyer shall have the option to: (a) accept such title as Seller is able to convey without reduction of the Purchase Price, or (b) cancel this Agreement and receive a return of all Deposits."

An examination of the public records revealed that the house did not have marketable title. Bucklin offered Morelli additional time to resolve the problem, and the closing did not occur as scheduled. Morelli decided that "the deal was over" and offered to return the deposit. Bucklin refused and, in mid-October, decided to exercise her option to accept the house without marketable title. She notified Morelli, who did not respond. She then filed a lawsuit against Morelli in a state court. (See *Damages*.)

(a) One group will discuss whether Morelli breached the contract and will decide in whose favor the court should rule.

(b) A second group will assume that Morelli did breach the contract and will determine what the appropriate remedy is in this situation.

The Commercial Environment

CHAPTER 13

Intellectual Property Rights

Intellectual property is any property that results from intellectual, creative processes—the products of an individual's mind. Although it is an abstract term for an abstract concept, intellectual property is nonetheless familiar to almost everyone. The apps for your iPhone, iPad, or Samsung Galaxy, the movies you see, and the music you listen to are all forms of intellectual property.

More than two hundred years ago, the framers of the U.S. Constitution recognized the importance of protecting creative works in Article I, Section 8. Statutory protection of these rights began in the 1940s and continues to evolve to meet the needs of modern society. In today's global economy, however, protecting intellectual property in one country is no longer sufficient. The United States is participating in various international agreements to secure ownership rights in intellectual property in other countries.

Whether locally or globally, businesspersons have a vital need to protect their rights in intellectual property, which may be more valuable than their physical property, such as machines and buildings. Consider, for instance, the importance of intellectual property rights to technology companies, such as Apple, Inc., and Samsung. These two companies have been involved in patent litigation over the designs of their smartphones for several years.

13–1 Trademarks and Related Property

A **trademark** is a distinctive mark, motto, device, or implement that a manufacturer stamps, prints, or otherwise affixes to the goods it produces so that they can be identified on the market and their origins made known. In other words, a trademark is a source indicator. At common law, the person who used a symbol or mark to identify a business or product was protected in the use of that trademark. Clearly, by using another's trademark, a business could lead consumers to believe that its goods were made by the other business. The law seeks to avoid this kind of confusion.

In the following classic case, the defendants argued that the Coca-Cola trademark was entitled to no protection under the law because the term did not accurately represent the product.

Classic Case 13.1

The Coca-Cola Co. v. The Koke Co. of America

Supreme Court of the United States, 254 U.S. 143, 41 S.Ct. 113, 65 L.Ed.189 (1920).

Company Profile *John Pemberton, an Atlanta pharmacist, invented a caramel-colored, carbonated soft drink in 1886. His bookkeeper, Frank Robinson, named the beverage Coca-Cola after two of the ingredients, coca leaves and kola nuts. Asa Candler bought the Coca-Cola Company in 1891, and within seven years, he had made the soft drink available throughout the United States, as well as in parts of Canada and Mexico. Candler continued to sell Coke aggressively and to open up new markets, reaching Europe before 1910. In doing so, however, he attracted numerous competitors, some of which tried to capitalize directly on the Coke name.*

Case 13.1 Continued

Background and Facts The Coca-Cola Company sought to enjoin (prevent) the Koke Company of America and other beverage companies from, among other things, using the word *Koke* for their products. The Koke Company of America and other beverage companies contended that the Coca-Cola trademark was a fraudulent representation and that Coca-Cola was therefore not entitled to any help from the courts. The Koke Company and the other defendants alleged that the Coca-Cola Company, by its use of the Coca-Cola name, represented that the beverage contained cocaine (from coca leaves), which it no longer did. The trial court granted the injunction against the Koke Company, but the appellate court reversed the lower court's ruling. Coca-Cola then appealed to the United States Supreme Court.

In the Language of the Court

Mr. Justice *HOLMES* delivered the opinion of the Court.

* * * *

* * * Before 1900 the beginning of [Coca-Cola's] good will was more or less helped by the presence of cocaine, a drug that, like alcohol or caffeine or opium, may be described as a deadly poison or as a valuable [pharmaceutical item, depending on the speaker's purposes]. The amount seems to have been very small,[a] but it may have been enough to begin a bad habit and after the Food and Drug Act of June 30, 1906, if not earlier, long before this suit was brought, it was eliminated from the plaintiff's compound.

* * * Since 1900 the sales have increased at a very great rate corresponding to a like increase in advertising. The name now characterizes a beverage to be had at almost any soda fountain. It means a single thing coming from a single source, and well known to the community. It hardly would be too much to say that the drink characterizes the name as much as the name the drink. In other words *Coca-Cola probably means to most persons the plaintiff's familiar product to be had everywhere rather than a compound of particular substances.* * * * Before this suit was brought the plaintiff had advertised to the public that it must not expect and would not find cocaine, and had eliminated everything tending to suggest cocaine effects except the name and the picture of [coca] leaves and nuts, which probably conveyed little or nothing to most who saw it. It appears to us that it would be going too far to deny the plaintiff relief against a palpable [readily evident] fraud because possibly here and there an ignorant person might call for the drink with the hope for incipient cocaine intoxication. The plaintiff's position must be judged by the facts as they were when the suit was begun, not by the facts of a different condition and an earlier time. [Emphasis added.]

Decision and Remedy *The district court's injunction was allowed to stand. The competing beverage companies were enjoined from calling their products Koke.*

Impact of This Case on Today's Law *In this early case, the United States Supreme Court made it clear that trademarks and trade names (and nicknames for those marks and names, such as the nickname "Coke" for "Coca-Cola") that are in common use receive protection under the common law. This holding is significant historically because it is the predecessor to the federal statute later passed to protect trademark rights—the Lanham Act of 1946. In many ways, this act represented a codification of common law principles governing trademarks.*

Critical Thinking

• **What If the Facts Were Different?** *Suppose that Coca-Cola had been trying to make the public believe that its product contained cocaine. Would the result in this case likely have been different? Why or why not?*

---

a. In reality, until 1903 the amount of active cocaine in each bottle of Coke was equivalent to one "line" of cocaine.

13–1a Statutory Protection of Trademarks

Statutory protection of trademarks and related property is provided at the federal level by the Lanham Act of 1946.[1] The Lanham Act was enacted, in part, to protect manufacturers from losing business to rival companies that used confusingly similar trademarks. The act incorporates the common law of trademarks and provides remedies for owners of trademarks who wish to enforce their claims in federal court. Many states also have trademark statutes.

Trademark Dilution   In 1995, Congress amended the Lanham Act by passing the Federal Trademark Dilution Act,[2] which allowed trademark owners to bring suits in federal court for trademark **dilution.** In 2006, Congress further amended the law on trademark dilution by passing the Trademark Dilution Revision Act (TDRA).[3]

Under the TDRA, to state a claim for trademark dilution, a plaintiff must prove the following:

1. The plaintiff owns a famous mark that is distinctive.
2. The defendant has begun using a mark in commerce that allegedly is diluting the famous mark.
3. The similarity between the defendant's mark and the famous mark gives rise to an *association* between the marks.
4. The association is likely to impair the distinctiveness of the famous mark or harm its reputation.

Trademark dilution laws protect "distinctive" or "famous" trademarks (such as Rolls Royce, McDonald's, Starbucks, and Apple) from certain unauthorized uses. Such a mark is protected even when the use is on noncompeting goods or is unlikely to cause confusion. More than half of the states have also enacted trademark dilution laws.

Marks Need Not Be Identical   Note that a famous mark may be diluted by the use of an *identical* mark or by the use of a *similar* mark.[4] A similar mark is more likely to lessen the value of a famous mark when the companies using the marks provide related goods or compete against each other in the same market.

■ **CASE IN POINT 13.1** Samantha Lundberg opened a business called "Sambuck's Coffeehouse," in Astoria, Oregon, even though she knew that "Starbucks" was one of the largest coffee chains in the nation. Starbucks

Corporation filed a dilution lawsuit, and a federal court ruled that use of the "Sambuck's" mark constituted trademark dilution because it created confusion for consumers. Not only was there a "high degree" of similarity between the marks, but also both companies provided coffee-related services and marketed their services through "stand-alone" retail stores. Therefore, the use of the similar mark (Sambuck's) reduced the value of the famous mark (Starbucks).[5] ■

13–1b Trademark Registration

Trademarks may be registered with the state or with the federal government. To register for protection under federal trademark law, a person must file an application with the U.S. Patent and Trademark Office in Washington, D.C. Under current law, a mark can be registered (1) if it is currently in commerce or (2) if the applicant intends to put it into commerce within six months.

In special circumstances, the six-month period can be extended by thirty months. Thus, the applicant would have a total of three years from the date of notice of trademark approval to make use of the mark and file the required use statement. Registration is postponed until the mark is actually used. During this waiting period, any applicant can legally protect his or her trademark against a third party who previously has neither used the mark nor filed an application for it.

Registration is renewable between the fifth and sixth years after the initial registration and every ten years thereafter (every twenty years for those trademarks registered before 1990).

13–1c Trademark Infringement

Registration of a trademark with the U.S. Patent and Trademark Office gives notice on a nationwide basis that the trademark belongs exclusively to the registrant. The registrant is also allowed to use the symbol ® to indicate that the mark has been registered. Whenever that trademark is copied to a substantial degree or used in its entirety by another, intentionally or unintentionally, the trademark has been *infringed* (used without authorization).

When a trademark has been infringed, the owner of the mark has a cause of action against the infringer. To succeed in a trademark infringement action, the owner must show that the defendant's use of the mark created a likelihood of confusion about the origin of the defendant's goods or services. The owner need not prove that

---

1. 15 U.S.C. Sections 1051–1128.
2. 15 U.S.C. Section 1125.
3. Pub. L. No. 103-312, 120 Stat. 1730 (2006).
4. See *Louis Vuitton Malletier S.A. v. Haute Diggity Dog, LLC*, 507 F.3d 252 (4th Cir. 2007); and *Moseley v. V Secret Catalogue, Inc.*, 537 U.S. 418, 123 S.Ct. 1115, 155 L.Ed.2d 1 (2003).
5. *Starbucks Corp. v. Lundberg*, 2005 WL 3183858 (D.Or. 2005).

the infringer acted intentionally or that the trademark was registered (although registration does provide proof of the date of inception of the trademark's use).

The most commonly granted remedy for trademark infringement is an *injunction* to prevent further infringement. Under the Lanham Act, a trademark owner that successfully proves infringement can recover actual damages, plus the profits that the infringer wrongfully received from the unauthorized use of the mark. A court can also order the destruction of any goods bearing the unauthorized trademark. In some situations, the trademark owner may also be able to recover attorneys' fees.

At the center of the following case was an injunction granted in an earlier dispute between two brothers prohibiting one of them from using trademarks owned by the other, including a mark featuring their shared last name.

Case 13.2

LFP IP, LLC v. Hustler Cincinnati, Inc.
United States Court of Appeals, Sixth Circuit, 810 F.3d 424 (2016).

Background and Facts Brothers Jimmy and Larry Flynt owned "The Hustler Club," a bar and nightclub in Cincinnati, Ohio. Larry opened Hustler clubs in other Ohio cities. Within a few years, he also began publishing *Hustler,* a sexually explicit magazine. Larry formed LFP IP, Inc., and other corporations to conduct his enterprises. Many of them used the trademarks "HUSTLER" and "LARRY FLYNT," which LFP owned. Jimmy opened his own store, Hustler Cincinnati, and paid LFP licensing fees to use the "HUSTLER" mark.

When the store stopped paying the fees, LFP filed a suit in a federal district court against the store's corporate owner, alleging trademark infringement. The court issued an injunction prohibiting Jimmy from using the "HUSTLER" mark. Later, he opened a store called "FLYNT Sexy Gifts." LFP claimed that this name was likely to cause confusion with the "LARRY FLYNT" mark. The court modified the injunction to limit Jimmy's use of the "Flynt" name without "Jimmy." Jimmy appealed.

In the Language of the Court
SUTTON, Circuit Judge.
* * * *

Courts * * * may exercise their sound judicial discretion to modify an injunction if the circumstances, whether of law or fact, obtaining at the time of its issuance have changed, or new ones have since arisen.

* * * The [district] court * * * applied the traditional test for trademark infringement under federal law, asking whether (1) Larry and his companies owned the LARRY FLYNT trademark, (2) Jimmy used the mark in commerce, and (3) the use was likely to cause confusion. The court found all three elements satisfied * * * . Because the original injunction was tailored to prevent trademark infringement by [Jimmy] and because Jimmy had committed new violations, the district court acted appropriately when it modified its initial grant of relief to cover Jimmy's conduct at the [new] outlet.

The district court's modified injunction was also suitably tailored to the changed circumstances. Balancing the competing interests of Larry and Jimmy, the court permitted Jimmy to use his full name while protecting Larry's interest in the LARRY FLYNT trademark.
* * * *

Jimmy * * * takes issue with some of the factual findings that the district court used to justify the modified injunction.

But none of the district court's factual findings is clearly erroneous. * * * Larry * * * presented evidence that he used the mark in connection with a wide range of adult entertainment products, including the kinds of products sold at Jimmy's store. Because *product use * * * marks the salient [most noticeable] indicator of ownership in trademark-infringement actions*, the district court reasonably found that Larry * * * owned the LARRY FLYNT trademark with respect to retail goods. The court also reasonably found that Larry began using the mark on adult entertainment products before Jimmy did. * * * And * * * Larry's company * * * continued to use that mark in commerce. [Emphasis added.]

In claiming an absence of evidence of consumer confusion, Jimmy missteps. Some of the evidence comes from Jimmy himself. When asked about instances where a consumer has been confused, in terms of whether or not Jimmy was the owner of the store, Jimmy responded, "I have experienced the

Case 13.2 Continues

Case 13.2 Continued

confusion in the names, you know. Jimmy and Larry Flynt, in this market area, is somewhat synonymous with Hustler or with Flynt. You're not going to get around that."

Decision and Remedy *The U.S. Court of Appeals for the Sixth Circuit affirmed the lower court's modification of the injunction. The injunction was initially tailored to prevent Jimmy's infringement of his brother's marks. When Jimmy committed a new violation by opening "FLYNT Sexy Gifts," the district court acted appropriately in modifying the injunction to cover this conduct.*

Critical Thinking
- **E-Commerce** *Could Jimmy use his last name—the name that he shares with his brother—as a domain name? Why or why not?*
- **What If the Facts Were Different?** *Suppose that Jimmy had used the marks at the center of this case on an entirely different line of goods, not adult entertainment products. Would the result have been the same? Explain.*

13–1d Distinctiveness of the Mark

A trademark must be sufficiently distinctive to enable consumers to identify the manufacturer of the goods easily and to distinguish between those goods and competing products.

Strong Marks Fanciful, arbitrary, or suggestive trademarks are generally considered to be the most distinctive (strongest) trademarks. These marks receive automatic protection because they serve to identify a particular product's source, as opposed to describing the product itself.

Fanciful and Arbitrary Trademarks. Fanciful trademarks use invented words, such as "Xerox" for one manufacturer's copiers and "Google" for a search engine. Arbitrary trademarks use common words in an uncommon way that is not descriptive of the product, such as "Dutch Boy" as a name for paint.

Even a single letter used in a particular style can be an arbitrary trademark. ■ **CASE IN POINT 13.2** Sports entertainment company ESPN sued Quiksilver, Inc., a maker of youth-oriented clothing, alleging trademark infringement. ESPN claimed that Quiksilver's clothing used the stylized "X" mark that ESPN uses in connection with the "X Games" ("extreme" sports competitions).

Quiksilver filed counterclaims for trademark infringement and dilution, arguing that it had a long history of using the stylized X on its products. ESPN had created the X Games in the mid-1990s, and Quiksilver had been using the X mark since 1994. ESPN asked the court to dismiss Quiksilver's counterclaims, but the court refused, holding that the X on Quiksilver's clothing is clearly an arbitrary mark. The court found that the two Xs are

"similar enough that a consumer might well confuse them." Therefore, Quicksilver could continue its claim for trademark infringement.[6] ■

Suggestive Trademarks. Suggestive trademarks indicate something about a product's nature, quality, or characteristics, without describing the product directly. These marks require imagination on the part of the consumer to identify the characteristic.

"Dairy Queen," for instance, suggests an association between its products and milk, but it does not directly describe ice cream. "Blu-ray" is a suggestive mark that is associated with the high-quality, high-definition video contained on a particular type of optical data storage disc. Although blue-violet lasers are used to read blu-ray discs, the term *blu-ray* does not directly describe the disc.

Secondary Meaning Descriptive terms, geographic terms, and personal names are not inherently distinctive and do not receive protection under the law until they acquire a secondary meaning. A secondary meaning may arise when customers begin to associate a specific term or phrase (such as *London Fog*) with specific trademarked items (coats with "London Fog" labels) made by a particular company.

Whether a secondary meaning becomes attached to a name usually depends on how extensively the product is advertised, the market for the product, the number of sales, and other factors. ■ **CASE IN POINT 13.3** Unity Health Plans Insurance Corporation has been a health maintenance organization (HMO) insurer in Wisconsin since 1955. In 2013, another health-care provider, Iowa

---

6. *ESPN, Inc. v. Quiksilver, Inc.*, 586 F.Supp.2d 219 (S.D.N.Y. 2008).

Health System, began rebranding itself (changing its name and marketing) as UnityPoint Health. When the company expanded into Wisconsin, where Unity Health already had an established presence, Unity Health filed a trademark infringement suit in federal court.

The court found that Unity Health was a descriptive mark, and thus not inherently distinctive. But the court also held that the Unity Health mark had acquired a secondary meaning, largely because it had been used for so long and so exclusively by one health insurer in Wisconsin. It made no difference to the court that only one part of the mark (Unity) was common to both trademarks. To allow Iowa Health Systems to use the mark UnityPoint Health in Wisconsin would likely create confusion for consumers. Therefore, the court issued an injunction and blocked Iowa Health from using the trademark Unity-Point Health.[7] ∎

Once a secondary meaning is attached to a term or name, a trademark is considered distinctive and is protected. Even a color can qualify for trademark protection, as did the color schemes used by some state university sports teams, including Ohio State University and Louisiana State University.[8]

∎ **CASE IN POINT 13.4** Federal Express Corporation (FedEx) provides transportation and delivery services worldwide using the logo FedEx in a specific color combination. FedEx sued a competitor, JetEx Management Services, Inc., for using the same color combination and a similar name and logo. JetEx also mimicked FedEx's trademarked slogan ("The World on Time" for FedEx, and "Keeping the World on Time" for JetEx). FedEx alleged trademark infringement and dilution, among other claims. A federal district court in New York granted a permanent injunction to block JetEx from using the infringing mark in FedEx colors.[9] ∎

Generic Terms Generic terms that refer to an entire class of products, such as *bicycle* and *computer,* receive no protection, even if they acquire secondary meanings. A particularly thorny problem arises when a trademark acquires generic use. For instance, *aspirin* and *thermos* were originally the names of trademarked products, but today the words are used generically. Other trademarks that have acquired generic use are *escalator, trampoline, raisin bran, dry ice, lanolin, linoleum, nylon,* and *cornflakes.*

A trademark does not become generic simply because it is commonly used, however. ∎ **CASE IN POINT 13.5** In 2014, David Elliot and Chris Gillespie sought to register numerous domain names, including "googledisney.com" and "googlenewstvs.com." (A *domain name* is part of an Internet address, such as "cengage.com.") They were unable to register the names because all of them used the word *google,* a trademark of Google, Inc.

Elliot and Gillespie brought an action in federal court to have the Google trademark cancelled because it had become a generic term. They argued that because most people now use *google* as a verb ("to google") when referring to searching the Internet with any search engine (not just Google), the term should no longer be protected. The court held that even if people do use the word *google* as a verb, it is still a protected trademark if consumers associate the noun with one company. The court concluded that "the primary significance of the word *google* to a majority of the public who utilize Internet search engines is a designation of the Google search engine."[10] ∎

13–1e Service, Certification, and Collective Marks

A **service mark** is essentially a trademark that is used to distinguish the *services* (rather than the products) of one person or company from those of another. For instance, each airline has a particular mark or symbol associated with its name. Titles and character names used in radio and television are frequently registered as service marks.

Other marks protected by law include certification marks and collective marks. A **certification mark** is used by one or more persons, other than the owner, to certify the region, materials, mode of manufacture, quality, or other characteristic of specific goods or services. Certification marks include "Good Housekeeping Seal of Approval" and "UL Tested."

When used by members of a cooperative, association, or other organization, a certification mark is referred to as a **collective mark.** ∎ **EXAMPLE 13.6** Collective marks appear at the ends of motion picture credits to indicate the various associations and organizations that participated in the making of the films. The union marks found on the tags of certain products are also collective marks. ∎

13–1f Trade Dress

The term **trade dress** refers to the image and overall appearance of a product. Trade dress is a broad concept

---

7. *Unity Health Plans Insurance Co. v. Iowa Health System,* 995 F.Supp.2d 874 (W.D.Wis. 2014).

8. *Board of Supervisors of Louisiana State University v. Smack Apparel Co.,* 438 F.Supp.2d 653 (E.D.La. 2006). See also *Abraham v. Alpha Chi Omega,* 781 F.Supp.2d 396 (N.D.Tex. 2011).

9. *Federal Express Corp. v. JetEx Management Services, Inc.,* 2014 WL 4628983 (E.D.N.Y. 2014).

10. *Elliot v. Google,* 45 F.Supp.3d 1156 (D.Ariz. 2014).

and can include either all or part of the total image or overall impression created by a product or its packaging.

■ **EXAMPLE 13.7** The distinctive decor, menu, layout, and style of service of a particular restaurant may be regarded as trade dress. Trade dress can also include the layout and appearance of a catalogue, the use of a lighthouse as part of the design of a golf hole, the fish shape of a cracker, or the G-shaped design of a Gucci watch. ■

Basically, trade dress is subject to the same protection as trademarks. In cases involving trade dress infringement, as in trademark infringement cases, a major consideration is whether consumers are likely to be confused by the allegedly infringing use.

13–1g Counterfeit Goods

Counterfeit goods copy or otherwise imitate trademarked goods, but they are not the genuine trademarked goods. The importation of goods that bear counterfeit (fake) trademarks poses a growing problem for U.S. businesses, consumers, and law enforcement. In addition to the negative financial effects on legitimate businesses, certain counterfeit goods, such as pharmaceuticals and nutritional supplements, can present serious public health risks.

The Stop Counterfeiting in Manufactured Goods Act The Stop Counterfeiting in Manufactured Goods Act[11] (SCMGA) was enacted to combat counterfeit goods. The act makes it a crime to traffic intentionally in or attempt to traffic in counterfeit goods or services, or to knowingly use a counterfeit mark on or in connection with goods or services.

Before this act, the law did not prohibit the creation or shipment of counterfeit labels that were not attached to any product. Therefore, counterfeiters would make labels and packaging bearing another's trademark, ship the labels to another location, and then affix them to an inferior product to deceive buyers. The SCMGA closed this loophole by making it a crime to knowingly traffic in counterfeit labels, stickers, packaging, and the like, regardless of whether the items are attached to any goods.

Penalties for Counterfeiting Persons found guilty of violating the SCMGA may be fined up to $2 million or imprisoned for up to ten years (or more if they are repeat offenders). If a court finds that the statute was violated, it must order the defendant to forfeit the counterfeit products (which are then destroyed), as well as any property used in the commission of the crime. The defendant must also pay restitution to the trademark holder or victim in an amount equal to the victim's actual loss.

■ **CASE IN POINT 13.8** Charles Anthony Jones pleaded guilty to trafficking of counterfeit prescription erectile dysfunction drugs. The court sentenced Jones to thirty-seven months in prison and ordered him to pay $633,019 in restitution. Jones appealed, arguing that the amount awarded was more than the pharmaceutical companies' actual losses. The court agreed. The pharmaceutical companies were entitled only to their lost net profits rather than the retail price of the genuine drugs.[12] ■

Combating Foreign Counterfeiters Although Congress has enacted statutes against counterfeit goods, the United States cannot prosecute foreign counterfeiters because our national laws do not apply to them. One effective tool that U.S. officials have used to combat online sales of counterfeit goods is to obtain a court order to close down the domain names of Web sites that sell such goods. For instance, U.S. agents have shut down hundreds of domain names on the Monday after Thanksgiving ("Cyber Monday"). Shutting down the Web sites, particularly on key shopping days, prevents some counterfeit goods from entering the United States. Europol, an international organization, has also used this tactic.

13–1h Trade Names

Trademarks apply to *products*. A **trade name** indicates part or all of a business's name, whether the business is a sole proprietorship, a partnership, or a corporation. Generally, a trade name is directly related to a business and its goodwill.

A trade name may be protected as a trademark if the trade name is also the name of the company's trademarked product—for example, Coca-Cola. Unless it is also used as a trademark or service mark, a trade name cannot be registered with the federal government. Trade names are protected under the common law, but only if they are unusual or fancifully used. The word *Safeway,* for example, was sufficiently fanciful to obtain protection as a trade name for a grocery chain.

13–1i Licensing

One way to avoid litigation and still make use of another's trademark or other form of intellectual property is to obtain a license to do so. A **license** in this context is an agreement, or contract, permitting the use of a

11. Pub. L. No. 109-181 (2006), which amended 18 U.S.C. Sections 2318–2320.

12. *United States v. Jones*, 616 Fed.Appx. 726 (5th Cir. 2015).

trademark, copyright, patent, or trade secret for certain purposes. The party that owns the intellectual property rights and issues the license is the *licensor,* and the party obtaining the license is the *licensee.* The licensee generally pays fees, or *royalties,* for the privilege of using the intellectual property.

A license grants only the rights expressly described in the license agreement. A licensor might, for example, allow the licensee to use the trademark as part of its company or domain name, but not otherwise use the mark on any products or services. Disputes frequently arise over licensing agreements, particularly when the license involves Internet uses.

■ **CASE IN POINT 13.9** George V Restauration S.A. and others owned and operated the Buddha Bar Paris, a restaurant with an Asian theme in Paris, France. One of the owners allowed Little Rest Twelve, Inc., to use the Buddha Bar trademark and its associated concept in New York City under the name *Buddha Bar NYC.* Little Rest paid royalties for its use of the Buddha Bar mark and advertised Buddha Bar NYC's affiliation with Buddha Bar Paris. This connection was also noted on its Web site and in the media.

When a dispute arose, the owners of Buddha Bar Paris withdrew their permission for Buddha Bar NYC's use of their mark, but Little Rest continued to use it. The owners of the mark filed a suit in a New York state court against Little Rest. The court granted an injunction to prevent Little Rest from using the mark.[13] ■

13-2 Patents

A **patent** is a grant from the government that gives an inventor the exclusive right to make, use, or sell his or her invention for a period of twenty years. Patents for designs, as opposed to those for inventions, are given for a fourteen-year period. The applicant must demonstrate to the satisfaction of the U.S. Patent and Trademark Office that the invention, discovery, process, or design is novel, useful, and not obvious in light of current technology.

Until recently, U.S. patent law differed from the laws of many other countries because the first person to invent a product obtained the patent rights rather than the first person to file for a patent. It was often difficult to prove who invented an item first, however, which prompted Congress to change the system in 2011 by passing the America Invents Act.[14] Now the first person to file an application for a patent on a product or process will receive patent protection. In addition, the new law established a nine-month limit for challenging a patent on any ground.

The period of patent protection begins on the date the patent application is filed, rather than when the patent is issued, which may sometimes be years later. After the patent period ends (either fourteen or twenty years later), the product or process enters the public domain, and anyone can make, sell, or use the invention without paying the patent holder.

13-2a Searchable Patent Databases

A significant development relating to patents is the availability online of the world's patent databases. The Web site of the U.S. Patent and Trademark Office (www.uspto.gov) provides searchable databases covering U.S. patents granted since 1976. The Web site of the European Patent Office (www.epo.org) provides online access to 50 million patent documents in more than seventy nations through a searchable network of databases.

Businesses use these searchable databases in many ways. Companies may conduct patent searches to list or inventory their patents, which are valuable assets. Patent searches may also be conducted to study trends and patterns in a specific technology or to gather information about competitors in the industry.

13-2b What Is Patentable?

Under federal law, "[w]hoever invents or discovers any new and useful process, machine, manufacture, or composition of matter, or any new and useful improvement thereof, may obtain a patent therefor, subject to the conditions and requirements of this title."[15] Thus, to be patentable, the applicant must prove that the invention, discovery, process, or design is *novel, useful,* and *not obvious* in light of current technology.

In sum, almost anything is patentable, except the laws of nature, natural phenomena, and abstract ideas (including algorithms[16]). Even artistic methods and works of art, certain business processes, and the structures of storylines

---

13. *George V Restauration S.A. v. Little Rest Twelve, Inc.*, 58 A.D.3d 428, 871 N.Y.S.2d 65 (2009).

14. The full title of this law is the Leahy-Smith America Invents Act, Pub. L. No. 112-29 (2011), which amended 35 U.S.C. Sections 1, 41, and 321.

15. 35 U.S.C. Section 101.

16. An *algorithm* is a step-by-step procedure, formula, or set of instructions for accomplishing a specific task. An example is the set of rules used by a search engine to rank the listings contained within its index in response to a query.

are patentable, provided that they are novel and not obvious.[17]

Plants that are reproduced asexually (by means other than from seed), such as hybrid or genetically engineered plants, are patentable in the United States, as are genetically engineered (or cloned) microorganisms and animals. ■ **CASE IN POINT 13.10** Monsanto, Inc., sells its patented genetically modified (GM) seeds to farmers to help them achieve higher yields from crops using fewer pesticides. It requires farmers who buy GM seeds to sign licensing agreements promising to plant the seeds for only one crop and to pay a technology fee for each acre planted. To ensure compliance, Monsanto has many full-time employees whose job is to investigate and prosecute farmers who use the GM seeds illegally. Monsanto has filed nearly 150 lawsuits against farmers in the United States and has been awarded more than $15 million in damages (not including out-of-court settlement amounts).[18] ■

13–2c Patent Infringement

If a firm makes, uses, or sells another's patented design, product, or process without the patent owner's permission, that firm commits the tort of patent infringement. Patent infringement may occur even though the patent owner has not put the patented product into commerce. Patent infringement may also occur even though not all features or parts of a product are copied. (To infringe the patent on a process, however, all steps or their equivalent must be copied.) To read about an important issue in patent infringement today, see this chapter's *Digital Update* feature.

Patent Infringement Lawsuits and High-Tech Companies Obviously, companies that specialize in developing new technology stand to lose significant profits if someone "makes, uses, or sells" devices that incorporate their patented inventions. Because these firms are the holders of numerous patents, they are frequently involved in patent infringement lawsuits (as well as other types of intellectual property disputes).

■ **CASE IN POINT 13.11** Apple sued Samsung in federal court alleging that Samsung's Galaxy smartphones and tablets that use Google's HTC Android operating system infringe on Apple's patents. Apple has design

patents that cover its devices' graphical user interface (the display of icons on the home screen), shell, and screen and button design. Apple has also patented the way information is displayed on iPhones and other devices, the way windows pop open, and the way information is scaled and rotated.

A jury found that Samsung had willfully infringed five of Apple's patents and awarded damages. The parties appealed. A judge later reduced the amount of damages awarded on the patent claims, but litigation between the two companies has continued. In 2015, a federal appellate court held that elements of the physical design of these two manufacturers' mobile devices and their on-screen icons were functional and thus not protected under the Lanham Act. A product feature is functional and not protected as trade dress if it is essential to the article's use or purpose or affects the cost or quality of the article.[19] ■

Patent Infringement and Foreign Sales Many companies that make and sell electronics and computer software and hardware are based in foreign nations (for instance, Samsung Electronics Company is a Korean firm). Foreign firms can apply for and obtain U.S. patent protection on items that they sell within the United States. Similarly, U.S. firms can obtain protection in foreign nations where they sell goods.

In the United States, the Supreme Court has narrowly construed patent infringement as it applies to exported software, however. As a general rule, under U.S. law, no patent infringement occurs when a patented product is made and sold in another country. ■ **CASE IN POINT 13.12** AT&T Corporation holds a patent on a device used to digitally encode, compress, and process recorded speech. AT&T brought an infringement case against Microsoft Corporation, which admitted that its Windows operating system incorporated software code that infringed on AT&T's patent.

The United States Supreme Court held that Microsoft was liable only for infringement in the United States and not for the Windows-based computers produced in foreign locations. The Court reasoned that Microsoft had not "supplied" the software for the computers but had only electronically transmitted a master copy, which the foreign manufacturers copied and loaded onto the computers.[20] ■

17. For a United States Supreme Court case discussing the obviousness requirement, see *KSR International Co. v. Teleflex, Inc.*, 550 U.S. 398, 127 S.Ct. 1727, 167 L.Ed.2d 705 (2007).

18. See, for example, *Monsanto Co. v. Bowman*, 657 F.3d 1341 (Fed.Cir. 2011); and *Monsanto Co. v. Scruggs*, 2009 WL 1228318 (Fed.Cir. 2009).

19. *Apple, Inc. v. Samsung Electronics Co.*, 926 F.Supp.2d 1110 (N.D.Cal. 2013); 786 F.3d 983 (Fed. Cir. 2015).

20. *Microsoft Corp. v. AT&T Corp.*, 550 U.S. 437, 127 S.Ct. 1746, 167 L.Ed.2d 737 (2007).

DIGITAL UPDATE   The Problem of Patent Trolls

In recent years, a huge number of patent infringement lawsuits have been filed against software and technology firms. Many patent cases involve companies defending real innovations, but some lawsuits are "shakedowns" by patent trolls.

Patent trolls—more formally called nonpracticing entities (NPEs) or patent assertion entities (PAEs)—are firms that do not make or sell products or services but are in the business of patent litigation. These firms buy patents and then try to enforce them against companies that *do* sell products or services, demanding licensing fees and threatening infringement lawsuits. Patent trolls usually target online businesses.

"I'm Going to Sue You Unless You Pay Me to Go Away"

Patent trolls literally bank on the fact that when threatened with infringement suits, most companies would rather pay to settle than engage in costly litigation, even if they believe they could win.

Consider an example. Soverain Software, LLC, sued dozens of online retailers, including Amazon, Avon, Home Depot, Macy's, Nordstrom, Kohl's, RadioShack, The Gap, and Victoria's Secret. Soverain claimed that it owned patents that covered nearly any use of online shopping-cart technology and that all these retailers had infringed on its patents. Amazon paid millions to settle with Soverain, as did most of the other defendants.

Interestingly, one online retailer, Newegg, Inc., refused to pay Soverain and ultimately won in court. In 2013, a federal appellate court held that the

shopping-cart patent claim was invalid on the ground of obviousness because the technology for it had already existed before Soverain obtained its patent.[a]

The Role of Software Patents

The patent troll problem is concentrated in software patents, which often include descriptions of what the software does rather than the computer code involved. Many software patents are vaguely worded and overly broad. In the United States, both the patent system and the courts have had difficulty evaluating and protecting such patents.

As a result, nearly any business that uses basic technology can be a target of patent trolls. In fact, *more than 60 percent of all new patent cases* are filed by patent trolls. The firms most commonly targeted by patent trolls are large technology companies, including AT&T, Google, Apple, Samsung, Amazon, and Verizon. In one recent year, "AT&T was sued for patent infringement by patent trolls 54 times—more than once a week."[b]

Critical Thinking *Some argue that the best way to stop patent trolls from taking advantage of the system would be to eliminate software patents completely and pass a law that makes software unpatentable. Would this be fair to software and technology companies? Why or why not?*

a. *Soverain Software, LLC v. Newegg, Inc.*, 728 F.3d 1332 (Fed. Cir. 2013), *cert.* denied, 134 S.Ct. 910 (2014).
b. Roger Parloff, "Taking on the Patent Trolls," *Fortune*, February 27, 2014.

13–2d Remedies for Patent Infringement

If a patent is infringed, the patent holder may sue for relief in federal court. The patent holder can seek an injunction against the infringer and can also request damages for royalties and lost profits. In some cases, the court may grant the winning party reimbursement for attorneys' fees and costs. If the court determines that the infringement was willful, the court can triple the amount of damages awarded (treble damages).

In the past, permanent injunctions were routinely granted to prevent future infringement. Today, however, according to the United States Supreme Court, a patent holder must prove that it has suffered irreparable injury and that the public interest would not be *disserved* by

a permanent injunction.[21] Thus, courts have discretion to decide what is equitable in the circumstances and to consider what is in the public interest rather than just the interests of the parties.

■ **CASE IN POINT 13.13** Cordance Corporation developed some of the technology and software that automates Internet communications. Cordance sued Amazon.com, Inc., for patent infringement, claiming that Amazon's one-click purchasing interface infringed on one of Cordance's patents. After a jury found Amazon guilty of infringement, Cordance requested the court to issue a permanent injunction against Amazon's infringement or,

21. *eBay, Inc. v. MercExchange, LLC*, 547 U.S. 388, 126 S.Ct. 1837, 164 L.Ed.2d 641 (2006).

alternatively, to order Amazon to pay Cordance an ongoing royalty.

The court refused to issue a permanent injunction because Cordance had not proved that it would otherwise suffer irreparable harm. Cordance and Amazon were not direct competitors in the relevant market. Cordance had never sold or licensed the technology infringed by Amazon's one-click purchasing interface and had presented no market data or evidence to show how the infringement negatively affected Cordance. The court also refused to impose an ongoing royalty on Amazon.[22] ■

13–3 Copyrights

A **copyright** is an intangible property right granted by federal statute to the author or originator of a literary or artistic production of a specified type. The Copyright Act of 1976,[23] as amended, governs copyrights. Works created after January 1, 1978, are automatically given statutory copyright protection for the life of the author plus 70 years. For copyrights owned by publishing houses, the copyright expires 95 years from the date of publication or 120 years from the date of creation, whichever comes first. For works by more than one author, the copyright expires 70 years after the death of the last surviving author.[24]

When copyright protection ends, works enter into the *public domain.* Intellectual property, such as songs and other published works, that have entered into the public domain belong to everyone and are not protected by copyright or patent laws.

■ **CASE IN POINT 13.14** The popular character Sherlock Holmes originated in stories written by Arthur Conan Doyle and published from 1887 through 1927. Over the years, elements of the characters and stories created by Doyle have appeared in books, movies, and television series, including *Elementary* on CBS and *Sherlock* on BBC.

Before 2013, those who wished to use the copyrighted Sherlock material had to pay a licensing fee to Doyle's estate. Then, in 2013, the editors of a book of Holmes-related stories filed a lawsuit in federal court claiming that the basic Sherlock Holmes story elements introduced before 1923 should no longer be protected. The

court agreed and ruled that these elements have entered the public domain—that is, the copyright has expired, and they can be used without permission.[25] ■

13–3a Registration

Copyrights can be registered with the U.S. Copyright Office (www.copyright.gov) in Washington, D.C. Registration is not required, however. A copyright owner no longer needs to place the symbol © or the term *Copr.* or *Copyright* on the work to have the work protected against infringement. Chances are that if somebody created it, somebody owns it.

Generally, copyright owners are protected against the following:

1. Reproduction of the work.
2. Development of derivative works.
3. Distribution of the work.
4. Public display of the work.

13–3b What Is Protected Expression?

Works that are copyrightable include books, records, films, artworks, architectural plans, menus, music videos, product packaging, and computer software. To be protected, a work must be "fixed in a durable medium" from which it can be perceived, reproduced, or communicated. As noted, protection is automatic, and registration is not required.

Section 102 of the Copyright Act explicitly states that it protects original works that fall into one of the following categories:

1. Literary works (including newspaper and magazine articles, computer and training manuals, catalogues, brochures, and print advertisements).
2. Musical works and accompanying words (including advertising jingles).
3. Dramatic works and accompanying music.
4. Pantomimes and choreographic works (including ballets and other forms of dance).
5. Pictorial, graphic, and sculptural works (including cartoons, maps, posters, statues, and even stuffed animals).
6. Motion pictures and other audiovisual works (including multimedia works).
7. Sound recordings.
8. Architectural works.

---

22. *Cordance Corp. v. Amazon.com, Inc.*, 730 F.Supp.2d 333 (D.Del. 2010).
23. 17 U.S.C. Sections 101 *et seq.*
24. These time periods reflect the extensions of the length of copyright protection enacted by Congress in the Copyright Term Extension Act of 1998, 17 U.S.C. Section 302. The United States Supreme Court upheld the constitutionality of the act in 2003. See *Eldred v. Ashcroft*, 537 U.S. 186, 123 S.Ct. 769, 154 L.Ed.2d 683 (2003).

25. *Klinger v. Conan Doyle Estate, Ltd.*, 988 F.Supp.2d 879 (N.D.Ill. 2013).

Section 102 Exclusions Generally, anything that is not an original expression will not qualify for copyright protection. Facts widely known to the public are not copyrightable. Page numbers are not copyrightable because they follow a sequence known to everyone. Mathematical calculations are not copyrightable.

Furthermore, it is not possible to copyright an *idea*. Section 102 of the Copyright Act specifically excludes copyright protection for any "idea, procedure, process, system, method of operation, concept, principle, or discovery, regardless of the form in which it is described, explained, illustrated, or embodied." Thus, anyone can freely use the underlying ideas or principles embodied in a work.

What is copyrightable is the particular way in which an idea is *expressed*. Whenever an idea and an expression are inseparable, the expression cannot be copyrighted. An idea and its expression, then, must be separable to be copyrightable. Thus, for the design of a useful item to be copyrightable, the way it looks must be separate from its utilitarian (functional) purpose.

■ **CASE IN POINT 13.15** Inhale, Inc., registered a copyright on a hookah—a device for smoking tobacco by filtering the smoke through water held in a container at the base. Starbuzz Tobacco, Inc., sold hookahs with water containers shaped exactly like the Inhale containers.

Inhale filed a suit in a federal district court against Starbuzz for copyright infringement. The court determined that the shape of the water container on Inhale's hookahs was not copyrightable. The U.S. Court of Appeals for the Ninth Circuit affirmed the judgment. "The shape of a container is not independent of the container's utilitarian function—to hold the contents within its shape—because the shape accomplishes the function."[26] ■

Compilations of Facts Unlike ideas, *compilations* of facts are copyrightable. Under Section 103 of the Copyright Act, a compilation is "a work formed by the collection and assembling of preexisting materials or data that are selected, coordinated, or arranged in such a way that the resulting work as a whole constitutes an original work of authorship."

The key requirement in the copyrightability of a compilation is originality. If the facts are selected, coordinated, or arranged in an original way, they can qualify for copyright protection. Therefore, the White Pages of a telephone directory do not qualify for copyright protection, because they simply list alphabetically names and telephone numbers. The Yellow Pages of a directory can be copyrightable, provided the information is selected, coordinated, or arranged in an original way. Similarly, a compilation of information about yachts listed for sale has qualified for copyright protection.[27]

13–3c Copyright Infringement

Whenever the form or expression of an idea is copied, an infringement of copyright has occurred. The reproduction does not have to be exactly the same as the original, nor does it have to reproduce the original in its entirety. If a substantial part of the original is reproduced, the copyright has been infringed.

In the following case, rapper Curtis Jackson—better known as "50 Cent"—was the defendant in a suit that claimed his album *Before I Self-Destruct,* and the film of the same name, infringed the copyright of Shadrach Winstead's book *The Preacher's Son—But the Streets Turned Me into a Gangster.*

---

26. *Inhale, Inc. v. Starbuzz Tobacco, Inc.,* 755 F.3d 1038 (2014).

27. *BUC International Corp. v. International Yacht Council, Ltd.,* 489 F.3d 1129 (11th Cir. 2007).

Case Analysis 13.3

Winstead v. Jackson

United States Court of Appeals, Third Circuit, 509 Fed.Appx. 139 (2013).

In the Language of the Court

PER CURIAM. [By the Whole Court]

* * * *

* * * Winstead filed his * * * complaint in the United States District Court for the District of New Jersey, claiming that Jackson's album/CD and film derived their contents from, and infringed the copyright of, his book.

* * * *

* * * The District Court dismissed Winstead's * * * complaint * * *, concluding that Jackson * * * did not improperly copy protected aspects of Winstead's book.

* * * *

Winstead appeals.

* * * *

Here, it is not disputed that Winstead is the owner of the copyrighted property * * * . However, *not all copying is copyright infringement, so even if actual copying is proven, the court must decide, by comparing the allegedly infringing work with the original work, whether the copying was unlawful. Copying may be proved inferentially by showing that the allegedly infringing work is substantially similar to the copyrighted*

Case 13.3 Continues

Case 13.3 Continued

work. A court compares the allegedly infringing work with the original work, and considers whether a "lay-observer" would believe that the copying was of protectable aspects of the copyrighted work. The inquiry involves distinguishing between the author's expression and the idea or theme that he or she seeks to convey or explore, because the former is protected and the latter is not. The court must determine whether the allegedly infringing work is similar because it appropriates the unique expressions of the original work, or merely because it contains elements that would be expected when two works express the same idea or explore the same theme. [Emphasis added.]

* * * A lay observer would not believe that Jackson's album/CD and film copied protectable aspects of Winstead's book. Jackson's album/CD is comprised of 16 individual songs, which explore drug-dealing, guns and money, vengeance, and other similar clichés of hip hop gangsterism. Jackson's fictional film is the story of a young man who turns to violence when his mother is killed in a drive-by shooting. The young man takes revenge by killing the man who killed his mother, and then gets rich by becoming an "enforcer" for a powerful criminal. He takes up with a woman who eventually betrays him, and is shot to death by her boyfriend, who has just been released from prison. The movie ends with his younger brother vowing to seek vengeance. Winstead's book purports to be autobiographical and tells the story of a young man whose beloved father was a Bishop in the church. The protagonist was angry as a child because his stepmother abused him, but he found acceptance and self-esteem on the streets of Newark because he was physically

powerful. He earned money robbing and beating people, went to jail, returned to crime upon his release, and then made even more money. The protagonist discusses his time at Rahway State Prison in great and compelling detail. The story ends when the protagonist learns that his father has passed away; he conveys his belief that this tragedy has led to his redemption, and he hopes that others might learn from his mistakes.

* * * Although Winstead's book and Jackson's works share similar themes and setting, the story of an angry and wronged protagonist who turns to a life of violence and crime has long been a part of the public domain [and is therefore not protected by copyright law]. Winstead argues * * * that a protagonist asking for God's help when his father dies, cutting drugs with mixing agents to maximize profits, and complaining about relatives who are addicts and steal the product, are protectable, but these things are not unique. To the extent that Jackson's works contain these elements, they are to be expected when two works express the same idea about "the streets" or explore the same theme. Winstead argues that not every protagonist whose story concerns guns, drugs, and violence in an urban setting winds up in prison or loses a parent, but this argument only serves to illustrate an important difference between his book and Jackson's film. Jackson's protagonist never spends any time in prison, whereas Winstead's protagonist devotes a considerable part of his story to his incarcerations.

In addition, Winstead's book and Jackson's works are different with respect to character, plot, mood, and sequence of events. Winstead's protagonist embarks on a life of crime at a very young age, but is redeemed by the death of his beloved

father. Jackson's protagonist turns to crime when he is much older and only after his mother is murdered. He winds up dead at a young age, unredeemed. Winstead's book is hopeful; Jackson's film is characterized * * * by moral apathy. It is true that both works involve the loss of a parent and the protagonist's recognition of the parent's importance in his life, but nowhere does Jackson appropriate anything unique about Winstead's expression of this generic topic.

Winstead contends that direct phrases from his book appear in Jackson's film. * * * He emphasizes these phrases: "Yo, where is my money at," "I would never have done no shit like that to you," "my father, my strength was gone," "he was everything to me," and "I did not know what to do," but, like the phrases "putting the work in," "get the dope, cut the dope," "let's keep it popping," and "the strong take from the weak but the smart take from everybody," they are either common in general or common with respect to hip hop culture, and do not enjoy copyright protection. The average person reading or listening to these phrases in the context of an overall story or song would not regard them as unique and protectable. Moreover, words and short phrases do not enjoy copyright protection. The similarity between Winstead's book and the lyrics to Jackson's songs on the album/CD is even more tenuous. "Stretching the dope" and "bloodshot red eyes" are common phrases that do not enjoy copyright protection. A side-by-side comparison of Winstead's book and the lyrics from Jackson's album/CD do not support a claim of copyright infringement.

For the foregoing reasons, we will affirm the order of the District Court dismissing [Winstead's] complaint.

Legal Reasoning Questions

1. Which expressions of an original work are protected by copyright law?

2. Is all copying copyright infringement? If not, what is the test for determining whether a creative work has been unlawfully copied?

3. How did the court in this case determine whether the defendant's work infringed on the plaintiff's copyright?

Remedies for Copyright Infringement Those who infringe copyrights may be liable for damages or criminal penalties. These range from actual damages or statutory damages, imposed at the court's discretion, to criminal proceedings for willful violations.

Actual damages are based on the harm caused to the copyright holder by the infringement, while statutory damages, not to exceed $150,000, are provided for under the Copyright Act. Criminal proceedings may result in fines and/or imprisonment. A court can also issue a permanent injunction against a defendant when the court deems it necessary to prevent future copyright infringement.

■ **CASE IN POINT 13.16** Rusty Carroll operated an online term paper business, R2C2, Inc., that offered up to 300,000 research papers for sale at nine Web sites. Individuals whose work was posted on these Web sites without their permission filed a lawsuit against Carroll for copyright infringement. Because Carroll had repeatedly failed to comply with court orders regarding discovery, the court found that the copyright infringement was likely to continue unless an injunction was issued. The court therefore issued a permanent injunction prohibiting Carroll and R2C2 from selling any term paper without sworn documentary evidence that the paper's author had given permission.[28] ■

The "Fair Use" Exception An exception to liability for copyright infringement is made under the "fair use" doctrine. In certain circumstances, a person or organization can reproduce copyrighted material without paying royalties. Section 107 of the Copyright Act provides as follows:

> [T]he fair use of a copyrighted work, including such use by reproduction in copies or phonorecords or by any other means specified by [Section 106 of the Copyright Act], for purposes such as criticism, comment, news reporting, teaching (including multiple copies for classroom use), scholarship, or research, is not an infringement of copyright. In determining whether the use made of a work in any particular case is a fair use the factors to be considered shall include—
>
> (1) the purpose and character of the use, including whether such use is of a commercial nature or is for nonprofit educational purposes;
> (2) the nature of the copyrighted work;
> (3) the amount and substantiality of the portion used in relation to the copyrighted work as a whole; and
> (4) the effect of the use upon the potential market for or value of the copyrighted work.

What Is Fair Use? Because these guidelines are very broad, the courts determine whether a particular use is fair on a case-by-case basis. Thus, anyone who reproduces copyrighted material may be committing a violation. In determining whether a use is fair, courts have often considered the fourth factor to be the most important.

■ **CASE IN POINT 13.17** A number of research universities, in partnership with Google, Inc., agreed to digitize books from their libraries and create a repository for them. Eighty member institutions (including many colleges and universities) contributed more than ten million works into the HathiTrust Digital Library. Some authors complained that this book scanning violated their rights and sued the HathiTrust and several associated entities for copyright infringement.

The court, however, sided with the defendants and held that making digital copies for the purposes of online search was a fair use. The library's searchable database enabled researchers to find terms of interest in the digital volumes—but not to read the volumes online. Therefore, the court concluded that the digitization did not provide a substitute that damaged the market for the original works.[29] ■

The First Sale Doctrine Section 109(a) of the Copyright Act provides that the owner of a particular item that is copyrighted can, without the authority of the copyright owner, sell or otherwise dispose of it. This rule is known as the first sale doctrine.

Under this doctrine, once a copyright owner sells or gives away a particular copy of a work, the copyright owner no longer has the right to control the distribution of that copy. Thus, for instance, a person who buys a copyrighted book can sell it to someone else. The first sale doctrine also applies to a person who receives promotional CDs, such as a music critic or radio programmer.[30]

■ **CASE IN POINT 13.18** Supap Kirtsaeng, a citizen of Thailand, was a graduate student at the University of Southern California. He enlisted friends and family in Thailand to buy copies of textbooks there and ship them to him in the United States. Kirtsaeng resold the textbooks on eBay, where he eventually made about $100,000.

John Wiley & Sons, Inc., had printed eight of those textbooks in Asia. Wiley sued Kirtsaeng in federal district court for copyright infringement. Kirtsaeng argued that Section 109(a) of the Copyright Act allows the first purchaser-owner of a book to sell it without the copyright owner's permission. The trial court held in favor of Wiley, and that decision was affirmed on appeal. Kirtsaeng then appealed to the United States Supreme Court, which ruled

---

28. *Weidner v. Carroll,* 2010 WL 310310 (S.D.Ill. 2010).

29. *Authors Guild, Inc., v. HathiTrust,* 755 F.3d 87 (2d Cir. 2014).
30. See, for example, *UMG Recordings, Inc. v. Augusto,* 628 F.3d 1175 (9th Cir. 2011).

in Kirtsaeng's favor. The first sale doctrine applies even to goods purchased abroad and resold in the United States.[31] ∎

13-3d Copyright Protection for Software

The Computer Software Copyright Act amended the Copyright Act to include computer programs in the list of creative works protected by federal copyright law.[32] Generally, copyright protection extends to those parts of a computer program that can be read by humans, such as the "high-level" language of a source code. Protection also extends to the binary-language object code, which is readable only by the computer, and to such elements as the overall structure, sequence, and organization of a program.

Not all aspects of software are protected, however. Courts typically have not extended copyright protection to the "look and feel"—the general appearance, command structure, video images, menus, windows, and other screen displays—of computer programs. (Note that copying the "look and feel" of another's product may be a violation of trade dress or trademark laws, however.) Sometimes it can be difficult for courts to decide which particular aspects of software are protected.

∎ **CASE IN POINT 13.19** Oracle America, Inc., is a software company that owns numerous application programming interfaces, or API packages. Oracle grants licenses to others to use these API packages to write applications in the Java programming language. Java is open and free for anyone to use, but using it requires an interface. When Google began using some of Oracle's API packages to run Java on its Android mobile devices, Oracle sued for copyright infringement. Google argued that the software packages were command structure and, as such, not protected under copyright law. Ultimately, a federal appellate court concluded that the API packages were source code and were entitled to copyright protection.[33] ∎

13-4 Trade Secrets

The law of trade secrets protects some business processes and information that are not, or cannot be, patented, copyrighted, or trademarked. A **trade secret** is basically information of commercial value, such as customer lists, plans, and research and development. Trade secrets may also include pricing information, marketing methods, production techniques, and generally anything that makes an individual company unique and that would have value to a competitor.

Unlike copyright and trademark protection, protection of trade secrets extends to both ideas and their expression. For this reason, and because there are no registration or filing requirements for trade secrets, trade secret protection may be well suited for software.

Of course, a company's trade secrets must be disclosed to some persons, particularly to key employees. Businesses generally attempt to protect their trade secrets by having all employees who use a protected process or information agree in their contracts, or in confidentiality agreements, never to divulge it.

13-4a State and Federal Law on Trade Secrets

Under Section 757 of the *Restatement of Torts,* those who disclose or use another's trade secret, without authorization, are liable to that other party if either of the following is true:

1. They discovered the secret by improper means.
2. Their disclosure or use constitutes a breach of a duty owed to the other party.

Stealing confidential business data by industrial espionage, such as by tapping into a competitor's computer, is a theft of trade secrets without any contractual violation and is actionable in itself.

Trade secrets have long been protected under the common law. Today, nearly every state has enacted trade secret laws based on the Uniform Trade Secrets Act.[34] Additionally, the Economic Espionage Act[35] makes the theft of trade secrets a federal crime.

13-4b Trade Secrets in Cyberspace

Computer technology is undercutting many business firms' ability to protect their confidential information, including trade secrets. For example, a dishonest employee could e-mail trade secrets in a company's computer to a competitor or a future employer. If e-mail is not an option, the employee might walk out with the information on a flash drive.

Misusing a company's social media account is yet another way in which employees may appropriate trade secrets. ∎ **CASE IN POINT 13.20** Noah Kravitz worked for a company called PhoneDog for four years as a product reviewer and video blogger. PhoneDog provided him with the Twitter account "@PhoneDog_Noah." Kravitz's popularity grew, and he had approximately 17,000

---

31. *Kirtsaeng v. John Wiley & Sons, Inc.*, ___ U.S. ___, 133 S.Ct. 1351, 185 L.Ed.2d 392 (2013).

32. Pub. L. No. 96-517 (1980), amending 17 U.S.C. Sections 101, 117.

33. *Oracle America, Inc. v. Google Inc.*, 750 F.3d 1339 (Fed.Cir. 2014).

34. The Uniform Trade Secrets Act, as drafted by the National Conference of Commissioners on Uniform State Laws (NCCUSL), can be found at uniformlaws.org.

35. 18 U.S.C. Sections 1831–1839.

followers by the time he quit. PhoneDog requested that Kravitz stop using the Twitter account. Although Kravitz changed his handle to "@noahkravitz," he continued to use the account. PhoneDog subsequently sued Kravitz for misappropriation of trade secrets, among other things. Kravitz moved for a dismissal, but the court found that the complaint adequately stated a cause of action for

misappropriation of trade secrets and allowed the suit to continue.[36] ■

Exhibit 13–1 outlines trade secrets and other forms of intellectual property discussed in this chapter.

36. *PhoneDog v. Kravitz*, 2011 WL 5415612 (N.D.Cal. 2011). See also *Mintel Learning Technology, Inc. v. Ambrow Education Holding Ltd.*, 2012 WL 762126 (N.D.Cal. 2012).

EXHIBIT 13–1 Forms of Intellectual Property

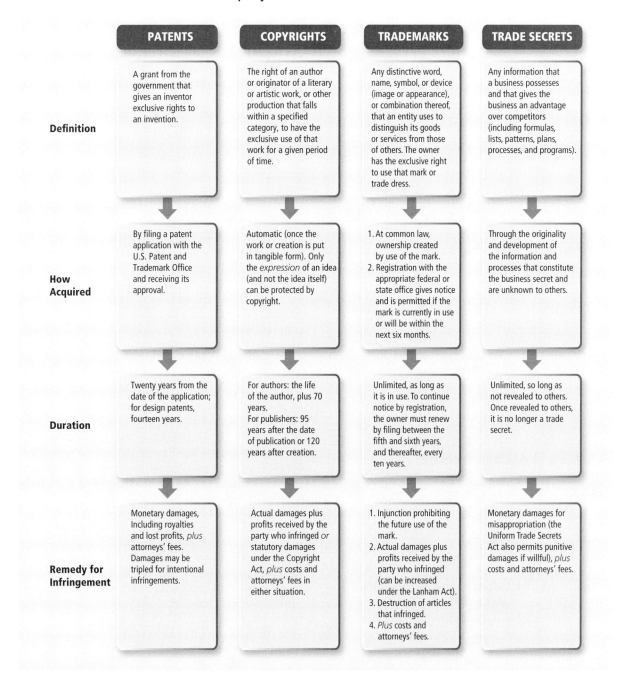

13–5 International Protection for Intellectual Property

For many years, the United States has been a party to various international agreements relating to intellectual property rights. For instance, the Paris Convention of 1883, to which almost 180 countries are signatory, allows parties in one country to file for patent and trademark protection in any of the other member countries. Other international agreements in this area include the Berne Convention, the Trade-Related Aspects of Intellectual Property Rights (known as the TRIPS agreement), the Madrid Protocol, and the Anti-Counterfeiting Trade Agreement.

13–5a The Berne Convention

Under the Berne Convention, if a U.S. citizen writes a book, every country that has signed the convention must recognize the U.S. author's copyright in the book. Also, if a citizen of a country that has not signed the convention first publishes a book in one of the 169 countries that have signed, all other countries that have signed the convention must recognize that author's copyright. Copyright notice is not needed to gain protection under the Berne Convention for works published after March 1, 1989.

In 2011, the European Union altered its copyright rules under the Berne Convention to extend the period of royalty protection for musicians from fifty years to seventy years. This decision aids major record labels as well as performers and musicians who previously faced losing royalties from sales of their older recordings. The profits of musicians and record companies have been shrinking for years because of the sharp decline in sales of compact discs and the rise in illegal downloads.

13–5b The TRIPS Agreement

The Berne Convention and other international agreements have given some protection to intellectual property on a worldwide level. None of them, however, has been as significant and far reaching in scope as the TRIPS agreement. Representatives from more than one hundred nations signed the TRIPS agreement in 1994.

Establishes Standards and Procedures The TRIPS agreement established, for the first time, standards for the international protection of intellectual property rights, including patents, trademarks, and copyrights for movies, computer programs, books, and music. Each member country of the World Trade Organization must include in its domestic laws broad intellectual property rights and effective remedies (including civil and criminal penalties) for violations of those rights.

Each member nation must also ensure that legal procedures are available for parties who wish to bring actions for infringement of intellectual property rights. Additionally, a related document established a mechanism for settling disputes among member nations.

Prohibits Discrimination Generally, the TRIPS agreement forbids member nations from discriminating against foreign owners of intellectual property rights in the administration, regulation, or adjudication of those rights. In other words, a member nation cannot give its own nationals (citizens) favorable treatment without offering the same treatment to nationals of all other member countries. ■ **EXAMPLE 13.21** A U.S. software manufacturer brings a suit for the infringement of intellectual property rights under Germany's national laws. Because Germany is a member of the TRIPS agreement, the U.S. manufacturer is entitled to receive the same treatment as a German manufacturer. ■

13–5c The Madrid Protocol

In the past, one of the difficulties in protecting U.S. trademarks internationally was the time and expense required to apply for trademark registration in foreign nations. The filing fees and procedures for trademark registration vary significantly among individual countries. The Madrid Protocol, which was signed into law in 2003, may help to resolve these problems.

The Madrid Protocol is an international treaty that has been signed by about a hundred countries. Under its provisions, a U.S. company wishing to register its trademark abroad can submit a single application and designate other member countries in which the company would like to register its mark. The treaty was designed to reduce the costs of international trademark protection by more than 60 percent.

Although the Madrid Protocol may simplify and reduce the cost of trademark registration in foreign countries, it remains to be seen whether it will provide significant benefits to trademark owners. Even with an easier registration process, there are still questions as to whether all member countries will enforce the law and protect the mark.

13–5d The Anti-Counterfeiting Trade Agreement

In 2011, Australia, Canada, Japan, Korea, Morocco, New Zealand, Singapore, and the United States signed the Anti-Counterfeiting Trade Agreement (ACTA), an international treaty to combat global counterfeiting and piracy. Other nations have since signed the agreement.

Goals and Provisions The goals of the treaty are to increase international cooperation, facilitate the best law enforcement practices, and provide a legal framework to combat counterfeiting. ACTA applies not only to counterfeit physical goods, such as medications, but also to pirated copyrighted works being distributed via the Internet. The idea is to create a new standard of enforcement for intellectual property rights that goes beyond the TRIPS agreement and encourages international cooperation and information sharing among signatory countries.

Border Searches Under ACTA, member nations are required to establish border measures that allow officials, on their own initiative, to search commercial shipments of imports and exports for counterfeit goods. The treaty neither requires nor prohibits random border searches of electronic devices, such as laptops, tablet devices, and smartphones, for infringing content.

If border authorities reasonably believe that any goods in transit are counterfeit, the treaty allows them to keep the suspect goods unless the owner proves that the items are authentic and noninfringing. The treaty allows member nations, in accordance with their own laws, to order online service providers to furnish information about suspected trademark and copyright infringers, including their identities.

Reviewing: Intellectual Property Rights

Two computer science majors, Trent and Xavier, have an idea for a new video game, which they propose to call Hallowed. They form a business and begin developing their idea. Several months later, Trent and Xavier run into a problem with their design and consult a friend, Brad, who is an expert in designing computer source codes. After the software is completed but before Hallowed is marketed, a video game called Halo 2 is released for both the Xbox and the Playstation systems. Halo 2 uses source codes similar to those of Hallowed and imitates Hallowed's overall look and feel, although not all the features are alike. Using the information presented in the chapter, answer the following questions.

1. Would the name *Hallowed* receive protection as a trademark or as trade dress? Explain.
2. If Trent and Xavier had obtained a patent on Hallowed, would the release of Halo 2 have infringed on their patent? Why or why not?
3. Based only on the facts described above, could Trent and Xavier sue the makers of Halo 2 for copyright infringement? Why or why not?
4. Suppose that Trent and Xavier discover that Brad took the idea of Hallowed and sold it to the company that produced Halo 2. Which type of intellectual property issue does this raise?

Debate This . . . *Congress has amended copyright law several times so that copyright holders now have protection for many decades. Was Congress right in extending these copyright time periods?*

Terms and Concepts

certification mark 251	intellectual property 246	trade dress 251
collective mark 251	license 252	trade name 252
copyright 256	patent 253	trade secret 260
dilution 248	service mark 251	trademark 246

Issue Spotters

1. Roslyn, a food buyer for Organic Cornucopia Food Company, decides to go into business for herself as Roslyn's Kitchen. She contacts Organic's suppliers, offering to buy their entire harvest for the next year. She also contacts Organic's customers, offering to sell her products at prices lower than Organic's prices. Has Roslyn violated any of the intellectual property rights discussed in this chapter? Explain. (See *Trade Secrets*.)

2. Global Products develops, patents, and markets software. World Copies, Inc., sells Global's software without the maker's permission. Is this patent infringement? If so, how might Global save the cost of suing World for infringement and at the same time profit from World's sales? (See *Patents*.)

• Check your answers to the Issue Spotters against the answers provided in Appendix B at the end of this text.

Business Scenarios

13–1. Fair Use. Professor Wise is teaching a summer seminar in business torts at State University. Several times during the course, he makes copies of relevant sections from business law texts and distributes them to his students. Wise does not realize that the daughter of one of the textbook authors is a member of his seminar. She tells her father about Wise's copying activities, which have taken place without her father's or his publisher's permission. Her father sues Wise for copyright infringement. Wise claims protection under the fair use doctrine. Who will prevail? Explain. (See *Copyrights*.)

13–2. Patent Infringement. John and Andrew Doney invented a hard-bearing device for balancing rotors. Although they obtained a patent for their invention from the U.S. Patent and Trademark Office, it was never used as an automobile wheel balancer. Some time later, Exetron Corp. produced an automobile wheel balancer that used a hard-bearing device with a support plate similar to that of the Doneys' device. Given that the Doneys had not used their device for automobile wheel balancing, does Exetron's use of a similar device infringe on the Doneys' patent? Why or why not? (See *Patents*.)

Business Case Problems

13–3. Spotlight on Macy's—Copyright Infringement.

United Fabrics International, Inc., bought a fabric design from an Italian designer and registered a copyright to it with the U.S. Copyright Office. When Macy's, Inc., began selling garments with a similar design, United filed a copyright infringement suit against Macy's. Macy's argued that United did not own a valid copyright to the design and so could not claim infringement. Does United have to prove that the copyright is valid to establish infringement? Explain. [*United Fabrics International, Inc. v. C&J Wear, Inc.,* 630 F.3d 1255 (9th Cir. 2011)] (See *Copyrights*.)

13–4. Theft of Trade Secrets. Hanjuan Jin, a citizen of China, worked as a software engineer for Motorola for many years in a division that created proprietary standards for cellular communications. Contrary to Motorola's policies, Jin also secretly began working as a consultant for Lemko Corp., as well as with Sun Kaisens, a Chinese software company, and with the Chinese military. She started corresponding with Sun Kaisens's management about a possible full-time job in China. Jin took several medical leaves of absence from Motorola to return to Beijing and work with Sun Kaisens and the military.

After one of these medical leaves, Jin returned to Motorola. Over a period of several days, Jin accessed and downloaded thousands of documents on her personal laptop and on pen drives. When, later, she attempted to board a flight to China from Chicago, she was randomly searched by U.S. Customs

and Border Protection officials at the airport. U.S. officials discovered the downloaded Motorola documents. Are there any circumstances under which Jin could avoid being prosecuted for theft of trade secrets? If so, what are these circumstances? Discuss fully. [*United States v. Hanjuan Jin,* 833 F.Supp.2d 977 (N.D.Ill. 2012)] (See *Trade Secrets*.)

13–5. Copyright Infringement. SilverEdge Systems Software hired Catherine Conrad to perform a singing telegram. SilverEdge arranged for James Bendewald to record Conrad's performance of her copyrighted song to post on its Web site. Conrad agreed to wear a microphone to assist in the recording, told Bendewald what to film, and asked for an additional fee only if SilverEdge used the video for a commercial purpose. Later, the company chose to post a video of a different performer's singing telegram instead. Conrad filed a suit in a federal district court against SilverEdge and Bendewald for copyright infringement. Are the defendants liable? Explain. [*Conrad v. Bendewald,* 500 Fed.Appx. 526 (7th Cir. 2013)] (See *Copyrights*.)

13–6. Business Case Problem with Sample Answer—Patents. The U.S. Patent and Trademark Office (PTO)

denied Raymond Gianelli's application for a patent for a "Rowing Machine"—an exercise machine on which a user *pulls* on handles to perform a rowing motion against a selected resistance. The PTO considered the device obvious in light of a previously patented "Chest Press Apparatus for Exercising

Regions of the Upper Body"—an exercise machine on which a user *pushes* on handles to overcome a selected resistance. On what ground might this result be reversed on appeal? Discuss. [*In re Gianelli,* 739 F.3d 1375 (Fed. Cir. 2014)] (See *Patents.*)

- **For a sample answer to Problem 13–6, go to Appendix C at the end of this text.**

13–7. Patents. Rodney Klassen was employed by the U.S. Department of Agriculture (USDA). Without the USDA's authorization, Klassen gave Jim Ludy, a grape grower, plant material for two unreleased varieties of grapes. For almost two years, most of Ludy's plantings bore no usable fruit, none of the grapes were sold, and no plant material was given to any other person. The plantings were visible from publicly accessible roads, but none of the vines were labeled, and the variety could not be identified by simply viewing the vines. Under patent law, an applicant may not obtain a patent for an invention that is in public use for more than one year before the date of the application. Could the USDA successfully apply for patents on the two varieties given to Ludy? Explain. [*Delano Farms Co. v. California Table Grape Commission,* 778 F.3d 1243 (Fed. Cir. 2015)] (See *Patents.*)

13–8. Copyright. Savant Homes, Inc., is a custom home designer and builder. Using what it called the "Anders Plan," Savant built a model house in Windsor, Colorado. This was a ranch house with two bedrooms on one side and a master suite on the other, separated by a combined family room, dining room, and kitchen. Ron and Tammie Wagner toured the Savant house. The same month, the Wagners hired builder Douglas Collins and his firm, Douglas Consulting, LLC, to build a house for them in Windsor. After it was built, Savant filed a suit in a federal district court against Collins for copyright infringement, alleging that the builder had copied the Anders Plan in the design and construction of the Wagner house. Collins showed that the Anders Plan consisted of standard elements and standard arrangements of elements. In these circumstances, has infringement occurred? Explain.

[*Savant Homes, Inc. v. Collins,* 809 F.3d 1133 (10th Cir. 2016)] (See *Copyrights.*)

13–9. A Question of Ethics—Copyright Infringement.

 *Custom Copies, Inc., prepares and sells coursepacks, which contain compilations of readings for college courses. A teacher selects the readings and delivers a syllabus to the copy shop, which obtains the materials from a library, copies them, and binds the copies. Blackwell Publishing, Inc., which owns the copyright to some of the materials, filed a suit, alleging copyright infringement. Custom Copies filed a motion to dismiss for failure to state a claim. [*Blackwell Publishing, Inc. v. Custom Copies, Inc., 2006 WL 1529503 (N.D.Fla. 2006)]* (See *Copyrights.*)

(a) Custom Copies argued, in part, that creating and selling did not "distribute" the coursepacks. Does a copy shop violate copyright law if it only copies materials for coursepacks? Does the copying fall under the "fair use" exception? Should the court grant the defendant's motion? Why or why not?

(b) What is the potential impact of copying and selling a book or journal without the permission of, and the payment of royalties or a fee to, the copyright owner? Explain.

13–10. Special Case Analysis—Copyright Infringement. Go to Case Analysis 13.3, *Winstead v. Jackson.* Read the excerpt, and answer the following questions. (See *Copyrights.*)

(a) Issue: This case focused on an allegation of copyright infringement involving what parties and which creative works?

(b) Rule of Law: What is the test for determining whether a creative work infringes the copyright of another work?

(c) Applying the Rule of Law: How did the court determine whether the claim of copyright infringement was supported in this case?

(d) Conclusion: Was the defendant liable for copyright infringement? Why or why not?

Legal Reasoning Group Activity

13–11. Patents. After years of research, your company develops a product that might revolutionize the green (environmentally conscious) building industry. The product is made from relatively inexpensive and widely available materials combined in a unique way that can substantially lower the heating and cooling costs of residential and commercial buildings. The company has registered the trademark it intends to use on the product and has filed a patent application with the U.S. Patent and Trademark Office. (See *Patents.*)

(a) One group should provide three reasons why this product does or does not qualify for patent protection.

(b) Another group should develop a four-step procedure for how your company can best protect its intellectual property rights (trademark, trade secret, and patent) and prevent domestic and foreign competitors from producing counterfeit goods or cheap knockoffs.

(c) Another group should list and explain three ways your company can utilize licensing.

CHAPTER 14

Internet Law, Social Media, and Privacy

The Internet has changed our lives and our laws. Technology has put the world at our fingertips and now allows even the smallest business to reach customers around the globe. At the same time, the Internet presents a variety of challenges for the law.

Courts are often in uncharted waters when deciding disputes that involve the Internet, social media, and online privacy. Judges may have no common law precedents to rely on when resolving a case. Long-standing principles of justice may be inapplicable. New rules are evolving, but often not as quickly as technology.

For instance, Facebook is confronting lawsuits over its facial recognition software, which scans the faces in uploaded photos and identifies them in other photos across the site. As a result of this technology, Facebook has collected and stored a huge amount of facial recognition data—data that some users claim violates their privacy. The situation has been complicated by DeepFace, a sophisticated new technology developed by Facebook that can recognize faces almost as well as humans. In fact, Facebook has already agreed not to use the facial recognition software in Europe due to privacy complaints. In the United States, however, privacy rights generally hinge on whether the person has a reasonable expectation of privacy, which might be lacking in photos posted online.

14–1 Internet Law

A number of laws specifically address issues that arise only on the Internet. Three such issues are unsolicited e-mail, domain names, and cybersquatting, as we discuss here. We also discuss how the law is dealing with problems of trademark infringement and dilution online.

14–1a Spam

Businesses and individuals alike are targets of **spam.**[1] Spam is the unsolicited "junk e-mail" that floods virtual mailboxes with advertisements, solicitations, and other messages. Considered relatively harmless in the early days of the Internet, by 2017 spam accounted for roughly 75 percent of all e-mails.

State Regulation of Spam In an attempt to combat spam, thirty-seven states have enacted laws that prohibit or regulate its use. Many state laws that regulate spam require the senders of e-mail ads to instruct the recipients on how they can "opt out" of further e-mail ads from the same sources. For instance, in some states, an unsolicited e-mail must include a toll-free phone number or return e-mail address that the recipient can use to ask the sender to send no more unsolicited e-mails.

The Federal CAN-SPAM Act In 2003, Congress enacted the Controlling the Assault of Non-Solicited Pornography and Marketing (CAN-SPAM) Act.[2] The legislation applies to any "commercial electronic mail messages" that are sent to promote a commercial product or service. Significantly, the statute preempts state antispam laws except for those provisions in state laws that prohibit false and deceptive e-mailing practices.

Generally, the act permits the sending of unsolicited commercial e-mail but prohibits certain types of spamming activities. Prohibited activities include the use of a false return address and the use of false, misleading, or deceptive information when sending e-mail. The statute also prohibits the use of "dictionary attacks"—sending messages to randomly generated e-mail addresses—and the "harvesting" of e-mail addresses from Web sites through the use of specialized software.

■ **EXAMPLE 14.1** Sanford Wallace, known as the "Spam King," is considered to be one of the world's most

---

1. The term *spam* is said to come from the lyrics of a Monty Python song that repeats the word *spam* over and over.

2. 15 U.S.C. Sections 7701 *et seq.*

prolific spammers. He has operated several businesses over the years that used *botnets* (automated spamming networks) to send out hundreds of millions of unwanted e-mails. Wallace also infected computers with spyware and then sold consumers the software to fix it. He infiltrated Facebook accounts to spam 27 million of its users. He has been sued by the Federal Trade Commission, Facebook, and MySpace, and ordered to pay millions of dollars in fines. The Federal Bureau of Investigation ultimately arrested Wallace and brought criminal charges. In 2015, he pleaded guilty to fraud, spam, and violating a court order not to access Facebook. Wallace was sentenced to serve thirty months in jail and pay $310,000 in fines. ■

Arresting prolific spammers, however, has done little to curb spam, which continues to flow at a rate of 70 billion messages per day. In effect, this means that the federal CAN-SPAM act has done little or nothing to reduce the amount of spam.

The U.S. Safe Web Act After the CAN-SPAM Act prohibited false and deceptive e-mails originating in the United States, spamming from servers located in other nations increased. These cross-border spammers generally were able to escape detection and legal sanctions because the Federal Trade Commission (FTC) lacked the authority to investigate foreign spamming.

Congress sought to rectify the situation by enacting the U.S. Safe Web Act (also known as the Undertaking Spam, Spyware, and Fraud Enforcement with Enforcers Beyond Borders Act).[3] The act allows the FTC to cooperate and share information with foreign agencies in investigating and prosecuting those involved in spamming, spyware, and various Internet frauds and deceptions.

The Safe Web Act also provides a "safe harbor" for **Internet service providers (ISPs)**—that is, organizations that provide access to the Internet. The safe harbor gives ISPs immunity from liability for supplying information to the FTC concerning possible unfair or deceptive conduct in foreign jurisdictions.

14–1b Domain Names

As e-commerce expanded worldwide, one issue that emerged involved the rights of a trademark owner to use the mark as part of a domain name. A **domain name** is part of an Internet address, such as "cengage.com."

Structure of Domain Names Every domain name ends with a top-level domain (TLD), which is the part of the name to the right of the period. The TLD often indicates the type of entity that operates the site. For instance, *com* is an abbreviation for *commercial,* and *edu* is short for *education.*

The second-level domain (SLD)—the part of the name to the left of the period—is chosen by the business entity or individual registering the domain name. Competition for SLDs among firms with similar names and products has led to numerous disputes. By using an identical or similar domain name, parties have attempted to profit from a competitor's **goodwill** (the nontangible value of a business).

Distribution System The Internet Corporation for Assigned Names and Numbers (ICANN), a nonprofit corporation, oversees the distribution of domain names and operates an online arbitration system. Due to numerous complaints, ICANN recently overhauled the domain name distribution system.

In 2012, ICANN started selling new generic top-level domain names (gTLDs) for an initial price of $185,000 plus an annual fee of $25,000. Whereas TLDs were limited to only a few terms (such as *com, net,* and *org*), gTLDs can take any form. By 2017, many companies and corporations had acquired gTLDs based on their brands, such as *aol, bmw, canon, target,* and *walmart.* Some companies have numerous gTLDs. Google's gTLDs, for instance, include *android, bing, chrome, gmail, goog,* and *YouTube.*

Because gTLDs have greatly increased the potential number of domain names, domain name registrars have proliferated. Registrar companies charge a fee to businesses and individuals to register new names and to renew annual registrations (often through automated software). Many of these companies also buy and sell expired domain names.

14–1c Cybersquatting

One of the goals of the new gTLD system was to address the problem of *cybersquatting*. **Cybersquatting** occurs when a person registers a domain name that is the same as, or confusingly similar to, the trademark of another and then offers to sell the domain name back to the trademark owner.

■ **CASE IN POINT 14.2** Apple, Inc., has repeatedly sued cybersquatters that registered domain names similar to its products, such as iphone4s.com and ipods.com. Apple won a judgment in litigation at the World Intellectual Property Organization against a company that was squatting on the domain name iPhone6s.com.[4] ■

---

3. Pub. L. No. 109-455, 120 Stat. 3372 (2006), codified in various sections of 15 U.S.C. and 12 U.S.C. Section 3412.

4. WIPO Case No. D2012-0951.

Anticybersquatting Legislation Because cybersquatting has led to so much litigation, Congress enacted the Anticybersquatting Consumer Protection Act (ACPA),[5] which amended the Lanham Act—the federal law protecting trademarks. The ACPA makes cybersquatting illegal when both of the following are true:

1. The domain name is identical or confusingly similar to the trademark of another.
2. The one registering, trafficking in, or using the domain name has a "bad faith intent" to profit from that trademark.

Despite the ACPA, cybersquatting continues to present a problem for businesses.

Frequent Changes in Domain Name Ownership Facilitates Cybersquatting All domain name registrars are supposed to relay information about their transactions to ICANN and other companies that keep a master list of domain names, but this does not always occur. The speed at which domain names change hands and the difficulty in tracking mass automated registrations have created an environment in which cybersquatting can flourish.

■ **CASE IN POINT 14.3** OnNet USA, Inc., owns the English-language rights to 9Dragons, a game with a martial arts theme, and operates a Web site for its promotion. When a party known as "Warv0x" began to operate a pirated version of the game at Play9D.com, OnNet filed an action under the ACPA in a federal court. OnNet was unable to obtain contact information for the owner of Play9D.com through its Australian domain name registrar, however, and thus could not complete service of process. Therefore, the federal court allowed OnNet to serve the defendant by publishing a notice of the suit in a newspaper in Gold Coast, Australia.[6] ■

Typosquatting Typosquatting is registering a name that is a misspelling of a popular brand, such as googl.com or appple.com. Because many Internet users are not perfect typists, Web pages using these misspelled names receive a lot of traffic. More traffic generally means increased profit (advertisers often pay Web sites based on the number of unique visits, or hits).

Typosquatting may sometimes fall beyond the reach of the ACPA. If the misspelling is significant, the trademark owner may have difficulty proving that the name is identical or confusingly similar to the trademark of another, as the ACPA requires.

Typosquatting adds costs for businesses seeking to protect their domain name rights. Companies must attempt to register not only legitimate variations of their domain names but also potential misspellings. Large corporations may have to register thousands of domain names across the globe just to protect their basic brands and trademarks.

Applicability and Sanctions of the ACPA The ACPA applies to all domain name registrations of trademarks. Successful plaintiffs in suits brought under the act can collect actual damages and profits, or they can elect to receive statutory damages ranging from $1,000 to $100,000.

Although some companies have been successful suing under the ACPA, there are roadblocks to pursuing such lawsuits. Some domain name registrars offer privacy services that hide the true owners of Web sites, making it difficult for trademark owners to identify cybersquatters. Thus, before bringing a suit, a trademark owner has to ask the court for a subpoena to discover the identity of the owner of the infringing Web site. Because of the high costs of court proceedings, discovery, and even arbitration, many disputes over cybersquatting are settled out of court.

To facilitate dispute resolution, ICANN now offers the Uniform Rapid Suspension (URS) system. URS allows trademark holders with clear-cut infringement claims to obtain rapid relief. ■ **EXAMPLE 14.4** In the first dispute filed involving gTLDs, IBM filed a complaint with URS against an individual who registered the domain names IBM.guru and IBM.ventures in February 2014. A week later, the URS panel decided in IBM's favor and suspended the two domain names. ■

14–1d Meta Tags

Meta tags are key words that give Internet browsers specific information about a Web page. Meta tags can be used to increase the likelihood that a site will be included in search engine results, even if the site has nothing to do with the key words. In effect, one site can appropriate the key words of other sites with more frequent hits so that the appropriating site will appear in the same search engine results as the more popular sites.

Using another's trademark in a meta tag without the owner's permission normally constitutes trademark infringement. Some uses of another's trademark as a meta tag may be permissible, however, if the use is reasonably

---

5. 15 U.S.C. Section 1129.
6. *OnNet USA, Inc. v. Play9D.com*, 2013 WL 120319 (N.D.Cal. 2013).

necessary and does not suggest that the owner authorized or sponsored the use.

■ **CASE IN POINT 14.5** Farzad and Lisa Tabari are auto brokers—the personal shoppers of the automotive world. They contact authorized dealers, solicit bids, and arrange for customers to buy from the dealer offering the best combination of location, availability, and price. The Tabaris offered this service at the Web sites buy-a-lexus.com and buyorleaselexus.com.

Toyota Motor Sales U.S.A., Inc., the exclusive distributor of Lexus vehicles and the owner of the Lexus mark, objected to the Tabaris' practices. The Tabaris removed Toyota's photographs and logo from their site and added a disclaimer in large type at the top, but they refused to give up their domain names. Toyota sued for infringement. The court forced the Tabaris to stop using any "domain name, service mark, trademark, trade name,

meta tag or other commercial indication of origin that includes the mark LEXUS."[7] ■

14–1e Trademark Dilution in the Online World

Trademark *dilution* occurs when a trademark is used, without authorization, in a way that diminishes the distinctive quality of the mark. Unlike trademark infringement, a claim of dilution does not require proof that consumers are likely to be confused by a connection between the unauthorized use and the mark. For this reason, the products involved need not be similar, as the following *Spotlight Case* illustrates.

---

7. *Toyota Motor Sales, U.S.A., Inc. v. Tabari*, 610 F.3d 171 (9th Cir. 2011).

Spotlight on Internet Porn

Case 14.1 Hasbro, Inc. v. Internet Entertainment Group, Ltd.
United States District Court, Western District of Washington, 1996 WL 84853 (1996).

Background and Facts In 1949, Hasbro, Inc.—then known as the Milton Bradley Company—published its first version of Candy Land, a children's board game. Hasbro is the owner of the trademark "Candy Land," which has been registered with the U.S. Patent and Trademark Office since 1951. Over the years, Hasbro has produced several versions of the game, including Candy Land puzzles, a travel version, a computer game, and a handheld electronic version. In the mid-1990s, Brian Cartmell and his employer, the Internet Entertainment Group, Ltd., used the term *candyland.com* as a domain name for a sexually explicit Internet site. Anyone who performed an online search using the word *candyland* was directed to this adult Web site. Hasbro filed a trademark dilution claim in a federal court, seeking a permanent injunction to prevent the defendants from using the Candy Land trademark.

In the Language of the Court
DWYER, U.S. District Judge
* * * *

2. Hasbro has demonstrated a probability of proving that defendants Internet Entertainment Group, Ltd., Brian Cartmell and Internet Entertainment Group, Inc. (collectively referred to as "defendants") have been diluting the value of Hasbro's CANDY LAND mark by using the name CANDYLAND to identify a sexually explicit Internet site, and by using the name string "candyland.com" as an Internet domain name which, when typed into an Internet-connected computer, provides Internet users with access to that site.
* * * *

4. Hasbro has shown that defendants' use of the CANDY LAND name and the domain name candyland.com in connection with their Internet site is causing irreparable injury to Hasbro.

5. *The probable harm to Hasbro from defendants' conduct outweighs any inconvenience that defendants will experience if they are required to stop using the CANDYLAND name.* [Emphasis added.]
* * * *

THEREFORE, IT IS HEREBY ORDERED that Hasbro's motion for preliminary injunction is granted.

Case 14.1 Continues

Case 14.1 Continued   **Decision and Remedy** *The federal district court granted Hasbro an injunction against the defendants, agreeing that the domain name* candyland *was "causing irreparable injury to Hasbro." The judge ordered the defendants to immediately remove all content from the* candyland.com *Web site and to stop using the Candy Land mark.*

Critical Thinking
- **Economic** *How can companies protect themselves from others who create Web sites that have similar domain names, and what limits each company's ability to be fully protected?*
- **What If the Facts Were Different?** *Suppose that the site using* candyland.com *had not been sexually explicit but had sold candy. Would the result have been the same? Explain.*

14–1f Licensing

A company may permit another party to use a trademark (or other intellectual property) under a license. A licensor might grant a license allowing its trademark to be used as part of a domain name, for instance.

Another type of license involves the use of a product such as software. This sort of licensing is ubiquitous in the online world. When you download an application on your smartphone, tablet, or other mobile device, for instance, you are typically entering into a license agreement. You are obtaining only a *license* to use that app and not ownership rights in it. Apps published on Google Play, for instance, may use its licensing service to prompt users to agree to a license at the time of installation and use.

Licensing agreements frequently include restrictions that prohibit licensees from sharing the file and using it to create similar software applications. The license may also limit the use of the application to a specific device or give permission to the user for a certain time period.

14–2 Copyrights in Digital Information

Copyright law is probably the most important form of intellectual property protection on the Internet. This is because much of the material on the Internet (including software and database information) is copyrighted, and in order to transfer that material online, it must be "copied." Generally, whenever a party downloads software or music into a computer's random access memory, or RAM, without authorization, a copyright is infringed.

Initially, criminal penalties for copyright violations could be imposed only if unauthorized copies were exchanged for financial gain. Then, Congress amended the law and extended criminal liability for the piracy of copyrighted materials to persons who exchange unauthorized copies of copyrighted works without realizing a profit.

14–2a Digital Millennium Copyright Act

In 1998, Congress enacted the Digital Millennium Copyright Act (DMCA).[8] The DMCA gave significant protection to owners of copyrights in digital information. Among other things, the act established civil and criminal penalties for anyone who circumvents (bypasses) encryption software or other technological antipiracy protection. Also prohibited are the manufacture, import, sale, and distribution of devices or services for circumvention.

Allows Fair Use The DMCA provides for exceptions to fit the needs of libraries, scientists, universities, and others. In general, the law does not restrict the "fair use" of circumvention methods for educational and other noncommercial purposes. For instance, circumvention is allowed to test computer security, to conduct encryption research, to protect personal privacy, and to enable parents to monitor their children's use of the Internet. The exceptions are to be reconsidered every three years.

One federal appellate court extended the situations in which the fair use doctrine applies. ■ **CASE IN POINT 14.6** Stephanie Lenz posted a short video on YouTube of her toddler son dancing with the Prince song "Let's Go Crazy" playing in the background. Universal Music Group (UMG) sent YouTube a take-down notice that stated that the video violated copyright law under the DMCA. YouTube removed the "dancing baby" video and

---

8. 17 U.S.C. Sections 512, 1201–1205, 1301–1332; and 28 U.S.C. Section 4001.

notified Lenz of the allegations of copyright infringement, warning her that repeated incidents of infringement could lead it to delete her account.

Lenz filed a lawsuit against UMG claiming that accusing her of infringement constituted a material misrepresentation (fraud) because UMG knew that Lenz's video was a fair use of the song. The district court held that UMG should have considered the fair use doctrine before sending the take-down notice. UMG appealed, and the U.S. Court of Appeals for the Ninth Circuit affirmed. Lenz was allowed to pursue nominal damages from UMG for sending the notice without considering whether her use was fair.[9] ■

Limits Liability of Internet Service Providers

The DMCA also limits the liability of Internet service providers (ISPs). Under the act, an ISP is not liable for copyright infringement by its customer *unless* the ISP is aware of the subscriber's violation. An ISP may be held liable only if it fails to take action to shut down the subscriber after learning of the violation. A copyright holder must act promptly, however, by pursuing a claim in court, or the subscriber has the right to be restored to online access.

14–2b File-Sharing Technology

Soon after the Internet became popular, a few enterprising programmers created software to compress large data files, particularly those associated with music. The best-known compression and decompression system is MP3, which enables music fans to download songs or entire CDs onto their computers or onto portable listening devices, such as smartphones and tablets. The MP3 system also made it possible for music fans to access other fans' files by engaging in file-sharing via the Internet.

Methods of File-Sharing File-sharing is accomplished through **peer-to-peer (P2P) networking.** The concept is simple. Rather than going through a central Web server, P2P networking uses numerous personal computers (PCs) that are connected to the Internet. Individuals on the same network can access files stored on one another's PCs through a **distributed network.** Parts of the network may be distributed all over the country or the world, which offers an unlimited number of uses. Persons scattered throughout the country or the world can work together on the same project by using file-sharing programs.

A newer method of sharing files via the Internet is **cloud computing,** which is essentially a subscription-based or pay-per-use service that extends a computer's software or storage capabilities. Cloud computing can deliver a single application through a browser to multiple users. Alternatively, cloud computing might be a utility program to pool resources and provide data storage and virtual servers that can be accessed on demand. Amazon, Facebook, Google, IBM, and Sun Microsystems are using and developing more cloud computing services.

Sharing Stored Music and Movies When file-sharing is used to download others' stored music files, copyright issues arise. Recording artists and their labels stand to lose large amounts of royalties and revenues if relatively few digital downloads or CDs are purchased and then made available on distributed networks. Anyone can get the music for free on these networks, which has prompted recording companies to pursue individuals for file-sharing copyrighted works.

■ **CASE IN POINT 14.7** Maverick Recording Company and other recording companies sued Whitney Harper in federal court for copyright infringement. Harper had used a file-sharing program to download a number of copyrighted songs from the Internet and had then shared the audio files with others via a P2P network. The plaintiffs sought $750 per infringed work—the minimum amount of statutory damages available under the Copyright Act.

Harper claimed that she was an "innocent" infringer because she was unaware that her actions constituted copyright infringement. Under the act, innocent infringement can result in a reduced penalty. The court, however, noted that a copyright notice appeared on all the songs that Harper had downloaded. She therefore could not assert the innocent infringer defense, and the court ordered her to pay damages of $750 per infringed work.[10] ■

Pirated Movies and Television File-sharing also creates problems for the motion picture and television industries, which lose significant amounts of revenue annually as a result of piracy. Numerous Web sites offer software that facilitates the illegal copying of movies and television programs. BitTorrent, for instance, is a P2P protocol that enables users to download and transfer high-quality files from the Internet. Popcorn Time is a BitTorent site that offers streaming services that enable users to watch pirated movies and television shows without downloading them.

---

9. *Lenz v. Universal Music Group,* 801 F.3d 1126 (9th Cir. 2015).

10. *Maverick Recording Co. v. Harper,* 598 F.3d 193 (2010).

14–3 Social Media

Social media provide a means by which people can create, share, and exchange ideas and comments via the Internet. Social networking sites, such as Facebook, Google+, LinkedIn, Pinterest, and Tumblr, have become ubiquitous. Studies show that Internet users spend more time on social networks than at any other sites. The amount of time people spend accessing social networks on their smartphones and other mobile devices has been increasing every year (by nearly 30 percent in 2016 alone).

■ **EXAMPLE 14.8** Facebook has more than 1.6 billion active monthly users. Individuals use Facebook to maintain social contacts, update friends on events, and distribute images to others. Facebook members often share common interests based on their school, location, or recreational affiliation, such as a sports team. ■

14–3a Legal Issues

The emergence of Facebook and other social networking sites has created a number of legal and ethical issues for businesses. For instance, a firm's rights in valuable intellectual property may be infringed if users post trademarked images or copyrighted materials on these sites without permission. Various aspects of the legal process may involve the content of social media, as discussed next. Employers' social media policies may also be at issue.

Impact on Litigation Social media posts now are routinely included in discovery in litigation because they can provide damaging information that establishes a person's intent or what she or he knew at a particular time. Like e-mail, posts on social networks can be the smoking gun that leads to liability.

Tweets and other social media posts can also be used to reduce damages awards. ■ **EXAMPLE 14.9** Jill Daniels sued for injuries she sustained in a car accident, claiming that her injuries made it impossible for her to continue working as a hairstylist. The jury initially determined that her damages were $237,000, but when the jurors saw tweets and photographs of Daniels partying in New Orleans and vacationing on the beach, they reduced the final award to $142,000. ■

Impact on Settlement Agreements Social media posts have been used to invalidate settlement agreements that contain confidentiality clauses. ■ **CASE IN POINT 14.10** Patrick Snay was the headmaster of Gulliver Preparatory School in Florida. When Gulliver did not renew

Snay's employment contract, Snay sued the school for age discrimination. During mediation, Snay agreed to settle the case for $80,000 and signed a confidentiality clause that required him and his wife not to disclose the "terms and existence" of the agreement. Nevertheless, Snay and his wife told their daughter, Dana, that the dispute had been settled and that they were happy with the results.

Dana, a college student, had recently graduated from Gulliver and, according to Snay, had suffered retaliation at the school. Dana posted a Facebook comment that said "Mama and Papa Snay won the case against Gulliver. Gulliver is now officially paying for my vacation to Europe this summer. SUCK IT." The comment went out to 1,200 of Dana's Facebook friends, many of whom were Gulliver students, and school officials soon learned of it. The school immediately notified Snay that he had breached the confidentiality clause and refused to pay the settlement amount. Ultimately, a state intermediate appellate court held that Snay had breached the confidentiality clause and therefore could not enforce the settlement agreement.[11] ■

Criminal Investigations Law enforcement uses social media to detect and prosecute criminals. A surprising number of criminals boast about their illegal activities on social media. ■ **EXAMPLE 14.11** A nineteen-year-old posts a message on Facebook bragging about how drunk he was on New Year's Eve and apologizing to the owner of the parked car that he hit. The next day, police officers arrest him for drunk driving and leaving the scene of an accident. ■

Some police departments now authorize officers to go undercover on social media sites. ■ **EXAMPLE 14.12** As part of Operation Crew Cut, New York Police Department (NYPD) officers routinely pretend to be young women in order to "friend" suspects on Facebook. Using these fake identities, officers are able to avoid the social media site's privacy settings and gain valuable information about illegal activities. ■

Administrative Agency Investigations Federal regulators also use social media posts in their investigations into illegal activities. ■ **EXAMPLE 14.13** Reed Hastings, the top executive of Netflix, stated on Facebook that Netflix subscribers had watched a billion hours of video the previous month. As a result, Netflix's stock price rose, which prompted a federal agency investigation. Under securities laws, such a statement is considered to be material information to investors. Thus, it must be disclosed to

---

11. *Gulliver Schools, Inc. v. Snay*, 137 So.3d 1045 (Fla.App. 2014).

all investors, not just a select group, such as those who had access to Hastings's Facebook post.

The agency ultimately concluded that it could not hold Hastings responsible for any wrongdoing because the agency's policy on social media use was not clear. The agency then issued new guidelines that allow companies to disclose material information through social media if investors have been notified in advance. ■

In addition, an administrative law judge can base her or his decision on the content of social media posts. ■ **CASE IN POINT 14.14** Jennifer O'Brien was a tenured teacher at a public school in New Jersey when she posted two messages on her Facebook page. "I'm not a teacher—I'm a warden for future criminals!" and "They had a scared straight program in school—why couldn't I bring first graders?" Not surprisingly, outraged parents protested. The deputy superintendent of schools filed a complaint against O'Brien with the state's commissioner of education, charging her with conduct unbecoming a teacher.

After a hearing, an administrative law judge (ALJ) ordered that O'Brien be removed from her teaching position. O'Brien appealed to a state court, claiming that her Facebook postings were protected by the First Amendment and could not be used by the school district to discipline or discharge her. The court found that O'Brien had failed to establish that her Facebook postings were protected speech and that the seriousness of O'Brien's conduct warranted removal from her position.[12] ■

Employers' Social Media Policies Many large corporations have established specific guidelines on using social media in the workplace. Employees who use social media in a way that violates their employer's stated policies may be disciplined or fired from their jobs. Courts and administrative agencies usually uphold an employer's right to terminate a person based on his or her violation of a social media policy.

■ **CASE IN POINT 14.15** Virginia Rodriquez worked for Wal-Mart Stores, Inc., for almost twenty years and had been promoted to management. Then she was disciplined for violating the company's policies by having a fellow employee use Rodriquez's password to alter the price of an item that she purchased. Under Wal-Mart's rules, another violation within a year would mean termination.

Nine months later, on Facebook, Rodriquez publicly chastised employees under her supervision for calling in sick to go to a party. The posting violated Wal-Mart's "Social Media Policy," which was "to avoid public comment that adversely affects employees." Wal-Mart

terminated Rodriquez. She filed a lawsuit, alleging discrimination, but the court issued a summary judgment in Wal-Mart's favor.[13] ■

14–3b The Electronic Communications Privacy Act

The Electronic Communications Privacy Act (ECPA)[14] amended federal wiretapping law to cover electronic forms of communications. Although Congress enacted the ECPA many years before social media networks existed, it nevertheless applies to communications through social media.

The ECPA prohibits the intentional interception of any wire, oral, or electronic communication. It also prohibits the intentional disclosure or use of the information obtained by the interception.

Exclusions Excluded from the ECPA's coverage are any electronic communications through devices that an employer provides for its employee to use "in the ordinary course of its business." Consequently, if a company provides the electronic device (cell phone, laptop, tablet) to the employee for ordinary business use, the company is not prohibited from intercepting business communications made on it. This "business-extension exception" permits employers to monitor employees' electronic communications made in the ordinary course of business. It does not, however, permit employers to monitor employees' personal communications.

Another exception to the ECPA allows an employer to avoid liability under the act if the employees consent to having their electronic communications monitored by the employer.

Stored Communications Part of the ECPA is known as the Stored Communications Act (SCA).[15] The SCA prohibits intentional and unauthorized access to *stored* electronic communications and sets forth criminal and civil sanctions for violators. A person can violate the SCA by intentionally accessing a stored electronic communication. The SCA also prevents "providers" of communication services (such as cell phone companies and social media networks) from divulging private communications to certain entities and individuals.

■ **CASE IN POINT 14.16** Two restaurant employees, Brian Pietrylo and Doreen Marino, were fired after their manager uncovered their password-protected MySpace group. The group's communications, stored on MySpace's

---

12. *In re O'Brien*, 2013 WL 132508 (N.J. Sup. 2013).

13. *Rodriquez v. Wal-Mart Stores, Inc.*, 2013 WL 102674 (N.D.Tex. 2013).
14. 18 U.S.C. Sections 2510–2521.
15. 18 U.S.C. Sections 2701–2711.

Web site, contained sexual remarks about customers and management, as well as comments about illegal drug use and violent behavior. One employee said the group's purpose was to "vent about any BS we deal with out of work without any outside eyes spying on us."

The restaurant learned about the private MySpace group when a hostess showed it to a manager who requested access. The hostess was not explicitly threatened with termination but feared she would lose her job if she did not comply.

After they were fired, Pietrylo and Marino filed a lawsuit against the restaurant. They claimed that their former employer had gained unauthorized access to their MySpace group communications in violation of the SCA. The court allowed the employees' SCA claim, and the jury awarded them $17,003 in compensatory and punitive damages.[16] ∎

14–3c Protection of Social Media Passwords

In recent years, employees and applicants for jobs or colleges have sometimes been asked to divulge their social media passwords. An employer or school may look at an individual's Facebook or other account to see if it includes controversial postings such as racially discriminatory remarks or photos of drug parties. Such postings can have a negative effect on a person's prospects even if they were made years earlier or are taken out of context.

By 2017, about half of the states had enacted legislation to protect individuals from having to disclose their social media passwords. Each state's law is slightly different. Some states, such as Michigan, prohibit employers from taking adverse action against an employee or job applicant based on what the person has posted online. Michigan's law also applies to e-mail and cloud storage accounts.

Legislation will not completely prevent employers and others from taking actions against a person based on his or her social network postings, though. Management and human resources personnel are unlikely to admit that they looked at someone's Facebook page and that it influenced their decision. They may not even have to admit to looking at the Facebook page if they use private browsing, which enables people to keep their Web browsing activities confidential. How, then, would a rejected job applicant be able to prove that she or he was rejected because the employer accessed social media postings? See this chapter's *Digital Update* feature for a discussion of employer monitoring of social media.

14–3d Company-wide Social Media Networks

Many companies, including Dell, Inc., and Nikon Instruments, form their own internal social media networks. Software companies offer a variety of systems, including Salesforce.com's Chatter, Microsoft's Yammer, and Cisco Systems' WebEx Social. Posts on these internal networks, or *intranets,* are quite different from the typical posts on Facebook, LinkedIn, and Twitter. Employees use these intranets to exchange messages about topics related to their work, such as deals that are closing, new products, production flaws, how a team is solving a problem, and the details of customer orders. Thus, the tone is businesslike.

Protection of Trade Secrets An important advantage to using an internal system for employee communications is that the company can better protect its trade secrets. The company usually decides which employees can see particular intranet files and which employees will belong to each specific "social" group within the company. Companies providing internal social media networks often keep the resulting data on their own servers in secure "clouds."

Other Advantages Internal social media systems also offer additional benefits. They provide real-time information about important issues, such as production glitches. Additionally, posts can include tips on how to best sell new products or deal with difficult customers, as well as information about competitors' products and services. Another major benefit is a significant reduction in e-mail. Rather than wasting fellow employees' time reading mass e-mailings, workers can post messages or collaborate on presentations via the company's social network.

14–4 Online Defamation

Cyber torts are torts that arise from online conduct. One of the most prevalent cyber torts is online defamation. Defamation is wrongfully hurting a person's reputation by communicating false statements about that person to others. Because the Internet enables individuals to communicate with large numbers of people simultaneously (via a blog or tweet, for instance), online defamation has become a problem in today's legal environment.

∎ **EXAMPLE 14.17** Singer-songwriter Courtney Love was sued for defamation based on remarks she posted

---

16. *Pietrylo v. Hillstone Restaurant Group*, 2009 WL 3128420 (D.N.J. 2009).

DIGITAL UPDATE — Monitoring Employees' Social Media—Right or Wrong?

Just about everyone seems to be using some form of social media. That, of course, includes employees. Increasingly, employees' social media use is being monitored by their employers. Sometimes, employees are even being fired over their social media posts.

Monitoring of Employees' Social Media Use

Employers have monitored their employees' Internet use for years. According to Gartner, Inc., an information technology advisory company, employers are now using the same technology to examine workers' social media use.

Companies have a number of concerns about how their employees use social media. For one thing, they may worry about security problems, such as employees' posting unauthorized videos of company activities. In addition, they do not wish to have their clients discussed on employees' social media posts. Finally, some companies are concerned that certain posts may violate the law. For instance, if hospital employees discuss patients, they not only are disregarding hospital regulations, but also are violating the federal Health Insurance Portability and Accountability Act (HIPAA).[a]

Restrictions on Access to Employees' Social Media Records

In disputes over discrimination, hostile work environment, and other employment situations, employers typically seek access to certain employees' complete social media records. The courts have not uniformly

accepted such access.[b] The general rule is that during any dispute, courts require employers to demonstrate a "reasonable" need for social media evidence. So-called fishing expeditions are rarely allowed.

But what about regular monitoring of employee online behavior? As long as an employee has no expectation of privacy on the social media site and is not part of a protected class, courts will side with employers. After all, social media posts are public, even when privacy settings are enabled. Note, though, that whenever employer monitoring involves obtaining information about religious affiliation, sexual orientation, or pregnancies, litigation may ensue.

The rule of thumb is that the more personal the information about any employee, the more problematic social media monitoring becomes. As one expert in the field stated, "Recent cases teach that when a company decides to monitor employee behavior online, uncertainty takes over."[c]

Critical Thinking *Some companies use internal social media networks for work-related employee communications. Would the same legal rules that apply to monitoring public social media platforms, such as Twitter and Facebook, also apply to company-provided social media platforms?*

---

a. Pub. L. No. 104-191 (1996); 29 U.S.C. Sections 1181 *et seq.*

b. *Ogden v. All-State Career School*, 299 F.R.D. 446 (2014). See also *Appler v. Mead Johnson & Co., LLC*, 2015 WL 5615038 (S.D.Ind. 2015), and *In re Milo's Kitchen Dog Treats Consol*, 307 F.R.D. 177 (2015).

c. Rodney Satterwhite, "'Friend' or Foe? Balancing the Litigation Risks of Monitoring Employees' Social Media Profiles at Various Stages of Employment," 2014 WL 5465794 (2014).

---

about fashion designer Dawn Simorangkir on Twitter. Love claimed that her statements were statements of opinion (rather than statements of fact, as required) and therefore were not actionable as defamation. Nevertheless, Love ended up paying $430,000 to settle the case out of court. ■

14–4a Identifying the Author of Online Defamation

An initial issue raised by online defamation is simply discovering who is committing it. In the real world,

identifying the author of a defamatory remark generally is an easy matter. It is more difficult if a business firm discovers that defamatory statements about its policies and products are being posted in an online forum, because the postings are anonymous. Therefore, a threshold barrier to anyone who seeks to bring an action for online defamation is discovering the identity of the person who posted the defamatory message.

An Internet service provider (ISP) can disclose personal information about its customers only when ordered to do so by a court. Consequently, businesses and individuals are increasingly bringing lawsuits against "John Does" (John Doe, Jane Doe, and the like are fictitious names used in lawsuits when the identity of a party is not known or when a party wishes to conceal his or her name for privacy reasons). Then, using the authority of the courts, the plaintiffs can obtain from the ISPs the identity of the persons responsible for the defamatory messages.

■ **CASE IN POINT 14.18** Seven users of Yelp, Inc.—a social networking Web site for consumer reviews—posted negative reviews of Hadeed Carpet Cleaning, Inc., in Alexandria, Virginia. Hadeed brought a defamation suit against the "John Doe" reviewers in a Virginia state court, claiming that because these individuals were not actual customers, their comments were false and defamatory. Yelp failed to comply with a court order to reveal the users' identities and was held in contempt.

Yelp appealed, claiming that releasing the identities would violate the defendants' First Amendment right to free speech. A state intermediate appellate court affirmed the lower court's judgment, noting that Hadeed could not move forward with its defamation lawsuit unless it knew the identities of the defendants. Revealing the identities of Yelp reviewers was not a violation of their First Amendment rights.[17] ■

14–4b Liability of Internet Service Providers

Recall that under tort law those who repeat or otherwise republish a defamatory statement are normally subject to liability. Thus, newspapers, magazines, and television and radio stations are subject to liability for defamatory content that they publish or broadcast, even though the content was prepared or created by others. Applying this rule to cyberspace, however, raises an important issue: Should ISPs be regarded as publishers and therefore be held liable for defamatory messages that are posted by their users?

General Rule The Communications Decency Act (CDA) states that "[n]o provider or user of an interactive computer service shall be treated as the publisher or speaker of any information provided by another information content provider."[18] Thus, under the CDA, ISPs usually are treated differently from publishers in print and other media and are not liable for publishing defamatory statements that come from a third party.

Exceptions Although the courts generally have construed the CDA as providing a broad shield to protect ISPs from liability for third party content, some courts have started establishing limits to this immunity. ■ **CASE IN POINT 14.19** Roommate.com, LLC, operates an online roommate-matching Web site that helps individuals find roommates based on their descriptions of themselves and their roommate preferences. Users respond to a series of online questions, choosing from answers in drop-down and select-a-box menus.

Some of the questions asked users to disclose their sex, family status, and sexual orientation—which is not permitted under the federal Fair Housing Act. When a nonprofit housing organization sued Roommate.com, the company claimed it was immune from liability under the CDA. A federal appellate court disagreed and ruled that Roommate.com was not immune from liability. By creating the Web site and the questionnaire and answer choices, Roommate.com prompted users to express discriminatory preferences and matched users based on these preferences in violation of federal law.[19] ■

14–5 Other Actions Involving Online Posts

Online conduct can give rise to a wide variety of legal actions. E-mails, tweets, posts, and every sort of online communication can form the basis for almost any type of tort. For example, in addition to defamation, suits relating to online conduct may involve allegations of wrongful interference or infliction of emotional distress.

Besides actions grounded in the common law, online conduct may give rise to a cause of action directed expressly at online communications by a statute. In the following case, the court was asked to issue an injunction to prohibit speech that was alleged to constitute *cyberstalking*. The applicable statute defined this term to require, in part, "substantial emotional distress."

---

17. *Yelp, Inc. v. Hadeed Carpet Cleaning, Inc.*, 62 Va.App. 678, 752 S.E.2d 554 (2014).
18. 47 U.S.C. Section 230.

19. *Fair Housing Council of San Fernando Valley v. Roommate.com, LLC*, 666 F.3d 1216 (9th Cir. 2012).

David v. Textor

District Court of Appeal of Florida, Fourth District, 41 Fla.L.Weekly D131, 189 So.3d 871 (2016).

In the Language of the Court

WARNER, J. [Judge].

* * * *

[Alkiviades] David and [John] Textor both have companies which produce holograms used in the music industry. * * * Shortly before the Billboard Music Awards show, it was announced that Textor's company, Pulse Entertainment, would show a Michael Jackson hologram performance. Immediately thereafter, David's company, Hologram USA, Inc., * * * filed suit for patent infringement against Pulse in the U.S. District Court in Nevada * * * . Pulse countered by filing a business tort suit against David in California.

[One month later,] Textor filed a petition [in a Florida state court against David under Florida Statutes] Sections 784.046 and 784.0485, which concern cyberstalking.

The alleged acts of cyberstalking were (1) a * * * text from David to Textor, demanding that Textor give credit to David's company at the Billboard Awards show for the hologram, for which David would drop his patent infringement suit; otherwise, he threatened to increase damages in that suit and stated, "You will be ruined I promise you"; (2) an e-mail from David to business associates (other than Textor) that he had more information about Textor that would be released soon, but not specifying what that information was; (3) an online article from July 2014 on Entrepreneur.com, in which David was quoted as saying that he "would have killed [Textor] if he could"; and (4) articles about Textor that David posted and reposted in various online outlets.

* * * *

The trial court [issued an injunction] prohibiting David from communicating with Textor or posting any information about him online, and ordering that

he remove any materials he already had posted.

David * * * moved to dissolve the * * * injunction. * * * The court denied the motion to dissolve and amended its order to prohibit David from communicating with Textor either through electronic means, in person, or through third parties. The amended order also provided:

> Respondent David shall immediately cease and desist from sending any text messages, e-mails, posting any tweets (including the re-tweeting or forwarding), posting any images or other forms of communication directed at John Textor without a legitimate purpose. Threats or warnings of physical or emotional harm or attempts to extort Textor or any entity associated with Textor by Respondent David, personally or through his agents, directed to John Textor, directly or by other means, are prohibited.

From this order, David appeals.

David claims that none of the allegations in the petition constitute cyberstalking, but are merely heated rhetoric over a business dispute. Further, he claims that the injunction constitutes a prior restraint on speech, which violates the First Amendment.

[Florida Statutes] Section 784.0485 allows an injunction against * * * cyberstalking. * * * Section 784.048 defines * * * cyberstalking:

> * * * "Cyberstalk" means to engage in a course of conduct to communicate, or to cause to be communicated, words, images, or language by or through the use of electronic mail or electronic communication, directed at a specific person, causing substantial emotional distress to that person and serving no legitimate purpose.

Whether a communication causes substantial emotional distress * * * is governed by the reasonable person standard. * * * Whether a communication serves a legitimate purpose * * * will cover a wide variety of conduct. * * * Where comments are made on an electronic medium to be read by others, they cannot be said to be directed to a particular person. [Emphasis added.]

In this case, Textor alleged that two communications came directly from David to him, both of which were demands that Textor drop his lawsuit. In neither of them did David make any threat to Textor's safety. From the full e-mail, David's threats that Textor would be "sorry" if he didn't settle must be taken in the context of the lawsuit and its potential cost to Textor. Because of the existence of the various lawsuits and the heated controversy over the hologram patents, these e-mails had a legitimate purpose in trying to get Textor to drop what David considered a spurious lawsuit. Moreover, nothing in the e-mails should have caused substantial emotional distress to Textor, himself a sophisticated businessman. Indeed, that they did not is reflected in Textor's refusal to settle or adhere to their terms.

The postings online are also not communications which would cause substantial emotional distress. Most of them are simply re-tweets of articles or headlines involving Textor. That they may be embarrassing to Textor is not at all the same as causing him substantial emotional distress sufficient to obtain an injunction.

Even the alleged physical threat made by David in an online interview, that David would have killed Textor if he could have, would not cause a reasonable person substantial emotional distress.

Case 14.2 Continues

Case 14.2 Continued

In the online article the author stated that "David joked" when stating that he would have killed Textor. Spoken to a journalist for publication, it hardly amounts to an actual and credible threat of violence to Textor.

In sum, none of the allegations in Textor's petition show acts constituting cyberstalking, in that a reasonable person would not suffer substantial emotional distress over them. Those communications made directly to Textor served a legitimate purpose.

An injunction in this case would also violate [the freedom of speech under the U.S. Constitution's First Amendment. An] injunction directed to speech is a classic example of prior restraint on speech triggering First Amendment concerns. * * * *Prior restraints on speech and publication are the most serious and the least tolerable infringement on First Amendment rights.* [Florida Statutes] Section 784.048 itself recognizes the First Amendment rights of individuals by concluding that a "course of conduct" for

purposes of the statute does not include protected speech. [Emphasis added.]

Here, the online postings simply provide information, gleaned from other sources, regarding Textor and the many lawsuits against him. The injunction prevents not only communications *to* Textor, but also communications *about* Textor. Such prohibition by prior restraint violates the Constitution.

For the foregoing reasons, we reverse the * * * injunction and remand with directions to dismiss the petition.

Legal Reasoning Questions

1. How is *cyberstalking* defined by the statute in this case, and what conduct by the defendant allegedly fit this definition?

2. What standard determines whether certain conduct meets the requirements of the cyberstalking statute? What law or legal principle limits an injunction that is directed at speech?

3. Why did the court in this case "reverse the . . . injunction and remand with directions to dismiss the petition"? Explain.

14–6 Privacy

Facebook, Google, and Yahoo have all been accused of violating users' privacy rights. The courts have held that the right to privacy is guaranteed by the Bill of Rights, and some state constitutions. To maintain a suit for the invasion of privacy, though, a person must have a reasonable expectation of privacy in the particular situation.

14–6a Reasonable Expectation of Privacy

People clearly have a reasonable expectation of privacy when they enter their personal banking or credit-card information online. They also have a reasonable expectation that online companies will follow their own privacy policies. But it is probably not reasonable to expect privacy in statements made on Twitter—or photos posted on Twitter, Flickr, or Instagram, for that matter.

Sometimes, to be sure, people mistakenly believe that they are making statements or posting photos in a private forum. ■ **EXAMPLE 14.20** Randi Zuckerberg, the older sister of Mark Zuckerberg (the founder of Facebook), used a mobile app called "Poke" to post a "private" photo on Facebook of their family gathering during the holidays. Poke allows the sender to decide how long the photo can be seen by others. Facebook allows users to configure their privacy settings to limit access to photos, which Randi thought she had done. Nonetheless, the photo showed up in the Facebook feed of Callie Schweitzer, who then put it on Twitter, where it eventually "went viral." Schweitzer apologized and removed the photo, but it had already gone public for the world to see. ■

In the following case, the court considered whether a Facebook user's expectation of privacy in photos that she posted on the site was reasonable.

Case 14.3

Nucci v. Target Corp.

District Court of Appeal of Florida, Fourth District, 162 So.3d 146 (2015).

Background and Facts Maria Nucci filed a suit in a Florida state court against Target Corporation, alleging that she suffered an injury when she slipped and fell on a "foreign substance" on the floor of a Target store. Target filed a motion to compel an inspection of Nucci's Facebook profile, which

Case 14.3 Continued

included 1,249 photos. Target argued that it was entitled to view the profile because Nucci's lawsuit put her physical and mental condition at issue.

Nucci responded that her Facebook page's privacy setting prevented the general public from having access to it. She claimed that she had a reasonable expectation of privacy in the profile and that Target's access would invade that privacy right. The court issued an order to compel discovery of certain photos, including some on Nucci's Facebook page, that were relevant to her physical and mental condition before and following the alleged injury. Nucci petitioned a state intermediate appellate court for relief from the order.

In the Language of the Court

GROSS, J. [Judge]

* * * *

*In a personal injury case * * * , the fact-finder is required to examine the quality of the plaintiff's life before and after the accident to determine the extent of the loss.* From testimony alone, it is often difficult for the fact-finder to grasp what a plaintiff's life was like prior to an accident. It would take a great novelist, a Tolstoy, a Dickens, or a Hemingway, to use words to summarize the totality of a prior life. If a photograph is worth a thousand words, *there is no better portrayal of what an individual's life was like than those photographs the individual has chosen to share through social media before the occurrence of an accident causing injury.* Such photographs are the equivalent of a "day in the life" slide show produced by the plaintiff before the existence of any motive to manipulate reality. [Emphasis added.]

* * * *

The Florida Constitution expressly protects an individual's right to privacy. * * * The right to privacy in the Florida Constitution ensures that individuals are able to determine for themselves when, how and to what extent information about them is communicated to others.

Before the right to privacy attaches, there must exist a legitimate expectation of privacy. * * *

* * * Social networking sites, such as Facebook, are free websites where an individual creates a "profile" which functions as a personal Web page and may include, at the user's discretion, numerous photos and a vast array of personal information including age, employment, education, religious and political views and various recreational interests. Once a user joins a social networking site, he or she can use the site to search for "friends" and create linkages to others based on similar interests.

* * * *

* * * *Generally, the photographs posted on a social networking site are neither privileged nor protected by any right of privacy, regardless of any privacy settings that the user may have established.* Such posted photographs are unlike medical records or communications with one's attorney, where disclosure is confined to narrow, confidential relationships. Facebook itself does not guarantee privacy. By creating a Facebook account, a user acknowledges that her personal information would be shared with others. Indeed, that is the very nature and purpose of these social networking sites else they would cease to exist. [Emphasis added.]

* * * The expectation that such information is private, in the traditional sense of the word, is not a reasonable one.

Decision and Remedy *The state intermediate appellate denied Nucci's petition for relief from the order to compel discovery of her Facebook photos. The court concluded that "the photographs sought were reasonably calculated to lead to the discovery of admissible evidence, and Nucci's privacy interest in them was minimal."*

Critical Thinking

- **What If the Facts Were Different?** *Suppose that Target had asked for a much broader range of Facebook material that concerned not just Nucci's physical and mental condition at the time of her alleged injury but also her personal relationships with her family, romantic partners, and significant others. Would the result have been the same? Discuss.*
- **Ethical** *Would a court also allow Target discovery of Facebook photos that were posted by Nucci's friends and family? Why or why not?*

14–6b Data Collection and Cookies

Whenever a consumer purchases items online from a retailer, such as Amazon.com or Best Buy, the retailer collects information about the consumer. **Cookies** are invisible files that computers, smartphones, and other mobile devices create to track a user's Web browsing activities. Cookies provide detailed information to marketers about an individual's behavior and preferences, which is then used to personalize online services.

Over time, a retailer can amass considerable data about a person's shopping habits. Does collecting this information violate a consumer's right to privacy? Should retailers be able to pass on the data they have collected to their affiliates? Should they be able to use the information to predict what a consumer might want and then create online "coupons" customized to fit the person's buying history?

■ **EXAMPLE 14.21** Facebook, Inc., once used a targeted advertising technique called "Sponsored Stories." An ad would display a Facebook friend's name and profile picture, along with a statement that the friend "likes" the company sponsoring the advertisement. A group of plaintiffs filed suit, claiming that Facebook had used their pictures for advertising without their permission. When a federal court refused to dismiss the case, Facebook agreed to settle. ■

14–6c Internet Companies' Privacy Policies

The Federal Trade Commission (FTC) investigates consumer complaints of privacy violations. The FTC has forced many companies, including Google, Facebook, Twitter, and MySpace, to enter a consent decree that gives the FTC broad power to review their privacy and data practices. It can then sue companies that violate the terms of the decree.

■ **EXAMPLE 14.22** In 2012, Google settled a suit brought by the FTC alleging that it had misused data from Apple's Safari users. Google allegedly had used cookies to trick the Safari browser on iPhones and iPads so that Google could monitor users who had blocked such tracking. This violated the company's consent decree with the FTC. Google agreed to pay $22.5 million to settle the suit without admitting liability. ■

Facebook has faced a number of complaints about its privacy policy and has changed its policy several times to satisfy its critics and ward off potential government investigations. Other companies, including mobile app developers, have also changed their privacy policies to provide more information to consumers. Consequently, it is frequently the companies, rather than courts or legislatures, that are defining the privacy rights of their online users.

Reviewing: Internet Law, Social Media, and Privacy

While he was in high school, Joel Gibb downloaded numerous songs to his smartphone from an unlicensed file-sharing service. He used portions of the copyrighted songs when he recorded his own band and posted videos on YouTube and Facebook. Gibb also used BitTorrent to download several movies from the Internet. Now he has applied to Boston University. The admissions office has requested access to his Facebook password, and he has complied. Using the information presented in the chapter, answer the following questions.

1. What laws, if any, did Gibb violate by downloading the music and videos from the Internet?
2. Was Gibb's use of portions of copyrighted songs in his own music illegal? Explain.
3. Can individuals legally post copyrighted content on their Facebook pages? Why or why not?
4. Did Boston University violate any laws when it asked Joel to provide his Facebook password? Explain.

Debate This . . .   *Internet service providers should be subject to the same defamation laws as newspapers, magazines, and television and radio stations.*

Terms and Concepts

cloud computing 271	distributed network 271	peer-to-peer (P2P) networking 271
cookie 280	domain name 267	social media 272
cybersquatting 267	goodwill 267	spam 266
cyber tort 274	Internet service provider (ISP) 267	typosquatting 268

Issue Spotters

1. Karl self-publishes a cookbook titled *Hole Foods*, in which he sets out recipes for donuts, Bundt cakes, tortellini, and other foods with holes. To publicize the book, Karl designs the Web site holefoods.com. Karl appropriates the key words of other cooking and cookbook sites with more frequent hits so that holefoods.com will appear in the same search engine results as the more popular sites. Has Karl done anything wrong? Explain. (See *Internet Law*.)

2. Eagle Corporation began marketing software in 2007 under the mark "Eagle." In 2017, Eagle.com, Inc., a different company selling different products, begins to use *eagle* as part of its URL and registers it as a domain name. Can Eagle Corporation stop this use of *eagle*? If so, what must the company show? (See *Internet Law*.)

• **Check your answers to the Issue Spotters against the answers provided in Appendix B at the end of this text.**

Business Scenarios

14–1. Internet Service Providers. CyberConnect, Inc., is an Internet service provider (ISP). Pepper is a CyberConnect subscriber. Market Reach, Inc., is an online advertising company. Using sophisticated software, Market Reach directs its ads to those users most likely to be interested in a particular product. When Pepper receives one of the ads, she objects to the content. Further, she claims that CyberConnect should pay damages for "publishing" the ad. Is the ISP regarded as a publisher and therefore liable for the content of Market Reach's ad? Why or why not? (See *Online Defamation*.)

14–2. Privacy. SeeYou, Inc., is an online social network. SeeYou's members develop personalized profiles to interact and share information—photos, videos, stories, activity updates, and other items—with other members. Members post the information that they want to share and decide with whom they want to share it. SeeYou launched a program to allow members to share with others what they do elsewhere online. For example, if a member rents a movie through Netflix, SeeYou will broadcast that information to everyone in the member's online network. How can SeeYou avoid complaints that this program violates its members' privacy? (See *Privacy*.)

Business Case Problems

14–3. Business Case Problem with Sample Answer—Privacy. Using special software, South Dakota law enforcement officers found a person who appeared to possess child pornography at a specific Internet address. The officers subpoenaed Midcontinent Communications, the service that assigned the address, for the personal information of its subscriber. With this information, the officers obtained a search warrant for the residence of John Rolfe, where they found a laptop that contained child pornography. Rolfe argued that the subpoenas violated his "expectation of privacy." Did Rolfe have a privacy interest in the information obtained by the subpoenas issued to Midcontinent? Discuss. [*State of South Dakota v. Rolfe*, 825 N.W.2d 901 (S.Dak. 2013)] (See *Privacy*.)

• **For a sample answer to Problem 14–3, go to Appendix C at the end of this text.**

14–4. File-Sharing. Dartmouth College professor M. Eric Johnson, in collaboration with Tiversa, Inc., a company that monitors peer-to-peer networks to provide security services, wrote an article titled "Data Hemorrhages in the Health-Care Sector." In preparing the article, Johnson and Tiversa searched the networks for data that could be used to commit medical or financial identity theft. They found a document that contained the Social Security numbers, insurance information, and treatment codes for patients of LabMD, Inc. Tiversa notified LabMD of the find in order to solicit its business. Instead of hiring Tiversa, however, LabMD filed a suit in a federal district court against the company, alleging trespass, conversion, and violations of federal statutes. What do these facts indicate about the security of private information? Explain. How should the court rule? [*LabMD, Inc. v. Tiversa, Inc.*, 509 Fed.Appx. 842 (11th Cir. 2013)] (See *Copyrights in Digital Information*.)

14–5. Social Media. Mohammad Omar Aly Hassan and nine others were indicted in a federal district court on charges of conspiring to advance violent jihad (holy war against enemies of Islam) and other offenses related to terrorism. The evidence at Hassan's trial included postings he made on Facebook concerning his adherence to violent jihadist ideology. Convicted, Hassan appealed, contending that the Facebook items had not been properly authenticated (established as his own comments). How might the government show the connection between postings on Facebook and those who post them? Discuss. [*United States v. Hassan*, 742 F.3d 104 (4th Cir. 2014)] (See *Social Media*.)

14–6. Social Media. Kenneth Wheeler was angry at certain police officers in Grand Junction, Colorado, because of a driving-under-the-influence arrest that he viewed as unjust. While in Italy, Wheeler posted a statement to his Facebook page urging his "religious followers" to "kill cops, drown them in the blood of their children, hunt them down and kill their entire bloodlines" and provided names. Later, Wheeler added a post to "commit a massacre in the

Stepping Stones preschool and day care, just walk in and kill everybody." Could a reasonable person conclude that Wheeler's posts were true threats? How might law enforcement officers use Wheeler's posts? Explain. [*United States v. Wheeler,* 776 F.3d 736 (10th Cir. 2015)] (See *Social Media.*)

14–7. Social Media. Irvin Smith was charged in a Georgia state court with burglary and theft. Before the trial, during the selection of the jury, the state prosecutor asked the prospective jurors whether they knew Smith. No one responded affirmatively. Jurors were chosen and sworn in, without objection. After the trial, during deliberations, the jurors indicated to the court that they were deadlocked. The court charged them to try again. Meanwhile, the prosecutor learned that "Juror 4" appeared as a friend on the defendant's Facebook page and filed a motion to dismiss her. The court replaced Juror 4 with an alternate. Was this an appropriate action, or was it an "abuse of discretion"? Should the court have admitted evidence that Facebook friends do not always actually know each other? Discuss. [*Smith v. State of Georgia,* 335 Ga.App. 497, 782 S.E.2d 305 (2016)] (See *Social Media.*)

14–8. A Question of Ethics—Criminal Investigations.

 After the unauthorized release and posting of classified U.S. government documents to WikiLeaks.org, allegedly involving Bradley Manning, a U.S. Army private first class, the U.S. government began a criminal investigation. The government obtained a court order to require Twitter, Inc., to turn over subscriber information and communications to and from the e-mail addresses of Birgitta Jonsdottir and others. The court sealed the order and the other documents in the case, reasoning that "there exists no right to public notice of all the types of documents filed in a . . . case." Jonsdottir and the others appealed this decision. [In re Application of the United States of America for an Order Pursuant to 18 U.S.C. Section 2703(d), *707 F.3d 283 (4th Cir. 2013)*] (See *Social Media.*)

(a) Why would the government want to "seal" the documents of an investigation? Why would the individuals under investigation want those documents to be "unsealed"? What factors should be considered in striking a balance between these competing interests?

(b) How does law enforcement use social media to detect and prosecute criminals? Is this use of social media an unethical invasion of individuals' privacy? Discuss.

Legal Reasoning Group Activity

14–9. File-Sharing. James, Chang, and Sixta are roommates. They are music fans and frequently listen to the same artists and songs. They regularly exchange MP3 music files that contain songs from their favorite artists. (See *Copyrights in Digital Information.*)

(a) One group of students will decide whether the fact that the roommates are transferring files among themselves for no monetary benefit precludes them from being subject to copyright law.

(b) The second group will consider an additional fact. Each roommate regularly buys CDs and rips (copies) them to his or her hard drive. Then the roommate gives the CDs to the other roommates to do the same.

CHAPTER 15

The Formation of Sales and Lease Contracts

When we turn to contracts for the sale and lease of goods, we move away from common law principles and into the area of statutory law. State statutory law governing sales and lease transactions is based on the Uniform Commercial Code (UCC), which has been adopted as law by all of the states.[1] Of all the

attempts to produce a uniform body of laws relating to commercial transactions in the United States, none has been as successful as the UCC.

The goal of the UCC is to simplify and to streamline commercial transactions. The UCC allows parties to form sales and lease contracts, including those entered into online, without observing the same degree of formality used in forming other types of contracts.

Today, businesses often engage in sales and lease transactions on a global scale. The United Nations Convention on Contracts for the International Sale of Goods (CISG) governs international sales contracts. The CISG is a model uniform law that applies only when a nation has adopted it, just as the UCC applies only to the extent that it has been adopted by a state.

---

1. Louisiana has not adopted Articles 2 and 2A, however.

15–1 The Uniform Commercial Code

In the early years of this nation, sales law varied from state to state, and this lack of uniformity complicated the formation of multistate sales contracts. The problems became especially troublesome in the late nineteenth century as multistate contracts became the norm. At that time, the National Conference of Commissioners on Uniform State Laws (NCCUSL) began drafting uniform laws relating to commercial transactions to address these problems.

In 1945, the NCCUSL began to work on the Uniform Commercial Code (UCC) to integrate various uniform acts into a single uniform law. The UCC was completed in 1949. Over the next several years, it was substantially accepted by almost every state in the nation.

15–1a Comprehensive Coverage of the UCC

The UCC is the single most comprehensive codification of the broad spectrum of laws involved in a total commercial transaction. The UCC views the entire "commercial transaction for the sale of and payment for goods" as a single legal occurrence having numerous facets. The

articles and sections of the UCC are periodically revised or supplemented to clarify certain aspects or to establish new rules as needed when the business environment changes.

You can gain an idea of the UCC's comprehensiveness by looking at the titles of the articles on the first page of Appendix A. Article 1, titled General Provisions, sets forth definitions and general principles applicable to commercial transactions. Article 1 thus provides the basic groundwork for the remaining articles, each of which focuses on a particular aspect of commercial transactions.

Article 1 sets forth an obligation to perform in "good faith" all contracts falling under the UCC [UCC 1–304]. Note, though, that many contracts do not fall under the UCC, because they do not involve commercial transactions. ■ **CASE IN POINT 15.1** Peter Amaya was a third-year medical student at Indiana University School of Medicine (IUSM) when three professors saw him cheating on an exam. He denied cheating and maintained that he was merely looking over at the clock on the wall. When he was dismissed from the school, Amaya filed suit in state court against the dean and IUSM, alleging breach of contract and breach of the duty of good faith.

The court granted IUSM's motion for summary judgment. Amaya appealed, but the reviewing court affirmed. Because a contract between a university and its students is not a sale of goods, the UCC's duty of good faith does not apply. The university's conclusion that Amaya failed to maintain acceptable professional standards was a "rational determination" arrived at after deliberation and after Amaya had numerous opportunities to be heard.[2] ∎

15–1b A Single, Integrated Framework for Commercial Transactions

The UCC attempts to provide a consistent and integrated framework of rules to deal with all the phases *ordinarily arising* in a commercial sales transaction from start to finish. Consider the following events, all of which may occur during a single transaction:

1. *A contract for the sale or lease of goods is formed and executed.* Article 2 and Article 2A of the UCC provide rules governing all aspects of this transaction.
2. *The transaction may involve a payment—by check, electronic fund transfer, or other means.* Article 3 (on negotiable instruments), Article 4 (on bank deposits and collections), Article 4A (on fund transfers), and Article 5 (on letters of credit) cover this part of the transaction.
3. *The transaction may involve a bill of lading or a warehouse receipt that covers goods when they are shipped or stored.* Article 7 (on documents of title) deals with this subject.
4. *The transaction may involve a demand by the seller or lender for some form of security for the remaining balance owed.* Article 9 (on secured transactions) covers this part of the transaction.

15–2 The Scope of Articles 2 (Sales) and 2A (Leases)

Article 2 of the UCC sets forth the requirements for *sales contracts,* as well as the duties and obligations of the parties involved in the sales contract. Article 2A covers similar issues for *lease contracts.* Bear in mind, however, that the parties to sales or lease contracts are free to agree to terms different from those stated in the UCC.

15–2a Article 2—The Sale of Goods

Article 2 of the UCC (as adopted by state statutes) governs **sales contracts,** or contracts for the sale of goods.

---

2. *Amaya v. Brater,* 981 N.E.2d 1235 (Ind.App. 2013).

To facilitate commercial transactions, Article 2 modifies some of the common law contract requirements that were discussed in the previous chapters.

To the extent that it has not been modified by the UCC, however, the common law of contracts also applies to sales contracts. In other words, the common law requirements for a valid contract—agreement consideration, capacity, and legality—are also applicable to sales contracts.

In general, the rule is that whenever a conflict arises between a common law contract rule and the state statutory law based on the UCC, the UCC controls. Thus, when a UCC provision addresses a certain issue, the UCC rule governs. When the UCC is silent, the common law governs. The relationship between general contract law and the law governing sales of goods is illustrated in Exhibit 15–1.

In regard to Article 2, keep two points in mind.

1. Article 2 deals with the sale of *goods.* It does not deal with real property (real estate), services, or intangible property such as stocks and bonds. Thus, if the subject matter of a dispute is goods, the UCC governs. If it is real estate or services, the common law applies.
2. In some situations, the rules can vary depending on whether the buyer or the seller is a *merchant.*

We look now at how the UCC defines a *sale, goods,* and *merchant status.*

What Is a Sale? The UCC defines a **sale** as "the passing of title [evidence of ownership rights] from the seller to the buyer for a price" [UCC 2–106(1)]. The price may be payable in cash or in other goods or services. (For a discussion of whether states can impose taxes on online sales, see this chapter's *Digital Update* feature.)

What Are Goods? To be characterized as a *good,* an item of property must be *tangible,* and it must be *movable.* **Tangible property** has physical existence—it can be touched or seen. **Intangible property**—such as corporate stocks and bonds, patents and copyrights, and ordinary contract rights—has only conceptual existence and thus does not come under Article 2. A *movable* item can be carried from place to place. Hence, real estate is excluded from Article 2.

Goods Associated with Real Estate. Goods *associated* with real estate often do fall within the scope of Article 2, however [UCC 2–107]. For instance, a contract for the sale of minerals, oil, or gas is a contract for the sale of goods if *severance, or separation, is to be made by the seller.* Similarly, a contract for the sale of growing crops or

EXHIBIT 15–1 The Law Governing Contracts

This exhibit graphically illustrates the relationship between general contract law and statutory law (UCC Articles 2 and 2A) governing contracts for the sale and lease of goods. Sales contracts are not governed exclusively by Article 2 of the UCC but are also governed by general contract law whenever it is relevant and has not been modified by the UCC.

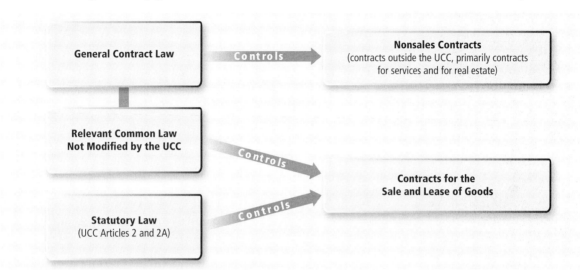

timber to be cut is a contract for the sale of goods *regardless of who severs them from the land.*

■ **CASE IN POINT 15.2** Perry Dan Cruse owned a business in Indiana that bought standing timber, cut it, and then resold it. Donald Freyberger had a contract with Cruse under which Cruse was to harvest 120 choice trees from Freyberger's land within six months. As payment, Freyberger would receive a percentage of the net proceeds from the sale of the cut timber. Cruse harvested and cut the trees but then filed for bankruptcy before the timber was sold. Freyberger filed a claim with the bankruptcy court, asserting that he had a "vendor's lien" on the timber because Cruse owed him $15,150 on the contract. (A lien would give Freyberger's claim priority over Cruse's other creditors.)

The bankruptcy court held that the timber was personal property (goods) under the UCC regardless of who cut it. Because no vendor's lien can arise on personal property under Indiana law, Freyberger's claim did not receive any special priority under bankruptcy law, and the debt could be discharged.[3] ■

Goods and Services Combined. When contracts involve a combination of goods and services, courts generally use the **predominant-factor test** to determine whether a contract is primarily for the sale of goods or the sale of

services.[4] If a court decides that a mixed contract is primarily a goods contract, *any* dispute, even a dispute over the services portion, will be decided under the UCC.

■ **CASE IN POINT 15.3** H & C Ag Services, LLC, entered into a contract with Ohio Fresh Eggs, LLC, that referred to "manure brokering services." H & C agreed to pay Ohio Fresh "service fees" for "all available tonnage per year of manure," which would then be resold to other parties. But the parties' contract did not specify the amount of manure. When Ohio Fresh did not carry out the contract, H & C sued for breach. A jury ruled that the primary purpose of the contract was for "manure brokering" (a service) rather than the "purchase of manure" (goods) and thus the UCC did not apply. The state trial court awarded H & C more than $2.5 million in damages. Ohio Fresh appealed.

The reviewing court held that the UCC governed the parties' contract under the predominant-factor test. The purpose of the contract was for the sale of goods—the manure—not the removal or resale of it. Despite the contract's use of the words *brokering* and *service fees,* H & C was clearly the buyer of manure from Ohio Fresh, who was the seller. Therefore, the UCC applied. Because the quantity term was left open, the parties had *not* agreed on

---

3. *In re Cruse,* 2013 WL 323275 (S.D. Indiana 2013).

4. UCC 2–314(1) does stipulate that serving food or drinks is a "sale of goods" for purposes of the implied warranty of merchantability, which will be discussed in the context of warranties. The UCC also specifies that selling unborn animals or rare coins qualifies as a "sale of goods."

DIGITAL UPDATE   Taxing Web Purchases

In 1992, the United States Supreme Court ruled that an individual state cannot compel an out-of-state business that lacks a substantial physical presence within that state to collect and remit state taxes.[a] Congress has the power to pass legislation requiring out-of-state corporations to collect and remit state sales taxes, but it has not yet done so. Thus, only online retailers that also have a physical presence within a state must collect state taxes on Web sales made to residents of that state. (State residents are supposed to self-report their purchases and pay use taxes to the state, which they rarely do.)

Redefining Physical Presence

A number of states have found a way to collect taxes on Internet sales made to state residents by out-of-state corporations—by redefining *physical presence.* New York started the trend in 2008 when it changed its tax laws in this manner. Now, an online retailer that pays any party within New York to solicit business for its products is considered to have a physical presence in the state and must collect state taxes. Since New York changed its law, around half of the states have made similar changes in an effort to increase their revenues by collecting sales tax from online retailers.

These new laws, often called the "Amazon tax" laws because they are largely aimed at Amazon.com, affect all online sellers, including Overstock.com and Drugstore.com. These laws especially affect retailers that pay affiliates to direct traffic to their Web sites. A federal appellate court in 2016 upheld the constitutionality of Colorado's so-called Amazon tax law, reasoning that the statute was necessary to avoid creating a tax shelter for online retailers.[b]

Local Governments Sue Online Travel Companies

Travelocity, Priceline.com, Hotels.com, and Orbitz.com are online travel companies (OTCs) that offer, among other things, hotel booking services. By 2018, more than twenty-five cities, including Atlanta, Charleston, Philadelphia, and San Antonio, had filed suits claiming that the OTCs owed taxes on hotel reservations that they had booked. All of the cities involved in the suits impose a hotel occupancy tax, which is essentially a sales tax.

Initially, some cities won their cases, but more recently, they have been losing in court.[c] As of 2018, courts in twenty-three states have concluded that the OTCs are not subject to hotel occupancy tax, and courts in six states have found the OTCs were liable for taxes. In Wyoming, for example, the state's highest court ruled that Travelocity, Priceline, Hotwire, Expedia, and Trip Network had to collect and remit sales tax.[d]

The Market Place Fairness Act

By the time you read this, online sales taxes may have become a reality for every online business that has annual revenues in excess of $1 million. For several years now, legislation called the Market Place Fairness Act has been introduced in the U.S. Senate. The act, if passed, would allow states to collect sales taxes from online retailers for in-state transactions.

A significant problem with such legislation is the complexity of collecting taxes for multiple jurisdictions. The current tax system involves 9,600 taxing jurisdictions. Even one zip code may cover multiple taxing entities, such as different cities and counties. Just consider that the Dallas–Fort Worth airport includes six separate taxing jurisdictions. Current software solutions for retailers that allow them to collect and remit sales taxes for different jurisdictions are extremely costly to install and operate. Overstock.com, for example, spent $1.3 million to add just one state to its sales tax collection system.

Critical Thinking *Some argue that if online retailers must pay sales taxes in jurisdictions in which they have no physical presence, they have no democratic way to fight high taxes in those places. Is this an instance of taxation without representation? Discuss.*

a. *Quill Corp. v. North Dakota,* 504 U.S. 298, 112 S.Ct. 1904, 119 L.Ed.2d 91 (1992).
b. *Direct Marketing Association v. Brohl,* 814 F.3d 1129 (10th Cir. 2016).

c. *Montana Dept. of Revenue v. Priceline.com, Inc.,* 380 Mont. 352, 354 P.3d 631 (2015); and *Travelscape, LLC v. South Carolina Dept. of Revenue,* 391 S.C. 89, 705 S.E.2d 28 (2011).
d. *Travelocity.com, LP v. Wyoming Dept. of Revenue,* 329 P.3d 131, 2014 -NMSC- 019 (2014). Also see *Expedia, Inc. v. District of Columbia,* 120 A.3d 623 (D.C.App. 2015).

an essential term. This meant that the contract was not enforceable under the UCC (open terms are discussed later in this chapter). Therefore, the appellate court reversed the lower court's decision and held in favor of Ohio Fresh.[5] ∎

Who Is a Merchant?   Article 2 governs the sale of goods in general. It applies to sales transactions between all buyers and sellers. In a limited number of instances, though, the UCC presumes that special business standards ought to be imposed because of merchants' relatively high degree of commercial expertise.[6] Such standards do not apply to the casual or inexperienced seller or buyer (consumer).

Section 2–104 sets forth three ways in which merchant status can arise:

1. A merchant is a person who *deals in goods of the kind* involved in the sales contract. Thus, a retailer, a wholesaler, or a manufacturer is a merchant of the goods sold in his or her business. A merchant for one type of goods is not necessarily a merchant for another type. For instance, a sporting goods retailer is a merchant when selling tennis rackets but not when selling a used computer.

2. A merchant is a person who, by occupation, *holds himself or herself out as having knowledge and skill* unique to the practices or goods involved in the transaction. This broad definition may include banks or universities as merchants.

3. A person who *employs a merchant as a broker, agent, or other intermediary* has the status of merchant in that transaction. Hence, if an art collector hires a broker to purchase or sell art for her, the collector is considered a merchant in the transaction.

In summary, a person is a **merchant** when she or he, acting in a mercantile capacity, possesses or uses an expertise specifically related to the goods being sold. This basic distinction is not always clear-cut. For instance, state courts appear to be split on whether farmers should be considered merchants.

15–2b   Article 2A—Leases

Leases of personal property (goods such as automobiles and industrial equipment) have become increasingly common. In this context, a lease is a transfer of the right to possess and use goods for a period of time in exchange for payment. Article 2A of the UCC was created to fill the need for uniform guidelines in this area.

Article 2A covers any transaction that creates a lease of goods or a sublease of goods [UCC 2A–102, 2A–103(1)(k)]. Article 2A is essentially a repetition of Article 2, except that it applies to leases of goods rather than sales of goods and thus varies to reflect differences between sales and lease transactions. (Note that Article 2A is not concerned with leases of real property, such as land or buildings.)

Definition of a Lease Agreement   Article 2A defines a **lease agreement** as a lessor's and lessee's bargain with respect to the lease of goods, as found in their language and as implied by other circumstances [UCC 2A–103(1)(k)]. A **lessor** is one who transfers the right to the possession and use of goods under a lease [UCC 2A–103(1)(p)]. A **lessee** is one who acquires the right to the possession and use of goods under a lease [UCC 2A–103(1)(o)]. In other words, the lessee is the party who is leasing the goods from the lessor.

Article 2A applies to all types of leases of goods. Special rules apply to certain types of leases, however, including consumer leases and finance leases.

Consumer Leases   A *consumer lease* involves three elements:

1. A lessor who regularly engages in the business of leasing or selling.

2. A lessee (except an organization) who leases the goods "primarily for a personal, family, or household purpose."

3. Total lease payments that are less than $25,000 [UCC 2A–103(1)(e)].

To ensure special protection for consumers, certain provisions of Article 2A apply only to consumer leases. For instance, one provision states that a consumer may recover attorneys' fees if a court determines that a term in a consumer lease contract is unconscionable [UCC 2A–108(4)(a)].

Finance Leases   A *finance lease* involves a lessor, a lessee, and a supplier. The lessor buys or leases goods from the supplier and leases or subleases them to the lessee [UCC 2A–103(1)(g)]. Typically, in a finance lease, the lessor is simply financing the transaction. ∎ **EXAMPLE 15.4** Marlin Corporation wants to lease a crane for use in its construction business. Marlin's bank agrees to purchase the equipment from Jenco, Inc., and lease the equipment to Marlin. In this situation, the bank is the lessor-financer, Marlin is the lessee, and Jenco is the supplier. ∎

---

5. *H & C Ag Services, LLC v. Ohio Fresh Eggs, LLC,* 41 N.E.3d 915, 2015 -Ohio- 3714 (Ohio App. 2015).

6. The provisions that apply only to merchants deal principally with the Statute of Frauds, firm offers, confirmatory memoranda, warranties, and contract modification. These special rules reflect expedient business practices commonly known to merchants in the commercial setting. They will be discussed later in this chapter.

Article 2A, unlike ordinary contract law, makes the lessee's obligations under a finance lease irrevocable and independent from the financer's obligations [UCC 2A–407]. In other words, the lessee must perform and continue to make lease payments even if the leased equipment turns out to be defective. The lessee must look almost entirely to the supplier for any recovery.

■ **EXAMPLE 15.5** McKessen Company obtains surgical ophthalmic equipment from a manufacturer and leases it to Vasquez for use at his medical eye center. When the equipment turns out to be defective, Vasquez stops making the lease payments. McKessen sues. Because the lease clearly qualifies as a finance lease under Article 2A, a court will hold in favor of McKessen. Vasquez is obligated to make all payments due under the lease regardless of the condition or performance of the leased equipment. Vasquez can sue the manufacturer of the defective equipment, however. ■

15–3 The Formation of Sales and Lease Contracts

In regard to the formation of sales and lease contracts, the UCC modifies the common law in several ways. We look here at how Articles 2 and 2A of the UCC modify common law contract rules. Remember, though, that parties to sales and lease contracts are basically free to establish whatever terms they wish.

The UCC comes into play when the parties either fail to provide certain terms in their contract or wish to change the effect of the UCC's terms in the contract's application. The UCC makes this very clear by its repeated use of such phrases as "unless the parties otherwise agree" and "absent a contrary agreement by the parties."

15–3a Offer

In general contract law, the moment a definite offer is met by an unqualified acceptance, a binding contract is formed. In commercial sales transactions, the verbal exchanges, correspondence, and actions of the parties may not reveal exactly when a binding contractual obligation arises. The UCC states that an agreement sufficient to constitute a contract can exist even if the moment of its making is undetermined [UCC 2–204(2), 2A–204(2)].

Open Terms According to general contract law, an offer must be definite enough for the parties (and the

courts) to ascertain its essential terms when it is accepted. In contrast, the UCC states that a sales or lease contract will not fail for indefiniteness even if one or more terms are left open as long as *both* of the following are true:

1. The parties intended to make a contract.
2. There is a reasonably certain basis for the court to grant an appropriate remedy [UCC 2–204(3), 2A–204(3)].

The UCC provides numerous *open-term* provisions (discussed next) that can be used to fill the gaps in a contract. Thus, if a dispute occurs, all that is necessary to prove the existence of a contract is an indication (such as a purchase order) that there is a contract. Missing terms can be proved by evidence, or a court can presume that the parties intended whatever is reasonable under the circumstances.

Keep in mind, though, that if too many terms are left open, a court may find that the parties did not intend to form a contract. Also, the *quantity* of goods involved usually must be expressly stated in the contract. If the quantity term is left open, the courts will have no basis for determining a remedy.

Open Price Term. If the parties have not agreed on a price, the court will determine a "reasonable price at the time for delivery" [UCC 2–305(1)]. If either the buyer or the seller is to determine the price, the price is to be decided in good faith [UCC 2–305(2)]. Under the UCC, *good faith* means honesty in fact and the observance of reasonable commercial standards of fair dealing in the trade [UCC 2–103(1)(b)]. The concepts of *good faith* and *commercial reasonableness* permeate the UCC.

Sometimes, the price fails to be set through the fault of one of the parties. In that situation, the other party can treat the contract as canceled or determine a reasonable price. ■ **EXAMPLE 15.6** Perez and Merrick enter into a contract for the sale of goods and agree that Perez will determine the price. Perez refuses to specify the price. Merrick can either treat the contract as canceled or set a reasonable price [UCC 2–305(3)]. ■

Open Payment Term. When the parties do not specify payment terms, payment is due at the time and place at which the buyer is to receive the goods [UCC 2–310(a)]. The buyer can tender payment using any commercially normal or acceptable means, such as a check or credit card. If the seller demands payment in cash, however, the buyer must be given a reasonable time to obtain it [UCC 2–511(2)].

■ **CASE IN POINT 15.7** H. Daya International Co. is a clothing manufacturer and wholesaler based in Hong

Kong. H. Daya sold and delivered nearly $2 million worth of goods to two companies owned by Salomon Murciano. The businesses' principal place of business was in New York City. The companies, Do Denim, LLC, and Reward Jean, made only partial payments on the amounts due. After receiving discount credits, Do Denim still owed $282,029, and Reward Jean owed $721,155. H. Daya filed suit in a federal district court in New York against both companies for breach of contract. The court found in favor of H. Daya and awarded damages for the amounts due under the contract, plus prejudgment interest.

Under a New York statute, prejudgment interest of 9 percent begins accruing from "the earliest ascertainable date the cause of action existed." Because the UCC specifies that payment is due at the time the buyer receives the goods, the court held that interest started accruing from the receipt of the final shipment. Therefore, Do Denim owed an additional $44,645 in interest, and Reward Jean owed $109,181 in interest to H. Daya.[7] ■

Open Delivery Term. When no delivery terms are specified, the buyer normally takes delivery at the seller's place of business [UCC 2–308(a)]. If the seller has no place of business, the seller's residence is used. When goods are located in some other place and both parties know it, delivery is made there. If the time for shipment or delivery is not clearly specified in the sales contract, then the court will infer a "reasonable" time for performance [UCC 2–309(1)].

Duration of an Ongoing Contract. A single contract might specify successive performances but not indicate how long the parties are required to deal with each other. In this situation, either party may terminate the ongoing contractual relationship. Nevertheless, principles of good faith and sound commercial practice call for reasonable notification before termination so as to give the other party sufficient time to seek a substitute arrangement [UCC 2–309(2), (3)].

Options and Cooperation with Regard to Performance. When the contract contemplates shipment of the goods but does not specify the shipping arrangements, the *seller* has the right to make these arrangements. The seller must make the arrangements in good faith, using commercial reasonableness in the situation [UCC 2–311].

When a sales contract omits terms relating to the assortment of goods, the *buyer* can specify the assortment. ■ **EXAMPLE 15.8** Petry Drugs agrees to purchase one thousand toothbrushes from Marconi's Dental Supply. The toothbrushes come in a variety of colors, but the contract does not specify color. Petry, the buyer, has the right to take six hundred blue toothbrushes and four hundred green ones if it wishes. Petry, however, must exercise good faith and commercial reasonableness in making the selection [UCC 2–311]. ■

Open Quantity Terms Normally, as mentioned earlier, if the parties do not specify a quantity, no contract is formed. A court will have no basis for determining a remedy, because there is almost no way to determine objectively what is a reasonable quantity of goods for someone to buy. (In contrast, a court can objectively determine a reasonable price for particular goods by looking at the market for like goods.) The UCC recognizes two exceptions to this rule in requirements and output contracts [UCC 2–306(1)].

Requirements Contracts. Requirements contracts are common in the business world and normally are enforceable. In a **requirements contract,** the buyer agrees to purchase and the seller agrees to sell all or up to a stated amount of what the buyer requires.

■ **EXAMPLE 15.9** Newport Cannery forms a contract with Victor Tu. The cannery agrees to purchase from Tu, and Tu agrees to sell to the cannery, all of the green beans that the cannery requires during the following summer. There is implicit consideration in this contract because the buyer (the cannery) gives up the right to buy goods (green beans) from any other seller. This forfeited right creates a legal *detriment*—that is, consideration. ■

If, however, the buyer promises to purchase only if he or she *wishes* to do so, the promise is illusory (without consideration) and unenforceable by either party. Similarly, if the buyer reserves the right to buy the goods from someone other than the seller, the promise is unenforceable (illusory) as a requirements contract.

Output Contracts. In an **output contract,** the seller agrees to sell and the buyer agrees to buy all or up to a stated amount of what the seller produces. ■ **EXAMPLE 15.10** Ruth Sewell has planted two acres of organic tomatoes. Bella Union, a local restaurant, agrees to buy all of the tomatoes that Sewell produces that year to use at the restaurant. Again, because the seller essentially forfeits the right to sell goods to another buyer, there is implicit consideration in an output contract. ■

The UCC imposes a *good faith limitation* on requirements and output contracts. The quantity under such contracts is the amount of requirements or the amount of output that occurs during a *normal* production period.

---

7. *H. Daya Inter. Co. v. Do Denim,* 2012 WL 2524729 (S.D.N.Y. 2012).

The actual quantity purchased or sold cannot be unreasonably disproportionate to normal or comparable prior requirements or output [UCC 2–306(1)].

Merchant's Firm Offer Under regular contract principles, an offer can be revoked at any time before acceptance. The major common law exception is an *option contract*, in which the offeree pays consideration for the offeror's irrevocable promise to keep the offer open for a stated period. The UCC creates a second exception for *firm offers* made by a merchant concerning the sale or lease of goods (regardless of whether or not the offeree is a merchant).

When a Merchant's Firm Offer Arises. A **firm offer** arises when a merchant-offeror gives *assurances in a signed writing* that the offer will remain open. The merchant's firm offer is irrevocable without the necessity of consideration[8] for the stated period or, if no definite period is stated, a reasonable period (neither to exceed three months) [UCC 2–205, 2A–205].

■ **EXAMPLE 15.11** Osaka, a used-car dealer, e-mails a letter to Gomez on January 1, stating, "I have a used 2016 Toyota RAV4 on the lot that I'll sell you for $22,000 any time between now and January 31." This e-mail creates a firm offer, and Osaka will be liable for breach of contract if he sells the RAV4 to another person before January 31. ■

Requirements for a Firm Offer. To qualify as a firm offer, the offer must be:

1. *Written* (or electronically recorded, such as in an e-mail).
2. *Signed* by the offeror.[9]

When a firm offer is contained in a form contract prepared by the offeree, the offeror must also sign a separate assurance of the firm offer. The requirement of a separate signature ensures that the offeror will be made aware of the firm offer.

For instance, an offeree might respond to an initial offer by sending its own form contract containing a clause stating that the offer will remain open for three months. If the firm offer is buried amid copious language on the last page of the offeree's form contract, the offeror may inadvertently sign the contract without realizing that it contains a firm offer. This would defeat the purpose of the rule—which is to give effect to a merchant's *deliberate* intent to be bound to a firm offer.

15–3b Acceptance

Acceptance of an offer to buy, sell, or lease goods generally may be made in any reasonable manner and by any reasonable means. The UCC permits acceptance of an offer to buy goods "either by a prompt *promise* to ship or by the prompt or current shipment of conforming or nonconforming goods" [UCC 2–206(1)(b)]. *Conforming goods* accord with the contract's terms, whereas *nonconforming goods* do not.

The prompt shipment of nonconforming goods constitutes both an acceptance, which creates a contract, and a breach of that contract. This rule does not apply if the seller **seasonably** (within a reasonable amount of time) notifies the buyer that the nonconforming shipment is offered only as an *accommodation,* or as a favor. The notice of accommodation must clearly indicate to the buyer that the shipment does not constitute an acceptance and that, therefore, no contract has been formed.

■ **EXAMPLE 15.12** McFarren Pharmacy orders five cases of Johnson & Johnson 3-by-5-inch gauze pads from H.T. Medical Supply, Inc. If H.T. ships five cases of Xeroform 3-by-5-inch gauze pads instead, the shipment acts as both an acceptance of McFarren's offer and a breach of the resulting contract. McFarren may sue H.T. for any appropriate damages. If, however, H.T. notifies McFarren that the Xeroform pads are being shipped *as an accommodation*—because H.T. has only Xeroform pads in stock—the shipment does not act as an acceptance. Instead, it constitutes a counteroffer, and a contract will be formed only if McFarren accepts the Xeroform gauze pads. ■

Communication of Acceptance Under the common law, because a unilateral offer invites acceptance by performance, the offeree need not notify the offeror of performance unless the offeror would not otherwise know about it. In other words, a unilateral offer can be accepted by beginning performance.

The UCC is more stringent than the common law in this regard because it requires notification. Under the UCC, if the offeror is not notified within a reasonable time that the offeree has accepted the contract by beginning performance, then the offeror can treat the offer as having lapsed before acceptance [UCC 2–206(2), 2A–206(2)].

Additional Terms Recall that under the common law, the mirror image rule requires that the terms of the

---

8. If the offeree pays consideration, then an option contract (not a merchant's firm offer) is formed.
9. *Signed* includes any symbol executed or adopted by a party with a present intention to authenticate a writing [UCC 1–201(37)]. A complete signature is not required.

acceptance exactly match those of the offer. ■ **EXAMPLE 15.13** Adderson e-mails an offer to sell twenty Samsung Galaxy tablet model S2 to Beale. If Beale accepts the offer but changes it to require model S4 tablets, then there is no contract if the mirror image rule applies. ■

To avoid such problems, the UCC dispenses with the mirror image rule. Under the UCC, a contract is formed if the offeree's response indicates a *definite* acceptance of the offer, *even if the acceptance includes terms additional to or different from those contained in the offer* [UCC 2–207(1)]. Whether the additional terms become part of the contract depends, in part, on whether the parties are nonmerchants or merchants.

Rules When One Party or Both Parties Are Nonmerchants.

If one (or both) of the parties is a *nonmerchant*, the contract is formed according to the terms of the original offer. The contract does not include any of the additional terms in the acceptance [UCC 2–207(2)].

■ **CASE IN POINT 15.14** OfficeSupplyStore.com sells office supplies on the Web. Employees of the Kansas City School District in Missouri ordered $17,642.54 worth of office supplies—without the authority or approval of their employer—from the Web site. The invoices accompanying the goods contained a *forum-selection clause* that required all disputes to be resolved in California.

When the goods were not paid for, Office Supply filed suit in California. The Kansas City School District objected, arguing that the forum-selection clause was not binding. The court held that the forum-selection clause was not part of the parties' contract. The clause was an additional term included in the invoices delivered to a nonmerchant buyer (the school district) with the purchased goods. Therefore, the clause did not become part of the contract unless the buyer expressly agreed, which did not happen in this case.[10] ■

Rules When Both Parties Are Merchants.

The UCC includes a special rule for merchants to avoid the "battle of the forms," which occurs when two merchants exchange separate standard forms containing different contract terms.

Under UCC 2–207(2), in contracts *between merchants,* the additional terms *automatically* become part of the contract *unless* one of the following conditions arises:

1. The original offer expressly limited acceptance to its terms.
2. The new or changed terms materially alter the contract.
3. The offeror objects to the new or changed terms within a reasonable period of time.

When determining whether an alteration is material, courts consider several factors. Generally, if the modification does not involve any unreasonable element of surprise or hardship for the offeror, a court will hold that the modification did not materially alter the contract. Courts also consider the parties' prior dealings. As shown in the following case, however, what constitutes a material alteration is frequently a question of fact that only a court can decide.

---

10. *OfficeSupplyStore.com v. Kansas City School Board*, 334 S.W.3d 574 (Kan. 2011).

Case 15.1

C. Mahendra (N.Y.), LLC v. National Gold & Diamond Center, Inc.

New York Supreme Court, Appellate Division, First Department, 125 A.D.3d 454, 3 N.Y.S.3d 27 (2015).

Background and Facts C. Mahendra (N.Y.), LLC, is a New York wholesaler of loose diamonds. National Gold & Diamond Center, Inc., is a California seller of jewelry. Over a ten-year period, National placed orders, totaling millions of dollars, with Mahendra by phoning and negotiating the terms. Mahendra shipped diamonds "on memorandum" for National to examine. Mahendra then sent invoices for the diamonds that National chose to keep. Both the memoranda and the invoices stated, "You consent to the exclusive jurisdiction of the . . . courts situated in New York County."

When two orders totaling $64,000 went unpaid, Mahendra filed a suit in a New York state court against National, alleging breach of contract. National filed a motion to dismiss the complaint for lack of personal jurisdiction, contending that the forum-selection clause was not binding. The court granted the motion. Mahendra appealed.

Case 15.1 Continues

Case 15.1 Continued

In the Language of the Court
SWEENY, P.J. [Presiding Judge], *MOSKOWITZ, DEGRASSE, MANZANET-DANIELS, CLARK*, JJ. [Judges]
* * * *

* * * Defendant argued the forum-selection clause in the * * * memorandums was not binding because its president never signed the memorandums' terms and conditions. Defendant thus maintained that it had not signed or agreed to the forum-selection clause, nor had it otherwise consented to being sued in New York. Likewise, defendant asserted that because it had negotiated for and ordered the diamonds from California and did not sign or agree to the forum-selection clause, the consent to jurisdiction contained in the memorandums would materially alter the parties' agreements in contravention of UCC 2–207(2)(b). Thus, defendant concluded, it was not bound by the unsigned provision on the back of the * * * memorandums.

* * * *

* * * The [lower] court found the forum-selection clause invalid, noting that defendant did not sign the invoices. The court further found that under UCC 2–207(2), forum-selection clauses are additional terms that materially alter a contract, and must be construed as mere proposals for additions to the contract. Thus, the court concluded, the forum-selection clause was non-binding absent an express agreement. Indeed, the court noted, the complaint did not allege that defendant affirmatively expressed consent, either orally or in writing, to the forum-selection clause when it retained the invoices.

* * * *

The [lower] court correctly found that defendant is not bound by the forum-selection clause on plaintiff's invoices. UCC 2–207 contemplates situations like the one here, where parties do business through an exchange of forms such as purchase orders and invoices. As the parties did here, *merchants frequently include terms in their forms that were not discussed with the other side. UCC 2–207(2) addresses that scenario, providing, "the additional terms are to be construed as proposals for addition to the contract. Between merchants such terms become part of the contract unless: * * * (b) they materially alter it."* [Emphasis added.]

Here, during telephone discussions, the parties negotiated the essential terms required for contract formation, and the invoices were merely confirmatory. Thus, the forum-selection clause is an additional term that materially altered the parties' oral contracts, and defendant did not give its consent to that additional term.

Decision and Remedy *A state intermediate appellate court agreed that "the forum-selection clause is an additional term that materially altered the parties' . . . contracts, and defendant did not give its consent to that additional term." But the court reversed the dismissal of Mahendra's complaint on the ground that National's phone calls with Mahendra were sufficient contacts to subject the defendant to personal jurisdiction in New York under the state's long-arm statute.*

Critical Thinking
- **Legal** *What is Mahendra's best argument that the forum-selection clause was, in fact, binding on National? Discuss.*

Prior Dealings between Merchants. In contracts between merchants, courts also consider the parties' prior dealings. ■ **CASE IN POINT 15.15** WPS, Inc., submitted a proposal to manufacture equipment for Expro Americas, LLC, and Surface Production Systems, Inc. (SPS). Expro and SPS then submitted two purchase orders. WPS accepted the first purchase order in part and the second order conditionally. Among other things, WPS's acceptance required that Expro and SPS give their "full release to proceed" and agree to "pay all valid costs associated

with any order cancellation." The parties' negotiations continued, and Expro and SPS eventually submitted a third purchase order.

Although the third purchase order did not comply with all of WPS's requirements, it did give WPS permission to proceed. It also specified that Expro and SPS would pay all cancellation costs. With Expro and SPS's knowledge, WPS began working on that order. Expro and SPS later canceled the order and refused to pay the cancellation costs. When the dispute ended in court,

Expro and SPS claimed that the additional terms in WPS's acceptance had materially altered the contract and rendered it unenforceable. The court found in favor of WPS. Expro and SPS had given a release to proceed that authorized WPS to go forward with manufacturing the equipment. Because "the parties operated as if they had additional time to resolve the outstanding differences," the court reasoned that Expro and SPS were contractually obligated to pay the cancellation costs.[11] ■

Conditioned on Offeror's Assent. The offeree's response is not an acceptance if it contains additional or different terms and is expressly *conditioned* on the offeror's assent to those terms [UCC 2–207(1)]. This is true whether or not the parties are merchants.

■ **EXAMPLE 15.16** Philips offers to sell Hundert 650 pounds of turkey thighs at a specified price and with specified delivery terms. Hundert responds, "I accept your offer for 650 pounds of turkey thighs *on the condition that you agree to give me ninety days to pay for them.*" Hundert's response will be construed not as an acceptance but as a counteroffer, which Philips may or may not accept. ■

Additional Terms May Be Stricken. The UCC provides yet another option for dealing with conflicting terms in the parties' writings. Section 2–207(3) states that conduct by both parties that recognizes the existence of a contract is sufficient to establish a contract for sale. This is so even if the writings of the parties do not otherwise establish a contract. In this situation, "the terms of the particular contract will consist of those terms on which the writings of the parties agree, together with any supplementary terms incorporated under any other provisions of this Act." In a dispute over contract terms, this provision allows a court simply to strike from the contract those terms on which the parties do not agree.

■ **EXAMPLE 15.17** SMT Marketing orders goods over the phone from Brigg Sales, Inc., which ships the goods to SMT with an acknowledgment form confirming the order. SMT accepts and pays for the goods. The parties' writings do not establish a contract, but there is no question that a contract exists. If a dispute arises over the terms, such as the extent of any warranties, UCC 2–207(3) provides the governing rule. ■

As noted previously, the fact that a merchant's acceptance frequently contains terms that add to or even conflict with those of the offer is often referred to as the "battle of the forms." Although the UCC tries to eliminate this battle, the problem of differing contract terms

still arises in commercial settings, particularly when standard forms (for placing and confirming orders) are used.

15–3c Consideration

The common law rule that a contract requires consideration also applies to sales and lease contracts. Unlike the common law, however, the UCC does not require a contract modification to be supported by new consideration. The UCC states that an agreement modifying a contract for the sale or lease of goods "needs no consideration to be binding" [UCC 2–209(1), 2A–208(1)]. Of course, any contract modification must be made in good faith [UCC 1–304].

In some situations, an agreement to modify a sales or lease contract without consideration must be in writing to be enforceable. For instance, if the contract itself specifies that any changes to the contract must be in a signed writing, only those changes agreed to in a signed writing are enforceable.

Sometimes, when a consumer (nonmerchant) is buying goods from a merchant-seller, the merchant supplies a form that contains a prohibition against oral modification. In those situations, the consumer must sign a separate acknowledgment of the clause for it to be enforceable [UCC 2–209(2), 2A–208(2)]. Also, any modification that makes a sales contract come under Article 2's writing requirement (its Statute of Frauds, discussed next) usually requires a writing (or electronic record) to be enforceable.

See Concept Summary 15.1 for a review of the UCC's rules on offer, acceptance, and consideration.

15–3d The Statute of Frauds

The UCC contains Statute of Frauds provisions covering sales and lease contracts. Under these provisions, sales contracts for goods priced at $500 or more and lease contracts requiring total payments of $1,000 or more must be in writing to be enforceable [UCC 2–201(1), 2A–201(1)]. (These low threshold amounts may eventually be raised.)

Sufficiency of the Writing A writing, including an e-mail or other electronic record, will be sufficient to satisfy the UCC's Statute of Frauds as long as it:

1. Indicates that the parties intended to form a contract.
2. Is signed by the party (or agent of the party) against whom enforcement is sought. (Remember that a typed name can qualify as a signature on an electronic record.)

---

11. *WPS, Inc. v. Expro Americas, LLC,* 369 S.W.3d 384 (Tex.App. 2012).

Concept Summary 15.1

Offer, Acceptance, and Consideration under the UCC

Offer	• Not all terms have to be included for a contract to be formed. • The price does not have to be included for a contract to be formed. • Particulars of performance can be left open. • An offer by a merchant in a signed writing with assurances that the offer will not be withdrawn is irrevocable without consideration (for up to three months).
Acceptance	• Acceptance may be made by any reasonable means of communication. It is effective when dispatched. • An offer can be made by a promise to ship or by the shipment of conforming goods, or by prompt shipment of nonconforming goods unless accompanied by a notice of accommodation. • Acceptance by performance requires notice within a reasonable time. Otherwise, the offer can be treated as lapsed. • A definite expression of acceptance creates a contract even if the terms of the acceptance differ from those of the offer (unless acceptance is expressly conditioned on consent to the additional or different terms).
Consideration	• A *modification* of a contract for the sale or lease of goods does not require consideration as long as it is made in good faith.

The contract normally will not be enforceable beyond the quantity of goods shown in the writing, however. All other terms can be proved in court by oral testimony. For leases, the writing must reasonably identify and describe the goods leased and the lease term.

Special Rules for Contracts between Merchants

The UCC provides a special rule for merchants in sales transactions (there is no corresponding rule that applies to leases under Article 2A). Merchants can satisfy the Statute of Frauds if, after the parties have agreed orally, one of the merchants sends a signed written confirmation to the other merchant within a reasonable time.

The communication must indicate the terms of the agreement, and the merchant receiving the confirmation must have reason to know of its contents. Unless the merchant who receives the confirmation gives written notice of objection to its contents within ten days after receipt, the writing is sufficient against the receiving merchant, even though she or he has not signed it [UCC 2–201(2)].

■ **EXAMPLE 15.18** Alfonso is a merchant-buyer in Cleveland. He contracts over the telephone to purchase $6,000 worth of spare aircraft parts from Goldstein, a merchant-seller in New York City. Two days later, Goldstein e-mails a signed confirmation detailing the terms of the oral contract, and Alfonso subsequently receives it. Alfonso does not notify Goldstein in writing that he objects to the contents of the confirmation within ten days of receipt. Therefore, Alfonso cannot raise the Statute of Frauds as a defense against the enforcement of the oral contract. ■

Exceptions The UCC defines three exceptions to the writing requirements of the Statute of Frauds. An oral contract for the sale of goods priced at $500 or more or the lease of goods involving total payments of $1,000 or more will be enforceable despite the absence of a writing in the circumstances described next [UCC 2–201(3), 2A–201(4)].

Specially Manufactured Goods. An oral contract for the sale or lease of custom-made goods will be enforceable if:

1. The goods are *specially manufactured* for a particular buyer or specially manufactured or obtained for a particular lessee.

2. The goods are *not suitable for resale or lease* to others in the ordinary course of the seller's or lessor's business.

3. The seller or lessor *has substantially started to manufacture* the goods or has made commitments for the manufacture or procurement of the goods.

In these situations, once the seller or lessor has taken action, the buyer or lessee cannot repudiate the agreement claiming the Statute of Frauds as a defense.

■ **EXAMPLE 15.19** Womach orders custom window treatments to use at a day spa business from Hunter Douglas for $6,000. The contract is oral. When Hunter Douglas manufactures the window coverings and tenders delivery to Womach, she refuses to pay for them, even though the job has been completed on time. Womach claims that she is not liable because the contract was oral. If the unique style, size, and color of the window treatments make it improbable that Hunter Douglas can find another buyer, Womach is liable to Hunter Douglas. ■

Admissions. An oral contract for the sale or lease of goods is enforceable if the party against whom enforcement is sought admits in pleadings, testimony, or other court proceedings that a sales or lease contract was made. In this situation, the contract will be enforceable even though it was oral, but enforceability will be limited to the quantity of goods admitted.

■ **CASE IN POINT 15.20** Gerald Lindgren, a farmer, agreed by phone to sell his crops to Glacial Plains Cooperative. The parties reached four oral agreements: two for the delivery of soybeans and two for the delivery of corn. Lindgren made the soybean deliveries and part of the first corn delivery, but he sold the rest of his corn to another dealer. Glacial Plains bought corn elsewhere, paying a higher price, and then sued Lindgren for breach of contract. In papers filed with the court, Lindgren acknowledged his oral agreements with Glacial Plains and admitted that he did not fully perform. The court applied the admissions exception and held that the four agreements were enforceable.[12] ■

Partial Performance. An oral contract for the sale or lease of goods is enforceable if payment has been made and accepted or goods have been received and accepted. This is the "partial performance" exception. The oral contract will be enforced at least to the extent that performance actually took place.

■ **EXAMPLE 15.21** Quality Meats buys food products and sells them to retail operations. Quality orally contracts with A1 Food Services, Inc., to ship three orders of beef to Choice Processing, for which A1 agrees to pay. Quality ships the goods to Choice and sends invoices to A1. A1 bills Choice for all three orders, but pays Quality only for the first two. Quality then files a suit against A1 to recover the cost of the third order.

A1 argues that because the parties did not have a written agreement, there was no enforceable contract. But a court could find that even though A1 had not signed a written contract or purchase order, it had partially performed the contract by paying for the first two shipments. A1's conduct is likely sufficient to prove the existence of a contract, and the court could require A1 to pay for the last shipment. ■

The exceptions just discussed and other ways in which sales law differs from general contract law are summarized in Exhibit 15–2.

15–3e Parol Evidence

Recall that parol evidence consists of evidence outside the contract, such as evidence of the parties' prior negotiations, prior agreements, or contemporaneous oral agreements. When a contract completely sets forth all the terms and conditions agreed to by the parties and is intended as a final statement of their agreement, it is considered fully *integrated*. The terms of a **fully integrated contract** cannot be contradicted by evidence of any prior agreements or contemporaneous oral agreements.

If, however, the writing contains some of the terms the parties agreed on but not others, then the contract is not fully integrated. When a court finds that a contract is *not fully integrated,* then the court may allow evidence of *consistent additional terms* to explain or supplement the terms in the contract. The court may also allow the parties to submit evidence of *course of dealing, usage of trade,* or *course of performance* [UCC 2–202, 2A–202].

Course of Dealing and Usage of Trade Under the UCC, the meaning of any agreement, evidenced by the language of the parties and their actions, must be interpreted in light of commercial practices and other surrounding circumstances. In interpreting a commercial agreement, a court will assume that the course of dealing between the parties and the general usage of trade were taken into account when the agreement was phrased.

Course of Dealing. A **course of dealing** is a sequence of actions and communications between the parties to a particular transaction that establishes a common basis for their understanding [UCC 1–303(b)]. A course of dealing is restricted to the sequence of conduct between the parties in their transactions prior to the agreement.

---

12. *Glacial Plains Cooperative v. Lindgren*, 759 N.W.2d 661 (Min.App. 2009).

EXHIBIT 15–2 Major Differences between Contract Law and Sales Law

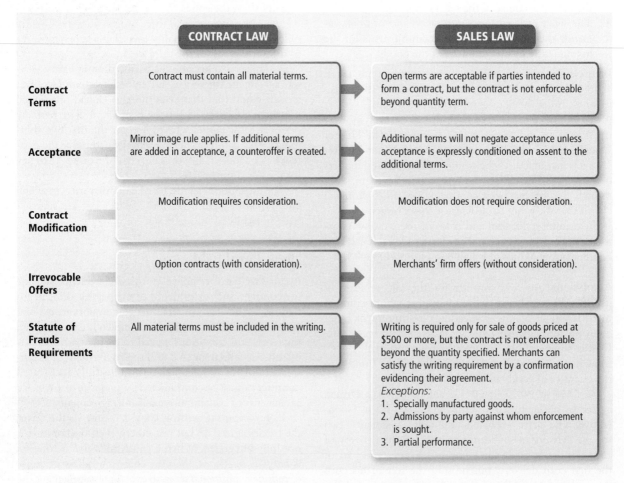

	CONTRACT LAW	SALES LAW
Contract Terms	Contract must contain all material terms.	Open terms are acceptable if parties intended to form a contract, but the contract is not enforceable beyond quantity term.
Acceptance	Mirror image rule applies. If additional terms are added in acceptance, a counteroffer is created.	Additional terms will not negate acceptance unless acceptance is expressly conditioned on assent to the additional terms.
Contract Modification	Modification requires consideration.	Modification does not require consideration.
Irrevocable Offers	Option contracts (with consideration).	Merchants' firm offers (without consideration).
Statute of Frauds Requirements	All material terms must be included in the writing.	Writing is required only for sale of goods priced at $500 or more, but the contract is not enforceable beyond the quantity specified. Merchants can satisfy the writing requirement by a confirmation evidencing their agreement. *Exceptions:* 1. Specially manufactured goods. 2. Admissions by party against whom enforcement is sought. 3. Partial performance.

Under the UCC, a course of dealing between the parties is relevant in ascertaining the meaning of the parties' agreement. It "may give particular meaning to specific terms of the agreement, and may supplement or qualify the terms of the agreement" [UCC 1–303(d)].

Usage of Trade. Some practices and methods of dealing are so regularly observed in a place, vocation, or trade that parties to contracts expect them to be observed in their transactions. Such a practice or method of dealing is known as a **usage of trade** [UCC 1–303(c)].

■ **EXAMPLE 15.22** Phat Khat Loans, Inc., hires Fleet Title Review Company to search the public records for prior claims on potential borrowers' assets. Fleet's invoice states, "Liability limited to amount of fee." In the title search industry, liability limits are common. After conducting many searches for Phat Khat, Fleet reports that there are no claims with respect to Main

Street Autos. Phat Khat lends $100,000 to Main, with payment guaranteed by Main's assets. When Main defaults on the loan, Phat Khat learns that another lender has priority to Main's assets under a previous claim. If Phat Khat sues Fleet for breach of contract, Fleet's liability will normally be limited to the amount of its fee. The statement in the invoice was part of the contract between Phat Khat and Fleet, according to the usage of trade in the industry and the parties' course of dealing. ■

Course of Performance The conduct that occurs under the terms of a particular agreement is called a **course of performance** [UCC 1–303(a)]. Presumably, the parties themselves know best what they meant by their words. Thus, the course of performance actually carried out under the parties' agreement is the best indication of what they meant [UCC 2–208(1), 2A–207(1)].

■ **EXAMPLE 15.23**   Janson's Lumber Company contracts with Lopez to sell Lopez a specified number of two-by-fours. The lumber in fact does not measure exactly 2 inches by 4 inches but rather 1⅞ inches by 3¾ inches. Janson's agrees to deliver the lumber in five deliveries, and Lopez, without objection, accepts the lumber in the first three deliveries. On the fourth delivery, however, Lopez objects that the two-by-fours do not measure precisely 2 inches by 4 inches.

The course of performance in this transaction—that is, Lopez's acceptance of three deliveries without objection—is relevant in determining that here a "two-by-four" actually means a "1⅞-by-3¾." Janson's can also prove that two-by-fours need not be exactly 2 inches by 4 inches by applying usage of trade, course of dealing, or both. Janson's can, for example, show that in previous transactions, Lopez took 1⅞-inch-by-3¾-inch lumber without objection. In addition, Janson's can show that in the trade, two-by-fours are commonly 1⅞ inches by 3¾ inches. ■

Rules of Construction   The UCC provides *rules of construction* for interpreting contracts. Express terms, course of performance, course of dealing, and usage of trade are to be construed to be consistent with each other whenever reasonable. When such a construction is unreasonable, however, the UCC establishes the following order of priority [UCC 1–303(e), 2–208(2), 2A–207(2)]:

1. Express terms.
2. Course of performance.
3. Course of dealing.
4. Usage of trade.

15–3f Unconscionability

An unconscionable contract is one that is so unfair and one sided that it would be unreasonable to enforce it. The UCC allows a court to evaluate a contract or any clause in a contract, and if the court deems it to have been unconscionable *at the time it was made,* the court can do any of the following [UCC 2–302, 2A–108]:

1. Refuse to enforce the contract.
2. Enforce the remainder of the contract without the unconscionable part.
3. Limit the application of the unconscionable term to avoid an unconscionable result.

The following classic case illustrates an early application of the UCC's unconscionability provisions.

Classic Case 15.2

Jones v. Star Credit Corp.

Supreme Court of New York, Nassau County, 59 Misc.2d 189, 298 N.Y.S.2d 264 (1969).

Background and Facts   The Joneses agreed to purchase a freezer for $900 as the result of a sales-person's visit to their home. Tax and financing charges raised the total price to $1,234.80. Later, the Joneses, who had made payments totaling $619.88, brought a suit in a New York state court to have the purchase contract declared unconscionable under the UCC. At trial, the freezer was found to have a maximum retail value of approximately $300.

In the Language of the Court

Sol M. *WACHTLER*, Justice.

* * * *

* * * [Section 2–302 of the UCC] authorizes the court to find, as a matter of law, that a contract or a clause of a contract was "unconscionable at the time it was made," and upon so finding the court may refuse to enforce the contract, excise the objectionable clause or limit the application of the clause to avoid an unconscionable result.

* * * *

* * * The question which presents itself is whether or not, under the circumstances of this case, the sale of a freezer unit having a retail value of $300 for $900 ($1,439.69 including credit charges and $18 sales tax) is unconscionable as a matter of law.

Concededly, deciding [this case] is substantially easier than explaining it. No doubt, the mathematical disparity between $300, which presumably includes a reasonable profit margin, and $900, which is exorbitant on its face, carries the greatest weight. Credit charges alone exceed by more than $100 the retail value of the freezer. These alone may be sufficient to sustain the decision. Yet, a caveat [warning]

Case 15.2 Continues

is warranted lest we reduce the import of Section 2–302 solely to a mathematical ratio formula. It may, at times, be that; yet it may also be much more. The very limited financial resources of the purchaser, known to the sellers at the time of the sale, is entitled to weight in the balance. Indeed, the value disparity itself leads inevitably to the felt conclusion that knowing advantage was taken of the plaintiffs. In addition, *the meaningfulness of choice essential to the making of a contract can be negated by a gross inequality of bargaining power.* [Emphasis added.]

* * * *

* * * The defendant has already been amply compensated. In accordance with the statute, the application of the payment provision should be limited to amounts already paid by the plaintiffs and the contract be reformed and amended by changing the payments called for therein to equal the amount of payment actually so paid by the plaintiffs.

Decision and Remedy *The court held that the contract was not enforceable and reformed the contract so that no further payments were required.*

Impact of This Case on Today's Law *This early classic case illustrates the approach that many courts take today when deciding whether a sales contract is unconscionable—an approach that focuses on "excessive" price and unequal bargaining power. Most of the litigants who have used UCC 2–302 successfully could demonstrate both an absence of meaningful choice and contract terms that were unreasonably favorable to the other party.*

Critical Thinking
- **Social** *Why would the seller's knowledge of the buyers' limited resources support a finding of unconscionability?*

15–4 Contracts for the International Sale of Goods

International sales contracts between firms or individuals located in different countries may be governed by the 1980 United Nations Convention on Contracts for the International Sale of Goods (CISG). The CISG governs international contracts only if the countries of the parties to the contract have ratified the CISG and if the parties have not agreed that some other law will govern their contract.

As of 2018, the CISG had been adopted by eighty-four countries, including the United States, Canada, some Central and South American countries, China, most European nations, Japan, and Mexico. That means that the CISG is the uniform international sales law of countries that account for more than two-thirds of all global trade.

Essentially, the CISG is to international sales contracts what Article 2 of the UCC is to domestic sales contracts. In domestic transactions, the UCC applies when the parties to a contract for a sale of goods have failed to specify in writing some important term, such as price or delivery. Similarly, whenever the parties to international transactions have adopted the CISG and failed to specify in writing the precise terms of a contract, the CISG will be applied.

Unlike the UCC, *the CISG does not apply to consumer sales.* Neither the UCC nor the CISG applies to contracts for services.

15–4a A Comparison of CISG and UCC Provisions

The provisions of the CISG, although similar for the most part to those of the UCC, differ from them in some respects. If the CISG and the UCC conflict, the CISG applies (because it is a treaty of the U.S. national government and therefore is supreme). We look here at some differences with respect to contract formation. CISG provisions relating to risk of loss, performance, remedies, and warranties will be discussed in other chapters as those topics are examined.

The Mirror Image Rule Under the UCC, a definite expression of acceptance that contains additional terms can still result in the formation of a contract, unless the additional terms are conditioned on the assent of the offeror. In other words, as we have seen, the UCC does away with the mirror image rule in domestic sales contracts.

Article 19 of the CISG provides that a contract can be formed even though the acceptance contains additional terms, unless the additional terms materially alter the contract. Under the CISG, however, the definition of a "material alteration" includes almost any change in the terms. If an additional term relates to payment, quality,

quantity, price, time and place of delivery, extent of one party's liability to the other, or the settlement of disputes, the CISG considers the added term a material alteration. In effect, then, the CISG requires that the terms of the acceptance mirror those of the offer.

The court in the following case applied the CISG's mirror image rule to eighteen contracts for sales of frozen potatoes from a supplier in Canada to a company in Illinois.

Case Analysis 15.3

VLM Food Trading International, Inc. v. Illinois Trading Co.

United States Court of Appeals, Seventh Circuit, 811 F.3d 247 (2016).

In the Language of the Court

SYKES, Circuit Judge.

* * * *

This [is a] contract dispute between plaintiff VLM Food Trading International, Inc., a Canadian agricultural supplier, and Illinois Trading Company, an Illinois produce reseller.

* * * *

* * * VLM sold frozen potatoes to Illinois Trading through nine separate transactions without incident. Illinois Trading then encountered financial difficulty and failed to pay for the next nine shipments from VLM. The parties agree that each transaction occurred the same way. First, Illinois Trading sent a purchase order specifying the item, quantity, price, and place of delivery for the potatoes. Second, VLM responded with an e-mail confirming the terms of the sale. Third, VLM shipped the order and Illinois Trading accepted it. Finally, VLM followed up by mail with an invoice. Importantly for us, the trailing invoices included a provision purporting to make Illinois Trading liable for * * * attorney's fees if it breached the contracts.

When Illinois Trading stopped paying its invoices, VLM sued Illinois Trading [in a federal district court].

* * * The answer admitted that the defendant owed VLM the purchase price for the produce * * * but contested liability for attorney's fees.

* * * The judge applied the [United Nations Convention on Contracts for

the International Sale of Goods] and held that the attorney's fees provision was *not* part of the contracts. [VLM appealed, challenging the court's analysis and application of the law to reach this conclusion.]

* * * *

The Convention's definition of the "loss" resulting from a breach of contract does not itself include attorney's fees. To succeed, VLM must show that its contracts with Illinois Trading expressly made Illinois Trading liable for VLM's attorney's fees in the event of a breach. To determine whether the fees provision was expressly accepted by Illinois Trading, we need to know when the terms of their agreement became binding. [Emphasis added.]

A contract is formed under the Convention when there is a valid offer and acceptance. An offer is valid if it is sufficiently definite and indicates the intention of the offeror to be bound in case of acceptance. An offer is sufficiently definite if it indicates the goods and expressly or implicitly fixes or makes provision for determining the quantity and price. Once a valid offer has been extended, the offeree can accept by words or conduct, but not by silence or inactivity. An acceptance becomes effective at the moment the indication of assent reaches the offeror. Acceptance can also be demonstrated through the offeree's conduct, if allowed as a result of practices which the parties have established between themselves or of usage.

So far so good— these contract principles are familiar and very similar to those expressed in the UCC. But * * * the Convention departs dramatically from the UCC by using the common-law "mirror image" rule * * * to resolve "battles of the forms." Under the mirror-image rule, as expressed in Article 19(1) of the Convention, "a reply to an offer which purports to be an acceptance but contains additions, limitations or other modifications is a rejection of the offer and constitutes a counter-offer."

Each Illinois Trading purchase order met all the Convention's criteria for an offer; they included sufficiently definite terms, were directed to VLM specifically, and indicated that Illinois Trading intended to be bound by VLM's acceptance. Each of VLM's confirmation e-mails was, in turn, an effective acceptance of Illinois Trading's offer because each one confirmed and accepted the terms of the purchase order. As such, the contracts were formed when Illinois Trading received VLM's confirmation e-mails. The attorney's fees provision was *not* part of the agreement described in the purchase orders and the e-mail confirmations; that term first appeared in the trailing invoices that were mailed to Illinois Trading *after* VLM delivered the produce.

Under the Convention VLM had already bound itself to the contracts proposed by Illinois Trading when it

Case 15.3 Continues

confirmed Illinois Trading's purchase offer by e-mail. The attorney's fees provision therefore could not have been a counteroffer. Rather, * * * the attorney's fees * * * provision would be a proposed modification to the contracts. Under the mirror-image rule, a party does not have to object to a proposed modification in order to keep it from being incorporated; any term that is not "mirrored" in the offer and acceptance is excluded. Contracts can only be modified by agreement of the parties.

Illinois Trading never made any statements indicating its acceptance of the proposed attorney's fees modification. Indeed, the only possible activity that could have indicated Illinois Trading's acceptance of the proposed modification was its payment of the invoices. But that conduct is just as consistent with Illinois Trading's obligations under the original agreement as it is with any new acceptance. Furthermore, since VLM had already completely performed its duties under the original proposed agreement, it had no performance left to offer in consideration for any (gratuitous) agreement by Illinois Trading to assume liability for VLM's attorney's fees in the event of breach.

* * * *

VLM contends that despite the contract-formation analysis prescribed by the Convention, the parties subjectively intended the attorney's fees provision to apply. In VLM's view the Convention "commands" judges to consider extrinsic evidence to illuminate the parties' intent. This argument relies largely on Article 8(3), which reads: "In determining the intent of a party * * * due consideration is to be given to all relevant circumstances of the case including the negotiations, any practices which the parties have established between themselves, usages and any subsequent conduct of the parties." But the purpose of this intent test is to help courts interpret the statements and conduct of parties according to their intent where the other party knew * * * what that intent was. Although VLM's conduct, sending trailing invoices containing an attorney's fees provision, clearly indicates that *VLM* intended Illinois Trading to be liable for collection fees, there was never any indication of *mutual* intent at the time of contracting. Fee-shifting was never mentioned during any negotiations, and none of Illinois Trading's subsequent conduct indicates that it agreed to pay VLM's attorney's fees.

* * * *

VLM also points to Article 9(1), which says that "parties are bound to any usage to which they have agreed and by any practices which they have established between themselves." This clause doesn't help for two reasons. First, there simply isn't any established "practice" between Illinois Trading and VLM regarding liability for attorney's fees. * * * Second, evidence of "usage" comes into play to clarify the meaning assigned to a contract term * * * . Here, no contract term is ambiguous and thus in need of clarification by evidence of usage. In other words, there's no disagreement about what the attorney's fees provision *means;* the only issue is whether it was part of the parties' agreement.

* * * *

Finally, the fact that some of Illinois Trading's contracts with other vendors included fee-shifting provisions is not relevant under the mirror-image rule, nor is the fact that Illinois Trading paid attorney's fees as part of its settlements with certain vendors. Nothing in the Convention indicates that common industry practices are automatically grafted onto contracts; rather, the content of each contract must be analyzed independently.

For all these reasons, the [district court] judge properly applied the Convention and held that the parties' contracts did not include the attorney's fees provision.

Legal Reasoning Questions

1. How did the CISG's rules regarding the formation of contracts affect the lower court's holding in this case?

2. Did the appellate court agree with the lower court's analysis and application of the CISG's rules? Why or why not?

3. What would have been the result if the court had applied the UCC instead of the CISG?

Irrevocable Offers UCC 2–205 provides that a merchant's firm offer is irrevocable, even without consideration, if the merchant gives assurances in a signed writing. In contrast, under the CISG, an offer can become irrevocable without a signed writing. Article 16(2) of the CISG provides that an offer will be irrevocable if:

1. The offeror states orally that the offer is irrevocable.

2. The offeree reasonably relies on the offer as being irrevocable.

In both of these situations, the offer will be irrevocable even without a writing and without consideration.

The Writing Requirement As discussed previously, the UCC has a Statute of Frauds provision. UCC 2–201 requires contracts for the sale of goods priced at $500 or more to be evidenced by a written or electronic record signed by the party against whom enforcement is sought.

Article 11 of the CISG, however, states that a contract of sale "need not be concluded in or evidenced by writing and is not subject to any other requirements as to form. It may be proved by any means, including witnesses." Article 11 of the CISG accords with the legal customs of most nations, which no longer require contracts to meet certain formal or writing requirements to be enforceable.

Time of Contract Formation Under the common law of contracts and the UCC, an acceptance is effective on dispatch, so a contract is created when the acceptance is transmitted. Under the CISG, in contrast, a contract is created not at the time the acceptance is transmitted but only on its *receipt* by the offeror. (The offer becomes *irrevocable,* however, when the acceptance is sent.)

Article 18(2) states that an acceptance by return promise (a unilateral contract) "becomes effective at the moment the indication of assent reaches the offeror." Under Article 18(3), the offeree may also bind the offeror by performance even without giving any notice to the offeror. The acceptance becomes effective "at the moment the act is performed." Thus, it is the offeree's reliance, rather than the communication of acceptance to the offeror, that creates the contract.

15–4b Special Provisions in International Contracts

Language and legal differences among nations can create various problems for parties to international contracts when disputes arise. It is possible to avoid these problems by including in a contract special provisions relating to choice of language, choice of forum, choice of law, and the types of events that may excuse the parties from performance.

Choice-of-Language Clause A deal struck between a U.S. company and a company in another country frequently involves two languages. One party may not understand complex contractual terms that are written in the other party's language. Translating the terms poses its own problems, as typically many phrases are not readily translatable into another language.

To make sure that no disputes arise out of this language problem, an international sales contract should include a **choice-of-language clause.** This clause will designate the official language by which the contract will be interpreted in the event of disagreement. The clause might also specify that the agreement is to be translated into, say, Spanish, and that the translation is to be approved by both parties. If arbitration is anticipated, an additional clause must be added to indicate the official language that will be used at the arbitration proceeding.

Forum-Selection Clause A **forum-selection clause** designates the forum (place, or court) in which any disputes that arise under the contract will be litigated. This clause should indicate the specific court that will have jurisdiction. The forum does not necessarily have to be within the geographic boundaries of either party's nation.

Including a forum-selection clause in an international contract is especially important because when several countries are involved, litigation may be sought in courts in different nations. There are no universally accepted rules regarding the jurisdiction of a particular court over subject matter or parties to a dispute, although the adoption of the 2005 Choice of Court Convention helped to resolve certain issues.

Under certain circumstances, a forum-selection clause will not be valid. Specifically, if the clause denies one party an effective remedy, or is the product of fraud or unconscionable conduct, the clause will not be enforced. Similarly, if the designated forum causes substantial inconvenience to one of the parties, or violates public policy, the clause may not be enforced.

Choice-of-Law Clause A contractual provision designating the applicable law, called a **choice-of-law clause,** is typically included in every international contract. At common law (and in European civil law systems), parties are allowed to choose the law that will govern their contractual relationship. There must normally be some connection between the chosen law and the contracting parties to show that the parties are not merely trying to avoid the laws of their own jurisdictions.

Under the UCC, parties may choose the law that will govern the contract as long as the choice is "reasonable." Article 6 of the CISG, however, imposes no limitation on the parties in their choice of what law will govern the contract. The 1986 Hague Convention on the Law Applicable to Contracts for the International Sale of Goods—often referred to as the Choice-of-Law Convention—allows unlimited autonomy in the choice of law. Whenever a choice of law is not specified in a contract, the Hague Convention indicates that the law of the country where the seller's place of business is located will govern.

***Force Majeure* Clause** Every contract, and particularly those involving international transactions, should have a ***force majeure* clause.** The French term *force majeure* means "impossible or irresistible force"—sometimes loosely defined as "an act of God." *Force majeure* clauses often stipulate that other events (in addition to acts of God) will excuse liability for nonperformance. Occurrences such as adverse governmental orders or regulations, embargoes, and extreme shortages of materials commonly excuse a party's nonperformance.

Note that some *force majeure* clauses require notice before a party's liability for nonperformance (or delay in performance) will be excused. **■ CASE IN POINT 15.24** Bigge Power Constructors manufactures cranes and other heavy equipment. Bigge contracted to purchase castings from a supplier, Rexnord Industries, LLC, for $4.5 million. Bigge needed the castings for the manufacture of two large derricks that were to be used in building nuclear power plants. The parties' contract set forth a delivery schedule for the castings, which Rexnord failed to meet. Although Bigge accepted and used all of the castings Rexnord supplied, it withheld $1 million from the purchase price for costs it had incurred as a result of the supplier's delay.

Rexnord sued for breach, claiming that the delay was a *force majeure* event, which the contract defined as any event "beyond a party's reasonable control." The court held that Rexnord's delay was not excused because Rexnord had never given Bigge the required notice that events constituting a *force majeure* had occurred. Thus, Bigge was entitled to damages for Rexnord's untimely delivery of goods. (If the supplier had given the required notice, its delay normally would have been excused.)[13] ■

---

13. *Rexnord Industries, LLC v. Bigge Power Constructors,* 947 F.Supp.2d 951 (E.D.Wis. 2013).

Reviewing: The Formation of Sales and Lease Contracts

Guy Holcomb owns and operates Oasis Goodtime Emporium, an adult entertainment establishment. Holcomb wanted to create an adult Internet system for Oasis that would offer customers adult-theme videos and "live" chat room programs using performers at the club. On May 10, Holcomb signed a work order authorizing Thomas Consulting Group (TCG) "to deliver a working prototype of a customer chat system, demonstrating the integration of live video and chatting in a Web browser." In exchange for creating the prototype, Holcomb agreed to pay TCG $64,697. On May 20, Holcomb signed an additional work order in the amount of $12,943 for TCG to install a customized firewall system. The work orders stated that Holcomb would make monthly installment payments to TCG, and both parties expected the work would be finished by September.

Due to unforeseen problems largely attributable to system configuration and software incompatibility, the project required more time than anticipated. By the end of the summer, the Web site was still not ready, and Holcomb had fallen behind in his payments to TCG. TCG threatened to cease work and file a suit for breach of contract unless the bill was paid. Rather than make further payments, Holcomb wanted to abandon the Web site project. Using the information presented in the chapter, answer the following questions.

1. Would a court be likely to decide that the transaction between Holcomb and TCG was covered by the Uniform Commercial Code (UCC)? Why or why not?
2. Would a court be likely to consider Holcomb a merchant under the UCC? Why or why not?
3. Did the parties have a valid contract under the UCC? Were any terms left open in the contract? If so, which terms? How would a court deal with open terms?
4. Suppose that Holcomb and TCG meet in October in an attempt to resolve their problems. At that time, the parties reach an oral agreement that TCG will continue to work without demanding full payment of the past due amounts and Holcomb will pay TCG $5,000 per week. Assuming the contract falls under the UCC, is the oral agreement enforceable? Why or why not?

Debate This . . . *The UCC should require the same degree of definiteness of terms, especially with respect to price and quantity, as contract law does.*

Terms and Concepts

choice-of-language clause 301
choice-of-law clause 301
course of dealing 295
course of performance 296
firm offer 290
force majeure clause 301
forum-selection clause 301

fully integrated contract 295
intangible property 284
lease agreement 287
lessee 287
lessor 287
merchant 287
output contract 289

predominant-factor test 285
requirements contract 289
sale 284
sales contract 284
seasonably 290
tangible property 284
usage of trade 296

Issue Spotters

1. E-Design, Inc., orders 150 computer desks. Fav-O-Rite Supplies, Inc., ships 150 printer stands. Is this an acceptance of the offer or a counteroffer? If it is an acceptance, is it a breach of the contract? Why or why not? What if Fav-O-Rite told E-Design it was sending the printer stands as "an accommodation"? (See *The Formation of Sales and Lease Contracts*.)

2. Truck Parts, Inc. (TPI), often sells supplies to United Fix-It Company (UFC), which services trucks. Over the phone, they negotiate for the sale of eighty-four sets of tires. TPI sends a letter to UFC detailing the terms and two weeks later ships the tires. Is there an enforceable contract between them? Why or why not? (See *The Formation of Sales and Lease Contracts*.)

• **Check your answers to the Issue Spotters against the answers provided in Appendix B at the end of this text.**

Business Scenarios

15–1. Merchant's Firm Offer. On May 1, Jennings, a car dealer, e-mails Wheeler and says, "I have a 1955 Thunderbird convertible in mint condition that I will sell you for $13,500 at any time before June 9. [Signed] Peter Jennings." By May 15, having heard nothing from Wheeler, Jennings sells the car to another. On May 29, Wheeler accepts Jennings's offer and tenders $13,500. When told Jennings has sold the car to another, Wheeler claims Jennings has breached their contract. Is Jennings in breach? Explain. (See *The Formation of Sales and Lease Contracts*.)

15–2. Additional Terms. Strike offers to sell Bailey one thousand shirts for a stated price. The offer declares that shipment will be made by Dependable truck line. Bailey replies, "I accept your offer for one thousand shirts at the price quoted. Delivery to be by Yellow Express truck line." Both Strike and Bailey are merchants. Three weeks later, Strike ships the shirts by Dependable truck line, and Bailey refuses to accept delivery. Strike sues for breach of contract. Bailey claims that there never was a contract because his reply, which included a modification of carriers, did not constitute an acceptance. Bailey further claims that even if there had been a contract, Strike would have been in breach because Strike shipped the shirts by Dependable, contrary to the contract terms. Discuss fully Bailey's claims. (See *The Formation of Sales and Lease Contracts*.)

Business Case Problems

15–3. Spotlight on Goods and Services—The Statute of Frauds. Fallsview Glatt Kosher Caterers ran a business that provided travel packages, including food, entertainment, and lectures on religious subjects, to customers during the Passover holiday at a New York resort. Willie Rosenfeld verbally agreed to pay Fallsview $24,050 for the Passover package for himself and his family. Rosenfeld did not appear at the resort and never paid the amount owed. Fallsview sued Rosenfeld for breach of contract. Rosenfeld claimed that the contract was unenforceable because it was not in writing and violated the UCC's Statute of Frauds. Is the contract valid? Explain. [*Fallsview Glatt Kosher Caterers, Inc. v. Rosenfeld*, 7 Misc. 3d 557,

794 N.Y.S.2d 790 (2005)] (See *The Formation of Sales and Lease Contracts*.)

15–4. Business Case Problem with Sample Answer—Additional Terms. B.S. International, Ltd. (BSI), makes costume jewelry. JMAM, LLC, is a wholesaler of costume jewelry. JMAM sent BSI a letter with the terms for orders, including the necessary procedure for obtaining credit for items that customers rejected. The letter stated, "By signing below, you agree to the terms." Steven Baracsi, BSI's owner, signed the letter and returned it. For six years, BSI made jewelry for JMAM, which resold it. Items rejected by customers were sent back to

JMAM, but were never returned to BSI. BSI filed a suit against JMAM, claiming $41,294.21 for the unreturned items. BSI showed the court a copy of JMAM's terms. Across the bottom had been typed a "PS" requiring the return of rejected merchandise. Was this "PS" part of the contract? Discuss. [*B.S. International, Ltd. v. JMAM, LLC,* 13 A.3d 1057 (R.I. 2011)] (See *The Formation of Sales and Lease Contracts.*)

• For a sample answer to Problem 15–4, go to Appendix C at the end of this text.

15–5. Partial Performance and the Statute of Frauds. After a series of e-mails, Jorge Bonilla, the sole proprietor of a printing company in Uruguay, agreed to buy a used printer from Crystal Graphics Equipment, Inc., in New York. Crystal Graphics, through its agent, told Bonilla that the printing press was fully operational, contained all of its parts, and was in excellent condition except for some damage to one of the printing towers. Bonilla paid $95,000. Crystal Graphics sent him a signed, stamped invoice reflecting this payment. The invoice was dated six days after Bonilla's conversation with the agent.

When the printing press arrived, Bonilla discovered that it was missing parts and was damaged. Crystal Graphics sent replacement parts, but they did not work. Crystal Graphics was never able to make the printer operational. Bonilla sued, alleging breach of contract, breach of the implied covenant of good faith and fair dealing, breach of express warranty, and breach of implied warranty. Crystal Graphics claimed that the contract was not enforceable because it did not satisfy the Statute of Frauds. Can Crystal Graphics prevail on this basis? Why or why not? [*Bonilla v. Crystal Graphics Equipment, Inc.,* 2012 WL 360145 (S.D.Fla. 2012)] (See *The Formation of Sales and Lease Contracts.*)

15–6. The Statute of Frauds. Kendall Gardner agreed to buy from B&C Shavings a specially built shaving mill to produce wood shavings for poultry processors. B&C faxed an invoice to Gardner reflecting a purchase price of $86,200, with a 30 percent down payment and the "balance due before shipment." Gardner paid the down payment. B&C finished the mill and wrote Gardner a letter telling him to "pay the balance due or you will lose the down payment." By then, Gardner had lost his customers for the wood shavings, could not pay the balance due, and asked for the return of his down payment. Did these parties have an enforceable contract under the Statute of Frauds? Explain. [*Bowen v. Gardner,* 2013 Ark. App. 52, 425 S.W.3d 875 (2013)] (See *The Formation of Sales and Lease Contracts.*)

15–7. Goods and Services Combined. Allied Shelving and Equipment, Inc., sells and installs shelving systems. National Deli, LLC, contracted with Allied to provide and install a parallel rack system (a series of large shelves) in National's warehouse. Both parties were dissatisfied with the result. National filed a suit in a Florida state court against

Allied, which filed a counterclaim. Each contended that the other had materially breached the contract. The court applied common law contract principles to rule in National's favor on both claims. Allied appealed, arguing that the court should have applied the UCC. When does a court apply common law principles to a contract that involves both goods and services? In this case, why might an appellate court rule that the UCC should be applied instead? Explain. [*Allied Shelving and Equipment, Inc. v. National Deli, LLC,* 40 Fla. L. Weekly D145, 154 So.3d 482 (2015)] (See *The Scope of Articles 2 and 2A.*)

15–8. Acceptance. New England Precision Grinding, Inc. (NEPG), sells precision medical parts in Massachusetts. NEPG agreed to supply Kyphon, Inc., with stylets and nozzles. NEPG contracted with Simply Surgical, LLC, to obtain the parts from Iscon Surgicals, Ltd. The contract did not mention Kyphon or require Kyphon's acceptance of the parts. Before shipping, Iscon would certify that the parts conformed to NEPG's specifications. On receiving the parts, NEPG would certify that they conformed to Kyphon's specifications. On delivery, Kyphon would also inspect the parts. After about half a dozen transactions, NEPG's payments to Simply Surgical lagged, and the seller refused to make further deliveries. NEPG filed a suit in a Massachusetts state court against Simply Surgical, alleging breach of contract. NEPG claimed that Kyphon had rejected some of the parts, which gave NEPG the right not to pay for them. Do the UCC's rules with respect to acceptance support or undercut the parties' actions? Discuss. [*New England Precision Grinding, Inc. v. Simply Surgical, LLC,* 89 Mass.App.Ct.176, 46 N.E.3d 590 (2016)] (See *The Formation of Sales and Lease Contracts.*)

15–9. A Question of Ethics—Contract Terms. Daniel

 Fox owned Fox & Lamberth Enterprises, Inc., a kitchen and bath remodeling business, in Dayton, Ohio. Fox leased a building from Carl and Bellulah Hussong. Craftsmen Home Improvement, Inc., also remodeled baths and kitchens. When Fox planned to close his business, Craftsmen expressed an interest in buying his showroom assets. Fox set a price of $50,000. Craftsmen's owners agreed and gave Fox a list of the desired items and "A Bill of Sale" that set the terms for payment. The parties did not discuss Fox's arrangement with the Hussongs, but Craftsmen expected to negotiate a new lease and extensively modified the premises, including removing some of the displays to its own showroom. When the Hussongs and Craftsmen could not agree on new terms, Craftsmen told Fox that the deal was off. *[*Fox & Lamberth Enterprises, Inc. v. Craftsmen Home Improvement, Inc., 2006 -Ohio- 1427 (2 Dist. 2006)]* (See *The Formation of Sales and Lease Contracts.*)

(a) In Fox's suit in an Ohio state court for breach of contract, Craftsmen raised the Statute of Frauds as a defense. What are the requirements of the Statute of Frauds? Did the deal between Fox and Craftsmen meet these requirements? Did it fall under one of the exceptions? Explain.

(b) Craftsmen also claimed that the predominant factor of its agreement with Fox was a lease for the Hussongs' building. What is the predominant-factor test? Does it apply here? In any event, is it fair to hold a party to a contract to buy a business's assets when the buyer cannot negotiate a favorable lease of the premises on which the assets are located? Discuss.

Legal Reasoning Group Activity

15–10. Parol Evidence. Mountain Stream Trout Co. agreed to buy "market size" trout from trout grower Lake Farms, LLC. Their five-year contract did not define *market size*. At the time, in the trade, *market size* referred to fish of one-pound live weight. After three years, Mountain Stream began taking fewer, smaller deliveries of larger fish, claiming that *market size* varied according to whatever its customers demanded and that its customers now demanded larger fish. Lake Farms filed a suit for breach of contract. (See *The Formation of Sales and Lease Contracts.*)

(a) The first group will decide whether parol evidence is admissible to explain the terms of this contract. Are there any exceptions that could apply?

(b) A second group will determine the impact of course of dealing and usage of trade on the interpretation of contract terms.

(c) A third group will discuss how parties to a commercial contract can avoid the possibility that a court will interpret the contract terms in accordance with trade usage.

CHAPTER 16

Performance, Breach, and Warranties in Sales and Lease Contracts

The performance that is required of the parties under a sales or lease contract consists of the duties and obligations each party has under the terms of the contract. The basic obligation of the seller or lessor is to *transfer and deliver conforming goods*. The basic obligation of the buyer or lessee is to *accept and pay for conforming goods* in accordance with the contract [UCC 2–301, 2A–516(1)].

Sometimes, circumstances make it difficult for a party to carry out the promised performance, leading to a breach of the contract. When a breach occurs, the aggrieved (wronged) party looks for remedies. Note that in contrast to the common law of contracts, remedies under the UCC are cumulative in nature—meaning that the aggrieved party is not limited to one exclusive remedy.

Note also that the UCC has numerous rules governing product warranties as they occur in sales and lease contracts. Articles 2 (on sales) and 2A (on leases) designate several types of warranties that can arise in a sales or lease contract, including warranties of title, express warranties, and implied warranties. In addition, federal law imposes certain requirements on warranties.

Because a warranty imposes a duty on the seller or lessor, a breach of warranty is a breach of the seller's or lessor's promise. Assuming that the parties have not agreed to limit or modify the remedies available, if the seller or lessor breaches a warranty, the buyer or lessee can sue to recover damages. Under some circumstances, a breach of warranty can allow the buyer or lessee to rescind (cancel) the agreement.

16–1 Performance Obligations

Overall performance of a sales or lease contract is controlled by the agreement between the parties. When the contract is unclear and disputes arise, the courts look to the UCC and impose standards of good faith and commercial reasonableness.

The obligations of good faith and commercial reasonableness underlie every sales and lease contract. The UCC's good faith provision, which can never be disclaimed, reads as follows: "Every contract or duty within this Act imposes an obligation of good faith in its performance or enforcement" [UCC 1–304]. *Good faith* means honesty in fact. For a merchant, it means honesty in fact and the observance of reasonable commercial standards of fair dealing in the trade [UCC 2–103(1)(b)]. In other words, merchants are held to a higher standard of performance or duty than are nonmerchants.

16–1a Obligations of the Seller or Lessor

The basic duty of the seller or lessor is to deliver the goods called for under the contract to the buyer or lessee. Goods that conform to the contract description in every way are called **conforming goods.** To fulfill the contract, the seller or lessor must either deliver or tender delivery of conforming goods to the buyer or lessee.

Tender of Delivery **Tender of delivery** occurs when the seller or lessor makes conforming goods available and gives the buyer or lessee whatever notification is reasonably necessary to enable the buyer or lessee to take delivery [UCC 2–503(1), 2A–508(1)].

Tender must occur at a *reasonable hour* and in a *reasonable manner*. For instance, a seller cannot call the buyer at 2:00 A.M. and say, "The goods are ready. I'll give you twenty minutes to get them." Unless the parties have agreed otherwise, the goods must be tendered for delivery at a reasonable hour and kept available for a reasonable time to enable the buyer to take possession [UCC 2–503(1)(a)].

Normally, all goods called for by a contract must be tendered in a single delivery unless the parties have agreed on delivery in several lots or *installments* (discussed shortly) [UCC 2–307, 2–612, 2A–510]. ■ **CASE IN POINT 16.1** Richard and Nancy Garziano contracted with Louisiana Log Home (LLH) Company for a log-cabin kit to be delivered to them in Pass Christian, Mississippi. The contract required three installment payments. The final payment, due at delivery, was to include the cost of transportation. Two days before delivery, LLH told the buyers that the final payment would be $7,686.43, plus the transportation cost of $2,625.60. The Garzianos replied that they thought they had paid off the balance for the cabin and that they expected the shipping costs to be lower. They refused to pay more, so LLH did not deliver the kit.

The Garzianos sued LLH for breach of contract, alleging that LLH had violated Mississippi's version of UCC 2–503(1) by failing to give them reasonable notice of the price of delivery. The lower court held in favor of LLH, and a federal appellate court affirmed. The parties' contract had clearly indicated that the buyer was to pay the costs of shipping the materials to the site. The contract had also stated the total price for the kit, so the Garzianos knew that they still owed a balance to LLH. They were given reasonable notice of the delivery date and price in compliance with the terms of the contract and the UCC. Therefore, LLH did not breach the contract.[1] ■

Place of Delivery The buyer and seller (or lessor and lessee) may agree that the goods will be delivered to a particular destination where the buyer or lessee will take possession. If the contract does not indicate where the goods will be delivered, then the place for delivery will be one of the following:

1. The *seller's place of business.*
2. The *seller's residence,* if the seller has no business location [UCC 2–308(a)].
3. The *location of the goods,* if both parties know at the time of contracting that the goods are located somewhere other than the seller's business [UCC 2–308(b)].

■ **EXAMPLE 16.2** Li Wan and Boyd both live in San Francisco. In San Francisco, Li Wan contracts to sell Boyd five used trucks, which both parties know are located in

a Chicago warehouse. If nothing more is specified in the contract, the place of delivery for the trucks is Chicago. ■

Delivery via Carrier In many instances, it is clear from the surrounding circumstances or delivery terms in the contract that the parties intended the goods to be moved by a carrier. In carrier contracts, the seller fulfills the obligation to deliver the goods through either a shipment contract or a destination contract.

Shipment Contracts. A *shipment contract* requires or authorizes the seller to ship goods by a carrier, rather than to deliver them at a particular destination [UCC 2–319, 2–509(1)(a)]. Under a shipment contract, unless otherwise agreed, the seller must do the following:

1. Place the goods into the hands of the carrier.
2. Make a contract for their transportation that is reasonable according to the nature of the goods and their value. (For instance, certain types of goods need refrigeration in transit.)
3. Obtain and promptly deliver or tender to the buyer any documents necessary to enable the buyer to obtain possession of the goods from the carrier.
4. Promptly notify the buyer that shipment has been made [UCC 2–504].

If the seller does not make a reasonable contract for transportation or notify the buyer of the shipment, the buyer can reject the goods, but only if a *material loss* or a *significant delay* results. ■ **EXAMPLE 16.3** Zigi's Organic Fruits sells strawberries to Lozier under a shipment contract. If Zigi's does not arrange for refrigerated transportation and the berries spoil during transport, a material loss to Lozier will likely result. ■ Of course, the parties are free to make agreements that alter the UCC's rules and allow the buyer to reject goods for other reasons.

Destination Contracts. In a *destination contract,* the seller agrees to deliver conforming goods to the buyer at a particular destination. The goods must be tendered at a reasonable hour and held at the buyer's disposal for a reasonable length of time. The seller must also give the buyer appropriate notice and any necessary documents to enable the buyer to obtain delivery from the carrier [UCC 2–503].

The Perfect Tender Rule The seller or lessor has an obligation to ship or tender *conforming goods.* The buyer or lessee is then obligated to accept and pay for the goods according to the contract terms [UCC 2–507].

---

1. *Garziano v. Louisiana Log Home Co.,* 569 Fed.Appx. 292 (5th Cir. 2014).

Under the common law, the seller was obligated to deliver goods that conformed with the terms of the contract in every detail (unless the doctrine of substantial performance applied). The UCC adopted the **perfect tender rule.** It states that if goods or tender of delivery fails *in any respect* to conform to the contract, the buyer or lessee may accept the goods, reject the entire shipment, or accept part and reject part [UCC 2–601, 2A–509].

The corollary to this rule is that if the goods conform in every respect, the buyer or lessee does not have a right to reject the goods. ■ **CASE IN POINT 16.4** U.S. Golf & Tennis Centers, Inc., agreed to buy 96,000 golf balls from Wilson Sporting Goods Company for a total price of $20,000. Wilson represented that U.S. Golf was receiving its lowest price ($5 per two-dozen unit).

Wilson shipped golf balls to U.S. Golf that conformed to the contract in quantity and quality, but it did not receive payment. U.S. Golf claimed that it had learned that Wilson had sold the product for $2 per unit to another buyer. U.S. Golf asked Wilson to reduce the contract price of the balls to $4 per unit. Wilson refused and filed a suit. The court ruled in favor of Wilson. Because it was undisputed that the shipment of golf balls conformed to the contract specifications, U.S. Golf was obligated to accept the goods and pay the agreed-on price.[2] ■

Exceptions to the Perfect Tender Rule

Because of the rigidity of the perfect tender rule, several exceptions to the rule have been created, some of which we discuss here.

Agreement of the Parties. Exceptions to the perfect tender rule may be established by agreement. The parties may agree, for instance, that defective goods or parts will not be rejected if the seller or lessor is able to repair or replace them within a reasonable period of time. In this situation, the perfect tender rule does not apply.

Cure. The UCC does not specifically define the term **cure,** but it refers to the right of the seller or lessor to repair, adjust, or replace defective or nonconforming goods [UCC 2–508, 2A–513].

The seller or lessor has a right to attempt to "cure" a defect when the following are true:

1. A delivery is rejected because the goods were nonconforming.
2. The time for performance has not yet expired.
3. The seller or lessor provides timely notice to the buyer or lessee of the intention to cure.

4. The cure can be made within the contract time for performance.

Even if the contract time for performance has expired, the seller or lessor can still cure if he or she had *reasonable grounds to believe that the nonconforming tender would be acceptable to the buyer or lessee* [UCC 2–508(2), 2A–513(2)].

■ **EXAMPLE 16.5** In the past, Rio Electronics has frequently allowed Topps Company to substitute grey keyboards when the silver keyboards that Rio ordered were not in stock. Under a new contract for keyboards, Rio rejects a shipment of grey keyboards. In this situation, Topps had reasonable grounds to believe that Rio would accept the grey keyboards as a substitute. Therefore, normally Topps can cure within a reasonable time even if the conforming delivery will occur after the contract time for performance. ■

A seller or lessor will sometimes tender nonconforming goods with some type of price allowance (discount). A discounted price can serve as the "reasonable grounds" to believe that the buyer or lessee will accept the nonconforming tender.

The right to cure substantially restricts the right of the buyer or lessee to reject goods. To reject, the buyer or lessee must inform the seller or lessor of the particular defect. If the defect is not disclosed, the buyer or lessee cannot later assert the defect as a defense if the defect is one that the seller or lessor could have cured. Generally, buyers and lessees must act in good faith and state specific reasons for refusing to accept goods [UCC 2–605, 2A–514].

Substitution of Carriers. Sometimes, an agreed-on manner of delivery (such as the use of a particular carrier) becomes impracticable or unavailable through no fault of either party. In that situation, if a commercially reasonable substitute is available, this substitute performance is sufficient tender to the buyer and must be used [UCC 2–614(1)]. The seller or lessor is required to arrange for a substitute carrier and normally is responsible for any additional shipping costs (unless the contract states otherwise).

■ **EXAMPLE 16.6** A sales contract calls for a large generator to be shipped by United Trucking on or before June 1. The contract terms clearly state the importance of the delivery date. The employees of United go on strike. The seller must make a reasonable substitute tender, by another trucking company or perhaps by rail, if such a substitute is available. ■

Installment Contracts. An **installment contract** is a single contract that requires or authorizes delivery in two

---

2. *Wilson Sporting Goods Co. v. U.S. Golf and Tennis Centers, Inc.,* 2012 WL 601804 (Tenn.App. 2012).

or more separate lots to be accepted and paid for separately. With an installment contract, a buyer or lessee can reject an installment *only if the nonconformity substantially impairs the value* of the installment and cannot be cured [UCC 2–307, 2–612(2), 2A–510(1)]. ■ **EXAMPLE 16.7** A seller is to deliver fifteen freezers in lots of five each. In the first lot, four of the freezers have defective cooling units that cannot be repaired. The buyer in these circumstances can reject the entire lot. ■ If the buyer or lessee fails to notify the seller or lessor of the rejection, however, and subsequently accepts a nonconforming installment, the contract is reinstated [UCC 2–612(3), 2A–510(2)].

Unless the contract provides otherwise, the entire installment contract is breached only when one or more nonconforming installments *substantially* impair the value of the *whole contract*. The point to remember is that the UCC significantly alters the right of the buyer or lessee to reject the entire contract if the contract requires delivery to be made in several installments. The UCC strictly limits rejection to instances of *substantial* nonconformity.

Commercial Impracticability. Occurrences unforeseen by either party when a contract was made may make performance commercially impracticable. When this occurs, the perfect tender rule no longer applies. The seller or lessor must, however, notify the buyer or lessee as soon as practicable that there will be a delay or nondelivery [UCC 2–615, 2A–405].

Commercial impracticability arises only when the parties, at the time the contract was made, had no reason to anticipate that the event would occur. It does not extend to problems that could have been foreseen, such as an increase in cost resulting from inflation.

■ **CASE IN POINT 16.8** In a classic 1970s case, Maple Farms, Inc., entered a contract to supply a school district in New York with milk for one school year. The contract price was the market price of milk in June, but by December, the price of raw milk had increased by 23 percent. Maple Farms stood to lose $7,350 on this contract (and more on similar contracts with other school districts). To avoid performing the contract, Maple Farms filed a suit and claimed that the unanticipated increases in its costs made performance "impracticable." A New York trial court disagreed. Because inflation and fluctuating prices could have been foreseen, they did not render performance of this contract impracticable. The court granted summary judgment in favor of the school district.[3] ■

---

3. *Maple Farms, Inc. v. City School District of Elmira,* 76 Misc.2d 1080, 352 N.Y.S.2d 784 (1974).

Sometimes, the unforeseen event only *partially* affects the capacity of the seller or lessor to perform. Therefore, the seller or lessor can *partially* fulfill the contract but cannot tender total performance. In this event, the seller or lessor is required to distribute any remaining goods or deliveries fairly and reasonably among the parties to whom it is contractually obligated [UCC 2–615(b), 2A–405(b)]. The buyer or lessee must receive notice of the allocation and has the right to accept or reject it [UCC 2–615(c), 2A–405(c)].

Destruction of Identified Goods. Sometimes, an unexpected event, such as a fire, totally destroys goods through no fault of either party before risk passes to the buyer or lessee. In such a situation, *if the goods were identified at the time the contract was formed,* the parties are excused from performance [UCC 2–613, 2A–221]. If the goods are only partially destroyed, however, the buyer or lessee can inspect them and either treat the contract as void or accept the damaged goods with a reduction in the contract price.

■ **EXAMPLE 16.9** Atlas Sporting Equipment agrees to lease to River Bicycles sixty bicycles of a particular model that has been discontinued. No other bicycles of that model are available. River specifies that it needs the bicycles to rent to tourists. Before Atlas can deliver the bicycles, they are destroyed by a fire. In this situation, Atlas is not liable to River for failing to deliver the bicycles. Through no fault of either party, the goods were destroyed before the risk of loss passed to the lessee. The loss was total, so the contract is avoided. Clearly, Atlas has no obligation to tender the bicycles, and River has no obligation to make the lease payments for them. ■

Assurance and Cooperation. If one party has "reasonable grounds" to believe that the other party will not perform, the first party may *in writing* "demand adequate assurance of due performance" from the other party. Until such assurance is received, the first party may "suspend" further performance without liability. What constitutes "reasonable grounds" is determined by commercial standards. If the requested assurances are not forthcoming within a reasonable time (not to exceed thirty days), the failure to respond may be treated as a repudiation of the contract [UCC 2–609, 2A–401].

Sometimes, the performance of one party depends on the cooperation of the other. When cooperation is not forthcoming, the first party can either proceed to perform the contract in any reasonable manner or suspend performance without liability and hold the uncooperative party in breach [UCC 2–311(3)].

■ **EXAMPLE 16.10** Aman is required by contract to deliver 1,200 LG washing machines to various locations in California on or before October 1. Friedman, the buyer, is to specify the locations for delivery. Aman repeatedly requests the delivery locations, but Friedman does not respond. The washing machines are ready for shipment on October 1, but Friedman still refuses to give Aman the delivery locations. If Aman does not ship on October 1, he cannot be held liable. Aman is excused for any resulting delay of performance because of Friedman's failure to cooperate. ■

Concept Summary 16.1 reviews the obligations of the seller.

16–1b Obligations of the Buyer or Lessee

The main obligation of the buyer or lessee under a sales or lease contract is to pay for the goods tendered. Once

---

Concept Summary 16.1

Obligations of the Seller or Lessor

Tender of Delivery	• Tender of delivery occurs when the seller or lessor makes *conforming goods* available and gives the buyer or lessee whatever notification is reasonably necessary to enable the buyer or lessee to take delivery [UCC 2–503(1), 2A–508(1)]. The seller may also tender delivery by placing conforming goods into the hands of a carrier in shipment or destination contracts. • Unless the parties have agreed otherwise, the conforming goods must be tendered for delivery at a *reasonable hour* and in a *reasonable manner* [UCC 2–503(1)(a)].
The Perfect Tender Rule	Under the perfect tender doctrine, the seller or lessor must tender goods that conform exactly to the terms of the contract. Exceptions to this rule can be established by agreement of the parties or as follows: • *Cure*—The right of the seller or lessor to *cure*—that is, repair, adjust, or replace—nonconforming goods within the contract time for performance [UCC 2–508, 2A–513]. • *Substitution of carriers*—If the agreed-on means of delivery becomes impracticable or unavailable, the seller must substitute an alternative carrier, if a reasonable one is available [UCC 2–614(1)]. • *Installment contracts*—Unless the contract provides otherwise, the entire installment contract is breached only when one or more nonconforming installments *substantially* impair the value of the *whole* contract [UCC 2–612(2), 2A–510(1)]. • *Commercial impracticability*—When performance becomes commercially impracticable owing to circumstances unforeseen when the contract was formed, the perfect tender rule no longer applies [UCC 2–615, 2A–405]. • *Destruction of identified goods*—When an unexpected event, such as a fire, totally destroys goods that were identified to the contract when it was formed, through no fault of either party, performance is excused [UCC 2–613, 2A–221]. • *Assurance and cooperation*—If a party has reasonable grounds to believe that the other party is not going to perform and demands assurances, the other party's failure to respond within a reasonable time may be treated as a repudiation (breach) and excuse further performance [UCC 2–609, 2A–401]. A party's failure to cooperate with the other party may also excuse the party from further performing [UCC 2–311(3)].

the seller or lessor has adequately tendered delivery, the buyer or lessee is obligated to accept conforming goods and pay for them according to the terms of the contract.

Payment In the absence of any specific agreements, the buyer or lessee must make payment at the time and place the goods are *received* [UCC 2–310(a), 2A–516(1)]. When a sale is made on credit, the buyer is obligated to pay according to the specified credit terms (for example, 60, 90, or 120 days), not when the goods are received. The credit period usually begins on the *date of shipment* [UCC 2–310(d)]. Under a lease contract, a lessee must make the lease payment that was specified in the contract [UCC 2A–516(1)].

Payment can be made by any means agreed on between the parties—cash or any other method generally acceptable in the commercial world. If the seller demands cash, the seller must give the buyer reasonable time to obtain it [UCC 2–511].

Right of Inspection Unless the parties otherwise agree, or for C.O.D. (collect on delivery) transactions, the buyer or lessee has an absolute right to inspect the goods before making payment. This right allows the buyer or lessee to verify that the goods tendered or delivered conform to the contract. If the goods are not as ordered, the buyer or lessee has no duty to pay. *An opportunity for inspection is therefore a condition precedent to the right of the seller or lessor to enforce payment* [UCC 2–513(1), 2A–515(1)].

Inspection can take place at any reasonable place and time and in any reasonable manner. Generally, what is reasonable is determined by custom of the trade, past practices of the parties, and the like. The buyer bears the costs of inspecting the goods but can recover the costs from the seller if the goods do not conform and are rejected [UCC 2–513(2)].

■ **CASE IN POINT 16.11** Jessie Romero offered to deliver two trade-in vehicles to Scoggin-Dickey Chevrolet Buick, Inc., in exchange for a 2006 Silverado pickup. Scoggin-Dickey agreed. The parties negotiated a price, including a value for the trade-in vehicles, plus cash. Romero paid the cash and took the 2006 Silverado (but the dealer kept the title to it). Several weeks later, Romero delivered the two trade-in vehicles.

On inspecting the trade-in vehicles, Scoggin-Dickey found that they had little value. One of them did not even run. The dealer repossessed the Silverado. Romero sued for breach of contract, claiming that the dealer had no right to reject the trade-in vehicles after the contract was signed. The court held that the contract for the sale was not completed until Romero traded in the two vehicles. Scoggin-Dickey had a right to inspect them and did

so within a reasonable time after they were delivered. The dealership was entitled to reject the trade-in vehicles and keep the 2006 Silverado, but it had to refund Romero's cash and return the trade-in vehicles.[4] ■

Acceptance After having had a reasonable opportunity to inspect the goods, the buyer or lessee can demonstrate acceptance in any of the following ways:

1. The buyer or lessee indicates (by words or conduct) to the seller or lessor that the goods are conforming or that he or she will retain them in spite of their nonconformity [UCC 2–606(1)(a), 2A–515(1)(a)].

2. The buyer or lessee fails to reject the goods within a reasonable period of time [UCC 2–602(1), 2–606(1)(b), 2A–515(1)(b)].

3. In sales contracts, the buyer will be deemed to have accepted the goods if he or she performs any act inconsistent with the seller's ownership. For instance, any use or resale of the goods—except for the limited purpose of testing or inspecting the goods—generally constitutes an acceptance [UCC 2–606(1)(c)].

The obligations of the buyer or lessee under the UCC are outlined in Exhibit 16–1.

Partial Acceptance If some of the goods delivered do not conform to the contract and the seller or lessor has failed to cure, the buyer or lessee can make a *partial* acceptance [UCC 2–601(c), 2A–509(1)]. The same is true if the nonconformity was not reasonably discoverable before acceptance. (In the latter situation, the buyer or lessee may be able to revoke the acceptance, as will be discussed later in this chapter.)

A buyer or lessee cannot accept less than a single commercial unit, however. The UCC defines a *commercial unit* as a unit of goods that, by commercial usage, is viewed as a "single whole" for purposes of sale. A commercial unit cannot be divided without materially impairing the character of the unit, its market value, or its use [UCC 2–105(6), 2A–103(1)(c)]. A commercial unit can be a single article (such as a machine), a set of articles (such as a suite of furniture), a quantity (such as a bale, a gross, or a carload), or any other unit treated in the trade as a single whole.

16–1c Anticipatory Repudiation

What if, before the time for contract performance, one party clearly communicates to the other the intention *not* to perform? Such an action is a breach of the contract by *anticipatory repudiation.*

---

4. *Romero v. Scoggin-Dickey Chevrolet Buick, Inc.,* 2010 WL 456910 (Tex. App.—Amarillo 2010).

EXHIBIT 16–1 Obligations of the Buyer or Lessee

THE PAYMENT FOR THE GOODS	THE RIGHT OF INSPECTION	THE ACCEPTANCE OF THE GOODS
• On tender of delivery by the seller or lessor, the buyer or lessee must pay for the goods at the time and place the goods are *received*, unless the sale is made on credit [UCC 2–310(a)]. • Payment can be made by any method generally acceptable in the commercial world, but the seller can demand cash [UCC 2–511].	• Unless otherwise agreed or in C.O.D. (collect on delivery) shipments, the buyer or lessee has an absolute right to inspect the goods before acceptance [UCC 2–513(1), 2A–515(1)].	• The buyer or lessee can manifest acceptance of delivered goods in words or by conduct [UCC 2–606(1), 2A–515(1)]. • A buyer or lessee who fails to reject goods within a reasonable time period will be deemed to have accepted them [UCC 2–606(1)(a), 2A–515(1)(b)]. • A buyer will be deemed to have accepted goods if he or she performs any act inconsistent with the seller's ownership [UCC 2–606(1)(c)].

Suspension of Performance Obligations When anticipatory repudiation occurs, the nonbreaching party has a choice of two responses:

1. Treat the repudiation as a final breach by pursuing a remedy.
2. Wait to see if the repudiating party will decide to honor the contract despite the avowed intention to renege [UCC 2–610, 2A–402].

In either situation, the nonbreaching party may suspend performance.

Retraction of Repudiation The UCC permits the breaching party to "retract" his or her repudiation (subject to some limitations). This can be done by any method that clearly indicates the party's intent to perform. Once retraction is made, the rights of the repudiating party under the contract are reinstated. There can be no retraction, however, if since the time of the repudiation the other party has canceled or materially changed position or otherwise indicated that the repudiation is final [UCC 2–611, 2A–403].

■ **EXAMPLE 16.12** On April 1, Cora Lyn, who owns a small inn, purchases a suite of furniture from Tom Horton, proprietor of Horton's Furniture Warehouse. The contract states that "delivery must be made on or before May 1." On April 10, Horton informs Lyn that he cannot make delivery until May 10 and asks her to consent to the modified delivery date.

In this situation, Lyn has two options. She can either treat Horton's notice of late delivery as a final breach of contract and pursue a remedy or agree to the later delivery date. Suppose that Lyn does neither for two weeks. On April 24, Horton informs Lyn that he will be able to deliver the furniture by May 1 after all. In effect, Horton has retracted his repudiation, reinstating the rights and obligations of the parties under the original contract. Note that if Lyn had told Horton that she was canceling the contract after he repudiated, he would not have been able to retract his repudiation. ■

16–2 Remedies of the Seller or Lessor

Note that remedies for breach under the UCC are *cumulative* in nature—meaning that the aggrieved (wronged) party is not limited to one exclusive remedy. When the buyer or lessee is in breach, the remedies available to the seller or lessor depend on the circumstances existing at the time of the breach. The most pertinent considerations are which party has possession of the goods, whether the goods are in transit, and whether the buyer or lessee has rejected or accepted the goods.

16–2a When the Goods Are in the Possession of the Seller or Lessor

If the buyer or lessee breaches the contract *before the goods have been delivered,* the seller or lessor has the right to pursue the following remedies:

1. Cancel (rescind) the contract.
2. Withhold delivery of the goods.
3. Resell or dispose of the goods and sue to recover damages.
4. Sue to recover the purchase price or lease payments due.
5. Sue to recover damages for the buyer's nonacceptance of goods.

The Right to Cancel the Contract If the buyer or lessee breaches the contract, the seller or lessor can choose to simply cancel the contract [UCC 2–703(f), 2A–523(1)(a)]. The seller or lessor must notify the buyer or lessee of the cancellation, and at that point all remaining obligations of the seller or lessor are discharged. The buyer or lessee is not discharged from all remaining obligations, however. She or he is in breach, and the seller or lessor can pursue remedies available under the UCC for breach.

The Right to Withhold Delivery In general, sellers and lessors can withhold delivery or discontinue performance of their obligations under sales or lease contracts when the buyers or lessees are in breach [UCC 2–703(a), 2A–523(1)(c)]. This is true whether a buyer or lessee has wrongfully rejected or revoked acceptance of contract goods (discussed later), failed to make a payment, or repudiated the contract. The seller or lessor can also refuse to deliver the goods to a buyer or lessee who is insolvent (unable to pay debts as they become due) unless the buyer or lessee pays in cash [UCC 2–702(1), 2A–525(1)].

The Right to Resell or Dispose of the Goods and Recover Damages When a buyer or lessee breaches or repudiates the contract while the seller or lessor is in possession of the goods, the seller or lessor can resell or dispose of the goods. Any resale of the goods must be made in good faith and in a commercially reasonable manner. The seller must give the original buyer reasonable notice of the resale, unless the goods are perishable or will rapidly decline in value [UCC 2–706(2), (3)].

The seller can retain any profits made as a result of the sale and can hold the buyer or lessee liable for any loss [UCC 2–703(d), 2–706(1), 2A–523(1)(e), 2A–527(1)]. (Here, a loss is any deficiency between the resale price and the contract price.) In lease transactions, the lessor can lease the goods to another party and recover damages from the original lessee. Damages include any unpaid lease payments up to the time the new lease begins. The lessor can also recover any deficiency between the lease payments due under the original lease and those due under the new lease, along with incidental damages [UCC 2A–527(2)].

When the goods contracted for are *unfinished at the time of the breach,* the seller or lessor can do either of the following:

1. Cease manufacturing the goods and resell them for scrap or salvage value.
2. Complete the manufacture and resell or dispose of the goods, and hold the buyer or lessee liable for any deficiency.

In choosing between these two alternatives, the seller or lessor must exercise reasonable commercial judgment in order to mitigate the loss and obtain maximum value from the unfinished goods [UCC 2–704(2), 2A–524(2)].

The Right to Recover the Purchase Price or Lease Payments Due Under the UCC, an unpaid seller or lessor can bring an action to recover the purchase price or the payments due under the lease contract, plus incidental damages [UCC 2–709(1), 2A–529(1)]. If a seller or lessor is unable to resell or dispose of the goods and sues for the contract price or lease payments due, the goods must be held for the buyer or lessee. The seller or lessor can resell the goods at any time before collecting the judgment from the buyer or lessee. If the goods are resold, the net proceeds from the sale must be credited to the buyer or lessee because of the duty to mitigate damages.

■ **EXAMPLE 16.13** Cascade School contracts with Stickme.com to purchase ten thousand bumper stickers with the school's name and logo on them. Stickme tenders delivery of the stickers, but Cascade wrongfully refuses to accept them. In this situation, Stickme can bring an action for the purchase price. Stickme has delivered conforming goods, and Cascade has refused to accept or pay for the goods. Obviously, Stickme will not likely be able to resell the stickers, so this situation falls under UCC 2–709. Stickme is required to make the bumper stickers available for Cascade. In the unlikely event that it can find another buyer, it can sell the stickers at any time prior to collecting the judgment from Cascade. ■

The Right to Recover Damages for the Buyer's Nonacceptance If a buyer or lessee repudiates a contract or wrongfully refuses to accept the goods, a seller or lessor can bring an action to recover the damages sustained. Ordinarily, the amount of damages equals the difference between the contract price or lease payments and the market price or lease payments at the time and place of tender of the goods, plus incidental damages [UCC 2–708(1), 2A–528(1)].

When the ordinary measure of damages is inadequate to put the seller or lessor in as good a position as the buyer's or lessee's performance would have, the UCC provides an alternative. In that situation, the proper measure of damages is the lost profits of the seller or lessor, including a reasonable allowance for overhead and other expenses [UCC 2–708(2), 2A–528(2)].

16–2b When the Goods Are in Transit

When the seller or lessor has delivered the goods to a carrier or a bailee but the buyer or lessee has not yet received them, the goods are said to be *in transit*.

Effect of Insolvency and Breach If the seller or lessor learns that the buyer or lessee is insolvent, the seller or lessor can stop the delivery of the goods still in transit, regardless of the quantity of goods shipped. A different rule applies if the buyer or lessee is in breach but is not insolvent. In this situation, the seller or lessor can stop the goods in transit only if the quantity shipped is at least a carload, a truckload, a planeload, or a larger shipment [UCC 2–705(1), 2A–526(1)].

Requirements for Stopping Delivery To stop delivery, the seller or lessor must *timely notify* the carrier or other bailee that the goods are to be returned or held for the seller or lessor. If the carrier has sufficient time to stop delivery, the goods must be held and delivered according to the instructions of the seller or lessor. The seller or lessor is liable to the carrier for any additional costs incurred [UCC 2–705(3), 2A–526(3)].

The seller or lessor has the right to stop delivery of the goods under UCC 2–705(2) and 2A–526(2) until the time when:

1. The buyer or lessee receives the goods.
2. The carrier or the bailee acknowledges the rights of the buyer or lessee in the goods (by reshipping or holding the goods for the buyer or lessee, for example).
3. A negotiable document of title covering the goods has been properly transferred to the buyer in a sales transaction, giving the buyer ownership rights in the goods [UCC 2–705(2)].

Once the seller or lessor reclaims the goods in transit, she or he can pursue the remedies allowed to sellers and lessors when the goods are in their possession.

16–2c When the Goods Are in the Possession of the Buyer or Lessee

When the buyer or lessee breaches the contract while the goods are in his or her possession, the seller or lessor can sue. The seller or lessor can recover the purchase price of the goods or the lease payments due, plus incidental damages [UCC 2–709(1), 2A–529(1)].

In some situations, a seller may also have a right to reclaim the goods from the buyer. For instance, in a sales contract, if the buyer has received the goods on credit and the seller discovers that the buyer is insolvent, the seller can demand the return of the goods [UCC 2–702(2)]. Ordinarily, the demand must be made within ten days of the buyer's receipt of the goods.[5] The seller's right to reclaim the goods is subject to the rights of a good faith purchaser or other subsequent buyer in the ordinary course of business who purchases the goods from the buyer before the seller reclaims them.

In regard to lease contracts, if the lessee is in default (fails to make payments that are due, for instance), the lessor may reclaim leased goods that are in the lessee's possession [UCC 2A–525(2)].

16–3 Remedies of the Buyer or Lessee

When the seller or lessor breaches the contract, the buyer or lessee has numerous remedies available under the UCC. Like the remedies available to sellers and lessors, the remedies available to buyers and lessees depend on the circumstances at the time of the breach. Relevant factors include whether the seller has refused to deliver conforming goods or has delivered nonconforming goods.

16–3a When the Seller or Lessor Refuses to Deliver the Goods

If the seller or lessor refuses to deliver the goods to the buyer or lessee, the basic remedies available to the buyer or lessee include the right to:

1. Cancel (rescind) the contract.
2. Obtain goods that have been paid for if the seller or lessor is insolvent.
3. Sue to obtain specific performance if the goods are unique or if damages are an inadequate remedy.

---

5. The seller can demand and reclaim the goods at any time if the buyer misrepresented his or her solvency in writing within three months prior to the delivery of the goods.

4. Buy other goods (obtain *cover*) and recover damages from the seller.
5. Sue to obtain identified goods held by a third party (*replevy* goods).
6. Sue to obtain damages.

The Right to Cancel the Contract When a seller or lessor fails to make proper delivery or repudiates the contract, the buyer or lessee can cancel, or rescind, the contract. The buyer or lessee is relieved of any further obligations under the contract but retains all rights to other remedies against the seller or lessor [UCC 2–711(1), 2A–508(1)(a)]. (The right to cancel the contract is also available to a buyer or lessee who has rightfully rejected goods or revoked acceptance, as will be discussed shortly.)

The Right to Obtain the Goods upon Insolvency If a buyer or lessee has partially or fully paid for goods that are in the possession of a seller or lessor who becomes insolvent, the buyer or lessee can obtain the goods. The seller or lessor must have become insolvent within ten days after receiving the first payment, and the goods must be identified to the contract. To exercise this right, the buyer or lessee must pay the seller or lessor any unpaid balance of the purchase price or lease payments [UCC 2–502, 2A–522].

The Right to Obtain Specific Performance A buyer or lessee can obtain specific performance if the goods are unique or the remedy at law (monetary damages) is inadequate [UCC 2–716(1), 2A–521(1)]. Ordinarily, an award of damages is sufficient to place a buyer or lessee in the position she or he would have occupied if the seller or lessor had fully performed.

When the contract is for the purchase of a particular work of art or a similarly unique item, however, damages may not be sufficient. Under these circumstances, equity requires that the seller or lessor perform exactly by delivering the particular goods identified to the contract (the remedy of specific performance).

■ **CASE IN POINT 16.14** Together, Doreen Houseman and Eric Dare bought a house and a pedigreed dog. When the couple separated, they agreed that Dare would keep the house (and pay Houseman for her interest in it) and that Houseman would keep the dog. Houseman allowed Dare to take the dog for visits, but after one visit, Dare kept the dog. Houseman filed a lawsuit seeking specific performance of their agreement. The court found that because pets have special subjective value to their owners, a dog can be considered a unique good. Thus, an award of specific performance was appropriate.[6] ■

The Right of Cover In certain situations, buyers and lessees can protect themselves by obtaining **cover**—that is, by buying or leasing substitute goods for those that were due under the contract. This option is available when the seller or lessor repudiates the contract or fails to deliver the goods, or when a buyer or lessee has rightfully rejected goods or revoked acceptance. In purchasing or leasing substitute goods, the buyer or lessee must act in good faith and without unreasonable delay [UCC 2–712, 2A–518].

After obtaining substitute goods, the buyer or lessee can recover from the seller or lessor:

1. The difference between the cost of cover and the contract price (or lease payments).
2. Incidental damages that resulted from the breach.
3. *Consequential damages* to compensate for indirect losses (such as lost profits) resulting from the breach that were reasonably foreseeable at the time of contract formation. The amount of consequential damages is reduced by any amount the buyer or lessee saved as a result of the breach. (For instance, the buyer might obtain cover without having to pay delivery charges that were part of the original sales contract.)

Buyers and lessees are not required to cover, and failure to do so will not bar them from using any other remedies available under the UCC. A buyer or lessee who fails to cover, however, risks collecting a lower amount of consequential damages. A court may reduce the consequential damages by the amount of the loss that could have been avoided had the buyer or lessee purchased or leased substitute goods.

The Right to Replevy Goods Buyers and lessees also have the right to replevy goods. **Replevin**[7] is an action to recover identified goods in the hands of a party who is unlawfully withholding them. Under the UCC, a buyer or lessee can replevy goods identified to the contract if the seller or lessor has repudiated or breached the contract. To maintain an action to replevy goods, buyers and lessees must usually show that they were unable to cover for the goods after making a reasonable effort [UCC 2–716(3), 2A–521(3)].

6. *Houseman v. Dare*, 405 N.J.Super. 538, 966 A.2d 24 (2009).
7. Pronounced ruh-*pleh*-vun, derived from the Old French word *plevir,* meaning "to pledge."

The Right to Recover Damages If a seller or lessor repudiates the contract or fails to deliver the goods, the buyer or lessee can sue for damages. For the buyer, the measure of recovery is the difference between the contract price and the market price of the goods at the time the buyer *learned* of the breach. For the lessee, the measure is the difference between the lease payments and the lease payments that could have been obtained for the goods at the time the lessee learned of the breach. The market price or market lease payments are determined at the place where the seller or lessor was supposed to deliver the goods. The buyer or lessee can also recover incidental and consequential damages less the expenses that were saved as a result of the breach [UCC 2–713, 2A–519].

■ **CASE IN POINT 16.15** Les Entreprises Jacques Defour & Fils, Inc., contracted to buy a thirty-thousand-gallon industrial tank from Dinsick Equipment Corporation for $70,000. Les Entreprises hired Xaak Transport, Inc., to pick up the tank, but when Xaak arrived at the pickup location, there was no tank. Les Entreprises paid Xaak $7,459 for its services and filed a suit against Dinsick.

The court awarded compensatory damages of $70,000 for the tank and incidental damages of $7,459 for the transport. To establish a breach of contract requires an enforceable contract, substantial performance by the nonbreaching party, a breach by the other party, and damages. In this case, Les Entreprises agreed to buy a tank and paid the price. Dinsick failed to tender or deliver the tank, or to refund the price. The shipping costs were a necessary part of performance, so this was a reasonable expense.[8] ■

16–3b When the Seller or Lessor Delivers Nonconforming Goods

When the seller or lessor delivers nonconforming goods, the buyer or lessee has several remedies available under the UCC.

The Right to Reject the Goods If either the goods or their tender fails to conform to the contract in any respect, the buyer or lessee can reject all of the goods or any commercial unit of the goods [UCC 2–601, 2A–509]. On rejecting the goods, the buyer or lessee may obtain cover or cancel the contract, and may seek damages just as if the seller or lessor had refused to deliver the goods.

Timeliness and Reason for Rejection Are Required. The buyer or lessee must reject the goods within a reasonable amount of time after delivery or tender of delivery and must seasonably notify the seller or lessor [UCC 2–602(1), 2A–509(2)]. If the buyer or lessee fails to reject the goods within a reasonable amount of time, acceptance will be presumed.

When rejecting goods, the buyer or lessee must also designate defects that are ascertainable by reasonable inspection. Failure to do so precludes the buyer or lessee from using such defects to justify rejection or to establish breach if the seller or lessor could have cured the defects [UCC 2–605, 2A–514].

Duties of Merchant-Buyers and Merchant-Lessees When Goods Are Rejected. Sometimes, a *merchant-buyer or lessee* rightfully rejects goods, and the seller or lessor has no agent or business at the place of rejection. In that situation, the merchant-buyer or lessee has a good faith obligation to follow any reasonable instructions received from the seller or lessor with respect to the goods [UCC 2–603, 2A–511]. The buyer or lessee is entitled to be reimbursed for the care and cost entailed in following the instructions. The same requirements apply if the buyer or lessee rightfully revokes her or his acceptance of the goods at some later time [UCC 2–608(3), 2A–517(5)]. (Revocation of acceptance will be discussed shortly.)

If no instructions are forthcoming and the goods are perishable or threaten to decline in value quickly, the buyer or lessee can resell the goods. The buyer or lessee must exercise good faith and can take appropriate reimbursement and a selling commission (not to exceed 10 percent of the gross proceeds) from the proceeds [UCC 2–603(1), (2); 2A–511(1)]. If the goods are not perishable, the buyer or lessee may store them for the seller or lessor or reship them to the seller or lessor [UCC 2–604, 2A–512].

Revocation of Acceptance Acceptance of the goods precludes the buyer or lessee from exercising the right of rejection. It does not necessarily prevent the buyer or lessee from pursuing other remedies, however. In certain circumstances, a buyer or lessee is permitted to *revoke* his or her acceptance of the goods.

Revoking Acceptance of a Commercial Unit. Acceptance of a lot or a commercial unit can be revoked if the nonconformity *substantially* impairs the value of the lot or unit *and* if one of the following factors is present:

1. Acceptance was based on the reasonable assumption that the nonconformity would be cured, and it has not been cured within a reasonable period of time [UCC 2–608(1)(a), 2A–517(1)(a)].

---

8. *Les Entreprises Jacques Defour & Fils, Inc. v. Dinsick Equipment Corp.*, 2011 WL 307501 (N.D.Ill. 2011).

2. The failure of the buyer or lessee to discover the nonconformity was reasonably induced either by the difficulty of discovery before acceptance or by assurances made by the seller or lessor [UCC 2–608(1)(b), 2A–517(1)(b)].

■ **CASE IN POINT 16.16** Armadillo Distribution Enterprises, Inc., is a major distributor of musical instruments. Armadillo contracted with a Chinese corporation, Hai Yun Musical Instruments Manufacture Co., Ltd., to manufacture one thousand drum kits. Hai Yun had made drums for Armadillo in the past. Hai Yun furnished samples for Armadillo's approval prior to manufacturing the kits. After Armadillo inspected and approved the samples, Hai Yun delivered five shipping containers of drum kits, and Armadillo began distribution.

Armadillo soon started receiving numerous complaints from its retail outlet customers concerning product returns due to cosmetic and structural defects in the drum kits. Armadillo immediately inspected the remaining four shipment containers and discovered that a high percentage of the drum kits were defective and unfit for commercial distribution. Armadillo revoked its acceptance of the kits and filed a suit in federal court for breach of contract. The district court ruled that Hai Yun had breached the contract by delivering nonconforming goods. The court awarded Armadillo nearly $90,000 in direct and incidental damages.[9] ■

Notice of Revocation. Revocation of acceptance is not effective until notice is given to the seller or lessor. Notice must occur within a reasonable time after the buyer or lessee either discovers or *should have discovered* the grounds for revocation. Additionally, revocation must occur before the goods have undergone any substantial change (such as spoilage) not caused by their own defects [UCC 2–608(2), 2A–517(4)]. Once acceptance is revoked, the buyer or lessee can pursue remedies, just as if the goods had been rejected.

To effectively revoke acceptance, a buyer must "relinquish dominion over the goods." This requires a buyer to return the goods or at least to stop using them, unless the use is necessary to avoid substantial hardship. At issue in the following case was whether the purchaser of lights for a commercial building sufficiently relinquished dominion over the goods to revoke acceptance.

---

9. *Armadillo Distribution Enterprises, Inc. v. Hai Yun Musical Instruments Manufacture Co. Ltd.*, 142 F.Supp.3d 1245 (M.D.Fla. 2015).

Genesis Health Clubs, Inc. v. LED Solar & Light Co.

United States Court of Appeals, Tenth Circuit, 639 Fed.Appx. 550 (2016).

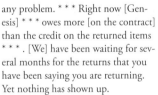

In the Language of the Court

HARRIS L. HARTZ, Circuit Judge.

* * * *

Genesis [Health Clubs, Inc.], based in Kansas, operates health clubs. LED Solar & Light Company], based in Virginia, manufactures and sells LED lighting.

* * * LED Solar submitted a proposed contract "to furnish the replacement lamps for Genesis's building" for $82,271.50. LED Solar "warranted watt for watt exchange a minimum of 35% deduction in wattage consumption." * * * Genesis executed the contract later that month.

Soon after installation began, Genesis encountered problems with the lights. [Genesis] complained that "the defect rate on these lamps is * * * 73% * * *," "the LED tubes * * * are not consistent in color," [and there are] multiple light failures throughout Genesis's facility.

* * * [LED Solar] found "no fault with [the] lamps" and instructed [Genesis] to return problem lights for a refund.

* * * Genesis returned a shipment of lights, seeking a $3,777 refund.

* * * [A later e-mail to LED Solar explained] that Genesis would be "returning all of the lights" one shipment at a time in exchange for a refund, "allowing Genesis to phase out the faulty lamps."

But the return/refund process never got off the ground because of a dispute regarding whether Genesis had been properly credited for its [previous] shipment of lights * * *. On the same day as [the] email saying that Genesis would return the lights one shipment at a time, [LED Solar] responded by email, telling [Genesis]:

* * * Everything you have shipped back that was not damaged in handling works fine. If you ship those items back not damaged we will credit the account without any problem. * * * Right now [Genesis] * * * owes more [on the contract] than the credit on the returned items * * *. [We] have been waiting for several months for the returns that you have been saying you are returning. Yet nothing has shown up.

[Genesis] replied * * *:

* * * You have not been prompt in your commitment to refund for returned items. * * * You have your money for the entire order that was pre-paid. * * * We are trying to replace the defective lights with the refund dollars for the product returned.

* * * [LED Solar] never paid Genesis the $3,777 and Genesis never returned any more lights.

Case 16.1 Continues

Case 16.1 Continued

* * * Genesis filed a * * * petition [in a Kansas state court] asserting claims of breach of * * * warranty. LED Solar removed the case to federal court based on diversity jurisdiction.

* * * *

* * * The court concluded that Genesis could not recover the purchase price because it failed to reject or revoke acceptance of the lights. [Genesis appealed.]

* * * *

Under the * * * Uniform Commercial Code, a buyer may cancel the contract and recover the purchase price by rightfully rejecting or justifiably revoking acceptance. *Rejection is available for goods that fail in any respect to conform to the contract, and it must be communicated to the seller within a reasonable time after the goods' delivery or tender. What constitutes a reasonable time depends on the nature, purpose, and circumstances of the action.* [Emphasis added.]

Even after the goods have been accepted, the buyer may revoke his acceptance of a lot or commercial unit whose nonconformity substantially impairs its value to him if he has accepted it * * * on the reasonable assumption that its nonconformity would be cured and it has not been seasonably cured. A buyer who revokes has

the same rights and duties with regard to the goods involved as if he had rejected them. Thus, revocation requires notification to the seller within a reasonable time after the buyer discovers or should have discovered the ground for it and before any substantial change in condition of the goods which is not caused by their own defects.

In the case of both remedies, the buyer's exercise of ownership or dominion over the goods may negate an attempt to cancel the contract and recover the purchase price. * * * *A buyer's act of dominion over the goods * * * is inconsistent with a claim by the buyer that acceptance has been revoked.* [Emphasis added.]

In the case before us, Genesis did not effectively reject or revoke acceptance of the lights because it never relinquished dominion over them. Despite allegedly agreeing with LED Solar to return all the lights in stages, it never returned any after reaching the agreement and continued to use them.

Genesis argues that without the $3,777 refund for an earlier (preagreement) shipment of lights to LED Solar, it was unable "to continue the return and replacement process. * * * [LED Solar] was aware that Genesis * * * would have to find and purchase new lights to

replace LED Solar's * * * bulbs prior to removing them all from the facility."

True, a buyer's continued use of the goods after the supposed revocation is not inconsistent with revocation if such use was necessary to avoid substantial hardship. But Genesis made no showing of substantial hardship. It offered no financial evidence that it could not afford to return any more lights without the $3,777 refund * * * . It cites no evidence that it attempted to resolve the impasse and reach some accommodation with LED Solar for future returns. It did not even produce evidence that LED Solar was incorrect in saying that the $3,777 had been credited toward what Genesis still owed. Nor does it explain why it could not afford to return lights that were not functioning. In short, no reasonable jury could find that Genesis reasonably continued using the lights after it informed LED Solar that it wanted to return them. Genesis had no excuse for using the bulbs until LED Solar accepted the * * * financial terms demanded by Genesis to govern the returns. There was no proper rejection or revocation of acceptance of the bulbs.

We conclude that summary judgment was properly entered on Genesis's claim for a refund of the purchase price.

Legal Reasoning Questions

1. According to the UCC, if delivered goods do not conform to a sales contract, how can the buyer revoke acceptance?

2. In this case, what was the dispute between the buyer and the seller? How did this dispute end in litigation?

3. On what key point did the lower and appellate courts agree? Why?

The Right to Recover Damages for Accepted Goods A buyer or lessee who has accepted nonconforming goods may also keep the goods and recover damages [UCC 2–714(1), 2A–519(3)]. To do so, the buyer or lessee must notify the seller or lessor of the breach within a reasonable time after the defect was or should have been discovered. Failure to give notice of the defects (breach) to the seller or lessor normally bars the buyer or lessee from pursuing any remedy [UCC 2–607(3), 2A–516(3)]. In addition, the parties to a sales or lease contract can insert into the contract a

provision requiring the buyer or lessee to give notice of any defects in the goods within a prescribed period.

When the goods delivered are not as promised, the measure of damages generally equals the difference between the value of the goods as accepted and their value if they had been delivered as warranted. An exception occurs if special circumstances show proximately caused damages of a different amount [UCC 2–714(2), 2A–519(4)]. The buyer or lessee is also entitled to incidental and consequential damages when appropriate

[UCC 2–714(3), 2A–519]. With proper notice to the seller or lessor, the buyer or lessee can also deduct all or any part of the damages from the price or lease payments still due under the contract [UCC 2–717, 2A–516(1)].

Is two years after a sale of goods a reasonable time period in which to discover a defect in those goods and notify the seller of a breach? That was the question in the following case.

Spotlight on Baseball Cards

Case 16.2 Fitl v. Strek

Supreme Court of Nebraska, 269 Neb. 51, 690 N.W.2d 605 (2005).

Background and Facts In 1995, James Fitl attended a sports-card show in San Francisco, California, where he met Mark Strek, doing business as Star Cards of San Francisco, an exhibitor at the show. Later, on Strek's representation that a certain 1952 Mickey Mantle Topps baseball card was in near-mint condition, Fitl bought the card from Strek for $17,750. Strek delivered it to Fitl in Omaha, Nebraska, and Fitl placed it in a safe-deposit box.

In May 1997, Fitl sent the card to Professional Sports Authenticators (PSA), a sports-card grading service. PSA told Fitl that the card was ungradable because it had been discolored and doctored. Fitl complained to Strek, who replied that Fitl should have initiated a return of the card sooner. According to Strek, "a typical grace period for the unconditional return of a card [was within] 7 days to 1 month" of its receipt. In August, Fitl sent the card to ASA Accugrade, Inc. (ASA), another grading service, for a second opinion of the value. ASA also concluded that the card had been refinished and trimmed. Fitl filed a suit in a Nebraska state court against Strek, seeking damages. The court awarded Fitl $17,750, plus his court costs. Strek appealed to the Nebraska Supreme Court.

In the Language of the Court

WRIGHT, J. [Judge]

* * * *

Strek claims that the [trial] court erred in determining that notification of the defective condition of the baseball card 2 years after the date of purchase was timely pursuant to [UCC] 2–607(3)(a).

* * * The [trial] court found that Fitl had notified Strek within a reasonable time after discovery of the breach. Therefore, our review is whether the [trial] court's finding as to the reasonableness of the notice was clearly erroneous.

Section 2–607(3)(a) states: "Where a tender has been accepted * * * the buyer must within a reasonable time after he discovers or should have discovered any breach notify the seller of breach or be barred from any remedy." [Under UCC 1–204(2),] *"what is a reasonable time for taking any action depends on the nature, purpose and circumstances of such action."* [Emphasis added.]

The notice requirement set forth in Section 2–607(3)(a) serves three purposes.

* * * The most important one is to enable the seller to make efforts to cure the breach by making adjustments or replacements in order to minimize the buyer's damages and the seller's liability. A second policy is to provide the seller a reasonable opportunity to learn the facts so that he may adequately prepare for negotiation and defend himself in a suit. A third policy * * * is the same as the policy behind statutes of limitation: to provide a seller with a terminal point in time for liability.

* * * *A party is justified in relying upon a representation made to the party as a positive statement of fact when an investigation would be required to ascertain its falsity.* In order for Fitl to have determined that the baseball card had been altered, he would have been required to conduct an investigation. We find that he was not required to do so. Once Fitl learned that the baseball card had been altered, he gave notice to Strek. [Emphasis added.]

* * * One of the most important policies behind the notice requirement * * * is to allow the seller to cure the breach by making adjustments or replacements to minimize the buyer's damages and the seller's liability. However, even if Fitl had learned immediately upon taking possession of the baseball card that it was not authentic and had notified Strek at that time, there is no evidence that Strek could have made any adjustment or taken any action that would have minimized his liability. In its altered condition, the baseball card was worthless.

Case 16.2 Continues

* * * Earlier notification would not have helped Strek prepare for negotiation or defend himself in a suit because the damage to Fitl could not be repaired. Thus, the policies behind the notice requirement, to allow the seller to correct a defect, to prepare for negotiation and litigation, and to protect against stale claims at a time beyond which an investigation can be completed, were not unfairly prejudiced by the lack of an earlier notice to Strek. Any problem Strek may have had with the party from whom he obtained the baseball card was a separate matter from his transaction with Fitl, and an investigation into the source of the altered card would not have minimized Fitl's damages.

Decision and Remedy *The state supreme court affirmed the decision of the lower court. Under the circumstances, notice of a defect in the card two years after its purchase was reasonable. The buyer had reasonably relied on the seller's representation that the card was "authentic" (which it was not), and when the defects were discovered, the buyer had given timely notice.*

Critical Thinking
- **What If the Facts Were Different?** *Suppose that Fitl and Strek had included in their deal a written clause requiring Fitl to give notice of any defect in the card within "7 days to 1 month" of its receipt. Would the result have been different? Why or why not?*
- **Legal Environment** *What might a court award to a buyer who prevails in a dispute such as the one in this case?*

16–3c Additional Provisions Affecting Remedies

The parties to a sales or lease contract can vary their respective rights and obligations by contractual agreement. For instance, a seller and buyer can expressly provide for remedies in addition to those offered by the UCC. They can also specify remedies in lieu of those provided in the UCC (including liquidated damages clauses), or they can change the measure of damages. A seller can provide that the buyer's only remedy on the seller's breach will be repair or replacement of the item. Alternatively, the seller can limit the buyer's remedy to return of the goods and refund of the purchase price.

In sales and lease contracts, an agreed-on remedy is in addition to those provided in the UCC unless the parties expressly agree that the remedy is exclusive of all others [UCC 2–719(1), 2A–503(1),(2)].

Exclusive Remedies If the parties state that a remedy is *exclusive,* then it is the sole remedy. ■ **EXAMPLE 16.17** Standard Tool Company agrees to sell a pipe-cutting machine to United Pipe & Tubing Corporation. The contract limits United's remedy exclusively to repair or replacement of any defective parts. Thus, repair or replacement of defective parts is the buyer's only remedy under this contract. ■

When circumstances cause an exclusive remedy to fail in its essential purpose, it is no longer exclusive, and the buyer or lessee may pursue other remedies available under

the UCC [UCC 2–719(2), 2A–503(2)]. In *Example 16.17,* suppose that Standard Tool Company was unable to repair a defective part, and no replacement parts were available. In this situation, because the exclusive remedy failed in its essential purpose (to provide recovery), the buyer could pursue other remedies available under the UCC.

Consequential Damages Consequential damages are special damages that compensate for indirect losses (such as lost profits) resulting from a breach of contract that were reasonably foreseeable. Under the UCC, parties to a contract can limit or exclude consequential damages, provided the limitation is not unconscionable.

When the buyer or lessee is a consumer, any limitation of consequential damages for personal injuries resulting from consumer goods is presumed to be unconscionable. The limitation of consequential damages is not necessarily unconscionable when the loss is commercial in nature—for instance, lost profits and property damage [UCC 2–719(3), 2A–503(3)].

Statute of Limitations An action for breach of contract under the UCC must be commenced *within four years after the cause of action accrues* [UCC 2–725(1)]. This means that a buyer or lessee must file the lawsuit within four years after the breach occurs.[10] Thus, the buyer or lessee has four years from the delivery date to file

---

10. For breach of warranty, the cause of action arises when the seller or lessor delivers the contracted goods [UCC 2–725(2), 2A–506(2)].

a suit for breach of warranty. The parties can agree in their contract to reduce this period to not less than one year but cannot extend it beyond four years [UCC 2–725(1), 2A–506(1)].

If a buyer or lessee has accepted nonconforming goods, that party has a reasonable time to notify the seller or lessor of the breach. Failure to provide notice will bar the buyer or lessee from pursuing any remedy [UCC 2–607(3)(a), 2A–516(3)].

16–4 Sales and Lease Warranties

Most goods are covered by some type of warranty designed to protect buyers. In sales and lease law, a warranty is an assurance or guarantee by the seller or lessor about the quality and features of the goods being sold or leased.

16–4a Warranties of Title

Under the UCC, three types of title warranties—*good title, no liens,* and *no infringements*—can automatically arise in sales and lease contracts [UCC 2–312, 2A–211]. Normally, a seller or lessor can disclaim or modify these title warranties only by including *specific language* in the contract. For instance, sellers may assert that they are transferring only such rights, title, and interest as they have in the goods.

Good Title In most sales, sellers warrant that they have good and valid title to the goods sold and that the transfer of the title is rightful [UCC 2–312(1)(a)]. If the buyer subsequently learns that the seller did not have valid title to the goods that were purchased, the buyer can sue the seller for breach of this warranty.

No Liens A second warranty of title protects buyers and lessees who are *unaware* of any encumbrances against goods at the time the contract is made [UCC 2–312(1)(b), 2A–211(1)]. (Such encumbrances—that is, claims, charges, or liabilities—are usually called *liens*.[11])

This warranty protects buyers who, for instance, unknowingly purchase goods that are subject to a creditor's security interest. (A *security interest* in this context is an interest in the goods that secures payment or performance of an obligation.) If a creditor legally repossesses the goods from a buyer *who had no actual knowledge of the security interest,* the buyer can recover from the seller for breach of warranty. (In contrast, a buyer who has *actual*

knowledge of a security interest has no recourse against a seller.)

■ **EXAMPLE 16.18** Henderson buys a used boat from Loring for cash. A month later, Barish proves that she has a valid security interest in the boat and that Loring, who has missed five payments, is in default. Barish then repossesses the boat from Henderson. Henderson demands his cash back from Loring. Under Section 2–312(1)(b), Henderson has legal grounds to recover from Loring. As a seller of goods, Loring warrants that the goods are delivered free from any security interest or other lien of which the buyer has no knowledge. ■

Article 2A affords similar protection for lessees. Section 2A–211(1) provides that during the term of the lease, no claim of any third party will interfere with the lessee's enjoyment of the leasehold interest.

No Infringements A third type of warranty of title arises automatically when the seller or lessor is a merchant. A merchant-seller or merchant-lessor warrants that the buyer or lessee takes the goods *free of infringements* from any copyright, trademark, or patent claims of a third person [UCC 2–312(3), 2A–211(2)].

If the buyer is subsequently sued by a third party holding copyright, trademark, or patent rights in the goods, then this warranty is breached. The buyer *must notify the seller* of the litigation within a reasonable time to enable the seller to decide whether to defend the lawsuit. The seller then decides whether to defend the buyer and bear all expenses in the action.

If the seller agrees in a writing to defend and to pay the expenses, then the buyer must turn over control of the litigation to the seller. Otherwise, the buyer is barred from any remedy against the seller for liability established by the litigation [UCC 2–607(3)(b), 2–607(5)(b)]. Thus, if a buyer wins at trial but did not notify the seller of the litigation, the buyer cannot sue the seller to recover the expenses of the lawsuit.

In situations that involve leases rather than sales, Article 2A provides for the same notice of infringement litigation [UCC 2A–516(3)(b), 2A–516(4)(b)]. Failure to provide notice normally bars any subsequent remedy against the lessor for liability established by the litigation (except for leases for consumer goods).

16–4b Express Warranties

A seller or lessor can create an **express warranty** by making representations concerning the quality, condition, description, or performance potential of the goods.

---

11. Pronounced *leens.*

Under UCC 2–313 and 2A–210, express warranties arise when a seller or lessor indicates any of the following:

1. That the goods conform to any *affirmation* (declaration that something is true) *of fact or promise* that the seller or lessor makes to the buyer or lessee about the goods. Such affirmations or promises are usually made during the bargaining process. ■ **EXAMPLE 16.19** D. J. Vladick, a salesperson at Home Depot, tells a customer, "These drill bits will easily penetrate stainless steel—and without dulling." Vladick's statement is an express warranty. ■

2. That the goods conform to any *description* of them. ■ **EXAMPLE 16.20** A label reads "Crate contains one Kawasaki Brute Force 750 4X4i EPS ATV," and a contract calls for the delivery of a "wool coat." Both statements create express warranties that the goods sold conform to the descriptions. ■

3. That the goods conform to any *sample or model* of the goods shown to the buyer or lessee. ■ **EXAMPLE 16.21** Melissa Faught orders a stainless steel 5500 Super Angel juicer for $1,100 after seeing a dealer demonstrate its use at a health fair. The Super Angel is shipped to her. When the juicer arrives, it is an older model, not the 5500 model. This is a breach of an express warranty because the dealer warranted that the juicer would be the same model used in the demonstration. ■

Express warranties can be found in a seller's or lessor's advertisement, brochure, or promotional materials, in addition to being made orally or in an express warranty provision in a sales or lease contract.

Basis of the Bargain

To create an express warranty, a seller or lessor does not have to use formal words, such as *warrant* or *guarantee*. It is only necessary that a reasonable buyer or lessee would regard the representation as being part of the basis of the bargain [UCC 2–313(2), 2A–210(2)].

The UCC does not explicitly define the phrase "basis of the bargain." Generally, it means that the buyer or lessee must have relied on the representation at the time of entering into the agreement. Therefore, a court must determine in each case whether a representation was made at such a time and in such a way that it induced the buyer or lessee to enter into the contract.

Statements of Opinion and Value

Only statements of fact create express warranties. A seller or lessor who states an opinion about or recommends the goods thus does not create an express warranty [UCC 2–313(2), 2A–210(2)].

■ **CASE IN POINT 16.22** Kathleen Arthur underwent a surgical procedure for neck pain. Her surgeon implanted an Infuse Bone Graft device made by Medtronic, Inc. Although the device was not approved for this use, a sales representative for Medtronic allegedly had told the surgeon that the Infuse device could be appropriate for this surgery. The surgery did not resolve Arthur's neck pain, and she developed numbness in her arm and fingers. She filed a breach of warranty claim against Medtronic, alleging that the salesperson's statements created an express warranty. The court dismissed Arthur's case, however. The alleged statements of a sales representative on whether it was "appropriate" to use the Infuse device in such a procedure were opinion and did not create an express warranty.[12] ■

Similarly, a seller or lessor who makes a statement about the value or worth of the goods does not create an express warranty. Thus, a statement such as "this is worth a fortune" or "anywhere else you'd pay $10,000 for it" usually does not create a warranty.

Opinions by Experts Ordinarily, statements of opinion do not create warranties. If the seller or lessor is an expert, however, and gives an opinion as an expert to a layperson, then a warranty may be created. ■ **EXAMPLE 16.23** Stephen is an art dealer and an expert in seventeenth-century paintings. If Stephen tells Lauren, a purchaser, that in his opinion a particular painting is by Rembrandt, Stephen has warranted the accuracy of his opinion. ■

Reasonable Reliance It is not always easy to determine whether a statement constitutes an express warranty or puffery ("seller's talk"). The reasonableness of the buyer's or lessee's reliance appears to be the controlling criterion in many cases. Additionally, the context in which a statement is made may be relevant in determining the reasonableness of a buyer's or lessee's reliance. For instance, a reasonable person is more likely to rely on a written statement made in an advertisement than on a statement made orally by a salesperson.

■ **CASE IN POINT 16.24** Lennox International, Inc., makes heating, ventilating, and air conditioning (HVAC) systems. T & M Solar and Air Conditioning, Inc., is a California corporation that contracts to install HVAC systems. T & M became interested in Lennox solar panel systems. Lennox advertised that the systems could run through the existing HVAC system, rather than through an electrical panel. This meant that the systems, unlike

---

12. *Arthur v. Medtronic, Inc.,* 123 F.Supp.3d 1145 (E.D.Mo. 2015).

traditional solar panel systems, could be installed without modifying the electrical panels in a residence.

Lennox representatives repeatedly assured T & M that their systems would operate as advertised and would pass National Electric Code requirements. Lennox sent representatives to California to advertise the systems to potential T & M clients. T & M ordered and paid for six Lennox systems for customers. The systems that Lennox supplied could not be operated or installed as promised, however, and T & M ultimately had to remove them from customers' homes at its own expense. T & M filed suit, alleging breach of an express warranty. The court found that T & M had ordered the Lennox systems precisely because they could operate through the HVAC system without modification of existing electrical panels. That was sufficient evidence of reasonable reliance to justify a trial.[13] ■

---

13. *T & M Solar and Air Conditioning, Inc. v. Lennox International, Inc.*, 83 F.Supp.3d 855 (N.D.Cal. 2015).

16–4c Implied Warranties

An **implied warranty** is one that *the law derives* by inference from the nature of the transaction or the relative situations or circumstances of the parties. Under the UCC, merchants impliedly warrant that the goods they sell or lease are merchantable and, in certain circumstances, fit for a particular purpose. In addition, an implied warranty may arise from a course of dealing or usage of trade. These three types of implied warranties are illustrated in Exhibit 16–2 and examined in the following subsections.

Implied Warranty of Merchantability Every sale or lease of goods made by a merchant who deals in goods of the kind sold or leased automatically gives rise to an **implied warranty of merchantability** [UCC 2–314, 2A–212]. Thus, a merchant who is in the business of selling ski equipment makes an implied warranty of merchantability every time he sells a pair of skis. A neighbor selling her skis at a garage sale does not (because she is not in the business of selling goods of this type).

EXHIBIT 16–2 Types of Implied Warranties

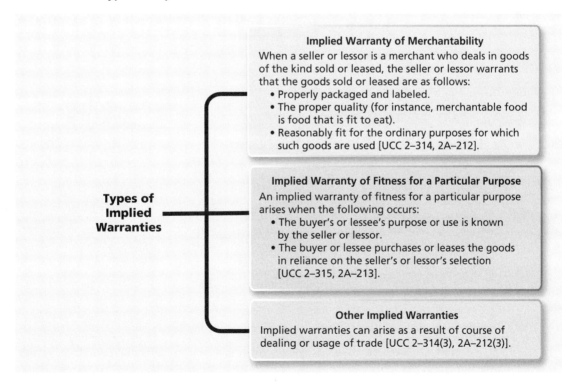

Merchantable Goods. To be *merchantable,* goods must be "reasonably fit for the ordinary purposes for which such goods are used." They must be of at least average, fair, or medium-grade quality. The quality must be comparable to quality that will pass without objection in the trade or market for goods of the same description. The warranty of merchantability may be breached even though the merchant did not know or could not have discovered that a product was defective (not merchantable).

To be merchantable, the goods must also be adequately packaged and labeled. In addition, they must conform to the promises or affirmations of fact made on the container or label, if any. Of course, merchants are not absolute insurers against *all* accidents arising in connection with the goods. A bar of soap is not unmerchantable merely because a user could slip and fall by stepping on it.

The implied warranty of merchantability may be breached when the warrantor has unsuccessfully attempted to repair or replace defective parts. ■ **CASE IN POINT 16.25** Ilan Brand leased a new Hyundai Genesis from Allen Hyundai. The next day, when he was driving on an interstate highway, the sunroof began opening and closing, although Brand was not pushing the sunroof buttons. He immediately returned the vehicle to the Hyundai dealer. He was told it had a defective sunroof switch, which would be repaired within 24 hours. In spite of the dealer's assurances, however, the problem was not repaired. Ten days later, Brand—who still had not been able to pick up the vehicle—attempted to rescind the lease. Hyundai would not allow him to do so.

Brand then filed an action for breach of the implied warranty of merchantability in state court. The trial court dismissed the case, but the appellate court reversed. The reviewing court held that a reasonable jury could conclude that the opening and closing of the sunroof constituted a safety hazard and therefore breached the implied warranty of merchantability. The court remanded the case for a jury trial.[14] ■

Merchantable Food. The serving of food or drink to be consumed on or off the premises is also treated as a sale of goods and subject to the implied warranty of merchantability [UCC 2–314(1)]. "Merchantable" food is food that is fit to eat.

Courts generally determine whether food is fit to eat on the basis of consumer expectations. Consumers should reasonably expect to find on occasion bones in fish fillets, cherry pits in cherry pie, a nutshell in a package of shelled nuts, and the like. Such substances are, after all, natural to the ingredients or the finished food product. In contrast, consumers would not reasonably expect to find an inchworm in a can of peas or a piece of glass in a soft drink.

In the following *Classic Case,* the court had to determine whether one should reasonably expect to find a fish bone in fish chowder.

---

14. *Brand v. Hyundai Motor America,* 226 Cal.App.4th 1538, 173 Cal.Rptr.3d 454 (4th Dist. 2014).

Classic Case **16.3**

Webster v. Blue Ship Tea Room, Inc.
Supreme Judicial Court of Massachusetts, 347 Mass. 421 198 N.E.2d 309 (1964).

Background and Facts Blue Ship Tea Room, Inc., was located in Boston in an old building overlooking the ocean. Priscilla Webster, who had been born and raised in New England, went to the restaurant and ordered fish chowder. The chowder was milky in color. After three or four spoonfuls, she felt something lodged in her throat. As a result, she underwent two esophagoscopies (procedures in which an instrument is used to look into the throat). In the second esophagoscopy, a fish bone was found and removed. Webster filed a suit against the restaurant in a Massachusetts state court for breach of the implied warranty of merchantability. The jury rendered a verdict for Webster, and the restaurant appealed to the state's highest court.

In the Language of the Court
REARDON, Justice.

    [The plaintiff] ordered a cup of fish chowder. Presently, there was set before her "a small bowl of fish chowder." * * * After 3 or 4 [spoonfuls] she was aware that something had lodged in her throat because she "couldn't swallow and couldn't clear her throat by gulping and she could feel it." This misadventure

Case 16.3 Continued

led to two esophagoscopies at the Massachusetts General Hospital, in the second of which, on April 27, 1959, a fish bone was found and removed. The sequence of events produced injury to the plaintiff which was not insubstantial.

We must decide whether a fish bone lurking in a fish chowder, about the ingredients of which there is no other complaint, constitutes a breach of implied warranty under applicable provisions of the Uniform Commercial Code * * * . As the judge put it in his charge [jury instruction], "Was the fish chowder fit to be eaten and wholesome? * * * Nobody is claiming that the fish itself wasn't wholesome. * * * But the bone of contention here—I don't mean that for a pun—but was this fish bone a foreign substance that made the fish chowder unwholesome or not fit to be eaten?"

* * * *

[We think that it] is not too much to say that a person sitting down in New England to consume a good New England fish chowder embarks on a gustatory [taste-related] adventure which may entail the removal of some fish bones from his bowl as he proceeds. We are not inclined to tamper with age-old recipes by any amendment reflecting the plaintiff's view of the effect of the Uniform Commercial Code upon them. We are aware of the heavy body of case law involving foreign substances in food, but we sense a strong distinction between them and those relative to unwholesomeness of the food itself, [for example,] tainted mackerel, and a fish bone in a fish chowder. * * * We consider that the joys of life in New England include the ready availability of fresh fish chowder. *We should be prepared to cope with the hazards of fish bones, the occasional presence of which in chowders is, it seems to us, to be anticipated, and which, in the light of a hallowed tradition, do not impair their fitness or merchantability.* [Emphasis added.]

Decision and Remedy *The Supreme Judicial Court of Massachusetts "sympathized with a plaintiff who has suffered a peculiarly New England injury" but entered a judgment for the defendant, Blue Ship Tea Room. A fish bone in fish chowder is not a breach of the implied warranty of merchantability.*

Impact of This Case on Today's Law *This classic case, phrased in memorable language, was an early application of the UCC's implied warranty of merchantability to food products. The case established the rule that consumers should expect to find, on occasion, elements of food products that are natural to the product (such as fish bones in fish chowder). Courts today still apply this rule.*

Critical Thinking

• **E-Commerce** *If Webster had made the chowder herself from a recipe that she had found on the Internet, could she have successfully brought an action against its author for a breach of the implied warranty of merchantability? Explain.*

Implied Warranty of Fitness for a Particular Purpose

The **implied warranty of fitness for a particular purpose** arises in the sale or lease of goods when a seller or lessor (merchant or nonmerchant) knows *both* of the following:

1. The particular purpose for which a buyer or lessee will use the goods.
2. That the buyer or lessee is relying on the skill and judgment of the seller or lessor to select suitable goods [UCC 2–315, 2A–213].

Particular versus Ordinary Purpose. A "particular purpose" of the buyer or lessee differs from the "ordinary purpose for which goods are used" (merchantability). Goods can be merchantable but unfit for a particular purpose.

■ **EXAMPLE 16.26** Sheryl needs a gallon of paint to match the color of her living room walls—a light shade somewhere between coral and peach. She takes a sample to Sherwin-Williams and requests a gallon of paint of that color. Instead, the salesperson gives her a gallon of bright blue paint. Here, the salesperson has not breached any warranty of implied merchantability—the bright blue paint is of high quality and suitable for interior walls. The salesperson has breached an implied warranty of fitness for a particular purpose, though, because the paint is not the right color for Sheryl's purpose (to match her living room walls). ■

Knowledge and Reliance Requirements. A seller or lessor need not have actual knowledge of the buyer's or lessee's particular purpose. It is sufficient if a seller or lessor "has reason to know" the purpose. For an implied warranty to be created, however, the buyer or lessee must have *relied* on the skill or judgment of the seller or lessor in selecting or furnishing suitable goods. Moreover, the seller or lessor must have reason to know that the buyer or lessee is relying on her or his judgment or skill.

Warranties Implied from Prior Dealings or Trade Custom

Implied warranties can also arise (or be excluded or modified) as a result of course of dealing or usage of trade [UCC 2–314(3), 2A–212(3)]. Without evidence to the contrary, when both parties to a sales or lease contract have knowledge of a well-recognized trade custom, the courts will infer that both parties intended for that custom to apply to their contract.

■ **EXAMPLE 16.27** Industry-wide custom is to lubricate a new car before it is delivered. If a dealer fails to lubricate a car, the dealer can be held liable to a buyer for damages resulting from the breach of an implied warranty. (This would also be negligence on the part of the dealer.) ■

Lemon Laws

Purchasers of defective automobiles—called "lemons"—may have remedies in addition to those offered by the UCC. All of the states and the District of Columbia have enacted *lemon laws*. Basically, state lemon laws provide remedies to consumers who buy automobiles that repeatedly fail to meet standards of quality and performance.

Although lemon laws vary by state, typically they apply to automobiles under warranty that are defective in a way that significantly affects their value or use. Lemon laws do not necessarily cover used-car purchases (unless the car is covered by a manufacturer's extended warranty) or vehicles that are leased.[15]

Generally, the car's owner must notify the dealer or manufacturer of the defect and give the dealer or manufacturer a number of opportunities to remedy it (usually four). If the seller fails to cure the problem despite a reasonable number of attempts (as specified by state law), the buyer may be entitled to a new car, replacement of defective parts, or return of all consideration paid. Buyers who prevail in a lemon-law dispute may also be entitled to reimbursement of their attorneys' fees.

Magnuson-Moss Warranty Act

The Magnuson-Moss Warranty Act[16] was designed to prevent deception in warranties by making them easier to understand. The act modifies UCC warranty rules to some extent when *consumer* transactions are involved. The warrantor must make certain disclosures to consumers fully and conspicuously in a single document in "readily understood language." (The UCC, however, remains the primary codification of warranty rules for commercial transactions.)

Under the Magnuson-Moss Act, no seller is *required* to give a written warranty for consumer goods sold. If a seller chooses to make an express written warranty, however, and the cost of the consumer goods is more than $25, the warranty must be labeled as either "full" or "limited."

A *full warranty* requires free repair or replacement of any defective part. If the product cannot be repaired within a reasonable time, the consumer has the choice of a refund or a replacement without charge. A full warranty can be for an unlimited or a limited time period, such as a "full twelve-month warranty."

A *limited warranty* is one in which the buyer's recourse is limited in some fashion, such as to replacement of an item. The fact that only a limited warranty is being given must be conspicuously stated.

16–4d Overlapping Warranties

Sometimes, two or more warranties are made in a single transaction. An implied warranty of merchantability, an implied warranty of fitness for a particular purpose, or both can exist in addition to an express warranty. ■ **EXAMPLE 16.28** A sales contract for a new car states that "this car engine is warranted to be free from defects for 36,000 miles or thirty-six months, whichever occurs first." This statement creates an express warranty against all defects, as well as an implied warranty that the car will be fit for normal use. ■

The rule under the UCC is that express and implied warranties are construed as *cumulative* if they are *consistent* with one another [UCC 2–317, 2A–215]. In other words, courts interpret two or more warranties as being in agreement with each other unless this construction is unreasonable. If it is unreasonable for the two warranties to be consistent, then the court looks at the intention of the parties to determine which warranty is dominant.

---

15. Note that in some states, such as California, these laws may extend beyond automobile purchases and apply to other consumer goods.

16. 15 U.S.C. Sections 2301–2312.

If the warranties are *inconsistent,* the courts usually apply the following rules to interpret which warranty is most important:

1. *Express* warranties displace inconsistent *implied* warranties, except implied warranties of fitness for a particular purpose.
2. Samples take precedence over inconsistent general descriptions.
3. Exact or technical specifications displace inconsistent samples or general descriptions.

16–4e Warranty Disclaimers and Limitations on Liability

The UCC generally permits warranties to be disclaimed or limited by specific and unambiguous language, provided that this is done in a manner that protects the buyer or lessee from surprise. Because each type of warranty is created in a different way, the manner in which a seller or lessor can disclaim warranties varies with the type of warranty.

Express Warranties A seller or lessor can disclaim all oral express warranties by including in the contract a written disclaimer. The disclaimer must be in language that is clear and conspicuous and must be called to a buyer's or lessee's attention [UCC 2–316(1), 2A–214(1)]. This allows the seller or lessor to avoid false allegations that oral warranties were made. It also ensures that only representations made by properly authorized individuals are included in the bargain.

Note that a buyer or lessee must be made aware of any warranty disclaimers or modifications *at the time the contract is formed.* In other words, the seller or lessor cannot modify any warranties or disclaimers made during the bargaining process without the consent of the buyer or lessee.

Implied Warranties Normally, unless circumstances indicate otherwise, the implied warranties of merchantability and fitness are disclaimed by an expression such as "as is" or "with all faults." Both parties must be able to clearly understand from the language used that there are no implied warranties [UCC 2–316(3)(a), 2A–214(3)(a)]. (Note, however, that some states have passed consumer protection statutes that forbid "as is" sales or make it illegal to disclaim warranties of merchantability on consumer goods.)

To specifically disclaim an implied warranty of merchantability, a seller or lessor must mention the word *merchantability.* The disclaimer need not be written, but if it is, the writing must be conspicuous [UCC 2–316(2), 2A–214(4)].

Under the UCC, a term or clause is conspicuous when it is written or displayed in such a way that a reasonable person would notice it. Conspicuous terms include words set in capital letters, in a larger font size, or in a different color so as to be set off from the surrounding text.

To disclaim an implied warranty of fitness for a particular purpose, the disclaimer must be in a writing and must be conspicuous. The writing does not have to mention the word *fitness.* It is sufficient if, for instance, the disclaimer states, "There are no warranties that extend beyond the description on the face hereof."

Buyer's or Lessee's Examination or Refusal to Inspect If a buyer or lessee examines the goods (or a sample or model) as fully as desired, there is no implied warranty with respect to defects that are found or that could be found on a reasonable examination [UCC 2–316(3)(b), 2A–214(2)(b)]. Also, if a buyer or lessee refuses to examine the goods on the seller's or lessor's request that he or she do so, there is no implied warranty with respect to reasonably evident defects.

Warranty Disclaimers and Unconscionability The UCC sections dealing with warranty disclaimers do not refer specifically to unconscionability as a factor. Ultimately, however, the courts will test warranty disclaimers with reference to the UCC's unconscionability standards [UCC 2–302, 2A–108]. Factors such as lack of bargaining position, "take-it-or-leave-it" choices, and a buyer's or lessee's failure to understand or know of a warranty disclaimer will be relevant to the issue of unconscionability.

Statutes of Limitations A cause of action for breach of contract under the UCC must be commenced within four years after the breach occurs (unless the parties agree to a shorter period). An action for breach of warranty accrues when the seller or lessor *tenders* delivery, even if the buyer or lessee is unaware of the breach at that time [UCC 2–725(2), 2A–506(2)]. In addition, the nonbreaching party usually must notify the breaching party within a reasonable time after discovering the breach or be barred from pursuing any remedy [UCC 2–607(3)(a), 2A–516(3)].

Reviewing: Performance, Breach, and Warranties in Sales and Lease Contracts

GFI, Inc., a Hong Kong company, makes audio decoder chips, an essential component in the manufacture of smartphones. Egan Electronics contracts with GFI to buy 10,000 chips on an installment contract, with 2,500 chips to be shipped every three months, F.O.B. Hong Kong, via Air Express. At the time for the first delivery, GFI delivers only 2,400 chips. GFI explains, however, that although the shipment is 4 percent short, the chips are of a higher quality than those specified in the contract and are worth 5 percent more. Egan accepts the shipment and pays GFI the contract price.

At the time for the second shipment, GFI makes a shipment identical to the first. Egan again accepts and pays for the chips. At the time for the third shipment, GFI ships 2,400 of the same chips, but this time GFI sends them via Hong Kong Air instead of Air Express. While in transit, the chips are destroyed. When it is time for the fourth shipment, GFI again sends 2,400 chips, but this time Egan rejects the chips without explanation. Using the information presented in the chapter, answer the following questions.

1. Did GFI have a legitimate reason to expect that Egan would accept the fourth shipment? Why or why not?
2. Did the substitution of carriers in the third shipment constitute a breach of the contract by GFI? Explain.
3. Suppose that the silicon used for the chips becomes unavailable for a period of time. Consequently, GFI cannot manufacture enough chips to fulfill the contract but does ship as many as it can to Egan. Under what doctrine might a court release GFI from further performance of the contract?
4. Under the UCC, does Egan have a right to reject the fourth shipment? Why or why not?

Debate This . . . *No express warranties should be created by the oral statements made by salespersons about a product.*

Terms and Concepts

conforming goods 306
cover 315
cure 308
express warranty 321
implied warranty 323

implied warranty of fitness for a
   particular purpose 325
implied warranty of
   merchantability 323
installment contract 308

perfect tender rule 308
replevin 315
tender of delivery 306

Issue Spotters

1. Country Fruit Stand orders eighty cases of peaches from Downey Farms. Without stating a reason, Downey delivers thirty cases instead of eighty and delivers at the wrong time. Does Country have the right to reject the shipment? Explain. (See *Performance Obligations*.)
2. Stella bought a cup of coffee at the Roasted Bean Drive-Thru. The coffee had been heated to 190 degrees and consequently had dissolved the inside of the cup. When Stella lifted the lid, the cup collapsed, spilling the contents on her lap. To recover for third-degree burns on her thighs, Stella filed a suit against the Roasted Bean. Can Stella recover for breach of the implied warranty of merchantability? Why or why not? (See *Sales and Lease Warranties*.)

• **Check your answers to the Issue Spotters against the answers provided in Appendix B at the end of this text.**

Business Scenarios

16–1. Anticipatory Repudiation. Moore contracted in writing to sell her 2017 Hyundai Santa Fe to Hammer for $18,500. Moore agreed to deliver the car on Wednesday, and Hammer promised to pay the $18,500 on the following

Friday. On Tuesday, Hammer informed Moore that he would not be buying the car after all. By Friday, Hammer had changed his mind again and tendered $18,500 to Moore. Moore, although she had not sold the car to another party, refused the tender and refused to deliver. Hammer claimed that Moore had breached their contract. Moore contended that Hammer's repudiation released her from her duty to perform under the contract. Who is correct, and why? (See *Performance Obligations*.)

16–2. Implied Warranties. Moon, a farmer, needs to install a two-thousand-pound piece of equipment in his barn. This will require lifting the equipment thirty feet up into a hayloft. Moon goes to Davidson Hardware and tells Davidson that he needs some heavy-duty rope to be used on his farm. Davidson recommends a one-inch-thick nylon rope, and Moon purchases two hundred feet of it. Moon ties the rope around the piece of equipment; puts the rope through a pulley; and, with a tractor, lifts the equipment off the ground. Suddenly, the rope breaks. The equipment crashes to the ground and is severely damaged. Moon files a suit against Davidson for breach of the implied warranty of fitness for a particular purpose. Discuss how successful Moon will be in his suit. (See *Sales and Lease Warranties*.)

Business Case Problems

16–3. Spotlight on Apple—Implied Warranties. Alan

Vitt purchased an iBook G4 laptop computer from Apple, Inc. Shortly after the one-year warranty expired, the laptop failed to work due to a weakness in the product manufacture. Vitt sued Apple, arguing that the laptop should have lasted "at least a couple of years," which Vitt believed was a reasonable consumer expectation for a laptop. Vitt claimed that Apple's descriptions of the laptop as "durable," "rugged," "reliable," and "high performance" were affirmative statements concerning the quality and performance of the laptop, which Apple did not meet. How should the court rule? Why? [*Vitt v. Apple Computer, Inc.,* 469 Fed.Appx. 605 (9th Cir. 2011)] (See *Sales and Lease Warranties*.)

16–4. Business Case Problem with Sample Answer—Nonconforming Goods. Padma Paper Mills, Ltd., converts

waste paper into usable paper. In 2007, Padma entered into a contract with Universal Exports, Inc., under which Universal Exports certified that it would ship white envelope cuttings. Padma paid $131,000 for the paper. When the shipment arrived, however, Padma discovered that Universal Exports had sent multicolored paper plates and other brightly colored paper products. Padma accepted the goods but notified Universal Exports that they did not conform to the contract. Can Padma recover even though it accepted the goods knowing that they were nonconforming? If so, how? [*Padma Paper Mills, Ltd. v. Universal Exports, Inc.,* 34 Misc.3d 1236(A), 950 N.Y.S. 2d 609 (2012)] (See *Remedies of the Buyer or Lessee*.)

• For a sample answer for Problem 16–4, go to Appendix C at the end of this text.

16–5. The Right of Rejection. Erb Poultry, Inc., is a distributor of fresh poultry products in Lima, Ohio. CEME, LLC, does business as Bank Shots, a restaurant in Trotwood, Ohio. CEME ordered chicken wings and "dippers" from Erb, which were delivered and for which CEME issued a check in payment. A few days later, CEME stopped payment on the check. When contacted by Erb, CEME alleged that the products were beyond their freshness date, mangled, spoiled, and the wrong sizes. CEME did not provide any evidence to support the claims or arrange to return the products. Is CEME entitled to a full refund of the amount paid for the chicken? Explain. [*Erb Poultry, Inc. v. CEME, LLC,* 20 N.E.3d 1228, 2014 -Ohio- 4504 (2014)] (See *Remedies of the Buyer or Lessee*.)

16–6. Remedies for Breach. LO Ventures, LLC, doing business as Reefpoint Brewhouse in Racine, Wisconsin, contracted with Forman Awnings and Construction, LLC, for the fabrication and installation of an awning system over an outdoor seating area. After the system was complete, Reefpoint expressed concerns about the workmanship but did not give Forman a chance to make repairs. The brewhouse used the awning for two months and then had it removed so that siding on the building could be replaced. The parties disagreed about whether cracked and broken welds observed after the removal of the system were due to shoddy workmanship. Reefpoint paid only $400 on the contract price of $8,161. Can Reefpoint rescind the contract and obtain a return of its $400? Is Forman entitled to recover the difference between Reefpoint's payment and the contract price? Discuss. [*Forman Awnings and Construction, LLC v. LO Ventures, LLC,* 360 Wis.2d 492, 864 N.W.2d 121 (2015)] (See *Remedies of the Buyer or Lessee*.)

16–7. Express Warranties. Charity Bell bought a used Toyota Avalon from Awny Gobran of Gobran Auto Sales, Inc. The odometer showed that the car had been driven 147,000 miles. Bell asked whether it had been in any accidents. Gobran replied that it was in good condition. The parties signed a warranty disclaimer that the vehicle was sold "as is." Problems with the car arose the same day as the purchase. Gobran made a few ineffectual attempts to repair it before refusing to do more. Meanwhile, Bell obtained a vehicle history report from Carfax, which showed that the Avalon had been damaged in an accident and that its last reported odometer reading was 237,271. Was the "as is" disclaimer sufficient to put Bell on notice that the odometer reading could be false and that the car might have been in an accident? Can Gobran avoid any liability that might otherwise be imposed because Bell did not obtain the Carfax report until *after* she bought the car? Discuss. [*Gobran Auto Sales Inc. v. Bell*, 335 Ga.App. 873, 783 S.E.2d 389 (2016)] (See *Sales and Lease Warranties*.)

16–8. Remedies of the Buyer or Lessee. M.C. and Linda Morris own a home in Gulfport, Mississippi, that was extensively damaged in Hurricane Katrina. The Morrises contracted with Inside Outside, Inc. (IO), to rebuild their kitchen. When the new kitchen cabinets were delivered, some defects were apparent, and as installation progressed, others were revealed. IO ordered replacement parts to cure the defects. Before the parts arrived, however, the parties' relationship deteriorated, and IO offered to remove the cabinets and refund the price. The Morrises also asked to be repaid for the installation fee. IO refused but emphasized that it was willing to fulfill its contractual obligations. At this point, are the Morrises entitled to revoke their acceptance of the cabinets? Why or why not? [*M.C. Morris v. Inside Outside, Inc.*, 185 So.3d 413 (Miss.App. 2016)] (See *Remedies of the Buyer or Lessee*.)

16–9. A Question of Ethics—Lemon Laws. *Randal Schwei-* *ger bought a 2008 Kia Spectra EX from Kia Motors America, Inc., for his stepdaughter, April Kirichkow. The cost was $17,231, plus sales tax, fees, and other items. April had trouble starting the car. The Kia dealership replaced various parts of the motor several times but was unable to fix the problem. Schweiger sought a refund under the state's lemon law. When they could not agree on the amount, Schweiger filed a suit in a Wisconsin state court against Kia. From a judgment in Schweiger's favor, Kia appealed. [Schweiger v. Kia Motors America, Inc., 347 Wis.2d 550, 830 N.W.2d 723 (2013)] (See Sales and Lease Warranties.)*

(a) Kia offered a refund of $3,306.24. Should this offer bar Schweiger's claim for a refund? Why or why not?

(b) Schweiger claimed that Kia's offer did not include the $1,301 cost of a service contract. Kia argued that the "payoff to the lender" of $13,060.16, which Schweiger agreed was the correct amount, "would by definition refund the cost of the service contract." The court found "no logical basis" for this argument. Is it ethical for a party to argue a position for which there is no logical basis? Discuss.

Legal Reasoning Group Activity

16–10. Warranties. Milan purchased saffron extract, marketed as "America's Hottest New Way to a Flat Belly," online from Dr. Chen. The Web site stated that recently published studies showed a significant weight loss (more than 25 percent) for people who used pure saffron extract as a supplement *without diet and exercise*. Dr. Chen said that the saffron suppresses appetite by increasing levels of serotonin, which reduces emotional eating. Milan took the extract as directed without any resulting weight loss. (See *Sales and Lease Warranties*.)

(a) The first group will determine whether Dr. Chen's Web site made any express warranty on the saffron extract or its effectiveness in causing weight loss.

(b) The second group will discuss whether the implied warranty of merchantability applies to the purchase of weight-loss supplements.

(c) The third group will decide if Dr. Chen's sale of saffron extract breached the implied warranty of fitness for a particular purpose.

Agency and Business Forms

CHAPTER 17

Agency Relationships in Business

One of the most common, important, and pervasive legal relationships is that of **agency.** In an agency relationship involving two parties, one of the parties, called the *agent,* agrees to represent or act for the other, called the *principal.* The principal has the right to control the agent's conduct in matters entrusted to the agent.

Agency relationships are crucial in the business world. By using agents, a principal can conduct multiple business operations at the same time in different locations. Indeed, the only way that certain business entities can function is through their agents. For instance, a corporate officer is an agent who serves in a representative capacity for the corporation. The officer has the authority to bind the corporation to a contract. Only through its officers can corporations enter into contracts.

Most employees are also considered to be agents of their employers.

Today, however, the United States is experiencing a trend toward a so-called *gig economy,* which centers on short-term, independent workers who are not employees. Companies like Uber and Lyft (discussed in this chapter's feature) provide evidence of this trend. This type of on-demand employment raises questions related to agency, making agency an increasingly important topic for students of business law and the legal environment to understand.

17-1 Agency Law

Section 1(1) of the *Restatement (Third) of Agency*[1] defines *agency* as "the fiduciary relation [that] results from the manifestation of consent by one person to another that the other shall act in his [or her] behalf and subject to his [or her] control, and consent by the other so to act." In other words, in a principal-agent relationship, the parties have agreed that the agent will act *on behalf and instead of* the principal in negotiating and transacting business with third parties.

The term **fiduciary** is at the heart of agency law. When this term is used as a noun, it refers to a person having a duty created by his or her undertaking to act primarily for another's benefit in matters connected with the undertaking. When used as an adjective, as in the phrase *fiduciary relationship,* it means that the relationship involves trust and confidence.

Agency relationships commonly exist between employers and employees. Agency relationships may sometimes

also exist between employers and independent contractors who are hired to perform special tasks or services.

17-1a Employer-Employee Relationships

Normally, all employees who deal with third parties are deemed to be agents. A salesperson in a department store, for instance, is an agent of the store's owner (the principal) and acts on the owner's behalf. Any sale of goods made by the salesperson to a customer is binding on the principal. Similarly, most representations of fact made by the salesperson with respect to the goods sold are binding on the principal.

Because employees who deal with third parties generally are deemed to be agents of their employers, agency law and employment law overlap considerably. Agency relationships, however, can exist outside an employer-employee relationship, so agency law has a broader reach than employment law. Additionally, agency law is based on the common law, whereas much employment law is statutory law.

Employment laws (state and federal) apply only to the employer-employee relationship. Statutes governing

---

1. The *Restatement (Third) of Agency* is an authoritative summary of the law of agency and is often referred to by judges in their decisions and opinions.

Social Security, withholding taxes, workers' compensation, unemployment compensation, workplace safety, and employment discrimination apply only if an employer-employee relationship exists. *These laws do not apply to independent contractors.*

17–1b Employer–Independent Contractor Relationships

Independent contractors are not employees because, by definition, those who hire them have no control over the details of their work performance. Section 2 of the *Restatement (Third) of Agency* defines an **independent contractor** as follows:

> [An independent contractor is] a person who contracts with another to do something for him [or her] but who is not controlled by the other nor subject to the other's right to control with respect to his [or her] physical conduct in the performance of the undertaking. He [or she] may or may not be an agent.

Building contractors and subcontractors are independent contractors. A property owner who hires a contractor and subcontractors to complete a project does not control the details of the way they perform their work. Truck drivers who own their vehicles and hire out on a per-job basis are independent contractors, but truck drivers who drive company trucks on a regular basis usually are employees. See this chapter's *Ethics Today* feature for a discussion of disputes involving the classification of drivers working for Uber and Lyft.

The relationship between a principal and an independent contractor may or may not involve an agency relationship. To illustrate: A homeowner who hires a real estate broker to sell her house has contracted with an independent contractor (the broker). The homeowner has also established an agency relationship with the broker for the specific purpose of selling the property. Similarly, an insurance agent is both an independent contractor and an agent of the insurance company for which he sells policies. (Note that an insurance *broker,* in contrast, normally is an agent of the person obtaining insurance and not of the insurance company.)

17–1c Determination of Employee Status

The courts are frequently asked to determine whether a particular worker is an employee or an independent contractor. How a court decides this issue can have a significant effect on the rights and liabilities of the parties.

Employers are required to pay certain taxes, such as Social Security and unemployment taxes, for employees but not for independent contractors. Therefore, workers may benefit from obtaining employee status in some situations.

Criteria Used by the Courts   In deciding whether a worker is categorized as an employee or an independent contractor, courts often consider the following questions:

1. *How much control does the employer exercise over the details of the work?* If the employer exercises considerable control over the details of the work and the day-to-day activities of the worker, this indicates employee status. This is perhaps the most important factor weighed by the courts in determining employee status.
2. *Is the worker engaged in an occupation or business distinct from that of the employer?* If so, this points to independent-contractor, not employee, status.
3. *Is the work usually done under the employer's direction or by a specialist without supervision?* If the work is usually done under the employer's direction, this indicates employee status.
4. *Does the employer supply the tools at the place of work?* If so, this indicates employee status.
5. *For how long is the person employed?* If the person is employed for a long period of time, this indicates employee status.
6. *What is the method of payment—by time period or at the completion of the job?* Payment by time period, such as once every two weeks or once a month, indicates employee status.
7. *What degree of skill is required of the worker?* If a great degree of skill is required, this may indicate that the person is an independent contractor hired for a specialized job and not an employee.

Whether a worker is an employee or an independent contractor can affect the employer's liability for the worker's actions. An employer normally is not responsible for the actions of an independent contractor. ■ **CASE IN POINT 17.1** Terence Pershad was a tow truck driver for Five Star Auto Service. Five Star had contracted to perform towing and auto repair services for AAA North Jersey, Inc. After one of its customers was involved in a car accident, AAA called Five Star for assistance, and Five Star sent a truck driven by Pershad. Pershad got into a fight with Nicholas Coker, a passenger in the car, and assaulted Coker with a knife.

Coker filed a suit in a New Jersey state court against Pershad, Five Star, and AAA. The court determined that

Is It Fair to Classify Uber and Lyft Drivers as Independent Contractors?

The transportation-for-hire world has changed dramatically since Uber, Lyft, and other transportation-sharing companies came onto the scene. Uber started in San Francisco in 2009. Today, its services are available in one form or another in about 60 countries and more than 300 cities worldwide. Its main competitor, Lyft, was launched in 2012 and operates in more than 200 U.S. cities. The growth in transportation sharing has not been without its set-backs, though. Most of them involve laws that have prohibited Uber and Lyft from operating in certain cities, as well as lawsuits by drivers claiming that they were misclassified.

Classification of Workers

Workers in the United States generally fall into two categories: employees and independent contractors. Employment laws, including minimum wage and anti-discrimination statutes, cover employees. Such laws do not cover most independent contractors. Enter the digital age of on-demand workers who obtain job assignments via apps.

Workers for Lyft, Uber, and similar companies choose when and where they will perform their duties. They do not choose how much they will be paid, however. For them, employment is a take-it-or-leave-it proposition. They electronically accept the platform terms of the apps, or they obtain no work assignments.

Some critics of this contractual system argue that there should be a new category of workers with "dependent-contractor" status who receive some of the protections traditionally given only to employees. Certain aspects of current labor law would be attached to the relationships between dependent contractors and their employers.

Worker Misclassification Lawsuits

A number of former or current Uber and Lyft drivers have pursued legal remedies to change their job classification and to obtain better benefits. In California, for instance, two federal court judges allowed separate lawsuits to go before juries on the question of whether on-demand drivers should be considered employees rather than independent contractors.[a]

In a similar case, rather than go to court, Lyft settled a worker misclassification lawsuit for $12.25 million. The suit, which was settled in 2016, had been brought in 2013. The settlement did not achieve a reclassification of Lyft drivers as employees. Basically, Lyft agreed to change its terms of service to conform to California's independent contractor status regulations. For instance, the company can no longer deactivate drivers' accounts without reason and without warning the drivers. Drivers have to be given a fair hearing first. Even though the lawsuit and the agreement were California based, the new terms of service will apply to all Lyft's drivers nationwide.

Competitors Sue Uber

In many cities, competitors, especially taxi drivers, have sued Uber. These lawsuits have involved claims of unfair competition, lack of minimum wages, and unsafe vehicles. A taxi driver sued Uber in northern California, for instance, but a federal district court ruled in favor of Uber's request for summary judgment.[b]

Another suit was brought in Pennsylvania. In this one, Checker Cab of Philadelphia claimed that Uber was violating Pennsylvania's unfair competition law. Checker Cab sought a preliminary injunction to prevent Uber from taking away its customers. The federal district court refused to grant an injunction, however, because Checker Cab failed to show irreparable harm. That decision was upheld on appeal.[c]

Critical Thinking *What choices do disgruntled Uber and Lyft drivers have?*

a. *Cotter v. Lyft, Inc.*, 60 F.Supp.3d 1067 (N.D.Cal. 2015); *O'Connor v. Uber Technologies, Inc., et al.*, Case No. C-13-3826 EMC (N.D.Cal. 2015).
b. *Rosen v. Uber Technologies, Inc.*, ___ F.Supp.3d ___, 2016 WL 704078 (N.D.Cal. 2016).
c. *Checker Cab of Philadelphia, Inc. v. Uber Technologies, Inc.*, 643 Fed.Appx. 229 (3d Cir. 2016).

Pershad was Five Star's employee and that Five Star was an independent contractor, not AAA's employee. Therefore, AAA was not liable (and Five Star was, so it entered into a settlement agreement with Coker). Coker appealed, but a state intermediate appellate court affirmed. AAA could not be held liable for the actions of Five Star, its independent contractor, because "AAA did not control the manner and means of Five Star's work."[2] ∎

Criteria Used by the IRS The Internal Revenue Service (IRS) has established its own criteria for determining

2. *Coker v. Pershad*, 2013 WL 1296271 (N.J.Sup.Ct. 2013).

whether a worker is an independent contractor or an employee. The most important factor is the degree of control the business exercises over the worker.

The IRS tends to closely scrutinize a firm's classification of its workers because, as mentioned, employers can avoid certain tax liabilities by hiring independent contractors instead of employees. Even when a firm has classified a worker as an independent contractor, the IRS may decide that the worker is actually an employee. If the IRS decides that an employee is misclassified, the employer will be responsible for paying any applicable Social Security, withholding, and unemployment taxes due for that employee.

Employee Status and "Works for Hire" Ordinarily, a person who creates a copyrighted work is the owner of it—unless it is a "work for hire." Under the Copyright Act, any copyrighted work created by an employee within the scope of her or his employment at the request of the employer is a "work for hire." The employer owns the copyright to the work.

In contrast, when an employer hires an independent contractor—such as a freelance artist, writer, or computer programmer—the independent contractor normally owns the copyright. An exception is made if the parties agree in writing that the work is a "work for hire" and the work falls into one of nine specific categories. The nine categories include audiovisual works, collective works (such as magazines), motion pictures, textbooks, tests, and translations.

■ **CASE IN POINT 17.2** As a freelance contractor, Brian Cooley created two sculptures of dinosaur eggs for the National Geographic Society for use in connection with an article in its magazine, *National Geographic*. Cooley spent hundreds of hours researching, designing, and constructing the sculptures. National Geographic hired Louis Psihoyos to photograph Cooley's sculptures for the article. Cooley and Psihoyos had separate contracts with National Geographic in which each transferred the copyrights in their works to National Geographic for a limited time.

The rights to the works were returned to the artists at different times after publication. Psihoyos then began licensing his photographs of Cooley's sculptures to third parties in return for royalties. He digitized the photographs and licensed them to various online stock photography companies, and they appeared in several books published by Penguin Group. Cooley sued Psihoyos for copyright infringement.

Psihoyos argued that he owned the photos and could license them however he saw fit, but a federal district court disagreed. The court found that Psihoyos did not have an unrestricted right to use and license the photos.

When Psihoyos reproduced an image of a Cooley sculpture, he reproduced the sculpture, which infringed on Cooley's copyright. Therefore, the court granted a summary judgment to Cooley.[3] ■

17–2 Formation of the Agency Relationship

Agency relationships normally are consensual. They come about by voluntary consent and agreement between the parties. Normally, the agreement need not be in writing, and consideration is not required.

A person must have contractual capacity to be a principal.[4] The idea is that those who cannot legally enter into contracts directly should not be allowed to do so indirectly through an agent. Any person can be an agent, however, regardless of whether he or she has the capacity to contract (including minors).

An agency relationship can be created for any legal purpose. An agency relationship created for a purpose that is illegal or contrary to public policy is unenforceable. ■ **EXAMPLE 17.3** Archer (as principal) contracts with Burke (as agent) to sell illegal narcotics. The agency relationship is unenforceable because selling illegal narcotics is a felony and is contrary to public policy. If Burke sells the narcotics and keeps the profits, Archer cannot sue to enforce the agency agreement. ■

An agency relationship can arise in four ways: by agreement of the parties, by ratification, by estoppel, and by operation of law.

17–2a Agency by Agreement

Most agency relationships are based on an express or implied agreement that the agent will act for the principal and that the principal agrees to have the agent so act. An agency agreement can take the form of an express written contract or be created by an oral agreement. ■ **EXAMPLE 17.4** Reese asks Grace, a gardener, to contract with others for the care of his lawn on a regular basis. If Grace agrees, an agency relationship exists between Reese and Grace for the lawn care. ■

An agency agreement can also be implied by conduct. ■ **CASE IN POINT 17.5** Gilbert Bishop was admitted to a nursing home, Laurel Creek Health Care Center, suffering from various physical ailments. He was not able to use his hands well enough to write but

---

3. *Cooley v. Penguin Group (USA), Inc.*, 31 F.Supp.3d 599 (S.D.N.Y. 2014).
4. Note that some states allow a minor to be a principal. When a minor is permitted to be a principal, any resulting contracts will be voidable by the minor principal but *not* by the adult third party.

was otherwise mentally competent. Because it was Laurel Creek's policy to have the patient's spouse sign the forms if the patient could not, Bishop's wife Anna signed the admission papers for him. The paperwork included a mandatory arbitration clause. Later, when the family filed a lawsuit against Laurel Creek, the nursing home sought to enforce the arbitration clause. Ultimately, a Kentucky appellate court held that Bishop was bound by the contract and the arbitration clause his wife had signed. Bishop's conduct had indicated that he was giving his wife authority to act as his agent in signing the admission papers.[5] ■

17–2b Agency by Ratification

On occasion, a person who is in fact not an agent (or who is an agent acting outside the scope of her or his authority) makes a contract on behalf of another (a principal). If the principal approves or affirms that contract by word or by action, an agency relationship is created by *ratification*. Ratification involves a question of intent, and intent can be expressed by either words or conduct.

17–2c Agency by Estoppel

Sometimes, a principal causes a third person to believe that another person is the principal's agent, and the third person acts to his or her detriment in reasonable reliance on that belief. When this occurs, the principal is "estopped to deny" (prevented from denying) the agency relationship. The principal's actions have created the *appearance* of an agency that does not in fact exist, creating an agency by estoppel.

The Third Party's Reliance Must Be Reasonable
The third person must prove that he or she *reasonably* believed that an agency relationship existed.[6] Facts and circumstances must show that an ordinary, prudent person familiar with business practice and custom would have been justified in concluding that the agent had authority.

Created by the Principal's Conduct
Note that the acts or declarations of a purported *agent* in and of themselves do not create an agency by estoppel. Rather,

it is the deeds or statements of the *principal* that create an agency by estoppel. ■ **CASE IN POINT 17.6** Francis Azur was president and chief executive officer of ATM Corporation of America. Michelle Vanek was Azur's personal assistant. Among other duties, she reviewed his credit-card statements. For seven years, Vanek took unauthorized cash advances from Azur's credit-card account with Chase Bank. The charges appeared on at least sixty-five monthly statements.

When Azur discovered Vanek's fraud, he fired her and closed the account. He filed a suit against Chase, arguing that the bank should not have allowed Vanek to take cash advances. The court concluded that Azur (the principal) had given the bank reason to believe that Vanek (the agent) had authority. Therefore, Azur was estopped from denying Vanek's authority.[7] ■

17–2d Agency by Operation of Law

The courts may find an agency relationship in the absence of a formal agreement in other situations as well. This may occur in family relationships, such as when one spouse purchases certain basic necessaries and charges them to the other spouse's account. The courts often rule that a spouse is liable for payment for the necessaries because of either a social policy or a legal duty to supply necessaries to family members.

Agency by operation of law may also occur in emergency situations. If an agent cannot contact the principal and failure to act would cause the principal substantial loss, the agent may take steps beyond the scope of her or his authority. For instance, a railroad engineer may contract on behalf of his or her employer for medical care for an injured motorist hit by the train.

17–3 Duties of Agents and Principals

Once the principal-agent relationship has been created, both parties have duties that govern their conduct. As discussed previously, the principal-agent relationship is *fiduciary*—based on trust. In a fiduciary relationship, each party owes the other the duty to act with the utmost good faith.

---

5. *Laurel Creek Health Care Center v. Bishop*, 2010 WL 985299 (Ky.App. 2010).
6. These concepts also apply when a person who is, in fact, an agent undertakes an action that is beyond the scope of her or his authority.

---

7. *Azur v. Chase Bank, USA, N.A.*, 601 F.3d 212 (3d Cir. 2010).

17–3a Agent's Duties to the Principal

Generally, the agent owes the principal five duties—performance, notification, loyalty, obedience, and accounting (see Exhibit 17–1).

Performance An implied condition in every agency contract is the agent's agreement to use reasonable diligence and skill in performing the work. When an agent fails to perform his or her duties, liability for breach of contract may result.

Standard of Care. The degree of skill or care required of an agent is usually that expected of a reasonable person under similar circumstances. Generally, this is interpreted to mean ordinary care. If an agent has represented herself or himself as possessing special skills, however, the agent is expected to exercise the degree of skill claimed. Failure to do so constitutes a breach of the agent's duty.

Gratuitous Agents. Not all agency relationships are based on contract. In some situations, an agent acts gratuitously—that is, without payment. A gratuitous agent cannot be liable for breach of contract because there is no contract. He or she is subject only to tort liability. Once a gratuitous agent has begun to act in an agency capacity, he or she has the duty to continue to perform in that capacity. A gratuitous agent must perform in an acceptable manner and is subject to the same standards of care and duty to perform as other agents.

■ **EXAMPLE 17.7** Bower's friend Alcott is a real estate broker. Alcott offers to sell Bower's vacation home at no charge. If Alcott never attempts to sell the home, Bower has no legal cause of action to force her to do so. If Alcott does attempt to sell the home to Friedman, but then performs so negligently that the sale falls through, Bower can sue Alcott for negligence. ■

Notification An agent is required to notify the principal of all matters that come to her or his attention concerning the subject matter of the agency. This is the *duty of notification,* or the duty to inform.

■ **EXAMPLE 17.8** Perez, an artist, is about to negotiate a contract to sell a series of paintings to Barber's Art Gallery for $25,000. Perez's agent learns that Barber is insolvent and will be unable to pay for the paintings. The agent has a duty to inform Perez of Barber's insolvency because it is relevant to the subject matter of the agency, which is the sale of Perez's paintings. ■

Generally, the law assumes that the principal is aware of any information acquired by the agent that is relevant to the agency—regardless of whether the agent actually passes on this information to the principal. It is a basic tenet of agency law that notice to the agent is notice to the principal.

Loyalty Loyalty is one of the most fundamental duties in a fiduciary relationship. Basically, the agent has the duty to act *solely for the benefit of his or her principal* and not in the interest of the agent or a third party. For instance, an agent cannot represent two principals in the same transaction unless both know of the dual capacity and consent to it.

EXHIBIT 17–1 Duties of the Agent

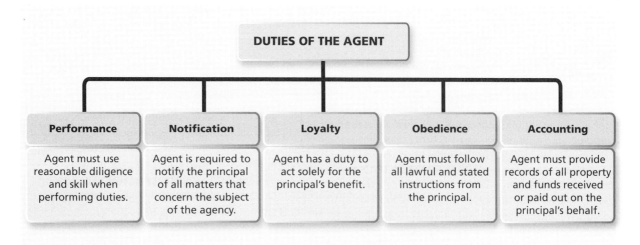

The duty of loyalty also means that any information or knowledge acquired through the agency relationship is confidential. It is a breach of loyalty to disclose such information either during the agency relationship or after its termination. Typical examples of confidential information are trade secrets and customer lists compiled by the principal.

The agent's loyalty must be undivided. The agent's actions must be strictly for the benefit of the principal and must not result in any secret profit for the agent.

In the following case, an employer alleged that a former employee had breached his duty of loyalty by planning a competing business while still working for the employer.

Spotlight on Taser International

Case 17.1 Taser International, Inc. v. Ward

Court of Appeals of Arizona, Division 1, 224 Ariz. 389, 231 P.3d 921 (2010).

Background and Facts Taser International, Inc., develops and makes electronic control devices, commonly called stun guns, as well as accessories for electronic control devices, including a personal video and audio recording device called the TASER CAM.

Steve Ward was Taser's vice president of marketing when he began to explore the possibility of developing and marketing devices of his own design, including a clip-on camera. Ward talked to patent attorneys and a product development company and completed most of a business plan. After he resigned from Taser, he formed Vievu, LLC, to market his clip-on camera.

Ten months after Ward resigned, Taser announced the AXON, a product that provides an audio-video record of an incident from the visual perspective of the person involved. Taser then filed a suit in an Arizona state court against Ward, alleging that he had breached his duty of loyalty to Taser. The court granted Taser's motion for a summary judgment in the employer's favor. Ward appealed.

In the Language of the Court

PORTLEY, Judge.

* * * *

* * * An agent is under the duty to act with entire good faith and loyalty for the furtherance of the interests of his principal in all matters concerning or affecting the subject of his agency.

One aspect of this broad principle is that an employee is precluded from actively competing with his or her employer during the period of employment.

Although an employee may not compete prior to termination, the employee may take action during employment, not otherwise wrongful, to prepare for competition following termination of the agency relationship. Preparation cannot take the form of acts in direct competition with the employer's business. [Emphasis added.]

* * * *

It is undisputed that, prior to his resignation, Ward did not solicit or recruit any Taser employees, distributors, customers, or vendors; he did not buy, sell, or incorporate any business; he did not acquire office space or other general business services; he did not contact or enter into any agreements with suppliers or manufacturers for his proposed clip-on camera; and he did not sell any products. However, Ward did begin developing a business plan, counseled with several attorneys, explored and abandoned the concept of an eyeglass-mounted camera device, and engaged, to some extent, in the exploration and development of a clip-on camera device.

Ward argues that his pre-termination activities did not constitute active competition but were merely lawful preparation for a future business venture. Taser contends, however, that "this case is * * * about developing a rival design during employment, knowing full well TASER has sold such a device and continues to develop a second-generation product."

* * * *

* * * Assuming Taser was engaged in the research and development of a recording device during Ward's employment, assuming Ward knew or should have known of those efforts, and assuming Taser's device would compete with Ward's concept, substantial design and development efforts by Ward during his employment would constitute direct competition with the business activities of Taser and

Case 17.1 Continued

would violate his duty of loyalty. In the context of a business which engages in research, design, development, manufacture, and marketing of products, we cannot limit "competition" to just actual sales of competing products.

Decision and Remedy *A state intermediate appellate court agreed with Taser that an employee may not actively compete with his employer before his employment is terminated. But the parties disputed the extent of Ward's pre-termination efforts, creating a genuine issue of material fact that could not be resolved on a motion for summary judgment. The appellate court thus reversed the lower court's decision in Taser's favor and remanded the case for further proceedings.*

Critical Thinking
- **Legal Environment** *Did Ward breach any duties owed to his employer in addition to his alleged breach of the duty of loyalty? Discuss.*
- **What If the Facts Were Different?** *Suppose that Ward's pre-termination activities focused on a product that was not designed to compete with Taser's products. Would these efforts have breached the duty of loyalty? Why or why not?*

Obedience When acting on behalf of the principal, an agent has a duty to follow all lawful and clearly stated instructions of the principal. Any deviation from such instructions is a violation of this duty.

During emergency situations, however, when the principal cannot be consulted, the agent may deviate from the instructions without violating this duty. Whenever instructions are not clearly stated, the agent can fulfill the duty of obedience by acting in good faith and in a manner reasonable under the circumstances.

Accounting Unless the agent and principal agree otherwise, the agent must keep and make available to the principal an account of all property and funds received

and paid out on the principal's behalf. This includes gifts from third parties in connection with the agency.

The agent has a duty to maintain a separate account for the principal's funds and must not intermingle these funds with the agent's personal funds. If a licensed professional (such as an attorney) violates this duty, he or she may be subject to disciplinary action by the licensing authority (such as the state bar association). Of course, the professional will also be liable to his or her client (the principal) for failure to account.

17–3b Principal's Duties to the Agent

The principal also has certain duties to the agent (as shown in Exhibit 17–2). These duties relate to compensation,

EXHIBIT 17–2 Duties of the Principal

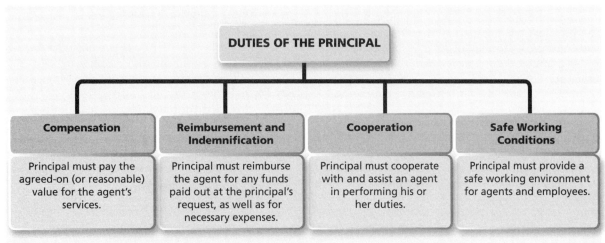

reimbursement and indemnification, cooperation, and safe working conditions.

Compensation In general, when a principal requests certain services from an agent, the agent reasonably expects payment. For instance, when an accountant or an attorney is asked to act as an agent, an agreement to compensate the agent for this service is implied. The principal therefore has a duty to pay the agent for services rendered.

Unless the agency relationship is gratuitous and the agent does not act in exchange for payment, the principal must pay the agreed-on value for the agent's services. If no amount has been expressly agreed on, then the principal owes the agent the customary compensation for such services. The principal also has a duty to pay that compensation in a timely manner.

■ **CASE IN POINT 17.9** Keith Miller worked as a sales representative for Paul M. Wolff Company, a subcontractor specializing in concrete-finishing services. Sales representatives at Wolff are paid a 15 percent commission on projects that meet a 35 percent gross profit threshold. The commission is paid after the projects are completed. When Miller resigned, he asked for commissions on fourteen projects for which he had secured contracts but which had not yet been completed. Wolff refused, so Miller sued.

The court found that "an agent is entitled to receive commissions on sales that result from the agent's efforts," even after the employment or agency relationship ends. Miller had met the gross profit threshold on ten of the unfinished projects, and therefore, he was entitled to more than $21,000 in commissions.[8] ■

Reimbursement and Indemnification Whenever an agent disburses funds at the request of the principal, the principal has a duty to reimburse the agent. The principal must also reimburse the agent (even a gratuitous agent) for any necessary expenses incurred in the course of the reasonable performance of her or his agency duties. Agents cannot recover for expenses incurred as a result of their own misconduct or negligence, though.

---

8. *Miller v. Paul M. Wolff Co.*, 178 Wash.App. 957, 316 P.3d 1113 (2014).

Subject to the terms of the agency agreement, the principal has the duty to *indemnify* (compensate) an agent for liabilities incurred because of authorized and lawful acts and transactions. For instance, if the agent, on the principal's behalf, forms a contract with a third party, and the principal fails to perform the contract, the third party may sue the agent for damages. In this situation, the principal is obligated to compensate the agent for any costs incurred by the agent as a result of the principal's failure to perform the contract.

Additionally, the principal must indemnify the agent for the value of benefits that the agent confers on the principal. The amount of indemnification usually is specified in the agency contract. If it is not, the courts will look to the nature of the business and the type of loss to determine the amount. Note that this rule applies to acts by gratuitous agents as well.

Cooperation A principal has a duty to cooperate with the agent and to assist the agent in performing his or her duties. The principal must do nothing to prevent that performance.

For instance, when a principal grants an agent an exclusive territory, the principal creates an **exclusive agency,** in which the principal cannot compete with the agent or appoint or allow another agent to compete. If the principal does so, he or she violates the exclusive agency and is exposed to liability for the agent's lost profits.

■ **EXAMPLE 17.10** Penny (the principal) creates an exclusive agency by granting Andrew (the agent) a territory within which only Andrew may sell Penny's organic skin care products. If Penny starts to sell the products herself within Andrew's territory—or permits another agent to do so—Penny has failed to cooperate with the agent. Because she has violated the exclusive agency, Penny can be held liable for Andrew's lost sales or profits. ■

In the following case, a pair of potential homebuyers entered into an agreement with a realtor to act as the buyers' exclusive agent in locating and purchasing property. Later, the buyers executed an exclusive agency agreement with a different realtor. Neither agent knew about the other until the buyers found a home that they liked and bought it.

NRT New England, LLC v. Jones

Appellate Court of Connecticut, 162 Conn.App. 840, 134 A.3d 632 (2016).

In the Language of the Court

HARPER, J. [Judge]

* * * *

The defendant [Christopher Jones] met Andrea Woolston, a licensed realtor working as an independent contractor [for NRT New England, LLC, doing business as Coldwell Banker Residential Brokerage], in October 2010. The defendant expressed to Woolston a desire to purchase a home for himself and his then fiancée, Katherine Wiltshire. One of the first things Woolston asked the defendant was whether he was represented by another agent. The defendant responded that he was not. After a number of conversations about the defendant's needs and wishes, the parties executed an exclusive right to represent buyer agreement (agreement), which established, among other things, that Woolston was the defendant's exclusive agent for finding, negotiating, and purchasing property. Over the next several months, Woolston devoted a substantial amount of time searching for properties for the defendant to purchase. Specifically, Woolston researched available properties at six town halls in the communities in which the defendant was interested. She showcased a number of properties personally to the defendant and Wiltshire and introduced many more to them through e-mail. Woolston and the defendant had at least twenty appointments where they viewed multiple properties. Additionally, Woolston visited many properties alone to determine if they were suitable for the defendant. Altogether, Woolston spent hundreds of hours seeking a suitable home for the defendant.

The agreement was in effect from January 11, 2011 until July 11, 2011, and set forth the geographical area that the defendant was interested in and the rate of compensation for the plaintiff's services. With respect to geographical area, the parties agreed that Woolston would seek properties in Killingworth, Guilford, Essex, Old Saybrook, Deep River, Lyme, and Old Lyme [Connecticut]. With respect to compensation, the defendant agreed to pay the plaintiff a commission equal to 2.5 percent of the purchase price of the property "if the [buyer] or any person or entity acting on the [buyer's] behalf purchases, options, exchanges, leases or trades any property, through the efforts of anyone, including the [buyer]." The agreement imposed the following duties on the defendant: "The [buyer] will not deal directly with any other broker, agent or licensee during the term of this agreement. The [buyer] will notify other brokers, agents or licensees at first contact that the [buyer] is being exclusively represented by [NRT]. The [buyer] will disclose to [NRT] any past and/or current contacts for any real property or with any other real estate broker or agent."

On May 10, 2011, the defendant informed Woolston via e-mail that he and Wiltshire purchased property at 300 Vineyard Point Road in Guilford for $1,375,000. The defendant learned of this property on May 4, 2011, from Mary Jane Burt, a realtor with H. Pearce Real Estate (H. Pearce), who previously had represented Wiltshire with the sale of her house in Hamden [Connecticut]. Woolston subsequently confronted the defendant and eventually learned that he

and Wiltshire previously had executed an exclusive right to represent buyer agreement with Burt and H. Pearce. This agreement was in effect from August 1, 2010, until August 1, 2011, and contained a provision designating Burt as the exclusive agent for the defendant and Wiltshire. Thus, at the time the defendant purchased the property in Guilford, he was under contract for exclusive agency with both Woolston and Burt. The defendant never told Woolston or Burt that he had two agreements in effect at the same time. Woolston notified her superiors of what had transpired.

* * * [NRT] filed a * * * complaint [in a Connecticut state court] against the defendant [for] breach of contract * * * . After a trial * * * , the court * * * found that the plaintiff had proven * * * breach of contract * * * and damages. * * * The court awarded the plaintiff $34,375 in damages [which represented 2.5 percent of the purchase price for the Vineyard Point property] plus attorney's fees and costs. This appeal followed.

* * * *

The defendant * * * claims that the agreement was unenforceable. Specifically, he argues that the court improperly * * * found that it was inequitable to deny the plaintiff recovery.

* * * *

There is ample evidence in the record to support the court's conclusion that denying the plaintiff relief would be inequitable. Woolston testified, and the defendant himself conceded, that she rendered a significant amount of services to the defendant over several months.

Case 17.2 Continues

Specifically, Woolston researched properties at town halls for availability and encumbrances, contacted property owners, arranged personal visits, prepared and presented literature to the defendant on available properties, and attended appointments with the defendant and Wiltshire. Woolston spent hundreds of hours working for the defendant in total.

The defendant, on the other hand, accepted Woolston's services while under contract with another agent in violation of the agreement. Indeed, the defendant acknowledged that he was untruthful with Woolston at the beginning of their relationship when he told her that he was not represented by another agent.

In fact, he was scheduling appointments and viewing properties with both Woolston and Burt at approximately the same time in May 2011. For example, the defendant e-mailed Woolston on May 2, 2011, thanking her for showing him a property. Approximately one week later, the defendant e-mailed Woolston to inform her that he viewed 300 Vineyard Point Road with Burt and had "put in an all cash bid that has been accepted."

The defendant nevertheless argues that it would not be inequitable to deny recovery to the plaintiff because Woolston performed no services in connection with his purchase of 300

Vineyard Point Road. We are not persuaded. *The defendant agreed to pay a commission "equal to 2.5% of the purchase price if the [buyer] or any person or entity acting on the [buyer's] behalf purchases * * * any property, through the efforts of anyone, including the [buyer], where an agreement to purchase the property was entered into during the term of this agreement."* However unjust this result may seem to the defendant in hindsight, we cannot say it is inequitable because it is precisely what he agreed to. [Emphasis added.]

* * * *

The judgment is affirmed.

Legal Reasoning Questions

1. What is the advantage to a principal of an exclusive agency agreement? What was the advantage to Jones of his agreement with Woolston? Discuss.

2. Why, in addition to damages, was the plaintiff awarded attorneys' fees and costs?

3. Jones's agreement with Woolston provided that on the purchase of the property, NRT "will, whenever feasible, seek compensation from the seller or the seller's agent." The court determined that it was not feasible. Why would it not be reasonable in this situation to ask the seller of the property to pay part of Woolston's commission?

Safe Working Conditions The common law requires the principal to provide safe working premises, equipment, and conditions for all agents and employees. The principal has a duty to inspect working areas and to warn agents and employees about any unsafe situations. When the agent is an employee, the employer's liability is frequently covered by state workers' compensation insurance. In addition, federal and state statutes often require the employer to meet certain safety standards.

17–3c Rights and Remedies of Agents and Principals

In general, for every duty of the principal, the agent has a corresponding right, and vice versa. When one party to the agency relationship violates his or her duty to the other party, the remedies available to the nonbreaching party arise out of contract and tort law. These remedies include monetary damages, termination of the agency relationship, injunctions, and required accountings.

The agent has the right to be compensated, to be reimbursed and indemnified, and to have a safe working environment. An agent also has the right to perform agency duties without interference by the principal. In addition, an agent can withhold further performance and demand that the principal give an accounting.

A principal has contract remedies for an agent's breach of fiduciary duties. The principal has tort remedies if the agent engages in misrepresentation, negligence, deceit, libel, slander, or trespass. In addition, any breach of a fiduciary duty by an agent may justify the principal's termination of the agency.

17–4 Agent's Authority

The liability of a principal to third parties with whom an agent contracts depends on whether the agent had the authority to enter into legally binding contracts on the principal's behalf. An agent's authority can be either *actual* (express or implied) or *apparent*. If an agent contracts outside the scope of his or her authority, the principal may still become liable by ratifying the contract.

17–4a Express Authority

Express authority is authority declared in clear, direct, and definite terms. Express authority can be given orally or in writing.

The Equal Dignity Rule In most states, the **equal dignity rule** requires that if the contract being executed is or must be in writing, then the agent's authority must also be in writing. (Recall that a writing includes an electronic record.) Failure to comply with the equal dignity rule can make a contract voidable *at the option of the principal.* The law regards the contract at that point as a mere offer. If the principal decides to accept the offer, the acceptance must be ratified, or affirmed, in writing.

■ **EXAMPLE 17.11** Paloma (the principal) orally asks Austin (the agent) to sell a ranch that Paloma owns. Austin finds a buyer and signs a sales contract on behalf of Paloma to sell the ranch. Because a contract for an interest in realty must be in writing, the equal dignity rule applies. The buyer cannot enforce the contract unless Paloma subsequently ratifies Austin's agency status *in a writing.* Once the sales contract is ratified, either party can enforce rights under the contract. ■

Modern business practice allows several exceptions to the equal dignity rule:

1. An executive officer of a corporation normally can conduct *ordinary* business transactions without obtaining written authority from the corporation.
2. When the agent acts in the presence of the principal, the rule does not apply.
3. When the agent's act of signing is merely a formality, then the agent does not need written authority to sign. ■ **EXAMPLE 17.12** Sandra Healy (the principal) negotiates a contract but is called out of town the day it is to be signed. If Healy orally authorizes Derek Santini to sign, the oral authorization is sufficient. ■

Power of Attorney Giving an agent a **power of attorney** confers express authority.[9] The power of attorney is a written document and is usually notarized. (A document is notarized when a **notary public**—a person authorized to attest to the authenticity of signatures—signs, dates, and imprints the document with her or his seal of authority.) Most states have statutory provisions for creating a power of attorney.

A power of attorney can be *special* (permitting the agent to perform specified acts only), or it can be *general* (permitting the agent to transact all business for the principal). Because a general power of attorney grants extensive authority to the agent, it should be used with great caution and usually only in exceptional circumstances. Ordinarily, a power of attorney terminates on the incapacity or death of the person giving the power.[10]

17–4b Implied Authority

An agent has the **implied authority** to do what is reasonably necessary to carry out express authority and accomplish the objectives of the agency. Authority can also be implied by custom or inferred from the position the agent occupies.

■ **EXAMPLE 17.13** Archer is employed by Packard Grocery to manage one of its stores. Packard has not expressly stated that Archer has authority to contract with third persons. Nevertheless, authority to manage a business implies authority to do what is reasonably required (as is customary or can be inferred from a manager's position) to operate the business. This includes forming contracts to hire employees, buying merchandise and equipment, and advertising the products sold in the store. ■

Note, however, that an agent's implied authority cannot contradict his or her express authority. Thus, if a principal has limited an agent's express authority, then the fact that the agent customarily would have such authority is irrelevant.

17–4c Apparent Authority

Actual authority (express or implied) arises from what the principal makes clear *to the agent.* Apparent authority, in contrast, arises from what the principal causes a third party to believe. An agent has **apparent authority** when the principal, by either word or action, causes a *third party* reasonably to believe that the agent has authority to act, even though the agent has no express or implied authority.

Apparent authority usually comes into existence through a principal's pattern of conduct over time. ■ **CASE IN POINT 17.14** Gilbert Church owned Church Farm, Inc., a horse-breeding farm in Illinois, which was managed by Herb Bagley. Church Farm's advertisements for the breeding rights to one of its stallions, Imperial Guard, directed all inquiries to "Herb Bagley, Manager." Vern and Gail Lundberg contacted Bagley and executed a preprinted contract giving them breeding rights to Imperial

---

9. An agent who holds a power of attorney is called an *attorney-in-fact* for the principal. The holder does not have to be an attorney-at-law (and often is not).

10. A *durable* power of attorney, however, continues to be effective despite the principal's incapacity or death. An elderly person, for instance, might grant a durable power of attorney to provide for the handling of property and investments or specific health-care needs should he or she become incompetent.

Guard "at Imperial Guard's location." Bagley handwrote a statement on the contract that guaranteed the Lundbergs "six live foals in the first two years." He then signed it "Gilbert G. Church by H. Bagley."

The Lundbergs bred four mares, which resulted in one live foal. Church then moved Imperial Guard from Illinois to Oklahoma. The Lundbergs sued Church for breaching the contract by moving the horse. Church claimed that Bagley was not authorized to sign contracts for Church or to change or add terms but only to present preprinted contracts to potential buyers. The jury found in favor of the Lundbergs and awarded $147,000 in damages. Church appealed, but the state appellate court affirmed the judgment. The court found that "an agent may bind his principal by acts which the principal has not given him actual authority to perform, but which he appears authorized to perform." Because Church allowed circumstances to lead the Lundbergs to believe Bagley had the authority, Church was bound by Bagley's actions.[11] ∎

17–4d Emergency Powers

When an unforeseen emergency demands action by the agent to protect or preserve the property and rights of the principal, but the agent is unable to communicate with the principal, the agent has emergency power. ∎ **EXAMPLE 17.15** Rob Fulsom is an engineer for Pacific Drilling Company. While Fulsom is acting within the scope of his employment, he is severely injured in an accident on an oil rig many miles from home. Acosta, the rig supervisor, directs Thompson, a physician, to give medical aid to Fulsom and to charge Pacific for the medical services.

Acosta, an agent, has no express or implied authority to bind the principal, Pacific Drilling, for Thompson's medical services. Because of the emergency situation, however, the law recognizes Acosta as having authority to act appropriately under the circumstances. ∎

17–4e Ratification

Ratification occurs when the principal affirms, or accepts responsibility for, an agent's *unauthorized* act. When ratification occurs, the principal is bound to the agent's act, and the act is treated as if it had been authorized by the principal *from the outset*. Ratification can be either express or implied.

If the principal does not ratify the contract, the principal is not bound, and the third party's agreement with the agent is viewed as merely an unaccepted offer. Because

the third party's agreement is an unaccepted offer, the third party can revoke it at any time, without liability, before the principal ratifies the contract. The agent, however, may be liable to the third party for misrepresenting her or his authority.

The requirements for ratification can be summarized as follows:

1. The agent must have acted on behalf of an identified principal who subsequently ratifies the action.
2. The principal must know all of the material facts involved in the transaction. If a principal ratifies a contract without knowing all of the facts, the principal can rescind (cancel) the contract.
3. The principal must affirm the agent's act in its entirety.
4. The principal must have the legal capacity to authorize the transaction at the time the agent engages in the act and at the time the principal ratifies. The third party must also have the legal capacity to engage in the transaction.
5. The principal's affirmation (ratification) must occur before the third party withdraws from the transaction.
6. The principal must observe the same formalities when ratifying the act as would have been required to authorize it initially.

17–5 Liability in Agency Relationships

Frequently, a question arises as to which party, the principal or the agent, should be held liable for contracts formed by the agent or for torts and crimes committed by the agent.

17–5a Liability for Contracts

Liability for contracts formed by an agent depends on how the principal is classified and on whether the actions of the agent were authorized or unauthorized. Principals are classified as disclosed, partially disclosed, or undisclosed.[12]

1. A **disclosed principal** is a principal whose identity is known by the third party at the time the contract is made by the agent.
2. A **partially disclosed principal** is a principal whose identity is not known by the third party. Nevertheless, the third party knows that the agent is or *may*

---

11. *Lundberg v. Church Farm, Inc.*, 502 N.E.2d 806, 151 Ill.App.3d (1986).

12. *Restatement (Third) of Agency*, Section 1.04(2).

be acting for a principal at the time the contract is made. ■ **EXAMPLE 17.16** Eileen has contracted with a real estate agent to sell certain property. She wishes to keep her identity a secret, but the agent makes it clear to potential buyers of the property that he is acting in an agency capacity. In this situation, Eileen is a partially disclosed principal. ■

3. An **undisclosed principal** is a principal whose identity is totally unknown by the third party. In addition, the third party has no knowledge that the agent is acting in an agency capacity at the time the contract is made.

Authorized Acts If an agent acts within the scope of her or his authority, normally the principal is obligated to perform the contract regardless of whether the principal was disclosed, partially disclosed, or undisclosed. Whether the *agent may also be held liable* under the contract, however, depends on the disclosed, partially disclosed, or undisclosed status of the principal.

Disclosed or Partially Disclosed Principal. A disclosed or partially disclosed principal is liable to a third party for a contract made by the agent. If the principal is disclosed, the agent has no contractual liability for the nonperformance of the principal or the third party. If the principal is partially disclosed, in most states the agent is also treated as a party to the contract. Thus, the third party can hold the agent liable for contractual nonperformance.[13]

■ **CASE IN POINT 17.17** Stonhard, Inc., makes epoxy and urethane flooring and installs it in industrial and commercial buildings. Marvin Sussman contracted with Stonhard to install flooring at a Blue Ridge Farms food-manufacturing facility in Brooklyn, New York. Sussman did not disclose that he was acting as an agent for the facility's owner, Blue Ridge Foods, LLC, at the time of the contract.

When Stonhard was not paid for the flooring it installed, it filed a suit against the facility, its owner, and Sussman to recover damages for breach of contract. The lower court dismissed the complaint against Sussman personally, but on appeal a reviewing court reversed that decision. The contract had been signed by Sussman "of Blue Ridge Farms." That evidence indicated that Sussman was acting as an agent for a partially disclosed principal, in that the agency relationship was known, but not the principal's identity. "As an agent for an undisclosed [or partially disclosed] principal, Sussman became personally liable under the contract."[14] ■

Undisclosed Principal. When neither the fact of an agency relationship nor the identity of the principal is disclosed, the undisclosed principal is bound to perform just as if the principal had been fully disclosed at the time the contract was made.

When a principal's identity is undisclosed and the agent is forced to pay the third party, the agent is entitled to be indemnified (compensated) by the principal. The principal had a duty to perform, even though his or her identity was undisclosed, and failure to do so will make the principal ultimately liable.

Once the undisclosed principal's identity is revealed, the third party generally can elect to hold either the principal or the agent liable on the contract. Conversely, the undisclosed principal can require the third party to fulfill the contract, *unless* one of the following is true:

1. The undisclosed principal was expressly excluded as a party in the written contract.
2. The contract is a negotiable instrument signed by the agent with no indication of signing in a representative capacity.[15]
3. The performance of the agent is personal to the contract, thus allowing the third party to refuse the principal's performance.

Unauthorized Acts If an agent has no authority but nevertheless contracts with a third party, the *principal* cannot be held liable on the contract. It does not matter whether the principal was disclosed, partially disclosed, or undisclosed. The *agent* is liable.

■ **EXAMPLE 17.18** Chu signs a contract for the purchase of a truck, purportedly acting as an agent under authority granted by Navarro. In fact, Navarro has not given Chu any such authority. Navarro refuses to pay for the truck, claiming that Chu had no authority to purchase it. The seller of the truck is entitled to hold Chu liable for payment. ■

If the principal is disclosed or partially disclosed, and the agent contracts with a third party without authorization, the agent is liable to the third party. The agent's liability here is based on his or her breach of the *implied warranty of authority,* not on the breach of the contract

---

13. *Restatement (Third) of Agency,* Section 6.02.

14. *Stonhard, Inc. v. Blue Ridge Farms, LLC,* 114 A.D.3d 757, 980 N.Y.S.2d 507 (2 Dept. 2014).

15. Under the Uniform Commercial Code (UCC), only the agent is liable if the instrument neither names the principal nor shows that the agent signed in a representative capacity [UCC 3–402(b)(2)].

itself.[16] An agent impliedly warrants that he or she has the authority to enter a contract on behalf of the principal. If the third party knows at the time the contract is made that the agent does not have authority—or if the agent expresses to the third party *uncertainty* as to the extent of her or his authority—the agent is not personally liable.

Actions by E-Agents Although in the past standard agency principles applied only to *human* agents, today these same agency principles also apply to e-agents. An electronic agent, or **e-agent,** is a semiautonomous software program that is capable of executing specific tasks, such as searching through many databases and retrieving relevant information for the user.

E-agents can enter into binding agreements on behalf of their principals. Thus, if consumers place an order over the Internet, and the company (principal) takes the order via an e-agent, the company cannot later claim that it did not receive the order.

17–5b Liability for Torts and Crimes

Obviously, any person, including an agent, is liable for his or her own torts and crimes. Whether a principal can also be held liable for an agent's torts and crimes depends on several factors, which we examine here. In some situations, a principal may be held liable not only for the torts of an agent but also for torts committed by an independent contractor.

Principal's Tortious Conduct A principal who acts through an agent may be liable for harm resulting from the principal's own negligence or recklessness. Thus, a principal may be liable if he or she gives improper instructions, authorizes the use of improper materials or tools, or establishes improper rules that result in the agent's committing a tort.

■ **EXAMPLE 17.19** Parker knows that Audrey's driver's license has been suspended but nevertheless tells her to use the company truck to deliver some equipment to a customer. If someone is injured as a result, Parker will be liable for his own negligence in instructing Audrey to drive without a valid license. ■

Principal's Authorization of Agent's Tortious Conduct Similarly, a principal who authorizes an agent to commit a tort may be liable to persons or property injured thereby, because the act is considered to be the principal's. ■ **EXAMPLE 17.20** Pedro directs his agent, Andy, to cut the corn on specific acreage, which neither of them has the right to do. The harvest is therefore a

trespass (a tort), and Pedro is liable to the owner of the corn. (Andy is also liable even if he did not know that Pedro lacked the right to harvest the corn.) ■

Liability for Agent's Misrepresentation A principal is exposed to tort liability whenever a third person sustains a loss due to the agent's misrepresentation. The principal's liability depends on whether the agent was actually or apparently authorized to make representations and whether the representations were made within the scope of the agency.

The principal is always directly responsible for an agent's misrepresentation made within the scope of the agent's authority. ■ **EXAMPLE 17.21** Ainsley is a demonstrator for Pavlovich's products. Pavlovich sends Ainsley to a home show to demonstrate the products and to answer questions from consumers. Pavlovich has given Ainsley authority to make statements about the products. If Ainsley makes only true representations, all is fine. But if he makes false claims, Pavlovich will be liable for any injuries or damages sustained by third parties in reliance on Ainsley's false representations. ■

When a principal has placed an agent in a position of apparent authority, the principal may also be liable for the agent's fraudulent acts. For instance, partners in a partnership generally have the apparent implied authority to act as agents of the firm. Thus, if one of the partners commits a tort or a crime, the partnership itself—and often the other partners personally—can be held liable for the loss.

Liability for Agent's Negligence An agent is liable for his or her own torts. A principal may also be liable for harm an agent causes to a third party under the doctrine of **respondeat superior,**[17] a Latin term meaning "let the master respond." Under the doctrine of *respondeat superior*, the principal-employer is liable for any harm caused to a third party by an agent-employee in the course or scope of employment. The doctrine imposes **vicarious liability,** or indirect liability, because the principal-employer is being held liable for torts committed by an agent-employee.

When an agent commits a negligent act in such a situation, *both* the agent and the principal are liable. ■ **EXAMPLE 17.22** Aegis hires SDI to provide landscaping services for its property. An herbicide sprayed by SDI employee David Hoggatt enters the Aegis building through the air-conditioning system and causes

---

16. The agent is not liable on the contract because the agent was never intended personally to be a party to the contract.

17. Pronounced ree-*spahn*-dee-uht soo-*peer*-ee-your. The doctrine of *respondeat superior* applies not only to employer-employee relationships but also to other principal-agent relationships in which the principal has the right of control over the agent.

Catherine Warner, an Aegis employee, to suffer a heart attack. If Warner sues, both SDI (principal) and Hoggatt (agent) can be held liable for negligence. ■

The doctrine of *respondeat superior* is similar to the theory of strict liability in that liability is imposed regardless of fault for reasons of public policy. Every person has a duty to manage his or her affairs so as not to injure another. This duty applies even when a person acts through an agent (controls the conduct of another).

Determining the Scope of Employment. The key to determining whether a principal may be liable for the torts of an agent under the doctrine of *respondeat superior* is whether the torts are committed within the scope of the agency. Courts may consider the following factors in determining whether a particular act occurred within the course and scope of employment:

1. Whether the employee's act was authorized by the employer.
2. The time, place, and purpose of the act.
3. Whether the act was one commonly performed by employees on behalf of their employers.
4. The extent to which the employer's interest was advanced by the act.
5. The extent to which the private interests of the employee were involved.
6. Whether the employer furnished the means or instrumentality (such as a truck or a machine) by which an injury was inflicted.
7. Whether the employer had reason to know that the employee would perform the act in question and whether the employee had done it before.
8. Whether the act involved the commission of a serious crime.

In the following case, the court had to determine whether or not a dump truck operator was the employee of a concrete services contractor.

Case 17.3

Asphalt & Concrete Services, Inc. v. Perry

Court of Special Appeals of Maryland, 221 Md.App. 235, 108 A.3d 558 (2015).

Background and Facts Asphalt & Concrete Services, Inc. (ACS), was working on a play pad at St. John Regional Catholic School in Frederick, Maryland. ACS project manager Blake Wood contacted William Johnson at Higher Power Trucking, LLC, to arrange for a dump truck to haul material from a quarry to the job site. One day, while Johnson was driving the dump truck between the job site and the quarry, the truck struck and injured Moran Perry, who was crossing an intersection.

To recover for his injuries, Perry filed a lawsuit in a Maryland state court against ACS. Perry alleged that Johnson's negligence in operating the dump truck was the proximate cause of his injuries and that Johnson was ACS's employee. ACS, however, claimed that Johnson was an independent contractor. A jury agreed with Perry and awarded him $529,500 in damages. The court issued a judgment in Perry's favor, and ACS appealed.

In the Language of the Court

GRAEFF, J. [Judge]

* * * *

* * * Pursuant to the doctrine of *respondeat superior,* an employer may be found liable for torts committed by its employee while acting in the scope of employment. ACS does not dispute this well-established rule, but it argues that the evidence showed that Mr. Johnson was not its employee.

* * * Maryland courts have traditionally considered five criteria in determining whether or not an employer/employee relationship exists between two parties. *These criteria, developed from the common law standard for determining the master/servant relationship, include (1) the power to select and hire the employee, (2) the payment of wages, (3) the power to discharge, (4) the power to control the employee's conduct, and (5) whether the work is part of the regular business of the employer.* [Emphasis added.]

Of the five factors, the factor of control stands out as the most important. * * * Whether the employer has the right to control and direct the employee in the performance of the work and in the manner in which the work is to be done is the decisive, or controlling, test.

* * * *

Case 17.3 Continues

Here, * * * the evidence indicated as follows: (1) ACS called Mr. Johnson directly to reserve his trucking services; (2) Mr. Wood spoke only to Mr. Johnson when calling Higher Power; (3) ACS directed Mr. Johnson to go to the * * * quarry to pick up materials for the play pad project and gave him the time to be there for the pick-up; (4) Mr. Johnson was required to bring the materials directly to the job site after his truck was loaded, and if Mr. Johnson did not deliver the materials promptly, ACS had the right to dock his pay or to no longer employ him; (5) ACS paid Mr. Johnson on an hourly basis from the time he picked up his first load until ACS dismissed him from the job site; (6) after Mr. Johnson delivered his first load of materials, ACS directed him to return to the quarry to pick up and bring back additional materials; and (7) at the job site, Mr. Johnson was obligated to follow ACS's directions in terms of where to drop the materials, how much material to drop, and how many times he would need to return to the quarry. Based on that evidence, a jury could find that Mr. Johnson was subject to ACS's control, and ACS was liable for Mr. Johnson's negligence pursuant to the doctrine of *respondeat superior.*

Decision and Remedy *The state intermediate appellate court affirmed the jury's finding with respect to Johnson's status as ACS's employee. The court disagreed, however, with the lower court's admission of certain evidence that may have influenced the jury's finding of proximate cause for Perry's injuries. As a result, the court reversed the judgment on this ground and remanded the case for a new trial.*

Critical Thinking
- **Economic** *Why did ACS contend that Johnson was not its employee? Discuss.*

The Distinction between a "Detour" and a "Frolic." A useful insight into the concept of "scope of employment" can be gained from Judge Baron Parke's classic distinction between a "detour" and a "frolic" in the case of *Joel v. Morison.*[18] In this case, the English court held that if a servant merely took a detour from his master's business, the master will be responsible. If, however, the servant was on a "frolic of his own" and not in any way "on his master's business," the master will not be liable.

■ **EXAMPLE 17.23** While driving his employer's vehicle to call on a customer, Mandel decides to stop at a store—which is three blocks off his route—to take care of a personal matter. As Mandel approaches the store, he negligently runs into a parked vehicle owned by Chan. In this situation, because Mandel's detour from the employer's business is not substantial, he is still acting within the scope of employment, and the employer is liable.

But suppose instead that Mandel decides to pick up a few friends in another city for cocktails and in the process negligently runs his vehicle into Chan's. In this situation, the departure from the employer's business is substantial—Mandel is on a "frolic" of his own. Thus, the employer normally will not be liable to Chan for damages. ■

An employee going to and from work or to and from meals usually is considered to be outside the scope of employment. If travel is part of a person's position, however, as it is for a traveling salesperson, then travel time is normally considered within the scope of employment.

Liability for Agent's Intentional Torts Most intentional torts that individuals commit have no relation to their employment, and their employers will not be held liable. Nevertheless, under the doctrine of *respondeat superior,* the employer can be liable for intentional torts that an employee commits within the course and scope of employment. For instance, a department store owner is liable when a security guard who is a store employee commits the tort of false imprisonment while acting within the scope of employment.

In addition, an employer who knows or should know that an employee has a propensity for committing tortious acts is liable for the employee's acts even if they would not ordinarily be considered within the scope of employment. ■ **EXAMPLE 17.24** Chaz, the owner of the Comedy Club, hires Alec as a bouncer for the club even though he knows that Alec has a history of arrests for criminal assault and battery. In this situation, Chaz may be liable if Alec viciously attacks a customer in the parking lot after hours. ■ An employer can also be liable for

---

18. 6 Car. & P. 501, 172 Eng.Rep. 1338 (1834).

permitting an employee to engage in reckless actions that can injure others.

Liability for Independent Contractor's Torts

Generally, an employer is not liable for physical harm caused to a third person by the negligent act of an independent contractor in the performance of the contract. This is because the employer does not have *the right to control* the details of an independent contractor's performance.

Courts make an exception to this rule when the contract involves unusually hazardous activities, such as blasting operations, the transportation of highly volatile chemicals, or the use of poisonous gases. In these situations, strict liability is imposed, and an employer cannot be shielded from liability merely by using an independent contractor.

Liability for Agent's Crimes

An agent is liable for his or her own crimes. A principal or employer normally is *not* liable for an agent's crime even if the crime was committed within the scope of authority or employment. An exception to this rule is made when the principal or employer participated in the crime by conspiracy or other action.

In addition, in some jurisdictions, a principal may be liable under specific statutes if an agent, in the course and scope of employment, violates certain regulations. For instance, a principal might be liable for an agent's violation of sanitation rules or regulations governing prices, weights, or the sale of liquor.

17–6 Termination of an Agency

Agency law is similar to contract law in that both an agency and a contract may be terminated by an act of the parties or by operation of law. Once the relationship between the principal and the agent has ended, the agent no longer has the right (*actual* authority) to bind the principal. For an agent's *apparent* authority to be terminated, though, third persons may also need to be notified that the agency has been terminated.

17–6a Termination by Act of the Parties

An agency may be terminated by certain acts of the parties, which are listed and described in Exhibit 17–3. When an agency agreement specifies the time period

EXHIBIT 17–3 Termination by Act of the Parties

METHOD	RULES	ILLUSTRATION
1. Lapse of Time.	Agency terminates automatically at the end of the stated time.	Page lists her property for sale with Alex, a real estate agent, for six months. The agency ends in six months.
2. Purpose Achieved.	Agency terminates automatically on the completion of the purpose for which it was formed.	Calvin, a cattle rancher, hires Abe as his agent in the purchase of fifty head of breeding stock. The agency ends when the cattle have been purchased.
3. Occurrence of a Specific Event.	Agency normally terminates automatically on the event's occurrence.	Meredith appoints Allen to handle her business affairs while she is away. The agency terminates when Meredith returns.
4. Mutual Agreement.	Agency terminates when both parties consent to end the agency relationship.	Linda and Greg agree that Greg will no longer be her agent in procuring business equipment.
5. At the Option of One Party (*revocation*, if by principal; *renunciation*, if by agent).	Either party normally has a right to terminate the agency relationship. Wrongful termination can lead to liability for breach of contract.	When Patrick becomes ill, he informs Alice that he is revoking her authority to be his agent.

during which the agency relationship will exist, the agency ends when that time period expires. If no definite time is stated, then the agency continues for a reasonable time and can be terminated at will by either party. What constitutes a reasonable time depends on the circumstances and the nature of the agency relationship.

The parties can, of course, mutually agree to end their agency relationship. In addition, as a general rule, either party can terminate the agency relationship without the agreement of the other. The act of termination is called *revocation* if done by the principal and *renunciation* if done by the agent. Note, however, that the terminating party may face liability if the termination is wrongful.

Wrongful Termination Although both parties have the *power* to terminate the agency, they may not always possess the *right* to do so. Wrongful termination can subject the canceling party to a lawsuit for breach of contract. ■ **EXAMPLE 17.25** Rawlins has a one-year employment contract with Munro to act as agent in return for $65,000. Munro has the *power* to discharge Rawlins before the contract period expires. But if he does so, he can be sued for breaching the contract, because he had no *right* to terminate the agency. ■

Even in an agency at will—in which either party may terminate at any time—the principal who wishes to terminate must give the agent *reasonable* notice. The notice must be at least sufficient to allow the agent to recoup his or her expenses and, in some situations, to make a normal profit.

Notice of Termination When the parties terminate an agency, it is the principal's duty to inform any third parties who know of the existence of the agency that it has been terminated. No particular form is required for notice of termination to be effective. The principal can personally notify the third party, or the party can learn of the termination through some other means. Although an agent's *actual authority* ends when the agency is terminated, an agent's *apparent authority* continues until the third party receives notice (from any source) that such authority has been terminated.

17–6b Termination by Operation of Law

Certain events terminate agency authority automatically because their occurrence makes it impossible for the agent to perform or improbable that the principal would continue to want performance. Note that when an agency terminates by operation of law, there is no duty to notify third persons.

1. *Death or insanity.* The general rule is that the death or insanity of either the principal or the agent automatically and immediately terminates an ordinary agency relationship.[19] Knowledge of the death or insanity is not required.
2. *Impossibility.* When the specific subject matter of an agency is destroyed or lost, the agency terminates. Similarly, when it is impossible for the agent to perform the agency lawfully because of a change in the law, the agency terminates.
3. *Changed circumstances.* Sometimes, an event occurs that has such an unusual effect on the subject matter of the agency that the agent can reasonably infer that the principal will not want the agency to continue. In such situations, the agency terminates. ■ **EXAMPLE 17.26** Baird hires Joslen to sell a tract of land for $40,000. Subsequently, Joslen learns that there is oil under the land and that the land is therefore worth $1 million. The agency and Joslen's authority to sell the land for $40,000 are terminated. ■
4. *Bankruptcy.* If either the principal or the agent petitions for bankruptcy, the agency is *usually* terminated. In certain circumstances, such as when the agent's financial status is irrelevant to the purpose of the agency, the agency relationship may continue.
5. *War.* When the principal's country and the agent's country are at war with each other, the agency is terminated.

---

19. An exception to this rule exists in the bank-customer relationship. A bank, as agent, can continue to exercise specific types of authority after the customer's death or insanity and can continue to pay checks drawn by the customer for ten days after death.

Reviewing: Agency Relationships in Business

James Blatt hired Marilyn Scott to sell insurance for the Massachusetts Mutual Life Insurance Company. Their contract stated, "Nothing in this contract shall be construed as creating the relationship of employer and employee." The contract was terminable at will by either party. Scott financed her own office and staff, was paid according to performance, had no taxes withheld from her checks, and could legally sell products of Massachusetts Mutual's competitors. Blatt learned that Scott was simultaneously selling insurance for Perpetual Life Insurance Corporation, one of Massachusetts Mutual's fiercest competitors. Blatt therefore withheld client contact information from Scott. Scott complained to Blatt that he was inhibiting her ability to sell insurance for Massachusetts Mutual. Blatt subsequently terminated their contract. Scott filed a suit in a New York state court against Blatt and Massachusetts Mutual. Scott claimed that she had lost sales for Massachusetts Mutual—and commissions—as a result of Blatt's withholding contact information from her. Using the information presented in the chapter, answer the following questions.

1. Who is the principal and who is the agent in this scenario? By which method was an agency relationship formed between Scott and Blatt?
2. What facts would the court consider most important in determining whether Scott was an employee or an independent contractor?
3. How would the court most likely rule on Scott's employee status? Why?
4. Which of the four duties that Blatt owed Scott in their agency relationship has probably been breached?

Debate This . . .   *The doctrine of* respondeat superior *should be modified to make agents solely liable for their tortious (wrongful) acts committed within the scope of employment.*

Terms and Concepts

agency 332	express authority 343	power of attorney 343
apparent authority 343	fiduciary 332	ratification 344
disclosed principal 344	implied authority 343	*respondeat superior* 346
e-agent 346	independent contractor 333	undisclosed principal 345
equal dignity rule 343	notary public 343	vicarious liability 346
exclusive agency 340	partially disclosed principal 344	

Issue Spotters

1. Winona contracted with XtremeCast, a broadcast media firm, to cohost an Internet-streaming sports program. Winona and XtremeCast signed a new contract for each episode. In each contract, Winona agreed to work a certain number of days for a certain salary. During each broadcast, Winona was free to improvise her performance. She had no other obligation to work for XtremeCast. Was Winona an independent contractor? (See *Agency Law.*)
2. Davis contracts with Estee to buy a certain horse on her behalf. Estee asks Davis not to reveal her identity. Davis makes a deal with Farmland Stables, the owner of the horse, and makes a down payment. Estee does not pay the rest of the price. Farmland Stables sues Davis for breach of contract. Can Davis hold Estee liable for whatever damages he has to pay? Why or why not? (See *Liability in Agency Relationships.*)

• **Check your answers to the Issue Spotters against the answers provided in Appendix B at the end of this text.**

Business Scenarios

17–1. Employee versus Independent Contractor. Stephen Hemmerling was a driver for the Happy Cab Co. Hemmerling paid certain fixed expenses and followed various rules relating to the use of the cab, the hours that could be worked, and the solicitation of fares, among other things. Rates were set by the state. Happy Cab did not withhold taxes from Hemmerling's pay. While driving the cab, Hemmerling was injured in an accident and filed a claim for workers' compensation benefits in a state court. Such benefits are not available to independent contractors. On what basis might the court hold that Hemmerling was an employee? Explain. (See *Agency Law.*)

17–2. *Respondeat Superior.* ABC Tire Corp. hires Arnez as a traveling salesperson and assigns him a geographic area and time schedule in which to solicit orders and service customers. Arnez is given a company car to use in covering the territory. One day, Arnez decides to take his personal car to cover part of his territory. It is 11:00 A.M., and Arnez has just finished calling on all customers in the city of Tarrytown. His next appointment is at 2:00 P.M. in the city of Austex, twenty miles down the road. Arnez starts out for Austex, but halfway there he decides to visit a former college roommate who runs a farm ten miles off the main highway. Arnez is enjoying his visit with his former roommate when he realizes that it is 1:45 P.M. and that he will be late for the appointment in Austex. Driving at a high speed down the country road to reach the main highway, Arnez crashes his car into a tractor, severely injuring Thomas, the driver of the tractor. Thomas claims that he can hold ABC Tire Corp. liable for his injuries. Discuss fully ABC's liability in this situation. (See *Liability in Agency Relationships.*)

Business Case Problems

17–3. Liability for Contracts. Thomas Huskin and his wife entered into a contract to have their home remodeled by House Medic Handyman Service. Todd Hall signed the contract as an authorized representative of House Medic. It turned out that House Medic was a fictitious name for Hall Hauling, Ltd. The contract did not indicate this, however, and Hall did not inform the Huskins about Hall Hauling. When a contract dispute later arose, the Huskins sued Todd Hall personally for breach of contract. Can Hall be held personally liable? Why or why not? [*Huskin v. Hall*, 2012 WL 553136 (Ohio Ct.App. 2012)] (See *Liability in Agency Relationships.*)

17–4. Agent's Duties to Principal. William and Maxine Miller were shareholders of Claimsco International, Inc. They filed a suit against the other shareholders, Michael Harris and Kenneth Hoxie, and the accountant who worked for all of them—John Verchota. Among other things, the Millers alleged that Verchota had breached a duty that he owed them. They claimed that at Harris's instruction, Verchota had taken various actions that placed them at a disadvantage to the other shareholders. Verchota had allegedly adjusted Claimsco's books to maximize the Millers' financial liabilities, for instance, and had falsely reported distributions of income to them without actually transferring that income. Which duty are the Millers referring to? If the allegations can be proved, did Verchota breach this duty? Explain. [*Miller v. Harris*, 2013 IL App (2d) 120512, 985 N.E.2d 671 (2 Dist. 2013)] (See *Duties of Agents and Principals.*)

17–5. Business Case Problem with Sample Answer—Determining Employee Status. Nelson Ovalles worked as a cable installer for Cox Rhode Island Telecom, LLC, under an agreement with a third party, M&M Communications, Inc. The agreement stated that no employer-employee relationship existed between Cox and M&M's technicians, including Ovalles. Ovalles was required to designate his affiliation with Cox on his work van, clothing, and identification badge. Cox had minimal contact with him, however, and had limited power to control how he performed his duties. Cox supplied cable wire and similar items, but the equipment was delivered to M&M, not to Ovalles. On a workday, while Ovalles was fulfilling a work order, his van rear-ended a car driven by Barbara Cayer. Is Cox liable to Cayer? Explain. [*Cayer v. Cox Rhode Island Telecom, LLC,* 85 A.3d 1140 (R.I. 2014)] (See *Agency Law.*)

- **For a sample answer to Problem 17–5, go to Appendix C at the end of this text.**

17–6. Agent's Authority. Terry Holden's stepmother, Rosie, was diagnosed with amyotrophic lateral sclerosis (ALS), and Terry's wife, Susan, became Rosie's primary caregiver. Rosie executed a durable power of attorney appointing Susan as her agent. Susan opened a joint bank account with Rosie at Bank of America, depositing $9,643.62 of Rosie's funds. Susan used some of the money to pay for "household expenses to keep us going while we were taking care of her." Rosie died three months later. Terry's father, Charles, as executor of Rosie's estate, filed a petition in a Texas state court against Susan for an accounting. What general duty did Susan owe Rosie as her agent? What does an agent's duty of accounting require? Did Susan breach either of these duties? Explain. [*Holden v. Holden,* 456 S.W.3d 642 (Tex.App.—Tyler 2015)] (See *Agent's Authority.*)

17–7. Scope of Agent's Authority. Kindred Nursing Centers East, LLC, owns and operates Whitesburg Gardens, a long-term care and rehabilitation facility, in Huntsville, Alabama. Lorene Jones was admitted to the facility following knee-replacement surgery. Jones's daughter, Yvonne Barbour, signed the admission forms required by Whitesburg Gardens as her mother's representative in her presence. Jones did not object. The forms included an "Alternative Dispute Resolution Agreement," which provided for binding arbitration in the event of a dispute between "the Resident" (Jones) and "the Facility" (Whitesburg Gardens). Six days later, Jones was transferred to a different facility. After recovering from the surgery, she filed a suit in an Alabama state court against Kindred, alleging substandard care on a claim of negligence. Can Jones be compelled to submit her claim to arbitration? Explain. [*Kindred Nursing Centers East, LLC v. Jones,* __ So.3d __, 2016 WL 762450 (Ala. 2016)] (See *Agent's Authority.*)

17–8. Agency Relationships. Standard Oil of Connecticut, Inc., sells home heating, cooling, and security systems. Standard schedules installation and service appointments with its customers and then contracts with installers and technicians to do the work. The company requires an installer or technician to complete a project by a certain time but to otherwise "exercise independent judgment and control in the execution of any work." The installers and technicians are licensed and certified by the state. Standard does not train them, provide instruction manuals, supervise them at customers' homes, or inspect their work. The installers and technicians use their own equipment and tools, and they can choose which days they work. Standard pays a set rate per project. According to criteria used by the courts, are these installers and technicians independent contractors or employees? Why?

[*Standard Oil of Connecticut, Inc. v. Administrator, Unemployment Compensation Act,* 320 Conn. 611, 134 A.3d 581 (2016)] (See *Agency Law.*)

17–9. A Question of Ethics—Vicarious Liability. *Jamie* *Paliath worked as a real estate agent for Home Town Realty of Vandalia, LLC (the principal, a real estate broker). Torri Auer, a California resident, relied on Paliath's advice and assistance to buy three rental properties in Ohio. Before the sales, Paliath had represented that each property was worth approximately twice as much as what Auer would pay and that there was a waiting list of prospective tenants. Paliath also stated that all of the property needed work and agreed to do the work for a specified price. Nearly a year later, substantial work was still needed, and only a few of the units had been rented. Auer sued Paliath and Home Town Realty for fraudulent misrepresentation. [Auer v. Paliath, 140 Ohio St.3d 276, 17 N.E.3d 561, 2014-Ohio-3632 (2014)]* (See *Liability for Torts and Crimes.*)

(a) Were Paliath's representations to Auer within the scope of her employment? Explain. Will the court hold the principal (Home Town Realty) liable for the misrepresentations of the agent (Paliath)?

(b) What is the ethical basis for imposing vicarious liability on a principal for an agent's tort?

Legal Reasoning Group Activity

17–10. Agent's Duties to Principal. John Warren wanted to buy a condominium in California. Hildegard Merrill was the agent for the seller. Because Warren's credit rating was poor, Merrill told him he needed a co-borrower to obtain a mortgage at a reasonable rate. Merrill said that her daughter Charmaine would "go on title" until the loan and sale were complete if Warren would pay her $10,000. Merrill also offered to defer her commission on the sale as a loan to Warren so that he could make a 20 percent down payment on the property. He agreed to both plans.

Merrill secured the mortgage in Charmaine's name alone by misrepresenting her daughter's address, business, and income.

To close the sale, Merrill had Warren remove his name from the title to the property. In October, Warren moved into the condominium, repaid Merrill the amount of her deferred commission, and began paying the mortgage. Within a few months, Merrill had Warren evicted. Warren subsequently filed a suit against Merrill and Charmaine. (See *Duties of Agents and Principals.*)

(a) The first group will determine who among these parties was in an agency relationship.

(b) The second group will discuss the basic duty that an agent owes a principal and decide whether that duty was breached here.

MILLER

CHAPTER 18

Small Businesses and Limited Liability Companies

A goal of many business students is to become an **entrepreneur,** one who initiates and assumes the financial risk of a new business enterprise and undertakes to provide or control its management. One of the first decisions an entrepreneur must make is which form of business organization will be most appropriate for the new endeavor.

In selecting an organizational form, the entrepreneur will consider a num-

ber of factors. These include (1) ease of creation, (2) the liability of the owners, (3) tax considerations, and (4) the ability to raise capital. Keep these factors in mind as you read this chapter and the next one and learn about the various forms of business organization. Remember, too, in considering these business forms that the primary motive of an entrepreneur is to make profits.

Traditionally, entrepreneurs have used three major business forms—the sole proprietorship, the partnership, and the corporation. In this chapter, we look at two of these—sole proprietorships and partnerships. We also examine the limited liability company, a relatively new and increasingly popular form of business enterprise.

18–1 General Considerations for Small Businesses

Most small businesses begin as sole proprietorships. Once the business is under way, the sole proprietorship form may become too limited. The owner and any additional investors may then want to establish a more formal organization, such as a partnership, a limited liability company (LLC), or a corporation. These forms of business limit the owner's personal liability, or legal responsibility, for business debts and obligations. Each business form has its own advantages and disadvantages, but legal limited liability generally is necessary for those who wish to raise outside capital.

18–1a Requirements for All Business Forms

Any business, whatever its form, has to meet a variety of legal requirements, which typically relate to the following:

1. Business name registration.
2. Occupational licensing.
3. State tax registration (for instance, to obtain permits for collecting and remitting sales taxes).

4. Health and environmental permits.
5. Zoning and building codes.
6. Import/export regulations.

If the business has employees, the owner must also comply with a host of laws governing the workplace.

18–1b Protecting Intellectual Property

Protecting rights in intellectual property is a central concern for many small businesses. For instance, software companies and app developers depend on their copyrights and patents to protect their investments in the research and development required to create new programs. Without copyright or patent protection, a competitor or a customer could simply copy the software or app.

Trademarks Choosing a trademark or service mark and making sure that it is protected under trademark law can be crucial to the success of a new business venture. Indeed, a factor to consider in choosing a name for a business entity is whether the business name will be used as a trademark. The general rule is that a trademark cannot be the same as another's mark or so similar that confusion might result.

For the most protection, trademarks should be registered with the U.S. Patent and Trademark Office (PTO). If the mark is federally registered, the owner may use the symbol ® with the mark. This well-known symbol puts others on notice of the registration and helps to prevent trademark infringement. An owner who has not registered can use the symbol ™. Registration with the PTO should be renewed five years after the initial registration and at ten-year intervals thereafter.

Trade Secrets Much of the value of a small business may lie in its trade secrets, such as information about product development, production processes and techniques, and customer lists. Preserving the secrecy of the information is necessary for legal protection.

As a practical matter, trade secrets must be divulged to key employees. Thus, any business runs the risk that those employees might disclose the secrets to competitors—or even set up competing businesses themselves.

To protect their trade secrets, companies may require employees who have access to trade secrets to agree in their employment contracts never to divulge those secrets. A small business may also choose to include a covenant not to compete in an employment contract. A noncompete clause will help to protect against the possibility that a key employee will go to work for a competitor or set up a competing business.

18–1c Obtaining Loans

Raising capital is critical to the growth of most small businesses. In the early days of a business, the sole proprietor may be able to contribute sufficient capital, but as the business becomes successful, more funds may be needed. The owner may want to raise capital from external sources to expand the business. One way to do this is to borrow funds.

Obtaining a bank loan is beneficial for small businesses because it allows the owner to retain full ownership and control of the business. Note, though, that the bank may place some restrictions on future business decisions as a condition of granting the loan. In addition, bank loans may not be available for some businesses. Banks are usually reluctant to lend significant sums to businesses that are not yet established. Even if a bank is willing to make such a loan, the bank may require personal guaranty contracts from the owner, putting the owner's personal assets at risk.

Loans with desirable terms may be available from the U.S. Small Business Administration (SBA). One SBA program provides loans of up to $25,000 to businesspersons who are women, low-income individuals, or members of minority groups. Be aware that the SBA requires business owners to put some of their own funds at risk in the business. In addition, many states offer small-business grants to individuals starting a business.

18–2 Sole Proprietorships

In the earliest stages, as mentioned, a small business may operate as a **sole proprietorship,** which is the simplest form of business. In this form, the owner is the business. Thus, anyone who does business without creating a separate business organization has a sole proprietorship. The law considers all new, single-owner businesses to be sole proprietorships unless the owner affirmatively adopts some other form.

More than two-thirds of all U.S. businesses are sole proprietorships. Sole proprietors can own and manage any type of business from an informal home-office or Web-based undertaking to a large restaurant or construction firm. About 99 percent of the sole proprietorships in the United States have revenues of less than $1 million per year.

18–2a Advantages of the Sole Proprietorship

A major advantage of the sole proprietorship is that the proprietor owns the entire business and receives all of the profits (because she or he assumes all of the risk). In addition, starting a sole proprietorship is easier and less costly than starting any other kind of business because few legal formalities are required. Generally, no documents need to be filed with the government to start a sole proprietorship.[1]

Taxes A sole proprietor pays only personal income taxes (including Social Security and Medicare taxes) on the business's profits. The profits are reported as personal income on the proprietor's personal income tax return. In other words, the business itself need not file an income tax return. Sole proprietors are allowed to establish retirement accounts that are tax-exempt until the funds are

---

1. Although starting a sole proprietorship involves fewer legal formalities than other business organizational forms, even a small sole proprietorship may need to comply with zoning requirements, obtain a state business license, and the like.

withdrawn. Like any form of business enterprise, a sole proprietorship can be liable for other taxes, such as those collected and applied to the disbursement of unemployment compensation.

Flexibility A sole proprietorship offers more flexibility than does a partnership or a corporation. The sole proprietor is free to make any decision she or he wishes concerning the business—including what kind of business to pursue, whom to hire, and when to take a vacation. The sole proprietor can sell or transfer all or part of the business to another party at any time without seeking approval from anyone else. In contrast, approval is typically required from partners in a partnership and from shareholders in a corporation.

18–2b Disadvantages of the Sole Proprietorship

The major disadvantage of the sole proprietorship is that the proprietor alone bears the burden of any losses or liabilities incurred by the business enterprise. In other words, the sole proprietor has unlimited liability for all obligations that arise in doing business. Any lawsuit against the business or its employees can lead to unlimited personal liability for the owner of a sole proprietorship.

■ **EXAMPLE 18.1** Aaron and Melissa Klein, owners of the Sweet Cakes by Melissa bakery, refused to bake a wedding cake for a same-sex couple's wedding. They claimed that their religious beliefs did not allow them to provide services for same-sex ceremonies. The Oregon State Bureau of Labor and Industries argued that their decision violated the law. In 2015, an administrative law judge ruled against the Kleins' motion to dismiss and ordered them to pay $135,000 in damages. As sole proprietors, the Kleins were personally responsible for paying the damages. ■

Creditors can pursue the owner's personal assets to satisfy any business debts. Although sole proprietors may obtain insurance to protect the business, liability can easily exceed policy limits. This unlimited liability is a major factor to be considered in choosing a business form.

The sole proprietorship also has the disadvantage of lacking continuity after the death of the proprietor. When the owner dies, so does the business—it is automatically dissolved.

Another disadvantage is that in raising capital, the proprietor is limited to his or her personal funds and any loans that he or she can obtain for the business. Lenders may be unwilling to make loans to sole proprietorships,

particularly start-ups, because the sole proprietor risks unlimited personal liability and may not be able to pay. (See this chapter's *Digital Update* feature for a discussion of one court's refusal to discharge a loan made to a sole proprietor who had declared bankruptcy.)

18–3 Partnerships

Partnerships are governed both by common law concepts—in particular, those relating to agency—and by statutory law. As in so many other areas of business law, the National Conference of Commissioners on Uniform State Laws has drafted uniform laws for partnerships, and these have been widely adopted by the states.

The Uniform Partnership Act (UPA) governs the operation of partnerships *in the absence of express agreement* and has done much to reduce controversies in the law relating to partnerships. A majority of the states have enacted the most recent version of the UPA (introduced in 1997 and last amended in 2013).

The UPA defines a **partnership** as "an association of two or more persons to carry on as co-owners a business for profit" [UPA 101(6)]. Note that the UPA's definition of *person* includes corporations, so a corporation can be a partner in a partnership [UPA 101(10)]. The *intent* to associate is a key element of a partnership, and one cannot join a partnership unless all other partners consent [UPA 401(i)].

18–3a Essential Elements of a Partnership

Conflicts sometimes arise over whether a business enterprise is a legal partnership, especially when there is no formal, written partnership agreement. To determine whether a partnership exists, courts usually look for the following three essential elements, which are implicit in the UPA's definition:

1. A sharing of profits or losses.
2. A joint ownership of the business.
3. An equal right to be involved in the management of the business.

If the evidence in a particular case is insufficient to establish all three factors, the UPA provides a set of guidelines to be used.

The Sharing of Profits and Losses The sharing of both profits and losses from a business creates a *presumption* that a partnership exists. ■ **EXAMPLE 18.2** Syd and Drake start a business that sells fruit smoothies near

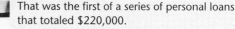

A Sole Proprietorship, Facebook Poker, and Bankruptcy

One major downside of a sole proprietorship is that it is more difficult for a sole proprietor to obtain funding for start-up and expansion. Moreover, if funding is obtained through loans, the sole proprietor is exposed to personal liability.

Personal Liability Exposure for an Online Startup

A case in point went before the United States bankruptcy court in Massachusetts in 2015.[a] Michael Dewhurst, living in Raynham, Massachusetts, sometimes did computer work for Gerald Knappik. Dewhurst decided to start a new business venture—the commercial development of a Facebook poker-playing application. Dewhurst envisioned an application that would enable multiple individuals to play poker together over the Internet through Facebook. Dewhurst informed Knappik of his business plan and predicted that his Facebook poker application "was going to be something very big."

Knappik initially loaned $50,000 to Dewhurst for the project. The loan agreement stated, "The sole purpose of this loan agreement is to provide funds on a personal level for the startup of said business project, in conjunction with borrower's personal funds, not limited to startup costs, operating expenses, advertising costs."

That was the first of a series of personal loans that totaled $220,000.

Dewhurst had repaid only $9,000 on the total outstanding debt when he filed for bankruptcy. Ultimately, the bankruptcy court ascertained that at least $120,000 of the loans that were supposed to be used exclusively for the Facebook poker project had been used for other activities. Furthermore, Dewhurst kept "no contemporaneous records of his disbursements and uses of this cash, no cash journal, ledger, or disbursement slips of any kind."

The Lender Objects to a Bankruptcy Discharge of Monies Owed

During bankruptcy proceedings, Knappik requested that the bankruptcy court deny discharge of Dewhurst's debts to him. Upon review, the court stated that "Dewhurst's failure to keep and preserve adequate records makes it impossible to reconstruct an accurate and complete account of financial affairs and business transactions." The bankruptcy judge ultimately denied discharge of $120,000 of the debt owed to Knappik. Thus, a sole proprietor's failed attempt to create an online poker-playing application led to personal liability even after he had filed for bankruptcy.

Critical Thinking *Sole proprietorships, as well as other businesses, routinely seek funding for online projects. How can the individuals involved avoid personal liability?*

a. *In re Dewhurst*, 528 Bankr. 211 (D.Mass. 2015).

---

a college campus. They open a joint bank account, from which they pay for supplies and expenses, and they share the proceeds (and losses) that the smoothie stand generates. If a conflict arises as to their business relationship, a court will assume that a partnership exists unless the parties prove otherwise. ∎

A court will not presume that a partnership exists, however, if shared profits were received as payment of any of the following [UPA 202(c)(3)]:

1. A debt by installments or interest on a loan.
2. Wages of an employee or compensation for the services of an independent contractor.
3. Rent to a landlord.
4. An annuity to a surviving spouse or representative of a deceased partner.

5. A sale of the **goodwill** (the valuable reputation of a business viewed as an intangible asset) of a business or property.

Joint Property Ownership Joint ownership of property does not in and of itself create a partnership [UPA 202(c)(1) and (2)]. The parties' intentions are key. ∎ **EXAMPLE 18.3** Chiang and Burke jointly own farmland and lease it to a farmer for a share of the profits from the farming operation in lieu of fixed rental payments. This arrangement normally would not make Chiang, Burke, and the farmer partners. ∎

At common law, a partnership was treated only as an aggregate of individuals and never as a separate legal entity. Today, in contrast, a majority of the states follow the UPA and treat a partnership as an entity for most purposes. As an entity, a partnership may hold the title to real or personal property in its name rather than in the names of the individual partners.

18–3b Tax Treatment of Partnerships

Modern law does treat a partnership as an aggregate of the individual partners rather than as a separate legal entity in one situation—for federal income tax purposes. The partnership is a pass-through entity and not a taxpaying entity. A **pass-through entity** is a business entity that has no tax liability. The entity's income is passed through to the owners, who pay income taxes on it.

Thus, the income or losses the partnership incurs are "passed through" the entity framework and attributed to the partners on their individual tax returns. The partnership itself pays no taxes and is responsible only for filing an **information return** with the Internal Revenue Service.

A partner's profit from the partnership (whether distributed or not) is taxed as individual income to the individual partner. Similarly, partners can deduct a share of the partnership's losses on their individual tax returns (in proportion to their partnership interests).

18–3c Partnership Formation

A partnership is a voluntary association of individuals. As such, it is formed by the agreement of the partners. As a general rule, agreements to form a partnership can be *oral, written,* or *implied by conduct.* Some partnership agreements, however, such as one authorizing partners to transfer interests in real property, must be in writing to be legally enforceable.

A partnership agreement, also known as **articles of partnership,** can include almost any terms that the parties wish, unless they are illegal or contrary to public policy or statute [UPA 103]. The rights and duties of partners are governed largely by the specific terms of their partnership agreement. In the absence of provisions to the contrary in the partnership agreement, the law imposes certain rights and duties, as discussed in the following subsections. The character and nature of the partnership business generally influence the application of these rights and duties.

Duration of the Partnership The partnership agreement can specify the duration of the partnership by stating that it will continue until a designated date or until the completion of a particular project. This is called a *partnership for a term.* If no fixed duration is specified, the partnership is a *partnership at will.* A partnership at will can be dissolved at any time without liability.

Partnership by Estoppel When a third person has reasonably and detrimentally relied on the representation that a nonpartner was part of a partnership, a court may conclude that a **partnership by estoppel** exists. In this situation, a court may impose liability—but not partnership rights—on the alleged partner.

A partnership by estoppel may also be imposed when a partner represents, expressly or impliedly, that a nonpartner is a member of the firm. In this situation, the nonpartner may be regarded as an agent whose acts are binding on the partnership [UPA 308].

■ **CASE IN POINT 18.4**   Jackson Paper Manufacturing Company made paper used by Stonewall Packaging, LLC. Jackson and Stonewall had officers and directors in common, and they shared employees, property, and equipment. In reliance on Jackson's business reputation, Best Cartage, Inc., agreed to provide transportation services for Stonewall and bought thirty-seven tractor-trailers to use in fulfilling the contract. Best provided the services until Stonewall terminated the agreement.

Best filed a suit for breach of contract against Stonewall and Jackson, seeking $500,678 in unpaid invoices and consequential damages of $1,315,336 for the tractor-trailers it had purchased. Best argued that Stonewall and Jackson had a partnership by estoppel. The court agreed, finding that "defendants combined labor, skills, and property to advance their alleged business partnership." Jackson had negotiated the agreement on Stonewall's behalf. Jackson also had bought real estate, equipment, and general supplies for Stonewall with no expectation that Stonewall would repay these expenditures. This was sufficient to prove a partnership by estoppel.[2] ■

18–3d Rights of Partners

The rights of partners in a partnership relate to the following areas: management, interest in the partnership, compensation, inspection of books, accounting, and property.

Management In a general partnership, all partners have equal rights in managing the partnership [UPA 401(f)]. Unless the partners agree otherwise, each partner has one vote in management matters *regardless of the proportional size of his or her interest in the firm.* In a large partnership, partners often agree to delegate daily management responsibilities to a management committee made up of one or more of the partners.

---

2. *Best Cartage, Inc. v. Stonewall Packaging, LLC,* 727 S.E.2d 291 (N.C.App. 2012).

The majority rule controls decisions on ordinary matters connected with partnership business, unless otherwise specified in the agreement. Decisions that significantly change the nature of the partnership or that are outside the ordinary course of the partnership business, however, require the *unanimous* consent of the partners [UPA 301(2), 401(i), 401(j)]. For instance, unanimous consent is likely required for a partnership to admit new partners, to amend the partnership agreement, or to enter a new line of business.

Interest in the Partnership Each partner is entitled to the proportion of business profits and losses that is specified in the partnership agreement. If the agreement does not apportion profits (indicate how the profits will be shared), the UPA provides that profits will be shared equally. If the agreement does not apportion losses, losses will be shared in the same ratio as profits [UPA 401(b)].

■ **EXAMPLE 18.5** The partnership agreement between Rick and Brett provides for capital contributions of $60,000 from Rick and $40,000 from Brett. If the agreement is silent as to how Rick and Brett will share profits or losses, they will share both profits and losses equally.

In contrast, if the agreement provides for profits to be shared in the same ratio as capital contributions, 60 percent of the profits will go to Rick, and 40 percent will go to Brett. Unless the agreement provides otherwise, losses will be shared in the same ratio as profits. ■

A partner's creditor can petition a court for a **charging order** to attach the partner's *interest* in the partnership to satisfy the partner's obligation [UPA 502]. A partner's interest in the partnership includes her or his proportionate share of any profits that are distributed. A partner can also assign her or his right to receive a share of the partnership profits to another to satisfy a debt.

Compensation Devoting time, skill, and energy to partnership business is a partner's duty and generally is not a compensable service. Rather, as mentioned, a partner's income from the partnership takes the form of a distribution of profits according to the partner's share in the business.

Partners can, of course, agree otherwise. For instance, the managing partner of a law firm often receives a salary—in addition to her or his share of profits—for performing special administrative or managerial duties.

Inspection of the Books Partnership books and records must be kept accessible to all partners. Each partner has the right to receive full and complete information concerning the conduct of all aspects of partnership business [UPA 403]. Partners have a duty to provide the

information to the firm, which has a duty to preserve it and to keep accurate records.

The partnership books must be kept at the firm's principal business office (unless the partners agree otherwise). Every partner is entitled to inspect all books and records on demand and can make copies of the materials. The personal representative of a deceased partner's estate has the same right of access to partnership books and records that the decedent would have had [UPA 403].

Accounting An accounting of partnership assets or profits is required to determine the value of each partner's share in the partnership. An accounting can be performed voluntarily, or it can be compelled by court order. Under UPA 405(b), a partner has the right to bring an action for an accounting during the term of the partnership, as well as on the partnership's dissolution.

Property Property acquired *by* a partnership is the property of the partnership and not of the partners individually [UPA 203]. Partnership property includes all property that was originally contributed to the partnership and anything later purchased by the partnership or in the partnership's name (except in rare circumstances) [UPA 204].

A partner may use or possess partnership property only on behalf of the partnership [UPA 401(g)]. A partner is *not* a co-owner of partnership property and has no right to sell, mortgage, or transfer partnership property to another [UPA 501]. Because partnership property is owned by the partnership and not by the individual partners, the property cannot be used to satisfy the personal debts of individual partners.

18–3e Duties and Liabilities of Partners

The duties and liabilities of partners are derived from agency law. Each partner is an agent of every other partner and acts as both a principal and an agent in any business transaction within the scope of the partnership agreement.

Each partner is also a general agent of the partnership in carrying out the usual business of the firm "or business of the kind carried on by the partnership" [UPA 301(1)]. Thus, every act of a partner concerning partnership business and "business of the kind" and every contract signed in the partnership's name bind the firm.

Fiduciary Duties The fiduciary duties that a partner owes to the partnership and to the other partners are the duty of care and the duty of loyalty [UPA 404(a)]. Under the UPA, a partner's *duty of care* is limited to refraining from "grossly negligent or reckless conduct, intentional misconduct, or a knowing violation of law" [UPA 404(c)]. A partner is not liable to the partnership for simple negligence or honest errors in judgment in conducting partnership business.

The *duty of loyalty* requires a partner to account to the partnership for "any property, profit, or benefit" derived by the partner in the conduct of the partnership's business or from the use of its property. A partner must also refrain from competing with the partnership in business or dealing with the firm as an adverse party [UPA 404(b)].

The duty of loyalty can be breached by self-dealing, misusing partnership property, disclosing trade secrets, or usurping a partnership business opportunity. The following case is a classic example.

Meinhard v. Salmon

Court of Appeals of New York, 249 N.Y. 458, 164 N.E. 545 (1928).

Background and Facts Walter Salmon negotiated a twenty-year lease for the Hotel Bristol in New York City. To pay for the conversion of the building into shops and offices, Salmon entered into an agreement with Morton Meinhard to assume half of the cost. They agreed to share the profits and losses from the joint venture. (A *joint venture* is similar to a partnership but typically is created for a single project.) Salmon was to have the sole power to manage the building, however.

Less than four months before the end of the lease term, the building's owner, Elbridge Gerry, approached Salmon about a project to raze the converted structure, clear five adjacent lots, and construct a single building across the whole property. Salmon agreed and signed a new lease in the name of his own business, Midpoint Realty Company, without telling Meinhard. When Meinhard learned of the deal, he filed a suit in a New York state court against Salmon. The court ruled in Meinhard's favor, and Salmon appealed.

In the Language of the Court

CARDOZO, C.J. [Chief Justice]
* * * *

Joint adventurers, like copartners, owe to one another, while the enterprise continues, the duty of the finest loyalty. Many forms of conduct permissible in a work-a-day world for those acting at arm's length are forbidden to those bound by fiduciary ties. * * * Not honesty alone, but the punctilio [strictness in observance of details] of an honor the most sensitive, is then the standard of behavior. As to this there has developed a tradition that is unbending and inveterate [entrenched]. Uncompromising rigidity has been the attitude of courts * * * when petitioned to undermine the rule of undivided loyalty.

* * * The trouble about [Salmon's] conduct is that he excluded his coadventurer from any chance to compete, from any chance to enjoy the opportunity for benefit.

* * * The very fact that Salmon was in control with exclusive powers of direction charged him the more obviously with the duty of disclosure, [because] only through disclosure could opportunity be equalized.

* * * Authority is, of course, abundant that one partner may not appropriate to his own use a renewal of a lease, though its term is to begin at the expiration of the partnership. The lease at hand with its many changes is not strictly a renewal. Even so, the standard of loyalty for those in trust relations is without the fixed divisions of a graduated scale. * * * *A man obtaining [an] * * * opportunity * * * by the position he occupies as a partner is bound by his obligation to his copartners in such dealings not to separate his interest from theirs, but, if he acquires any benefit, to communicate it to them. Certain it is also that there may be no abuse of special opportunities growing out of a special trust as manager or agent.* [Emphasis added.]

* * * Very likely [Salmon] assumed in all good faith that with the approaching end of the venture he might ignore his coadventurer and take the extension for himself. He had given to the enterprise time

Case 18.1 Continued

and labor as well as money. He had made it a success. Meinhard, who had given money, but neither time nor labor, had already been richly paid. * * * [But] Salmon had put himself in a position in which thought of self was to be renounced, however hard the abnegation [self-denial]. He was much more than a coadventurer. He was a managing coadventurer. For him and for those like him the rule of undivided loyalty is relentless and supreme.

Decision and Remedy *The Court of Appeals of New York held that Salmon had breached his fiduciary duty by failing to inform Meinhard of the business opportunity and secretly taking advantage of it himself. The court granted Meinhard an interest "measured by the value of half of the entire lease."*

Impact of This Case on Today's Law *This classic case involved a joint venture, not a partnership. At the time, a member of a joint venture had only the duty to refrain from actively subverting the rights of the other members. The decision in this case imposed the highest standard of loyalty on joint-venture members. The duty is now the same in both joint ventures and partnerships. Courts today frequently quote the eloquent language used in this opinion when describing the standard of loyalty that applies to partnerships.*

Critical Thinking

* **What If the Facts Were Different?** *Suppose that Salmon had disclosed Gerry's proposal to Meinhard, who had said that he was not interested. Would the result in this case have been different? Explain.*

Waiver of Fiduciary Duties A partner's fiduciary duties may not be waived or eliminated in the partnership agreement. In fulfilling them, each partner must act consistently with the obligation of good faith and fair dealing [UPA 103(b), 404(d)]. The agreement can specify acts that the partners agree will violate a fiduciary duty.

Note that a partner may pursue his or her own interest without automatically violating these duties [UPA 404(e)]. The key is whether the partner disclosed the interest to the other partners. ■ **EXAMPLE 18.6** Jayne Trell, a partner at Jacoby & Meyers, owns a shopping mall. Trell may vote against a partnership proposal to open a competing mall, provided that she has fully disclosed her interest in the existing shopping mall to the other partners at the firm. ■ A partner cannot make secret profits or put self-interest before his or her duty to the interest of the partnership, however.

Authority of Partners The UPA affirms general principles of agency law that pertain to a partner's authority to bind a partnership in contract. If a partner acts within the scope of her or his authority, the partnership is legally bound to honor the partner's commitments to third parties.

A partner may also subject the partnership to tort liability under agency principles. When a partner is carrying on partnership business with third parties in the usual way, apparent authority exists, and both the partner and the firm share liability. The partnership will not be liable, however, if the third parties *know* that the partner has no such authority.

Limitations on Authority. A partnership may limit a partner's capacity to act as the firm's agent or transfer property on its behalf by filing a "statement of partnership authority" in a designated state office [UPA 105, 303]. Such limits on a partner's authority normally are effective only with respect to third parties who are notified of the limitation. (An exception is made in real estate transactions when the statement of authority has been recorded with the appropriate state office.)

The Scope of Implied Powers. The agency concepts relating to apparent authority, actual authority, and ratification apply to partnerships. The extent of implied authority generally is broader for partners than for ordinary agents, however.

In an ordinary partnership, the partners can exercise all implied powers reasonably necessary and customary to carry on that particular business. Some customarily implied powers include the authority to make warranties on goods in the sales business and the power to enter into contracts consistent with the firm's regular course of business.

■ **EXAMPLE 18.7** Jamie Schwab is a partner in a firm that operates a retail tire store. He regularly promises that "each tire will be warranted for normal wear for 40,000 miles." Because Schwab has authority to make warranties, the partnership is bound to honor the warranty. Schwab would not, however, have the authority to sell the partnership's office equipment or other property without the consent of all of the other partners. ■

Liability of Partners One significant disadvantage associated with a traditional partnership is that the partners are *personally* liable for the debts of the partnership. In most states, the liability is essentially unlimited, because the acts of one partner in the ordinary course of business subject the other partners to personal liability [UPA 305]. Note that normally the partnership's assets must be exhausted before creditors can reach the partners' individual assets, however.

Joint Liability. Each partner in a partnership generally is jointly liable for the partnership's obligations. **Joint liability** means that a third party must sue all of the partners as a group, but each partner can be held liable for the full amount. If, for instance, a third party sues one partner on a partnership contract, that partner has the right to demand that the other partners be sued with her or him. In fact, if the third party does not name all of the partners in the lawsuit, the assets of the partnership cannot be used to satisfy the judgment.

Joint and Several Liability. In the majority of the states, under UPA 306(a), partners are both jointly and severally (separately, or individually) liable for all partnership obligations. **Joint and several liability** means that a third party has the option of suing all of the partners together (jointly) or one or more of the partners separately (severally). All partners in a partnership can be held liable even if a particular partner did not participate in, know about, or ratify the conduct that gave rise to the lawsuit.

A judgment against one partner severally (separately) does not extinguish the others' liability. (Similarly, a release of one partner does not discharge the partners' several liability.) Those not sued in the first action normally may be sued subsequently, unless the court in the first action held that the partnership was in no way liable. If a plaintiff is successful in a suit against a partner or partners, he or she may collect on the judgment only against the assets of those partners named as defendants.

Indemnification. With joint and several liability, a partner who commits a tort can be required to indemnify (reimburse) the partnership for any damages it pays. Indemnification will typically be granted *unless* the tort was committed in the ordinary course of the partnership's business.

■ **EXAMPLE 18.8** Nicole Martin, a partner at Patti's Café, is working in the café's kitchen one day when her young son suffers serious injuries to his hands from a dough press. Her son, through his father, files a negligence lawsuit against the partnership. Even if the suit is successful and the partnership pays damages to Martin's son, the firm is not entitled to indemnification. Martin would not be required to indemnify the partnership because her negligence occurred in the ordinary course of the partnership's business (making food for customers). ■

Liability of Incoming Partners. A partner newly admitted to an existing partnership is not personally liable for any partnership obligations incurred *before* the person became a partner [UPA 306(b)]. In other words, the new partner's liability to existing creditors of the partnership is limited to her or his capital contribution to the firm.

■ **EXAMPLE 18.9** Smartclub, an existing partnership with four members, admits a new partner, Alex Jaff. He contributes $100,000 to the partnership. Smartclub has debts amounting to $600,000 at the time Jaff joins the firm. Although Jaff's capital contribution of $100,000 can be used to satisfy Smartclub's obligations, Jaff is not personally liable for partnership debts incurred before he became a partner. If, however, the partnership incurs additional debts after Jaff becomes a partner, he will be personally liable for those amounts, along with all the other partners. ■

18–3f Dissociation of a Partner

Dissociation occurs when a partner ceases to be associated in the carrying on of the partnership business. Dissociation normally entitles the partner to have his or her interest purchased by the partnership. It also terminates the partner's actual authority to act for the partnership and to participate in running its business.

Once dissociation occurs, the partnership may continue to do business without the dissociated partner.[3] If the partners no longer wish to (or are unable to) continue the business, the partnership may be terminated (dissolved).

Events That Cause Dissociation Under UPA 601, a partner can be dissociated from a partnership in any of the following ways:

1. By the partner's voluntarily giving notice of an "express will to withdraw." (When a partner gives notice of intent to withdraw, the remaining partners must decide whether to continue the partnership business. If they decide not to continue, the voluntary dissociation of a partner will dissolve the firm [UPA 801(1)].)

---

3. Under the previous version of the UPA, when a partner withdrew from a partnership, the partnership was considered dissolved, and the business had to end. The amended UPA dramatically changed the law governing partnership breakups by no longer requiring that a partnership end if one partner dissociates.

2. By the occurrence of an event specified in the partnership agreement.

3. By a unanimous vote of the other partners under certain circumstances, such as when a partner transfers substantially all of her or his interest in the partnership.

4. By order of a court or arbitrator if the partner has engaged in wrongful conduct that affects the partnership business. The court can order dissociation if a partner breached the partnership agreement or violated a duty owed to the partnership or to the other partners. Dissociation may also be ordered if the partner engaged in conduct that makes it "not reasonably practicable to carry on the business in partnership with the partner" [UPA 601(5)].

5. By the partner's declaring bankruptcy, assigning his or her interest in the partnership for the benefit of creditors, or becoming physically or mentally incapacitated, or by the partner's death.

Wrongful Dissociation A partner has the *power* to dissociate from a partnership at any time, but she or he may not have the *right* to do so. If the partner lacks the right to dissociate, then the dissociation is considered wrongful under the law [UPA 602]. When a partner's dissociation breaches a partnership agreement, for instance, it is wrongful.

A partner who wrongfully dissociates is liable to the partnership and to the other partners for damages caused by the dissociation. This liability is in addition to any other obligation of the partner to the partnership or to the other partners.

Effects of Dissociation On a partner's dissociation, his or her right to participate in the management and conduct of the partnership business terminates [UPA 603]. The partner's duty of loyalty also ends. A partner's duty of care continues only with respect to events that occurred before dissociation, unless the partner participates in winding up the partnership's business (discussed shortly).

Buyouts. After a partner's dissociation, his or her interest in the partnership must be purchased according to the rules in UPA 701. The **buyout price** is based on the amount that would have been distributed to the partner if the partnership had been wound up on the date of dissociation. Offset against the price are amounts owed by the partner to the partnership, including damages for wrongful dissociation.

Before entering into a partnership, partners may agree on how the assets will be valued and divided in the event that the partnership dissolves. This is called a **buy-sell agreement.** Such an agreement may eliminate costly negotiations or litigation later. Under UPA 701(a), if a partner's dissociation does not result in a dissolution of the partnership, a buyout of the partner's interest is mandatory.

Liability to Third Parties. For two years after a partner dissociates from a continuing partnership, the partnership may be bound by the acts of the dissociated partner based on apparent authority [UPA 702]. If a third party reasonably believed at the time of a transaction that the dissociated partner was still a partner, the partnership may be liable. Similarly, a dissociated partner may be liable for partnership obligations entered into during the two-year period following dissociation [UPA 703].

To avoid this possible liability, a partnership should notify its creditors, customers, and clients of a partner's dissociation. In addition, either the partnership or the dissociated partner can file a statement of dissociation in the appropriate state office to limit the dissociated partner's authority to ninety days after the filing [UPA 704]. Filing this statement helps to minimize the firm's potential liability for the former partner and vice versa.

18–3g Partnership Termination

The same events that cause dissociation can result in the end of the partnership if the remaining partners no longer wish to (or are unable to) continue the partnership business. A partner's departure will not necessarily end the partnership, though. Generally, the partnership can continue if the remaining partners consent [UPA 801].

The termination of a partnership is referred to as **dissolution,** which essentially means the commencement of the winding up process. **Winding up** is the actual process of collecting, liquidating, and distributing the partnership assets.

Dissolution Dissolution of a partnership generally can be brought about by acts of the partners, by operation of law, or by judicial decree [UPA 801]. Any partnership (including one for a fixed term) can be dissolved by the partners' agreement. If the partnership agreement states that it will dissolve on a certain event, such as a partner's death or bankruptcy, then the occurrence of that event will dissolve the partnership. A partnership for a fixed term or a particular undertaking is dissolved by operation of law at the expiration of the term or on the completion of the undertaking.

■ **CASE IN POINT 18.10** Clyde Webster, James Theis, and Larry Thomas formed T&T Agri-Partners Company to own and farm 180 acres in Christian County, Illinois. Under the partnership agreement, the firm was to continue until January 31, 2010, unless it was dissolved. The death of any partner would dissolve the partnership.

Webster died in 2002, but Theis and Thomas did not liquidate T&T and distribute its assets. Webster's estate, through its personal representative, Joseph Webster, filed a complaint in state court seeking to dissolve the partnership. The court ordered the partnership to be dissolved, but Theis and Thomas did not dissolve it.

In 2011, after a trial, the court found that the partnership had expired by its own terms on January 31, 2010, and again ordered the partnership dissolved. Theis and Thomas appealed, but the reviewing court affirmed. A partnership business cannot continue after one partner dies when the partnership agreement specified that the death of one partner would terminate the business.[4] ■

Any event that makes it unlawful for the partnership to continue its business will result in dissolution [UPA 801(4)]. Under the UPA, a court may order dissolution when it becomes obviously impractical for the firm to continue—for instance, if the business can only be operated at a loss [UPA 801(5)]

Winding Up and Distribution of Assets After dissolution, the partnership continues for the limited purpose of winding up the business. Each partner must exercise good faith. The partners cannot create new obligations on behalf of the partnership. They have authority only to complete transactions begun but not finished at the time of dissolution and to wind up the business of the partnership [UPA 803, 804(1)].

Duties and Compensation. Winding up includes collecting and preserving partnership assets, discharging liabilities (paying debts), and accounting to each partner for the value of his or her interest in the partnership. Partners continue to have fiduciary duties to one another and to the firm during this process.

UPA 401(h) provides that a partner is entitled to compensation for services in winding up partnership affairs above and apart from his or her share in the partnership profits. A partner may also receive reimbursement for expenses incurred in the process.

Creditors' Claims. Both creditors of the partnership and creditors of the individual partners can make claims on the partnership's assets. In general, partnership creditors share proportionately with the partners' individual creditors in the partners' assets, which include their interests in the partnership.

A partnership's assets are distributed according to the following priorities [UPA 807]:

1. Payment of debts, including those owed to partner and nonpartner creditors.
2. Return of capital contributions and distribution of profits to partners.

If the partnership's liabilities are greater than its assets, the partners bear the losses in the same proportion in which they shared the profits unless they have agreed otherwise.

18–4 The Limited Liability Company

A **limited liability company (LLC)** is a hybrid that combines the limited liability aspects of a corporation and the tax advantages of a partnership. The LLC has been available for only a few decades, but it has become the preferred structure for many small businesses.

LLCs are governed by state statutes, which vary from state to state. In an attempt to create more uniformity, the National Conference of Commissioners on Uniform State Laws issued the Uniform Limited Liability Company Act (ULLCA). Less than one-fifth of the states have adopted it, however. Thus, the law governing LLCs remains far from uniform.

Nevertheless, some provisions are common to most state statutes. We base our discussion of LLCs on these common elements.

18–4a The Nature of the LLC

LLCs share many characteristics with corporations. Like corporations, LLCs must be formed and operated in compliance with state law. Like the shareholders of a corporation, the owners of an LLC, who are called **members,** enjoy limited liability [ULLCA 303].[5]

Limited Liability of Members Members of LLCs are shielded from personal liability in most situations. In other words, the liability of members is normally limited to the amount of their investments.

An exception arises when a member has significantly contributed to the LLC's tortious conduct. ■ **CASE IN POINT 18.11** Randy Coley, the sole member and manager

---

4. *Estate of Webster v. Thomas,* 2013 IL App (5th) 120121-U, 2013 WL 164041 (2013).

5. Members of an LLC can also bring derivative actions, which you will read about in regard to corporations, on behalf of the LLC [ULLCA 101]. As with a corporate shareholder's derivative suit, any damages recovered go to the LLC, not to the members personally.

of East Coast Cablevision, LLC, installed cable television systems for many hotels and resorts. Coley established a DIRECTV Satellite Master Antenna Television (SMATV) account in the name of Massanutten Resort. The system provided programming to 168 timeshare units, as well as to the resort's bar, golf shop, lobbies, and waterpark. The bill for the resort's account was sent to (and paid by) East Coast Cablevision, which in turn billed the customers.

Over time, East Coast Cablevision began providing cable services to additional customers using the resort's SMATV account but did not pay DIRECTV for these other customers. Ultimately, another cable dealer affiliated with DIRECTV sued Coley for not paying for all of the DIRECTV programming transmissions that East Coast's customers had received. The court held that because Coley had played a direct role in the unauthorized transmissions, he could be held personally liable for them.[6] ■

When Liability May Be Imposed   The members of an LLC, like the shareholders in a corporation, can lose their limited personal liability in certain circumstances. For instance, when an individual guarantees payment of a business loan to the LLC, that individual is personally liable for the business's obligation. In addition, if an LLC member fails to comply with certain formalities, such as by commingling personal and business funds, a court can impose personal liability.

Under various principles of corporate law, courts may hold the owners of a business liable for its debts. On rare occasions, for instance, courts ignore the corporate structure ("pierce the corporate veil") to expose the shareholders to personal liability when it is required to achieve justice.

Similarly, courts will occasionally pierce the veil of an LLC to hold its members personally liable in circumstances that are clearly extraordinary. There must normally be some flagrant disregard of the LLC formalities, as well as fraud or malfeasance on the part of the LLC member.

■ **CASE IN POINT 18.12**   Tom and Shannon Brown purchased a new home in Hattiesburg, Mississippi, from Ray Richard and Nick Welch. Richard had hired Waldron Properties, LLC (WP), to build the home. Several years later, cracks began to develop in the walls of the Browns' home as a result of defects in the construction of the foundation. The Browns sued Murray Waldron, the sole member of WP, for breach of warranty under the state's New Home Warranty Act (NHWA). Because the required NHWA notice they had received when they

bought the home was signed by Waldron personally, they claimed that Waldron was liable personally.

The trial court found that WP, not Waldron individually, was the builder of the Browns' home. The Browns appealed. They contended that even if WP was the builder, the court should pierce the veil of the LLC and hold Waldron personally liable. The state appellate court disagreed and affirmed the lower court's ruling. The Browns had not entered into a contract with either Waldron or WP. There was not sufficient evidence that Waldron had disregarded LLC formalities or had engaged in fraud or other misconduct to justify piercing the LLC's veil to hold him personally liable.[7] ■

Other Similarities to Corporations   Another similarity between corporations and LLCs is that LLCs are legal entities apart from their owners. As a legal person, the LLC can sue or be sued, enter into contracts, and hold title to property [ULLCA 201]. The terminology used to describe LLCs formed in other states or nations is also similar to that used in corporate law. For instance, an LLC formed in one state but doing business in another state is referred to in the second state as a *foreign LLC.*

18–4b The Formation of the LLC

LLCs are creatures of statute and thus must follow state statutory requirements.

Articles of Organization   To form an LLC, **articles of organization** must be filed with a central state agency—usually the secretary of state's office [ULLCA 202].[8] Typically, the articles must include the name of the business, its principal address, the name and address of a registered agent, the members' names, and how the LLC will be managed [ULLCA 203]. The business's name must include the words *Limited Liability Company* or the initials *LLC* [ULLCA 105(a)]. Although a majority of the states permit one-member LLCs, some states require at least two members.

Preformation Contracts   Businesspersons sometimes enter into contracts on behalf of a business organization that is not yet formed. Persons who are forming a corporation, for instance, may enter into contracts during the process of incorporation but before the corporation becomes a legal entity. These contracts are referred to as

---

6. *Sky Cable, LLC v. Coley,* ___ F.Supp.2d ___, 2013 WL 3517337 (W.D.Va. 2013).

7. *Brown v. Waldron,* 186 So.3d 955 (Miss.Ct.App. 2016).
8. In addition to requiring articles of organization to be filed, a few states require that a notice of the intention to form an LLC be published in a local newspaper.

preincorporation contracts. The individual promoters who sign the contracts are bound to their terms. Once the corporation is formed and adopts the preincorporation contracts (by means of a *novation,* which substitutes a new contract for the old contract), it can enforce the contract terms.

In dealing with the preorganization contracts of LLCs, courts may apply the well-established principles of corporate law relating to preincorporation contracts. That is to say, when the promoters of an LLC enter preformation contracts, the LLC, once formed, can adopt the contracts by a novation and then enforce them.

■ **CASE IN POINT 18.13** 607 South Park, LLC, entered into an agreement to sell a hotel to 607 Park View Associates, Ltd., which then assigned the rights to the purchase to another company, 02 Development, LLC. At the time, 02 Development did not yet exist—it was legally created several months later. 607 South Park subsequently refused to sell the hotel to 02 Development, and 02 Development sued for breach of the purchase agreement.

A California appellate court ruled that LLCs should be treated the same as corporations with respect to preorganization contracts. Although 02 Development did not exist when the agreement was executed, once it came into existence, it could enforce any preorganization contract made on its behalf.[9] ■

18–4c Jurisdictional Requirements

As we have seen, LLCs and corporations share several characteristics, but a significant difference between these organizational forms involves federal jurisdictional requirements. Under the federal jurisdiction statute, a corporation is deemed to be a citizen of the state where it is incorporated and maintains its principal place of

---

9. *02 Development, LLC v. 607 South Park, LLC,* 159 Cal.App.4th 609, 71 Cal.Rptr.3d 608 (2008). See also, *Davis Wine Co. v. Vina Y Bodega Estampa, S.A.,* 823 F.Supp.2d 1159 (D.Or. 2011).

business. The statute does not mention the state citizenship of partnerships, LLCs, and other unincorporated associations. The courts, however, have tended to regard these entities as citizens of every state of which their members are citizens.

The state citizenship of an LLC may come into play when a party sues the LLC based on diversity of citizenship. Remember that when parties to a lawsuit are from different states and the amount in controversy exceeds $75,000, a federal court can exercise diversity jurisdiction. *Total* diversity of citizenship must exist, however.

■ **EXAMPLE 18.14** Jen Fong, a citizen of New York, wishes to bring a suit against Skycel, an LLC formed under the laws of Connecticut. One of Skycel's members also lives in New York. Fong will not be able to bring a suit against Skycel in federal court on the basis of diversity jurisdiction because the defendant LLC is also a citizen of New York. The same would be true if Fong was bringing a suit against multiple defendants and one of the defendants lived in New York. ■

18–4d Advantages of the LLC

The LLC offers many advantages to businesspersons, which is why this form of business organization has become increasingly popular.

Limited Liability A key advantage of the LLC is the limited liability of its members. The LLC as an entity can be held liable for any loss or injury caused by the wrongful acts or omissions of its members. As we have seen, however, members themselves generally are not personally liable.

In the following case, a consumer died as a result of using an allegedly defective product made and sold by an LLC. The consumer's children sought to hold the LLC's sole member and manager personally liable for the firm's actions.

Case 18.2

Hodge v. Strong Built International, LLC

Court of Appeal of Louisiana, Third Circuit, 159 So.3d 1159 (2015).

Background and Facts Donald Hodge was hunting in a deer stand when its straps—which held Hodge high up in a tree—failed. When the straps failed, Hodge and the deer stand fell to the ground, killing Hodge. Louisiana-based Strong Built International, LLC, was the maker and seller of the deer stand, and Ken Killen was Strong Built's sole member and manager.

Hodge's children, Donald and Rachel Hodge, filed a lawsuit in a Louisiana state court against Strong Built and Killen. They sought damages on a theory of product liability for the injury and death

Case 18.2 Continued

of their father caused by the allegedly defective deer stand. Killen filed a motion for summary judgment, asserting that he was not personally liable to the Hodges. The court granted the motion and issued a summary judgment in Killen's favor, dismissing the claims against him. The Hodges appealed.

In the Language of the Court
AMY, Judge.

* * * *

* * * An LLC member or manager's liability to third parties is delineated in [Louisiana Revised Statute (La.R.S.)] 12:1320, which states:

* * * *

* * * no member, manager, employee, or agent of a limited liability company is liable in such capacity for a debt, obligation, or liability of the limited liability company.

* * * *

* * * That protection is not unlimited. Pursuant to La.R.S. 12:1320(D), *a member or manager may be subjected to personal liability for claims involving * * * breach of a professional duty or other negligent or wrongful act.* [Emphasis added.]

* * * In an affidavit, Mr. Killen asserted that he is "not an engineer, nor a licensed professional in any profession in Louisiana or any other state." Mr. Killen also asserts that he:

was a participant in the creation of the deer stand which * * * Strong Built International, L.L.C. manufactured and sold, but he never personally dictated or participated in the design, selection of materials used in the manufacture, or the manufacture of, or the selection of any warnings to any deer stand for the use or consumption by any consumer beyond my input and work as a manager * * * and member of * * * Strong Built International, L.L.C.

The plaintiffs offered no evidence to contradict Mr. Killen's affidavit in this regard. Accordingly, we find no basis for Mr. Killen's personal liability under the "breach of professional duty" exception.

Neither do we find sufficient evidence in the record to create a genuine issue of material fact with regard to the "other negligent or wrongful act" exception.

* * * With regard to [this exception], the member (or manager) must have a duty of care to the plaintiff. * * * That duty must be "something more" than the duties arising out of the LLC's contract with the plaintiff.

* * * *

* * * Mr. Killen states in his affidavit that not only was he not personally responsible for the design and manufacture of the deer stands while involved with Strong Built International * * * but that any involvement that he may have had was in his capacity as a member and manager. *The plaintiffs have submitted nothing to show that Mr. Killen's actions are "something more" than his duties as a member/manager of the LLC.* [Emphasis added.]

Decision and Remedy *A state intermediate appellate court affirmed the judgment in Killen's favor. Under the applicable Louisiana state LLC statute, no member or manager of an LLC is liable in that capacity for the liability of the company. There are exceptions, but the Hodges failed to show that Killen's actions went beyond his duties as a member and manager of Strong Built.*

Critical Thinking
- **Economic** *Why does the law allow—and even encourage—limits to the liability of a business organization's owners and managers for the firm's actions? Discuss.*

Flexibility in Taxation Another advantage of the LLC is its flexibility in regard to taxation. An LLC that has *two or more members* can choose to be taxed as either a partnership or a corporation. A corporate entity normally must pay income taxes on its profits, and the shareholders must then pay personal income taxes on any of those profits that are distributed as dividends. An LLC that wants to distribute profits to its members almost always prefers to be taxed as a partnership to avoid the "double taxation" that is characteristic of the corporate entity.

Unless an LLC indicates that it wishes to be taxed as a corporation, the Internal Revenue Service (IRS) automatically taxes it as a partnership. This means that the LLC, as an entity, pays no taxes. Rather, as in a partnership, profits are "passed through" the LLC to the members, who then personally pay taxes on the profits. If an LLC's members want to reinvest profits in the business rather than distribute the profits to members, however, they may prefer to be taxed as a corporation. Corporate income tax rates may be lower than personal tax rates. Part of the attractiveness of the LLC is this flexibility with respect to taxation.

An LLC that has only *one member* cannot be taxed as a partnership. For federal income tax purposes, one-member LLCs are automatically taxed as sole proprietorships unless they indicate that they wish to be taxed as corporations. With respect to state taxes, most states follow the IRS rules.

Flexibility in Management and Foreign Investors Another advantage of the LLC for businesspersons is the flexibility it offers in terms of business operations and management, as will be discussed shortly. Foreign investors are allowed to become LLC members, so organizing as an LLC can enable a business to attract investors from other countries. (Many nations—including France, Germany, Japan, and places in Latin America—have particular business forms that provide for limited liability, much like an LLC.)

18-4e Disadvantages of the LLC

The main disadvantage of the LLC is that state LLC statutes are not uniform. Therefore, businesses that operate in more than one state may not receive consistent treatment in these states.

Generally, most states apply to a foreign LLC (an LLC formed in another state) the law of the state where the LLC was formed. Difficulties can arise, though, when one state's court must interpret and apply another state's laws.

18-4f LLC Management

Basically, LLC members have two options for managing the firm, as shown in Exhibit 18–1. The firm can be either a "member-managed" LLC or a "manager-managed" LLC. Most state LLC statutes and the ULLCA provide that unless the articles of organization specify otherwise, an LLC is assumed to be member managed [ULLCA 203(a)(6)].

In a *member-managed* LLC, all of the members participate in management, and decisions are made by majority

EXHIBIT 18–1 Management of an LLC

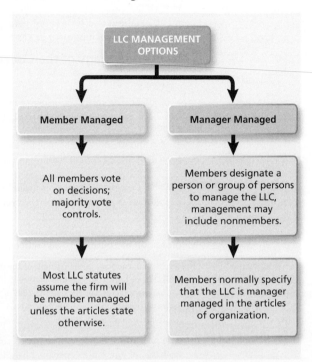

vote [ULLCA 404(a)]. In a *manager-managed* LLC, the members designate a group of persons to manage the firm. The management group may consist of only members, both members and nonmembers, or only nonmembers.

18-4g Fiduciary Duties

Under the ULLCA, managers in a manager-managed LLC owe fiduciary duties (the duty of loyalty and the duty of care) to the LLC and its members [ULLCA 409(a), 409(h)]. (This same rule applies in corporate law—corporate directors and officers owe fiduciary duties to the corporation and its shareholders.) Because not all states have adopted the ULLCA, though, some state statutes provide that managers owe fiduciary duties only to the LLC and not to the LLC's members.

18-4h The LLC Operating Agreement

The members of an LLC have considerable flexibility in managing and operating the business. The members of an LLC can decide how to operate the various aspects of the business by forming an **operating agreement** [ULLCA 103(a)]. In many states, an operating agreement is not required for an LLC to exist, and if there is one, it need not be in writing. Generally, though, LLC members should protect their interests by creating a written operating agreement.

Operating agreements typically contain provisions relating to the following areas:

1. Management and how future managers will be chosen or removed. (Although most LLC statutes are silent on this issue, the ULLCA provides that members may choose and remove managers by majority vote [ULLCA 404(b)(3)].)
2. How profits will be divided.
3. How membership interests may be transferred.
4. Whether the dissociation of a member, such as by death or departure, will trigger dissolution of the LLC.
5. Whether formal members' meetings will be held.
6. How voting rights will be apportioned. (If the agreement does not cover voting, LLC statutes in most states provide that voting rights are apportioned according to each member's capital contributions.[10] Some states provide that, in the absence of an agreement to the contrary, each member has one vote.)

■ **CASE IN POINT 18.15** Green Cab Taxi and Disabled Service Association LLC ("Green Cab") is a taxi service company in King County, Washington. The operating agreement requires the members to pay weekly fees. Members who do not pay are in default and must return their taxi licenses to the company. In addition, a member in default cannot hold a seat on the board or withdraw from the company without the consent of all of the members.

When a disagreement arose among the members concerning the company's management, several members, including Shumet Mekonen, withdrew from the company without the consent of the other members. Both sides continued to drive under the Green Cab name.

Mekonen's group filed a suit in a Washington state court against a group of members who had not withdrawn, including Dessie Zewdu. In part, the Mekonen group sought the right to operate as Green Cab. The court held that the plaintiffs could not represent themselves as Green Cab and ordered them to return their taxi licenses to the company. A state intermediate appellate court affirmed. Under the provisions of the company's operating agreement, the plaintiffs, as "defaulting members," had no right to retain and use the licenses.[11] ■

If a dispute arises and there is no agreement covering the topic under dispute, the state LLC statute will govern the outcome. For instance, most LLC statutes provide that if the members have not specified how profits will be divided, they will be divided equally among the members. When an issue is not covered by an operating agreement or by an LLC statute, the courts often apply principles of partnership law.

18–4i Dissociation in an LLC

Recall that in a partnership, *dissociation* occurs when a partner ceases to be associated in the carrying on of the partnership business. The same concept applies to LLCs. And like a partner in a partnership, a member of an LLC has the *power* to dissociate at any time but may not have the *right* to dissociate.

Under the ULLCA, the events that trigger a member's dissociation from an LLC are similar to the events causing a partner to be dissociated under the Uniform Partnership Act (UPA). These include voluntary withdrawal, expulsion by other members, court order, incompetence, bankruptcy, and death. Generally, if a member dies or otherwise dissociates from an LLC, the other members may continue to carry on the LLC business unless the operating agreement provides otherwise.

When a member dissociates from an LLC, he or she loses the right to participate in management and the right to act as an agent for the LLC. The member's duty of loyalty to the LLC also terminates, and the duty of care continues only with respect to events that occurred before dissociation. If the member's dissociation violates the LLC's operating agreement, it is considered legally wrongful, and the dissociated member can be held liable for damages caused by the dissociation.

Generally, the dissociated member has a right to have his or her interest in the LLC bought out by the other members. The LLC's operating agreement may contain provisions establishing a buyout price. If it does not, the member's interest is usually purchased at fair value. In states that have adopted the ULLCA, the LLC must purchase the interest at fair value within 120 days after the dissociation.

18–4j Dissolution of an LLC

Regardless of whether a member's dissociation was wrongful or rightful, normally the dissociated member has no right to force the LLC to dissolve. The remaining

---

10. In contrast, partners in a partnership generally have equal rights in management and equal voting rights unless they specify otherwise in their partnership agreement.
11. *MeKonen v. Zewdu,* 179 Wash.App. 1042 (2014).

members can opt either to continue or to dissolve the business.

Members can also stipulate in their operating agreement that certain events will cause dissolution, or they can agree that they have the power to dissolve the LLC by vote. As with partnerships, a court can order an LLC to be dissolved in certain circumstances. For instance, a court might order dissolution when the members have engaged in illegal or oppressive conduct, or when it is no longer feasible to carry on the business.

■ **CASE IN POINT 18.16**   Three men—Walter Perkins, Gary Fordham, and David Thompson—formed Venture Sales, LLC, to develop a subdivision in Petal, Mississippi. Each of them contributed land and funds, resulting in total holdings of 466 acres of land and about $158,000 in cash.

Perkins, who was working as an assistant coach for the Cleveland Browns, trusted Fordham and Thompson to develop the property. More than ten years later, however, they still had not done so, although they had formed two other LLCs and developed two other subdivisions in the area.

Fordham and Thompson claimed that they did not know when they could develop Venture's property and suggested selling it at a discounted price, but Perkins disagreed. Perkins then sought a judicial dissolution of Venture Sales. The court ordered the dissolution. Because Venture Sales was not meeting the economic purpose for which it was established (developing a subdivision), continuing the business was impracticable.[12] ■

A judge's exercise of discretion to order the dissolution of an LLC was disputed in the following case.

---

12. *Venture Sales, LLC v. Perkins,* 86 So.3d 910 (Miss.Sup. 2012).

Case Analysis 18.3

Reese v. Newman

District of Columbia Court of Appeals, 131 A.3d 880 (2016).

In the Language of the Court

KING, Senior Judge:

* * * Allison Reese and * * * Nicole Newman were co-owners of ANR Construction Management, LLC * * *. Following disputes over management of the company, Newman notified Reese in writing that she intended to * * * dissolve and wind-up the LLC. Reese did not want to dissolve the LLC but preferred that Newman simply be dissociated so that Reese could continue the business herself. Newman filed an action for judicial dissolution in [a District of Columbia court against Reese]. Reese filed a counterclaim for Newman's dissociation * * *. Following a jury trial, the jury * * * found grounds for both judicial dissolution and forced dissociation of Newman; the court, thereafter, ordered judicial dissolution of the LLC. * * * Reese appeals.

* * * *

Reese argues that the trial court erred when it purported to use discretion in

choosing between dissolution of the LLC, as proposed by Newman, and forcing dissociation of Newman from the LLC, as proposed by Reese. Reese argues that the [District of Columbia (D.C.)] statute [governing dissociation from an LLC] does not allow for any discretion by the court, and that, in fact, the statute mandates that the court order dissociation of Newman based on the jury's findings.

In matters of statutory interpretation, we review the trial court's decision *de novo.* Our analysis starts with the plain language of the statute, as the general rule of statutory interpretation is that the intent of the lawmaker is to be found in the language that he has used. To that end, *the words of the statute should be construed according to their ordinary sense and with the meaning commonly attributed to them.* [Emphasis added.]

Reese argues that the court was required to dissociate Newman from the LLC under [D.C. Code] Section

29–806.02(5) which reads:

> A person *shall* be dissociated as a member from a limited liability company when:
> * * * *
> (5) On application by the company, the person is expelled as a member by judicial order because the person has:
> (A) Engaged, or is engaging, in wrongful conduct that has adversely and materially affected, or will adversely and materially affect, the company's activities and affairs;
> (B) Willfully or persistently committed, or is willfully and persistently committing, a material breach of the operating agreement or the person's duties or obligations under Section 29–804.09; or
> (C) Engaged, or is engaging, in conduct relating to the company's activities which makes it not reasonably practicable to carry on the activities with the person as a member.

Case 18.3 Continued

Reese's interpretation of the statute is that, upon application to the court by a company, a judge shall dissociate a member of an LLC, when that member commits any one of the actions described in subsections (5)(A)–(C).

* * * While the introductory language of Section 29–806.02 does use the word "shall"—that command is in no way directed at the trial judge. It reads, "a person shall be dissociated * * * when," and then goes on to recite fifteen separate circumstances describing different occasions when a person shall be dissociated from an LLC. That is to say, when one of the events described in subparagraphs (1) through (15) occurs, the member shall be dissociated. Subparagraph (5), however, is merely one instance for which a person shall be dissociated; that is, when and if a judge has ordered a member expelled because she finds that any conditions under (5)(A)–(C) have been established. In other words, the command in the introductory language is not directed at the trial judge, it is directed at all the circumstances set forth in subparagraphs (1) through (15) * * * . There is nothing in the language of Section 29–806.02(5) that strips a judge of her discretion because it does not require the judge to expel the member if any of the enumerated conditions are established.

In short, Section 29–806.02(5) means: *when a judge has used her discretion to expel a member of an LLC by judicial order, under any of the enumerated circumstances in (5)(A)–(C), that member shall be dissociated.*

* * * Although Reese argues that the language of the "dissociation" section of the District's code should be read as forcing the hand of a trial judge who finds grounds for dissociation, Reese attempts to read the "dissolution" section differently.

Reese differentiates the sections by pointing to the dissolution section's express authorization to order a remedy other than dissolution in Section 29–807.01(b) which provides: "in a proceeding brought under subsection (a)(5) of this section, the * * * Court may order a remedy other than dissolution." While we are satisfied that judicial dissolution of an LLC is discretionary under this statute, Reese's attempt to buttress [reinforce] her argument that Section 29–806.02(5) is compulsory by pointing to this express provision in the dissolution section and the absence of a similar express provision in the dissociation section is unavailing. First, * * * the only "shall" in the dissociation section is in the introductory language, and the same "shall" can be found in the same

place, in the dissolution section: "a limited liability company is dissolved, and its activities and affairs *shall be wound up,* upon the occurrence of any of the following." If that language does not make the rest of the section mandatory in the dissolution section, and we are persuaded that it does not, it cannot be said that the "shall" in the introduction of the dissociation section does the opposite.

* * * *

In sum, we hold that Section 29–806.02(5) can only be interpreted to mean: when a judge finds that any of the events in (5)(A)–(C) have taken place, she may (*i.e.,* has discretion to) expel by judicial order a member of an LLC, and when a judge has done so the member shall be dissociated. *Moreover, when both grounds for dissociation of a member and dissolution of the LLC exist, the trial judge has discretion to choose either alternative.* [Emphasis added.]

Here, the jury * * * found that grounds were present for either outcome. The trial judge acknowledged that both options were on the table and then exercised her discretion in ordering that dissolution take place. We find no reason to disturb that order.

* * * *

Accordingly, the judgment in this appeal is therefore affirmed.

Legal Reasoning Questions

1. What dispute gave rise to the action filed in the court in this case? How did that dispute lead to the issue on appeal?

2. What is the role of an appellate court when reviewing the exercise of discretion by a trial court?

3. Newman alleged that after she delivered her notice to dissolve ANR, Reese locked her out of the LLC's bank accounts, blocked her access to the LLC's files and e-mail, and ended her salary and health benefits. Did any of the jury's findings support these allegations? Explain.

18–4k Winding Up

When an LLC is dissolved, any members who did not wrongfully dissociate may participate in the winding up process. To wind up the business, members must collect, liquidate, and distribute the LLC's assets.

Members may preserve the assets for a reasonable time to optimize their return, and they continue to have the authority to perform reasonable acts in conjunction with

winding up. In other words, the LLC will be bound by the reasonable acts of its members during the winding up process.

Once all of the LLC's assets have been sold, the proceeds are distributed. Debts to creditors are paid first (including debts owed to members who are creditors of the LLC). The members' capital contributions are returned next, and any remaining amounts are then distributed to members in equal shares or according to their operating agreement.

Reviewing: Small Businesses and Limited Liability Companies

The city of Papagos, Arizona, had a deteriorating bridge in need of repair on a prominent public roadway. The city posted notices seeking proposals for an artistic bridge design and reconstruction. Davidson Masonry, LLC, which was owned and managed by Carl Davidson and his wife, Marilyn Rowe, decided to submit a bid to create a decorative concrete structure that incorporated artistic metalwork. They contacted Shana Lafayette, a local sculptor who specialized in large-scale metal creations, to help them design the bridge. The city selected their bridge design and awarded them the contract for a commission of $184,000.

Davidson Masonry and Lafayette then entered into an agreement to work together on the bridge project. Davidson Masonry agreed to install and pay for concrete and structural work, and Lafayette agreed to install the metalwork at her expense. They agreed that overall profits would be split, with 25 percent going to Lafayette and 75 percent going to Davidson Masonry. Lafayette designed numerous metal sculptures of trout that were incorporated into colorful decorative concrete forms designed by Rowe. Davidson performed the structural engineering. The group worked together successfully until the completion of the project. Using the information presented in the chapter, answer the following questions.

1. Would Davidson Masonry automatically be taxed as a partnership or a corporation?
2. Is Davidson Masonry member managed or manager managed?
3. Suppose that during construction, Lafayette asked Carl Davidson to rent space in a warehouse that was close to the bridge so that she could work on her sculptures near the site where they would eventually be installed. Carl Davidson signed the rental contract in his own name rather than the name of the LLC. The other members of Davidson Masonry were not aware of the rental agreement. In this situation, would a court likely hold that Davidson Masonry was liable on the contract that Carl Davidson had entered? Why or why not?
4. Now suppose that Rowe has an argument with her husband and wants to withdraw from being a member of Davidson Masonry. What is the term for such a withdrawal, and what effect would it have on the LLC?

Debate This . . . *A partnership should automatically end when one partner dissociates from the firm.*

Terms and Concepts

articles of organization 365	entrepreneur 354	member 364
articles of partnership 358	goodwill 357	operating agreement 368
buyout price 363	information return 358	partnership 356
buy-sell agreement 363	joint and several liability 362	partnership by estoppel 358
charging order 359	joint liability 362	pass-through entity 358
dissociation 362	limited liability company	sole proprietorship 355
dissolution 363	(LLC) 364	winding up 363

Issue Spotters

1. Frank plans to open a sporting goods store and to hire Gogi and Hap. Frank will invest only his own funds. He expects that he will not make a profit for at least eighteen months and will make only a small profit in the three years after that. He hopes to expand eventually. Would a sole proprietorship be an appropriate form for Frank's business? Why or why not? (See *Sole Proprietorships*.)

2. Darnell and Eliana are partners in D&E Designs, an architectural firm. When Darnell dies, his widow claims that as Darnell's heir, she is entitled to take his place as Eliana's partner or to receive a share of the firm's assets. Is she right? Why or why not? (See *Partnerships*.)

• **Check your answers to the Issue Spotters against the answers provided in Appendix B at the end of this text.**

Business Scenarios

18–1. Partnership Formation. Daniel is the owner of a chain of shoe stores. He hires Rubya to be the manager of a new store, which is to open in Grand Rapids, Michigan. Daniel, by written contract, agrees to pay Rubya a monthly salary and 20 percent of the profits. Without Daniel's knowledge, Rubya represents himself to Classen as Daniel's partner and shows Classen the agreement to share profits. Classen extends credit to Rubya. Rubya defaults. Discuss whether Classen can hold Daniel liable as a partner. (See *Partnerships.*)

18–2. Limited Liability Companies. John, Lesa, and Tabir form a limited liability company. John contributes 60 percent of the capital, and Lesa and Tabir each contribute 20 percent. Nothing is decided about how profits will be divided. John assumes that he will be entitled to 60 percent of the profits, in accordance with his contribution. Lesa and Tabir, however, assume that the profits will be divided equally. A dispute over the profits arises, and ultimately a court has to decide the issue. What law will the court apply? In most states, what will result? How could this dispute have been avoided in the first place? Discuss fully. (See *The Limited Liability Company.*)

Business Case Problems

18–3. LLC Dissolution. Walter Van Houten and John King formed 1545 Ocean Avenue, LLC, with each managing 50 percent of the business. Its purpose was to renovate an existing building and construct a new commercial building. Van Houten and King quarreled over many aspects of the work on the properties. King claimed that Van Houten paid the contractors too much for the work performed. As the projects neared completion, King demanded that the LLC be dissolved and that Van Houten agree to a buyout. Because the parties could not agree on a buyout, King sued for dissolution. The trial court enjoined (prevented) further work on the projects until the dispute was settled. As the ground for dissolution, King cited the fights over management decisions. There was no claim of fraud or frustration of purpose. The trial court ordered that the LLC be dissolved, and Van Houten appealed. Should either of the owners be forced to dissolve the LLC before the completion of its purpose—that is, before the building projects are finished? Explain. [*In re 1545 Ocean Avenue, LLC,* 893 N.Y.S.2d 590 (N.Y.A.D. 2 Dept. 2010)] (See *The Limited Liability Company.*)

18–4. Business Case Problem with Sample Answer— LLC Operation. After Hurricane Katrina struck the Gulf Coast, James Williford, Patricia Mosser, Marquetta Smith, and Michael Floyd formed Bluewater Logistics, LLC, to bid on construction contracts. Under Mississippi law, every member of a member-managed LLC is entitled to participate in managing the business. The operating agreement provided for a "super majority" 75 percent vote to remove a member who "has either committed a felony or under any other circumstances that would jeopardize the company status" as a contractor. After Bluewater had completed more than $5 million in contracts, Smith told Williford that she, Mosser, and Floyd were exercising their "super majority" vote to fire him. No reason was provided. Williford sued Bluewater and the other members. Did Smith, Mosser, and Floyd breach the state LLC statute, their fiduciary duties, or the Bluewater operating agreements?

Discuss. [*Bluewater Logistics, LLC v. Williford,* 55 So.3d 148 (Miss. 2011)] (See *The Limited Liability Company.*)

• For a sample answer to Problem 18–4, go to Appendix C at the end of this text.

18–5. Formation of a Partnership. Leisa Reed and Randell Thurman lived together in Spring City, Tennessee. Randell and his father, Leroy, formed a cattle-raising operation and opened a bank account in the name of L&R Farm. Within a few years, Leroy quit the operation. Leisa and Randell each wrote a personal check for $5,000 to buy his cattle. Leisa picked up supplies, fed and administered medicine to cattle, collected hay, and participated in the bookkeeping for L&R. Later, checks drawn on her personal account for $12,000 to buy equipment and $35,000 to buy cattle were deposited into the L&R account. After several years, Leisa decided that she no longer wanted to associate with Randell, but they could not agree on a financial settlement. Was Leisa a partner in L&R? Is she entitled to half of the value of L&R's assets? Explain. [*Reed v. Thurman,* ___ S.W.3d ___, 2015 WL 1119449 (Tenn. Ct.App. 2015)] (See *Partnerships.*)

18–6. Jurisdictional Requirements in an LLC. Siloam Springs Hotel, LLC, operates a Hampton Inn in Siloam Springs, Arkansas. Siloam bought insurance from Century Surety Co. to cover the hotel. When guests suffered injuries due to a leak of carbon monoxide from the heating element of an indoor swimming pool, Siloam filed a claim with Century. Century denied coverage, which Siloam disputed. Century asked a federal district court to resolve the dispute. In asserting that the federal court had jurisdiction, Century noted that the amount in controversy exceeded $75,000 and that the parties had complete diversity of citizenship. Century is "a corporation organized under the laws of Ohio, with its principal place of business in Michigan," and Siloam is "a corporation organized under the laws of Oklahoma, with its principal place of business in Arkansas." Can the court exercise diversity jurisdiction in this case? Discuss. [*Siloam Springs Hotel, L.L.C. v. Century Surety Co.,* 781 F.3d 1233 (10th Cir. 2015)] (See *The Limited Liability Company.*)

18–7. Partnership Formation and Operation. FS Partners is a general partnership whose partners are Jerry Stahlman, a professional engineer, and Fitz & Smith, Inc., a corporation in the business of excavating and paving. Timothy Smith signed the partnership agreement on Fitz & Smith's behalf and deals with FS matters on Fitz & Smith's behalf. Stahlman handles the payment of FS's bills, including its tax bills, and is the designated partner on FS's federal tax return. FS was formed to buy and develop twenty acres of unoccupied, wooded land in York County, Pennsylvania. The deed to the property lists the owner as "FS Partners, a general partnership." When the taxes on the real estate were not paid, the York County Tax Claim Bureau published notice that the property would be sold at a tax sale. The bureau also mailed a notice to FS's address of record and posted a notice on the land. Is this sufficient notice of the tax sale? Discuss. [*FS Partners v. York County Tax Claim Bureau,* 132 A.3d 577 (Pa. 2016)] (See *Partnerships.*)

18–8. A Question of Ethics—Wrongful Dissociation.

Elliot Willensky and Beverly Moran formed a partnership to buy, renovate, and sell a house. Moran agreed to finance the effort, which was to cost no more than $60,000. Willensky agreed to oversee the work, which was to be done in six months. Willensky lived in the house during the renovation. As the project progressed, Willensky incurred excessive and unnecessary expenses, misappropriated funds for his personal use, did not pay bills on time, and did not

keep Moran informed of the costs. More than a year later, the renovation was still not completed, and Willensky walked off the project. Moran completed the renovation, which ultimately cost $311,222, and sold the house. Moran then sued to dissolve the partnership and recover damages from Willensky for breach of contract and wrongful dissociation. [Moran v. Willensky, 339 S.W.3d 651 (Tenn.Ct.App.2010)] (See *Partnerships.*)

(a) Moran alleged that Willensky had wrongfully dissociated from the partnership. When did this dissociation occur? Why was his dissociation wrongful?

(b) Which of Willensky's actions simply represent unethical behavior or bad management, and which constitute a breach of the agreement?

18–9. Special Case Analysis—LLC Dissolution. Go to Case Analysis 18.3, *Reese v. Newman.* Read the excerpt and answer the following questions.

(a) **Issue:** Which party's choice between two alternatives was at the heart of the issue on the appeal of the *Reese* case?

(b) **Rule of Law:** What rules of interpretation did the appellate court use to construe the language of the statutes that created those alternatives?

(c) **Applying the Rule of Law:** How did the court construe the language of those statutes?

(d) **Conclusion:** How did the court's construction of that language lead to the result?

Legal Reasoning Group Activity

18–10. Fiduciary Duties in LLCs. Newbury Properties Group owns, manages, and develops real property. Jerry Stoker and the Stoker Group, Inc. (the Stokers), also develop real property. Newbury entered into agreements with the Stokers concerning a large tract of property in Georgia. The parties formed Bellemare, LLC, to develop various parcels of the tract for residential purposes. The operating agreement of Bellemare indicated that "no Member shall be accountable to the LLC or to any other Member with respect to any other business or activity even if the business or activity competes with the LLC's business." Later, when the Newbury group

contracted with other parties to develop parcels within the tract in competition with Bellemare, LLC, the Stokers sued, alleging breach of fiduciary duty. (See *The Limited Liability Company.*)

(a) The first group will discuss and outline the fiduciary duties that the members of an LLC owe to each other.

(b) The second group will determine whether the terms of an operating agreement can alter these fiduciary duties.

(c) The third group will decide in whose favor the court should rule in this situation.

CHAPTER 19

Corporations

The corporation is a creature of statute. A corporation is an artificial being, existing only in law and being neither tangible nor visible. Its existence generally depends on state law, although some corporations, especially public organizations, are created under federal law. Each state has its own body of corporate law, and these laws are not entirely uniform.

The Model Business Corporation Act (MBCA) is a codification of modern corporation law. This model uniform law has been influential in shaping state corporation statutes. Today, the majority of state statutes are guided by the most recent version of the MBCA, often referred to as the Revised Model Business Corporation Act (RMBCA).

Keep in mind, however, that there is considerable variation among the laws of states that have used the MBCA or the RMBCA as a basis for their statutes. In addition, several states do not follow either act. Consequently, individual state corporation laws should be relied on to determine corporate law rather than the MBCA or RMBCA.

19-1 Nature and Classification

A corporation is a legal entity created and recognized by state law. This business entity can have one or more owners (called shareholders), and it operates under a name distinct from the names of its owners. Both individuals and other businesses can be shareholders. The corporation substitutes itself for its shareholders when conducting corporate business and incurring liability. Its authority to act and the liability for its actions, however, are separate and apart from the shareholders who own it.

A corporation is recognized under U.S. law as a person—an artificial *legal person,* as opposed to a *natural person.* As a "person," it enjoys many of the same rights and privileges under state and federal law that U.S. citizens enjoy. For instance, corporations possess the same right of access to the courts as citizens and can sue or be sued. The constitutional guarantees of due process, free speech, and freedom from unreasonable searches and seizures also apply to corporations.

19-1a Corporate Personnel

In a corporation, the responsibility for the overall management of the firm is entrusted to a *board of directors,* whose members are elected by the shareholders. The board of directors makes the policy decisions and hires *corporate officers* and other employees to run the daily business operations.

When an individual purchases a share of stock in a corporation, that person becomes a shareholder and an owner of the corporation. Unlike the partners in a partnership, the body of shareholders can change constantly without affecting the continued existence of the corporation. A shareholder can sue the corporation, and the corporation can sue a shareholder. Additionally, under certain circumstances, a shareholder can sue on behalf of a corporation.

19-1b The Limited Liability of Shareholders

One of the key advantages of the corporate form is the limited liability of its owners. Normally, corporate shareholders are not personally liable for the obligations of the corporation beyond the extent of their investments.

In certain limited situations, however, a court can *pierce the corporate veil* and impose liability on shareholders for the corporation's obligations. Additionally, creditors often will not extend credit to small companies unless the shareholders assume personal liability, as guarantors, for corporate obligations.

19–1c Corporate Earnings and Taxation

When a corporation earns profits, it can either pass them on to shareholders in the form of **dividends** or retain them as profits. These **retained earnings,** if invested properly, will yield higher corporate profits in the future. In theory, higher profits will cause the price of the company's stock to rise. Individual shareholders can then reap the benefits in the capital gains they receive when they sell their stock.

Whether a corporation retains its profits or passes them on to the shareholders as dividends, those profits are subject to income taxation by various levels of government. Failure to pay taxes can lead to severe consequences. The state can suspend the organization's corporate status until the taxes are paid and can even dissolve the corporation for failing to pay taxes.

Another important aspect of corporate taxation is that corporate profits can be subject to double taxation. The company pays tax on its profits. Then, if the profits are passed on to the shareholders as dividends, the shareholders must also pay income tax on them. (This is true unless the dividends represent distributions of capital, which are returns of holders' investments in the stock of the company.) The corporation normally does not receive a tax deduction for dividends it distributes. This double-taxation feature is one of the major disadvantages of the corporate form.

Some U.S. corporations use holding companies to reduce or defer their U.S. income taxes. At its simplest, a **holding company** (sometimes referred to as a *parent company*) is a company whose business activity consists of holding shares in another company. Typically, the holding company is established in a low-tax or no-tax offshore jurisdiction, such as the Cayman Islands, Dubai, Hong Kong, Luxembourg, Monaco, or Panama.

19–1d Criminal and Tort Liability

A corporation may be held liable for the criminal acts of its agents and employees. Although corporations cannot be imprisoned, they can be fined. (Of course, corporate directors and officers can be imprisoned.) In addition, under sentencing guidelines for crimes committed by corporate employees, corporations can face fines amounting to hundreds of millions of dollars.

A corporation is also liable for the torts committed by its agents or officers within the course and scope of their employment under the doctrine of *respondeat superior.* ■ **CASE IN POINT 19.1** Mark Bloom was an officer and a director of MB Investment Partners, Inc. (MB), at the time that he formed North Hills, LP, a stock investment fund. Bloom and other MB employees used MB's offices and equipment to administer investments in North Hills.

Later, investors in North Hills requested a full redemption of their investments. By that time, however, most of the funds that had been invested were gone. North Hills had, in fact, been a Ponzi scheme that Bloom had used to finance his lavish personal lifestyle, taking at least $20 million from North Hills for his personal use.

Barry Belmont and other North Hills investors filed a suit in a federal district court against MB, alleging fraud. The court held that MB was liable for Bloom's fraud. MB appealed, and the appellate court affirmed. Tort liability can be attributed to a corporation for the acts of its agent that were committed within the scope of the agent's employment.[1] ■

19–1e Classification of Corporations

The classification of a corporation normally depends on its location, purpose, and ownership characteristics, as described in the following subsections.

Domestic, Foreign, and Alien Corporations A corporation is referred to as a **domestic corporation** by its home state (the state in which it incorporates). A corporation formed in one state but doing business in another is referred to in the second state as a **foreign corporation.** A corporation formed in another country (say, Mexico) but doing business in the United States is referred to in the United States as an **alien corporation.**

A corporation does not have an automatic right to do business in a state other than its state of incorporation. In some instances, it must obtain a *certificate of authority* in any state in which it plans to do business. Once the certificate has been issued, the corporation generally can exercise in that state all of the powers conferred on it by its home state. If a foreign corporation does business in a state without obtaining a certificate of authority, the state can impose substantial fines and sanctions on that corporation.

Note that most state statutes specify certain activities, such as soliciting orders via the Internet, that are not considered "doing business" within the state. For instance, a foreign corporation normally does not need a certificate of authority to sell goods or services via the Internet or by mail.

What constitutes doing business within a state? In the following case, the court answered that question.

---

1. *Belmont v. MB Investment Partners, Inc.,* 708 F.3d 470 (3d Cir. 2013).

Drake Manufacturing Co. v. Polyflow, Inc.

Superior Court of Pennsylvania, 2015 PA Super 16, 109 A.3d 250 (2015).

Background and Facts   Drake Manufacturing Company, a Delaware corporation, entered into a contract to sell certain products to Polyflow, Inc., headquartered in Pennsylvania. Drake promised to ship the goods from Drake's plant in Sheffield, Pennsylvania, to Polyflow's place of business in Oaks, Pennsylvania, as well as to addresses in California, Canada, and Holland.

When Polyflow withheld payment of about $300,000 for some of the goods, Drake filed a breach of contract suit in a Pennsylvania state court against Polyflow seeking to collect the unpaid amount. But Drake had failed to obtain a certificate of authority to do business in Pennsylvania as a foreign corporation. Polyflow asserted that this failure to register with the state deprived Drake of the capacity to bring an action against Polyflow in the state's courts. The court issued a judgment in Drake's favor. Polyflow appealed.

In the Language of the Court

Opinion by *JENKINS*, J. [Judge]:
* * * *

[15 Pennsylvania Consolidated Statutes (Pa.C.S.)] Section 4121 provides: "A foreign business corporation, before doing business in this Commonwealth, shall procure a certificate of authority to do so from the Department of State."

* * * Typical conduct requiring a certificate of authority includes maintaining an office to conduct local intrastate business [and] entering into contracts relating to local business or sales.

A corporation is not "doing business" solely because it resorts to the courts of this Commonwealth to recover an indebtedness. [Emphasis added.]
* * * *

[15 Pa.C.S.] Section 4141(a) provides in relevant part that "a nonqualified foreign business corporation doing business in this Commonwealth * * * shall not be permitted to maintain any action or proceeding in any court of this Commonwealth until the corporation has obtained a certificate of authority."
* * * *

* * * The evidence demonstrates that Drake failed to submit a certificate of authority into evidence prior to the verdict in violation of 15 Pa.C.S. Section 4121. Therefore, the trial court should not have permitted Drake to prosecute its action.

The trial court contends that Drake is exempt from the certificate of authority requirement because it merely commenced suit in Pennsylvania to collect a debt * * * . Drake did much more, however, than file suit or attempt to collect a debt. Drake maintains an office in Pennsylvania to conduct local business, conduct which typically requires a certificate of authority. Drake also entered into a contract with Polyflow, and * * * shipped couplings and portable swaging machines to Polyflow's place of business in Pennsylvania * * * . In short, *Drake's conduct was * * * regular, systematic, and extensive, * * * thus constituting the transaction of business and requiring Drake to obtain a certificate of authority.* [Emphasis added.]

We also hold that Drake needed a certificate of authority to sue Polyflow in Pennsylvania for Polyflow's failure to pay for out-of-state shipments in California, Canada and Holland. A foreign corporation that "does business" in Pennsylvania * * * must obtain a certificate in order to prosecute a lawsuit in this Commonwealth, regardless of whether the lawsuit itself concerns in-state conduct or out-of-state conduct.

Decision and Remedy   *A state intermediate appellate court reversed the judgment in Drake's favor. Under Pennsylvania state statutes, Drake was required to obtain a certificate of authority to do business in that state. Drake failed to do so. The court should not have allowed Drake to prosecute its action against Polyflow.*

Critical Thinking

- **Legal Environment**   *Why would the appellate court permit Polyflow to get away with not paying for delivered and presumably merchantable goods?*

Close Corporations Most corporate enterprises in the United States fall into the category of close corporations. A **close corporation** is one whose shares are held by relatively few persons, often members of a family. Close corporations are also referred to as *closely held, family,* or *privately held* corporations.

Usually, the members of the small group constituting the shareholders of a close corporation are personally known to each other. Because the number of shareholders is so small, there is no trading market for the shares. In practice, a close corporation is often operated like a partnership.

The statutes in many states allow close corporations to depart significantly from certain formalities required by traditional corporation law.[2] Under the RMBCA, close corporations have considerable flexibility in determining their operating rules [RMBCA 7.32]. If all of a corporation's shareholders agree in writing, the corporation can operate without directors and bylaws. In addition, the corporation can operate without annual or special shareholders' or directors' meetings, stock certificates, or formal records of shareholders' or directors' decisions.[3]

Management of Close Corporations. Management of a close corporation resembles that of a sole proprietorship or a partnership, in that control is held by a single shareholder or a tightly knit group of shareholders. As a corporation, however, the firm must meet all specific legal requirements set forth in state statutes.

To prevent a majority shareholder from dominating the company, a close corporation may require that more than a simple majority of the directors approve any action taken by the board. In a larger corporation, such a requirement would typically apply only to extraordinary actions (such as selling all the corporate assets) and not to ordinary business decisions.

Transfer of Shares in Close Corporations. By definition, a close corporation has a small number of shareholders. Thus, the transfer of one shareholder's shares to someone else can cause serious management problems. The other shareholders may find themselves required to share control with someone they do not know or like. ■ **EXAMPLE 19.2** Three siblings, Sherry, Karen, and Henry Johnson, are the only shareholders of Johnson's Car Wash, Inc. Henry wants to sell his shares, but Sherry and Karen do not want him to sell the shares to a third person unknown to them. ■

To avoid this situation, a close corporation can restrict the transferability of shares to outside persons. Shareholders can be required to offer their shares to the corporation or to the other shareholders before selling them to an outside purchaser. In fact, in a few states close corporations must transfer shares in this manner under state statutes.

One way the close corporation can effect restrictions on transferability is by spelling them out in a **shareholder agreement.** A shareholder agreement can also provide for proportional control when one of the original shareholders dies. The decedent's shares of stock in the corporation can be divided in such a way that the proportionate holdings of the survivors, and thus their proportionate control, will be maintained.

Misappropriation of Close Corporation Funds. Sometimes, a majority shareholder in a close corporation takes advantage of his or her position and misappropriates company funds. In such situations, the normal remedy for the injured minority shareholders is to have their shares appraised and to be paid the fair market value for them.

S Corporations A close corporation that meets the qualifying requirements specified in Subchapter S of the Internal Revenue Code can choose to operate as an **S corporation.** (A corporation will automatically be taxed under Subchapter C unless it elects S corporation status.)

If a corporation has S corporation status, it can avoid the imposition of income taxes at the corporate level while retaining many of the advantages of a corporation, particularly limited liability. Among the numerous requirements for S corporation status, the following are the most important:

1. The corporation must be a domestic corporation.
2. The corporation must not be a member of an affiliated group of corporations.
3. The shareholders must be individuals, estates, or certain trusts and tax-exempt organizations. Partnerships and nonqualifying trusts cannot be shareholders. Corporations can be shareholders under certain circumstances.
4. The corporation must have no more than one hundred shareholders.
5. The corporation must have only one class of stock, although it is not necessary that all shareholders have the same voting rights.
6. No shareholder of the corporation may be a nonresident alien.

---

2. In some states, such as Maryland, a close corporation need not have a board of directors.
3. Shareholders cannot agree, however, to eliminate certain rights of shareholders, such as the right to inspect corporate records or the right to bring *derivative actions* (lawsuits on behalf of the corporation).

An S corporation is treated differently than a regular corporation for tax purposes. An S corporation is taxed like a partnership, so the corporate income passes through to the shareholders, who pay personal income tax on it. This treatment enables the S corporation to avoid the double taxation imposed on regular corporations. In addition, the shareholders' tax brackets may be lower than the tax bracket that the corporation would have been in if the tax had been imposed at the corporate level.

In spite of these benefits, the S corporation has lost much of its appeal. The newer limited liability business forms, such as LLCs, offer similar tax advantages and greater flexibility.

Public and Private Corporations A **public corporation** is a corporation formed by the government to meet some political or governmental purpose. Cities and towns that incorporate are common examples. In addition, many federal government organizations, such as the U.S. Postal Service, the Tennessee Valley Authority, and AMTRAK, are public corporations.

Note that a public corporation is not the same as a **publicly held corporation**. A publicly held corporation (often called a *public company*) is any corporation whose shares are publicly traded in a securities market, such as the New York Stock Exchange or the NASDAQ stock market.

Private corporations, in contrast, are created either wholly or in part for private benefit—that is, for profit. Most corporations are private. Although they may serve a public purpose, as a public electric or gas utility does, they are owned by private persons rather than by a government.

Nonprofit Corporations Corporations formed for purposes other than making a profit are called *nonprofit* or *not-for-profit* corporations. Private hospitals, educational institutions, charities, and religious organizations, for instance, are frequently organized as nonprofit corporations. The nonprofit corporation is a convenient form of organization that allows various groups to own property and to form contracts without exposing the individual members to personal liability.

In some circumstances, a nonprofit corporation and its members may also be immune from liability for a personal injury caused by its negligence. Whether those circumstances were present in the following case was the question before the court.

Case Analysis 19.2

Pantano v. Newark Museum

Superior Court of New Jersey, Appellate Division, __ A.3d __, 2016 WL 528771 (2016).

In the Language of the Court

PER CURIAM.

* * * *

* * * Plaintiff [Loredana Pantano] slipped and fell on icy steps at an entrance to the [Newark] Museum, suffering injuries to her back. At the time, plaintiff was employed as an immigration attorney by La Casa de Don Pedro (La Casa), a nonprofit organization located in Newark [New Jersey]. Upon arrival at her office that day, plaintiff was told by La Casa's Director of Personal Development to go to the Museum for an educational panel discussion being held as part of La Casa's fortieth anniversary celebration.

* * * The event was one of several organized to celebrate and commemorate the organization's history and role in the development of Newark. Staff members were not directly engaged in fundraising, but they were told to mingle with those attending the event, some of whom were contributors to La Casa. The Museum charged La Casa a fee for the use of the facility, specifically an auditorium to be used by the panel and those in attendance.

The Museum is a nonprofit association organized exclusively for charitable, artistic, scientific, educational, historical and cultural purposes * * * . It does, on occasion, rent its facilities to the public in order to generate income.

Plaintiff filed suit [in a New Jersey state court against the Museum] alleging the Museum was negligent in its maintenance of the premises. * * * The Museum moved for summary judgment, contending that plaintiff was a direct beneficiary of its charitable endeavors.

* * * *

* * * The judge granted the Museum's motion, and this appeal followed.

Plaintiff contends that she was not a beneficiary of the Museum's charitable purposes at the time of her fall because she was on the premises at the direction of her employer. We agree that pursuant to the [New Jersey Supreme] Court's holding in *Mayer v. Fairlawn Jewish Center*, 38 N.J. 549, 186 A.2d 274 (1962), plaintiff was not a direct recipient of the Museum's good works.

* * * *

In pertinent part, the [state Charitable Immunity Act (CIA)] provides:

Case 19.2 Continues

Case 19.2 Continued

No nonprofit corporation * * * shall * * * be liable to respond in damages to any person who shall suffer damage from the negligence * * * of such corporation * * * where such person is a beneficiary, to whatever degree, of the works of such nonprofit corporation * * * ; provided, however, that such immunity from liability shall not extend to any person * * * where such person is one unconcerned in and unrelated to and outside of the benefactions of such corporation.

The CIA serves two primary purposes. *First, immunity preserves a charity's assets. Second, immunity recognizes that a beneficiary of the services of a charitable organization has entered into a relationship that exempts the benefactor from liability.* [Emphasis added.]

* * * The established test for determining whether a party is a beneficiary of the works of a charity has two prongs. The first is that the institution pleading the immunity, at the time in question, was engaged in the performance of the charitable objectives it was organized to advance. The second is that the injured party must have been a direct recipient of those good works.

* * * *

As to the first prong, * * * a qualifying organization does not lose its statutory immunity merely because it charges money for its services, unless it makes a profit or collects fees for services totally unrelated to its organizational pursuits. * * * Hosting an educational panel discussion in the auditorium was entirely consistent with the Museum's charitable endeavors.

The second prong of the test * * * distinguishes between persons benefiting from the charity, and persons who contribute to the charity by virtue of their attendance or participation.

* * * *

In *Mayer*, * * * an employee of the Development Corporation for Israel was promoting the sale of bonds at a dinner on the premises of [Fairlawn Jewish Center, the defendant, when he sustained an injury].

* * * *

* * * He was there in fulfillment of his function and obligation as an employee to engage in the employer's work at the direction of the employer, and not for the purpose of receiving personally the philanthropy of the Center. Under the circumstances present he was a stranger to the charity and the [CIA did] not stand in the way of recovery.

* * * *

* * * *[Thus, under the CIA,] to be a beneficiary under the second prong, the injured party must be a direct recipient of the Museum's good works. Only those unconcerned in and unrelated to the benefactions of the organization are not beneficiaries.* [Emphasis added.]

* * * *

As an intermediate appellate court, we are bound to follow and enforce the decisions of the Supreme Court. Under [*Mayer*], plaintiff, as an employee of La Casa who was ordered on the day of her fall to attend the panel discussion at the Museum, was not a direct beneficiary of the Museum's charitable endeavors.

We therefore reverse the order granting summary judgment to the Museum and remand the matter.

Legal Reasoning Questions

1. How do the purposes of the Charitable Immunity Act (CIA) support each other?

2. Can a person be a direct beneficiary of a nonprofit's good works even though the person is on the nonprofit's premises under the direction of a third party? Explain.

3. Suppose that the museum had not been hosting an educational panel in its auditorium but instead had rented the facility to an organization for a sales conference. Would the result have been different? Discuss.

Professional Corporations Professionals such as physicians, lawyers, dentists, and accountants can incorporate. A professional corporation is typically identified by the letters *P.C.* (professional corporation), *S.C.* (service corporation), or *P.A.* (professional association).

In general, the laws governing the formation and operation of professional corporations are similar to those governing ordinary business corporations. There are some differences in terms of liability, however. For liability purposes, some courts treat professional corporations somewhat like partnerships and hold each professional liable for malpractice committed within the scope of the business by others in the firm.

Benefit Corporations A growing number of states have enacted legislation that creates a relatively new corporate form called a *benefit corporation*. A **benefit corporation** is a for-profit corporation that seeks to have a material positive impact on society and the environment. Benefit corporations differ from traditional corporations in the following ways:

1. *Purpose.* Although the corporation is designed to make a profit, its purpose is to benefit the public as a whole. (In contrast, the purpose of an ordinary business corporation is to provide long-term shareholder value.) The directors of a benefit corporation must, during

the decision-making process, consider the impact of their decisions on society and the environment.

2. *Accountability.* Shareholders of a benefit corporation determine whether the company has achieved a material positive impact. Shareholders also have a right of private action, called a *benefit enforcement proceeding,* enabling them to sue the corporation if it fails to pursue or create public benefit.

3. *Transparency.* A benefit corporation must issue an annual benefit report on its overall social and environmental performance that uses a recognized third-party standard to assess its performance. The report must be delivered to the shareholders and posted on a public Web site.

19–2 Formation and Powers

Many of today's largest companies started as sole proprietorships or partnerships. They converted to corporate entities as they grew because they needed to obtain additional capital by issuing shares of stock. Incorporating a business is much simpler today than it was twenty years ago, and many states allow businesses to incorporate via the Internet.

19–2a Promotional Activities

In the past, preliminary steps were taken to organize and promote a business prior to incorporating. Contracts were made with investors and others on behalf of the future corporation. Today, due to the relative ease of forming a corporation in most states, persons incorporating their business rarely, if ever, engage in preliminary promotional activities.

Nevertheless, businesspersons should understand that they are personally liable for any preincorporation contracts made with investors, accountants, or others on behalf of the future corporation. Personal liability continues until the newly formed corporation assumes liability for the preincorporation contracts through a novation.

19–2b Incorporation Procedures

Each state has its own set of incorporation procedures. Most often, they are listed on the secretary of state's Web site. Generally, however, all incorporators follow several basic steps, discussed next.

Select the State of Incorporation Because state corporate laws differ, individuals seeking to incorporate a business may look for the states that offer the most advantageous tax or other provisions. Many corporations, for instance, have chosen to incorporate in Delaware because it has historically had the least restrictive laws, along with provisions that favor corporate management. For reasons of convenience and cost, though, businesses often choose to incorporate in the state in which the corporation's business will primarily be conducted.

Secure the Corporate Name The choice of a corporate name is subject to state approval to ensure against duplication or deception. Most state statutes require a search to confirm that the chosen corporate name is available. A new corporation's name cannot be the same as, or deceptively similar to, the name of an existing corporation doing business within the state. All states require the corporation's name to include the word *Corporation (Corp.), Incorporated (Inc.), Company (Co.),* or *Limited (Ltd.).*

Prepare the Articles of Incorporation The primary document needed to incorporate a business is the **articles of incorporation**. The articles include basic information about the corporation and serve as a primary source of authority for its future organization and business functions. The person or persons who execute (sign) the articles are the *incorporators.*

Articles of incorporation vary widely depending on the jurisdiction and the size and type of the corporation. Generally, though, the articles *must* include the following information [RMBCA 2.02]:

1. The name of the corporation.
2. The number of shares of stock the corporation is authorized to issue [RMBCA 2.02(a)]. (Large corporations often also state a par value for each share, such as $0.20 per share, and specify the various types or classes of stock authorized for issuance.)
3. The name and street address of the corporation's initial registered agent and registered office. The registered agent is the person who can receive legal documents (such as orders to appear in court) on behalf of the corporation. The registered office is usually the main corporate office.
4. The name and address of each incorporator.

In addition, the articles *may* set forth other information, such as the names and addresses of the initial members of the board of directors and the duration and purpose of the corporation. A corporation has perpetual existence unless the articles state otherwise.

A corporation can be formed for any lawful purpose. The RMBCA does not require the articles to include a specific statement of purpose. Consequently, the articles often include only a general statement of purpose. By not mentioning specifics, the corporation avoids the need for future amendments to the corporate articles [RMBCA 2.02(b)(2)(i), 3.01]. Similarly, the articles do not provide much detail about the firm's operations, which are spelled out in the company's *bylaws* (discussed shortly).

File the Articles with the State   Once the articles of incorporation have been prepared and signed, they are sent to the appropriate state official, usually the secretary of state, along with the required filing fee. In most states, the secretary of state then stamps the articles "Filed" and returns a copy of the articles to the incorporators. Once this occurs, the corporation officially exists.

19–2c First Organizational Meeting to Adopt Bylaws

After incorporation, the first organizational meeting must be held. If the articles of incorporation named the initial board of directors, then the directors, by majority vote, call the meeting. If the articles did not name the directors (as is typical), then the incorporators hold the meeting to elect the directors and complete any other business necessary.

Usually, the most important function of this meeting is the adoption of **bylaws,** which are the internal rules of management for the corporation. The bylaws cannot conflict with the state corporation statute or the articles of incorporation [RMBCA 2.06]. Under the RMBCA, the shareholders may amend or repeal the bylaws. The board of directors may also amend or repeal the bylaws, unless the articles of incorporation or provisions of the state corporation statute reserve this power to the shareholders [RMBCA 10.20].

The bylaws typically describe such matters as voting requirements for shareholders, the election of the board of directors, and the methods of replacing directors. Bylaws also frequently outline the manner and time of holding shareholders' and board meetings.

19–2d Improper Incorporation

The procedures for incorporation are very specific. If they are not followed precisely, others may be able to challenge the existence of the corporation. Errors in incorporation procedures can become important when, for instance, a third party who is attempting to enforce a contract or bring a suit for a tort injury learns of them.

De Jure Corporations   If a corporation has substantially complied with all conditions precedent to incorporation, the corporation is said to have *de jure* (rightful and lawful) existence. In most states and under RMBCA

2.03(b), the secretary of state's filing of the articles of incorporation is conclusive proof that all mandatory statutory provisions have been met [RMBCA 2.03(b)].

Sometimes, the incorporators fail to comply with all statutory mandates. If the defect is minor, such as an incorrect address listed on the articles of incorporation, most courts will overlook the defect and find that a *de jure* corporation exists.

De Facto Corporations   If the defect in formation is substantial, such as a corporation's failure to hold an organizational meeting to adopt bylaws, the outcome will vary depending on the jurisdiction. Some states, including Mississippi, New York, Ohio, and Oklahoma, recognize the common law doctrine of *de facto* corporation. In those states, the courts will treat a corporation as a legal corporation despite a defect in its formation if the following three requirements are met:

1. A state statute exists under which the corporation can be validly incorporated.
2. The parties have made a good faith attempt to comply with the statute.
3. The parties have already undertaken to do business as a corporation.

Many state courts, however, have interpreted their states' version of the RMBCA as abolishing the common law doctrine of *de facto* corporations. These states include Alaska, Arizona, Minnesota, New Mexico, Oregon, South Dakota, Tennessee, Utah, and Washington, as well as the District of Columbia. In those jurisdictions, if there is a substantial defect in complying with the incorporation statute, the corporation does not legally exist, and the incorporators are personally liable.

Corporation by Estoppel   Sometimes, a business association holds itself out to others as being a corporation when it has made no attempt to incorporate. In those situations, the firm normally will be estopped (prevented) from denying corporate status in a lawsuit by a third party. The estoppel doctrine most commonly applies when a third party contracts with an entity that claims to be a corporation but has not filed articles of incorporation. It may also apply when a third party contracts with a person claiming to be an agent of a corporation that does not in fact exist.

When justice requires, courts in some states will treat an alleged corporation as if it were an actual corporation for the purpose of determining rights and liabilities in particular circumstances. Recognition of corporate status does not extend beyond the resolution of the problem at hand.

■ **CASE IN POINT 19.3** W.P. Media, Inc., and Alabama MBA, Inc., agreed to form a wireless Internet services company. W.P. Media was to create a wireless network, and Alabama MBA was to contribute the capital. Hugh Brown signed the parties' contract on behalf of Alabama MBA as the chair of its board. At the time, however, Alabama MBA's articles of incorporation had not yet been filed. Brown filed the articles of incorporation the following year.

Later, Brown and Alabama MBA filed a suit alleging that W.P. Media had breached their contract by not building the wireless network. W.P. Media contended that Alabama MBA had not existed as a corporation when the agreement was signed and thus the agreement was void. The Supreme Court of Alabama held that because W.P. Media had treated Alabama MBA as a corporation, W.P. Media was estopped from denying Alabama MBA's corporate existence.[4] ■

19–2e Corporate Financing

Part of the process of corporate formation involves corporate financing. Corporations normally are financed by the issuance and sale of corporate **securities**, which include stocks and bonds. **Stocks**, or *equity securities*, represent the purchase of ownership in the business firm. **Bonds**, or *debt securities*, represent the borrowing of funds by firms (and governments).

Stocks Issuing stocks is a standard way that corporations obtain financing. Basically, stocks represent ownership in a business firm. The true ownership of a corporation is represented by **common stock**, which provides a proportionate interest in the corporation with regard to (1) control (voting rights), (2) earnings, and (3) net assets. A shareholder's interest is generally in proportion to the number of shares he or she owns out of the total number of shares issued.

The issuing firm is not obligated to return a principal amount per share to each holder of common stock, because no firm can ensure that the market price per share of its common stock will not decline over time. The issuing firm also does not have to guarantee a dividend. Indeed, some corporations never pay dividends. Holders of common stock are investors who assume a *residual* position in the overall financial structure of a business. In terms of receiving payment for their investments, they are last in line.

Preferred stock is stock with *preferences*. Holders of preferred stock usually have priority over holders of common stock as to dividends and payment on dissolution of the corporation but frequently do not have the right to vote. Holders of preferred stock have a stronger position than common shareholders with respect to dividends and claims on assets, but they will not share in the full prosperity of the firm if it grows successfully over time. Preferred stockholders do receive fixed dividends periodically, however, and they may benefit to some extent from changes in the market price of the shares.

Bonds Bonds are issued by business firms and by governments at all levels as evidence of the funds they are borrowing from investors. Bonds normally have a designated *maturity date*—the date when the principal, or face amount, of the bond is returned to the investor. They are sometimes referred to as *fixed-income securities* because their owners (that is, the creditors) receive fixed-dollar interest payments, usually semiannually, during the period of time before maturity. Because debt financing represents a legal obligation on the part of the corporation, various features and terms of a particular bond issue are specified in a lending agreement.

Venture Capital Start-up businesses and high-risk enterprises often obtain venture capital financing. **Venture capital** is capital provided to new business ventures by professional, outside investors (*venture capitalists*, usually groups of wealthy investors and securities firms). Venture capital investments are high risk—the investors must be willing to lose all of their invested funds—but offer the potential for well-above-average returns at some point in the future.

To obtain venture capital financing, the start-up business typically gives up a share of its ownership to the venture capitalists. Venture capitalists also may provide managerial and technical expertise, and they nearly always are given some control over the new company's decisions. Many Internet-based companies, such as Google, were initially financed by venture capital.

Private Equity Capital Private equity firms obtain their capital from wealthy investors in private markets. The firms use their **private equity capital** to invest in existing—often, publicly traded—corporations. Usually, they buy an entire corporation and then reorganize it. Sometimes, divisions of the purchased company are sold off to pay down debt. Ultimately, the private equity firm may sell shares in the reorganized (and perhaps more profitable) company to the public in an *initial public offering* (IPO). In this way, the private equity firm can make profits by selling its shares in the company.

---

4. *Brown v. W.P. Media, Inc.*, 17 So.3d 1167 (Ala. 2009).

Crowdfunding Start-up businesses can also attempt to obtain financing through *crowdfunding*. **Crowdfunding** is a cooperative activity in which people network and pool funds and other resources via the Internet to assist a cause or invest in a venture. Sometimes, crowdfunding is used to raise funds for charitable purposes, such as disaster relief, but increasingly it is being used to finance budding entrepreneurs.

In 2016, new Securities and Exchange Commission (SEC) rules went into effect to allow companies to offer and sell securities through crowdfunding. The rules removed a decades-old ban on public solicitation for private investments, which means that companies can advertise investment opportunities to the general public. According to the SEC, the new rules are intended to help smaller companies raise capital while providing investors with additional protections. Companies are required to make specific disclosures and are limited to raising $1 million a year through crowdfunding.

19–2f Corporate Powers

When a corporation is created, the express and implied powers necessary to achieve its purpose also come into existence.

Express Powers The express powers of a corporation are found in its articles of incorporation, in the law of the state of incorporation, and in the state and federal constitutions. Corporate bylaws and the resolutions of the corporation's board of directors also establish express powers.

The following order of priority is used if a conflict arises among the various documents involving a corporation:

1. The U.S. Constitution.
2. State constitutions.
3. State statutes.
4. The articles of incorporation.
5. Bylaws.
6. Resolutions of the board of directors.

It is important that the bylaws set forth the specific operating rules of the corporation. State corporation statutes frequently provide default rules that apply if the company's bylaws are silent on an issue.

On occasion, the U.S. government steps in to challenge what a corporation may consider one of its express powers. This chapter's *Global Insight* discusses a dispute between the government and Microsoft Corporation over a demand that the company provide the government with access to e-mail stored in servers on foreign soil.

Implied Powers When a corporation is created, it acquires certain implied powers. Barring express constitutional, statutory, or other prohibitions, the corporation has the implied power to perform all acts reasonably necessary to accomplish its corporate purposes. For this reason, a corporation has the implied power to borrow and lend funds within certain limits and to extend credit to parties with whom it has contracts.

Most often, the president or chief executive officer of the corporation signs the necessary documents on behalf of the corporation. Corporate officers such as these have the implied power to bind the corporation in matters directly connected with the *ordinary* business affairs of the enterprise.

There is a limit to what a corporate officer can do, though. A corporate officer does not have the authority to bind the corporation to an action that will greatly affect the corporate purpose or undertaking, such as the sale of substantial corporate assets.

Ultra Vires Doctrine The term **ultra vires** means "beyond the power." In corporate law, acts of a corporation that are beyond its express or implied powers are *ultra vires* acts. In the past, most cases dealing with *ultra vires* acts involved contracts made for unauthorized purposes. Now, because the articles of incorporation of most private corporations do not state a specific purpose, the *ultra vires* doctrine has declined in importance.

Today, cases that allege *ultra vires* acts usually involve nonprofit corporations or municipal (public) corporations. ■ **CASE IN POINT 19.4** Four men formed a nonprofit corporation to create the Armenian Genocide Museum & Memorial (AGM&M). The bylaws appointed them as trustees (similar to corporate directors) for life. One of the trustees, Gerard L. Cafesjian, became the chair and president of AGM&M. Eventually, the relationship among the trustees deteriorated, and Cafesjian resigned.

The corporation then brought a suit claiming that Cafesjian had engaged in numerous *ultra vires* acts, self-dealing, and mismanagement. Although the bylaws required an 80 percent affirmative vote of the trustees to take action, Cafesjian had taken many actions without the board's approval. He had also entered into contracts for real estate transactions in which he had a personal interest. Because Cafesjian had taken actions that exceeded his authority and had failed to follow rules set forth in the bylaws, the court ruled that the corporation could go forward with its suit.[5] ■

---

5. *Armenian Assembly of America, Inc. v. Cafesjian*, 692 F.Supp.2d 20 (D.C. Cir. 2010).

GLOBAL INSIGHT

Does Cloud Computing Have a Nationality?

Everyone has heard of "the cloud," and most people use it for the storage of their digital data—photos, e-mails, music, documents, and just about anything else. Not surprisingly, major global digital players like Apple, Amazon, Google, and Microsoft have spent billions to create "clouds" of servers all over the world. In the clouds are stored confidential, organized, and secure data. The revenues generated by the U.S. cloud computing industry exceed $100 billion a year. But is the long-term picture for such revenues in doubt?

Microsoft Battles and the Global Cloud Industry Waits

The U.S. government issued a warrant to Microsoft to produce e-mails related to a narcotics case from a Hotmail account. That account was hosted in a Microsoft cloud location in Ireland. Microsoft refused, but a magistrate judge in the Southern District of New York confirmed the government's right to the Ireland-located e-mails.[a] On appeal to a U.S. district court, Microsoft again lost.[b] Microsoft appealed to the U.S. Court of Appeals for the Second Circuit and won in 2016.[c]

Microsoft maintained that "the power to embark on unilateral law enforcement incursions into a foreign sovereign country—directly or indirectly—has profound policy consequences. Worse still, it threatens the privacy of U.S. citizens." According to Microsoft's deputy general counsel, David Howard, "The U.S. government doesn't have the power to search a home in another country, nor should it have the power search the content of e-mails stored overseas."

A number of organizations apparently agreed with Microsoft. The ACLU, Apple, eBay, the Electronic Frontier Foundation, Fox News, the Irish government, and National Public Radio all filed "friend of the court" briefs in support of Microsoft's position. The federal appellate court was persuaded that the warrant could not be enforced extraterritorially.

Impact on the Industry

More was at stake in this case than the issues Microsoft identified. If Microsoft had ultimately lost, some industry experts predicted that U.S. technology companies would lose up to $35 billion a year from their cloud storage business. Foreign corporations and individuals would no longer trust U.S. companies to keep their data secret.

a. *In re Warrant to Search a Certain E-Mail Account Controlled and Maintained by Microsoft Corp.*, 15 F.Supp.3d 466 (S.D.N.Y. 2014).
b. *In re Warrant to Search a Certain E-Mail Account Controlled and Maintained by Microsoft Corp.*, 2014 WL 4629624 (S.D.N.Y. 2014).
c. *In Matter of Warrant to Search a Certain E-Mail Account Controlled and Maintained by Microsoft Corp.*, 829 F.3d 197 (2d Cir. 2016).

Critical Thinking *The law underlying the case against Microsoft is the Electronic Communications Privacy Act, which was enacted three years before the invention of the World Wide Web. Should that law still apply today? Why or why not?*

Remedies for *Ultra Vires* Acts Under Section 3.04 of the RMBCA, shareholders can seek an injunction from a court to prevent (or stop) the corporation from engaging in *ultra vires* acts. The attorney general in the state of incorporation can also bring an action to obtain an injunction against the *ultra vires* transactions or to seek dissolution of the corporation. The corporation or its shareholders (on behalf of the corporation) can seek damages from the officers and directors who were responsible for the *ultra vires* acts.

19–3 Piercing the Corporate Veil

Occasionally, the owners use a corporate entity to perpetrate a fraud, circumvent the law, or in some other way accomplish an illegitimate objective. In these situations, the courts will ignore the corporate structure by **piercing the corporate veil** and exposing the shareholders to personal liability [RMBCA 2.04].

Generally, courts pierce the veil when the corporate privilege is abused for personal benefit or when the corporate business is treated so carelessly that it is indistinguishable from that of a controlling shareholder. When the facts show that great injustice would result from a shareholder's use of a corporation to avoid individual responsibility, a court will look behind the corporate structure to the individual shareholders.

19–3a Factors That Lead Courts to Pierce the Corporate Veil

The following are some of the factors that frequently cause the courts to pierce the corporate veil:

1. A party is tricked or misled into dealing with the corporation rather than the individual.
2. The corporation is set up never to make a profit or always to be insolvent. Alternatively, it is too thinly capitalized—that is, it has insufficient capital at the time it is formed to meet its prospective debts or potential liabilities.
3. The corporation is formed to evade an existing legal obligation.
4. Statutory corporate formalities, such as holding required corporation meetings, are not followed.
5. Personal and corporate interests are mixed together, or **commingled,** to such an extent that the corporation has no separate identity.

■ **CASE IN POINT 19.5** Dog House Investments, LLC, operated a dog "camp" in Nashville, Tennessee. Dog House leased the property from Teal Properties, Inc., which was owned by Jerry Teal, its sole shareholder. Under the lease, Teal Properties promised to repair damage from fire or other causes that rendered the property "untenantable" (unusable). Following a flood, Dog House notified Jerry that the property was untenantable. Jerry assured Dog House that the flood damage was covered by insurance but took no steps to restore the property. The parties then agreed that Dog House would undertake the repairs and be reimbursed by Teal Properties.

Dog House spent $39,000 to repair the damage and submitted invoices for reimbursement. Teal Properties recovered $40,000 from its insurance company but did not pay Dog House. Close to bankruptcy, Dog House filed a suit in a Tennessee state court against Teal Properties and Jerry. The court pierced the corporate veil and held Jerry personally liable for the repair costs. Jerry appealed, but a state intermediate appellate court affirmed. The reviewing court found that piercing the corporate veil was appropriate because Jerry did not maintain an arms-length relationship with the corporation. Teal Properties owned no property and had no assets—it merely received rent that was immediately paid to Jerry Teal.[6] ■

State corporation codes usually do not prohibit a shareholder from lending funds to her or his corporation. Courts will scrutinize such a transaction closely if the loan comes from an officer, director, or majority shareholder, however. Loans from persons who control the corporation must be made in good faith and for fair value.

19–3b A Potential Problem for Close Corporations

The potential for corporate assets to be used for personal benefit is especially great in a close corporation. In such a corporation, the separate status of the corporate entity and the shareholders (often family members) must be carefully preserved. Practices that invite trouble for a close corporation include the commingling of corporate and personal funds and the shareholders' continuous personal use of corporate property (for instance, vehicles).

Typically, courts are reluctant to hold shareholders in close corporations personally liable for corporate obligations unless there is some evidence of fraud or wrongdoing. ■ **CASE IN POINT 19.6** Pip, Jimmy, and Theodore Brennan are brothers and shareholders of Brennan's, Inc., which owns and operates New Orleans's famous Brennan's Restaurant. As a close corporation, Brennan's, Inc., did not hold formal corporate meetings with agendas and minutes, but it did maintain corporate books, hold corporate bank accounts, and file corporate tax returns.

The Brennan brothers retained attorney Edward Colbert to represent them in a family matter, and the attorney's bills were sent to the restaurant and paid from the corporate account. Later, when Brennan's, Inc., sued Colbert for malpractice, Colbert argued that the court should pierce the corporate veil because the Brennan brothers did not observe corporate formalities. The court refused to do so, however, because there was no evidence of fraud, malfeasance, or other wrongdoing by the Brennan brothers. There is no requirement for small, close corporations to operate with the formality usually expected of larger corporations.[7] ■

19–3c The Alter-Ego Theory

Sometimes, courts pierce the corporate veil under the theory that the corporation was not operated as a separate entity. Rather, it was just another side (the *alter ego*) of the individual or group that actually controlled the corporation. This is called the *alter-ego theory*.

The alter-ego theory is applied when a corporation is so dominated and controlled by an individual (or group) that the separate identities of the person (or group) and the corporation are no longer distinct. Courts use the alter-ego theory to avoid injustice or fraud that would result if wrongdoers were allowed to hide behind the protection of limited liability.

■ **CASE IN POINT 19.7** Steiner Electric Company (Steiner) is an Illinois corporation that sells electrical

6. *Dog House Investments, LLC v. Teal Properties, Inc.*, 448 S.W.3d 905 (Tenn.Ct.App. 2014).

7. *Brennan's, Inc. v. Colbert*, 85 So.3d 787 (La.Ct.App. 2012).

products. Steiner sold goods to Delta Equipment Company and Sackett Systems, Inc., on credit. Both Delta and Sackett were owned and controlled by a single shareholder—Leonard J. Maniscalco. Steiner was not fully paid for the products it sold on credit to Delta and Sackett. Eventually, Steiner sued Delta and won a default judgment, but by that time, Delta had been dissolved. Steiner then asked a state court to pierce the corporate veil and hold Maniscalco liable for the debts of the two companies, claiming the companies were merely Maniscalco's alter egos.

The court agreed and held Maniscalco liable. Delta and Sackett were inadequately capitalized, transactions were not properly documented, funds were commingled, and corporate formalities were not observed. Maniscalco had consistently treated both companies in such a manner that they were, in practice, his alter egos.[8] ■

19–4 Directors and Officers

Corporate directors, officers, and shareholders all play different roles within the corporate entity, and it is important to know the rights and duties of each.

19–4a Directors

The board of directors is the ultimate authority in every corporation. Directors have responsibility for all policy-making decisions necessary to the management of all corporate affairs. No *individual* director, however, can act to bind the corporation. The directors must act as a body in carrying out routine corporate business.

The board selects and removes the corporate officers, determines the capital structure of the corporation, and declares dividends. Each director has one vote, and customarily the majority rules.

Few qualifications are required for directors. Only a handful of states impose minimum age and residency requirements.

Election of Directors Subject to statutory limitations, the number of directors is set forth in the corporation's articles or bylaws. Historically, the minimum number of directors has been three, but today many states permit fewer. Normally, the incorporators appoint the first board of directors at the time the corporation is created, or the directors are named in the articles of incorporation. The initial board serves until the first annual shareholders' meeting. Subsequent directors are elected by a majority vote of the shareholders.

A director usually serves for a term of one year—from annual meeting to annual meeting. Most state statutes permit longer and staggered terms. A common practice is to elect one-third of the board members each year for a three-year term. In this way, there is greater management continuity.

A director can be removed *for cause*—that is, for failing to perform a required duty—either as specified in the articles or bylaws or by shareholder action. When a vacancy on the board occurs, such as if a director dies or resigns, either the shareholders or the board itself can fill the vacant position, depending on state law and the bylaws. Note that even when an election is authorized, a court can invalidate the results if the directors have attempted to manipulate the election in order to reduce the shareholders' influence.

Compensation of Directors In the past, corporate directors were rarely compensated. Today, directors are often paid at least nominal sums. In large corporations, they may receive more substantial compensation because of the time, work, effort, and especially risk involved.

Most states permit the corporate articles or bylaws to authorize compensation for directors. In fact, the RMBCA states that unless the articles or bylaws provide otherwise, the board itself may set the directors' compensation [RMBCA 8.11]. Directors also receive indirect benefits, such as business contacts and prestige, and other rewards, such as stock options.

In many corporations, directors are also chief corporate officers (such as president or chief executive officer) and receive compensation in their managerial positions. A director who is also an officer of the corporation is referred to as an **inside director,** whereas a director who does not hold a management position is an **outside director.** Typically, a corporation's board of directors includes both inside and outside directors.

Board of Directors' Meetings The board of directors conducts business by holding formal meetings with recorded minutes. The dates of regular meetings are usually established in the articles or bylaws or by board resolution, and ordinarily no further notice is required. Special meetings can be called as well, with notice sent to all directors.

Most states allow directors to participate in board of directors' meetings from remote locations. Directors can participate via telephone, Web conferencing, or Skype,

---

8. *Steiner Electric Co. v. Maniscalco,* 51 N.E.3d 45, 2016 IL App (1st) 132023 (2016).

provided that all the directors can simultaneously hear one another during the meeting [RMBCA 8.20].

Quorum of Directors. Unless the articles of incorporation or bylaws specify a greater number, a majority of the board of directors normally constitutes a *quorum* [RMBCA 8.24]. (A **quorum** is the minimum number of members of a body of officials or other group that must be present for business to be validly transacted.) Some state statutes specifically allow corporations to set a quorum at less than a majority but not less than one-third of the directors.[9]

Voting. Once a quorum is present, the directors transact business and vote on issues affecting the corporation. Each director present at the meeting has one vote.[10] Ordinary matters generally require a simple majority vote, but certain extraordinary issues may require a greater-than-majority vote.

Committees of the Board of Directors

When a board of directors has a large number of members and must deal with myriad complex business issues, meetings can become unwieldy. Therefore, the boards of large, publicly held corporations typically create committees of directors and delegate certain tasks to these committees. By focusing on specific subjects, committees can increase the efficiency of the board.

Two common types of committees are the *executive committee* and the *audit committee*. An executive committee handles interim management decisions between board meetings. It is limited to dealing with ordinary business matters and does not have the power to declare dividends, amend the bylaws, or authorize the issuance of stock. The audit committee is responsible for the selection, compensation, and oversight of the independent public accountants that audit the firm's financial records. *The Sarbanes-Oxley Act requires all publicly held corporations to have an audit committee.*

Rights of Directors

A corporate director must have certain rights to function properly in that position, including those of participation, inspection, and indemnification.

Right to Participation. The *right to participation* means that directors are entitled to participate in all board of directors' meetings and have a right to be notified of these meetings. Because the dates of regular board meetings are usually specified in the bylaws, no notice of these meetings is required. If special meetings are called, however, notice is required unless waived by the director [RMBCA 8.23].

Right of Inspection. A director also has a *right of inspection,* which means that each director can access the corporation's books and records, facilities, and premises. Inspection rights are essential for directors to make informed decisions and to exercise the necessary supervision over corporate officers and employees. This right of inspection is almost absolute and cannot be restricted (by the articles, bylaws, or any act of the board of directors).

■ **CASE IN POINT 19.8** NavLink, Inc., a Delaware corporation, provides high-end data management for customers and governments in Saudi Arabia, Qatar, Lebanon, and the United Arab Emirates. NavLink's co-founders, George Chammas and Laurent Delifer, served on its board of directors.

Chammas and Delifer were concerned about the company's 2015 annual budget and three-year operating plan. Despite repeated requests, Chammas was never given the meeting minutes from several board meetings in 2015. Chammas and Delifer believed that the other directors were withholding information and holding secret "pre-board meetings" at which plans and decisions were being made without them. They filed suit in a Delaware state court seeking inspection rights.

The court ordered NavLink to provide the plaintiffs with board meeting minutes and with communications from NavLink's secretary regarding the minutes. The plaintiffs were also entitled to inspect corporate documents and communications concerning NavLink's 2015 budget and three-year plan.[11] ■

Right to Indemnification. When a director becomes involved in litigation by virtue of her or his position, the director may have a *right to indemnification* (reimbursement) for the legal costs, fees, and damages incurred. Most states allow corporations to indemnify and purchase liability insurance for corporate directors [RMBCA 8.51].

19–4b Corporate Officers and Executives

Corporate officers and other executive employees are hired by the board of directors. At a minimum, most corporations have a president, one or more vice presidents, a secretary,

---

9. See, for example, Delaware Code Annotated Title 8, Section 141(b); and New York Business Corporation Law Section 707.
10. Note that Louisiana allows a director to vote by proxy under certain circumstances.

11. *Chammas v. NavLink, Inc.,* 2016 WL 767714 (Del.Ch. 2016).

and a treasurer. In most states, an individual can hold more than one office, such as president and secretary, and can be both an officer and a director of the corporation.

In addition to carrying out the duties articulated in the bylaws, corporate and managerial officers act as agents of the corporation. Therefore, the ordinary rules of agency normally apply to their employment.

Corporate officers and other high-level managers are employees of the company, so their rights are defined by employment contracts. Nevertheless, the board of directors normally can remove a corporate officer at any time with or without cause. If the directors remove an officer in violation of the terms of an employment contract, however, the corporation may be liable for breach of contract.

19–4c Duties and Liabilities of Directors and Officers

The duties of corporate directors and officers are similar because both groups are involved in decision making and are in positions of control. Directors and officers are considered to be fiduciaries of the corporation because their relationship with the corporation and its shareholders is one of trust and confidence. As fiduciaries, directors and officers owe ethical—and legal—duties to the corporation and to the shareholders as a group. These fiduciary duties include the duty of care and the duty of loyalty.

Duty of Care Directors and officers must exercise due care in performing their duties. The standard of *due care* has been variously described in judicial decisions and codified in many state corporation codes. Generally, it requires a director or officer to:

1. Act in good faith (honestly).
2. Exercise the care that an ordinarily prudent (careful) person would exercise in similar circumstances.
3. Do what she or he believes is in the best interests of the corporation [RMBCA 8.30(a), 8.42(a)].

If directors or officers fail to exercise due care and the corporation or its shareholders suffer harm as a result, the directors or officers can be held liable for negligence. (An exception is made if the *business judgment rule* applies, as will be discussed shortly.)

Duty to Make Informed Decisions. Directors and officers are expected to be informed on corporate matters and to conduct a reasonable investigation of the situation before making a decision. They must, for instance, attend meetings and presentations, ask for information from those who have it, read reports, and review other written materials. In other words, directors and officers must investigate, study, and discuss matters and evaluate alternatives before making a decision. They cannot decide on the spur of the moment without adequate research.

Although directors and officers are expected to act in accordance with their own knowledge and training, they are also normally entitled to rely on information given to them by certain other persons. Under the laws of most states and Section 8.30(b) of the RMBCA, such persons include competent officers or employees, professionals such as attorneys and accountants, and committees of the board of directors. (The committee must be one on which the director does not serve, however.) The reliance must be in good faith to insulate a director from liability if the information later proves to be inaccurate or unreliable.

Duty to Exercise Reasonable Supervision. Directors are also expected to exercise a reasonable amount of supervision when they delegate work to corporate officers and employees. ■ **EXAMPLE 19.9** Dana, a corporate bank director, fails to attend any board of directors' meetings for five years. In addition, Dana never inspects any of the corporate books or records and generally fails to supervise the activities of the bank president and the loan committee. Meanwhile, Brennan, the bank president, who is a corporate officer, makes various improper loans and permits large overdrafts. In this situation, Dana (the corporate director) can be held liable to the corporation for losses resulting from the unsupervised actions of the bank president and the loan committee. ■

Dissenting Directors. Directors' votes at board of directors' meetings should be entered into the minutes. Sometimes, an individual director disagrees with the majority's vote (which becomes an act of the board of directors). Unless a dissent is entered in the minutes, the director is presumed to have assented. If the directors are later held liable for mismanagement as a result of a decision, dissenting directors are rarely held individually liable to the corporation. For this reason, a director who is absent from a given meeting sometimes registers a dissent with the secretary of the board regarding actions taken at the meeting.

The Business Judgment Rule Directors and officers are expected to exercise due care and to use their best judgment in guiding corporate management, but they are not insurers of business success. Under the **business judgment rule,** a corporate director or officer will not be liable to the corporation or to its shareholders for honest mistakes of judgment and bad business decisions.

Courts give significant deference to the decisions of corporate directors and officers, and consider the reasonableness of a decision at the time it was made, without the benefit of hindsight. Thus, corporate decision makers are not subjected to second-guessing by shareholders or others in the corporation.

When the Rule Applies. The business judgment rule will apply as long as the director or officer:

1. Took reasonable steps to become informed about the matter.
2. Had a rational basis for her or his decision.
3. Did not have a conflict between her or his personal interest and the interest of the corporation.

Provides Broad Protections. The business judgment rule provides broad protections to corporate decision makers. In fact, most courts will apply the rule unless there is evidence of bad faith, fraud, or a clear breach of fiduciary duties.

■ **CASE IN POINT 19.10**   The board of directors of the Chugach Alaska Corporation (CAC) voted to remove Sheri Buretta as the chair and install Robert Henrichs. During his term, Henrichs acted without board approval, made decisions with only his supporters present, retaliated against directors who challenged his decisions, and ignored board rules for conducting meetings. He refused to comply with bylaws that required a special shareholders' meeting in response to a shareholder petition and personally mistreated directors, shareholders, and employees. After six months, the board voted to reinstall Buretta.

CAC filed a suit in an Alaska state court against Henrichs, alleging a breach of fiduciary duty. A jury found Henrichs liable, and the court barred him from serving on CAC's board for five years. The appellate court affirmed. Given the nature and seriousness of Henrichs's misconduct, the business judgment rule did not protect him.[12] ■

Duty of Loyalty   *Loyalty* can be defined as faithfulness to one's obligations and duties. In the corporate context, the duty of loyalty requires directors and officers to subordinate their personal interests to the welfare of the corporation. For instance, a director should not oppose a transaction that is in the corporation's best interest simply because pursuing it may cost the director his or her position. Directors cannot use corporate funds or confidential corporate information for personal advantage and must refrain from self-dealing.

Cases dealing with the duty of loyalty typically involve one or more of the following:

1. Competing with the corporation.
2. Usurping (taking personal advantage of) a corporate opportunity.
3. Pursuing an interest that conflicts with that of the corporation.
4. Using information that is not available to the public to make a profit trading securities (insider trading).
5. Authorizing a corporate transaction that is detrimental to minority shareholders.
6. Selling control over the corporation.

The following *Classic Case* illustrates the conflict that can arise between a corporate officer's personal interest and his or her duty of loyalty.

---

12. *Henrichs v. Chugach Alaska Corp.*, 250 P.3d 531 (Alaska 2011).

Guth v. Loft, Inc.
Supreme Court of Delaware, 23 Del.Ch. 255, 5 A.2d 503 (1939).

Background and Facts   In 1930, Charles Guth became the president of Loft, Inc., a candy-and-restaurant chain. Guth and his family also owned Grace Company, which made syrups for soft drinks. Coca-Cola Company supplied Loft with cola syrup. Unhappy with what he felt was Coca-Cola's high price, Guth entered into an agreement with Roy Megargel to acquire the trademark and formula for Pepsi-Cola and form Pepsi-Cola Corporation. Neither Guth nor Megargel could finance the new venture, however, and Grace Company was insolvent.

Without the knowledge of Loft's board, Guth used Loft's capital, credit, facilities, and employees to further the Pepsi enterprise. At Guth's direction, a Loft employee made the concentrate for the syrup, which was sent to Grace to add sugar and water. Loft charged Grace for the concentrate but allowed forty months' credit. Grace charged Pepsi for the syrup but also granted substantial credit. Grace sold the syrup to Pepsi's customers, including Loft, which paid on delivery or within thirty days. Loft also paid for Pepsi's advertising. Finally, with profits declining as a result of switching from Coca-Cola, Loft filed a suit in a Delaware state court against Guth, Grace, and Pepsi, seeking their Pepsi stock and an accounting. The court entered a judgment in the plaintiff's favor. The defendants appealed to the Delaware Supreme Court.

Case 19.3 Continued

In the Language of the Court

LAYTON, Chief Justice, delivering the opinion of the court:
* * * *

Corporate officers and directors are not permitted to use their position of trust and confidence to further their private interests. * * * They stand in a fiduciary relation to the corporation and its stockholders. A public policy, existing through the years, and derived from a profound knowledge of human characteristics and motives, has established *a rule that demands of a corporate officer or director, peremptorily [not open for debate] and inexorably [unavoidably], the most scrupulous observance of his duty, not only affirmatively to protect the interests of the corporation committed to his charge, but also to refrain from doing anything that would work injury to the corporation* * * * . The rule that requires an undivided and unselfish loyalty to the corporation demands that there shall be no conflict between duty and self-interest. [Emphasis added.]
* * * *

* * * *If there is presented to a corporate officer or director a business opportunity which the corporation is financially able to undertake [that] is * * * in the line of the corporation's business and is of practical advantage to it * * * and, by embracing the opportunity, the self-interest of the officer or director will be brought into conflict with that of his corporation, the law will not permit him to seize the opportunity for himself.* * * * In such circumstances, * * * the corporation may elect to claim all of the benefits of the transaction for itself, and the law will impress a trust in favor of the corporation upon the property, interests and profits so acquired. [Emphasis added.]
* * * *

* * * The appellants contend that no conflict of interest between Guth and Loft resulted from his acquirement and exploitation of the Pepsi-Cola opportunity [and] that the acquisition did not place Guth in competition with Loft * * * . [In this case, however,] Guth was Loft, and Guth was Pepsi. He absolutely controlled Loft. His authority over Pepsi was supreme. As Pepsi, he created and controlled the supply of Pepsi-Cola syrup, and he determined the price and the terms. What he offered, as Pepsi, he had the power, as Loft, to accept. Upon any consideration of human characteristics and motives, he created a conflict between self-interest and duty. He made himself the judge in his own cause. * * * Moreover, a reasonable probability of injury to Loft resulted from the situation forced upon it. Guth was in the same position to impose his terms upon Loft as had been the Coca-Cola Company.

* * * The facts and circumstances demonstrate that Guth's appropriation of the Pepsi-Cola opportunity to himself placed him in a competitive position with Loft with respect to a commodity essential to it, thereby rendering his personal interests incompatible with the superior interests of his corporation; and this situation was accomplished, not openly and with his own resources, but secretly and with the money and facilities of the corporation which was committed to his protection.

Decision and Remedy   *The Delaware Supreme Court upheld the judgment of the lower court. The state supreme court was "convinced that the opportunity to acquire the Pepsi-Cola trademark and formula, goodwill and business belonged to [Loft], and that Guth, as its President, had no right to appropriate the opportunity to himself."*

Impact of This Case on Today's Law   *This early Delaware decision was one of the first to set forth a test for determining when a corporate officer or director has breached the duty of loyalty. The test has two basic parts: Was the opportunity reasonably related to the corporation's line of business, and was the corporation financially able to undertake the opportunity? The court also considered whether the corporation had an interest or expectancy in the opportunity. It recognized that when the corporation had "no interest or expectancy, the officer or director is entitled to treat the opportunity as his own."*

Critical Thinking
- **What If the Facts Were Different?**   *Suppose that Loft's board of directors had approved Pepsi-Cola's use of its personnel and equipment. Would the court's decision have been different? Discuss.*

Conflicts of Interest Corporate directors often have many business affiliations, and a director may sit on the board of more than one corporation. Of course, directors are precluded from entering into or supporting businesses that operate in direct competition with corporations on whose boards they serve. Their fiduciary duty requires them to make a full disclosure of any potential conflicts of interest that might arise in any corporate transaction [RMBCA 8.60].

Sometimes, a corporation enters into a contract or engages in a transaction in which an officer or director has a personal interest. The director or officer must make a *full disclosure* of the nature of the conflicting interest and all facts pertinent to the transaction. He or she must also abstain from voting on the proposed transaction. When these rules are followed, the transaction can proceed. Otherwise, directors would be prevented from ever having financial dealings with the corporations they serve.

■ **EXAMPLE 19.11** Ballo Corporation needs office space. Stephanie Colson, one of its five directors, owns the building adjoining the corporation's headquarters. Colson can negotiate a lease for the space to Ballo if she fully discloses her conflicting interest and any facts known to her about the proposed transaction to Ballo and the other four directors. If the lease arrangement is fair and reasonable, Colson abstains from voting on it, and the other directors unanimously approve it, the contract is valid. ■

Liability of Directors and Officers Directors and officers are exposed to liability on many fronts. They can be held liable for negligence in certain circumstances, as previously discussed. They may also be held liable for the crimes and torts committed by themselves or by corporate employees under their supervision.

Additionally, if shareholders perceive that the corporate directors are not acting in the best interests of the corporation, they may sue the directors on behalf of the corporation. (This is known as a *shareholder's derivative suit*, which will be discussed later in this chapter.) Directors and officers can also be held personally liable under a number of statutes, such as statutes enacted to protect consumers or the environment.

19–5 Shareholders

The acquisition of a share of stock makes a person an owner and a shareholder in a corporation. Shareholders thus own the corporation. Although they have no legal title to corporate property, such as buildings and

equipment, they do have an equitable (ownership) interest in the firm.

As a general rule, shareholders have no responsibility for the daily management of the corporation, although they are ultimately responsible for choosing the board of directors, which does have such control. Ordinarily, corporate officers and other employees owe no direct duty to individual shareholders (unless some contract or special relationship exists between them in addition to the corporate relationship). The duty of officers and directors is to act in the best interests of the corporation and its shareholder-owners *as a whole*. In turn, as you will read later in this chapter, controlling (majority) shareholders owe a fiduciary duty to minority shareholders.

19–5a Shareholders' Powers

Shareholders must approve fundamental changes affecting the corporation before the changes can be implemented. Hence, shareholder approval normally is required to amend the articles of incorporation or bylaws, to conduct a merger or dissolve the corporation, and to sell all or substantially all of the corporation's assets. Some of these powers are subject to prior board approval. Shareholder approval may also be requested (though it is not required) for certain other actions, such as to approve an independent auditor.

Shareholders also have the power to vote to elect or remove members of the board of directors. As described earlier, the first board of directors is either named in the articles of incorporation or chosen by the incorporators to serve until the first shareholders' meeting. From that time on, selection and retention of directors are exclusively shareholder functions.

19–5b Shareholders' Meetings

Shareholders' meetings must occur at least annually. In addition, special meetings can be called to deal with urgent matters. A corporation must notify its shareholders of the date, time, and place of an annual or special shareholders' meeting at least ten days, but not more than sixty days, before the meeting date [RMBCA 7.05].[13] (The date and time of the annual meeting can be specified in the bylaws.) Notice of a special meeting must include a statement of the purpose of the meeting, and business transacted at the meeting is limited to that purpose. Most

---

13. The shareholder can waive the requirement of notice by signing a waiver form [RMBCA 7.06]. A shareholder who does not receive notice but who learns of the meeting and attends without protesting the lack of notice is said to have waived notice by such conduct.

corporations specify in their bylaws the acceptable methods of notifying shareholders about meetings.

Proxies It usually is not practical for owners of only a few shares of stock of publicly traded corporations to attend a shareholders' meeting. Therefore, the law allows stockholders to appoint another person as their agent to vote their shares at the meeting. The agent's formal authorization to vote the shares is called a **proxy** (from the Latin *procurare,* meaning "to manage or take care of"). Proxy materials are sent to all shareholders before shareholders' meetings.

Management often solicits proxies, but any person can solicit proxies to concentrate voting power. Proxies have been used by groups of shareholders as a device for taking over a corporation. Proxies normally are revocable (can be withdrawn), unless they are specifically designated as irrevocable and coupled with an interest. A proxy is coupled with an interest when, for instance, the person receiving the proxies from shareholders has agreed to buy their shares. Under RMBCA 7.22(c), proxies are valid for eleven months, unless the proxy agreement mandates a longer period.

Shareholder Proposals When shareholders want to change a company policy, they can put their ideas up for a shareholder vote. They do this by submitting a shareholder proposal to the board of directors and asking the board to include the proposal in the proxy materials that are sent to all shareholders before meetings.

Rules for Proxies and Shareholder Proposals
The Securities and Exchange Commission (SEC) regulates the purchase and sale of securities. The SEC has special provisions relating to proxies and shareholder proposals. SEC Rule 14a-8 provides that all shareholders who own stock worth at least $1,000 are eligible to submit proposals for inclusion in corporate proxy materials. The corporation is required to include information on whatever proposals will be considered at the shareholders' meeting along with proxy materials. Only those proposals that relate to significant policy considerations, not ordinary business operations, must be included.

Under the SEC's e-proxy rules,[14] all public companies must post their proxy materials on the Internet and notify shareholders how to find that information. Although the law requires proxy materials to be posted online, public companies may also send the materials to shareholders by other means, including paper documents and DVDs sent by mail.

---

14. 17 C.F.R. Parts 240, 249, and 274.

19–5c Shareholder Voting

Shareholders exercise ownership control through the power of their votes. Corporate business matters are presented in the form of *resolutions,* which shareholders vote to approve or disapprove. Each common shareholder normally is entitled to one vote per share.

The articles of incorporation can exclude or limit voting rights, particularly for certain classes of shares. For instance, owners of preferred shares are usually denied the right to vote [RMBCA 7.21]. If a state statute requires specific voting procedures, the corporation's articles or bylaws must be consistent with the statute.

The corporation prepares a voting list before each shareholders' meeting. Ordinarily, only persons whose names appear on the corporation's stockholder records as owners are entitled to vote.

Quorum Requirements For shareholders to act during a meeting, a quorum must be present. Generally, a quorum exists when shareholders holding more than 50 percent of the outstanding shares are present. State laws often permit the articles of incorporation to set higher or lower quorum requirements, however. In some states, obtaining the unanimous written consent of shareholders is a permissible alternative to holding a shareholders' meeting [RMBCA 7.25].

Once a quorum is present, voting can proceed. A majority vote of the shares represented at the meeting usually is required to pass resolutions. At times, more than a simple majority vote is required, either by a state statute or by the corporate articles. Extraordinary corporate matters, such as a merger, consolidation, or dissolution of the corporation, require approval by a higher percentage of all corporate shares entitled to vote [RMBCA 7.27].

Cumulative Voting Most states permit, and many require, shareholders to elect directors by *cumulative voting,* a voting method designed to allow minority shareholders to be represented on the board of directors.

Formula. With cumulative voting, each shareholder is entitled to a total number of votes equal to the number of board members to be elected multiplied by the number of voting shares that the shareholder owns. The shareholder can cast all of these votes for one candidate or split them among several nominees for director. All candidates stand for election at the same time.

How Cumulative Voting Works. Cumulative voting can best be understood by example. ■ **EXAMPLE 19.12** A corporation has 10,000 shares issued and outstanding. The minority shareholders hold 3,000 shares, and the majority shareholders hold the other 7,000 shares. Three members of the board are to be elected. The majority shareholders' nominees are Alvarez, Beasley, and Caravel. The minority shareholders' nominee is Dovrik. Can Dovrik be elected to the board by the minority shareholders?

If cumulative voting is allowed, the answer is yes. The minority shareholders have 9,000 votes among them (the number of directors to be elected times the number of shares, or $3 \times 3,000 = 9,000$ votes). All of these votes can be cast to elect Dovrik. The majority shareholders have 21,000 votes ($3 \times 7,000 = 21,000$ votes), but these votes must be distributed among their three nominees.

The principle of cumulative voting is that no matter how the majority shareholders cast their 21,000 votes, they will not be able to elect all three directors if the minority shareholders cast all of their 9,000 votes for Dovrik, as illustrated in Exhibit 19–1. ■ In contrast, when cumulative voting is not required, the entire board can be elected by a majority of shares.

19–5d Rights of Shareholders

Shareholders possess numerous rights in addition to the right to vote their shares, and we examine several here.

Stock Certificates In the past, corporations commonly issued **stock certificates** that evidenced ownership of a specified number of shares in the corporation. Only a few jurisdictions still require physical stock certificates, and shareholders there have the right to demand that the corporation issue certificates (or replace those that were lost or destroyed). In most states and under RMBCA 6.26, a board of directors may provide that shares of stock will be uncertificated, or "paperless"—that is, no actual, physical stock certificates will be issued.

Preemptive Rights Sometimes, the articles of incorporation grant preemptive rights to shareholders [RMBCA 6.30]. With **preemptive rights,** a shareholder receives a preference over all other purchasers to subscribe to or purchase a prorated share of a new issue of stock. Generally, preemptive rights must be exercised within a specific time period (usually thirty days).

A shareholder who is given preemptive rights can purchase a percentage of the new shares being issued that is equal to the percentage of shares she or he already holds in the company. This allows each shareholder to maintain her or his proportionate control, voting power, and financial interest in the corporation. ■ **EXAMPLE 19.13** Katlin is a shareholder who owns 10 percent of a company. Because she also has preemptive rights, she can buy 10 percent of any new issue (to maintain her 10 percent position). Thus, if the corporation issues 1,000 more shares, Katlin can buy 100 of the new shares. ■

EXHIBIT 19–1 Results of Cumulative Voting

Ballot	Majority Shareholder Votes			Minority Shareholder Votes	Directors Elected
	Alvarez	*Beasley*	*Caravel*	*Dovrik*	
1	10,000	10,000	1,000	9,000	Alvarez, Beasley, Dovrik
2	9,001	9,000	2,999	9,000	Alvarez, Beasley, Dovrik
3	6,000	7,000	8,000	9,000	Beasley, Caravel, Dovrik

Preemptive rights are most important in close corporations because each shareholder owns a relatively small number of shares but controls a substantial interest in the corporation. Without preemptive rights, it would be possible for a shareholder to lose his or her proportionate control over the firm. Nevertheless, preemptive rights do not exist unless provided for in the articles of incorporation.

Stock Warrants Stock warrants are rights given by a company to buy stock at a stated price by a specified date. Usually, when preemptive rights exist and a corporation is issuing additional shares, it gives its shareholders stock warrants. Warrants are often publicly traded on securities exchanges.

Dividends As mentioned, a *dividend* is a distribution of corporate profits or income *ordered by the directors* and paid to the shareholders in proportion to their shares in the corporation. Dividends can be paid in cash, property, stock of the corporation that is paying the dividends, or stock of other corporations.[15]

State laws vary, but each state determines the general circumstances and legal requirements under which dividends are paid. State laws also control the sources of revenue to be used. All states allow dividends to be paid from the undistributed net profits earned by the corporation, for instance. A number of states allow dividends to be paid out of any surplus.

Illegal Dividends. Dividends are illegal if they are improperly paid from an unauthorized account or if their payment causes the corporation to become insolvent. Generally, shareholders must return illegal dividends only if they knew that the dividends were illegal when the payment was received (or if the dividends were paid when the corporation was insolvent). Whenever dividends are illegal or improper, the board of directors can be held personally liable for the amount of the payment.

The Directors' Failure to Declare a Dividend. When directors fail to declare a dividend, shareholders can ask a court to compel the directors to do so. To succeed, the shareholders must show that the directors have acted so unreasonably in withholding the dividend that their conduct is an abuse of their discretion.

Often, a corporation accumulates large cash reserves for a legitimate corporate purpose, such as expansion or research. The mere fact that the firm has sufficient earnings or surplus available to pay a dividend normally is not enough to compel the directors to declare a dividend. The courts are reluctant to interfere with corporate operations and will not compel directors to declare dividends unless abuse of discretion is clearly shown.

Inspection Rights Shareholders in a corporation enjoy both common law and statutory inspection rights. The RMBCA provides that every shareholder is entitled to examine specified corporate records, including voting lists [RMBCA 7.20, 16.02]. The shareholder may inspect in person, or an attorney, accountant, or other authorized assistant can do so as the shareholder's agent.

A shareholder has a right to inspect and copy corporate books and records only for a *proper purpose,* and the request to inspect must be made in advance. A shareholder who is denied the right of inspection can seek a court order to compel the inspection.

■ **CASE IN POINT 19.14** Trading Block Holdings, Inc., offers online brokerage services. On April 1, 2013, some shareholders of Trading Block, through an attorney, sent a letter asking to inspect specific items in the corporation's books and records. The letter indicated that the purpose was to determine the financial condition of the company, how it was being managed, and whether the company's financial practices were appropriate. It also stated that the shareholders wanted to know whether Trading Block's management had engaged in any self-dealing that had negatively impacted the company as a whole.

On April 30, Trading Block responded with a letter stating that the plaintiffs were on a "fishing expedition" and did not have a proper purpose for inspecting the corporate records. Eventually, the shareholders filed a motion to compel inspection in an Illinois state court. The trial court denied the plaintiffs' motion. On appeal, the reviewing court held that the plaintiffs' allegations of self-dealing by directors and officers constituted a proper purpose for their inspection request. The trial court's decision was reversed.[16] ■

Transfer of Shares Corporate stock represents an ownership right in intangible personal property. The law

---

15. On one occasion, a distillery declared and paid a dividend in bonded whiskey.

16. *Sunlitz Holding Co., W.L.L. v. Trading Block Holdings, Inc.,* 2014 IL App (1st) 133938, 17 N.E.3d 715, 384 Ill.Dec. 733 (2014).

generally recognizes the owner's right to transfer stock to another person unless there are valid restrictions on its transferability, such as frequently occur with close corporation stock.

When shares are transferred, a new entry is made in the corporate stock book to indicate the new owner. Until the corporation is notified and the entry is complete, all rights—including voting rights, notice of shareholders' meetings, and the right to dividend distributions—remain with the current record owner.

The Shareholder's Derivative Suit When the corporation is harmed by the actions of a third party, the directors can bring a lawsuit in the name of the corporation against that party. If the corporate directors fail to bring a lawsuit, shareholders can do so "derivatively" in what is known as a **shareholder's derivative suit.**

The right of shareholders to bring a derivative action is especially important when the wrong suffered by the corporation results from the actions of the corporate directors and officers. For obvious reasons, the directors and officers would probably be unwilling to take any action against themselves.

Before shareholders can bring a derivative suit, they must submit a written demand to the corporation, asking the board of directors to take appropriate action [RMBCA 7.40]. The directors then have ninety days in which to act. Only if they refuse to do so can the derivative suit go forward. In addition, a court will dismiss a derivative suit if a majority of the directors or an independent panel determines in good faith that the lawsuit is not in the best interests of the corporation [RMBCA 7.44].

When shareholders bring a derivative suit, they are not pursuing rights or benefits for themselves personally but are acting as guardians of the corporate entity. Therefore, if the suit is successful, any damages recovered normally go into the corporation's treasury, not to the shareholders personally.

19–5e Duties of Majority Shareholders

In some instances, a majority shareholder is regarded as having a fiduciary duty to the corporation and to the minority shareholders. This duty arises when a single shareholder (or a few shareholders acting in concert) owns a sufficient number of shares to exercise *de facto* control over the corporation. In these situations, the majority shareholder owes a fiduciary duty to the minority shareholders.

When a majority shareholder breaches her or his fiduciary duty to a minority shareholder, the minority shareholder can sue for damages. A breach of fiduciary duties by those who control a close corporation normally constitutes what is known as *oppressive conduct.* A common example of a breach of fiduciary duty occurs when the majority shareholders "freeze out" the minority shareholders and exclude them from certain benefits of participating in the firm.

■ **EXAMPLE 19.15** Brodie, Jordan, and Barbara form a close corporation to operate a machine shop. Brodie and Jordan own 75 percent of the shares in the company, but all three are directors. After disagreements arise, Brodie asks the company to purchase his shares, but his requests are refused. A few years later, Brodie dies, and his wife, Ella, inherits his shares. Jordan and Barbara refuse to perform a valuation of the company, deny Ella access to corporate information, do not declare any dividends, and refuse to elect Ella as a director. In this situation, the majority shareholders have violated their fiduciary duty to Ella. ■

19–6 Major Business Forms Compared

When deciding which form of business organization to choose, businesspersons normally consider several factors, including ease of creation, the liability of the owners, tax considerations, and the ability to raise capital. Each major form of business organization offers distinct advantages and disadvantages with respect to these and other factors.

Exhibit 19–2 summarizes the essential advantages and disadvantages of each of the forms of business organization discussed in this text.

EXHIBIT 19–2 Major Forms of Business Compared

SOLE PROPRIETORSHIP	PARTNERSHIP	CORPORATION	LIMITED LIABILITY COMPANY
Created at will by owner.	Created by agreement of the parties.	Authorized by the state under the state's corporation law.	Created by an agreement of the member-owners of the company. Articles of organization are filed. Charter must be issued by the state.
Not a separate entity; owner is the business.	A general partnership is a separate legal entity in most states.	Always a legal entity separate and distinct from its owners—a legal fiction for the purposes of owning property and being a party to litigation.	Treated as a legal entity.
Unlimited liability.	Unlimited liability.	Limited liability of shareholders—shareholders are not liable for the debts of the corporation.	Member-owners' liability is limited to the amount of capital contributions or investments.
Determined by owner; automatically dissolved on owner's death.	Terminated by agreement of the partners, but can continue to do business even when a partner dissociates from the partnership.	Can have perpetual existence.	Unless a single-member LLC, can have perpetual existence (same as a corporation).
Interest can be transferred, but individual's proprietorship then ends.	Although partnership interest can be assigned, assignee does not have full rights of a partner.	Shares of stock can be transferred.	Member interests are freely transferable.
Completely at owner's discretion.	Each partner has a direct and equal voice in management unless expressly agreed otherwise in the partnership agreement.	Shareholders elect directors, who set policy and appoint officers.	Member-owners can fully participate in management or can designate a group of persons to manage on behalf of the members.
Owner pays personal taxes on business income.	Each partner pays proportional share of income taxes on net profits, whether or not they are distributed.	Double taxation—corporation pays income tax on net profits, with no deduction for dividends, and shareholders pay income tax on disbursed dividends they receive.	LLC is not taxed, and members are taxed personally on profits "passed through" the LLC.
None or minimal.	None or minimal.	All required.	Organizational fee required. Others vary with states.
Generally no limitation.	Generally no limitation.[a]	Normally must qualify to do business and obtain certificate of authority.	Generally no limitations, but may vary depending on state.

a. A few states have enacted statutes requiring that foreign partnerships qualify to do business there.

Reviewing: Corporations

David Brock was on the board of directors of Firm Body Fitness, Inc., which owned a string of fitness clubs in New Mexico. Brock owned 15 percent of the Firm Body stock and was also employed as a tanning technician at one of the fitness clubs. After the January financial report showed that Firm Body's tanning division was operating at a substantial net loss, the board of directors, led by Marty Levinson, discussed terminating the tanning operations. Brock successfully convinced a majority of the board that the tanning division was necessary to market the clubs' overall fitness package. By April, the tanning division's financial losses had risen. The board hired a business analyst, who conducted surveys and determined that the tanning operations did not significantly increase membership.

A shareholder, Diego Peñada, discovered that Brock owned stock in Sunglow, Inc., the company from which Firm Body purchased its tanning equipment. Peñada notified Levinson, who privately reprimanded Brock. Shortly thereafter, Brock and Mandy Vail, who owned 37 percent of the Firm Body stock and also held shares of Sunglow, voted to replace Levinson on the board of directors. Using the information presented in the chapter, answer the following questions.

1. What duties did Brock, as a director, owe to Firm Body?
2. Does the fact that Brock owned shares in Sunglow establish a conflict of interest? Why or why not?
3. Suppose that Firm Body brought an action against Brock claiming that he had breached the duty of loyalty by not disclosing his interest in Sunglow to the other directors. What theory might Brock use in his defense?
4. Now suppose that Firm Body did not bring an action against Brock. What type of lawsuit might Peñada be able to bring based on these facts?

Debate This . . .   *The sole shareholder of an S corporation should not be able to avoid liability for the torts of her or his employees.*

Terms and Concepts

alien corporation 376
articles of incorporation 381
benefit corporation 380
bond 383
business judgment rule 389
bylaws 382
close corporation 378
commingle 386
common stock 383
crowdfunding 384
dividends 376
domestic corporation 376

foreign corporation 376
holding company 376
inside director 387
outside director 387
pierce the corporate veil 385
preemptive rights 394
preferred stock 383
private equity capital 383
proxy 393
public corporation 379
publicly held corporation 379
quorum 388

retained earnings 376
S corporation 378
securities 383
shareholder agreement 378
shareholder's derivative suit 396
stock 383
stock certificate 394
stock warrant 395
ultra vires 384
venture capital 383

Issue Spotters

1. Northwest Brands, Inc., is a small business incorporated in Minnesota. Its one class of stock is owned by twelve members of a single family. Ordinarily, corporate income is taxed at the corporate and shareholder levels. Is there a way for Northwest Brands to avoid this double taxation? Explain your answer. (See *Nature and Classification.*)

2. Nico is Omega Corporation's majority shareholder. He owns enough stock in Omega that if he were to sell it, the sale would be a transfer of control of the firm. Discuss whether Nico owes a duty to Omega or the minority shareholders in selling his shares. (See *Shareholders.*)

• **Check your answers to the Issue Spotters against the answers provided in Appendix B at the end of this text.**

Business Scenarios

19–1. Preincorporation. Cummings, Okawa, and Taft are recent college graduates who want to form a corporation to manufacture and sell digital tablets. Peterson tells them he will set in motion the formation of their corporation. First, Peterson makes a contract with Owens for the purchase of a piece of land for $20,000. Owens does not know of the prospective corporate formation at the time the contract is signed. Second, Peterson makes a contract with Babcock to build a small plant on the property being purchased. Babcock's contract is conditional on the corporation's formation. Peterson secures contracts with investors and necessary capitalization, and he files the articles of incorporation. (See *Formation and Powers.*)

(a) Discuss whether the newly formed corporation, Peterson, or both are liable on the contracts with Owens and Babcock.

(b) Discuss whether the corporation is automatically liable to Babcock on formation.

19–2. Conflicts of Interest. Oxy Corp. is negotiating with Wick Construction Co. for the renovation of Oxy's corporate headquarters. Wick, the owner of Wick Construction Co., is also one of the five members of Oxy's board of directors. The contract terms are standard for this type of contract. Wick has previously informed two of the other directors of his interest in the construction company. Oxy's board approves the contract by a three-to-two vote, with Wick voting with the majority. Discuss whether this contract is binding on the corporation. (See *Directors and Officers.*)

Business Case Problems

19–3. Spotlight on Smart Inventions—Piercing the Corporate Veil. Thomas Persson and Jon Nokes founded Smart Inventions, Inc., to market household consumer products. The success of their first product, the Smart Mop, continued with later products, which were sold through infomercials and other means. Persson and Nokes were the firm's officers and equal shareholders. Persson was responsible for product development, and Nokes was in charge of day-to-day operations. In time, they became dissatisfied with each other's efforts. Nokes represented the firm as financially "dying," "in a grim state, . . . worse than ever," and offered to buy all of Persson's shares for $1.6 million. Persson accepted.

On the day that they signed the agreement to transfer the shares, Smart Inventions began marketing a new product—the Tap Light. It was an instant success, generating millions of dollars in revenues. In negotiating with Persson, Nokes had intentionally kept the Tap Light a secret. Persson sued Smart Inventions, asserting fraud and other claims. Under what principle might Smart Inventions be liable for Nokes's fraud? Is Smart Inventions liable in this case? Explain. [*Persson v. Smart Inventions, Inc.,* 125 Cal.App.4th 1141, 23 Cal. Rptr.3d 335 (2 Dist. 2005)] (See *Piercing the Corporate Veil.*)

19–4. Duty of Loyalty. Kids International Corp. produced children's wear for Walmart and other retailers. Gila Dweck was a Kids director and its chief executive officer. Because she felt that she was not paid enough, she started Success Apparel to compete with Kids. Success operated out of Kids' premises, used its employees, borrowed on its credit, took advantage of its business opportunities, and capitalized on its customer relationships. As an "administrative fee," Dweck paid Kids 1 percent of Success's total sales. Did Dweck breach any fiduciary duties? Explain. [*Dweck v. Nasser,* 2012 WL 3194069 (Del.Ch. 2012)] (See *Directors and Officers.*)

19–5. Business Case Problem with Sample Answer— Piercing the Corporate Veil. Scott Snapp contracted with Castlebrook Builders, Inc., which was owned by Stephen Kappeler, to remodel a house. Kappeler estimated that the remodeling would cost around $500,000. Eventually, however, Snapp paid Kappeler more than $1.3 million. Snapp filed a suit in an Ohio state court against Castlebrook, alleging breach of contract and fraud, among other things.

During the trial, it was revealed that Castlebrook had issued no shares of stock and that personal and corporate funds had been commingled. The minutes of the corporate meetings all looked exactly the same. In addition, Kappeler could not provide an accounting for the Snapp project. In particular, he could not explain evidence of double and triple billing nor demonstrate that the amount Snapp paid had actually been spent on the remodeling project. Are these sufficient grounds to pierce the corporate veil? Explain. [*Snapp v. Castlebrook Builders, Inc.*, 2014 -Ohio- 163, 7 N.E.3d 574 (2014)] (See *Formation and Powers.*)

- **For a sample answer to Problem 19–5, go to Appendix C at the end of this text.**

19–6. Business Judgment Rule. Country Contractors, Inc., contracted to provide excavation services for A Westside Storage of Indianapolis, Inc., but did not complete the job and later filed for bankruptcy. Stephen Songer and Jahn Songer were Country's sole shareholders. The Songers had not misused the corporate form to engage in fraud. The firm had not been undercapitalized, personal and corporate funds had not been commingled, and Country had kept accounting records and minutes of its annual board meetings. Are the Songers personally liable for Country's failure to complete its contract? Explain. [*Country Contractors, Inc. v. A Westside Storage of Indianapolis, Inc.*, 4 N.E.3d 677 (Ind.App. 2014)] (See *Directors and Officers.*)

19–7. Torts. Jennifer Hoffman took her cell phone to a store owned by R&K Trading, Inc., for repairs. Later, Hoffman filed a suit in a New York state court against R&K, Verizon Wireless, Inc., and others. Hoffman sought to recover damages for a variety of torts, including infliction of emotional distress and negligent hiring and supervision. She alleged that an R&K employee, Keith Press, had examined her phone in a back room, accessed private photos of her stored on her phone, and disseminated the photos to the public. Hoffman testified that "after the incident, she learned from another R&K employee that personal information and pictures had been removed from the phones of other customers." Can R&K be held liable for the torts of its employees? Explain. [*Hoffman v. Verizon Wireless, Inc.*, 5 N.Y.S.3d 123, 125 A.D.3d 806 (2015)] (See *Nature and Classification.*)

19–8. Rights of Shareholders. FCR Realty, LLC, and Clifford B. Green & Sons, Inc., were co-owned by three brothers—Frederick, Clifford Jr., and Richard Green. Each brother was a shareholder of the corporation. Frederick was a controlling shareholder, as well as president. Each brother owned a one-third interest in the LLC. Clifford believed that Frederick had misused LLC and corporate funds to pay nonexistent debts and liabilities and had diverted LLC assets to the corporation. He also contended that Frederick had disbursed about $1.8 million in corporate funds to Frederick's own separate business. Clifford hired an attorney and filed an action on behalf of the two companies against Frederick for breach of fiduciary duty. Frederick argued that Clifford lacked the knowledge necessary to adequately represent the companies' interest because he did not understand financial statements. Can Clifford maintain the action against Frederick? If so, and if the suit is successful, who recovers the damages? Explain. [*FCR Realty, LLC v. Green*, __ A.3d __, 2016 WL 571449 (Conn.Sup.Ct. 2016)] (See *Shareholders.*)

19–9. A Question of Ethics—Piercing the Corporate Veil. *In New York City, 2406-12 Amsterdam Associates LLC* *brought an action in a New York state court against Alianza Dominicana and Alianza LLC to recover unpaid rent. The plaintiff asserted cause to pierce the corporate veil, alleging that Alianza Dominicana had made promises to pay its rent while discreetly forming Alianza LLC to avoid liability for it. According to 2406-12, Alianza LLC was 90 percent owned by Alianza Dominicana, had no employees, and had no function but to hold Alianza Dominicana's assets away from its creditors. The defendants filed a motion to dismiss the plaintiff's claim. [2406-12 Amsterdam Associates, LLC v. Alianza, LLC, 136 A.D.3d 512, 25 N.Y.S.2d 167 (1 Dept. 2016)] (See Piercing the Corporate Veil.)*

(a) Assuming that 2406-12's allegations are true, are there sufficient grounds to pierce Alianza LLC's corporate veil? Discuss.

(b) Suppose that the parties to this dispute were small, close corporations. How might that circumstance affect the result in this case?

Legal Reasoning Group Activity

19–10. Corporate versus LLC Form of Business. The limited liability company (LLC) may be the best organizational form for most businesses. For a significant number of firms, however, the corporate form or some other form of organization may be better. (See *Nature and Classification.*)

(a) The first group will outline several reasons why a firm might be better off as a corporation than as an LLC.

(b) The second group will discuss the differences between corporations and LLCs in terms of their management structures.

Article 2 of the Uniform Commercial Code

(Adopted in fifty-two jurisdictions—all fifty States, although Louisiana has adopted only Articles 1, 3, 4, 7, 8, and 9; the District of Columbia; and the Virgin Islands.)

The Code consists of the following articles:

Article
1. General Provisions
2. Sales
2A. Leases
3. Negotiable Instruments
4. Bank Deposits and Collections
4A. Funds Transfers
5. Letters of Credit
6. Repealer of U.C.C.—Article 6: Bulk Transfers and [Revised] Article 6: Bulk Sales
7. Warehouse Receipts, Bills of Lading and Other Documents of Title
8. Investment Securities
9. Secured Transactions

ARTICLE 2: SALES

Part 1—Short Title, General Construction and Subject Matter

§ 2–101. Short Title.

This Article shall be known and may be cited as Uniform Commercial Code—Sales.

§ 2–102. Scope; Certain Security and Other Transactions Excluded From This Article.

Unless the context otherwise requires, this Article applies to transactions in goods; it does not apply to any transaction which although in the form of an unconditional contract to sell or present sale is intended to operate only as a security transaction nor does this Article impair or repeal any statute regulating sales to consumers, farmers or other specified classes of buyers.

§ 2–103. Definitions and Index of Definitions.

(1) In this Article unless the context otherwise requires

(a) "Buyer" means a person who buys or contracts to buy goods.
(b) "Good faith" in the case of a merchant means honesty in fact and the observance of reasonable commercial standards of fair dealing in the trade.
(c) "Receipt" of goods means taking physical possession of them.
(d) "Seller" means a person who sells or contracts to sell goods.
(2) Other definitions applying to this Article or to specified Parts thereof, and the sections in which they appear are:
"Acceptance". Section 2–606.
"Banker's credit". Section 2–325.
"Between merchants". Section 2–104.
"Cancellation". Section 2–106(4).
"Commercial unit". Section 2–105.
"Confirmed credit". Section 2–325.
"Conforming to contract". Section 2–106.
"Contract for sale". Section 2–106.
"Cover". Section 2–712.
"Entrusting". Section 2–403.
"Financing agency". Section 2–104.
"Future goods". Section 2–105.
"Goods". Section 2–105.
"Identification". Section 2–501.
"Installment contract". Section 2–612.
"Letter of Credit". Section 2–325.
"Lot". Section 2–105.
"Merchant". Section 2–104.
"Overseas". Section 2–323.
"Person in position of seller". Section 2–707.
"Present sale". Section 2–106.
"Sale". Section 2–106.
"Sale on approval". Section 2–326.
"Sale or return". Section 2–326.
"Termination". Section 2–106.
(3) The following definitions in other Articles apply to this Article:
"Check". Section 3–104.
"Consignee". Section 7–102.
"Consignor". Section 7–102.
"Consumer goods". Section 9–109.
"Dishonor". Section 3–507.
"Draft". Section 3–104.
(4) In addition Article 1 contains general definitions and principles of construction and interpretation applicable throughout this Article.
As amended in 1994 and 1999.

§ 2–104. Definitions: "Merchant"; "Between Merchants"; "Financing Agency".

(1) "Merchant" means a person who deals in goods of the kind or otherwise by his occupation holds himself out as having knowledge or skill peculiar to the practices or goods involved in the transaction or to whom such knowledge or skill may be attributed by his employment of an agent or broker or other intermediary who by his occupation holds himself out as having such knowledge or skill.

(2) "Financing agency" means a bank, finance company or other person who in the ordinary course of business makes advances against goods or documents of title or who by arrangement with either the seller or the buyer intervenes in ordinary course to make or collect payment due or claimed under the contract for sale, as by purchasing or paying the seller's draft or making advances against it or by merely taking it for collection whether or not documents of title accompany the draft. "Financing agency" includes also a bank or other person who similarly intervenes between persons who are in the position of seller and buyer in respect to the goods (Section 2–707).

(3) "Between merchants" means in any transaction with respect to which both parties are chargeable with the knowledge or skill of merchants.

§ 2–105. Definitions: Transferability; "Goods"; "Future" Goods; "Lot"; "Commercial Unit".

(1) "Goods" means all things (including specially manufactured goods) which are movable at the time of identification to the contract for sale other than the money in which the price is to be paid, investment securities (Article 8) and things in action. "Goods" also includes the unborn young of animals and growing crops and other identified things attached to realty as described in the section on goods to be severed from realty (Section 2–107).

(2) Goods must be both existing and identified before any interest in them can pass. Goods which are not both existing and identified are "future" goods. A purported present sale of future goods or of any interest therein operates as a contract to sell.

(3) There may be a sale of a part interest in existing identified goods.

(4) An undivided share in an identified bulk of fungible goods is sufficiently identified to be sold although the quantity of the bulk is not determined. Any agreed proportion of such a bulk or any quantity thereof agreed upon by number, weight or other measure may to the extent of the seller's interest in the bulk be sold to the buyer who then becomes an owner in common.

(5) "Lot" means a parcel or a single article which is the subject matter of a separate sale or delivery, whether or not it is sufficient to perform the contract.

(6) "Commercial unit" means such a unit of goods as by commercial usage is a single whole for purposes of sale and division of which materially impairs its character or value on the market or in use. A commercial unit may be a single article (as a machine) or a set of articles (as a suite of furniture or an assortment of sizes) or a quantity (as a bale, gross, or carload) or any other unit treated in use or in the relevant market as a single whole.

§ 2–106. Definitions: "Contract"; "Agreement"; "Contract for Sale"; "Sale"; "Present Sale"; "Conforming" to Contract; "Termination"; "Cancellation".

(1) In this Article unless the context otherwise requires "contract" and "agreement" are limited to those relating to the present or future sale of goods. "Contract for sale" includes both a present sale of goods and a contract to sell goods at a future time. A "sale" consists in the passing of title from the seller to the buyer for a price (Section 2–401). A "present sale" means a sale which is accomplished by the making of the contract.

(2) Goods or conduct including any part of a performance are "conforming" or conform to the contract when they are in accordance with the obligations under the contract.

(3) "Termination" occurs when either party pursuant to a power created by agreement or law puts an end to the contract otherwise than for its breach. On "termination" all obligations which are still executory on both sides are discharged but any right based on prior breach or performance survives.

(4) "Cancellation" occurs when either party puts an end to the contract for breach by the other and its effect is the same as that of "termination" except that the cancelling party also retains any remedy for breach of the whole contract or any unperformed balance.

§ 2–107. Goods to Be Severed From Realty: Recording.

(1) A contract for the sale of minerals or the like (including oil and gas) or a structure or its materials to be removed from realty is a contract for the sale of goods within this Article if they are to be severed by the seller but until severance a purported present sale thereof which is not effective as a transfer of an interest in land is effective only as a contract to sell.

(2) A contract for the sale apart from the land of growing crops or other things attached to realty and capable of severance without material harm thereto but not described in subsection (1) or of timber to be cut is a contract for the sale of goods within this Article whether the subject matter is to be severed by the buyer or by the seller even though it forms part of the realty at the time of contracting, and the parties can by identification effect a present sale before severance.

(3) The provisions of this section are subject to any third party rights provided by the law relating to realty records, and the contract for sale may be executed and recorded as a document transferring an interest in land and shall then constitute notice to third parties of the buyer's rights under the contract for sale.

As amended in 1972.

Part 2—Form, Formation and Readjustment of Contract

§ 2–201. Formal Requirements; Statute of Frauds.

(1) Except as otherwise provided in this section a contract for the sale of goods for the price of $500 or more is not enforceable by way of action or defense unless there is some writing sufficient to indicate that a contract for sale has been made between the parties and signed by the party against whom enforcement is sought or by his authorized agent or broker. A writing is not insufficient because it omits or incorrectly states a term agreed upon but the contract is not enforceable under this paragraph beyond the quantity of goods shown in such writing.

(2) Between merchants if within a reasonable time a writing in confirmation of the contract and sufficient against the sender is received and the party receiving it has reason to know its contents, its satisfies the requirements of subsection (1) against such party unless written notice of objection to its contents is given within ten days after it is received.

(3) A contract which does not satisfy the requirements of subsection (1) but which is valid in other respects is enforceable

> **(a)** if the goods are to be specially manufactured for the buyer and are not suitable for sale to others in the ordinary course of the seller's business and the seller, before notice of repudiation is received and under circumstances which reasonably indicate that the goods are for the buyer, has made either a substantial beginning of their manufacture or commitments for their procurement; or
>
> **(b)** if the party against whom enforcement is sought admits in his pleading, testimony or otherwise in court that a contract for sale was made, but the contract is not enforceable under this provision beyond the quantity of goods admitted; or
>
> **(c)** with respect to goods for which payment has been made and accepted or which have been received and accepted (Sec. 2–606).

§ 2–202. Final Written Expression: Parol or Extrinsic Evidence.

Terms with respect to which the confirmatory memoranda of the parties agree or which are otherwise set forth in a writing intended by the parties as a final expression of their agreement with respect to such terms as are included therein may not be contradicted by evidence of any prior agreement or of a contemporaneous oral agreement but may be explained or supplemented

> **(a)** by course of dealing or usage of trade (Section 1–205) or by course of performance (Section 2–208); and
>
> **(b)** by evidence of consistent additional terms unless the court finds the writing to have been intended also as a complete and exclusive statement of the terms of the agreement.

§ 2–203. Seals Inoperative.

The affixing of a seal to a writing evidencing a contract for sale or an offer to buy or sell goods does not constitute the writing a sealed instrument and the law with respect to sealed instruments does not apply to such a contract or offer.

§ 2–204. Formation in General.

(1) A contract for sale of goods may be made in any manner sufficient to show agreement, including conduct by both parties which recognizes the existence of such a contract.

(2) An agreement sufficient to constitute a contract for sale may be found even though the moment of its making is undetermined.

(3) Even though one or more terms are left open a contract for sale does not fail for indefiniteness if the parties have intended to make a contract and there is a reasonably certain basis for giving an appropriate remedy.

§ 2–205. Firm Offers.

An offer by a merchant to buy or sell goods in a signed writing which by its terms gives assurance that it will be held open is not revocable, for lack of consideration, during the time stated or if no time is stated for a reasonable time, but in no event may such period of irrevocability exceed three months; but any such term of assurance on a form supplied by the offeree must be separately signed by the offeror.

§ 2–206. Offer and Acceptance in Formation of Contract.

(1) Unless other unambiguously indicated by the language or circumstances

> **(a)** an offer to make a contract shall be construed as inviting acceptance in any manner and by any medium reasonable in the circumstances;
>
> **(b)** an order or other offer to buy goods for prompt or current shipment shall be construed as inviting acceptance either by a prompt promise to ship or by the prompt or current shipment of conforming or nonconforming goods, but such a shipment of non-conforming goods does not constitute an acceptance if the seller seasonably notifies the buyer that the shipment is offered only as an accommodation to the buyer.

(2) Where the beginning of a requested performance is a reasonable mode of acceptance an offeror who is not notified of acceptance within a reasonable time may treat the offer as having lapsed before acceptance.

§ 2–207. Additional Terms in Acceptance or Confirmation.

(1) A definite and seasonable expression of acceptance or a written confirmation which is sent within a reasonable time operates as an acceptance even though it states terms additional to or different from those offered or agreed upon, unless acceptance is expressly made conditional on assent to the additional or different terms.

(2) The additional terms are to be construed as proposals for addition to the contract. Between merchants such terms become part of the contract unless:

> **(a)** the offer expressly limits acceptance to the terms of the offer;

(b) they materially alter it; or

(c) notification of objection to them has already been given or is given within a reasonable time after notice of them is received.

(3) Conduct by both parties which recognizes the existence of a contract is sufficient to establish a contract for sale although the writings of the parties do not otherwise establish a contract. In such case the terms of the particular contract consist of those terms on which the writings of the parties agree, together with any supplementary terms incorporated under any other provisions of this Act.

§ 2–208. Course of Performance or Practical Construction.

(1) Where the contract for sale involves repeated occasions for performance by either party with knowledge of the nature of the performance and opportunity for objection to it by the other, any course of performance accepted or acquiesced in without objection shall be relevant to determine the meaning of the agreement.

(2) The express terms of the agreement and any such course of performance, as well as any course of dealing and usage of trade, shall be construed whenever reasonable as consistent with each other; but when such construction is unreasonable, express terms shall control course of performance and course of performance shall control both course of dealing and usage of trade (Section 1–205).

(3) Subject to the provisions of the next section on modification and waiver, such course of performance shall be relevant to show a waiver or modification of any term inconsistent with such course of performance.

§ 2–209. Modification, Rescission and Waiver.

(1) An agreement modifying a contract within this Article needs no consideration to be binding.

(2) A signed agreement which excludes modification or rescission except by a signed writing cannot be otherwise modified or rescinded, but except as between merchants such a requirement on a form supplied by the merchant must be separately signed by the other party.

(3) The requirements of the statute of frauds section of this Article (Section 2–201) must be satisfied if the contract as modified is within its provisions.

(4) Although an attempt at modification or rescission does not satisfy the requirements of subsection (2) or (3) it can operate as a waiver.

(5) A party who has made a waiver affecting an executory portion of the contract may retract the waiver by reasonable notification received by the other party that strict performance will be required of any term waived, unless the retraction would be unjust in view of a material change of position in reliance on the waiver.

§ 2–210. Delegation of Performance; Assignment of Rights.

(1) A party may perform his duty through a delegate unless otherwise agreed or unless the other party has a substantial interest in having his original promisor perform or control the acts required by the contract. No delegation of performance relieves the party delegating of any duty to perform or any liability for breach.

(2) Except as otherwise provided in Section 9–406, unless otherwise agreed, all rights of either seller or buyer can be assigned except where the assignment would materially change the duty of the other party, or increase materially the burden or risk imposed on him by his contract, or impair materially his chance of obtaining return performance. A right to damages for breach of the whole contract or a right arising out of the assignor's due performance of his entire obligation can be assigned despite agreement otherwise.

(3) The creation, attachment, perfection, or enforcement of a security interest in the seller's interest under a contract is not a transfer that materially changes the duty of or increases materially the burden or risk imposed on the buyer or impairs materially the buyer's chance of obtaining return performance within the purview of subsection (2) unless, and then only to the extent that, enforcement actually results in a delegation of material performance of the seller. Even in that event, the creation, attachment, perfection, and enforcement of the security interest remain effective, but (i) the seller is liable to the buyer for damages caused by the delegation to the extent that the damages could not reasonably by prevented by the buyer, and (ii) a court having jurisdiction may grant other appropriate relief, including cancellation of the contract for sale or an injunction against enforcement of the security interest or consummation of the enforcement.

(4) Unless the circumstances indicate the contrary a prohibition of assignment of "the contract" is to be construed as barring only the delegation to the assignee of the assignor's performance.

(5) An assignment of "the contract" or of "all my rights under the contract" or an assignment in similar general terms is an assignment of rights and unless the language or the circumstances (as in an assignment for security) indicate the contrary, it is a delegation of performance of the duties of the assignor and its acceptance by the assignee constitutes a promise by him to perform those duties. This promise is enforceable by either the assignor or the other party to the original contract.

(6) The other party may treat any assignment which delegates performance as creating reasonable grounds for insecurity and may without prejudice to his rights against the assignor demand assurances from the assignee (Section 2–609).

As amended in 1999.

Part 3—General Obligation and Construction of Contract

§ 2–301. General Obligations of Parties.

The obligation of the seller is to transfer and deliver and that of the buyer is to accept and pay in accordance with the contract.

§ 2–302. Unconscionable Contract or Clause.

(1) If the court as a matter of law finds the contract or any clause of the contract to have been unconscionable at the time it was made the court may refuse to enforce the contract, or it may enforce the remainder of the contract without the unconscionable clause, or it may so limit the application of any unconscionable clause as to avoid any unconscionable result.

(2) When it is claimed or appears to the court that the contract or any clause thereof may be unconscionable the parties shall be afforded a reasonable opportunity to present evidence as to its commercial setting, purpose and effect to aid the court in making the determination.

§ 2–303. Allocations or Division of Risks.

Where this Article allocates a risk or a burden as between the parties "unless otherwise agreed", the agreement may not only shift the allocation but may also divide the risk or burden.

§ 2–304. Price Payable in Money, Goods, Realty, or Otherwise.

(1) The price can be made payable in money or otherwise. If it is payable in whole or in part in goods each party is a seller of the goods which he is to transfer.

(2) Even though all or part of the price is payable in an interest in realty the transfer of the goods and the seller's obligations with reference to them are subject to this Article, but not the transfer of the interest in realty or the transferor's obligations in connection therewith.

§ 2–305. Open Price Term.

(1) The parties if they so intend can conclude a contract for sale even though the price is not settled. In such a case the price is a reasonable price at the time for delivery if

(a) nothing is said as to price; or

(b) the price is left to be agreed by the parties and they fail to agree; or

(c) the price is to be fixed in terms of some agreed market or other standard as set or recorded by a third person or agency and it is not so set or recorded.

(2) A price to be fixed by the seller or by the buyer means a price for him to fix in good faith.

(3) When a price left to be fixed otherwise than by agreement of the parties fails to be fixed through fault of one party the other may at his option treat the contract as cancelled or himself fix a reasonable price.

(4) Where, however, the parties intend not to be bound unless the price be fixed or agreed and it is not fixed or agreed there is no contract. In such a case the buyer must return any goods already received or if unable so to do must pay their reasonable value at the time of delivery and the seller must return any portion of the price paid on account.

§ 2–306. Output, Requirements and Exclusive Dealings.

(1) A term which measures the quantity by the output of the seller or the requirements of the buyer means such actual output or requirements as may occur in good faith, except that no quantity unreasonably disproportionate to any stated estimate or in the absence of a stated estimate to any normal or otherwise comparable prior output or requirements may be tendered or demanded.

(2) A lawful agreement by either the seller or the buyer for exclusive dealing in the kind of goods concerned imposes unless otherwise agreed an obligation by the seller to use best efforts to supply the goods and by the buyer to use best efforts to promote their sale.

§ 2–307. Delivery in Single Lot or Several Lots.

Unless otherwise agreed all goods called for by a contract for sale must be tendered in a single delivery and payment is due only on such tender but where the circumstances give either party the right to make or demand delivery in lots the price if it can be apportioned may be demanded for each lot.

§ 2–308. Absence of Specified Place for Delivery.

Unless otherwise agreed

(a) the place for delivery of goods is the seller's place of business or if he has none his residence; but

(b) in a contract for sale of identified goods which to the knowledge of the parties at the time of contracting are in some other place, that place is the place for their delivery; and

(c) documents of title may be delivered through customary banking channels.

§ 2–309. Absence of Specific Time Provisions; Notice of Termination.

(1) The time for shipment or delivery or any other action under a contract if not provided in this Article or agreed upon shall be a reasonable time.

(2) Where the contract provides for successive performances but is indefinite in duration it is valid for a reasonable time but unless otherwise agreed may be terminated at any time by either party.

(3) Termination of a contract by one party except on the happening of an agreed event requires that reasonable notification be received by the other party and an agreement dispensing with notification is invalid if its operation would be unconscionable.

§ 2–310. Open Time for Payment or Running of Credit; Authority to Ship Under Reservation.

Unless otherwise agreed

(a) payment is due at the time and place at which the buyer is to receive the goods even though the place of shipment is the place of delivery; and

(b) if the seller is authorized to send the goods he may ship them under reservation, and may tender the documents of title, but the buyer may inspect the goods after their arrival before payment is due unless such inspection is inconsistent with the terms of the contract (Section 2–513); and

(c) if delivery is authorized and made by way of documents of title otherwise than by subsection (b) then payment is due at the time and place at which the buyer is to receive the documents regardless of where the goods are to be received; and

(d) where the seller is required or authorized to ship the goods on credit the credit period runs from the time of shipment but post-dating the invoice or delaying its dispatch will correspondingly delay the starting of the credit period.

§ 2–311. Options and Cooperation Respecting Performance.

(1) An agreement for sale which is otherwise sufficiently definite (subsection (3) of Section 2–204) to be a contract is not made invalid by the fact that it leaves particulars of performance to be specified by one of the parties. Any such specification must be made in good faith and within limits set by commercial reasonableness.

(2) Unless otherwise agreed specifications relating to assortment of the goods are at the buyer's option and except as otherwise provided in subsections (1)(c) and (3) of Section 2–319 specifications or arrangements relating to shipment are at the seller's option.

(3) Where such specification would materially affect the other party's performance but is not seasonably made or where one party's cooperation is necessary to the agreed performance of the other but is not seasonably forthcoming, the other party in addition to all other remedies

(a) is excused for any resulting delay in his own performance; and

(b) may also either proceed to perform in any reasonable manner or after the time for a material part of his own performance treat the failure to specify or to cooperate as a breach by failure to deliver or accept the goods.

§ 2–312. Warranty of Title and Against Infringement; Buyer's Obligation Against Infringement.

(1) Subject to subsection (2) there is in a contract for sale a warranty by the seller that

(a) the title conveyed shall be good, and its transfer rightful; and

(b) the goods shall be delivered free from any security interest or other lien or encumbrance of which the buyer at the time of contracting has no knowledge.

(2) A warranty under subsection (1) will be excluded or modified only by specific language or by circumstances which give the buyer reason to know that the person selling does not claim title in himself or that he is purporting to sell only such right or title as he or a third person may have.

(3) Unless otherwise agreed a seller who is a merchant regularly dealing in goods of the kind warrants that the goods shall be delivered free of the rightful claim of any third person by way of infringement or the like but a buyer who furnishes specifications to the seller must hold the seller harmless against any such claim which arises out of compliance with the specifications.

§ 2–313. Express Warranties by Affirmation, Promise, Description, Sample.

(1) Express warranties by the seller are created as follows:

(a) Any affirmation of fact or promise made by the seller to the buyer which relates to the goods and becomes part of the basis of the bargain creates an express warranty that the goods shall conform to the affirmation or promise.

(b) Any description of the goods which is made part of the basis of the bargain creates an express warranty that the goods shall conform to the description.

(c) Any sample or model which is made part of the basis of the bargain creates an express warranty that the whole of the goods shall conform to the sample or model.

(2) It is not necessary to the creation of an express warranty that the seller use formal words such as "warrant" or "guarantee" or that he have a specific intention to make a warranty, but an affirmation merely of the value of the goods or a statement purporting to be merely the seller's opinion or commendation of the goods does not create a warranty.

§ 2–314. Implied Warranty: Merchantability; Usage of Trade.

(1) Unless excluded or modified (Section 2–316), a warranty that the goods shall be merchantable is implied in a contract for their sale if the seller is a merchant with respect to goods of that kind. Under this section the serving for value of food or drink to be consumed either on the premises or elsewhere is a sale.

(2) Goods to be merchantable must be at least such as

(a) pass without objection in the trade under the contract description; and

(b) in the case of fungible goods, are of fair average quality within the description; and

(c) are fit for the ordinary purposes for which such goods are used; and

(d) run, within the variations permitted by the agreement, of even kind, quality and quantity within each unit and among all units involved; and

(e) are adequately contained, packaged, and labeled as the agreement may require; and

(f) conform to the promises or affirmations of fact made on the container or label if any.

(3) Unless excluded or modified (Section 2–316) other implied warranties may arise from course of dealing or usage of trade.

§ 2–315. Implied Warranty: Fitness for Particular Purpose.

Where the seller at the time of contracting has reason to know any particular purpose for which the goods are required and that the buyer is relying on the seller's skill or judgment to select or furnish suitable goods, there is unless excluded or modified under the next section an implied warranty that the goods shall be fit for such purpose.

§ 2–316. Exclusion or Modification of Warranties.

(1) Words or conduct relevant to the creation of an express warranty and words or conduct tending to negate or limit warranty shall be construed wherever reasonable as consistent with each other; but subject to the provisions of this Article on parol or extrinsic evidence (Section 2–202) negation or limitation is inoperative to the extent that such construction is unreasonable.

(2) Subject to subsection (3), to exclude or modify the implied warranty of merchantability or any part of it the language must mention merchantability and in case of a writing must be conspicuous, and to exclude or modify any implied warranty of fitness the exclusion must be by a writing and conspicuous. Language to exclude all implied warranties of fitness is sufficient if it states, for example, that "There are no warranties which extend beyond the description on the face hereof."

(3) Notwithstanding subsection (2)

    (a) unless the circumstances indicate otherwise, all implied warranties are excluded by expressions like "as is", "with all faults" or other language which in common understanding calls the buyer's attention to the exclusion of warranties and makes plain that there is no implied warranty; and

    (b) when the buyer before entering into the contract has examined the goods or the sample or model as fully as he desired or has refused to examine the goods there is no implied warranty with regard to defects which an examination ought in the circumstances to have revealed to him; and

    (c) an implied warranty can also be excluded or modified by course of dealing or course of performance or usage of trade.

(4) Remedies for breach of warranty can be limited in accordance with the provisions of this Article on liquidation or limitation of damages and on contractual modification of remedy (Sections 2–718 and 2–719).

§ 2–317. Cumulation and Conflict of Warranties Express or Implied.

Warranties whether express or implied shall be construed as consistent with each other and as cumulative, but if such construction is unreasonable the intention of the parties shall determine which warranty is dominant. In ascertaining that intention the following rules apply:

    (a) Exact or technical specifications displace an inconsistent sample or model or general language of description.

    (b) A sample from an existing bulk displaces inconsistent general language of description.

    (c) Express warranties displace inconsistent implied warranties other than an implied warranty of fitness for a particular purpose.

§ 2–318. Third Party Beneficiaries of Warranties Express or Implied.

Note: If this Act is introduced in the Congress of the United States this section should be omitted. (States to select one alternative.)

Alternative A

A seller's warranty whether express or implied extends to any natural person who is in the family or household of his buyer or who is a guest in his home if it is reasonable to expect that such person may use, consume or be affected by the goods and who is injured in person by breach of the warranty. A seller may not exclude or limit the operation of this section.

Alternative B

A seller's warranty whether express or implied extends to any natural person who may reasonably be expected to use, consume or be affected by the goods and who is injured in person by breach of the warranty. A seller may not exclude or limit the operation of this section.

Alternative C

A seller's warranty whether express or implied extends to any person who may reasonably be expected to use, consume or be affected by the goods and who is injured by breach of the warranty. A seller may not exclude or limit the operation of this section with respect to injury to the person of an individual to whom the warranty extends. As amended 1966.

§ 2–319. F.O.B. and F.A.S. Terms.

(1) Unless otherwise agreed the term F.O.B. (which means "free on board") at a named place, even though used only in connection with the stated price, is a delivery term under which

    (a) when the term is F.O.B. the place of shipment, the seller must at that place ship the goods in the manner provided in this Article (Section 2–504) and bear the expense and risk of putting them into the possession of the carrier; or

    (b) when the term is F.O.B. the place of destination, the seller must at his own expense and risk transport the goods to that place and there tender delivery of them in the manner provided in this Article (Section 2–503);

    (c) when under either (a) or (b) the term is also F.O.B. vessel, car or other vehicle, the seller must in addition at his own expense and risk load the goods on board. If the term is F.O.B. vessel the buyer must name the vessel and in an appropriate case the seller must comply with the provisions of this Article on the form of bill of lading (Section 2–323).

(2) Unless otherwise agreed the term F.A.S. vessel (which means "free alongside") at a named port, even though used only in connection with the stated price, is a delivery term under which the seller must

(a) at his own expense and risk deliver the goods alongside the vessel in the manner usual in that port or on a dock designated and provided by the buyer; and

(b) obtain and tender a receipt for the goods in exchange for which the carrier is under a duty to issue a bill of lading.

(3) Unless otherwise agreed in any case falling within subsection (1)(a) or (c) or subsection (2) the buyer must seasonably give any needed instructions for making delivery, including when the term is F.A.S. or F.O.B. the loading berth of the vessel and in an appropriate case its name and sailing date. The seller may treat the failure of needed instructions as a failure of cooperation under this Article (Section 2–311). He may also at his option move the goods in any reasonable manner preparatory to delivery or shipment.

(4) Under the term F.O.B. vessel or F.A.S. unless otherwise agreed the buyer must make payment against tender of the required documents and the seller may not tender nor the buyer demand delivery of the goods in substitution for the documents.

§ 2–320. C.I.F. and C. & F. Terms.

(1) The term C.I.F. means that the price includes in a lump sum the cost of the goods and the insurance and freight to the named destination. The term C. & F. or C.F. means that the price so includes cost and freight to the named destination.

(2) Unless otherwise agreed and even though used only in connection with the stated price and destination, the term C.I.F. destination or its equivalent requires the seller at his own expense and risk to

(a) put the goods into the possession of a carrier at the port for shipment and obtain a negotiable bill or bills of lading covering the entire transportation to the named destination; and

(b) load the goods and obtain a receipt from the carrier (which may be contained in the bill of lading) showing that the freight has been paid or provided for; and

(c) obtain a policy or certificate of insurance, including any war risk insurance, of a kind and on terms then current at the port of shipment in the usual amount, in the currency of the contract, shown to cover the same goods covered by the bill of lading and providing for payment of loss to the order of the buyer or for the account of whom it may concern; but the seller may add to the price the amount of the premium for any such war risk insurance; and

(d) prepare an invoice of the goods and procure any other documents required to effect shipment or to comply with the contract; and

(e) forward and tender with commercial promptness all the documents in due form and with any indorsement necessary to perfect the buyer's rights.

(3) Unless otherwise agreed the term C. & F. or its equivalent has the same effect and imposes upon the seller the same obligations and risks as a C.I.F. term except the obligation as to insurance.

(4) Under the term C.I.F. or C. & F. unless otherwise agreed the buyer must make payment against tender of the required documents and the seller may not tender nor the buyer demand delivery of the goods in substitution for the documents.

§ 2–321. C.I.F. or C. & F.: "Net Landed Weights"; "Payment on Arrival"; Warranty of Condition on Arrival.

Under a contract containing a term C.I.F. or C. & F.

(1) Where the price is based on or is to be adjusted according to "net landed weights", "delivered weights", "out turn" quantity or quality or the like, unless otherwise agreed the seller must reasonably estimate the price. The payment due on tender of the documents called for by the contract is the amount so estimated, but after final adjustment of the price a settlement must be made with commercial promptness.

(2) An agreement described in subsection (1) or any warranty of quality or condition of the goods on arrival places upon the seller the risk of ordinary deterioration, shrinkage and the like in transportation but has no effect on the place or time of identification to the contract for sale or delivery or on the passing of the risk of loss.

(3) Unless otherwise agreed where the contract provides for payment on or after arrival of the goods the seller must before payment allow such preliminary inspection as is feasible; but if the goods are lost delivery of the documents and payment are due when the goods should have arrived.

§ 2–322. Delivery "Ex-Ship".

(1) Unless otherwise agreed a term for delivery of goods "ex-ship" (which means from the carrying vessel) or in equivalent language is not restricted to a particular ship and requires delivery from a ship which has reached a place at the named port of destination where goods of the kind are usually discharged.

(2) Under such a term unless otherwise agreed

(a) the seller must discharge all liens arising out of the carriage and furnish the buyer with a direction which puts the carrier under a duty to deliver the goods; and

(b) the risk of loss does not pass to the buyer until the goods leave the ship's tackle or are otherwise properly unloaded.

§ 2–323. Form of Bill of Lading Required in Overseas Shipment; "Overseas".

(1) Where the contract contemplates overseas shipment and contains a term C.I.F. or C. & F. or F.O.B. vessel, the seller unless otherwise agreed must obtain a negotiable bill of lading stating that the goods have been loaded on board or, in the case of a term C.I.F. or C. & F., received for shipment.

(2) Where in a case within subsection (1) a bill of lading has been issued in a set of parts, unless otherwise agreed if the documents are not to be sent from abroad the buyer may demand tender of the full set; otherwise only one part of the bill of lading need be tendered. Even if the agreement expressly requires a full set

(a) due tender of a single part is acceptable within the provisions of this Article on cure of improper delivery (subsection (1) of Section 2–508); and

(b) even though the full set is demanded, if the documents are sent from abroad the person tendering an incomplete set may nevertheless require payment upon furnishing an indemnity which the buyer in good faith deems adequate.

(3) A shipment by water or by air or a contract contemplating such shipment is "overseas" insofar as by usage of trade or agreement it is subject to the commercial, financing or shipping practices characteristic of international deep water commerce.

§ 2–324. "No Arrival, No Sale" Term.

Under a term "no arrival, no sale" or terms of like meaning, unless otherwise agreed,

(a) the seller must properly ship conforming goods and if they arrive by any means he must tender them on arrival but he assumes no obligation that the goods will arrive unless he has caused the non-arrival; and

(b) where without fault of the seller the goods are in part lost or have so deteriorated as no longer to conform to the contract or arrive after the contract time, the buyer may proceed as if there had been casualty to identified goods (Section 2–613).

§ 2–325. "Letter of Credit" Term; "Confirmed Credit".

(1) Failure of the buyer seasonably to furnish an agreed letter of credit is a breach of the contract for sale.

(2) The delivery to seller of a proper letter of credit suspends the buyer's obligation to pay. If the letter of credit is dishonored, the seller may on seasonable notification to the buyer require payment directly from him.

(3) Unless otherwise agreed the term "letter of credit" or "banker's credit" in a contract for sale means an irrevocable credit issued by a financing agency of good repute and, where the shipment is overseas, of good international repute. The term "confirmed credit" means that the credit must also carry the direct obligation of such an agency which does business in the seller's financial market.

§ 2–326. Sale on Approval and Sale or Return; Rights of Creditors.

(1) Unless otherwise agreed, if delivered goods may be returned by the buyer even though they conform to the contract, the transaction is

(a) a "sale on approval" if the goods are delivered primarily for use, and

(b) a "sale or return" if the goods are delivered primarily for resale.

(2) Goods held on approval are not subject to the claims of the buyer's creditors until acceptance; goods held on sale or return are subject to such claims while in the buyer's possession.

(3) Any "or return" term of a contract for sale is to be treated as a separate contract for sale within the statute of frauds section of this Article (Section 2–201) and as contradicting the sale aspect of the contract within the provisions of this Article or on parol or extrinsic evidence (Section 2–202).

As amended in 1999.

§ 2–327. Special Incidents of Sale on Approval and Sale or Return.

(1) Under a sale on approval unless otherwise agreed

(a) although the goods are identified to the contract the risk of loss and the title do not pass to the buyer until acceptance; and

(b) use of the goods consistent with the purpose of trial is not acceptance but failure seasonably to notify the seller of election to return the goods is acceptance, and if the goods conform to the contract acceptance of any part is acceptance of the whole; and

(c) after due notification of election to return, the return is at the seller's risk and expense but a merchant buyer must follow any reasonable instructions.

(2) Under a sale or return unless otherwise agreed

(a) the option to return extends to the whole or any commercial unit of the goods while in substantially their original condition, but must be exercised seasonably; and

(b) the return is at the buyer's risk and expense.

§ 2–328. Sale by Auction.

(1) In a sale by auction if goods are put up in lots each lot is the subject of a separate sale.

(2) A sale by auction is complete when the auctioneer so announces by the fall of the hammer or in other customary manner. Where a bid is made while the hammer is falling in acceptance of a prior bid the auctioneer may in his discretion reopen the bidding or declare the goods sold under the bid on which the hammer was falling.

(3) Such a sale is with reserve unless the goods are in explicit terms put up without reserve. In an auction with reserve the auctioneer may withdraw the goods at any time until he announces completion of the sale. In an auction without reserve, after the auctioneer calls for bids on an article or lot, that article or lot cannot be withdrawn unless no bid is made within a reasonable time. In either case a bidder may retract his bid until the auctioneer's announcement of completion of the sale, but a bidder's retraction does not revive any previous bid.

(4) If the auctioneer knowingly receives a bid on the seller's behalf or the seller makes or procures such as bid, and notice has not been given that liberty for such bidding is reserved, the buyer may at his option avoid the sale or take the goods at the price of the last good faith bid prior to the completion of the sale. This subsection shall not apply to any bid at a forced sale.

Part 4—Title, Creditors and Good Faith Purchasers

§ 2–401. Passing of Title; Reservation for Security; Limited Application of This Section.

Each provision of this Article with regard to the rights, obligations and remedies of the seller, the buyer, purchasers or other third parties applies irrespective of title to the goods except where the provision refers to such title. Insofar as situations are not covered by the other provisions of this Article and matters concerning title became material the following rules apply:

(1) Title to goods cannot pass under a contract for sale prior to their identification to the contract (Section 2–501), and unless otherwise explicitly agreed the buyer acquires by their identification a special property as limited by this Act. Any retention or reservation by the seller of the title (property) in goods shipped or delivered to the buyer is limited in effect to a reservation of a security interest. Subject to these provisions and to the provisions of the Article on Secured Transactions (Article 9), title to goods passes from the seller to the buyer in any manner and on any conditions explicitly agreed on by the parties.

(2) Unless otherwise explicitly agreed title passes to the buyer at the time and place at which the seller completes his performance with reference to the physical delivery of the goods, despite any reservation of a security interest and even though a document of title is to be delivered at a different time or place; and in particular and despite any reservation of a security interest by the bill of lading

    (a) if the contract requires or authorizes the seller to send the goods to the buyer but does not require him to deliver them at destination, title passes to the buyer at the time and place of shipment; but

    (b) if the contract requires delivery at destination, title passes on tender there.

(3) Unless otherwise explicitly agreed where delivery is to be made without moving the goods,

    (a) if the seller is to deliver a document of title, title passes at the time when and the place where he delivers such documents; or

    (b) if the goods are at the time of contracting already identified and no documents are to be delivered, title passes at the time and place of contracting.

(4) A rejection or other refusal by the buyer to receive or retain the goods, whether or not justified, or a justified revocation of acceptance revests title to the goods in the seller. Such revesting occurs by operation of law and is not a "sale".

§ 2–402. Rights of Seller's Creditors Against Sold Goods.

(1) Except as provided in subsections (2) and (3), rights of unsecured creditors of the seller with respect to goods which have been identified to a contract for sale are subject to the buyer's rights to recover the goods under this Article (Sections 2–502 and 2–716).

(2) A creditor of the seller may treat a sale or an identification of goods to a contract for sale as void if as against him a retention of possession by the seller is fraudulent under any rule of law of the state where the goods are situated, except that retention of possession in good faith and current course of trade by a merchant-seller for a commercially reasonable time after a sale or identification is not fraudulent.

(3) Nothing in this Article shall be deemed to impair the rights of creditors of the seller

    (a) under the provisions of the Article on Secured Transactions (Article 9); or

    (b) where identification to the contract or delivery is made not in current course of trade but in satisfaction of or as security for a pre-existing claim for money, security or the like and is made under circumstances which under any rule of law of the state where the goods are situated would apart from this Article constitute the transaction a fraudulent transfer or voidable preference.

§ 2–403. Power to Transfer; Good Faith Purchase of Goods; "Entrusting".

(1) A purchaser of goods acquires all title which his transferor had or had power to transfer except that a purchaser of a limited interest acquires rights only to the extent of the interest purchased. A person with voidable title has power to transfer a good title to a good faith purchaser for value. When goods have been delivered under a transaction of purchase the purchaser has such power even though

    (a) the transferor was deceived as to the identity of the purchaser, or

    (b) the delivery was in exchange for a check which is later dishonored, or

    (c) it was agreed that the transaction was to be a "cash sale", or

    (d) the delivery was procured through fraud punishable as larcenous under the criminal law.

(2) Any entrusting of possession of goods to a merchant who deals in goods of that kind gives him power to transfer all rights of the entruster to a buyer in ordinary course of business.

(3) "Entrusting" includes any delivery and any acquiescence in retention of possession regardless of any condition expressed between the parties to the delivery or acquiescence and regardless of whether the procurement of the entrusting or the possessor's disposition of the goods have been such as to be larcenous under the criminal law.

(4) The rights of other purchasers of goods and of lien creditors are governed by the Articles on Secured Transactions (Article 9), Bulk Transfers (Article 6) and Documents of Title (Article 7).

As amended in 1988.

Part 5—Performance

§ 2–501. Insurable Interest in Goods; Manner of Identification of Goods.

(1) The buyer obtains a special property and an insurable interest in goods by identification of existing goods as goods to which the contract refers even though the goods so identified are nonconforming and he has an option to return or reject them. Such identification can be made at any time and in any manner explicitly agreed to by the parties. In the absence of explicit agreement identification occurs

    (a) when the contract is made if it is for the sale of goods already existing and identified;

    (b) if the contract is for the sale of future goods other than those described in paragraph (c), when goods are shipped, marked or otherwise designated by the seller as goods to which the contract refers;

(c) when the crops are planted or otherwise become growing crops or the young are conceived if the contract is for the sale of unborn young to be born within twelve months after contracting or for the sale of crops to be harvested within twelve months or the next normal harvest season after contracting whichever is longer.

(2) The seller retains an insurable interest in goods so long as title to or any security interest in the goods remains in him and where the identification is by the seller alone he may until default or insolvency or notification to the buyer that the identification is final substitute other goods for those identified.

(3) Nothing in this section impairs any insurable interest recognized under any other statute or rule of law.

§ 2–502. Buyer's Right to Goods on Seller's Insolvency.

(1) Subject to subsections (2) and (3) and even though the goods have not been shipped a buyer who has paid a part or all of the price of goods in which he has a special property under the provisions of the immediately preceding section may on making and keeping good a tender of any unpaid portion of their price recover them from the seller if:

(a) in the case of goods bought for personal, family, or household purposes, the seller repudiates or fails to deliver as required by the contract; or

(b) in all cases, the seller becomes insolvent within ten days after receipt of the first installment on their price.

(2) The buyer's right to recover the goods under subsection (1) (a) vests upon acquisition of a special property, even if the seller had not then repudiated or failed to deliver.

(3) If the identification creating his special property has been made by the buyer he acquires the right to recover the goods only if they conform to the contract for sale.

As amended in 1999.

§ 2–503. Manner of Seller's Tender of Delivery.

(1) Tender of delivery requires that the seller put and hold conforming goods at the buyer's disposition and give the buyer any notification reasonably necessary to enable him to take delivery. The manner, time and place for tender are determined by the agreement and this Article, and in particular

(a) tender must be at a reasonable hour, and if it is of goods they must be kept available for the period reasonably necessary to enable the buyer to take possession; but

(b) unless otherwise agreed the buyer must furnish facilities reasonably suited to the receipt of the goods.

(2) Where the case is within the next section respecting shipment tender requires that the seller comply with its provisions.

(3) Where the seller is required to deliver at a particular destination tender requires that he comply with subsection (1) and also in any appropriate case tender documents as described in subsections (4) and (5) of this section.

(4) Where goods are in the possession of a bailee and are to be delivered without being moved

(a) tender requires that the seller either tender a negotiable document of title covering such goods or procure acknowledgment by the bailee of the buyer's right to possession of the goods; but

(b) tender to the buyer of a non-negotiable document of title or of a written direction to the bailee to deliver is sufficient tender unless the buyer seasonably objects, and receipt by the bailee of notification of the buyer's rights fixes those rights as against the bailee and all third persons; but risk of loss of the goods and of any failure by the bailee to honor the non-negotiable document of title or to obey the direction remains on the seller until the buyer has had a reasonable time to present the document or direction, and a refusal by the bailee to honor the document or to obey the direction defeats the tender.

(5) Where the contract requires the seller to deliver documents

(a) he must tender all such documents in correct form, except as provided in this Article with respect to bills of lading in a set (subsection (2) of Section 2–323); and

(b) tender through customary banking channels is sufficient and dishonor of a draft accompanying the documents constitutes non-acceptance or rejection.

§ 2–504. Shipment by Seller.

Where the seller is required or authorized to send the goods to the buyer and the contract does not require him to deliver them at a particular destination, then unless otherwise agreed he must

(a) put the goods in the possession of such a carrier and make such a contract for their transportation as may be reasonable having regard to the nature of the goods and other circumstances of the case; and

(b) obtain and promptly deliver or tender in due form any document necessary to enable the buyer to obtain possession of the goods or otherwise required by the agreement or by usage of trade; and

(c) promptly notify the buyer of the shipment.

Failure to notify the buyer under paragraph (c) or to make a proper contract under paragraph (a) is a ground for rejection only if material delay or loss ensues.

§ 2–505. Seller's Shipment under Reservation.

(1) Where the seller has identified goods to the contract by or before shipment:

(a) his procurement of a negotiable bill of lading to his own order or otherwise reserves in him a security interest in the goods. His procurement of the bill to the order of a financing agency or of the buyer indicates in addition only the seller's expectation of transferring that interest to the person named.

(b) a non-negotiable bill of lading to himself or his nominee reserves possession of the goods as security but except in a case of conditional delivery (subsection (2) of Section 2–507) a non-negotiable bill of lading naming the buyer as consignee reserves no security interest even though the seller retains possession of the bill of lading.

(2) When shipment by the seller with reservation of a security interest is in violation of the contract for sale it constitutes an improper contract for transportation within the preceding section but impairs neither the rights given to the buyer by shipment and identification of the goods to the contract nor the seller's powers as a holder of a negotiable document.

§ 2–506. Rights of Financing Agency.

(1) A financing agency by paying or purchasing for value a draft which relates to a shipment of goods acquires to the extent of the payment or purchase and in addition to its own rights under the draft and any document of title securing it any rights of the shipper in the goods including the right to stop delivery and the shipper's right to have the draft honored by the buyer.

(2) The right to reimbursement of a financing agency which has in good faith honored or purchased the draft under commitment to or authority from the buyer is not impaired by subsequent discovery of defects with reference to any relevant document which was apparently regular on its face.

§ 2–507. Effect of Seller's Tender; Delivery on Condition.

(1) Tender of delivery is a condition to the buyer's duty to accept the goods and, unless otherwise agreed, to his duty to pay for them. Tender entitles the seller to acceptance of the goods and to payment according to the contract.

(2) Where payment is due and demanded on the delivery to the buyer of goods or documents of title, his right as against the seller to retain or dispose of them is conditional upon his making the payment due.

§ 2–508. Cure by Seller of Improper Tender or Delivery; Replacement.

(1) Where any tender or delivery by the seller is rejected because non-conforming and the time for performance has not yet expired, the seller may seasonably notify the buyer of his intention to cure and may then within the contract time make a conforming delivery.

(2) Where the buyer rejects a non-conforming tender which the seller had reasonable grounds to believe would be acceptable with or without money allowance the seller may if he seasonably notifies the buyer have a further reasonable time to substitute a conforming tender.

§ 2–509. Risk of Loss in the Absence of Breach.

(1) Where the contract requires or authorizes the seller to ship the goods by carrier

   (a) if it does not require him to deliver them at a particular destination, the risk of loss passes to the buyer when the goods are duly delivered to the carrier even though the shipment is under reservation (Section 2–505); but

   (b) if it does require him to deliver them at a particular destination and the goods are there duly tendered while in the possession of the carrier, the risk of loss passes to the buyer when the goods are there duly so tendered as to enable the buyer to take delivery.

(2) Where the goods are held by a bailee to be delivered without being moved, the risk of loss passes to the buyer

   (a) on his receipt of a negotiable document of title covering the goods; or

   (b) on acknowledgment by the bailee of the buyer's right to possession of the goods; or

   (c) after his receipt of a non-negotiable document of title or other written direction to deliver, as provided in subsection (4)(b) of Section 2–503.

(3) In any case not within subsection (1) or (2), the risk of loss passes to the buyer on his receipt of the goods if the seller is a merchant; otherwise the risk passes to the buyer on tender of delivery.

(4) The provisions of this section are subject to contrary agreement of the parties and to the provisions of this Article on sale on approval (Section 2–327) and on effect of breach on risk of loss (Section 2–510).

§ 2–510. Effect of Breach on Risk of Loss.

(1) Where a tender or delivery of goods so fails to conform to the contract as to give a right of rejection the risk of their loss remains on the seller until cure or acceptance.

(2) Where the buyer rightfully revokes acceptance he may to the extent of any deficiency in his effective insurance coverage treat the risk of loss as having rested on the seller from the beginning.

(3) Where the buyer as to conforming goods already identified to the contract for sale repudiates or is otherwise in breach before risk of their loss has passed to him, the seller may to the extent of any deficiency in his effective insurance coverage treat the risk of loss as resting on the buyer for a commercially reasonable time.

§ 2–511. Tender of Payment by Buyer; Payment by Check.

(1) Unless otherwise agreed tender of payment is a condition to the seller's duty to tender and complete any delivery.

(2) Tender of payment is sufficient when made by any means or in any manner current in the ordinary course of business unless the seller demands payment in legal tender and gives any extension of time reasonably necessary to procure it.

(3) Subject to the provisions of this Act on the effect of an instrument on an obligation (Section 3–310), payment by check is conditional and is defeated as between the parties by dishonor of the check on due presentment.

As amended in 1994.

§ 2–512. Payment by Buyer Before Inspection.

(1) Where the contract requires payment before inspection non-conformity of the goods does not excuse the buyer from so making payment unless

   (a) the non-conformity appears without inspection; or

(b) despite tender of the required documents the circumstances would justify injunction against honor under this Act (Section 5–109(b)).

(2) Payment pursuant to subsection (1) does not constitute an acceptance of goods or impair the buyer's right to inspect or any of his remedies.

As amended in 1995.

§ 2–513. Buyer's Right to Inspection of Goods.

(1) Unless otherwise agreed and subject to subsection (3), where goods are tendered or delivered or identified to the contract for sale, the buyer has a right before payment or acceptance to inspect them at any reasonable place and time and in any reasonable manner. When the seller is required or authorized to send the goods to the buyer, the inspection may be after their arrival.

(2) Expenses of inspection must be borne by the buyer but may be recovered from the seller if the goods do not conform and are rejected.

(3) Unless otherwise agreed and subject to the provisions of this Article on C.I.F. contracts (subsection (3) of Section 2–321), the buyer is not entitled to inspect the goods before payment of the price when the contract provides

    (a) for delivery "C.O.D." or on other like terms; or

    (b) for payment against documents of title, except where such payment is due only after the goods are to become available for inspection.

(4) A place or method of inspection fixed by the parties is presumed to be exclusive but unless otherwise expressly agreed it does not postpone identification or shift the place for delivery or for passing the risk of loss. If compliance becomes impossible, inspection shall be as provided in this section unless the place or method fixed was clearly intended as an indispensable condition failure of which avoids the contract.

§ 2–514. When Documents Deliverable on Acceptance; When on Payment.

Unless otherwise agreed documents against which a draft is drawn are to be delivered to the drawee on acceptance of the draft if it is payable more than three days after presentment; otherwise, only on payment.

§ 2–515. Preserving Evidence of Goods in Dispute.

In furtherance of the adjustment of any claim or dispute

    (a) either party on reasonable notification to the other and for the purpose of ascertaining the facts and preserving evidence has the right to inspect, test and sample the goods including such of them as may be in the possession or control of the other; and

    (b) the parties may agree to a third party inspection or survey to determine the conformity or condition of the goods and may agree that the findings shall be binding upon them in any subsequent litigation or adjustment.

Part 6—Breach, Repudiation and Excuse

§ 2–601. Buyer's Rights on Improper Delivery.

Subject to the provisions of this Article on breach in installment contracts (Section 2–612) and unless otherwise agreed under the sections on contractual limitations of remedy (Sections 2–718 and 2–719), if the goods or the tender of delivery fail in any respect to conform to the contract, the buyer may

    (a) reject the whole; or

    (b) accept the whole; or

    (c) accept any commercial unit or units and reject the rest.

§ 2–602. Manner and Effect of Rightful Rejection.

(1) Rejection of goods must be within a reasonable time after their delivery or tender. It is ineffective unless the buyer seasonably notifies the seller.

(2) Subject to the provisions of the two following sections on rejected goods (Sections 2–603 and 2–604),

    (a) after rejection any exercise of ownership by the buyer with respect to any commercial unit is wrongful as against the seller; and

    (b) if the buyer has before rejection taken physical possession of goods in which he does not have a security interest under the provisions of this Article (subsection (3) of Section 2–711), he is under a duty after rejection to hold them with reasonable care at the seller's disposition for a time sufficient to permit the seller to remove them; but

    (c) the buyer has no further obligations with regard to goods rightfully rejected.

(3) The seller's rights with respect to goods wrongfully rejected are governed by the provisions of this Article on Seller's remedies in general (Section 2–703).

§ 2–603. Merchant Buyer's Duties as to Rightfully Rejected Goods.

(1) Subject to any security interest in the buyer (subsection (3) of Section 2–711), when the seller has no agent or place of business at the market of rejection a merchant buyer is under a duty after rejection of goods in his possession or control to follow any reasonable instructions received from the seller with respect to the goods and in the absence of such instructions to make reasonable efforts to sell them for the seller's account if they are perishable or threaten to decline in value speedily. Instructions are not reasonable if on demand indemnity for expenses is not forthcoming.

(2) When the buyer sells goods under subsection (1), he is entitled to reimbursement from the seller or out of the proceeds for reasonable expenses of caring for and selling them, and if the expenses include no selling commission then to such commission as is usual in the trade or if there is none to a reasonable sum not exceeding ten per cent on the gross proceeds.

(3) In complying with this section the buyer is held only to good faith and good faith conduct hereunder is neither acceptance nor conversion nor the basis of an action for damages.

§ 2–604. Buyer's Options as to Salvage of Rightfully Rejected Goods.

Subject to the provisions of the immediately preceding section on perishables if the seller gives no instructions within a reasonable time after notification of rejection the buyer may store the rejected goods for the seller's account or reship them to him or resell them for the seller's account with reimbursement as provided in the preceding section. Such action is not acceptance or conversion.

§ 2–605. Waiver of Buyer's Objections by Failure to Particularize.

(1) The buyer's failure to state in connection with rejection a particular defect which is ascertainable by reasonable inspection precludes him from relying on the unstated defect to justify rejection or to establish breach

(a) where the seller could have cured it if stated seasonably; or

(b) between merchants when the seller has after rejection made a request in writing for a full and final written statement of all defects on which the buyer proposes to rely.

(2) Payment against documents made without reservation of rights precludes recovery of the payment for defects apparent on the face of the documents.

§ 2–606. What Constitutes Acceptance of Goods.

(1) Acceptance of goods occurs when the buyer

(a) after a reasonable opportunity to inspect the goods signifies to the seller that the goods are conforming or that he will take or retain them in spite of their nonconformity; or

(b) fails to make an effective rejection (subsection (1) of Section 2–602), but such acceptance does not occur until the buyer has had a reasonable opportunity to inspect them; or

(c) does any act inconsistent with the seller's ownership; but if such act is wrongful as against the seller it is an acceptance only if ratified by him.

(2) Acceptance of a part of any commercial unit is acceptance of that entire unit.

§ 2–607. Effect of Acceptance; Notice of Breach; Burden of Establishing Breach After Acceptance; Notice of Claim or Litigation to Person Answerable Over.

(1) The buyer must pay at the contract rate for any goods accepted.

(2) Acceptance of goods by the buyer precludes rejection of the goods accepted and if made with knowledge of a non-conformity cannot be revoked because of it unless the acceptance was on the reasonable assumption that the non-conformity would be seasonably cured but acceptance does not of itself impair any other remedy provided by this Article for non-conformity.

(3) Where a tender has been accepted

(a) the buyer must within a reasonable time after he discovers or should have discovered any breach notify the seller of breach or be barred from any remedy; and

(b) if the claim is one for infringement or the like (subsection (3) of Section 2–312) and the buyer is sued as a result of such a breach he must so notify the seller within a reasonable time after he receives notice of the litigation or be barred from any remedy over for liability established by the litigation.

(4) The burden is on the buyer to establish any breach with respect to the goods accepted.

(5) Where the buyer is sued for breach of a warranty or other obligation for which his seller is answerable over

(a) he may give his seller written notice of the litigation. If the notice states that the seller may come in and defend and that if the seller does not do so he will be bound in any action against him by his buyer by any determination of fact common to the two litigations, then unless the seller after seasonable receipt of the notice does come in and defend he is so bound.

(b) if the claim is one for infringement or the like (subsection (3) of Section 2–312) the original seller may demand in writing that his buyer turn over to him control of the litigation including settlement or else be barred from any remedy over and if he also agrees to bear all expense and to satisfy any adverse judgment, then unless the buyer after seasonable receipt of the demand does turn over control the buyer is so barred.

(6) The provisions of subsections (3), (4) and (5) apply to any obligation of a buyer to hold the seller harmless against infringement or the like (subsection (3) of Section 2–312).

§ 2–608. Revocation of Acceptance in Whole or in Part.

(1) The buyer may revoke his acceptance of a lot or commercial unit whose non-conformity substantially impairs its value to him if he has accepted it

(a) on the reasonable assumption that its nonconformity would be cured and it has not been seasonably cured; or

(b) without discovery of such non-conformity if his acceptance was reasonably induced either by the difficulty of discovery before acceptance or by the seller's assurances.

(2) Revocation of acceptance must occur within a reasonable time after the buyer discovers or should have discovered the ground for it and before any substantial change in condition of the goods which is not caused by their own defects. It is not effective until the buyer notifies the seller of it.

(3) A buyer who so revokes has the same rights and duties with regard to the goods involved as if he had rejected them.

§ 2–609. Right to Adequate Assurance of Performance.

(1) A contract for sale imposes an obligation on each party that the other's expectation of receiving due performance will not be impaired. When reasonable grounds for insecurity arise with respect to the performance of either party the other may in writing demand adequate assurance of due performance and until he receives such assurance may if commercially reasonable suspend any performance for which he has not already received the agreed return.

(2) Between merchants the reasonableness of grounds for insecurity and the adequacy of any assurance offered shall be determined according to commercial standards.

(3) Acceptance of any improper delivery or payment does not prejudice the party's right to demand adequate assurance of future performance.

(4) After receipt of a justified demand failure to provide within a reasonable time not exceeding thirty days such assurance of due performance as is adequate under the circumstances of the particular case is a repudiation of the contract.

§ 2–610. Anticipatory Repudiation.

When either party repudiates the contract with respect to a performance not yet due the loss of which will substantially impair the value of the contract to the other, the aggrieved party may

> **(a)** for a commercially reasonable time await performance by the repudiating party; or
>
> **(b)** resort to any remedy for breach (Section 2–703 or Section 2–711), even though he has notified the repudiating party that he would await the latter's performance and has urged retraction; and
>
> **(c)** in either case suspend his own performance or proceed in accordance with the provisions of this Article on the seller's right to identify goods to the contract notwithstanding breach or to salvage unfinished goods (Section 2–704).

§ 2–611. Retraction of Anticipatory Repudiation.

(1) Until the repudiating party's next performance is due he can retract his repudiation unless the aggrieved party has since the repudiation cancelled or materially changed his position or otherwise indicated that he considers the repudiation final.

(2) Retraction may be by any method which clearly indicates to the aggrieved party that the repudiating party intends to perform, but must include any assurance justifiably demanded under the provisions of this Article (Section 2–609).

(3) Retraction reinstates the repudiating party's rights under the contract with due excuse and allowance to the aggrieved party for any delay occasioned by the repudiation.

§ 2–612. "Installment Contract"; Breach.

(1) An "installment contract" is one which requires or authorizes the delivery of goods in separate lots to be separately accepted, even though the contract contains a clause "each delivery is a separate contract" or its equivalent.

(2) The buyer may reject any installment which is nonconforming if the non-conformity substantially impairs the value of that installment and cannot be cured or if the non-conformity is a defect in the required documents; but if the non-conformity does not fall within subsection (3) and the seller gives adequate assurance of its cure the buyer must accept that installment.

(3) Whenever non-conformity or default with respect to one or more installments substantially impairs the value of the whole contract there is a breach of the whole. But the aggrieved party reinstates the contract if he accepts a non-conforming installment without seasonably notifying of cancellation or if he brings an action with respect only to past installments or demands performance as to future installments.

§ 2–613. Casualty to Identified Goods.

Where the contract requires for its performance goods identified when the contract is made, and the goods suffer casualty without fault of either party before the risk of loss passes to the buyer, or in a proper case under a "no arrival, no sale" term (Section 2–324) then

> **(a)** if the loss is total the contract is avoided; and
>
> **(b)** if the loss is partial or the goods have so deteriorated as no longer to conform to the contract the buyer may nevertheless demand inspection and at his option either treat the contract as voided or accept the goods with due allowance from the contract price for the deterioration or the deficiency in quantity but without further right against the seller.

§ 2–614. Substituted Performance.

(1) Where without fault of either party the agreed berthing, loading, or unloading facilities fail or an agreed type of carrier becomes unavailable or the agreed manner of delivery otherwise becomes commercially impracticable but a commercially reasonable substitute is available, such substitute performance must be tendered and accepted.

(2) If the agreed means or manner of payment fails because of domestic or foreign governmental regulation, the seller may withhold or stop delivery unless the buyer provides a means or manner of payment which is commercially a substantial equivalent. If delivery has already been taken, payment by the means or in the manner provided by the regulation discharges the buyer's obligation unless the regulation is discriminatory, oppressive or predatory.

§ 2–615. Excuse by Failure of Presupposed Conditions.

Except so far as a seller may have assumed a greater obligation and subject to the preceding section on substituted performance:

> **(a)** Delay in delivery or non-delivery in whole or in part by a seller who complies with paragraphs (b) and (c) is not a breach of his duty under a contract for sale if performance as agreed has been made impracticable by the occurrence of a contingency the nonoccurrence of which was a basic assumption on which the contract was made or by compliance in good faith with any applicable foreign or domestic governmental regulation or order whether or not it later proves to be invalid.
>
> **(b)** Where the causes mentioned in paragraph (a) affect only a part of the seller's capacity to perform, he must allocate production and deliveries among his customers but may at his option include regular customers not then under contract as well as his own requirements for further manufacture. He may so allocate in any manner which is fair and reasonable.

(c) The seller must notify the buyer seasonably that there will be delay or non-delivery and, when allocation is required under paragraph (b), of the estimated quota thus made available for the buyer.

§ 2–616. Procedure on Notice Claiming Excuse.

(1) Where the buyer receives notification of a material or indefinite delay or an allocation justified under the preceding section he may by written notification to the seller as to any delivery concerned, and where the prospective deficiency substantially impairs the value of the whole contract under the provisions of this Article relating to breach of installment contracts (Section 2–612), then also as to the whole,

> **(a)** terminate and thereby discharge any unexecuted portion of the contract; or

> **(b)** modify the contract by agreeing to take his available quota in substitution.

(2) If after receipt of such notification from the seller the buyer fails so to modify the contract within a reasonable time not exceeding thirty days the contract lapses with respect to any deliveries affected.

(3) The provisions of this section may not be negated by agreement except in so far as the seller has assumed a greater obligation under the preceding section.

Part 7—Remedies

§ 2–701. Remedies for Breach of Collateral Contracts Not Impaired.

Remedies for breach of any obligation or promise collateral or ancillary to a contract for sale are not impaired by the provisions of this Article.

§ 2–702. Seller's Remedies on Discovery of Buyer's Insolvency.

(1) Where the seller discovers the buyer to be insolvent he may refuse delivery except for cash including payment for all goods theretofore delivered under the contract, and stop delivery under this Article (Section 2–705).

(2) Where the seller discovers that the buyer has received goods on credit while insolvent he may reclaim the goods upon demand made within ten days after the receipt, but if misrepresentation of solvency has been made to the particular seller in writing within three months before delivery the ten day limitation does not apply. Except as provided in this subsection the seller may not base a right to reclaim goods on the buyer's fraudulent or innocent misrepresentation of solvency or of intent to pay.

(3) The seller's right to reclaim under subsection (2) is subject to the rights of a buyer in ordinary course or other good faith purchaser under this Article (Section 2–403). Successful reclamation of goods excludes all other remedies with respect to them.

§ 2–703. Seller's Remedies in General.

Where the buyer wrongfully rejects or revokes acceptance of goods or fails to make a payment due on or before delivery or repudiates

with respect to a part or the whole, then with respect to any goods directly affected and, if the breach is of the whole contract (Section 2–612), then also with respect to the whole undelivered balance, the aggrieved seller may

(a) withhold delivery of such goods;

(b) stop delivery by any bailee as hereafter provided (Section 2–705);

(c) proceed under the next section respecting goods still unidentified to the contract;

(d) resell and recover damages as hereafter provided (Section 2–706);

(e) recover damages for non-acceptance (Section 2–708) or in a proper case the price (Section 2–709);

(f) cancel.

§ 2–704. Seller's Right to Identify Goods to the Contract Notwithstanding Breach or to Salvage Unfinished Goods.

(1) An aggrieved seller under the preceding section may

> **(a)** identify to the contract conforming goods not already identified if at the time he learned of the breach they are in his possession or control;

> **(b)** treat as the subject of resale goods which have demonstrably been intended for the particular contract even though those goods are unfinished.

(2) Where the goods are unfinished an aggrieved seller may in the exercise of reasonable commercial judgment for the purposes of avoiding loss and of effective realization either complete the manufacture and wholly identify the goods to the contract or cease manufacture and resell for scrap or salvage value or proceed in any other reasonable manner.

§ 2–705. Seller's Stoppage of Delivery in Transit or Otherwise.

(1) The seller may stop delivery of goods in the possession of a carrier or other bailee when he discovers the buyer to be insolvent (Section 2–702) and may stop delivery of carload, truckload, planeload or larger shipments of express or freight when the buyer repudiates or fails to make a payment due before delivery or if for any other reason the seller has a right to withhold or reclaim the goods.

(2) As against such buyer the seller may stop delivery until

> **(a)** receipt of the goods by the buyer; or

> **(b)** acknowledgment to the buyer by any bailee of the goods except a carrier that the bailee holds the goods for the buyer; or

> **(c)** such acknowledgment to the buyer by a carrier by reshipment or as warehouseman; or

> **(d)** negotiation to the buyer of any negotiable document of title covering the goods.

(3) (a) To stop delivery the seller must so notify as to enable the bailee by reasonable diligence to prevent delivery of the goods.

> **(b)** After such notification the bailee must hold and deliver the goods according to the directions of the seller but

the seller is liable to the bailee for any ensuing charges or damages.

(c) If a negotiable document of title has been issued for goods the bailee is not obliged to obey a notification to stop until surrender of the document.

(d) A carrier who has issued a non-negotiable bill of lading is not obliged to obey a notification to stop received from a person other than the consignor.

§ 2–706. Seller's Resale Including Contract for Resale.

(1) Under the conditions stated in Section 2–703 on seller's remedies, the seller may resell the goods concerned or the undelivered balance thereof. Where the resale is made in good faith and in a commercially reasonable manner the seller may recover the difference between the resale price and the contract price together with any incidental damages allowed under the provisions of this Article (Section 2–710), but less expenses saved in consequence of the buyer's breach.

(2) Except as otherwise provided in subsection (3) or unless otherwise agreed resale may be at public or private sale including sale by way of one or more contracts to sell or of identification to an existing contract of the seller. Sale may be as a unit or in parcels and at any time and place and on any terms but every aspect of the sale including the method, manner, time, place and terms must be commercially reasonable. The resale must be reasonably identified as referring to the broken contract, but it is not necessary that the goods be in existence or that any or all of them have been identified to the contract before the breach.

(3) Where the resale is at private sale the seller must give the buyer reasonable notification of his intention to resell.

(4) Where the resale is at public sale

    (a) only identified goods can be sold except where there is a recognized market for a public sale of futures in goods of the kind; and

    (b) it must be made at a usual place or market for public sale if one is reasonably available and except in the case of goods which are perishable or threaten to decline in value speedily the seller must give the buyer reasonable notice of the time and place of the resale; and

    (c) if the goods are not to be within the view of those attending the sale the notification of sale must state the place where the goods are located and provide for their reasonable inspection by prospective bidders; and

    (d) the seller may buy.

(5) A purchaser who buys in good faith at a resale takes the goods free of any rights of the original buyer even though the seller fails to comply with one or more of the requirements of this section.

(6) The seller is not accountable to the buyer for any profit made on any resale. A person in the position of a seller (Section 2–707) or a buyer who has rightfully rejected or justifiably revoked acceptance must account for any excess over the amount of his security interest, as hereinafter defined (subsection (3) of Section 2–711).

§ 2–707. "Person in the Position of a Seller".

(1) A "person in the position of a seller" includes as against a principal an agent who has paid or become responsible for the price of goods on behalf of his principal or anyone who otherwise holds a security interest or other right in goods similar to that of a seller.

(2) A person in the position of a seller may as provided in this Article withhold or stop delivery (Section 2–705) and resell (Section 2–706) and recover incidental damages (Section 2–710).

§ 2–708. Seller's Damages for Non-Acceptance or Repudiation.

(1) Subject to subsection (2) and to the provisions of this Article with respect to proof of market price (Section 2–723), the measure of damages for non-acceptance or repudiation by the buyer is the difference between the market price at the time and place for tender and the unpaid contract price together with any incidental damages provided in this Article (Section 2–710), but less expenses saved in consequence of the buyer's breach.

(2) If the measure of damages provided in subsection (1) is inadequate to put the seller in as good a position as performance would have done then the measure of damages is the profit (including reasonable overhead) which the seller would have made from full performance by the buyer, together with any incidental damages provided in this Article (Section 2–710), due allowance for costs reasonably incurred and due credit for payments or proceeds of resale.

§ 2–709. Action for the Price.

(1) When the buyer fails to pay the price as it becomes due the seller may recover, together with any incidental damages under the next section, the price

    (a) of goods accepted or of conforming goods lost or damaged within a commercially reasonable time after risk of their loss has passed to the buyer; and

    (b) of goods identified to the contract if the seller is unable after reasonable effort to resell them at a reasonable price or the circumstances reasonably indicate that such effort will be unavailing.

(2) Where the seller sues for the price he must hold for the buyer any goods which have been identified to the contract and are still in his control except that if resale becomes possible he may resell them at any time prior to the collection of the judgment. The net proceeds of any such resale must be credited to the buyer and payment of the judgment entitles him to any goods not resold.

(3) After the buyer has wrongfully rejected or revoked acceptance of the goods or has failed to make a payment due or has repudiated (Section 2–610), a seller who is held not entitled to the price under this section shall nevertheless be awarded damages for non-acceptance under the preceding section.

§ 2–710. Seller's Incidental Damages.

Incidental damages to an aggrieved seller include any commercially reasonable charges, expenses or commissions incurred in stopping delivery, in the transportation, care and custody of goods after the buyer's breach, in connection with return or resale of the goods or otherwise resulting from the breach.

§ 2–711. Buyer's Remedies in General; Buyer's Security Interest in Rejected Goods.

(1) Where the seller fails to make delivery or repudiates or the buyer rightfully rejects or justifiably revokes acceptance then with respect to any goods involved, and with respect to the whole if the breach goes to the whole contract (Section 2–612), the buyer may cancel and whether or not he has done so may in addition to recovering so much of the price as has been paid

> (a) "cover" and have damages under the next section as to all the goods affected whether or not they have been identified to the contract; or

> (b) recover damages for non-delivery as pro-vided in this Article (Section 2–713).

(2) Where the seller fails to deliver or repudiates the buyer may also

> (a) if the goods have been identified recover them as provided in this Article (Section 2–502); or

> (b) in a proper case obtain specific performance or replevy the goods as provided in this Article (Section 2–716).

(3) On rightful rejection or justifiable revocation of acceptance a buyer has a security interest in goods in his possession or control for any payments made on their price and any expenses reasonably incurred in their inspection, receipt, transportation, care and custody and may hold such goods and resell them in like manner as an aggrieved seller (Section 2–706).

§ 2–712. "Cover"; Buyer's Procurement of Substitute Goods.

(1) After a breach within the preceding section the buyer may "cover" by making in good faith and without unreasonable delay any reasonable purchase of or contract to purchase goods in substitution for those due from the seller.

(2) The buyer may recover from the seller as damages the difference between the cost of cover and the contract price together with any incidental or consequential damages as hereinafter defined (Section 2–715), but less expenses saved in consequence of the seller's breach.

(3) Failure of the buyer to effect cover within this section does not bar him from any other remedy.

§ 2–713. Buyer's Damages for Non-Delivery or Repudiation.

(1) Subject to the provisions of this Article with respect to proof of market price (Section 2–723), the measure of damages for non-delivery or repudiation by the seller is the difference between the market price at the time when the buyer learned of the breach and the contract price together with any incidental and consequential damages provided in this Article (Section 2–715), but less expenses saved in consequence of the seller's breach.

(2) Market price is to be determined as of the place for tender or, in cases of rejection after arrival or revocation of acceptance, as of the place of arrival.

§ 2–714. Buyer's Damages for Breach in Regard to Accepted Goods.

(1) Where the buyer has accepted goods and given notification (subsection (3) of Section 2–607) he may recover as damages for any non-conformity of tender the loss resulting in the ordinary course of events from the seller's breach as determined in any manner which is reasonable.

(2) The measure of damages for breach of warranty is the difference at the time and place of acceptance between the value of the goods accepted and the value they would have had if they had been as warranted, unless special circumstances show proximate damages of a different amount.

(3) In a proper case any incidental and consequential damages under the next section may also be recovered.

§ 2–715. Buyer's Incidental and Consequential Damages.

(1) Incidental damages resulting from the seller's breach include expenses reasonably incurred in inspection, receipt, transportation and care and custody of goods rightfully rejected, any commercially reasonable charges, expenses or commissions in connection with effecting cover and any other reasonable expense incident to the delay or other breach.

(2) Consequential damages resulting from the seller's breach include

> (a) any loss resulting from general or particular requirements and needs of which the seller at the time of contracting had reason to know and which could not reasonably be prevented by cover or otherwise; and

> (b) injury to person or property proximately resulting from any breach of warranty.

§ 2–716. Buyer's Right to Specific Performance or Replevin.

(1) Specific performance may be decreed where the goods are unique or in other proper circumstances.

(2) The decree for specific performance may include such terms and conditions as to payment of the price, damages, or other relief as the court may deem just.

(3) The buyer has a right of replevin for goods identified to the contract if after reasonable effort he is unable to effect cover for such goods or the circumstances reasonably indicate that such effort will be unavailing or if the goods have been shipped under reservation and satisfaction of the security interest in them has been made or tendered. In the case of goods bought for personal, family, or household purposes, the buyer's right of replevin vests upon acquisition of a special property, even if the seller had not then repudiated or failed to deliver.

As amended in 1999.

§ 2–717. Deduction of Damages From the Price.

The buyer on notifying the seller of his intention to do so may deduct all or any part of the damages resulting from any breach of the contract from any part of the price still due under the same contract.

§ 2–718. Liquidation or Limitation of Damages; Deposits.

(1) Damages for breach by either party may be liquidated in the agreement but only at an amount which is reasonable in the light of the anticipated or actual harm caused by the breach, the difficulties of proof of loss, and the inconvenience or nonfeasibility of otherwise obtaining an adequate remedy. A term fixing unreasonably large liquidated damages is void as a penalty.

(2) Where the seller justifiably withholds delivery of goods because of the buyer's breach, the buyer is entitled to restitution of any amount by which the sum of his payments exceeds

   (a) the amount to which the seller is entitled by virtue of terms liquidating the seller's damages in accordance with subsection (1), or

   (b) in the absence of such terms, twenty per cent of the value of the total performance for which the buyer is obligated under the contract or $500, whichever is smaller.

(3) The buyer's right to restitution under subsection (2) is subject to offset to the extent that the seller establishes

   (a) a right to recover damages under the provisions of this Article other than subsection (1), and

   (b) the amount or value of any benefits received by the buyer directly or indirectly by reason of the contract.

(4) Where a seller has received payment in goods their reasonable value or the proceeds of their resale shall be treated as payments for the purposes of subsection (2); but if the seller has notice of the buyer's breach before reselling goods received in part performance, his resale is subject to the conditions laid down in this Article on resale by an aggrieved seller (Section 2–706).

§ 2–719. Contractual Modification or Limitation of Remedy.

(1) Subject to the provisions of subsections (2) and (3) of this section and of the preceding section on liquidation and limitation of damages,

   (a) the agreement may provide for remedies in addition to or in substitution for those provided in this Article and may limit or alter the measure of damages recoverable under this Article, as by limiting the buyer's remedies to return of the goods and repayment of the price or to repair and replacement of nonconforming goods or parts; and

   (b) resort to a remedy as provided is optional unless the remedy is expressly agreed to be exclusive, in which case it is the sole remedy.

(2) Where circumstances cause an exclusive or limited remedy to fail of its essential purpose, remedy may be had as provided in this Act.

(3) Consequential damages may be limited or excluded unless the limitation or exclusion is unconscionable. Limitation of consequential damages for injury to the person in the case of consumer goods is *prima facie* unconscionable but limitation of damages where the loss is commercial is not.

§ 2–720. Effect of "Cancellation" or "Rescission" on Claims for Antecedent Breach.

Unless the contrary intention clearly appears, expressions of "cancellation" or "rescission" of the contract or the like shall not be construed as a renunciation or discharge of any claim in damages for an antecedent breach.

§ 2–721. Remedies for Fraud.

Remedies for material misrepresentation or fraud include all remedies available under this Article for non-fraudulent breach. Neither rescission or a claim for rescission of the contract for sale nor rejection or return of the goods shall bar or be deemed inconsistent with a claim for damages or other remedy.

§ 2–722. Who Can Sue Third Parties for Injury to Goods.

Where a third party so deals with goods which have been identified to a contract for sale as to cause actionable injury to a party to that contract

(a) a right of action against the third party is in either party to the contract for sale who has title to or a security interest or a special property or an insurable interest in the goods; and if the goods have been destroyed or converted a right of action is also in the party who either bore the risk of loss under the contract for sale or has since the injury assumed that risk as against the other;

(b) if at the time of the injury the party plaintiff did not bear the risk of loss as against the other party to the contract for sale and there is no arrangement between them for disposition of the recovery, his suit or settlement is, subject to his own interest, as a fiduciary for the other party to the contract;

(c) either party may with the consent of the other sue for the benefit of whom it may concern.

§ 2–723. Proof of Market Price: Time and Place.

(1) If an action based on anticipatory repudiation comes to trial before the time for performance with respect to some or all of the goods, any damages based on market price (Section 2–708 or Section 2–713) shall be determined according to the price of such goods prevailing at the time when the aggrieved party learned of the repudiation.

(2) If evidence of a price prevailing at the times or places described in this Article is not readily available the price prevailing within any reasonable time before or after the time described or at any other place which in commercial judgment or under usage of trade would serve as a reasonable substitute for the one described may be used, making any proper allowance for the cost of transporting the goods to or from such other place.

(3) Evidence of a relevant price prevailing at a time or place other than the one described in this Article offered by one party is not admissible unless and until he has given the other party such notice as the court finds sufficient to prevent unfair surprise.

§ 2–724. Admissibility of Market Quotations.

Whenever the prevailing price or value of any goods regularly bought and sold in any established commodity market is in issue, reports in official publications or trade journals or in newspapers or periodicals of general circulation published as the reports of such market shall be admissible in evidence. The circumstances of the preparation of such a report may be shown to affect its weight but not its admissibility.

§ 2–725. Statute of Limitations in Contracts for Sale.

(1) An action for breach of any contract for sale must be commenced within four years after the cause of action has accrued. By the original agreement the parties may reduce the period of limitation to not less than one year but may not extend it.

(2) A cause of action accrues when the breach occurs, regardless of the aggrieved party's lack of knowledge of the breach. A breach of warranty occurs when tender of delivery is made, except that where a warranty explicitly extends to future performance of the goods and discovery of the breach must await the time of such performance the cause of action accrues when the breach is or should have been discovered.

(3) Where an action commenced within the time limited by subsection (1) is so terminated as to leave available a remedy by another action for the same breach such other action may be commenced after the expiration of the time limited and within six months after the termination of the first action unless the termination resulted from voluntary discontinuance or from dismissal for failure or neglect to prosecute.

(4) This section does not alter the law on tolling of the statute of limitations nor does it apply to causes of action which have accrued before this Act becomes effective.

APPENDIX B

Answers to the *Issue Spotters*

CHAPTER 1

1. *Under what circumstances might a judge rely on case law to determine the intent and purpose of a statute?* Case law includes courts' interpretations of statutes, as well as constitutional provisions and administrative rules. Statutes often codify common law rules. For these reasons, a judge might rely on the common law as a guide to the intent and purpose of a statute.

2. *Assuming that these convicted war criminals had not disobeyed any law of their country and had merely been following their government's orders, what law had they violated? Explain.* At the time of the Nuremberg trials, "crimes against humanity" were new international crimes. The laws criminalized such acts as murder, extermination, enslavement, deportation, and other inhumane acts committed against any civilian population. These international laws derived their legitimacy from "natural law."

Natural law, which is the oldest and one of the most significant schools of jurisprudence, holds that governments and legal systems should reflect the moral and ethical ideals that are inherent in human nature. Because natural law is universal and discoverable by reason, its adherents believe that all other law is derived from natural law. Natural law therefore supersedes laws created by humans (national, or "positive," law), and in a conflict between the two, national or positive law loses its legitimacy.

The Nuremberg defendants asserted that they had been acting in accordance with German law. The judges dismissed these claims, reasoning that the defendants' acts were commonly regarded as crimes and that the accused must have known that the acts would be considered criminal. The judges clearly believed the tenets of natural law and expected that the defendants, too, should have been able to realize that their acts ran afoul of it. The fact that the "positivist law" of Germany at the time required them to commit these acts is irrelevant. Under natural law theory, the international court was justified in finding the defendants guilty of crimes against humanity.

CHAPTER 2

1. *Can a state, in the interest of energy conservation, ban all advertising by power utilities if conservation could be accomplished by less restrictive means? Why or why not?* No. Even if commercial speech is neither related to illegal activities nor misleading, it may be restricted if a state has a substantial interest that cannot be achieved by less restrictive means. In this case, the interest in energy conservation is substantial, but it could be achieved by less restrictive means. That would be the utilities' defense against the enforcement of this state law.

2. *Is this a violation of equal protection if the only reason for the tax is to protect the local firms from out-of-state competition? Explain.* Yes. The tax would limit the liberty of some persons (out-of-state businesses), so it is subject to a review under the equal protection clause. Protecting local businesses from out-of-state competition is not a legitimate government objective. Thus, such a tax would violate the equal protection clause.

CHAPTER 3

1. *Does the court in Sue's state have jurisdiction over Tipton? What factors will the court consider in determining jurisdiction?* Yes, the court in Sue's state has jurisdiction over Tipton on the basis of the company's minimum contacts with the state.

Courts look at the following factors in determining whether minimum contacts exist: the quantity of the contacts, the nature and quality of the contacts, the source and connection of the cause of action to the contacts, the interest of the forum state, and the convenience of the parties. Attempting to exercise jurisdiction without sufficient minimum contacts would violate the due process clause. Generally, courts have found that jurisdiction is proper when there is substantial business conducted online (with contracts, sales, and so on). Even when there is only some interactivity through a Web site, courts have sometimes held that jurisdiction is proper. Jurisdiction is not proper when there is merely passive advertising.

Here, all of these factors suggest that the defendant had sufficient minimum contacts with the state to justify the exercise of jurisdiction over the defendant. Two especially important factors were that the plaintiff sold the security system to a resident of the state and that litigating in the defendant's state would be relatively inconvenient for the plaintiff.

2. *If the dispute is not resolved, or if either party disagrees with the decision of the mediator or arbitrator, will a court hear the case? Explain.* Yes, if the dispute is not resolved, or if either party disagrees with the decision of the mediator or arbitrator, a court will hear the case. It is required that the dispute be submitted to mediation or arbitration, but this outcome is not binding.

CHAPTER 4

1. *Can Lou recover from Jana? Why or why not?* Probably. To recover on the basis of negligence, the injured party as a plaintiff must show that the truck's owner owed the plaintiff a duty of care, that the owner breached that duty, that the plaintiff was injured, and that the breach caused the injury.

In this situation, the owner's actions breached the duty of reasonable care. The billboard falling on the plaintiff was the direct cause of the injury, not the plaintiff's own negligence. Thus, liability turns on whether the plaintiff can connect the breach of duty to the injury. This involves the test of proximate cause—the question of foreseeability. The consequences to the injured party must have been a foreseeable result of the owner's carelessness.

2. *What might the firm successfully claim in defense?* The company might defend against this electrician's claim by asserting that the electrician should have known of the risk and, therefore, the company had no duty to warn. According to the problem, the danger is common knowledge in the electrician's field and should have been apparent to this electrician, given his years of training and experience. In other words, the company most likely had no need to warn the electrician of the risk.

The firm could also raise comparative negligence. Both parties' negligence, if any, could be weighed and the liability distributed proportionally. The defendant could also assert assumption of risk, claiming that the electrician voluntarily entered into a dangerous situation, knowing the risk involved.

CHAPTER 5

1. *With respect to the gas station, has she committed a crime? If so, what is it?* Yes. With respect to the gas station, she has obtained goods by false pretenses. She might also be charged with larceny and forgery, and most states have special statutes covering illegal use of credit cards.

2. *Has Ben committed a crime? If so, what is it?* Yes. The Counterfeit Access Device and Computer Fraud and Abuse Act provides that a person who accesses a computer online, without permission, to obtain classified data—such as consumer credit files in a credit agency's database—is subject to criminal prosecution. The crime has two elements: accessing the computer without permission and taking data. It is a felony if done for private financial gain. Penalties include fines and imprisonment for up to twenty years. The victim of the theft can also bring a civil suit against the criminal to obtain damages and other relief.

CHAPTER 6

1. *Does this raise an ethical conflict between Acme's employees? Between Acme and its employees? Between Acme and its shareholders? Explain your answers.* When a corporation decides to respond to what it sees as a moral obligation to correct for past discrimination by adjusting pay differences among its employees, an ethical conflict is raised between the firm and its employees and between the firm and its shareholders. This dilemma arises directly out of the effect such a decision has on the firm's profits. If satisfying this obligation increases profitability, then the dilemma is easily resolved in favor of "doing the right thing."

2. *Does Delta have an ethical duty to remove this product from the market, even if the injuries result only from misuse? Why or why not?* Maybe. On the one hand, it is not the company's "fault" when a product is misused. Also, keeping the product on the market is not a violation of the law, and stopping sales would hurt profits. On the other hand, suspending sales could reduce suffering and could stop potential negative publicity.

CHAPTER 7

1. *Can Ed recover? Why or why not?* No. This contract, although not fully executed, is for an illegal purpose and therefore is void. A void contract gives rise to no legal obligation on the part of any party. A contract that is void is no contract. There is nothing to enforce.

2. *Can Alison recover from Jerry the amount that she paid? Why or why not?* Yes, because a person who is unjustly enriched at the expense of another can be required to account for the benefit under the theory of quasi contract. The parties here did not have a contract, but the law will impose one to avoid the unjust enrichment.

CHAPTER 8

1. *Do Fidelity and Ron have a contract? Why or why not?* No. Revocation of an offer may be implied by conduct inconsistent with the offer. When the corporation hired someone else, and the offeree learned of the hiring, the offer was revoked. The acceptance was too late.

2. *Under the Uniform Electronic Transactions Act, what determines the effect of the electronic documents evidencing the parties' deal? Is a party's "signature" necessary? Explain.* First, it might be noted that the UETA does not apply unless the parties to a contract agree to use e-commerce in their transaction. In this deal, of course, the parties used e-commerce. The UETA removes barriers to e-commerce by giving the same legal effect to e-records and e-signatures as to paper documents and signatures. The UETA does not include rules for those transactions, however.

CHAPTER 9

1. *Can Kenwood enforce the lease against Joan? Why or why not?* No. Joan is a minor and may disaffirm this contract. Because the apartment was a necessary, however, she remains liable for the reasonable value of her occupancy of the apartment.

2. *Is Fred's promise binding? Explain.* Yes. Under the doctrine of detrimental reliance, or promissory estoppel, the promisee is entitled to payment of $5,000 from the promisor on graduation. There was a promise, on which the promisee relied, the reliance was substantial and definite (the promisee went to college for the full term, incurring considerable expenses, and will likely graduate), and it would only be fair to enforce the promise.

CHAPTER 10

1. *Can she rescind the deal? Why or why not?* Yes. Rescission may be granted on the basis of fraudulent misrepresentation.

The elements of fraudulent misrepresentation include intent to deceive, or *scienter*. *Scienter* exists if a party makes a statement recklessly, without regard to whether it is true or false, or if a party says or implies that a statement is made on some basis such as personal knowledge or personal investigation when it is not.

2. *Can Midstate enforce a deal for the full $800? Explain your answer.* No. Under the UCC, a contract for a sale of goods priced at $500 or more must be in writing to be enforceable. In this case, the contract is not enforceable beyond the quantity already delivered and paid for.

CHAPTER 11

1. *Can Jeff successfully sue Ed for the $100? Why or why not?* Yes. When one person makes a promise with the intention of benefiting a third person, the third person can sue to enforce it. This is a third party beneficiary contract. The third party in this problem is an intended beneficiary.

2. *Before Ready or Stealth starts performing, can the parties call off the deal? What if Stealth has already shipped the pizzas? Explain your answers.* Contracts that are executory on both sides—contracts on which neither party has performed—can be rescinded solely by agreement. Contracts that are executed on one side—contracts on which one party has performed—can be rescinded only if the party who has performed receives consideration for the promise to call off the deal.

CHAPTER 12

1. *If Haney sues Greg, what will be the measure of recovery?* A nonbreaching party is entitled to his or her benefit of the bargain under the contract. Here, the innocent party is entitled to be put in the position she would have been in if the contract had been fully performed. The measure of the benefit is the cost to complete the work ($500). These are compensatory damages.

2. *Is Lyle liable for Marley's expenses in providing for the cattle? Why or why not?* No. To recover damages that flow from the consequences of a breach but that are caused by circumstances beyond the contract (consequential damages), the breaching party must know, or have reason to know, that special circumstances will cause the nonbreaching party to suffer the additional loss. That was not the circumstance in this problem.

CHAPTER 13

1. *Has Roslyn violated any of the intellectual property rights discussed in this chapter? Explain.* Yes, Roslyn has committed theft of trade secrets. Lists of suppliers and customers cannot be patented, copyrighted, or trademarked, but the information they contain is protected against appropriation by others as trade secrets. And most likely, Roslyn signed a contract agreeing not to use this information outside her employment by Organic. But even without this contract, Organic could make a convincing case against its ex-employee for a theft of trade secrets.

2. *Is this patent infringement? If so, how might Global save the cost of suing World for infringement and at the same time profit from World's sales?* This is patent infringement. A software maker in this situation might best protect its product, save litigation costs, and profit from its patent by the use of a license. In the context of this problem, a license would grant permission to sell a patented item. (A license can be limited to certain purposes and to the licensee only.)

CHAPTER 14

1. *Has Karl done anything wrong? Explain.* Karl may have committed trademark infringement. A site that appropriates the key words of other sites with more frequent hits will appear in the same search engine results as the more popular sites. But using another's trademark as a key word without the owner's permission normally constitutes trademark infringement. Of course, some uses of another's trademark as a meta tag may be permissible if the use is reasonably necessary and does not suggest that the owner authorized or sponsored the use.

2. *Can Eagle Corporation stop this use of* eagle*? If so, what must the company show? Explain.* Yes. This may be an instance of trademark dilution. Dilution occurs when a trademark is used, without permission, in a way that diminishes the distinctive quality of the mark. Dilution does not require proof that consumers are likely to be confused by the use of the unauthorized mark. The products involved do not have to be similar. Dilution does require, however, that a mark be famous when the dilution occurs.

CHAPTER 15

1. *Is this an acceptance of the offer or a counteroffer? If it is an acceptance, is it a breach of the contract? Why or why not? What if Fav-O-Rite told E-Design it was sending the printer stands as "an accommodation"?* A shipment of nonconforming goods constitutes an acceptance of the offer and a breach, unless the seller seasonably notifies the buyer that the nonconforming shipment does not constitute an acceptance and is offered only as an accommodation. Thus, since there was no notification here, the shipment was both an acceptance and a breach. If, however, Fav-O-Rite had notified E-Design that it was sending the printer stands as an accommodation, the shipment would not constitute an acceptance, and Fav-O-Rite would not be in breach.

2. *Is there an enforceable contract between them? Why or why not?* Yes. In a transaction between merchants, the requirement of a writing is satisfied if one of them sends to the other a signed written confirmation that indicates the terms of the agreement, and the merchant receiving it has reason to know of its contents. If the merchant who receives the confirmation does not object in writing within ten days after receipt, the writing will be enforceable against him or her even though he or she has not signed anything.

CHAPTER 16

1. *Does Country have the right to reject the shipment? Explain.* Yes. A seller is obligated to deliver goods in conformity with a contract in every detail. This is the perfect tender rule. The exception of the seller's right to cure does not apply here, because the seller delivered too little too late to take advantage of this exception.

2. *Can Stella recover for breach of the implied warranty of merchantability? Why or why not?* Yes, Stella can recover from Roasted Bean for breach of the implied warranty of merchantability. An implied warranty of merchantability arises in every sale of goods sold by a merchant who deals in goods of the kind. Goods that are merchantable are fit for the ordinary purposes for which such goods are used. A sale of food or drink is a sale of goods. Merchantable food is food that is fit to eat or drink on the basis of consumer expectations. A consumer should reasonably expect hot coffee to be hot, but not to be so scalding that it causes third-degree burns.

CHAPTER 17

1. *Was Winona an independent contractor?* Yes. An independent contractor is a person who contracts with another—the principal—to do something but who is neither controlled by the other nor subject to the other's right to control with respect to the performance. Independent contractors are not employees, because those who hire them have no control over the details of their performance.

2. *Can Davis hold Estee liable for whatever damages he has to pay? Why or why not?* Yes. A principal has a duty to indemnify an agent for liabilities incurred because of authorized and lawful acts and transactions and for losses suffered because of the principal's failure to perform his or her duties.

CHAPTER 18

1. *Would a sole proprietorship be an appropriate form for Frank's business? Why or why not?* Yes. When a business is relatively small and is not diversified, employs relatively few people, has modest profits, and is not likely to expand significantly or require extensive financing in the immediate future, the most appropriate form for doing business may be a sole proprietorship.

2. *When Darnell dies, his widow claims that as Darnell's heir, she is entitled to take his place as Eliana's partner or to receive a share of the firm's assets. Is she right? Why or why not?* No. A widow (or widower) has no right to take a dead partner's place. A partner's death causes dissociation, after which the partnership must purchase the dissociated partner's partnership interest. Therefore, the surviving partners must pay the decedent's estate (for his widow) the value of the deceased partner's interest in the partnership.

CHAPTER 19

1. *Is there a way for Northwest Brands to avoid this double taxation? Explain your answer.* Yes. Small businesses that meet certain requirements can qualify as S corporations, created specifically to permit small businesses to avoid double taxation. The six requirements of an S corporation are (1) the firm must be a domestic corporation, (2) the firm must not be a member of an affiliated group of corporations, (3) the firm must have less than a certain number of shareholders, (4) the shareholders must be individuals, estates, or qualified trusts (or corporations in some cases), (5) there can be only one class of stock, and (6) no shareholder can be a nonresident alien.

2. *Discuss whether Nico owes a duty to Omega or the minority shareholders in selling his shares.* Yes. A single shareholder—or a few shareholders acting together—who owns enough stock to exercise *de facto* control over a corporation owes the corporation and minority shareholders a fiduciary duty when transferring those shares.

APPENDIX C

Sample Answers for *Business Case Problems with Sample Answer*

Problem 1–5. *Reading Citations.* The court's opinion in this case—*Equal Employment Opportunity Commission v. Autozone, Inc.,* 809 F.3d 916 (7th Cir. 2016)—can be found in Volume 809 of *Federal Reporter, Third Series* on page 916. The U.S. Court of Appeals for the Seventh Circuit issued this opinion in 2016.

Problem 2–4. *The Dormant Commerce Clause.* The court ruled that, like a state, Puerto Rico generally may not enact policies that discriminate against out-of-state commerce. The law requiring companies that sell cement in Puerto Rico to place certain labels on their products is clearly an attempt to regulate the cement market. The law imposed labeling regulations that affect transactions between the citizens of Puerto Rico and private companies. State laws that on their face discriminate against foreign commerce are almost always invalid, and this Puerto Rican law is such a law. The discriminatory labeling requirement placed sellers of cement manufactured outside Puerto Rico at a competitive disadvantage. This law therefore contravenes the dormant commerce clause.

Problem 3–7. *Corporate Contacts.* No, the defendants' motion to dismiss the suit for lack of personal jurisdiction should not be granted. A corporation normally is subject to jurisdiction in a state in which it is doing business. A court applies the minimum-contacts test to determine whether it can exercise jurisdiction over an out-of-state corporation. This requirement is met if the corporation sells its products within the state or places its goods in the "stream of commerce" with the intent that the goods be sold in the state.

In this problem, the state of Washington filed a suit in a Washington state court against LG Electronics, Inc., and nineteen other foreign companies that participated in the global market for cathode ray tube (CRT) products. The state alleged a conspiracy to raise prices and set production levels in the market for CRTs in violation of a state consumer protection statute. The defendants filed a motion to dismiss the suit for lack of personal jurisdiction. These goods were sold for many years in high volume in the United States, including the state of Washington. In other words, the corporations purposefully established minimum contacts in the state of Washington. This is a sufficient basis for a Washington state court to assert personal jurisdiction over the defendants.

In the actual case on which this problem is based, the court dismissed the suit for lack of personal jurisdiction. On appeal, a state intermediate appellate court reversed on the reasoning stated above.

Problem 4–5. *Negligence.* Negligence requires proof that (1) the defendant owed a duty of care to the plaintiff, (2) the defendant breached that duty, (3) the defendant's breach caused the plaintiff's injury, and (4) the plaintiff suffered a legally recognizable injury. With respect to the duty of care, a business owner has a duty to use reasonable care to protect business invitees. This duty includes an obligation to discover and correct or warn of unreasonably dangerous conditions that the owner of the premises should reasonably foresee might endanger an invitee. Some risks are so obvious that an owner need not warn of them. But even if a risk is obvious, a business owner may not be excused from the duty to protect its customers from foreseeable harm.

Because Lucario was the Weatherford's business invitee, the hotel owed her a duty of reasonable care to make its premises safe for her use. The balcony ran nearly the entire width of the window in Lucario's room. She could have reasonably believed that the window was a means of access to the balcony. The window/balcony configuration was dangerous, however, because the window opened wide enough for an adult to climb out, but the twelve-inch gap between one side of the window and the balcony was unprotected. This unprotected gap opened to a drop of more than three stories to a concrete surface below.

Should the hotel have anticipated the potential harm to a guest who opened the window in Room 59 and attempted to access the balcony? The hotel encouraged guests to "step out onto the balcony" to smoke. The dangerous condition of the window/balcony configuration could have been remedied at a minimal cost. These circumstances could be perceived as creating an "unreasonably dangerous" condition. And it could be concluded that the hotel created or knew of the condition and failed to take reasonable steps to warn of it or correct it. Of course, the Weatherford might argue that the window/balcony configuration was so obvious that the hotel was not liable for Lucario's fall.

In the actual case on which this problem is based, the court concluded that the Weatherford did not breach its duty of care to Lucario. On McMurtry's appeal, a state intermediate appellate court held that this conclusion was in error, vacated the lower court's judgment in favor of the hotel on this issue, and remanded the case.

Problem 5–4. *Criminal Liability.* Yes, Green exhibited the required mental state to establish criminal liability. A wrongful mental state (*mens rea*) is one of the elements typically required to establish criminal liability. The required mental state, or intent, is indicated in an applicable statute or law. For example, for murder, the required mental state is the intent to take another's life. A court can also find that the required mental state is present when a defendant's acts are reckless or criminally negligent. A defendant is criminally reckless if he or she consciously disregards a substantial and unjustifiable risk.

In this problem, Green was clearly aware of the danger to which he was exposing people on the street below. Although he did not indicate that he specifically intended to harm anyone, the risk of death created by his conduct was obvious. He must have known what was likely to happen if a bottle or plate thrown from the height of twenty-six stories hit a pedestrian or the windshield of an occupied motor vehicle on the street below. Despite his claim that he was intoxicated, he was sufficiently aware to stop throwing things from the balcony when he saw police in the area, and he later recalled what he had done and what had happened.

In the actual case on which this problem is based, after a jury trial, Green was convicted of reckless endangerment. On appeal, a state intermediate appellate court affirmed the conviction, based in part on the reasoning stated above.

Problem 6–3. *Online Privacy.* Facebook created a program that makes decisions for users. Using duty-based ethics, many believe that privacy is an extremely important right that should be fiercely protected. Accordingly, any program that has a default of giving out information is unethical. Facebook should create the program as an opt-in program. In addition, under the Kantian categorical imperative, if every company created opt-out programs that disclosed potentially personal information, the concept of privacy may be reduced to a theoretical concept only. One could argue that this reduction or elimination of privacy would not make the world a better place. From a utilitarian or outcome-based approach, the benefits of an opt-out program might be in ease of creation and start up, as well as ease of recruiting partner programs. The detriment is the elimination of choice on the part of users to disclose information about themselves. An opt-in program maintains that user control but may be harder to start, as it requires more marketing up front in order to convince users to opt in.

Problem 7–4. *Quasi Contract.* Gutkowski does not have a valid claim for payment, nor should he recover on the basis of a quasi contract. Quasi contracts are imposed by courts on parties in the interest of fairness and justice. Usually, a quasi contract is imposed to avoid the unjust enrichment of one party at the expense of another. Gutkowski was compensated as a consultant. For him to establish a claim that he is due more compensation based on unjust enrichment, he must have proof. As it is, he has only his claim that there were discussions about his being a part owner of YES. Discussions and negotiations are not a basis for recovery on a quasi contract. In the actual case on which this problem is based, the court dismissed Gutkowski's claim for payment.

Problem 8–4. *Online Acceptances.* No. A shrink-wrap agreement is an agreement whose terms are expressed inside the box in which the goods are packaged. The party who opens the box may be informed that he or she agrees to the terms by keeping whatever is in the box. In many cases, the courts have enforced the terms of shrink-wrap agreements just as they enforce the terms of other contracts. But not all of the terms presented in shrink-wrap agreements have been enforced by the courts. One important consideration is whether the buyer had adequate notice of the terms.

A click-on agreement is formed when a buyer, completing a transaction on a computer, is required to indicate his or her assent to be bound by the terms of an offer by clicking on a button that says, for example, "I agree." In Reasonover's situation, no such agreement was formed with respect to Clearwire's "Terms of Service" (TOS). The e-mail did not give adequate notice of the TOS. It did not contain a direct link to the terms—accessing them required clicks on further links through the firm's homepage. The written, shrink-wrap materials accompanying the modem did not provide adequate notice of the TOS. There was only a reference to Clearwire's Web site in small print at the bottom of one page. Similarly, Reasonover's access to an "I accept terms" box did not establish notice of the terms. She did not click on the box but quit the page. Even if any of these references was sufficient notice, Reasonover kept the modem only because Clearwire told her that she could not return it.

In the actual case on which this problem is based, the court refused to compel arbitration on the basis of the clause in Clearwire's TOS.

Problem 9–6. *Consideration.* Citynet's employee incentive plan was an offer for a unilateral contract. A Citynet employee who stayed on the job when he or she was under no obligation to do so could be considered to have accepted Citynet's offer and to have provided sufficient consideration to make the offer a binding and enforceable promise. Consideration has two elements—it must consist of something of legal value and must provide the basis for the bargain between the parties. A unilateral contract involves a promise in return for performance. The promisor becomes bound to the contract when the promisee performs—or, in many cases, begins to perform—the act. Both the promise and the performance have legal value.

Here, Citynet set up an employee incentive plan "to attract and retain experienced individuals." The plan provided that a participant who left Citynet's employ could "cash out" his or her entire vested balance. When Ray Toney terminated his employment and asked to redeem his vested balance, however, Citynet refused. But Toney had long stayed on the job when he did not have to. This was sufficient consideration to make Citynet's offer under the incentive plan a binding and enforceable contract with Toney.

In the actual case on which this problem is based, a West Virginia state court issued a judgment in Toney's favor. The West Virginia Supreme Court of Appeals affirmed, on the reasoning and principles stated above.

Problem 10–8. *Fraudulent Misrepresentation.* Yes, the facts in this problem evidence fraud. There are three elements to fraud: (1) the misrepresentation of a material fact, (2) an intent to deceive, and (3) an innocent party's justifiable reliance on the misrepresentation. To collect damages, the innocent party must suffer an injury.

Here, Pervis represented to Pauley that no further commission would be paid by Osbrink. This representation was false—despite Pervis's statement to the contrary, Osbrink continued to send payments to Pervis. Pervis knew the representation was false, as shown by the fact that she made it more than once during the time that she was continuing to receive payments from Osbrink. Each time Pauley asked about commissions, Pervis replied that she was not receiving any. Pauley's reliance on her business associate's statements was justified and reasonable. And for the purpose of recovering damages, Pauley suffered an injury in the amount of her share of the commissions that Pervis received as a result of the fraud.

In the actual case on which this problem is based, Pauley filed a suit in a Georgia state court against Pervis, who filed for bankruptcy in a federal bankruptcy court to stay the state action. The federal court held Pervis liable on the ground of fraud for the amount of the commissions that were not paid to Pauley and denied Pervis a discharge of the debt.

Problem 11–3. *Third Party Beneficiary.* Yes, the Kincaids can bring an action against the Desses for breach of their contract with Sirva. A third person becomes an intended third party beneficiary of a contract when the original parties to the contract expressly agree that the performance should be rendered to or directly benefit a third person. As the intended beneficiary of a contract, a third party has legal rights and can sue the promisor directly for breach of the contract.

Here, the Desses agreed in their contract with Sirva to disclose all information about their property. They further agreed that Sirva and "other prospective buyers" could rely on the Desses' disclosure in deciding "whether and on what terms to purchase the Property." The Kincaids were not direct parties to the contract between Sirva and the Desses, but the Kincaids were "other prospective buyers." Thus, the language of the contract indicated that the Kincaids were intended by Sirva and the Desses to be third party beneficiaries of it. As intended beneficiaries of the contract, the Kincaids could sue the Desses directly for its breach.

In the actual case on which this problem is based, the Kincaids filed a suit in a Kansas state court against the Desses. From a judgment in the Desses' favor (for lack of privity), the Kincaids appealed. A state intermediate appellate court reversed on the basis of the reasoning stated above and remanded the case for trial.

Problem 12–5. *Consequential Damages.* Simard is liable only for the losses and expenses related to the first resale. Simard could reasonably have anticipated that his breach would require another sale and that the sales price might be less than what he had agreed to pay. Therefore, he should be liable for the difference between his sales price and the first resale price ($29,000), plus any expenses arising from the first resale. Simard is not liable, however, for any expenses and losses related to the second resale. After all, Simard did not cause the second purchaser's default, and he could not reasonably have foreseen that default as a probable result of his breach.

Problem 13–6. *Patents.* One ground on which the denial of the patent application in this problem could be reversed on appeal is that the design of Raymond Gianelli's "Rowing Machine" is *not obvious* in light of the design of the "Chest Press Apparatus for Exercising Regions of the Upper Body."

To obtain a patent, an applicant must demonstrate to the satisfaction of the U.S. Patent and Trademark Office (PTO) that the invention, discovery, process, or design is novel, useful, and not obvious in light of current technology. In this problem, the PTO denied Gianelli's application for a patent for his "Rowing Machine"—an exercise machine on which a user *pulls* on handles to perform a rowing motion against a selected resistance to strengthen the back muscles. The PTO considered the device obvious in light of a patented "Chest Press Apparatus for Exercising Regions of the Upper Body"—a chest press exercise machine on which a user *pushes* on handles to overcome a selected resistance. But it can be easily argued that it is *not* obvious to modify a machine with handles designed to be *pushed* into one with handles designed to be *pulled*. In fact, anyone who has used exercise machines knows that a way to cause injury is to use a machine in a manner not intended by the manufacturer.

In the actual case on which this problem is based, the U.S. Court of Appeals for the Federal Circuit reversed the PTO's denial of Gianelli's application for a patent, based on the reasoning stated above.

Problem 14–3. *Privacy.* No, Rolfe did not have a privacy interest in the information obtained by the subpoenas issued to Midcontinent Communications. The right to privacy is guaranteed by at least one interpretation of the U.S. Constitution's Bill of Rights and by some state constitutions. A person must have a reasonable expectation of privacy, though, to maintain a suit or to assert a successful defense for an invasion of privacy. People clearly have a reasonable expectation of privacy when they enter their personal banking or credit card information online. They also have a reasonable expectation that online companies will follow their own privacy policies. But people do not have a reasonable expectation of privacy in statements made on Twitter and other data that they publicly disseminate. In other words, there is no violation of a subscriber's right to privacy when a third-party Internet provider receives a subpoena and discloses the subscriber's information.

Here, Rolfe supplied his e-mail address and other personal information, including his Internet protocol address, to Midcontinent. In other words, Rolfe publicly disseminated this information. Law enforcement officers obtained this information from Midcontinent through the subpoenas issued by the South Dakota state court. Rolfe provided his information to Midcontinent—he had no legitimate expectation of privacy in that information.

In the actual case on which this problem is based, Rolfe was charged with, and convicted of, possessing, manufacturing, and distributing child pornography, as well as other crimes. As part of the proceedings, the court found that Rolfe had no expectation of privacy in the information that he made available to

Midcontinent. On appeal, the South Dakota Supreme Court upheld the conviction.

Problem 15–4. ***Additional Terms.*** No. Under the common law, variations in terms between the offer and the offeree's acceptance violate the mirror image rule, which requires that the terms of an acceptance exactly mirror the terms of the offer. The UCC dispenses with this rule. Under the UCC, a contract is formed if the offeree makes a definite expression of acceptance even though the terms of the acceptance modify or add to the terms of the offer. When both parties to the contract are merchants, the additional terms become part of their contract unless (1) the original offer expressly required acceptance of its terms, (2) the new or changed terms materially alter the contract, or (3) the offeror rejects the new or changed terms within a reasonable time.

In this problem, the UCC applies because the transactions involve sales of goods. The original offer stated, "By signing below, you agree to the terms." This statement could be construed to expressly require acceptance of the terms to make the offer a binding contract (Exception 1 above). The contract stated that JMAM was to receive credit for any rejected merchandise. Nothing indicated that the merchandise would be returned to BSI. Baracsi, BSI's owner (the offeree), signed JMAM's (the offeror's) letter in the appropriate location. This indicated BSI's agreement to the terms. Thus, BSI made a definite expression of acceptance. The practice of the parties—for six years rejected items were not returned—further supports the conclusion that their contract did not contemplate the return of those items. The "PS" could be interpreted as materially altering the contract (Exception 2 above).

In the actual case on which this problem is based, the court dismissed BSI's complaint.

Problem 16–4. ***Nonconforming Goods.*** Padma notified Universal Exports about its breach, so Padma has two ways to recover even though it accepted the goods. Padma's first option is to argue that it revoked its acceptance, giving it the right to reject the goods. To revoke acceptance, Padma would have to show that (1) the nonconformity substantially impaired the value of the shipment, (2) it predicated its acceptance on a reasonable assumption that Universal Exports would cure the nonconformity, and (3) Universal Exports did not cure the nonconformity within a reasonable time. Padma's second option is to keep the goods and recover for the damages caused by Universal Exports' breach. Under this option, Padma could recover at least the difference between the value of the goods as promised and their value as accepted.

Problem 17–5. ***Determining Employee Status.*** No, Cox is not liable to Cayer for any injuries or damage that she sustained in the accident with Ovalles. Generally, an employer is not liable for physical harm caused to a third person by the negligent act of an independent contractor in the performance of a contract. This is be cause the employer does not have the right to control the details of the performance. In determining whether a worker

has the status of an independent contractor, how much control the employer can exercise over the details of the work is the most important factor weighed by the courts.

In this problem, Ovalles worked as a cable installer for Cox under an agreement with M&M. The agreement disavowed any employer-employee relationship between Cox and M&M's installers. Ovalles was required to designate his affiliation with Cox on his van, clothing, and an ID badge. But Cox had minimal contact with Ovalles and limited power to control the manner in which he performed his work. Cox supplied cable wire and other equipment, but these items were delivered to M&M, not Ovalles. These facts indicate that Ovalles was an independent contractor, not an employee. Thus, Cox was not liable to Cayer for the harm caused to her by Ovalles when his van rear-ended Cayer's car.

In the actual case on which this problem is based, the court issued a judgment in Cox's favor. The Rhode Island Supreme Court affirmed, applying the principles stated above to arrive at the same conclusion.

Problem 18–4. ***LLC Operation.*** Part of the attractiveness of an LLC as a form of business enterprise is its flexibility. The members can decide how to operate the business through an operating agreement. For example, the agreement can set forth procedures for choosing or removing members or managers.

Here, the Bluewater operating agreement provided for a "super majority" vote to remove a member under circumstances that would jeopardize the firm's contractor status. Thus, one Bluewater member could not unilaterally "fire" another member without providing a reason. In fact, a majority of the members could not terminate the other's interest in the firm without providing a reason. Moreover, the only acceptable reason would be a circumstance that undercut the firm's status as a contractor.

The flexibility of the LLC business form relates to its framework, not to its members' capacity to violate its operating agreement. In the actual case on which this problem is based, Smith attempted to "fire" Williford without providing a reason. In Williford's suit, the court issued a judgment in his favor.

Problem 19–5. ***Piercing the Corporate Veil.*** Yes, there are sufficient grounds in the facts of this problem to support piercing the corporate veil and holding Kappeler personally liable to Snapp. First, in a case in which a plaintiff seeks to pierce a corporate veil, there must be a fraud or other injustice to be remedied. In that situation, the factors that a court will consider in determining whether to pierce the corporate veil include (1) a party is tricked or misled into dealing with the corporation rather than the individual, (2) the corporation has insufficient capital to meet its prospective debts or other potential liabilities, (3) corporate formalities, such as holding required corporate meetings, are not followed, and (4) personal and corporate interests are commingled.

In this problem, the amount that Snapp ultimately paid the builder exceeded the original estimate by nearly $1 million—and the project was still unfinished. Kappeler could not provide an accounting for the Snapp project—he could not explain double and triple charges nor whether the amount that Snapp paid had actually been spent on the project. These facts support a conclusion of fraud. And they also indicate that Kappeler may have tricked or misled Snapp into dealing with the corporation rather than with Kappeler as an individual. Castlebrook had issued no shares of stock, which indicates insufficient capitalization. The minutes of the corporate meetings "all looked exactly the same," indicating that in fact the required corporate meetings had not been held. And Kappeler had commingled personal and corporate funds.

In the actual case on which this problem is based, in Snapp's suit against the builder, the court pierced the corporate veil and held Kappeler personally liable. A state intermediate appellate court affirmed.

Glossary

A

acceptance In contract law, the offeree's notification to the offeror that the offeree agrees to be bound by the terms of the offeror's proposal.

accord and satisfaction An agreement for payment (or other performance) between two parties, one of whom has a right of action against the other. After the payment has been accepted or other performance has been made, the "accord and satisfaction" is complete, and the obligation is discharged.

actionable Capable of serving as the basis of a lawsuit.

actual malice A condition that exists when a person makes a statement with either knowledge of its falsity or reckless disregard for the truth. In a defamation suit, a statement made about a public figure normally must be made with actual malice for liability to be incurred.

actus reus (pronounced *ak*-tus *ray*-uhs) A guilty (prohibited) act. The commission of a prohibited act and the intent to commit a crime are the two essential elements required for criminal liability.

administrative agency A federal or state government agency created by the legislature to perform a specific function, such as to make and enforce rules pertaining to the environment.

administrative law The body of law created by administrative agencies in order to carry out their duties and responsibilities.

administrative law judge (ALJ) One who presides over an administrative agency hearing and has the power to administer oaths, take testimony, rule on questions of evidence, and make determinations of fact.

age of majority The age at which an individual is considered legally capable of conducting himself or herself responsibly. A person of this age is entitled to the full rights of citizenship, including the right to vote. In contract law, the age at which one is no longer an infant and can no longer disaffirm a contract.

agency A relationship between two parties in which one party (the agent) agrees to represent or act for the other (the principal).

agreement A meeting of two or more minds in regard to the terms of a contract; usually broken down into two events—an offer by one party to form a contract, and an acceptance of the offer by the person to whom the offer is made.

alien corporation A corporation formed in another country but doing business in the United States.

alienation In real property law, the voluntary transfer of property from one person to another (as opposed to a transfer by operation of law).

allege To state, recite, assert, or charge.

alternative dispute resolution (ADR) The resolution of disputes in ways other than those involved in the traditional judicial process. Negotiation, mediation, and arbitration are forms of ADR.

anticipatory repudiation An assertion or action by a party indicating that he or she will not perform an obligation that he or she is contractually obligated to perform at a future time.

apparent authority Authority that is only apparent, not real. An agent's apparent authority arises when the principal causes a third party to believe that the agent has authority, even though she or he does not.

appellant The party who takes an appeal from one court to another.

appellee The party against whom an appeal is taken—that is, the party who opposes setting aside or reversing the judgment.

arbitration The settling of a dispute by submitting it to a disinterested third party (other than a court), who renders a decision. The decision may or may not be legally binding.

arbitration clause A clause in a contract that provides that, in the event of a dispute, the parties will submit the dispute to arbitration rather than litigate the dispute in court.

arson The malicious burning of another's dwelling. Some statutes have expanded arson to include any real property, regardless of ownership, and the destruction of property by other means—for example, by explosion.

articles of incorporation The document that is filed with the appropriate state official, usually the secretary of state, when a business is incorporated and that contains basic information about the corporation.

articles of organization The document filed with a designated state official by which a limited liability company is formed.

articles of partnership A written agreement that sets forth each partner's rights and obligations with respect to the partnership.

assault Any word or action intended to make another person fearful of immediate physical harm; a reasonably believable threat.

assignee The person to whom contract rights are assigned.

assignment The act of transferring to another all or part of one's rights arising under a contract.

assignor The person who assigns contract rights.

assumption of risk A defense against negligence that can be used when the plaintiff was aware of a danger and voluntarily assumed the risk of injury from that danger.

award In the context of litigation, the amount of money awarded to a plaintiff in a civil lawsuit as damages. In the context of arbitration, the arbitrator's decision.

B

bankruptcy court A federal court of limited jurisdiction that handles only bankruptcy proceedings.

battery The unprivileged, intentional touching of another.

benefit corporation A type of for-profit corporation, available by statute in a number of states, that seeks to have a material positive impact on society and the environment.

beyond a reasonable doubt The standard used to determine the guilt or innocence of a person criminally charged. To be guilty of a crime, one must be proved guilty "beyond and to the exclusion of every reasonable doubt." A reasonable doubt is one that would cause a prudent person to hesitate before acting in matters important to him or her.

bilateral contract A type of contract that arises when a promise is given in exchange for a promise.

bilateral mistake A mistake that occurs when both parties to a contract are mistaken about the same material fact.

Bill of Rights The first ten amendments to the U.S. Constitution.

binding authority Any source of law that a court must follow when deciding a case.

bond A security that evidences a corporate (or government) debt.

botnet Short for robot network—a group of computers that run an application controlled and manipulated only by the software source. Usually, the term is reserved for computers that have been infected by malicious robot software.

breach To violate a law, by an act or an omission, or to break a legal obligation that one owes to another person or to society.

breach of contract The failure, without legal excuse, of a promisor to perform the obligations of a contract.

browse-wrap terms Terms and conditions of use that are presented to an Internet user at the time a product, such as software, is downloaded but that need not be agreed to before the product is installed or used.

burglary The unlawful entry into a building with the intent to commit a felony. Some state statutes have expanded burglary to include the intent to commit any crime.

business ethics Ethics in a business context; a consensus of what constitutes right or wrong behavior in the world of business and the application of moral principles to situations that arise in a business setting.

business invitees Those people, such as customers or clients, who are invited onto business premises by the owner of those premises for business purposes.

business judgment rule A rule under which courts will not hold corporate officers and directors liable for honest mistakes of judgment and bad business decisions that were made in good faith.

buy-sell agreement In the context of partnerships, an express agreement made at the time of partnership formation for one or more of the partners to buy out the other or others should the situation warrant.

buyout price The amount payable to a partner on his or her dissociation from a partnership, based on the amount distributable to that partner if the firm were wound up on that date, and offset by any damages for wrongful dissociation.

bylaws The internal rules of management adopted by a corporation at its first organizational meeting.

C

case law The rules of law announced in court decisions. Case law interprets statutes, regulations, constitutional provisions, and other case law.

case on point A previous case involving factual circumstances and issues that are similar to those in the case before the court.

categorical imperative A concept developed by the philosopher Immanuel Kant as an ethical guideline for behavior. In deciding whether an action is right or wrong, or desirable or undesirable, a person should evaluate the action in terms of what would happen if everybody else in the same situation, or category, acted the same way.

causation in fact An act or omission without ("but for") which an event would not have occurred.

certification mark A mark used by one or more persons, other than the owner, to certify the region, materials, mode of manufacture, quality, or accuracy of the owner's goods or services. Examples of certification marks include the "Good Housekeeping Seal of Approval" and "UL Tested."

charging order In partnership law, an order granted by a court to a judgment creditor that entitles the creditor to attach a partner's interest in the partnership.

checks and balances The system by which each of the three branches of the national government (executive, legislative, and judicial) exercises checks on the powers of the other branches.

choice-of-language clause A clause in a contract designating the official language by which the contract will be interpreted in the event of a future disagreement over the contract's terms.

choice-of-law clause A clause in a contract designating the law (such as the law of a particular state or nation) that will govern the contract.

citation A reference to a publication in which a legal authority—such as a statute or a court decision—or other source can be found.

civil law system A system of law derived from that of the Roman Empire and based on a code rather than case law; the predominant system of law in the nations of continental Europe and the nations that were once their colonies. In the United States, Louisiana is the only state that has a civil law system.

click-on agreement An agreement that arises when a buyer, engaging in a transaction on a computer, indicates his or her assent to be bound by the terms of an offer by clicking on a button that says, for example, "I agree"; sometimes referred to as a *click-on license* or a *click-wrap agreement.*

close corporation A corporation whose shareholders are limited to a small group of persons, often family members.

cloud computing The delivery to users of on-demand services from third-party servers over a network.

collateral promise A secondary promise that is ancillary (subsidiary) to a principal transaction or primary contractual relationship, such as a promise made by one person to pay the debts of another if the latter fails to perform. A collateral promise normally must be in writing to be enforceable.

collective mark A mark used by members of a cooperative, association, or other organization to certify the region, materials, mode of manufacture, quality, or accuracy of the specific goods or services. Examples of collective marks include the labor union marks found on tags of certain products and the credits of movies, which indicate the various associations and organizations that participated in the making of the movies.

commerce clause The provision in Article I, Section 8, of the U.S. Constitution that gives Congress the power to regulate interstate commerce.

commercial impracticability A doctrine under which a seller may be excused from performing a contract when (1) a contingency occurs, (2) the contingency's occurrence makes performance impracticable, and (3) the nonoccurrence of the contingency was a basic assumption on which the contract was made.

commingle To put funds or goods together into one mass so that they are mixed to such a degree that they no longer have separate identities.

common law The body of law developed from custom or judicial decisions in English and U.S. courts, not attributable to a legislature.

common stock A security that evidences ownership in a corporation. A share of common stock gives the owner a proportionate interest in the corporation with regard to control, earnings, and net assets. Common stock is lowest in priority with respect to payment of dividends and distribution of the corporation's assets on dissolution.

comparative negligence A theory in tort law under which the liability for injuries resulting from negligent acts is shared by all parties who were negligent (including the injured party) on the basis of each person's proportionate negligence.

compelling government interest A test of constitutionality that requires the government to have compelling reasons for passing any law that restricts fundamental rights, such as free speech, or distinguishes between people based on a suspect trait.

compensatory damages A money award equivalent to the actual value of injuries or damages sustained by the aggrieved party.

computer crime Any violation of criminal law that involves knowledge of computer technology for its perpetration, investigation, or prosecution.

concurrent conditions Conditions in a contract that must occur or be performed at the same time; they are mutually dependent. No obligations arise until these conditions are simultaneously performed.

concurrent jurisdiction Jurisdiction that exists when two different courts have the power to hear a case. For example, some cases can be heard in either a federal or a state court.

concurring opinion A court opinion by one or more judges or justices who agree with the majority but want to make or emphasize a point that was not made or emphasized in the majority's opinion.

condition A possible future event, the occurrence or nonoccurrence of which will trigger the performance of a legal obligation or terminate an existing obligation under a contract.

condition precedent A condition in a contract that must be met before a party's promise becomes absolute.

condition subsequent A condition in a contract that operates to terminate a party's absolute promise to perform.

conforming goods Goods that conform to contract specifications.

consequential damages Special damages that compensate for a loss that is not direct or immediate (for example, lost profits). The special damages must have been reasonably foreseeable at the time the breach or injury occurred in order for the plaintiff to collect them.

consideration Generally, the value given in return for a promise or a performance. The consideration, which must be present to make the contract legally binding, must be something of legally sufficient value and must be bargained for.

constitutional law Law that is based on the U.S. Constitution and the constitutions of the various states.

contract An agreement that can be enforced in court; formed by two or more parties, each of whom agrees to perform or to refrain from performing some act now or in the future.

contractual capacity The legal ability to enter into contracts; the threshold mental capacity required by law for a party who enters into a contract to be bound by that contract.

contributory negligence A theory in tort law under which a complaining party's own negligence contributed to or caused his or her injuries. Contributory negligence is an absolute bar to recovery in a minority of jurisdictions.

conversion The wrongful taking, using, or retaining possession of personal property that belongs to another.

cookie A small file sent from a Web site and stored in a user's Web browser to track the user's Web browsing activities.

copyright The exclusive right of authors to publish, print, or sell an intellectual production for a statutory period of time. A copyright has the same monopolistic nature as a patent or trademark, but it differs in that it applies exclusively to works of art, literature, and other works of authorship, including computer programs.

corporate social responsibility The concept that corporations can and should act ethically, and be accountable to society for their actions.

cost-benefit analysis A decision-making technique that involves weighing the costs of a given action against the benefits of the action.

counteroffer An offeree's response to an offer in which the offeree rejects the original offer and at the same time makes a new offer.

course of dealing Prior conduct between parties to a contract that establishes a common basis for their understanding.

course of performance The conduct that occurs under the terms of a particular agreement. Such conduct indicates what the parties to an agreement intended it to mean.

court of equity A court that decides controversies and administers justice according to the rules, principles, and precedents of equity.

court of law A court in which the only remedies that could be granted were things of value, such as money damages. In the early English king's courts, courts of law were distinct from courts of equity.

covenant not to compete A contractual promise to refrain from competing with another party for a certain period of time and within a certain geographic area. Although covenants not to compete restrain trade, they are commonly found in partnership agreements, business sale agreements, and employment contracts. If they are ancillary to such agreements, covenants not to compete will normally be enforced by the courts unless the time period or geographic area is deemed unreasonable.

covenant not to sue An agreement to substitute a contractual obligation for some other type of legal action based on a valid claim.

cover A buyer's or lessee's purchase on the open market of goods to substitute for those promised but never delivered by the seller or lessor. Under the Uniform Commercial Code, if the cost of cover exceeds the cost of the contract goods, the buyer or lessee can recover the difference, plus incidental and consequential damages.

crime A wrong against society proclaimed in a statute and punishable by society through fines and/or imprisonment—or, in some cases, death.

criminal law The branch of law that defines and punishes wrongful actions committed against the public.

crowdfunding A cooperative activity in which people network and pool funds and other resources via the Internet to assist a cause (such as disaster relief) or invest in a business venture (such as a startup).

cure Under the Uniform Commercial Code, the right of a party who tenders nonconforming performance to correct his or her performance within the contract period.

cyber crime A crime that occurs online, in the virtual community of the Internet, as opposed to the physical world.

cyber fraud Fraud that involves the online theft of credit-card information, banking details, and other information for criminal use.

cyber tort A tort committed via the Internet.

cyberlaw An informal term used to refer to all laws governing electronic communications and transactions, particularly those conducted via the Internet.

cybersquatting Registering a domain name that is the same as, or confusingly similar to, the trademark of another and then offering to sell that domain name back to the trademark owner.

D

damages A monetary award sought as a remedy for a breach of contract or a tortious act.

defamation Any published or publicly spoken false statement that causes injury to another's good name, reputation, or character.

defendant One against whom a lawsuit is brought, or the accused person in a criminal proceeding.

defense Reasons that a defendant offers in an action or suit as to why the plaintiff should not obtain what he or she is seeking.

delegatee One to whom contract duties are delegated by another, called the delegator.

delegation The transfer of a contractual duty to a third party. The party delegating the duty (the delegator) to the third party (the delegatee) is still obliged to perform on the contract should the delegatee fail to perform.

delegator One who delegates his or her duties under a contract to another, called the delegatee.

dilution With respect to trademarks, a doctrine under which distinctive or famous trademarks are protected from certain unauthorized uses of the marks regardless of a showing of competition or a likelihood of confusion. Congress created a federal cause of action for dilution in 1995 with the passage of the Federal Trademark Dilution Act.

disaffirmance The legal avoidance, or setting aside, of a contractual obligation.

discharge The termination of an obligation, such as occurs when the parties to a contract have fully performed their contractual obligations.

discharge in bankruptcy The release of a debtor from all debts that are provable, except those specifically excepted from discharge by statute.

disclosed principal A principal whose identity is known to a third party at the time the agent makes a contract with the third party.

disparagement of property An economically injurious false statement made about another's product or property. A general term for torts that are more specifically referred to as *slander of quality* or *slander of title*.

dissenting opinion A court opinion that presents the views of one or more judges or justices who disagree with the majority's decision.

dissociation The severance of the relationship between a partner and a partnership.

dissolution The formal disbanding of a partnership, corporation, or other business entity. For instance, partnerships can be dissolved by acts of the partners, by operation of law, or by judicial decree.

distributed network A network that can be used by persons located (distributed) around the country or the globe to share computer files.

diversity of citizenship Under Article III, Section 2, of the U.S. Constitution, a basis for federal court jurisdiction over a lawsuit between (1) citizens of different states, (2) a foreign country and citizens of a state or of different states, or (3) citizens of a state and citizens or subjects of a foreign country. The amount in controversy must be more than $75,000 before a federal court can take jurisdiction in such cases.

dividend A distribution of corporate profits to the corporation's shareholders in proportion to the number of shares held.

domain name The series of letters and symbols used to identify a site operator on the Internet; an Internet "address."

domestic corporation In a given state, a corporation that is organized under the law of that state.

double jeopardy A situation occurring when a person is tried twice for the same criminal offense; prohibited by the Fifth Amendment to the U.S. Constitution.

dram shop act A state statute that imposes liability on the owners of bars and taverns, as well as those who serve alcoholic drinks to the public, for injuries resulting from accidents caused by intoxicated persons when the sellers or servers of alcoholic drinks contributed to the intoxication.

due process clause The provisions of the Fifth and Fourteenth Amendments to the U.S. Constitution that guarantee that no person shall be deprived of life, liberty, or property without due process of law. Similar clauses are found in most state constitutions.

duress Unlawful pressure brought to bear on a person, causing the person to perform an act that he or she would not otherwise perform (or refrain from doing something the person would otherwise have done).

duty of care The duty of all persons, as established by tort law, to exercise a reasonable amount of care in their dealings with others. Failure to exercise due care, which is normally determined by the "reasonable person standard," constitutes the tort of negligence.

duty-based ethics An ethical philosophy rooted in the idea that every person has certain duties to others, including both humans and the planet. Those duties may be derived from religious principles or from other philosophical reasoning.

E

e-agent A semiautonomous computer program that is capable of executing specific tasks.

e-contract A contract that is entered into in cyberspace and is evidenced only by electronic impulses (such as those that make up a computer's memory), rather than, for example, a typewritten form.

e-signature As defined by the Uniform Electronic Transactions Act, "an electronic sound, symbol, or process attached to or logically associated with a record and executed or adopted by a person with the intent to sign the record."

early neutral case evaluation A form of alternative dispute resolution in which a neutral third party evaluates the strengths and weakness of the disputing parties' positions. The evaluator's opinion forms the basis for negotiating a settlement.

emancipation In regard to minors, the act of being freed from parental control; occurs when a child's parent or legal guardian relinquishes the legal right to exercise control over the child. Normally, a minor who leaves home to support himself or herself is considered emancipated.

embezzlement The fraudulent appropriation of money or other property by a person to whom the money or property has been entrusted.

entrapment In criminal law, a defense in which the defendant claims that he or she was induced by a public official—usually an undercover agent or police officer—to commit a crime that he or she would otherwise not have committed.

entrepreneur One who initiates and assumes the financial risk of a new business enterprise and undertakes to provide or control its management.

equal dignity rule A rule requiring that an agent's authority be in writing if the contract to be made on behalf of the principal must be in writing.

equal protection clause The provision in the Fourteenth Amendment to the U.S. Constitution that guarantees that no state will "deny to any person within its jurisdiction the equal protection of the laws." This clause mandates that state governments treat similarly situated individuals in a similar manner.

equitable maxims General propositions or principles of law that have to do with fairness (equity).

establishment clause The provision in the First Amendment to the U.S. Constitution that prohibits Congress from creating any law "respecting an establishment of religion."

estopped Barred, impeded, or precluded.

ethical reasoning A reasoning process in which an individual links his or her moral convictions or ethical standards to the particular situation at hand.

ethics Moral principles and values applied to social behavior.

exclusionary rule In criminal procedure, a rule under which any evidence that is obtained in violation of the accused's constitutional rights guaranteed by the Fourth, Fifth, and Sixth Amendments, as well as any evidence derived from illegally obtained evidence, will not be admissible in court.

exclusive agency An agency in which a principal grants an agent an exclusive territory and does not allow another agent to compete in that territory.

exclusive jurisdiction Jurisdiction that exists when a case can be heard only in a particular court or type of court, such as a federal court or a state court.

exculpatory clause A clause that releases a contractual party from liability in the event of monetary or physical injury, no matter who is at fault.

executed contract A contract that has been completely performed by both parties.

executive agency An administrative agency within the executive branch of government. At the federal level, executive agencies are those within the cabinet departments.

executory contract A contract that has not yet been fully performed.

express authority Authority expressly given by one party to another. In agency law, an agent has express authority to act for a principal if both parties agree, orally or in writing, that an agency relationship exists in which the agent has the power (authority) to act in the place of, and on behalf of, the principal.

express contract A contract in which the terms of the agreement are fully and explicitly stated in words, oral or written.

express warranty A seller's or lessor's oral or written promise, ancillary to an underlying sales or lease agreement, as to the quality, description, or performance of the goods being sold or leased.

extrinsic evidence Evidence that relates to a contract but is not contained within the document itself, including the testimony of the parties, the testimony of witnesses, and additional agreements and communications. A court may consider extrinsic evidence only when a contract term is ambiguous and the evidence does not contradict the express terms of the contract.

F

federal form of government A system of government in which the states form a union and the sovereign power is divided between a central government and the member states.

federal question A question that pertains to the U.S. Constitution, acts of Congress, or treaties. A federal question provides a basis for federal jurisdiction.

felony A crime—such as arson, murder, rape, or robbery—that carries the most severe sanctions, usually ranging from one year in a state or federal prison to the forfeiture of one's life.

fiduciary As a noun, a person having a duty created by his or her undertaking to act primarily for another's benefit in matters connected with the undertaking; as an adjective, a relationship founded on trust and confidence.

filtering software A computer program that screens incoming data according to rules built into the software and blocks access to Web sites with content not consistent with these rules.

firm offer An offer (by a merchant) that is irrevocable without consideration for a period of time (not longer than three months). A firm offer by a merchant must be in writing and must be signed by the offeror.

forbearance The act of refraining from exercising a legal right.

force majeure (pronounced _mah_-zhure) **clause** A provision in a contract stipulating that certain unforeseen events—such as war, political upheavals, acts of God, and the like—will excuse a party from liability for nonperformance of contractual obligations.

foreign corporation In a given state, a corporation that does business in that state but is not incorporated there.

forgery The fraudulent making or altering of any writing in a way that changes the legal rights and liabilities of another.

formal contract A contract that by law requires a specific form, such as being executed under seal, to be valid.

forum-selection clause A provision in a contract designating the court, jurisdiction, or tribunal that will decide any disputes arising under the contract.

fraudulent misrepresentation (fraud) Any misrepresentation, either by misstatement or omission of a material fact, knowingly made with the intention of deceiving another and on which a reasonable person would and does rely to his or her detriment.

free exercise clause The provision in the First Amendment to the U.S. Constitution that prohibits Congress from making any law "prohibiting the free exercise" of religion.

frustration of purpose A court-created doctrine under which a party to a contract will be relieved of his or her duty to perform when the objective purpose for performance no longer exists (due to reasons beyond that party's control).

full faith and credit clause A clause in Article IV, Section 1, of the U.S. Constitution that provides that "Full Faith and Credit shall be given in each State to the public Acts, Records, and Judicial Proceedings of every other State." The clause ensures that rights established under deeds, wills, contracts, and the like in one state will be honored by the other states and that any judicial decision with respect to such property rights will be honored and enforced in all states.

fully integrated contract A contract that completely sets forth all the terms and conditions agreed to by the parties and is intended as a final statement of their agreement.

G

general damages In a tort case, an amount awarded to compensate individuals for the nonmonetary aspects of the harm suffered, such as pain and suffering; not available to companies.

Good Samaritan statute A state statute that provides that persons who rescue or provide emergency services to others in peril—unless they do so recklessly, thus causing further harm—cannot be sued for negligence.

goodwill In the business context, the valuable reputation of a business viewed as an intangible asset.

grand jury A group of citizens called to decide, after hearing the state's evidence, whether a reasonable basis (probable cause) exists for believing that a crime has been committed and whether a trial ought to be held.

H

hacker A person who uses one computer to break into another.

historical school A school of legal thought that looks to the past to determine what the principles of contemporary law should be.

holding company A company whose business activity is holding shares in another company.

I

identity theft The act of stealing another's identifying information—such as a name, date of birth, or Social Security number—and using that information to access the victim's financial resources.

implied authority Authority that is created not by an explicit oral or written agreement but by implication. In agency law, implied authority (of the agent) can be conferred by custom, inferred from the position the agent occupies, or implied by virtue of being reasonably necessary to carry out express authority.

implied contract A contract formed in whole or in part from the conduct of the parties (as opposed to an express contract).

implied warranty A warranty that the law derives by implication or inference from the nature of the transaction or the relative situation or circumstances of the parties.

implied warranty of fitness for a particular purpose A warranty that goods sold or leased are fit for a particular purpose. The warranty arises when any seller or lessor knows the particular purpose for which a buyer or lessee will use the goods and knows that the buyer or lessee is relying on the skill and judgment of the seller or lessor to select suitable goods.

implied warranty of merchantability A warranty that goods being sold or leased are reasonably fit for the ordinary purpose for which they are sold or leased, are properly packaged and labeled, and are of fair quality. The warranty automatically arises in every sale or lease of goods made by a merchant who deals in goods of the kind sold or leased.

impossibility of performance A doctrine under which a party to a contract is relieved of his or her duty to perform when performance becomes impossible or totally impracticable (through no fault of either party).

in personam jurisdiction Court jurisdiction over the "person" involved in a legal action; personal jurisdiction.

in rem jurisdiction Court jurisdiction over a defendant's property.

incidental beneficiary A third party who incidentally benefits from a contract but whose benefit was not the reason the contract was formed. An incidental beneficiary has no rights in a contract and cannot sue to have the contract enforced.

incidental damages Damages that compensate for expenses directly incurred because of a breach of contract, such as those incurred to obtain performance from another source.

independent contractor One who works for, and receives payment from, an employer but whose working conditions and methods are not controlled by the employer. An independent contractor is not an employee but may be an agent.

independent regulatory agency An administrative agency that is not considered part of the government's executive branch and is not subject to the authority of the president. Independent agency officials cannot be removed without cause.

indictment (pronounced in-*dyte*-ment) A charge by a grand jury that a reasonable basis (probable cause) exists for believing that a crime has been committed and that a trial should be held.

informal contract A contract that does not require a specified form or formality in order to be valid.

information A formal accusation or complaint (without an indictment) issued in certain types of actions (usually criminal actions involving lesser crimes) by a law officer, such as a magistrate.

information return A tax return submitted by a partnership that reports the business's income and losses. The partnership itself does not pay taxes on the income, but each partner's share of the profit (whether distributed or not) is taxed as individual income to that partner.

innocent misrepresentation A false statement of fact or an act made in good faith that deceives and causes harm or injury to another.

inside director A person on a corporation's board of directors who is also an officer of the corporation.

installment contract Under the Uniform Commercial Code, a contract that requires or authorizes delivery in two or more separate lots to be accepted and paid for separately.

intangible property Property that is incapable of being apprehended by the senses (such as by sight or touch). Intellectual property is an example of intangible property.

integrated contract A written contract that constitutes the final expression of the parties' agreement. If a contract is integrated, evidence extraneous to the contract that contradicts or alters the meaning of the contract in any way is inadmissible.

intellectual property Property resulting from intellectual, creative processes. Patents, trademarks, and copyrights are examples of intellectual property.

intended beneficiary A third party for whose benefit a contract is formed; an intended beneficiary can sue the promisor if such a contract is breached.

intentional tort A wrongful act knowingly committed.

Internet service provider (ISP) A business or organization that offers users access to the Internet and related services.

J

joint and several liability In partnership law, a doctrine under which a plaintiff may sue, and collect a judgment from, all of the partners together (jointly) or one or more of the partners separately (severally, or individually). A partner can be held liable even if she or he did not participate in, ratify, or know about the conduct that gave rise to the lawsuit.

joint liability In partnership law, the partners' shared liability for partnership obligations and debts. A third party must sue all of the partners as a group, but each partner can be held liable for the full amount.

judicial review The process by which courts decide on the constitutionality of legislative enactments and actions of the executive branch.

jurisdiction The authority of a court to hear a case and decide a specific action.

jurisprudence The science or philosophy of law.

L

laches The equitable doctrine that bars a party's right to legal action if the party has neglected for an unreasonable length of time to act on his or her rights.

larceny The wrongful taking and carrying away of another person's personal property with the intent to permanently deprive the owner of the property. Some states classify larceny as either grand or petit, depending on the property's value.

latent defect A defect that is not obvious or cannot readily be ascertained.

law A body of enforceable rules governing relationships among individuals and between individuals and their society.

lease agreement In regard to the lease of goods, an agreement in which one person (the lessor) agrees to transfer the right to the possession and use of property to another person (the lessee) in exchange for rental payments.

legal positivism A school of legal thought centered on the assumption that there is no law higher than the laws created by a national government. Laws must be obeyed, even if they are unjust, to prevent anarchy.

legal realism A school of legal thought that holds that the law is only one factor to be considered when deciding cases and that social and economic circumstances should also be taken into account.

legal reasoning The process of reasoning by which a judge harmonizes his or her opinion with the judicial decisions in previous cases.

lessee A person who pays for the use or possession of another's property.

lessor A property owner who allows others to use his or her property in exchange for the payment of rent.

liability The state of being legally responsible (liable) for something, such as a debt or obligation.

libel Defamation in writing or in some other form (such as in a digital recording) having the quality of permanence.

license In the context of intellectual property, a contract permitting the use of a trademark, copyright, patent, or trade secret of certain purposes. In the context of real property, a revocable right or privilege of a person to come on another person's land.

licensee One who receives a license to use, or enter onto, another's property.

limited liability company (LLC) A hybrid form of business enterprise that offers the limited liability of a corporation and the tax advantages of a partnership.

liquidated damages An amount, stipulated in the contract, that the parties to a contract believe to be a reasonable estimation of the damages that will occur in the event of a breach.

liquidated debt A debt that is due and certain in amount.

litigation The process of resolving a dispute through the court system.

long arm statute A state statute that permits a state to obtain personal jurisdiction over nonresident defendants. A defendant must have "minimum contacts" with that state for the statute to apply.

M

mailbox rule A rule providing that an acceptance of an offer becomes effective on dispatch.

majority opinion A court opinion that represents the views of the majority (more than half) of the judges or justices deciding the case.

malpractice Professional misconduct or the failure to exercise the requisite degree of skill as a professional. Negligence—the failure to exercise due care—on the part of a professional, such as a physician or an attorney, is commonly referred to as malpractice.

malware Malicious software programs designed to disrupt or harm a computer, network, smartphone, or other device.

mediation A method of settling disputes outside of court by using the services of a neutral third party, called a mediator. The mediator acts as a communicating agent between the parties and suggests ways in which the parties can resolve their dispute.

member A person who has an ownership interest in a limited liability company.

mens rea (pronounced *mehns ray*-uh) Criminal intent. The commission of a prohibited act and the intent to commit a crime are the two essential elements required for criminal liability.

merchant A person who is engaged in the purchase and sale of goods. Under the Uniform Commercial Code, a person who deals in goods of the kind involved in the sales contract; for further definitions, see UCC 2–104.

meta tag Word inserted into a Web site's key-words field to increase the site's appearance in search engine results.

mini-trial A private proceeding in which each party to a dispute argues its position before the other side. A neutral third party may be present and act as an adviser if the parties fail to reach an agreement.

mirror image rule A common law rule that requires, for a valid contractual agreement, that the terms of the offeree's acceptance adhere exactly to the terms of the offeror's offer.

misdemeanor A lesser crime than a felony, punishable by a fine or imprisonment for up to one year in other than a state or federal penitentiary.

mitigation of damages A rule requiring a plaintiff to have done whatever was reasonable to minimize the damages caused by the defendant.

money laundering Falsely reporting income that has been obtained through criminal activity as income obtained through a legitimate business enterprise—in effect, "laundering" the "dirty money."

moral minimum The minimum degree of ethical behavior expected of a business firm, which is usually defined as compliance with the law.

mutual rescission An agreement between the parties to cancel their contract, releasing the parties from further obligations under the contract. The object of the agreement is to restore the parties to the positions they would have occupied had no contract ever been formed.

N

natural law The oldest school of legal thought, based on the belief that the legal system should reflect universal ("higher") moral and ethical principles that are inherent in human nature.

necessaries Necessities required for life, such as food, shelter, clothing, and medical attention; may include whatever is believed to be necessary to maintain a person's standard of living or financial and social status.

necessity In criminal law, a defense against liability. Under Section 3.02 of the Model Penal Code, this defense is justifiable if "the harm or evil sought to be avoided" by a given action "is greater than that sought to be prevented by the law defining the offense charged." In real property law, a way of creating an easement when one party must have the easement in order to have access to his or her property.

negligence The failure to exercise the standard of care that a reasonable person would exercise in similar circumstances.

negligent misrepresentation Any manifestation through words or conduct that amounts to an untrue statement of fact made in circumstances in which a reasonable and prudent person would not have done that which led to the misrepresentation. A representation made with an honest belief in its truth may still be negligent due to (1) a lack of reasonable care in ascertaining the facts, (2) the manner of expression, or (3) the absence of the skill or competence required by a particular business or profession.

negotiation In regard to dispute settlement, a process in which parties attempt to settle their dispute without going to court, with or without attorneys to represent them. In regard to negotiable instruments, the transfer of an instrument in such a way that the transferee (the person to whom the instrument is transferred) becomes a holder.

nominal damages A small monetary award (often one dollar) granted to a plaintiff when no actual damage was suffered or when the plaintiff is unable to show such loss with sufficient certainty.

notary public A public official authorized to attest to the authenticity of signatures.

novation The substitution, by agreement, of a new contract for an old one, with the rights under the old one being terminated. Typically, there is a substitution of a new person who is responsible for the contract and the removal of an original party's rights and duties under the contract.

O

objective theory of contracts A theory under which the intent to form a contract will be judged by outward, objective facts as interpreted by a reasonable person, rather than by the party's own secret, subjective intentions. Objective facts might include what a party said when entering into the contract, how a party acted or appeared, and the circumstances surrounding the transaction.

offer A promise or commitment to perform or refrain from performing some specified act in the future.

offeree A person to whom an offer is made.

offeror A person who makes an offer.

online dispute resolution (ODR) The resolution of disputes with the assistance of organizations that offer dispute-resolution services via the Internet.

operating agreement An agreement in which the members of a limited liability company set forth the details of how the business will be managed and operated.

opinion A statement by a court expressing the reasons for its decision in a case.

option contract A contract under which the offeror cannot revoke his or her offer for a stipulated time period and the offeree can accept or reject the offer at any time during this period. The offeree must give consideration for the option to be enforceable.

ordinance A law passed by a local governing unit, such as a city or a county.

outcome-based ethics An ethical philosophy that focuses on the impacts of a decision on society or on key stakeholders.

output contract An agreement in which a seller agrees to sell and a buyer agrees to buy all or up to a stated amount of what the seller produces.

outside director A person on a corporation's board of directors who does not hold a management position at the corporation.

P

parol evidence rule A substantive rule of contracts under which a court will not receive into evidence the parties' prior negotiations, prior agreements, or contemporaneous oral agreements if that evidence contradicts or varies the terms of the parties' written contract.

partially disclosed principal A principal whose identity is unknown by a third party, but the third party knows that the agent is or may be acting for a principal at the time the agent and the third party form a contract.

partnering agreement An agreement between a seller and a buyer who frequently do business with each other on the terms and conditions that will apply to all subsequently formed electronic contracts.

partnership An agreement by two or more persons to carry on, as co-owners, a business for profit.

partnership by estoppel A partnership imposed by a court when nonpartners have held themselves out to be partners, or have allowed themselves to be held out as partners, and others have detrimentally relied on their misrepresentations.

pass-through entity A business entity that has no tax liability. The entity's income is passed through to the owners, and they pay taxes on the income.

past consideration Something given or some act done in the past, which cannot ordinarily be consideration for a later bargain.

patent A government grant that gives an inventor the exclusive right or privilege to make, use, or sell his or her invention for a limited time period.

peer-to-peer (P2P) networking The sharing of resources (such as files, hard drives, and processing styles) among multiple computers without the requirement of a central network server.

penalty A sum inserted into a contract not as a measure of compensation for its breach but rather as punishment for a default. The agreement as to the amount will not be enforced, and recovery will be limited to actual damages.

per curiam **opinion** By the whole court; a court opinion written by the court as a whole instead of being authored by a judge or justice.

perfect tender rule A common law rule under which a seller was required to deliver to the buyer goods that conformed perfectly to the requirements stipulated in the sales contract. A tender of nonconforming goods would automatically constitute a breach of contract. Under the Uniform Commercial Code, the rule has been greatly modified.

performance In contract law, the fulfillment of one's duties arising under a contract with another; the normal way of discharging one's contractual obligations.

persuasive authority Any legal authority or source of law that a court may look to for guidance but need not follow when making its decision.

petitioner In equity practice, a party that initiates a lawsuit.

petty offense In criminal law, the least serious kind of criminal offense, such as a traffic or building-code violation.

phishing Online fraud in which criminals pretend to be legitimate companies by using e-mails or malicious Web sites that trick individuals and companies into providing useful information, such as bank account numbers, Social Security numbers, and credit-card numbers.

piercing the corporate veil The action of a court to disregard the corporate entity and hold the shareholders personally liable for corporate debts and obligations.

plaintiff A party that initiates a lawsuit.

plea bargaining The process by which a criminal defendant and the prosecutor in a criminal case work out a mutually satisfactory disposition of the case, subject to court approval; usually involves the defendant's pleading guilty to a lesser offense in return for a lighter sentence.

plurality opinion A court opinion that is joined by the largest number of the judges or justices hearing the case, but fewer than half of the total number.

police powers Powers possessed by states as part of their inherent sovereignty. These powers may be exercised to protect or promote the public order, health, safety, morals, and general welfare.

power of attorney Authorization for another to act as one's agent or attorney either in specified circumstances (special) or in all situations (general).

precedent A court decision that furnishes an example or authority for deciding subsequent cases involving identical or similar facts.

predominant-factor test A test courts use to determine whether a contract is primarily for the sale of goods or for the sale of services.

preemption A doctrine under which certain federal laws preempt, or take precedence over, conflicting state or local laws.

preemptive rights The right of a shareholder in a corporation to have the first opportunity to purchase a new issue of that corporation's stock in proportion to the amount of stock already owned by the shareholder.

preferred stock A security that entitles the holder to payment of fixed dividends and that has priority over common stock in the distribution of assets on the corporation's dissolution.

prenuptial agreement An agreement made before marriage that defines each partner's ownership rights in the other partner's property. Prenuptial agreements must be in writing to be enforceable.

principle of rights The principle that human beings have certain fundamental rights (to life, freedom, and the pursuit of happiness, for example). A key factor in determining whether a business decision is ethical under this theory is how that decision affects the rights of others, such as employees, consumers, suppliers, and the community.

private equity Capital funds invested by a private equity firm in an existing corporation, usually to purchase and reorganize it.

privilege In tort law, the ability to act contrary to another person's right without that person's having legal redress for such acts. Privilege may be raised as a defense to defamation.

privileges and immunities clause Article IV, Section 2, of the U.S. Constitution requires states not to discriminate against one another's citizens. A resident of one state cannot be treated as an alien when in another state; he or she may not be denied such privileges and immunities as legal protection, access to courts, travel rights, and property rights.

privity of contract The relationship that exists between the promisor and the promisee of a contract.

probable cause Reasonable grounds for believing that a search should be conducted or that a person should be arrested.

probate court A state court of limited jurisdiction that conducts proceedings relating to the settlement of a deceased person's estate.

procedural law Law that establishes the methods of enforcing the rights established by substantive law.

promise A person's assurance that he or she will or will not do something.

promisee A person to whom a promise is made.

promisor A person who makes a promise.

promissory estoppel A doctrine that applies when a promisor makes a clear and definite promise on which the promisee justifiably relies. Such a promise is binding if justice will be better served by the enforcement of the promise.

proximate cause Legal cause; exists when the connection between an act and an injury is strong enough to justify imposing liability.

proxy Authorization to represent a corporate shareholder to serve as his or her agent and vote his or her shares in a certain manner.

public corporation A corporation owned by a federal, state, or municipal government—not to be confused with a publicly held corporation.

public figure An individual in the public limelight. Public figures include government officials and politicians, movie stars, well-known businesspersons, and generally anybody who becomes known to the public because of his or her position or activities.

publicly held corporation A corporation whose shares are publicly traded in securities markets, such as the New York Stock Exchange or the NASDAQ.

puffery A salesperson's exaggerated claims concerning the quality of goods offered for sale. Such claims involve opinions rather than facts and are not considered to be legally binding promises or warranties.

punitive damages Money damages that may be awarded to a plaintiff to punish the defendant and deter future similar conduct.

Q

quantum meruit A Latin phrase, meaning "as much as he deserves," that describes the extent of compensation owed under a quasi contract.

quasi contract A fictional contract imposed on parties by a court in the interests of fairness and justice; usually, quasi contracts are imposed to avoid the unjust enrichment of one party at the expense of another.

question of fact In a lawsuit, an issue involving a factual dispute. A question of fact can be decided by a judge or a jury.

question of law In a lawsuit, an issue involving the application or interpretation of a law. Only a judge, and not a jury, can decide a question of law.

quorum The number of members of a decision-making body that must be present before business may be transacted.

R

ratification The act of accepting and giving legal force to an obligation that previously was not enforceable.

reasonable person standard The standard of behavior expected of a hypothetical "reasonable person." The standard against which negligence is measured and that must be observed to avoid liability for negligence.

record According to the Uniform Electronic Transactions Act, information that is either inscribed on a tangible medium or stored in an electronic or other medium, and that is retrievable.

reformation A court-ordered correction of a written contract so that it reflects the true intentions of the parties.

release A contract in which one party forfeits the right to pursue a legal claim against the other party.

remedy The relief given to an innocent party to enforce a right or compensate for the violation of a right.

remedy at law A remedy available in a court of law. Money damages are awarded as a remedy at law.

remedy in equity A remedy allowed by courts in situations where remedies at law are not appropriate. Remedies in equity include injunction, specific performance, rescission and restitution, and reformation.

replevin (pronounced rih-*pleh*-vin) An action to recover specific goods in the hands of a party who is wrongfully withholding them from the other party.

reporter A publication in which court cases are published, or reported.

requirements contract An agreement in which a buyer agrees to purchase and the seller agrees to sell all or up to a stated amount of what the buyer needs or requires.

rescission (pronounced rih-*sih*-zhen) A remedy whereby a contract is canceled and the parties are returned to the positions they occupied before the contract was made; may be effected through the mutual consent of the parties, by their conduct, or by court decree.

respondeat superior A doctrine under which a principal-employer is liable for any harm caused to a third party by an agent-employee in the course or scope of employment.

respondent In equity practice, the party who answers a complaint or other proceeding.

restitution An equitable remedy under which a person is restored to his or her original position prior to loss or injury, or placed in the position he or she would have been in had the breach not occurred.

retained earnings The portion of a corporation's profits that has not been paid out as dividends to shareholders.

revocation In contract law, the withdrawal of an offer by an offeror. Unless an offer is irrevocable, it can be revoked at any time prior to acceptance without liability.

robbery The act of forcefully and unlawfully taking personal property of any value from another; force or intimidation is usually necessary for an act of theft to be considered a robbery.

rule of four A rule of the United States Supreme Court under which the Court will not issue a writ of *certiorari* unless at least four justices agree to do so.

S

S corporation A close business corporation that has most of the attributes of a corporation, including limited liability, but qualifies under the Internal Revenue Code to be taxed as a partnership.

sale The passing of title (evidence of ownership rights) from a seller to a buyer for a price.

sales contract A contract for the sale of goods under which the ownership of goods is transferred from a seller to a buyer for a price.

scienter (pronounced sy-*en*-ter) Knowledge by the misrepresenting party that material facts have been falsely represented or omitted with an intent to deceive.

search warrant An order granted by a public authority, such as a judge, that authorizes law enforcement personnel to search particular premises or property.

seasonably Within a specified time period. If no period is specified, within a reasonable time.

securities Generally, stocks, bonds, or other items that represent an ownership interest in a corporation or a promise of repayment of debt by a corporation.

self-defense The legally recognized privilege to protect one's self or property against injury by another. The privilege of self-defense protects only acts that are reasonably necessary to protect one's self or property.

self-incrimination Giving testimony in a trial or other legal proceeding that could expose the person testifying to criminal prosecution.

service mark A mark used in the sale or the advertising of services, such as to distinguish the services of one person from the services of others. Titles, character names, and other distinctive features of radio and television programs may be registered as service marks.

shareholder agreement An agreement between shareholders that restricts the transferability of shares, often entered into for the purpose of maintaining proportionate control of a close corporation.

shareholder's derivative suit A suit brought by a shareholder to enforce a corporate cause of action against a third person.

shrink-wrap agreement An agreement whose terms are expressed in a document located inside a box in which goods (usually software) are packaged; sometimes called a *shrink-wrap license*.

slander Defamation in oral form.

slander of quality The publication of false information about another's product, alleging that it is not what its seller claims.

slander of title The publication of a statement that denies or casts doubt on another's legal ownership of any property causing financial loss to that property's owner; also called *trade libel*.

small claims court Special courts in which parties may litigate small claims (usually, claims involving $2,500 or less). Attorneys are not required in small claims courts and in many states are not allowed to represent the parties.

social media Forms of communication through which users create and share information, ideas, messages, and other content via the Internet.

sociological school A school of legal thought that views the law as a tool for promoting justice in society.

sole proprietorship The simplest form of business organization, in which the owner is the business. The owner reports business income on his or her personal income tax return and is legally responsible for all debts and obligations incurred by the business.

sovereignty The quality of having independent authority over a geographic area. For instance, state governments have the authority to regulate affairs within their borders.

spam Bulk, unsolicited (junk) e-mail.

special damages In a tort case, an amount awarded to compensate the plaintiff for quantifiable monetary losses, such as medical expenses, property damage, and lost wages and benefits (now and in the future).

specific performance An equitable remedy requiring the breaching party to perform as promised under the contract; usually granted only when money damages would be an inadequate remedy and the subject matter of the contract is unique (for example, real property).

stakeholders Groups, other than the company's shareholders, that are affected by corporate decisions. Stakeholders include employees, customers, creditors, suppliers, and the community in which the corporation operates.

standing to sue The requirement that an individual must have a sufficient stake in a controversy before he or she can bring a lawsuit. The plaintiff must demonstrate that he or she has been either injured or threatened with injury.

stare decisis A common law doctrine under which judges are obligated to follow the precedents established in prior decisions.

Statute of Frauds A state statute under which certain types of contracts must be in writing to be enforceable.

statute of limitations A federal or state statute setting the maximum time period during which a certain action can be brought or certain rights enforced.

statutory law The body of law enacted by legislative bodies (as opposed to constitutional law, administrative law, or case law).

stock An ownership (equity) interest in a corporation, measured in units of shares.

stock certificate A certificate issued by a corporation evidencing the ownership of a specified number of shares in the corporation.

stock warrant A certificate that grants the owner the option to buy a given number of shares of stock, usually within a set time period.

substantive law Law that defines, describes, regulates, and creates legal rights and obligations.

summary jury trial A method of settling disputes in which a trial is held, but the jury's verdict is not binding. The verdict acts only as a guide to both sides in reaching an agreement during the mandatory negotiations that immediately follow the summary jury trial.

superseding cause An intervening force or event that breaks the connection between a wrongful act and an injury to another; in negligence law, a defense to liability.

supremacy clause The provision in Article VI of the U.S. Constitution that provides that the Constitution, laws, and treaties of the United States are "the supreme Law of the Land." Under this clause, state and local laws that directly conflict with federal law will be rendered invalid.

symbolic speech Nonverbal conduct that expresses opinions or thoughts about a subject. Symbolic speech is protected under the First Amendment's guarantee of freedom of speech.

T

tangible property Property that has physical existence and can be distinguished by the senses of touch, sight, and so on. A car is tangible property.

tender An unconditional offer to perform an obligation by a person who is ready, willing, and able to do so.

tender of delivery Under the Uniform Commercial Code, a seller's or lessor's act of placing conforming goods at the disposal of the buyer or lessee and giving the buyer or lessee whatever notification is reasonably necessary to enable the buyer or lessee to take delivery.

third party beneficiary One for whose benefit a promise is made in a contract but who is not a party to the contract.

tort A civil wrong not arising from a breach of contract. A breach of a legal duty that proximately causes harm or injury to another.

tortfeasor One who commits a tort.

trade dress The image and overall appearance of a product—for example, the distinctive decor, menu, layout, and style of service of a particular restaurant. Basically, trade dress is subject to the same protection as trademarks.

trade libel The publication of false information about another's product, alleging that it is not what its seller claims; also referred to as *slander of quality.*

trade name A term that is used to indicate part or all of a business's name and that is directly related to the business's reputation and goodwill. Trade names are protected under the common law (and under trademark law, if the name is the same as the firm's trademark).

trade secret Information or a process that gives a business an advantage over competitors who do not know the information or process.

trademark A distinctive mark, motto, device, or implement that a manufacturer stamps, prints, or otherwise affixes to the goods it produces so that they may be identified on the market and their origins made known. Once a trademark is established (under the common law or through registration), the owner is entitled to its exclusive use.

transferred intent A legal principle under which a person who intends to harm one individual, but unintentionally harms a different individual, can be liable to the second victim for an intentional tort.

trespass to land The entry onto, above, or below the surface of land owned by another without the owner's permission or legal authorization.

trespass to personal property The unlawful taking or harming of another's personal property; interference with another's right to the exclusive possession of his or her personal property.

triple bottom line The idea that investors and others should consider not only corporate profits, but also the corporation's impact on people and on the planet in assessing the firm. (The bottom line is people, planet, and profits.)

typosquatting A form of cybersquatting that relies on mistakes, such as typographical errors, made by Internet users when inputting information into a Web browser.

U

***ultra vires* acts** Acts of a corporation that are beyond its express and implied powers to undertake (the Latin phrase means "beyond the powers").

unconscionable (pronounced un-*kon*-shun-uh-bul) **contract or clause** A contract or clause that is void on the basis of public policy because one party, as a result of his or her disproportionate bargaining power, is forced to accept terms that are unfairly burdensome and that unfairly benefit the dominating party.

undisclosed principal A principal whose identity is unknown by a third party, and that person has no knowledge that the agent is acting for a principal at the time the agent and the third party form a contract.

undue influence Persuasion that is less than actual force but more than advice and that induces a person to act according to the will or purposes of the dominating party.

unenforceable contract A valid contract rendered unenforceable by some statute or law.

uniform law A model law created by the National Conference of Commissioners on Uniform State Laws and/or the American Law Institute for the states to consider adopting. If the state adopts the law, it becomes statutory law in that state. Each state has the option of adopting or rejecting all or part of a uniform law.

unilateral contract A contract that results when an offer can be accepted only by the offeree's performance.

unilateral mistake A mistake that occurs when one party to a contract is mistaken as to a material fact.

unliquidated debt A debt that is uncertain in amount.

usage of trade Any practice or method of dealing having such regularity of observance in a place, vocation, or trade as to justify an expectation that it will be observed with respect to the transaction in question.

usury Charging an illegal rate of interest.

utilitarianism An approach to ethical reasoning in which ethically correct behavior is related to an evaluation of the consequences of a given action on those who will be affected by it. In utilitarian reasoning, a "good" decision is one that results in the greatest good for the greatest number of people affected by the decision.

V

valid contract A contract that results when the elements necessary for contract formation (agreement, consideration, contractual capacity, and legality) are present.

venture capital Financing provided by professional, outside investors—that is, *venture capitalists,* usually groups of wealthy investors and securities firms—to new business ventures.

venue (pronounced *ven-*yoo) The geographical district in which an action is tried and from which the jury is selected.

vicarious liability Indirect liability imposed on a supervisory party (such as an employer) for the actions of a subordinate (such as an employee) because of the relationship between the two parties.

virus A type of malware that is transmitted between computers and attempts to do deliberate damage to systems and data.

void contract A contract having no legal force or binding effect.

voidable contract A contract that may be legally avoided (canceled) at the option of one of the parties.

voluntary consent Knowing and voluntary agreement to the terms of a contract. If voluntary consent is lacking, the contract will be voidable.

W

waiver An intentional, knowing relinquishment of a legal right.

white-collar crime Nonviolent crime committed by individuals or corporations to obtain a personal or business advantage.

winding up The second of two stages in the termination of a partnership or corporation, in which the firm's assets are collected, liquidated, and distributed, and liabilities are discharged.

worm A type of malware that is designed to copy itself from one computer to another without human interaction. A worm can copy itself automatically and can replicate in great volume and with great speed.

writ of *certiorari* (pronounced sur-shee-uh-*rah*-ree) A writ from a higher court asking the lower court for the record of a case.

Table of Cases

Following is a list of all the cases mentioned in this text, including those within the footnotes, features, and case problems. Any case that was an excerpted case for a chapter is given special emphasis by having its title **boldfaced**.

Index